The Archaeology of Mediterranean Landscapes

Series Editors
Graeme Barker and David Mattingly

1. Reconstructing Past Population Trends in Mediterranean Europe (3000 BC – AD 1800)
Edited by John Bintliff and Kostas Sbonias

2. Environmental Reconstruction in Mediterranean Landscape Archaeology
Edited by Philippe Leveau, Kevin Walsh, Frédéric Trément and Graeme Barker

3. Geographical Information Systems and Landscape Archaeology
Edited by Mark Gillings, David Mattingly and Jan van Dalen

4. Non-Destructive Techniques Applied to Landscape Archaeology
Edited by Marinella Pasquinucci and Frédéric Trément

5. Extracting Meaning from Ploughsoil Assemblages
Edited by Riccardo Francovich and Helen Patterson

General Editors' Introduction: The POPULUS Project

Graeme Barker and David Mattingly

This is one of five volumes being published by the POPULUS project, a European research network funded by the EU Human Capital and Mobility programme (Contract ERB CHRXCT930305) to address a series of methodological issues in Mediterranean landscape archaeology.

THE RESEARCH CONTEXT

Without a long historical perspective, research on changing demographic patterns in modern day Europe can only assess the impact of recurrent or perennial environmental and socio-economic aspects by constructing hypothetical models. The more empirically-based such models are, the greater their relevance to contemporary situations. This is particularly true of the less industrialized regions of Mediterranean Europe, where farming remains the principal economic focus and where the last decades have witnessed considerable migration of population to the cities or other more favoured economic regions. The problems facing these areas of the EU have an historic as well as a contemporary dimension and there is obvious importance in seeking to gain a clearer understanding of their long-term demographic trends.

Long-term demographic changes can be studied from many different perspectives and using many techniques, including history and the natural and social sciences. Numerous factors can be advanced to explain population growth and contraction (economic, environmental, social), but all research is hampered by the absence of detailed census records for much of the pre-modern period. However, landscape archaeology – a constellation of approaches and methodologies bridging the natural and social sciences, applied to both rural and urban contexts – has the potential to provide a major source of new information on the *longue durée* of human settlement in Mediterranean Europe. In recent years advances in field survey and excavation techniques, air photography, remote sensing, GIS (Geographical Information Systems), ceramic provenancing and dating have led to the accumulation of a wealth of new evidence on past settlement patterns. Potentially, therefore, the techniques of landscape archaeology offer the best opportunity significantly to advance our knowledge of European human demography in pre-industrial times, *c.* 3000 BC–AD 1800.

Despite this potential contribution of landscape archaeology, however, development has been uneven across Europe. In Mediterranean countries in particular, the traditional dominance of art historical approaches in archaeology, compounded by the strength of academic boundaries in other disciplines, has mitigated against the development of an approach to landscape analysis and demographic modelling that by definition demands an inter-disciplinary framework linking the natural and social sciences. Fieldwork in landscape archaeology has been the exception, not the rule. Moreover, where pioneering research has taken place, each team has tended to develop and use its own special methods (often reflecting a particular national tradition of archaeological research), with too little attention being paid to the necessity of achieving greater standardization of data sets. There are also specific problems relating to the interpretation of the status, size and length of occupation of the many sites that have been discovered. Scientific techniques can assist in refining the data so that more reliable demographic assessments can be made, but many interesting and important projects have not been able to make use of the full range of scientific techniques because the appropriate expertise is not available at the regional level. If landscape archaeology is to realize its potential to contribute significantly to debates on long-term demographic trends in Mediterranean Europe, it has to overcome the present lack of agreement on approaches and methods that makes meaningful comparisons between regional data difficult or impossible.

THE POPULUS OBJECTIVES

The aim of the POPULUS project, therefore, was to

investigate the feasibility of establishing a common series of research goals and standards in Mediterranean landscape archaeology so as to advance the study of the ancient demography of the region on a broad comparative front. A research network was established at five EU universities, each hosting a Working Party and training a trans-national Research Fellow in a specific sub-discipline within Landscape Archaeology, as follows:

- Prof Graeme Barker (School of Archaeological Studies, University of Leicester, UK) coordinated the overall project, and his colleague Dr David Mattingly co-ordinated the work of Working Party 1, and the training of the Research Fellow, in **Geographical Information Systems**;
- Dr John Bintliff (Department of Archaeology, University of Durham, UK) coordinated the work of Working Party 2, and the training of the Research Fellow, in **Demographic Modelling**;
- Prof Philippe Leveau (Centre Camille Julian, Université de Provence, France) coordinated the work of Working Party 3, and the training of the Research Fellow, in **Geoarchaeology**;
- Prof Riccardo Francovich (Dipartimento di Archeologia e Storia delle Arti, Università degli Studi di Siena, Italy) coordinated the work of Working Party 4, and the training of the Research Fellow, in **Field-survey Methodologies**, with particular emphasis on ceramic recording, provenancing and dating;
- Prof Marinella Pasquinucci (Dipartimento di Scienze Storiche del Mondo Antico, Università degli Studi di Pisa, Italy) coordinated the work of Working Party 5, and the training of the Research Fellow, in **Remote Sensing**, with particular emphasis on non-invasive techniques of archaeological survey.

The Working Parties were to bring together relevant expertise to define key issues in the methodologies of their research area, with a particular emphasis on the comparison of different research traditions and methods in different European countries. Each Working Party was to organise a Colloquium that would review methodologies and demonstrate best practice. The Research Fellows were to assist in the organisation of the Colloquia, and also to undertake research within their area of expertise and present their results to the relevant Colloquium. In addition, the Research Fellows and other members of the network were to collaborate in a programme of joint fieldwork to demonstrate the practical integration of improved and standardised methodologies in landscape archaeology. The principal outcome of POPULUS was to be the publication of the five colloquia, including the results of the joint fieldwork, together with a technical manual identifying best practice.

THE WORK PROGRAMME

The project started in January 1994 with the first meeting of the Steering Committee, composed of the coordinators in each of the partner universities. The Research Fellows were appointed through 1994: Leicester in January, Durham in April, Aix-en-Provence in April, Siena from February, and Pisa from June. The Working Parties met through 1994 and 1995, and the Research Fellows' training and field research were also undertaken during 1994 and 1995. In 1995 the project was expanded and strengthened with the addition of a team from the Department of Archaeology at the University of Ljubljana in Slovenia coordinated by Dr Predrag Novaković, under a supplementary EU grant (Contract ERBCIPD940624). The Colloquia took place in the autumn of 1995 and spring of 1996, the papers being revised by their authors through 1996, and then being edited at the five universities by the local coordinators and finally at Leicester (including several that were also translated into English after the main editing) by the General Editors during 1997.

THE WORKING PARTIES

The Working Parties were deliberately set up in terms of personnel from the network and from other universities and institutions to reflect the diversity of Community traditions and methodologies in each of the five main areas addressed. Working Party 1 had members from Britain, France, Greece, Holland, Italy, and Slovenia. Working Party 2 had members from Britain, France, Germany, Greece, Holland, Italy, and Slovenia. Working Party 3 had members from Britain, France, Italy, Spain and Slovenia. Working Party 4 had members from Britain, France, Holland, Italy, Spain and Slovenia. Working Party 5 had members from Britain, France, Greece, Italy and Slovenia.

THE RESEARCH FELLOWS

Under the terms of the Human Capital and Mobility programme, the Research Fellows were to be appointed from EU countries other than the designated place of work. This requirement of the Human Capital and Mobility programme was also seen as an extremely positive contribution to the goals of POPULUS, because the mobility of young archaeologists from one Community country to another was an important part of the process of integrating the different European intellectual and methodological traditions in landscape archaeology. The partner institutions proposed individuals where suitable qualified personnel were available, and the posts were also advertized widely through EU universities, museums and state archaeological services. The Leicester Research Fellow in GIS was Dr Jan van Dalen, a Dutch national with a first and second degree at Leiden University, who was working for the Dutch Archaeological Service on a programme developing GIS for predictive modelling of site distributions to aid their strategies of heritage management. The Durham Research Fellow in Demographic Modelling was Dr Kostas Sbonias, a Greek national with a first degree at Athens University in archaeology, a PhD from Heidelberg University, and extensive postgraduate experience in Greek landscape archaeology projects. The Aix-en-Provence Research Fellow in Geoarchaeology was Dr Kevin Walsh, a British national with a first degree in archaeology and geography at Lampeter University and an MA and a PhD in environmental archaeology at Leicester University. The Siena Research Fellow in Field Survey Methodologies was a British national, Dr Helen Patterson, who had a first degree in archaeology at Reading University and a PhD in ceramic analysis at Sheffield University, the latter with a primary focus on the analysis of medieval ceramics from a field survey and excavation project in Italy. The Pisa Research Fellow in Remote Sensing was a French national, Dr Frédéric Trément, who had a first degree in archaeology at the University of Lille and a PhD at the University of Aix-en-Provence in landscape archaeology. The Ljubljana Research Fellow was a Greek national, Mrs Helene Simoni, with a first degree in classical archaeology at the University of Athens and an MA in Landscape Studies at the University of Leicester. Her MA had included training in GIS, and she was appointed to Ljubljana to receive further training, and then to undertake research, in GIS.

The Research Fellows prepared discussion documents for each meeting of their respective Working Party. For the first meetings they gathered information about current archaeological research in the Mediterranean relevant to the activities of their Working Party, to help define the key issues for the subsequent Working Party meetings and the themes of the Colloquia, and to suggest names of appropriate speakers. In subsequent meetings they reported further developments in this data-gathering exercise, and also reported on their own field research. Supported by their supervisor (the regional coordinator), they were charged with the primary responsibility for the organization of their respective Colloquia including the soliciting of papers, the circulation of pre-prints to discussants, the running of the Colloquia, and liaison with speakers afterwards to secure finalized versions of papers. They also undertook as much of the preliminary editing of the proceedings as possible before the cessation of their contracts. Dr Trément in particular undertook much of the editing of the Aix as well as the Pisa Colloquia after the Aix Research Fellow left the project before the end of his contract for another post, Dr Trément transfering from Pisa to Leicester from February to June 1995 for this purpose. Each Research Fellow contributed an introductory paper to their Colloqium identifying the major strengths and weakness of current methodologies in their area of specialism, and has provided the supplementary information for the Manual of Best Practice. They also undertook field research that is published as separate Colloquia contributions and/or in publications on specific projects.

THE POPULUS COLLOQUIA

The five Colloquia took place on 13–16 October (Aix), 6–8 November (Leicester), 25–26 November (Durham), 1–3 December (Siena) and 4–6 December (Pisa) in 1995. Each Working Party coordinator was successful in obtaining limited additional funds locally (university, local administration etc) or nationally to augment the POPULUS budget for the travel and accommodation costs of speakers, and the Project Coordinator also secured a grant of £500 from the British Academy towards the travel costs of a speaker from the US attending the Leicester and Durham Colloquia. The Colloquia were structured to enhance debate amongst the different EU traditions of landscape archaeology. All papers were pre-circulated, and the main focus for each paper at most of the Colloquia was a presentation not by the authors of the paper but by a discussant from another country, followed by a brief response by the author(s) and then an open debate amongst the Colloquium participants. All five colloquia were characterized by vigorous but positive and friendly debate, and the papers were re-written by their authors in the light of the discussions and the general themes and issues that emerged.

THE POPULUS VOLUMES

The five Colloquia are being published as a series by Oxbow Books under the title *Mediterranean Landscapes,* with Graeme Barker and David Mattingly as Series Editors. The five volumes are: *1. Reconstructing Past Population Trends in Mediterranean Europe (3000 BC – AD 1800)* edited by John Bintliff and Kostas Sbonias; *2. Environmental Reconstruction in Mediterranean Landscape Archaeology* edited by Philippe Leveau, Frédéric Trément, Kevin Walsh and Graeme Barker; *3. Geographical Information Systems and Landscape Archaeology* edited by Mark Gillings, David Mattingly and Jan van Dalen; *4. Non-Destructive Techniques Applied to Landscape Archaeology* edited by Marinella Pasquinucci and Frédéric Trément; and *5. Extracting Meaning from Ploughsoil Assemblages* edited by Riccardo Francovich and Helen Patterson. The POPULUS volumes bring together a remarkable array of EU expertise in current approaches to Mediterranean landscape archaeology: the papers present the researches of 30 British, 4 German, 6 Dutch, 27 French, 4 Greek, 35 Italian, 8 Slovenian, and 6 Spanish scholars, as well as those of 11 Canadian/US scholars working in the region. They bridge the disciplinary and national boundaries that have mitigated against the development of a coherent methodology in Mediterranean landscape archaeology. The contents are as follows:

1. Reconstructing Past Population Trends in Mediterranean Europe (3000 BC – AD 1800)

edited by John Bintliff and Kostas Sbonias

ARCHAEOLOGICAL SURVEY AND DEMOGRAPHY:

1. *Introduction to issues in demography and survey.* Kostas Sbonias.
2. *Regional field surveys and population cycles.* John Bintliff.
3. *Counting people in an artefact-poor landscape: the Langadas case, Macedonia, Greece.* Stelios Andreou and Kostas Kotsakis.
4. *Demographic trends from archaeological survey: case studies from the Levant and Near East.* Tony Wilkinson.
5. *Archaeological proxy-data for demographic reconstructions: facts, factoids or fiction?* John Chapman.
6. *An attempt at the demographic interpretation of long-term settlement processes in the prehistory of Slovenia: the case of the 'archaeological map of Slovenia'.* Predrag Novaković.
7. *Prospection archéologique et démographie en Provence: approche paléodémographique de la Rive Occidentale de l'Etang de Berre sur la longue durée.* Frédéric Trément.
8. *Demography and Romanization in central Italy.* Franco Cambi.
9. *Beyond historical demography: the contribution of archaeological survey.* Simon Stoddart.

INTERDISCIPLINARY APPROACHES:

10. *Chance and the human population: population growth in the Mediterranean.* Ezra Zubrow and Jennifer Robinson.
11. *The potential of historical demography for regional studies.* Malcolm Smith.
12. *Clearing away the cobwebs: a critical perspective on historical sources for Roman population history.* Tim Parkin.
13. *The population of Roman Italy in town and country.* Elio Lo Cascio.
14. *Documentary sources for the history of medieval settlements in Tuscany.* Maria Ginatempo and Andrea Giorgi.
15. *The Ottoman Imperial Registers: central Greece and northern Bulgaria in the 15th–19th centuries – the demographic development of two areas compared.* Machiel Kiel.
16. *Investigating the interface between regional survey, historical demography and palaeodemography.* Kostas Sbonias.
17. *The contribution of palaeoanthropology to regional demographic history.* C. A. Marlow.
18. *Problems and prospects in palaeodemography.* Claude Masset.
19. *Relating cemetery studies to regional survey: Rocca San Silvestro, a case study.* Riccardo Francovich and Kathy Gruspier.
20. *Counting heads: an overview.* Jeremy Paterson.

2. Environmental Reconstruction in Mediterranean Landscape Archaeology

edited by Philippe Leveau, Frédéric Trément, Kevin Walsh and Graeme Barker

1. *Mediterranean landscape archaeology and environmental reconstruction.* K. Walsh
2. *Landscape archaeology and reconstruction of the Mediterranean environment based on palynology.* S. Bottema
3. *A computerized database for the palynological recording of human activity in the Mediterranean basin.* V. Andrieu, E. Brugiapaglia, R. Cheddadi, M. Reille and J.-L. de Beaulieu
4. *Reconstructing vegetation and landscapes in the Mediterranean: the contribution of anthracology.* J.-L. Vernet
5. *Some examples of climatic reconstruction in the Mediterranean using dendroclimatology.* F. Guibal
6. *Geomorphological techniques in Mediterranean landscape archaeology.* A. G. Brown
7. *L'apport de la micromorphologie des sols à la reconstitution des paléopaysages (Application au bassin méditerranéen pour la période 3000 av. J. C. – 1800 ap. J. C.).* N. Fédoroff
8. *Reconstructing past soil environments in the Mediterranean region.* R. S. Shiel
9. *Energy dispersive X-ray micro-analysis and the geochemistry of soil sediments.* D. D. Gilbertson and J. P. Grattan
10. *Searching for the ports of Troy.* E. Zangger, M. Timpson, S. Yazvenko and H. Leiermann
11. *Case studies from the Pontine region in central Italy on settlement and environmental change in the first millennium BC.* P. Attema, J. Delvigne and B. J. Haagsma
12. *Karst dolinas: evidence of population pressure and exploitation of agricultural resources in karstic landscapes.* P. Novaković, H. Simoni and B. Mušič
13. *Archeologia ambientale padana: un caso di studio – la pianura padana centrale tra il Bronzo medio ed il Bronzo finale (xvi–xiii sec. a. C.).* M. Cremaschi.
14. *Human impacts and natural characteristics of the ancient ports of Marseille and Fos, Provence, southern France.* C. Vella, C. Morhange and M. Provansal
15. *Developing a methodological approach to the evolution of field systems in the middle Rhône valley.* J.-F. Berger and C. Jung

16. *Progradación fluvial y cambios en la línea de costa en época histórica en el Golfo de Valencia (España).* P. Carmona
17. *The integration of historical, archaeological and palaeoenvironmental data at the regional scale: the Vallée des Baux, southern France.* P. Leveau
18. *The integration of historical, archaeological and palaeoenvironmental data at the regional scale: the Étang de Berre, southern France.* F. Trément
19. *Geoarchaeology in Mediterranean landscape archaeology: Concluding comments.* G. Barker and J. Bintliff.

3. Geographical Information Systems and Landscape Archaeology

edited by Mark Gillings, David Mattingly and Jan van Dalen

1. *Introduction* Mark Gillings and David Mattingly.

GIS AND ARCHAEOLOGY

2. *Geographical Information Systems: today and tomorrow?* Peter F. Fisher.

GIS AND ARCHAEOLOGICAL THEORY

3. *GIS and landscapes of perception* Robert Witcher
4. *Cartography and landscape perception: a case study from central Italy* Peter Attema.

THEORY AND METHOD

5. *Regional survey and GIS: the Boeotia Project* Mark Gillings and Kostas Sbonias
6. *Towards a methodology for modelling surface survey data: the Sangro Valley Project* Gary Lock, Tyler Bell and John Lloyd
7. *Between spaces: interpolation in archaeology* Jennifer M. Robinson and Ezra Zubrow.

GIS AND FIELD SURVEY DATA

8. *GIS-based analysis of the population trends on the island of Brač in central Dalmatia* Zoran Stančič and Vincent Gaffney
9. *Analyzing Rome's hinterland* Martin Belcher, Andrew Harrison and Simon Stoddart
10. *Reconstructing the population history of the Albegna Valley and Ager Cosanus, Tuscany, Italy, in the Etruscan period* Philip Perkins.

DEVELOPING TECHNIQUES AND APPROACHES:

11. *Probability modelling: a Bayesian and a geometric example* Jan van Dalen
12. *Multispectral classification of satellite images* Krištof Oštir, Zoran Stančič and Majda Trušnovec
13. *Geographic Information Systems and archaeology: methodological aspects of the presentation and display of results* Javier Baena Preysler, Concepcion Blasco, Javier Espiago, Alberto Rio

4. Non-Destructive Techniques Applied to Landscape Archaeology

edited by Marinella Pasquinucci and Frédéric Trément

1. *L'apport des méthodes non destructives à l'analyse des sites archéologiques: le point de vue de l'archéologue.* F. Trément.

REMOTE SENSING

2. *Télédétection et archéologie. Concepts fondamentaux, état de l'art et exemples.* B. Marcolongo and E. Barisano.
3. *Environmental studies through active and passive airborne remote sensing systems.* R. M. Cavalli, C. M. Marino and S. Pignatti.
4. *Metodi di telerilevamento in archeometria e nella diagnostica non invasiva.* A. Tonelli.
5. *Aerial archaeology around the Mediterranean.* B. Jones.
6. *Détection aérienne des camps néolithiques en Languedoc occidental.* J. Vaquer.
7. *La restitution des parcellaires anciens et des limitations antiques à partir des techniques de la télédétection et du traitement d'images.* D. Charraut and F. Favory.
8. *Digital classification and visualization systems of archaeological landscapes.* M. Forte.

GEOPHYSICS

9. *The IGAPS Project: integrated geophysical acquisition and processing system for cultural heritage.* D. Patella, S. Piro, L. Versino, F. Cammarano, R. Di Maio and P. Mauriello.
10. *La mesure de la résistivité (ou de la conductivité) électrique du sol en prospection archéologique.* A. Hesse.
11. *Magnetic techniques applied to archaeological survey.* D. Jordan.

5. Extracting Meaning from Ploughsoil Assemblages

edited by Riccardo Francovich and Helen Patterson

18. *Terracotta and its territory: a tormented relationship.* Franco Cambi.
19. *The Adriatic Islands Project: contact, commerce and commercialization.* Vincent Gaffney, Branco Kirigin, John W. Hayes, and Peter Leach.
20. *De la fouille à la prospection, et retour: céramologie et histoire du peuplement dans la cité de Nimes.* Claude Raynaud.
21. *Il rapporto fra superficie e sottosuolo; dal survey allo scavo: insediamento e circolazione ceramica fra V e X secolo nella Toscana centro-meridionale.* Riccardo Francovich and Marco Valenti.
22. *Reconstructing the classical landscape with figures: some interpretive explorations in North-West Keos.* Todd Whitelaw.
23. *Demographic trends: the contribution of regional survey data.* John Bintliff and Kostas Sbonias.
24. *Conclusion.* Susan E. Alcock, Franco Cambi, Simon Keay, and Claude Raynaud.

SCIENTIFIC OUTCOMES

All five working groups in the POPULUS network were able to agree on areas of best practice, whilst eschewing the idea of a 'cookbook' approach to methodologies in landscape archaeology, the results of which have been incorporated into the Manual of Best Practice that is currently in the final stages of completion. Its future use by Community archaeologists working in Mediterranean landscape archaeology will be the ultimate test of the effectiveness of the POPULUS project in integrating the best of the diversity of current methodologies in the discipline.

During the discussions of the Working Parties, several alternative views were expressed about the way regional archaeological research and landscape archaeology should be conducted. At one end of the spectrum were some archaeologists who advocated that they (the archaeologists) should enlist a battery of natural scientists and tap into their results for the purpose of understanding the environmental context of an excavation or survey record. At the other end of the spectrum were some geographers who proposed that they (the scientists) should run the regional archaeological projects, the head scientist being partnered by an archaeologist. As Graeme Barker and John Bintliff comment at the end of the Aix-en-Provence volume *Mediterranean Landscape Archaeology 2*, the conclusion from the Colloquia is that both these positions lack one fundamental component: where do we find the interpretative approaches for the human-landscape interaction that constitutes the prime reason that these many specialists are working alongside each other? The work of the POPULUS network has emphasized the enormous potential of effective partnerships between broad-based teams of geoarchaeologists and modern intensive survey teams. Reconstructing the history of Mediterranean landscape change and demography certainly needs natural scientists to analyze the changing forms of the landscape, and archaeologists to analyze changing settlement morphologies and systems. To *understand* that history, however, in terms of the interactions between landscape and people, and the perceptions, choices and adaptations that have underpinned human actions, will need effective partnerships between broad-based teams of archaeologists, geoarchaeologists, historians, and anthropologists. The greatest challenge of inter-disciplinary landscape archaeology in the Mediterranean in the coming years will be how to bridge the divide between the ecological approaches of the natural sciences to past landscapes, on the one hand, and the concerns of social archaeologists on the other with the interface between human actions and landscape.

In terms of modelling major trends in Mediterranean landscape history, one consistent theme for teams working in the eastern and western Mediterranean emerging from the POPULUS network is evidence for settlement shifts, population increase and agricultural intensification in the third millennium BC, and the extent to which these changes coincide with and are related to marked increases in the scale of human impact on sediments and vegetation and/or with climatic change. Regional inter-disciplinary landscape projects are also contributing as profoundly to our understanding of the impact of Roman imperial expansion and subsequent Romanization on the human and natural landscapes of the Mediterranean. Another central concern is the relative impact of climatic fluctuations and human impact in terms of dramatic environmental change: here, one significant weakness of current work is the lack of emphasis on investigating the prehistory and history of Mediterranean uplands. Some of the major landscape changes we can now detect in the Mediterranean region were the result of gradual long-term processes, others may have been caused by catastrophic events of short duration and very long recurrence intervals. The widespread application of dating techniques such as luminescence and palaeomagnetism in the coming years is likely to have an enormous impact in this respect: more refined chronologies seem likely to emphasize different rates of landscape change rather than uniformity, with profound implications for our understanding of human interactions with their landscape.

ENVIRONMENTAL RECONSTRUCTION IN MEDITERRANEAN LANDSCAPE ARCHAEOLOGY

Environmental Reconstruction in Mediterranean Landscape Archaeology

Edited by
Philippe Leveau, Frédéric Trément,
Kevin Walsh and Graeme Barker

Oxbow Books
1999

Published by
Oxbow Books, Park End Place, Oxford OX1 1HN

ISBN 1 900188 63 5

This book is available direct from

Oxbow Books, Park End Place, Oxford OX1 1HN
(Phone: 01865–241249; Fax: 01865–794449)

and

The David Brown Book Company
PO Box 511, Oakville, CT 06779, USA
(Phone: 860–945–9329; Fax: 860–945–9468)

or from our website

www.oxbowbooks.com

Printed in Great Britain at
The Alden Press
Oxford

Contents

List of Figures

List of Tables

Addresses of Contributors

Valérie Andrieu, Institut Méditerranéen d'Ecologie et de Paléoécologie (I.M.E.P.), U.R.A. C.N.R.S. 1152, Case 451, F - 13397 Marseille Cedex 20, France

Peter Attema, Rijksuniversiteit Groningen (RUG), Department of Archaeology, Poststraat 6, 9712 ER Groningen, Netherlands

Marcel Barbero, Institut Méditerranéen d'Ecologie et de Paléoécologie (I.M.E.P.), U.R.A. C.N.R.S. 1152, Case 451, F - 13397 Marseille Cedex 20 , France

Graeme Barker, School of Archaeological Studies, University of Leicester, Leicester LE1 7RH, UK

Jacques-Louis de Beaulieu, Institut Méditerranéen d'Ecologie et de Paléoécologie (I.M.E.P.), U.R.A. C.N.R.S. 1152, Case 451, F - 13397 Marseille Cedex 20, France

Jean-François Berger, AFAN-TGV Méditerranée and USR 708, CRA du CNRS, Sophia-Antipolis, Avenue A. Einstein, 06560 Valbonne, France

John Bintliff, Department of Archaeology, University of Durham, South Road, Durham DH1 3LE, UK

Sytze Bottema, Rijksuniversiteit Groningen, Biologisch Archaeologisch Instituut, Poststraat 6, 9712 ER Groningen, Netherlands

Anthony Brown, Department of Geography, University of Exeter, Exeter EX4 4RJ, UK

Elisabetta Brugiapaglia, Institut Méditerranéen d'Ecologie et de Paléoécologie (I.M.E.P.), U.R.A. C.N.R.S. 1152, Case 451, F - 13397 Marseille Cedex 20, France

Pilar Carmona, Departamento de Geografía, Universitat de València, Apdo. 22060, 46080 Valencia, Spain

Rachid Cheddadi, Institut Méditerranéen d'Ecologie et de Paléoécologie (I.M.E.P.), U.R.A. C.N.R.S. 1152, Case 451, F - 13397 Marseille Cedex 20 , France

Mauro Cremaschi, Centro di Geodinamica Alpina e Quaternaria, Dipartimento di Scienze della Terra, Via Mangiagalli 34, 20133 Milan, Italy

Jan Delvigne, Rijksuniversiteit Groningen (RUG), Department of Physical Geography, Kerklaan 30, 9751 NN, Haren, Netherlands

Nicolas Féderoff, Science des Sols et Hydrologie, INA P-G, 78850 Thiverval-Grignon, France

David Gilbertson, Institute of Geography and Earth Sciences, University of Wales Aberystwyth, Penglais, Aberystwyth, Dyfed SY23 3DB, Wales, UK

John Grattan, Institute of Geography and Earth Sciences, University of Wales Aberystwyth, Penglais, Aberystwyth, Dyfed SY23 3DB, Wales, UK

Frédéric Guibal, Institut Méditerranéen d'Ecologie et de Paléoécologie, E.R.S. 6100 CNRS, Case 451, Avenue Escadrille Normandie-Niemen, 13397 Marseille Cedex 20, France

Berndt-Jan Haagsma, Rijksuniversiteit Groningen (RUG), Department of Archaeology, Poststraat 6, 9712 ER Groningen, Netherlands

Antoinette Hesnard, Centre Camille Jullian (Unité Mixte de Recherche 6573 Université de Provence-CNRS), Maison Méditerranéenne des Sciences de l'Homme, 5 Rue du Château de l'Horloge, BP 647, 13094 Aix-en-Provence, France

Cécile Jung, AFAN-TGV Méditerranée and UMR 9966, University of Tours, Place A. France, 37000 Tours, France

Jacques Laborel, Laboratoire de Biologie Marine et d'Ecologie du Benthos, EP CNRS 75 Département des Sciences de la Mer, Luminy, 13288 Marseille, France

Horst Leiermann, W.-Bernsau-Weg 56, D–45239 Essen-Werden, Germany

Philippe Leveau, Centre Camille Jullian (Unité Mixte de Recherche 6573 Université de Provence-CNRS), Maison Méditerranéenne des Sciences de l'Homme, 5 Rue du Château de l'Horloge, BP 647, 13094 Aix-en-Provence, France

David Mattingly, School of Archaeological Studies, University of Leicester, Leicester LE1 7RH, UK

Christophe Morhange, CEREGE CNRS, Institut de Géographie, Université Aix-Marseille, Marseille, France

Branko Mušič, Department of Archaeology, University of Ljubljana, PP 580, 1001 Ljubljana, Slovenia

Predrag Novaković, Department of Archaeology, University of Ljubljana, PP 580, 1001 Ljubljana, Slovenia

Philippe Ponel, Institut Méditerranéen d'Ecologie et de Paléoécologie (I.M.E.P.), U.R.A. C.N.R.S. 1152, Case 451, F - 13397 Marseille Cedex 20, France

Mireille Provansal, CEREGE CNRS, Institut de Géographie, Université Aix-Marseille, Marseille, France

Maurice Reille, Institut Méditerranéen d'Ecologie et de Paléoécologie (I.M.E.P.), U.R.A. C.N.R.S. 1152, Case 451, F - 13397 Marseille Cedex 20, France

Robert Shiel, Agriculture Department, University of Newcastle upon Tyne, Newcastle upon Tyne NE1 7RU, UK

Helene Simoni, Department of Archaeology, University of Ljubljana, PP 580, 1001 Ljubljana, Slovenia

Michael E. Timpson, 305 Eagandale Place, #338, Eagan, MN 55121, USA

Frédéric Trément, Département d'Histoire, Université Blaise-Pascal (Clermont-Ferrand II), 29 Bd Gergovia, 63037 Clermont Ferrand, France

Claude Vella, URA 903 CNRS, Institut de Géographie, Université Aix-Marseille, Marseille, France

Jean-Louis Vernet, Laboratoire de Paléoenvironnements, Anthracologie et Action de l'Homme, Institut de Botanique, Université de Montpellier II Sciences et Techniques du Languedoc, 34095 Montpellier Cedex 05, France

Kevin Walsh, Centre Camille Jullian (Unité Mixte de Recherche 6573 Université de Provence-CNRS), Maison Méditerranéenne des Sciences de l'Homme, 5 Rue du Château de l'Horloge, BP 647, 13094 Aix-en-Provence, France

Sergei B. Yazvenko, LGL Limited, Environmental Research Associates, 9768 Second Street, Sidney V8L 3Y8, British Columbia, Canada

Eberhardt Zangger, Geoarchaeology International, Fliederstr. 21, CH-8006 Zürich, Switzerland

1. Mediterranean Landscape Archaeology and Environmental Reconstruction

Kevin Walsh

INTRODUCTION

This chapter is by way of an introduction to the proceedings of the POPULUS colloquium on environmental reconstruction in Mediterranean landscape archaeology. It considers briefly some of the foundations of the subject, and then goes onto discuss some general approaches and problematics that are dealt with in greater detail in the subsequent chapters.

This part of the POPULUS project was concerned primarily with the reconstruction of past environments (i.e. past geomorphological and palaeoecological processes) rather than the specific reconstruction of economic and subsistence strategies through the study of faunal remains. However, it is obviously realized that certain types of faunal evidence do yield important ecological evidence (Vigne and Vallades, 1996).

The POPULUS project is primarily concerned with the application of methodologies in *landscape* archaeology. This part of the project concentrates on those areas of environmental archaeology that aim to 'reconstruct' natural landscapes. At its most simplistic level we can say that we are not concerned with single, spatial and temporal, point-studies or even site-based archaeology, although such operations do constitute elements within landscape projects. In reality, we are concerned with environmental and human (cultural, ideological, economic) processes that are both diachronic and cover an often undefinable spatial area. In many ways it is the indeterminacy of our spatial boundaries that is our greatest problem, as well as the more fundamental definition of landscape itself. However, for the archaeologist, we can broadly define landscape as a spatial and temporal context in which the vestiges of historically-connected communities existed. Such communities interacted with one another at ideological, cultural and economic levels. All of these human processes had, and continue to have, a direct impact on the natural environment. This definition of 'a landscape' is open to debate, and is considered to some extent later in this chapter.

LANDSCAPE RECONSTRUCTION IN THE MEDITERRANEAN

Environmental archaeology (which employs and integrates palaeoecology and geomorphology among other environmental sciences) enjoyed its early successes in northern European and American countries and despite the fact that we can learn a lot from the strategies employed therein, the problems of environmental reconstruction in the Mediterranean often require a different approach. At a fundamental level there is a taphonomic question that is radically different from that in more northern latitudes. This taphonomic phenomenon is a direct function of climatic and geomorphological processes (and their related floral and faunal communities) that are peculiar to this region.

What I offer here is a very generalized introduction to the proceedings. This chapter considers the principal methodologies used in environmental reconstruction in Mediterranean landscape archaeology. It then goes on to discuss some of the fundamental issues that relate to our research area.

Site Catchment Analysis

There can be little doubt that one of the most influential approaches in modern Mediterranean landscape archaeology has been that of Site Catchment Analysis (SCA). In their discussion of SCA, Vita-Finzi and Higgs (1970) promoted the investigation of resource potential within a spatial context that would have been easily accessible to its occupants. Crucial to the SCA approach is the assessment of the characteristics of the natural resources extant within the catchment area (Fig. 1.1). This approach to understanding settlement patterns and the nature of environmental exploitation during the past (especially during the prehistoric period) has been extremely influential. Many of the strategies employed by landscape archaeologists in the Mediterranean have been either explicitly or implicitly directed by this approach. As Ammerman observes, site catchment analysis should not be considered as a technique or a method, it should in fact be considered as a model in disguise (1985: 29).

Land quality or potential

An important element of the SCA approach is the soil and vegetation survey. These have been very popular in Mediterranean landscape archaeology. More often than not, soil surveys commence with basic taxonomic classification. Often this classification includes the identification of the order, i.e. Alfisols through to Vertisols, and the identification of the soil type, e.g. Rendzina. Such an approach will usually include a description of the related geomorphology. Rudimentary chemical analyses of soils are also carried out, such as the measurements of pH and organic content for example (for a discussion of pedological approaches in landscape archaeology see Shiel, Chapter 8 in this volume, and for an equivalent discussion of geomorphological methodologies see Brown, Chapter 6).

Probably the most sophisticated example of a soil survey (or land potential) approach is the research carried out by Chapman and Shiel (1993). This project aimed to understand the nature of environmental change and human settlement in northern Dalmatia during the last 12,000 years. As with many other landscape projects, the environmental work considered the modern characteristics of soils in the survey area. The interpretation of this data included analyses of climatic changes for the study period and discussions of the probable effects of these climatic variations on the region's soils. Patterns of settlement for the different chronological periods (from the Mesolithic through to the Roman period) were then related to the (possible) variations in quality of the different soil types in the study area.

A complimentary approach to the soil survey is the vegetation survey. Examples of this approach can be found in many Mediterranean surveys (see Hope-Simpson, 1983, for an example). The vegetation survey usually comprises the mapping of present species across the survey area. As well as giving ecological information it can also indicate the potential of floral resources within an area. Certain types of vegetation patterning may also indicate the presence of archaeological sites, as buried remains may influence growth patterns.

It is obvious that a study of the modern environment is important as its state should be treated as the most recent succession phase in that environment's history. However, the study of the modern environment does not always inform us as to the precise nature of earlier stages in that locality's environmental history. We need to consider the *differences* between modern land potential and past land potential. For example, if we were to carry out a survey in a recently formed dune system and classify the land quality and use patterns accordingly, what could this tell us about past exploitation of this locality? Emphasis needs to be placed on the study of environmental change, or the reconstruction of past environmental contexts.

Palaeoecological studies

More and more landscape projects during the last twenty years or so have included work on palaeoenvironmental reconstruction. However, even a cursory review of the literature would reveal that the majority of the environmental archaeological research carried out in recent years in the Mediterranean has been geomorphological. Pure palaeoecological research (usually palynological) is widespread, but much of this palaeoecological work has been carried out in isolation from archaeological research. There are many reasons for this. For example, much of the palynological work in the Mediterranean up until relatively recently, has been more concerned with the study of vegetation sequences during the Pleistocene and the transition to the Holocene without recourse to anthropogenic influences (for a review of some of the palynological work carried out in the Mediterranean, see Andrieu *et al.,* Chapter 3). Another problem has been (and still is to a certain extent) that palynologists have been reluctant to carry out work on pollen from archaeological sediments which are considered as being too disturbed. Therefore, the possibility of making comparisons between 'natural' and archaeological pollen assemblages has been limited. However, the utility of such an approach has been well demonstrated in northern Europe where a number of projects have included the comparison of pollen assemblages from orthodox lake cores with specific pollen assemblages from dated buried soils (for examples see Bradshaw, 1991, and also Edwards, 1991a,1991b).

One other important area of debate is the role of pollen indicators. Many practitioners explicitly use the indicators as originally defined by Behre (1981). In many instances these are undoubtedly useful. However, in southern Europe the usefulness of anthropogenic indicators as initially outlined by Behre is debatable: Behre was originally discussing their use in central Europe where many of the species considered as indicators were actually introduced by humans from the Mediterranean area. However, subsequently Behre has completed similar research for part of the Mediterranean (1990) (see also Bottema, Chapter 2).

There are of course other forms of palaeoecological study which are useful to landscape archaeology. In the Mediterranean, which is well known for its limestone landscapes, molluscan analysis is potentially very important. Despite the obvious potential for this discipline, it has been surprisingly underexploited in the region. Where studies have been carried out they have often been within the context of pure (palaeo)ecological research. Molluscan analyses carried out in association with landscape archaeological survey have been very rare. One exception is the work carried out in the Montagnola Senese, Italy, where molluscan studies were carried out in conjunction with research into erosion histories (Hunt *et al.*, 1992).

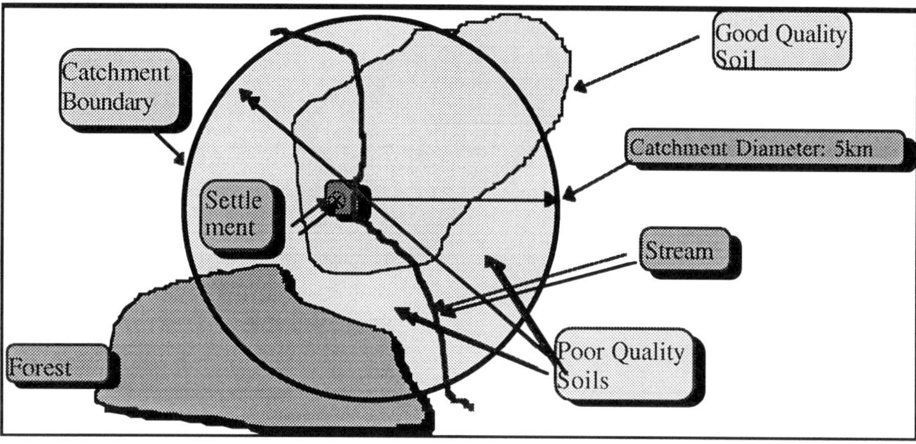

Figure 1.1. Representations of a Site Catchment.

Geomorphological studies

There can be little doubt that geomorphological studies have been the basis of much of the environmental reconstruction carried out in Mediterranean landscape archaeology. It is important that we consider the reasons for the supremacy of this type of environmental study. At one level there are the taphonomic reasons: palaeoecological evidence (mainly pollen) is not preserved as extensively as in more northern latitudes. Secondly, sedimentation processes are of major significance in most Mediterranean environments, and in many ways, such processes are the most obvious and dramatic of all the environmental processes in the regions under consideration.

Much of the geomorphological work carried out in the Mediterranean (especially that which is integrated with archaeological survey) has been profoundly influenced by the original work of Vita-Finzi. His book *The Mediterranean Valleys: Geological Changes in Historical Times* (1969) is arguably the most influential work on Mediterranean palaeoenvironments. This is not the place to re-cover the well-trodden ground of the debate regarding the nature and causes of the Younger Fill, but it must be said that this debate has in some ways influenced the direction (both in terms of strategies and methodologies) of geomorphological and geoarchaeological research in the Mediterranean. Questions relating to periods of soil and sediment stability and instability, and the possibility of either climatic or anthropogenic causes (or both) for these varying states, are key in our area of research. These debates relate directly to POPULUS' fundamental theme, that of demographic change, and the nature of environmental and human-population dynamics.

Geomorphological approaches are an important element of environmental reconstruction in the Mediterranean and consequently constitute an important part of this volume. The contribution of geographers from the Université d'Aix-Marseille in this field is well known within the Mediterranean and is also increasingly recognized in the English-speaking scientific community.

The geoarchaeological work carried out in the Mediterranean has been crucial to our understanding of human/environment interactions. The nature and timing of stability and instability in Mediterranean sediment regimes have been elucidated by the work carried out as a part of landscape archaeology projects. There is a thriving debate regarding this problem, with many practitioners now questioning the original scheme of Vita-Finzi's Younger Fill hypothesis. For example, van Andel *et al.* (1990) have demonstrated that erosional events Greece are far more varied across time and space than was originally thought. The role of human action in the landscape is considered as the key element rather than changes in climate.

Geomorphological and geoarchaeological work has become such an important part of Mediterranean landscape archaeology that it is now recognized that many fundamental archaeological questions cannot be answered without a coherent geoarchaeological programme. Zangger *et al.* (Chapter 10) demonstrate this point effectively.

Archaeozoology

Despite the fact we are concerned largely with palaeoenvironmental reconstruction, archaeozoology does make a contribution to this endeavour. Archaeozoological research can inform us as to the nature of certain types of human impact on an environment. The introduction of domesticates, and the appearance of 'wild' mammals associated with agro-pastoral systems, are clearly crucial developments in any environment's history (see Vigne and Vallades, 1996; Vigne *et al.*, 1994: 242–3). In a northern European context, Evans and Rose have shown how small vertebrate bones (extracted from raptor pellets) can compliment molluscan data, which tend to be relevant only for the ecologies of microhabitats (1992).

A DIVERSITY OF APPROACHES

Part of the rationale behind the POPULUS project was the comparison of the different approaches used by the various teams of researchers working in the Mediterranean. The aim of this study is to demonstrate the potential of different approaches and allow us to propose a set of 'best practices'. Obviously, there is no one group of researchers that has a monopoly on 'best practices'. What we do have at the moment is a series of practices that differ to a certain extent and possess different strengths and weaknesses. One of the main problems is the lack of a coherent approach where methodologies and consequently, data, are always compatible and/or comparable across different research projects.

One important difference that exists between some countries is the presence and absence of environmental archaeology as a coherent discipline, whether as an academic subject taught in universities, or as a discipline practised in the field. For example, much French environmental archaeology and geoarchaeology is based on co-operation between archaeologists and specialists such as physical geographers, palaeoecologists, palaeoentomologists etc.. This is true everywhere, but the point is that the lack of an established, coherent bridging discipline (in this instance environmental archaeology) may bring about conflicts of interest if specialists have no background in archaeology itself. More often than not environmental scientists have a different agenda to that of landscape archaeologists: temporal and spatial scales of interest are often different. For example, an archaeologist interested in an iron age landscape may be working with a geomorphologist who is interested in the identification of the transition to the Holocene in the sedimentary record.

There are, however, environmental specialisms which are strongly (if not, entirely) oriented towards archaeological problems. One such discipline is anthracology, the study of carbonized wood remains which has been applied with enormous success by French specialists in the south of France (see Vernet, 1991 and Chapter 4).

Many archaeological projects carried out in the Mediterranean have derived scientific competence as a result of multi-national co-operation. This is certainly true of a number of projects that have taken place in Italy and Greece. One such example is the Thermopylae Geoarchaeological Project which shows how the pass (the site of the famous battle between the Spartans and the Persians) has changed greatly since this event, and indeed before. The study included the analysis of material from seven core holes and the consideration of local sea- level data (Kraft *et al.*, 1987).

Much Italian geoarchaeology employs similar strategies and methods to those used by northern European practitioners. Any differences that do exist are those based on the exigencies posed by different taphonomic problems. Cremaschi's work is a good example of the Italian approach to geoarchaeology. Cremaschi's work on the Po plain has also been concerned with the study of Roman land surfaces and the development of centuriation. The most interesting study undertaken as part of this work is the analysis of the Santa Rosa ditch fill (1992: 127). The geomorphological work revealed increased sedimentation rates during the early medieval period, whilst the pollen work indicated forest regeneration in a wet environment.

In Spain environmental archaeology has been extensively employed on prehistoric projects. Lopez and Lopez' palynological study of material from archaeological sediments from megalithic tombsof the 4th-3rd millennia BC is an important example of the utility of archaeological palynology (1993). These studies give us a clear idea of the vegetational characteristics of an archaeological site just prior to, and probably contemporary with, its use. It should be pointed out that, unlike much palynology in the Mediterranean, this study is concerned with pollen from *archaeological* sediments. In terms of Spanish geoarchaeological research, the work of Carmona is clearly important, as she has worked a great deal with archaeologists including those researching classical antiquity and the early historic period (see for example Carmona, 1991 and Chapter 15).

It is apparent that certain techniques are more popular with different groups of researchers. For example, a number of Italian studies has made excellent use of micromorphology, while this technique has not been used as extensively in Spain. Archaeological palynology has been used with great success in a number of Spanish examples but has not been exploited to the same extent in other Mediterranean countries. One technique which seems to be absent in Spanish and Italian research is anthracology (charcoal analysis), a technique which along with malacology (molluscan analysis), is important in Southern France.

What is clear from this review is that the aims of most researchers are very similar. More often than not, environmental research is concerned with an assessment of sedimentary regimes (erosion/stability phases), the study of soil quality or potential, and the reconstruction of past vegetation patterns. Ultimately, the aim of such work is to assess the nature of the human/environment dialectic during the past: the impact of humans on the environment and of the environment on humans. However, despite having broadly similar aims, there are obvious differences in terms of the strategies and methodologies exploited for environmental reconstruction. A key issue for the POPULUS project was to identify strategies and methods which can be of utility in landscape archaeology and to demonstrate to archaeologists who are not involved in environmental research the potential of such an approach. As noted earlier, the absence of a clearly defined discipline (whether it be called environmental archaeology or not) in most of the countries in our study area is an issue. There is no one country which has a monopoly on 'excellent' environmental archaeology. Broadly speaking, most researchers involved in Mediterranean projects adopt similar methodologies, though certain methodologies are more refined and/or popular with certain groups of researchers than with others. However, what we must avoid is the homogenization of methodologies across the Mediterranean, as we may neglect the fact that certain approaches are more suitable than others in specific contexts. This discussion of the nature of environmental archaeology as it exists in different countries is important as we need to recognize that the environmental sciences as applied in archaeology do have particular problems to deal with that are not always the same as those, say, in mainstream physical geography or palaeoecology. One of the most important issues or problems in our subject is that of temporal and spatial scale.

LANDSCAPE ARCHAEOLOGY AND PROBLEMS OF SCALE

One of the key problems for Mediterranean landscape archaeology is the integration of different types of data, especially if we are trying to produce synthetic regional landscape studies where a wide range of methodological approaches (or even strategies) has been used. The final part of this chapter considers a fundamental issue for environmental reconstruction in landscape archaeology: that is, the recognition of the variation in the temporal and spatial scales at which different data types operate. Related to this problem is the problem of data compatibility and incompatibility.

An uncritical integration of varied data types is potentially dangerous. In certain situations such integration could involve the use of one type of data to reinforce another 'weaker' piece of evidence. For example, there are clear problems in integrating molluscan data with palynological evidence, as the two types of fossil operate at different spatial scales. Pollen can be transported over relatively great distances, whilst molluscs tend to remain within a confined area. A more fundamental problem is the relationship between these different data types and the archaeologist's definition of a landscape. Basically, we need to be sure of what it is that we are trying to reconstruct. It is this definition that will then influence the strategies and the range of methods that we ultimately go on to use.

Definitions of landscape

In defining 'landscape archaeology' Barker observes that there is no single accepted definition, but considers 'that for most British archaeologists the term has come to mean the archaeological study of the relationship of people to land in antiquity and more particularly of the relationships between people to land in the context of the environment they inhabited' (Barker, 1985: 1). In order to expand such a description, we might ask if a landscape ecological paradigm can be of utility in our attempts to define landscape in archaeology. Forman and Godron define an ecological landscape as '...a heterogeneous land area composed of a cluster of interacting ecosystems that is repeated in similar form throughout. Landscapes vary in size down to a few kilometres in diameter' (1986: 11). In essence a landscape is characterized by the repetition of ecosystem types that interact with one another across space (and logically also time). In contrast, a region 'is determined by a complex of climatic, physiographic, biological, economic, social and cultural characteristics....A region therefore almost always contains a number of landscapes' (Forman and Godron, 1986: 13). A region could contain a littoral zone, a flood plain zone or zones, prairie areas, agricultural zones and a mountainous zone. There is a major problem in adopting a landscape ecological approach in the study of archaeological/historical landscapes. If we are interested in past patterns of environmental exploitation and interaction, we cannot work with a definition of landscape which limits human activity to an area determined by the ecological characteristics described above. Humans tend to cross ecological/geomorphological boundaries for many different reasons. It is also recognized that 'ecological objects, however, continually move or flow between these landscape elements' (Forman and Godron, 1986: 25). Landscapes are defined by our own intuition, and whilst the patterning of environmental data (whether it be ecological and/or geomorphological) may be definable, and in some sense formal, it does not necessarily follow that the archaeological landscape and therefore past human behaviour are patterned in the same manner. Our definition of spatial boundaries and the different chronological periods of activity identified in such landscapes needs to be flexible and non-geometric.

If we accept that we cannot rigidly define our spatial and temporal limits when embarking on a landscape archaeological project, it is reasonable to attempt some kind of definition of these parameters, as we need to choose the methods which are most applicable to our project: the problem is often one of resolution. For example, a pollen diagram from a large lake with a concomitantly large catchment may be of little use to an archaeological project covering a small spatial area beyond the catchment of this lake. We need to recognize that we are employing methodologies from other disciplines whose scales of operation (both temporal and spatial) are very different from those aimed at by archaeologists. Very few environmental sciences are concerned with reconstructing spatial and temporal processes at the human scale. Some of these problems are considered by a number of contributors to this volume – Trément, for exampl((Chapter 17), considers the problems of integration and the problems of dating and the nature of spatial scales in landscape archaeology.

The issue of scale is clearly related to questions of

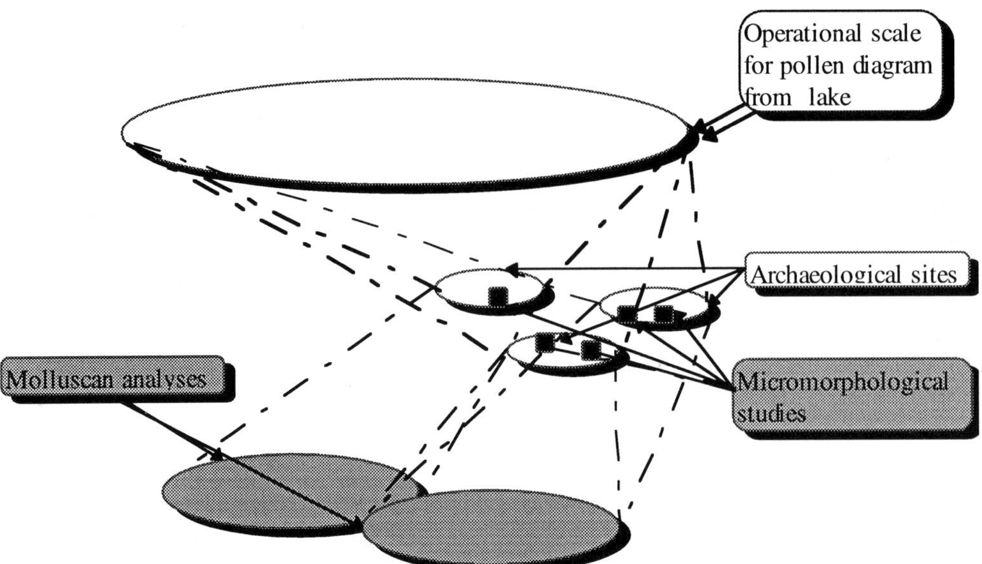

Figure 1.2. Abstract representations of the scale of operation of certain data types in relation to one another.

methodology: which techniques are suitable for what size of landscape or site? Issues of scale are also key to the integration of different data types: can a molluscan diagram from one study site be directly compared with a pollen diagram from a lake with a large catchment area (Fig. 1.2)?

One approach includes micro-scale studies of pollen from buried soils adjacent to the site as well as other types of proxy data from the micro-scale. Reliable regional environmental reconstruction '... can only be achieved through the compilation of numbers of detailed local studies' (Dincauze, 1987: 267). (For a discussion on spatial scale and palynology see Bradshaw, 1991, and also Edwards, 1991a and 1991b.) An equivalent pedological/ geomorphological technique that allows us to focus on such processes at this refined scale is micromorphology: this technique is discussed by Fédoroff (Chapter 7) and by Berger *et al.* (Chapter 14).

Temporal scales

As well as the problems of spatial scale and resolution, there are of course problems of temporal scale and resolution.

The nature of the chronological resolution available dictates to a certain extent the types of human/environmental processes that we can investigate. For example, there is the problem of recognising seasonal variations in climate, agricultural regimes and other seasonal impacts on the environment. Can we identify responses to short-term, high-magnitude events such as extreme storms or floods? There are some who consider that such extreme events are not important in the longer-term. However, there can be little doubt that human communities do respond to extreme events in some way. Even if a group of people return to a locality after an extreme event such as a flood or landslide, their returning is a calculated response and needs to be understood. Decisions to exploit the environment in a different manner after a high-magnitude event may have been taken and we need to identify these. But there is a problem in that we cannot easily identify such events and responses, or even the precise nature of the climatic cycles which are undoubtedly important in terms of human/environment interactions. Often, we can only identify cumulative processes and effects. One pertinent technique here in terms of climate reconstruction with a tight chronological resolution is dendro-climatology and chronology (see Guibal, Chapter 5). The work of Serre-Bachet *et al.* is of interest here, although most of their results only stretch to *c.*950 AD (1992). One interesting result of this work is the absence of evidence for the Little Ice Age in Spain (Serre-Brachet *et al.*, 1992: 361).

In many ways the problems of dating and scale are far more important than those of space. The advent of scientific dating methods after the war has led many archaeologists to believe that we now operate on the same level as the 'hard sciences'. Isotopic methods have given us a certain level of scientific maturity and even, complacency. However, we must question the ways in which such methods are employed and more importantly, how they are integrated with other data types. The ways in which we use isotopic dates are an important area for discussion. The problems of calibration and the statistical distributions of dates are of extreme importance, especially if we are researching the historical period, or making intra-site comparisons.

INTEGRATION AND THE REINFORCEMENT SYNDROME

An important issue for a discipline which exploits many varied methods and is truly multi-disciplinary, is that of data integration. The problem of the variation in spatial coverage and resolution of different data types used in landscape reconstruction has already been discussed. The issue of temporal scale has also been touched upon. Both of these issues become even more critical if we are employing documentary evidence in our research. In many ways written evidence is often the most attractive as it is usually securely dated, but it is in some ways the most dangerous type of data when we come to integrate it with other data types.

Palaeoenvironmental evidence can only provide generalized models of possible human activity in any given environment. Documentary evidence, on the other hand, is often too specific in as far as it cannot always be directly correlated spatially or temporally with proxy-environmental data. Documentary evidence can confirm or contradict any inferences made from the palaeoenvironmental data. Documents often relate to non-environmental interests, such as economic or political interests, and as such they cannot be used to support or even contradict proxy environmental data. Without going into a lengthy discussion of the problems associated with this form of data integration, all that we can say here is that such integration needs to be carried out in a rigorous and critical manner.

A number of the contributions to this volume discuss field projects that have integrated many varied data types. Leveau in Chapter 16 discusses the multi-disciplinary work that has been carried out across a number of sites from different periods in the Vallée des Baux in Provence, France.

Landscape types and methodological approaches

As well as considering the relationship between our methodologies and the scales at which we work, we should also be aware that certain landscape types (i.e. coast, mountain, karst, floodplain etc.) demand certain methodological approaches. At the outset of a landscape project we need to design our environmental strategy with the landscape type in mind. For example, the utility of planning for extensive palynological work for a dry karst area is questionable. However, as with any archaeological project, we need to prepare for unpredictability! We cannot anticipate with any real accuracy the range of methods that we will be able to apply to a given landscape type, but we can be reasonably sure of what 'stock-in-trade' methods are going to be useful.

The second part of this volume consists of a set of case studies, many of which consider environmental reconstruction in specific environment types. Attema *et al.* (Chapter 10) discuss their approach to a wetland zone (the Pontine region in central Italy). Novaković *et al.* (Chapter 12) discuss a landscape archaeological project that was undertaken in a karstic landscape. Berger and Jung (Chapter 14) discuss the application of a range of techniques (including micromorphology) to a complex mixed Mediterranean landscape that includes alluvial plains and Quaternary terraces amongst others.

The contribution by Vella *et al.* (Chapter 13) is representative of much of the work carried out by the geomorphologists from the Université de Provence, whose research on coastal change has continuously integrated and enhanced archaeological research in the French Mediterranean. Their discussion of approaches to Mediterranean coastlines (specifically ancient ports) is complimented by the contribution of Carmona (Chapter 15) who considers coastal change during the historic period in the Gulf of Valencia, Spain.

Although these case studies do not include all of the potential environment types that we might find in the Mediterranean, a broad range of methodological approaches is discussed and the range of procedures currently adopted by practitioners working in the European Mediterranean is represented.

CONCLUSIONS

The second part of this chapter has discussed some of the problems of data integration and the associated issues of spatial and temporal scales in landscape archaeology. The exploitation of data types that operate at a number of scales and different resolutions is in fact crucial to successful environmental reconstruction. What we need to be aware of is the uncritical integration of such data. The most important advantage of considering two very different types of data together is the fact that they allow us to consider processes at different scales. An approach which integrates data types from varied spatial scales is crucial to landscape archaeology: human activity takes place at different intensities, with varying impacts over different types of locality. Such a critique must include the analysis of problems of temporal and spatial scales, which in turn demands a thorough reflection on the strengths and weaknesses of each methodology exploited. A layered approach to landscape reconstruction is required, and as different problems are recognized during the period of a research programme we need to apply the relevant method that allows us to focus on specific questions. Flexibility in our methodological approaches is the key: if we decide at the planning stage of a project that we will carry out geomorphological and pedological mapping and take a pollen core if possible, and that is to be the extent of our environmental work, then we never answer all of the questions that a landscape poses. In fact we may never discover all of the questions!

During the colloquium a number of contributors discussed a wide range of approaches to landscape reconstruction. What became apparent during this meeting was that we require a framework or paradigm within which these methods of environmental reconstruction can be exploited usefully by archaeologists. At the moment there does not appear to be a strong cohesion between the different research groups and in the methods that they adopt. This may well impede useful dialogue between the different groups of researchers and retard the development of useful regional syntheses. As stated earlier, we are not arguing for an homogenization of methodological approaches, but rather a critical recognition of the strengths and weaknesses of different approaches and also a recognition of the importance of environmental reconstruction at the outset of all landscape archaeology projects.

REFERENCES

Ammerman, A.J. (1985) Modern land use versus the past: a case study from Calabria. In C. Malone and S. Stoddart (eds) *Papers in Italian Archaeology, part i, The Human Landscape*: 27–40. Oxford, British Archaeological Reports, International Series 243.

Barker, G. (1985) *Prehistoric Farming in Europe*. Cambridge, Cambridge University Press.

Behre, K.E. (1981) The interpretation of anthropogenic indicators in pollen diagrams. *Pollen et Spores* 23: 225–45.

Behre, K.E. (1990) Some reflections on anthropogenic indicators and the record of prehistoric occupation phases in pollen diagrams from the Near East. In S. Bottema, G. Entjes-Nieborg and W. van Zeist (eds) *Man's Role in the Shaping of the Eastern Mediterranean Landscape*: 219–230. Rotterdam, Balkema.

Bradshaw, R. (1991) Spatial scale in the pollen record. In D.R. Harris and K.D. Thomas (eds) *Modeling Ecological Change*, 41–52. London, Institute of Archaeology, UCL.

Carmona Gonzalez, P. (1991) Interpretataciùn paleohidrolùgica y geoarqueolùgica del substrato Romano y Musulmçn de la ciudad de Valencia. *Cuad de Geogr.* 49: 1–14.

Chapman, J. and Shiel, R. (1993) Social change and land use in prehistoric Dalmatia. *Proceedings of the Prehistoric Society* 59: 61–104.

Cremaschi, M., Marchetti, M. and Ravazzi, C. (1992) Gemorphological evidence for land surfaces cleared from forest in the central Po plain (northern Italy) during the Roman period. In B. Frenzel (ed.) *Evaluation of Land Surfaces Cleared from Forests in the Mediterranean Region during the Time of the Roman Empire* (ESF project European Palaeoclimate and Man 5): 119–132. Stuttgart, Fischer.

Dincauze, D.F. (1987) Strategies for palaeoenvironmental reconstruction in archaeology, *Advances in Archaeological Method and Theory* 11: 250–83. New York, Academic Press.

Edwards, K.J. (1991a) Spatial scale and palynology: a commentary on Bradshaw. In D.R. Harris and K.D. Thomas (eds) *Modelling Ecological Change*: 53–9. London, Institute of Archaeology, UCL.

Edwards, K.J. (1991b) Using space in cultural palaynology: the value of the off-site pollen record. InD.R. Harris and K.D. Thomas (eds) *Modelling Ecological Change:* 61–73. London, Institute of Archaeology, UCL.

Evans, J.G., and Rose, A.G. (1992) Small vertebrate and molluscan analysis from the same site. *Circaea* 8(2) 75–84

Foreman, R.T.T. and Godron, M. (1986) *Landscape Ecology*. New York, John Wiley.

Hope-Simpson, R. (1983) Archaeological survey of the Kommos area (south Crete) 1970 – 1980. In D.R. Keller and D.W. Rupp, *Archaeological Survey in the Mediterranean Area*: 297–99. Oxford, British Archaeological Reports, International Series 155.

Hunt, C.O., Gilbertson, D.D. and Donahue, R.E. (1992) Palaeoenvironmental evidence for agricultural soil erosion from late Holocene deposits in the Montagnola Senese, Italy. In M. Bell and J. Boardman (eds) *Past and Present Soil Erosion: Archaeological and Geographical Perspectives*: 163–74. Oxford, Oxbow,Oxbow Monograph 22.

Jahns, S. (1993) On the Holocene vegetation history of the Argive Plain (Peloponnese, southern Greece). *Vegetation History and Archaeobotany* 2(4): 187–203.

Kraft, J.C., Rapp, G., Szemler, G.J., Tziavos, C. and Kase, E.W. (1987) The pass at Thermopylae, Greece. *Journal of Field Archaeology* 14: 181–98.

Lopez, P. & Lopez, A. (1993) Estudio polinico de cuatro tumulos megaliticos en la cuenca del rio Ladra (Lugo, Galicia). *Trabajos de Prehistoria* 50: 235–47.

Serre-Brachet, F. Guiot, J. and Tessier, L. (1992) Dendroclimatic evidence from southwestern Europe and northwestern Africa. In R.S. Bradley and P.D. Jones (eds) *Climate Since AD 1500*. London, Routledge.

van Andel, T.H., Zangger, E. and Demitrack, A. (1990) Land use and soil erosion in prehistoric and historical Greece. *Journal of Field Archaeology* 17: 379–96.

Vernet, J-L., (1991) L'histoire du milieu mèditerranéen humanisé rèvélèee par les charbons de bois. In J. Guilane (ed) *Pour une Archéologie Agraire*. Paris, Armand Colin.

Vigne, J-D. and Valladas, H. (1996) Small mammal fossil assemblages as indicators of environmental change in Northern Corsica during the last 2500 years. *Journal of Archaeological Science* 23: 199–215.

Vigne, J.D., Thibault, J.C. and Cheylan, G. (1994) Les effets des activités humaines sur certaines peuplements de l'öle Lavezzi: Mammifères, Oiseux, Invertébrés. In J.D. Vigne (ed) *L'île Lavezzi: Hommes, Animaux, Archéologie et Marginalité (XIIIe-XXe Siécles, Bonifacio, Corse)*. Paris, CNRS Editions.

Vita-Finzi, C. (1969) *The Mediterranean Valleys: Geological Changes in Historical Times*. Cambridge, Cambridge University Press.

Vita-Finzi, C. and Higgs, E.S. (1970) Prehistoric economy in the Mount Carmel area of Palestine. *Proceedings of the Prehistoric Society* 36: 1–37.

2. Landscape Archaeology and Reconstruction of the Mediterranean Environment based on Palynology

Sytze Bottema

INTRODUCTION

This paper consists of two parts. The first part deals with a discussion on the definition of terms stemming from the discussions by the POPULUS working party on environmental reconstruction. Part two deals with palynology, one of the tools used in environmental reconstructions of past landscape. In this part technical, practical and theoretical aspects of palynology in connection with Mediterranean archaeology are discussed.

Investigations into the past environment of prehistoric and early historic communities became almost standard in excavations during the seventies and eighties. They were mostly undertaken by botanists and zoologists who had close connections with archaeology. Since then archaeologists are partly taking over, discovering the term landscape and explaining and defining it for purposes that differ from the way natural scientists regarded this complex field. Archaeologists and biologists differ in the way they define landscape and the relation of landscape to mankind. For (Mediterranean) archaeologists, landscape seems to be exclusively designed for humans, for instance as a resource area. Latest developments in the relation of mankind and the environment is the so-called perception of the landscape by its inhabitants. The more the 'outdoor scenery' starts to play a role in the discussion, the more the need for a definition of the term landscape is felt. The question is whether this aim will be reached.

DEFINITION OF THE TERM LANDSCAPE

The need to define terms such as landscape, region, area, becomes obvious when an increasing number of scientists of various disciplines starts to use them. This need is, however, no proof of these man-made terms being fit for definition. The frantic search for a proper definition of the concept 'nature' is illustrative of such a quest. At the same time that nature conservancy and politics wanted to define the conception of nature, the well-defined term 'ecology' (McIntosh, 1986; see also Dimbleby, 1977) started to replace the term nature or natural history, especially in political and bureaucratic circles. In my opinion the definition of 'landscape' will meet the same problems as the attempt to define nature. Even if some brilliant people make a good definition, sooner or later it will appear that the majority of researchers did not follow the proper definition as was the case with the term ecology.

These initial words do not mean that I consider a discussion on the definition of landscape out of place or redundant. The discussion emphasises the problems that exist if several people use a term that does not cover the same item. Walsh (1995) was right in stating that 'the indeterminacy of our spatial boundaries is our greatest problem, as well as the more fundamental definition of the landscape itself'. This statement was followed by the remark: 'however, for the archaeologist, we can broadly define landscape as a spatial and temporal context in which the vestiges of historically-connected communities exist'. For an archaeologist originating from the humanities, this would seem to be a reasonable approach to work with. An archaeologist originating from the natural sciences, however, would point at the space where the historically-connected communities do not exist. Are these the white patches that have no landscape?

Definitions of landscape

The discussion on the definition of landscape, e.g. what it is and how large it is, seems to suffer from the restricted knowledge of the outdoor scenery of most people. In modern geography everything is a 'landscape', including industrial towns. In this way the term clashes with the colloquial language. For instance in the Saxon dialect from the northeastern Netherlands as well as in colloquial Dutch, the terms land and landscape point at outdoor situations. For that reason the term environment is more suitable because this word simply tries to demonstrate everything present spatially at a certain time with no further statement on anthropogenic or natural assignments.

In Chapter 1 the fear is expressed that archaeologists from the Mediterranean world cannot work with a definition of 'human landscape' which limits human activity to an area determined by the ecological characteristics described by Foreman and Godron (1986). It is the fear of people of a faculty of humanities not being able to compete with natural scientists when it comes to defining landscape. For the first category mankind cannot be part of an ecological unit. The reality is that even Foreman and Godron are defining a humanly-created landscape because Europe and/or the Mediterranean do not have parts that have not been influenced by people.

Is there a need to include human activity or influence in the basic definition of the term landscape? I would hesitate to do so, because this would create an artificial boundary between environment and landscape both in time and space. For instance, the Allerød period would witness landscapes because there were palaeolithic hunters during that time, whereas in the same part of northwestern Europe the Younger Dryas would only know environment and have no landscape because we cannot prove human habitation at that time.

I do not consider a suggested 'human landscape' a better definition than the Foreman and Godron 'ecological landscape'. The term 'ecological definition' is not a proper term because it suggests that in other landscapes ecology plays no role. Furthermore, the Foreman and Godron definition will of course never be used even by the natural scientists in archaeology. If we come to a reasonable reconstruction of the past environment it will always be a fragmentary picture and a small part of past reality and hopefully not too much off the road. If we have to squeeze that in the Foreman and Godron definition, we will meet serious problems. I wonder if any archaeologist could translate the modern outdoor area or next-door landscape into that definition. If we want definitions or models, we will meet these problems. With regard to our wishes, it may be wise to look at the palaeo-data, see in what simple definitions and scales they fit and to try to construct a practical definition which is understood and even used by many people.

THE STUDY OF ENVIRONMENTAL CHANGE: THE PRESENT-DAY STATE OF ARCHAEOLOGY-ORIENTED PALYNOLOGY IN THE MEDITERRANEAN AREA

It is stated in the introductory chapter that much of the palynological work in the Mediterranean until relatively recently has been concerned with the study of vegetation sequences during the Pleistocene and the transition to the Holocene without recourse to anthropogenic influences. It is true that not much anthropogenic influence is concluded from the study of vegetation sequences in the Pleistocene and the transition to the Holocene. The reason is obvious. Apart from the Natufian in the Levant of the Eastern Mediterranean, there are no indications that settled people played any active role in the Mediterranean landscape. Hunter-gatherers may of course have influenced their environment, including the vegetation, for instance by fire. However, palynology up to now has not been able to demonstrate such impacts. The aim of palynology was not only directed to this period but also to the Holocene and even more to the younger part of it, especially in relation to human habitation (Bottema, 1982). For instance in 1963, I started palynological investigations in Greece in connection with the site of Nea Nikomedeia, Greece, on request of the excavator (Rodden, 1962). Comparable work was already started by van Zeist in Iran in connection with the archaeological investigations by Braidwood (van Zeist, 1967). As an example of the possibilities of the application of palynological investigations in connection with archaeology of the Mediterranean area, the value of two selected pollen diagrams will be discussed.

The palynology of Gomolava, Yugoslavia

In 1979, a 2x2 m column within the large-scale excavation of the site of Gomolava, Hrtkovci, Yugoslavia, was excavated to test sampling methods (Bottema and Ottaway, 1982). Tell Gomolava contains settlement occupation layers from the Vinča Pločnik and younger periods. The 5.50 m thick layers were sampled by flotation and sieving and studied culturally, malacologically, agrobotanically and palynologically in order to establish zones for comparison and subsequently to find out if any correlation between these zones existed. It is not the aim of this paper to discuss the results brought forward by Bottema and Ottaway (1982) but to draw the attention to the palynological part of that study (Fig. 2.1).

From the 5.50 m accumulation of settlement debris, only seven soil samples out of 50 contained pollen. The results are shown in a simple summarised diagram, partly showing pollen taxa, partly groups of pollen taxa. Spectrum 8, a surface sample collected along the river Sava about 1000 m from the dwelling mound, has been added. The fact that only seven out of 50 samples from the profile of the accumulated material yielded pollen illustrates that pollen analysis of archaeological sites is a hazardous investigation that needs to be explained (Bottema, 1975). One may question the formation of settlement deposits in the first place. How regular are they? Is there a fairly constant sedimentation or are there important hiatuses? Are the conditions for suitable pollen preservation properly fulfilled? In this respect one has to keep in mind that, if the inhabitants of Gomolava used clay for house building, for instance wattle and daub, the clay may have been collected at the side of the river. Such clay contains pollen that had precipitated at the time of the river side formation, perhaps a long time before the Vinča people erected their farms in Gomolava. This pollen (if preserved) will not give information on the archaeological period we are interested in, but on a preceding period. Experience has taught us that pollen in mudbrick is altogether oxidized rapidly, but it is

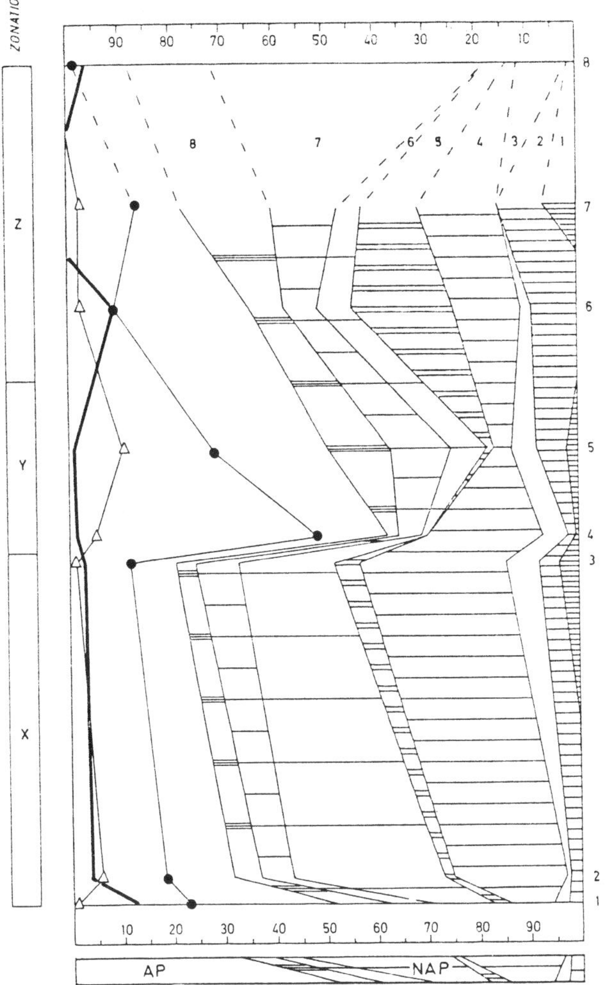

Simplified pollen diagram of Gomolava. 1, Chenopodiaceae; 2, *Centaurea solstitialis*-type; 3, *Plantago lanceolata*; 4, Tubuliflorae; 5, Liguliflorae; 6, Cerealia-type; 7, Gramineae; 8, other herb types. ●, *Pinus*; —, *Quercus*; △, *Picea*; AP, arboreal pollen; NAP, non-arboreal pollen.

Figure 2.1. Simplified summary diagram from the prehistoric settlement mound of Gomolava (Hrtkovci, Vojvodina, Yugoslavia) showing pollen taxa or groups of pollen taxa for seven levels (1–7). The topmost spectrum 8 represents the modern pollen precipitation along the Sava River. (After Bottema and Ottaway, 1982)

very difficult to prove if this is true for all pollen in clay.

In case of the Gomolava archaeological deposits, one can easily see that the latter can be answered negatively. During the Vinča period two metres of debris were deposited in which no pollen was found. The discovery of pollen in some samples of the settlement mound does only partly inform us about the vegetation around Gomolava or the impact of prehistoric people, but is specially indicative for local conditions, for instance pollen-preserving soil formations. Spectra 1 and 2 are samples from the soil on which the settlement was founded. Spectra 3 and 4 are samples from a soil that was formed after the settlement was abandoned, a fact also indicated by the archaeological investigations (Brukner, 1965). The increase of the *Pinus* pollen value from 15 to 50% (Fig. 2.1) cannot be explained by an increase of pine in the vegetation of the Sava valley and bordering uplands, but may be the result of grazing on the mound. Grazing reduced the local biomass and prevented flowering, so that the local pollen production was reduced very much and the relative effect of long distance pine pollen became felt strongly. The meagre results of the palynological investigation contribute very little to a reconstruction of the vegetation of the river valley and the upland around Gomolava and its relation to prehistory.

Beyşehir Gölü (Turkey)

As a contrast, one pollen diagram has been chosen from *c.*50 diagrams that have been constructed from cores collected in the Eastern Mediterranean area by the Biologisch-Archaeologisch Instituut in Groningen. In the respective catchment basins, pollen preservational conditions are often very well fulfilled, but it must be stated that human habitation is very rarely directly connected with the wet conditions in the marshes and lakes but must be looked for at some distance. The selected diagram originates from the west side of the lake of Beyşehir in southwestern Anatolia and covers the last 6000 years (Fig. 2.2). The results of the study of the complete investigations in Lake Beyşehir cover a period of 15,000 years and are given in van Zeist *et al.* (1975) and Bottema and Woldring (1984).

The diagram of Beyşehir results from a sediment core with the same length as that of the Gomolava settlement accumulation, but from the lake sediment 39 samples were produced (Fig. 2.2). The diagram is divided in zones and subzones on the basis of characteristic changes in the pollen curves. If necessary, such sediment can be investigated in more detail, as is shown in Figure 2.3, where the part representing zone 3 in Figure 2.2 has been analysed every 2.5 cm, thus producing 59 samples (Bottema and Woldring, 1984).

The interpretation of the Beyşehir diagram can be read in various publications (see literature list in van Zeist and Bottema, 1991). Here it is stressed that the palaeobotanical information of this site enables us to reconstruct the vegetation of this area and the Beyşehir diagram is confirmed by other diagrams from southwestern Turkey. For the late third millennium clear signs of human activity can be detected. The appearance of pollen of *Olea*, *Castanea*, *Juglans*, *Fraxinus ornus* and other indicative types visible in the pollen curves of zone 3a–e, dated to start about 3200 BP (uncalibrated radiocarbon years), has been found in many other southwestern Turkish sites and is ascribed to human impact. This characteristic phase has been published as the Beyşehir Occupation Phase, an action of prehistoric people in southwestern Turkey and northern Greece that is described in various publications. The evidence from the Beyşehir sediment is of far better quality than the meagre results of the samples of the settlement of Gomolava.

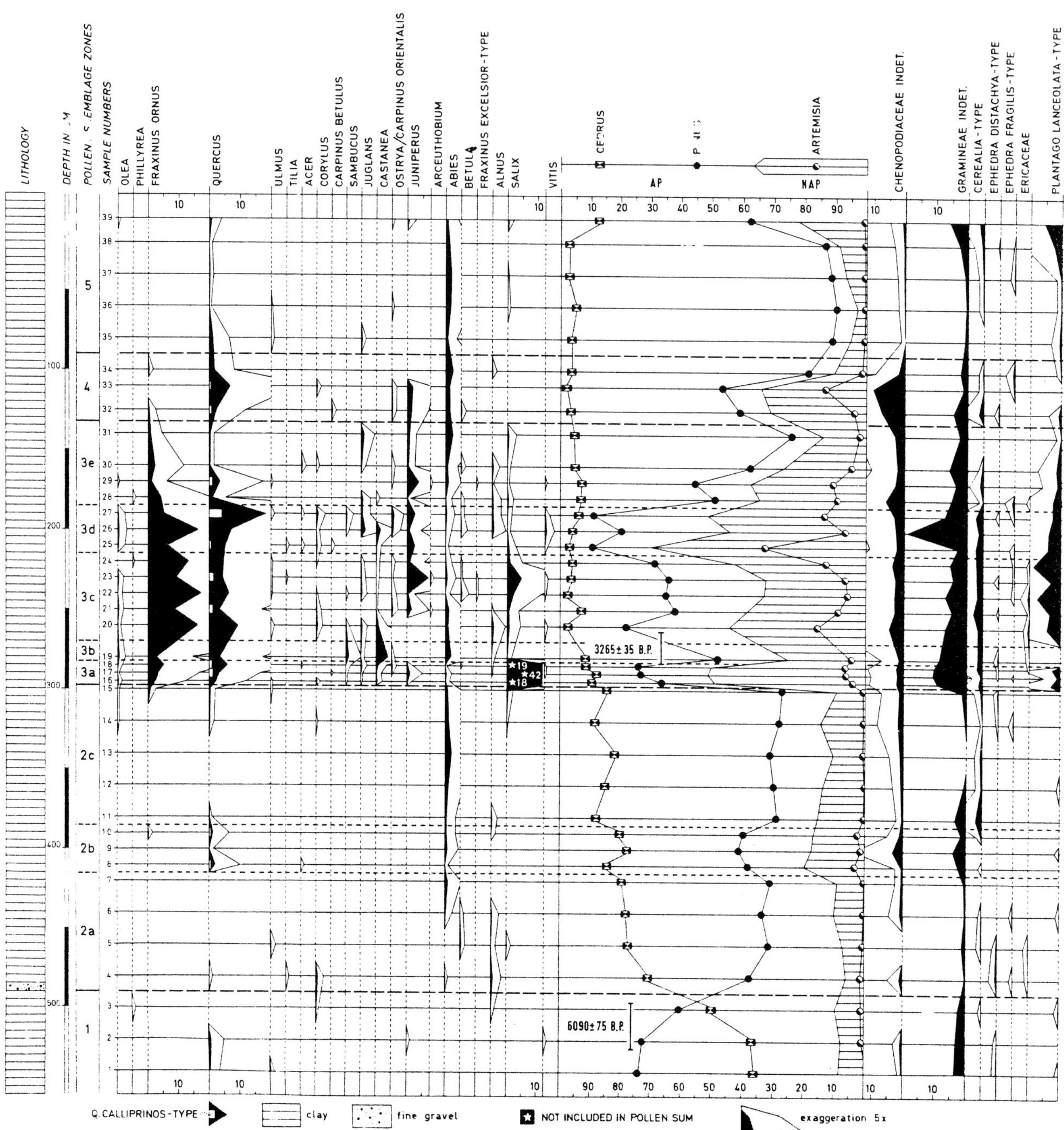

Figure 2.2. Selection of pollen curves from a diagram of Lake Beyşehir. (After van Zeist et al.*, 1975)*

The general contribution of palynology to environmental archaeology in the Eastern Mediterranean area

To what extent did palynology contribute to our knowledge of landscape in relation to prehistoric man ? The history of the vegetation of the Eastern Mediterranean from Greece to the Iranian Zagros mountains is discussed in relation to human activities in a series of articles of which the bibliographical sources can be found in Bottema and Woldring (1984) and van Zeist and Bottema (1991). In this respect the discussion in Chapter 1 on the value of the pollen indicators requires some comment. It seems reasonable to question the validity of primary and secondary European pollen indicators that have been discussed by Behre (1981) for their use in the Mediterranean area (Behre, 1990). Of course, there are cultivars that must be considered as typical Mediterranean species, such as olive (*Olea*

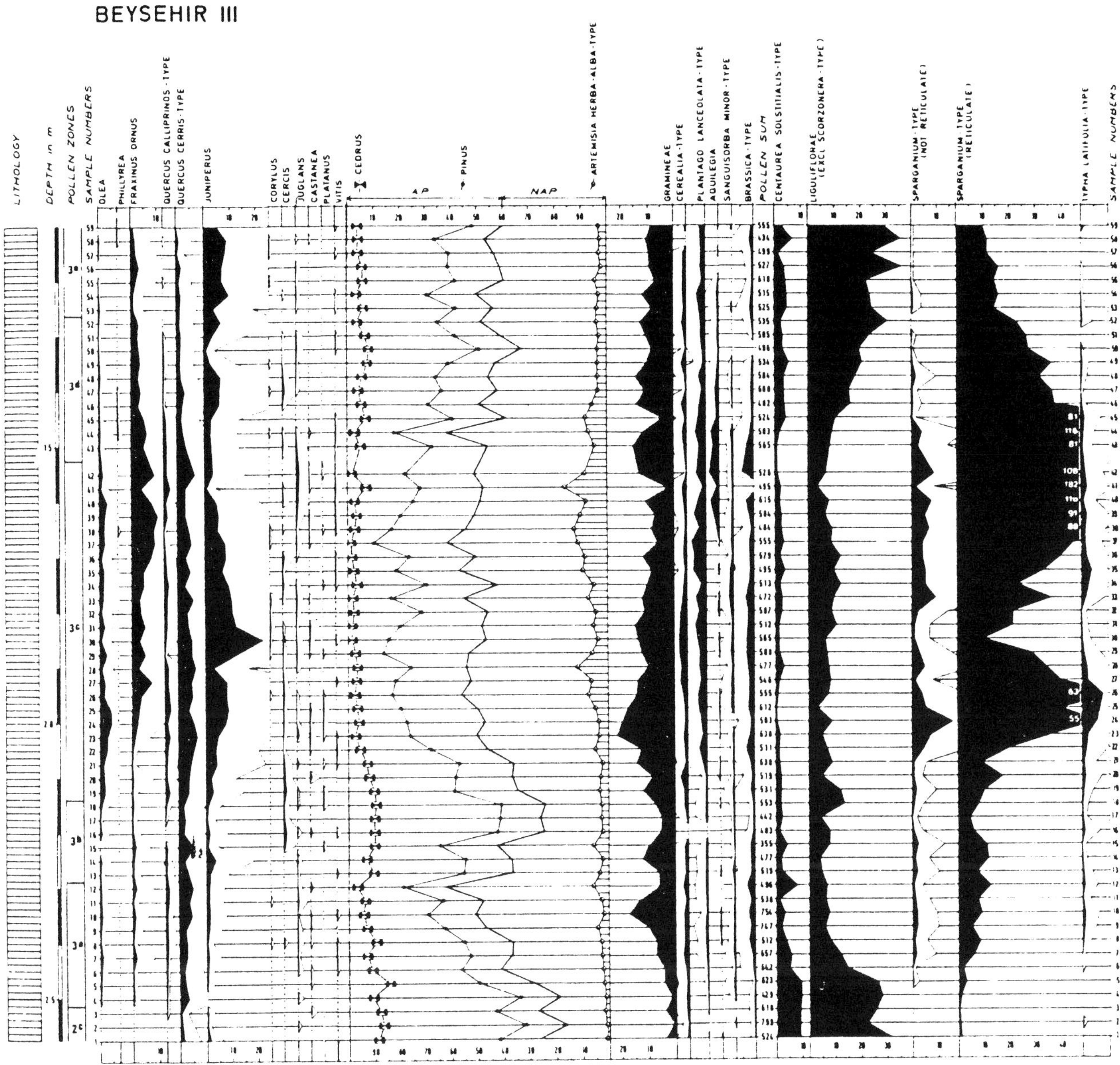

Figure 2.3. Selection of pollen curves from a detailed analysis of zone 3 of the pollen diagram of Lake Beyşehir (Fig. 2.2). (After Bottema and Woldring, 1984)

europaea) and carob (*Ceratonia siliqua*). They are so typical for the Mediterranean that phytosociologists consider them as character species (the Oleo-Ceratonion). It is, however, very difficult to assign them to a natural vegetation: they appeared during the period that people created maquis in the second millennium. For the carob it is very unclear where this species originally grew and it is not even impossible that the Romans brought it from Ethiopia to the Mediterranean. It is unlikely that both species spread with the maquis as is suggested by Jahns (1993). Wild-looking olives may be abandoned fruit trees which after close inspection may even appear to stand in rows. Many primitive olive trees turn out to be the sprouting root stock while the original cultivated and grafted part has died. From the study on the behaviour of olive it appears that the majority of the pollen, if not all, was produced by cultivated trees. A reason to consider Behre's work to a large part valid for the Mediterranean results from the comparison of human influence on the Eastern Mediterranean landscape including the Near East with that of northwestern Europe. In the search for indicator pollen types in diagrams obtained for the Near East, we have to realize that the origin of agriculture was located in an open landscape presumably covered by forest-steppe. The domesticates that were developed from the wild ancestors, grew in, or were closely connected with, open landscape. That may be the reason why human impact is not visible in pollen diagrams from those parts, because the vegetation was not fundamentally changed during the early developments of farming. Behre's indicator types are not present and no other types are known up to now that serve this purpose. However, from the moment that agriculture moved from the open landscape to landscapes that were covered with forest, characteristic indicators appear. A number of them is included in the indicators brought forward by Behre.

The palynological method

Mediterranean palynology is, like palynology in other parts of the globe, the study of subfossil pollen grains and spores from sediments and in our case the aim is the reconstruction of the past vegetation and climate in connection with human habitation. A crucial fact in palynology that is often overlooked is the identification reliability. Identification of pollen by individual researchers can hardly or not at all be controlled. Furthermore the identification level of pollen types depends on the identifiability itself. The identification can be on family, genus, or more rarely, species level.

From northern Europe towards the Mediterranean an increasing number of plant species is found, but the number of types identified in practice or in theory is not increasing likewise. For the Balkans the number of plant species nowadays is *c.*6000, whereas for the Netherlands 1100 species are listed. The number of pollen types found in past and present situations in the Balkans does not exceed that of the Netherlands six times, but less than two times (Bottema, 1984).

To produce a record of subfossil pollen in a certain area in the Mediterranean, one has to look for suitable sediments and one must even organize intensive surveys to find conditions that contain suitable pollen archives. Pollen-bearing sediments are sediments in which pollen is preserved in anaerobic conditions. In general this means very wet conditions such as perennial lakes, swamps or peat bogs. The sediments should have grown regularly, thus providing a suitable resolution in time with regard to the pollen precipitation. The presence of pollen archives in reasonable numbers well covering space and time would be the most ideal situation to study past landscape.

In practice the number of pollen diagrams is limited by unsuitable conditions. Areas that receive less than 300 mm precipitation annually seldom have pollen-bearing sediments. This does not mean that pollen-bearing sediments are guaranteed if precipitation is more than 300 mm. In limestone regions water rapidly disappears. The accumulation of organic material is hindered by the presence of lime. Thus Greek isles, including Crete, seldom offer suitable conditions for pollen preservation.

The demands for pollen preservation as described above indicate the limits of this method in connection with archaeology. The conditions in settlements differ considerably from those in sedimentary basins. Generally in archaeological sites there is irregular accumulation under aerobic circumstances where pollen rapidly decays (Bottema, 1975; Turner, 1985). Only under special conditions, which are seldom met with in the Mediterranean area, pollen will be preserved, for instance under burial mounds, in cesspits etc.

When all conditions are fulfilled, a pollen diagram can be produced that has to be dated, for instance by radiocarbon, to obtain information on the age and the time resolution respectively. In those parts of the Mediterranean where lime is common, the possibility of hard water effect in dates from sediments must be guarded against.

In the Eastern Mediterranean we have the subfossil pollen precipitation from an often three-dimensional (mountainous) system. In northwestern Europe, however, this system is in general flat. The behaviour of the vegetation and the interpretation of the pollen assemblages will differ in both situations. Plant or tree species which migrated northward after the ice age, travelled considerable distances, especially compared with the travelling routes taken by Mediterranean species under such circumstances. The latter category only has to move vertically along the slopes of the mountains at the moment that the temperature increases. The higher one climbs the mountain, the colder it gets (*c.*0.6°C each 100 m) and temperature forms a limit for the occurrence of plants. In case of a rise in temperature, a plant species or a complete vegetation belt may move upward but does not cover large distances.

If all demands are met with, a pollen diagram is produced that supplies us with the past pollen precipitation in a sedimentary basin. Our objective is to reconstruct the vegetal landscape, the stage for human habitation including eventual human impact upon this vegetation. To obtain that picture we have to translate the pollen evidence into plant cover and this is in fact the difficult task of palynology.

Calculation and presentation of the pollen data; comparison with pollen evidence from modern situations

The pollen precipitation is very seldom measured in pollen grains per time and surface unit, because we are not suitably informed on the amount of sediment per year. For the Mediterranean the datability of sediments is very low because of the absence of organic material in the predominantly clay sediments. What we can calculate is the number of pollen grains per cc sediment. Assuming a constant pollen production per year, information on the sedimentation rate can be gathered. Actually, we cannot assume a constant pollen production. It is likely that the annual pollen production was and is varying. Thus, we have to realize that we are always dealing with two variables in one equation. Conclusions on pollen production or sedimentation rate have to be based upon solid proof from modern evidence on pollen precipitation and radiocarbon-dated sediment.

Finally we reach our aim: the translation of our subfossil pollen precipitation. We should not speak of pollen rain because there may be a difference between pollen precipitation and pollen rain (Spieksma *et al.*, 1993). Spieksma *et al.* demonstrated that a Burkard machine that was used to sample airborne pollen for allergy research, produced a pollen spectrum that differed from the contents of natural pollen traps (moss cushions) growing under the machine.

The information on modern pollen precipitation in connection with the extant vegetation is important. Such a study informs us about the relation between a plant species and its pollen, representation, and pollen transport.

The surface sample, the modern pollen precipitation, is measured mostly from 'natural' pollen traps, moss cushions that are thought to catch pollen and preserve it. The age of moss patches is generally not known but should at least cover several years to smooth the effect of flowering and non-flowering years. The upper part of sediment cores should not be taken as a surface sample, especially if cores are taken under water because of the uncertainty of the age of such samples.

The catchment

It is very difficult to trace the original growing places of the plants that have produced the pollen that is collected in a certain spot, the catchment area. The past behaviour of the plant species/taxa is discussed on the basis of the 'actuality principle'. We assume that the plant species producing the subfossil pollen had the same ecological demands as their modern counterpart, the living plants of today. On the basis of this assumption we reconstruct habitats around the catchment, some nearby, some further away.

It is difficult to attribute the pollen types, which are identified on family or genus level, to a certain vegetation. Some of the representatives may have grown in or around the marsh, whereas the pollen may also have been produced by a related species that grew in the so-called upland vegetation.

The contents of the surface samples are composed by a variety of pollen taxa produced by types with a rather well-known (modern) ecological demand and many others that can in theory be attributed to many biotopes, as the type represents a large number of species. The number of plants, shrubs or trees that produced the pollen, their distance to the catchment basin, the way in which the vegetation was composed (in mixture or in mosaic), this all forms part of the study.

To what extent does palynology contribute to archaeology and more specifically to the landscape archaeology of the Eastern Mediterranean ? If we describe the aim of archaeology as a retrieval of the complete picture of the past, we can evaluate the contribution of palynology in this respect. Some of the problems described in Chapter 1 that hold for landscape archaeology in general, also hold for landscape/environment as concluded from pollen diagrams. The pollen signal originates from many parts in the landscape and is composed from them. Janssen (1966) has tried to define the origin of pollen and vegetation in terms of local (marsh/swamp/lake), extralocal and regional. In practice it is very difficult to express these terms in kilometres from the pollen catchment. Pollen is ascribed to this distance classification in a rather intuitive way, often without solid proof. Thus, the reconstruction of the surrounding area, even its limits, is based upon arbitrary decisions and is heavily leaning on the knowledge of the actual vegetation. In practice the terms local, regional and long distance, sometimes extended to extra local and supra-regional, even when defined in concrete measures, are not always identical. A study by Andersen (1976) demonstrates the variation in local and regional conditions which influences the parameters for modelling.

As is stated above we have to deal with two categories of pollen archives. The first category is the subfossil pollen in archives that cover a period of time and that are shown in pollen diagrams. The second category is the modern pollen precipitation collected from moss cushions, the so-called natural pollen traps. Information on modern pollen precipitation is used to study climate from pollen assemblages (Guiot, 1990). In such studies a key-set of the modern pollen precipitation is compared with data of weather stations. From this comparison a relation of pollen types with climate is developed. The validity of this method for the Eastern Mediterranean is tested by Lutgerink (1995).

Do surface samples represent the pollen precipitation of the modern period, for instance the last ten years, as we expect them to do? After years of rather uncritical use it turns out that the nature of the surface sample, collected from a patch of moss, can be centuries older than the present ten years. Pollen can be preserved in acid soils for centuries, whereas additional, younger, periods are missing from the same soil (Bottema, 1995). To catch and classify the modern pollen precipitation, modern standards have been developed by scientists and launched at an international meeting of the European Pollen Database in Arles in 1994.

CONCLUDING REMARKS

Palynology is a highly suitable tool for the general vegetation reconstruction of the Late-Quaternary period and is very useful to demonstrate differences or similarities in conditions in time and space. Palynology has its limits where it concerns the detailed attribution of all different floral elements to the surrounding landscape.

By translating the pollen evidence into vegetation and thus into visual landscape, the hazards of such action can be illustrated with the following example. In the northern Netherlands, the bone remains of three mammoths were found in a depression and a profile was sampled for pollen analysis; the aim was to reconstruct the Middle-Würm landscape around the find spot (Cappers *et al.*, 1993). In this case the palynological evidence, if based on the 'actuality principle', pointed to Siberian tundra conditions. During the excavation of the bones, large samples for macrofossil studies were taken. The macroremains concerned seeds and to a minor extent leaves which gave a picture different from that of the pollen study. The 60 plant species that were found are still present in the Netherlands, and are not of a tundra character. The only conspicuous difference between the present situation and that of the Middle Würm is the absence of trees in the latter period. The expectations were fixed and based upon ideas of arctic surroundings connected with mammoths and they were supported by the pollen studies. These studies gave no wrong information, but pollen was as usually identified to family or genus level. The pollen types were translated into plant taxa and attributed to arctic conditions because of the already existing mental picture of the arctic landscape as being the common (but wrong) idea about this period. The macrofossil evidence clearly demonstrated that the Würm landscape was not identical with modern tundra.

REFERENCES

Andersen, S.T. (1970) The relative pollen productivity and pollen representation of North European trees, and correction factors for tree pollen spectra. *Danmarks Geol. Undersøgelse, II. Raekke* 96: 1–99.

Behre, K.-E. (1981) The interpretation of anthropogenic pollen indicators in pollen diagrams. *Pollen et Spores* 23: 225–45.

Behre, K.-E. (1990) Some reflections on anthropogenic indicators and the record of prehistoric occupation phases in pollen diagrams from the Near East. In S. Bottema, G. Entjes-Nieborg and W. van Zeist (eds) *Man's Role in the Shaping of the Eastern Mediterranean Landscape*: 219–31. Rotterdam/Brookfield, Balkema.

Bottema, S. (1975) The interpretation of pollen spectra from prehistoric settlements (with special attention to Liguliflorae). *Palaeohistoria* 17: 17–35.

Bottema, S. (1982) Palynological investigations in Greece with special reference to pollen as an indicator of human activity. *Palaeohistoria* 24: 257–89.

Bottema, S. (1984) Pollen stratigraphical investigations in the Mediterranean area (with special emphasis on the problems of sampling and interpretation of the results). *Webbia* 38: 465–72.

Bottema, S. (1995) Het oppervlaktemonster : de relatie tussen stuifmeelregen en vegetatie. *Paleo-Aktueel* 6: 99–101.

Bottema, S. and Ottaway, B.S. (1982) Botanical, malacological and archaeological zonation of settlement deposits at Gomolava. *Journal of Archaeological Science* 9: 221–46.

Bottema, S. and Woldring, H. (1984) Late Quaternary vegetation and climate of southwestern Turkey, Part II. *Palaeohistoria* 26: 123–49.

Brukner, B. (1965) Neolithic and early Eneolithic layers at Gomolava. *Rad Vojvodinaski Muzeia* 14: 137–75.

Cappers, R.T.J. and Bosch, J.H.A., Bottema, S., Coope, G.R., van Geel, B., Mook-Kamps and E. Woldring, H. (1993) De reconstructie van het landschap. In *Mens en mammoet. De mammoeten van Orvelte en de vroegste bewoning van Noord-Nederland.* Archeologische Monografieën van het Drents Museum, deel 5, Assen.

Dimbleby, G.W. (1977) *Ecology and Archaeology*. London, Edward Arnold.

Foreman, R.T.T. and Godron, M. (1986) *Landscape Ecology*. New York, John Wiley.

Guiot, J. (1990) Methodology of the last climatic cycle reconstruction in France from pollen data. *Palaeogeography, Palaeoclimatology, Palaeoecology* 80: 49–69.

Jahns, S. (1993) On the Holocene vegetation history of the Argive Plain (Peloponnese, southern Greece). *Vegetation History and Archaeobotany* 2(4): 187–203.

Janssen, C.R. (1966) Recent pollen spectra from the deciduous and coniferous-deciduous forests of Northeastern Minnesota : a study in pollen dispersal. *Ecology* 47/5.

Lutgerink, R.H.P. (1995) Paleoclimate reconstructions for the Eastern Mediterranean area based on pollen data: constrain or not constrain? EUG 8 poster presentation. *Terra Nova* 7, abstract supplement 1: 218.

McIntosh, R.P. (1986) *The Background of Ecology. Concept and Theory.* Cambridge, Cambridge Unbiversity Press, Cambridge Studies in Ecology.

Rodden, J. (1962) Excavations at the Early Neolithic site at Nea Nikomedeia, Greek Macedonia (1961 season). *Proceedings of the Prehistoric Society* 28: 267–88.

Spieksma, F.T.M., Nikkels, B.H. and Bottema, S. (1994) Relationship between recent pollen deposition and airborne pollen concentration. *Review of Palaeobotany and Palynology* 82: 141–5.

Turner, C. (1985) Problems and pitfalls in the application of palynology to Pleistocene archaeological sites in western Europe. In J. Renault-Miskovski, M. Bui-Thi-Mai and M. Girard (eds) *Palynologie Archéologique*: 347–73. Paros, CNRS Notes et Monographies Techniques 17.

Walsh, K. (1995) Landscape Archaeology and Environmental Reconstruction. Paper to the *Populus Aix-en-Provence Colloquium (14–15th October 1995)*, Centre Camille Jullian, Université de Provence.

Zeist, W. van (1967) Late Quaternary vegetation history of western Iran. *Review of Palaeobotany and Palynology* 2: 301–11.

Zeist, W. van and Bottema, S. (1991) Late Quaternary vegetation of the Near East. *Beihefte zum Tübinger Atlas des Vorderen Orients*, Reihe A, 18. Wiesbaden.

Zeist, W. van, Woldring, H. and Stapert, D. (1975) Late Quaternary vegetation and climate of Southwestern Turkey. *Palaeohistoria* 17: 31–43.

3. A Computerized Data Base for the Palynological Recording of Human Activity in the Mediterranean Basin

Valérie Andrieu, Elisabetta Brugiapaglia, Rachid Cheddadi, Philippe Ponel, Maurice Reille, Jacques-Louis de Beaulieu, and Marcel Barbero

ABSTRACT

A synthesis has been made of bibliographic data relating to pollen evidence for human activity in the Mediterranean basin during the Holocene. It is based on the examination of 205 publications from between 1940 and 1994, covering twelve countries from around the Mediterranean. This assessment is followed by a presentation of pollen sequences in which the typical features of anthropic intervention in a natural environment were clearly recorded. This synthetic study has made it possible to propose the following three conclusions. First, due to reasons linked to the difficulties of pollen and taphonomic production and dispersion, only a limited number of anthropic activities is recorded by pollen sequences. Second, the anthropic activity recorded by the pollen profiles was rarely dated using carbon-14 dating; this situation explains the difficulties in correlating regional pollen data with local archaeological data at a local scale. Third, in order to bring human activity to the fore within a natural environment, it is necessary to use a multi-disciplinary palaeoecological approach, based simultaneously on a study of the pollen content and on the plant and insect macroremains from sedimentary sequences extracted from wet environments near archaeological sites.

BIBLIOGRAPHICAL SYNTHESIS

A total of 205 publications on the Holocene in twelve Mediterranean countries was analysed (Fig. 3.1). The publications which have been examined are those which propose palaeoecological reconstruction for the last 10,000 years based on data from pollen analyses of continental sites (marshes, peat bogs, lakes) or of sequences taken from coastal sites (lagoons).

Palynological data acquired on archaeological sites, in marine sequences and from the continental plateau, were not retained. On archaeological sites located in caves, shelter-caves or in other such settlements, the pollen record was disturbed: 1) by the very presence of human popu-

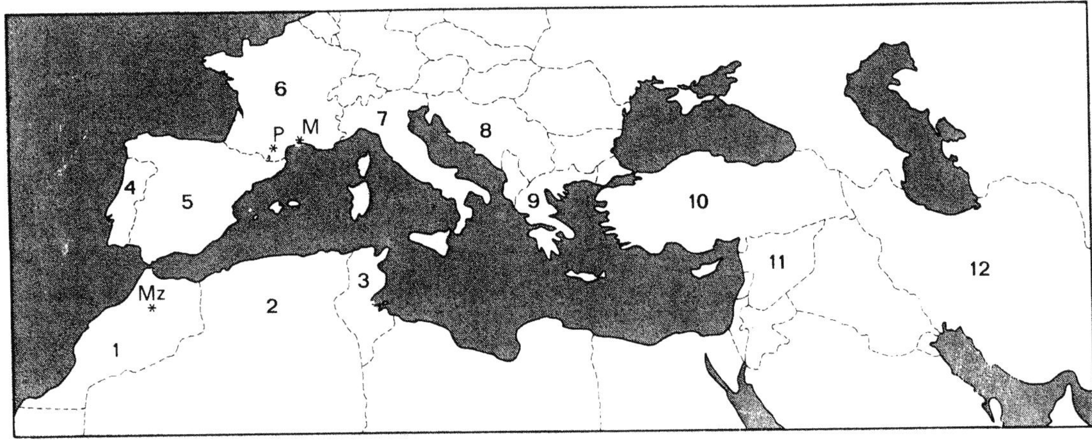

Figure 3.1. Map of the countries around the Mediterranean for which palynological publications were analyzed.
1. Morocco; 2. Algeria; 3. Tunisia; 4. Portugal; 5. Spain; 6. France; 7. Italy; 8. Ex-Yugoslavia; 9. Greece; 10. Turkey; 11. Syria; 12. Iran. M: Marsillargues; P: Pinet; Mz: Marzine.

lations in their settlements; 2) by the mode of pollen deposition in oxidized environments, which favour a preferential destruction of pollen; 3) by the inclusion of exogenous pollens from groundwater runoff along the walls of the caves: these phenomena result in mixed pollen flora. With deposits in marine environments (continental plateaux and abysses), the sedimentation of atmospheric pollen is disturbed as much by the action of marine currents as by the bioturbulent activity of benthic organisms; both of these phenomena result in a mixture of pollen flora and in a disturbance of the stratigraphy.

Finally it must be pointed out that articles based on data from fields other than pollinical analysis (carpology, paleoentomology and so on) are not presented in this bibliographic synthesis. The aim of this section is to determine to what extent pollen data can be used to detect human activity in the natural environment.

Classification of the publications

Two categories of publication have been distinguished (Table 3.1): regional monographs in which the original pollen data is presented; and synthetic publications that present compilations of original data published in regional monographs. The articles examined are those which have been published in journals. Doctoral theses have been excluded from this synthesis, with the exception of those for which their data has not yet been published in its entirety (Bottema, 1974; Triat-Laval, 1978; and so on). Of the 205 publications examined, 140 are regional monographs and 66 are syntheses. The largest number of publications concerns the French Mediterranean regions, a factor reflecting the long established and dynamic nature of the paleoecological teams working in this area.

The relevance of these publications

The quality of the regional monographs was assessed using purely objective criteria. Amongst these criteria, the most important are those related to the quality of the pollen data, such as : (1) the number of pollen sequences used as a basis for interpretation; (2) the number of pollen spectra per diagram and the resolution of the sampling (the number of spectra per metre of sediment); (3) the number of grains of pollen and spores counted as well as the number of taxa identified per pollen spectrum; (4) the type of graphic representation of data: partial pollen diagrams in which only a selection of taxa is published, or complete pollen diagrams. Other equally-determining criteria include the number of recorded anthropic events within the pollen sequences and the number of these events dated by radiocarbon dating.

According to their relevance, the regional monographs are classified into four categories numbered from 1 to 4: 1 = 'not informative', 2 = 'not interesting', 3 = 'interesting' and 4 = 'fundamental'. The 'not interesting' and 'not informative' publications are those based on the pollen data lacking in information on the anthropization of the natural environment, either due to the fact that the site has not

Countries	Regional monographs	Synthesis	Total number of publications
Algeria	2	0	2
ex-Yugoslavia	2	0	2
France	39	38	77
Greece	5	1	1
Iran	2	0	2
Italy	39	0	39
Morocco	6	0	6
Portugal	8	0	8
Spain	20	1	21
Syria	3	2	5
Tunisia	9	2	11
Turkey	5	1	6
General synthesis	0	21	21
Total	140	66	205

Table 3.1. The number of regional monographs and syntheses per country.

recorded this type of event, or because there is only a partial graphic representation of pollen data (limited to significant taxons from an ecological, climatic or stratigraphic point of view), thus making it impossible to determine the impact of human activity on the vegetation. The 'interesting' and 'fundamental' publications are those in which the anthropic pollen events are clearly featured and dated.

This qualitative analysis illustrates that the 140 regional monographs thus analysed, 52 are estimated to be 'interesting' and 'fundamental' (Table 3.2), and are therefore rich in pollen data attesting to human impact on the natural environment. France furnished the largest number of regional monographs (39), but only 13 have been found to be 'interesting' or 'fundamental'. Less than half of the publications examined, therefore, contain information on the history and the chronology of the anthropization of the natural environment.

Organization of the data-base

Bibliographic references were incorporated into an analytical database created using Paradox (Borland) software. This database was organized in such a way as to enable various analysts to insert the results of their own analyses of the publications. The data is archived in a non hierarchical system so that it is easily accessible for inquiries.

Each bibliographical entry consists of three fields linked by a key (Table. 3.3) :

- 1st field: bibliographical reference of each article analyzed (Table 3.3: a)
- 2nd field: general information on the scientific content of the article (Table 3.3: b). Article by Planchais (1982), analysed by...('the name of the critic'), a 'Regional Monograph' (MR) based on the pollen analysis of the Marsillargues sequence (shown in Figure 3.2). It is from the Subboreal and Subatlantic periods. This article is considered to be 'interesting' ('Publication interest'=

Countries	Regional monographs	Not informative + not interesting	Interesting	Fundamental	Interesting + Fundamental
Algeria	2	1	1	0	1
ex-Yugoslavia	2	2	0	0	0
France	39	26	9	4	13
Greece	5	3	1	1	2
Iran	2	2	0	0	0
Italy	39	22	13	4	17
Morocco	6	2	3	1	4
Portugal	8	3	4	1	5
Spain	20	19	1	0	1
Syria	3	1	2	0	2
Tunisia	9	5	4	0	4
Turkey	5	2	2	1	3
Total	140	88	40	12	52

Table 3.2. The quality of the publications analyzed.

```
Ref#:        211
Auteurs: PLANCHAIS N.
Date:    1982
Titre: Palynologie lagunaire de l'étang de Mauguio. Paléoenvironnement
Vol:      XXIV,1                 Pp:  93-118
Edition: Pollen et Spores
```
a

```
Nom du Critique:                               Type Publication MR
Période couverte: Subboréal à l'actuel
Début Anthropisation Subboréal            Intérêt publication:       3
Commentaires:           Très bel article de synthèse sur
          l'anthropisation fondé sur un diagramme pollinique
```
b

```
Diagram  Marsillargues                          Age Sup.
Type anthropisation  CB  Age Med.                  Age Inf.1300±60
Biostratigraphie  SA      Technique  C    Validité           0
```
c

Table 3.3. Example of a bibliographic entry.

3). Remarks on the scientific importance of the article can be made in the 'Comments' column: the number of anthropic events that is recorded by the pollen sequence, their age, and if it did occur, the nature of the impact of human activity on the natural environment.

- 3rd field: information on human activity recorded in pollen sequences (Table 3.3: c). In the Marsillargues diagram, a phase of cultivation of *Castanea* (CB) is recorded. This episode is contemporary with the Subatlantic (SA) and the beginning of it is dated by the radiocarbon dating ('Method' = C) to 1300 ± 60 BP ('Inferior age' = 1300 ± 60). According to the analyst, this date is valid ('Validity'= 0). For the same date, five other anthropic events are recorded in the Marsillargues sequence (Table 3.4): a deforestation episode (DF) followed by cultivation of *Cerealia* (CC), *Juglans* (CJ), *Olea* (CO) and *Vitis* (CV).

PALYNOLOGICAL EVIDENCE OF ANTHROPIC ACTION: SOME EXAMPLES

The sequences from Marsillargues (Planchais, 1982; Fig. 3.2), Pinet (Reille, 1991; Fig. 3.3) and Marzine (Reille, 1977; Fig. 3.4) were chosen because the recording of anthropic action is clear. The anthropic events are dated by Carbon 14 in the Marsillargues sequence only. In the other two sequences, pollen markers place the recorded anthropic events within a timescale.

The Marsillargues diagram

The Marsillargues sequence (Fig. 3. 2) was obtained by coring in a lagoon site (l'Etang de Maurio) in Languedoc (France). The appearance of *Juglans* in a continual curve is dated to 2270 ± 70 B.P., a dating that may be a little old, especially in comparison with a coherent ensemble of dates obtained for this event in the Western Mediterranean (Beug, 1975; Bottema, 1980) and which associates the appearance of walnut with the founding of Roman colonies in these areas towards 2000 BP. Above the '*Juglans* line' (Beug, 1975), an initial stage of woodland clearing is recorded. It affects the beech forest and is indicated in pollen assemblages by the collapse in the frequency of *Fagus*. Increased human intervention in Mediterranean woodlands is regis-

Phase of Deforestation: DF

Diagram	Marsillargues			Age Sup.	
Type anthropisation	DF	Age Med.		Age Inf.	1300±60
Biostratigraphie	SA	Technique	C	Validité	0

Phase of *Cerealia* Cultivation: CC

Diagram	Marsillargues			Age Sup.	
Type anthropisation	CC	Age Med.		Age Inf.	1300±60
Biostratigraphie	SA	Technique	C	Validité	0

Phase of *Castanea* Cultivation: CB

Diagram	Marsillargues			Age Sup.	
Type anthropisation	CB	Age Med.		Age Inf.	1300±60
Biostratigraphie	SA	Technique	C	Validité	0

Phase of *Juglans* Cultivation: CJ

Diagram	Marsillargues			Age Sup.	
Type anthropisation	CJ	Age Med.		Age Inf.	1300±60
Biostratigraphie	SA	Technique	C	Validité	0

Phase of *Olea* Cultivation: CO

Diagram	Marsillargues			Age Sup.	
Type anthropisation	CO	Age Med.		Age Inf.	1300±60
Biostratigraphie	SA	Technique	C	Validité	0

Phase of *Vitis* Cultivation: CV

Diagram	Marsillargues			Age Sup.	
Type anthropisation	CV	Age Med.		Age Inf.	1300±60
Biostratigraphie	SA	Technique	C	Validité	0

Table 3.4. List of anthropic events recorded in the Marsillarges sequence during the Subatlantic (SA).

tered around 1300 ± 60 BP and is evident in the pollen record by the collapse in the frequencies of *Quercus ilex* (which includes *Q. ilex* and *Q. coccifera)* pollen. This event relates to a deforestation episode which affects the evergreen oak forest. Local human populations clear the land in order to increase agricultural land. This was confirmed by the simultaneous appearance of cultivated taxa in pollen curves: *Cerealia, Castanea, Vitis* and *Olea.*

The results of the pollen analysis for the Marsillargues site as well as for the rest of the pollen sequences in the articles analyzed have been put into a synthetic table (Table 3.5). This table includes all of the anthropic events recorded by the pollen sites, together with the age of these events dated either by radiocarbon dating, by biostratigraphic correlation, or by historical texts. The grey-tinted events are the ones that are radiocarbon-dated.

The Pinet diagram

The Pinet sequence (Reille, 1991; Fig. 3.3) was obtained by coring in the middle of a peat bog situated at 880 m altitude on the karstic plateau of Sault (in the Pyrénées in the department of the Aude). This sequence clearly illustrates, to the same degree as that of Marsillargues, evidence of human intervention within the natural environment. In the pollen diagram from Pinet this remains undated.

Above the '*Juglans* line' (Beug, 1975), we note a collapse

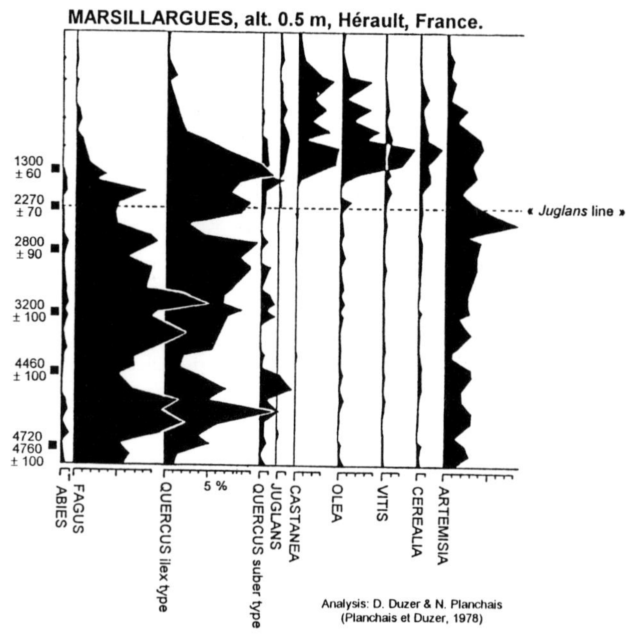

Figure 3.2. Simplified pollen diagram from Marsillargues. (After Planchais and Duzer, 1978)

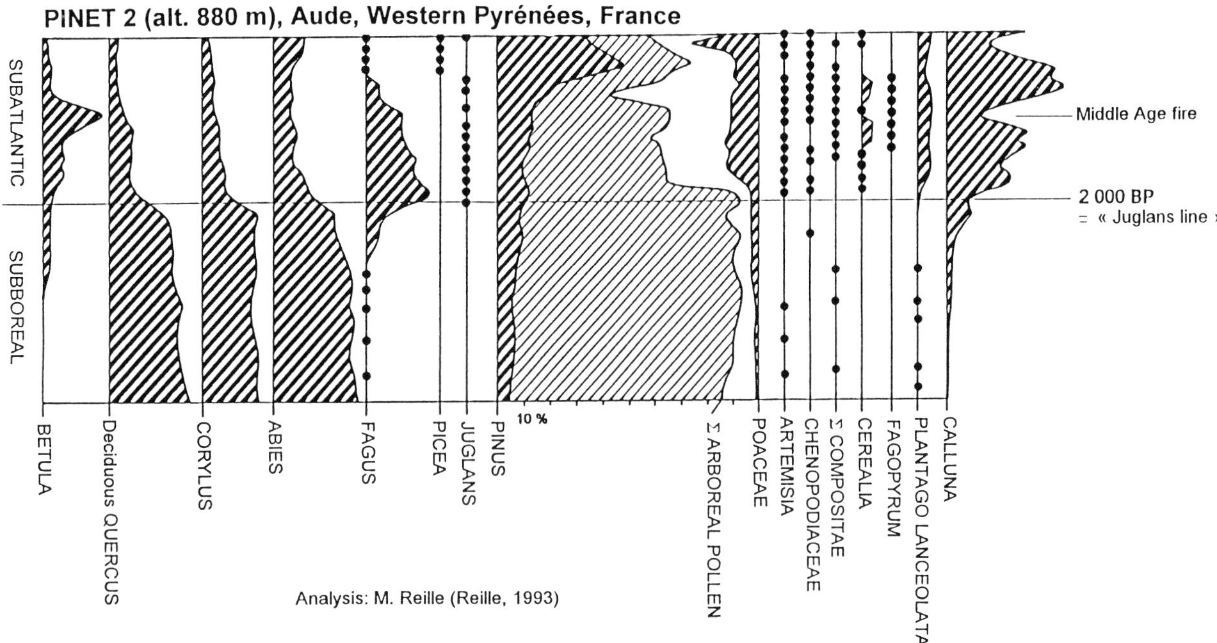

Figure 3.3. Simplified pollen diagram from Pinet. (After Reille, 1991)

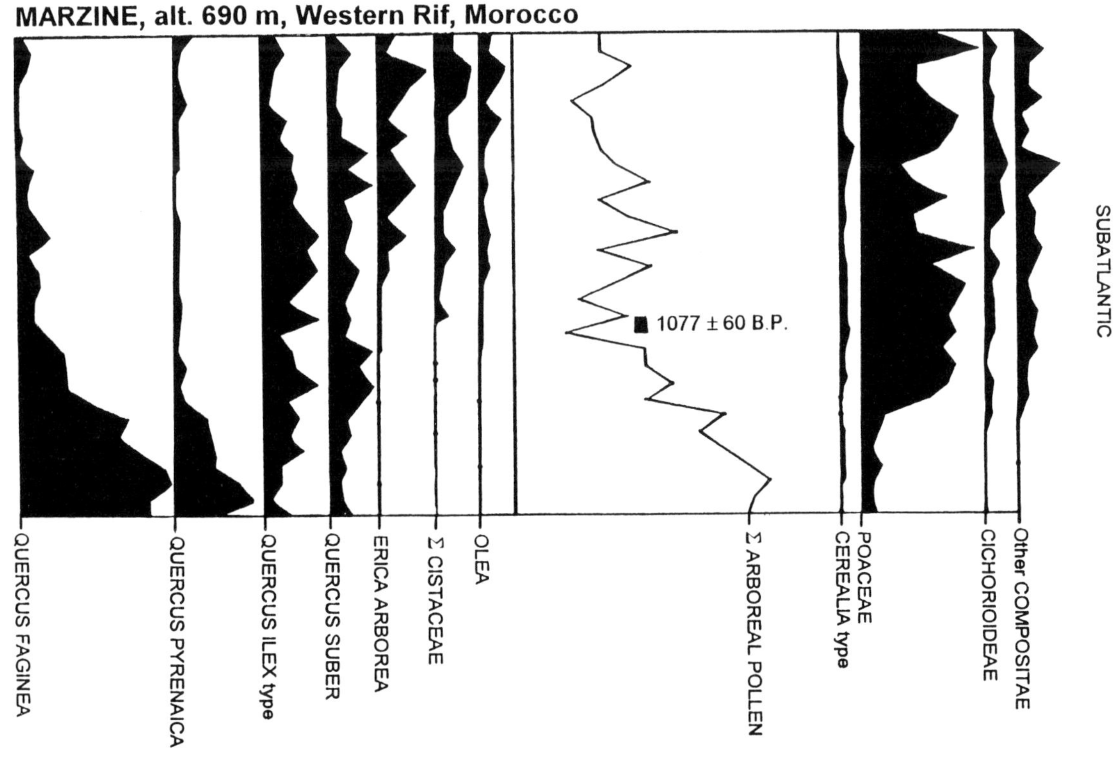

Figure 3.4. Simplified pollen diagram for Marzine. (After Reille, 1977)

in the frequency of arboreal pollen. The taxa concerned are those of the oak forest (deciduous *Quercus, Corylus*) and of the beech-fir forest (*Fagus, Abies*). These pollen events represent a land-clearing episode. They are not of climatic origin as they are either contemporary with the appearance or with an improved representation in the pollen assemblages of anthropic markers. The increase in the percentages of Poaceae and *Plantago lancealata,* as well as the continuous occurrences of Chenopodiaceae, illustrate that land was cleared to make way for pasture. Plots of land were also planted with crops, as has been shown by the increase in the frequency of cultivated plants (Cerealia, *Fagopyrum)* and ruderal plants (*Artemisia* and other Compositae). *Fagopyrum* is a cereal from central Asia, introduced to Europe in the Middle Ages (Bonnier, 1990). *Fagopyrum* is therefore a useful marker for determining that it was during the Middle Ages that local populations burnt the Pinet peat bog. This event is conveyed in pollen assemblages by a collapse of the *Calluna* present in the peat bog, and by a transitional increase in the frequencies of *Betula*, the germinal capacity of which is increased in ashy soils.

The Marzine diagram

The Marzine sequence (Reille, 1977; Fig. 3.4) comes from a peat bog situated at 690 metres altitude in the Western Rif (Morocco). In this pollen diagram, we note that during the Subatlantic, a period of deforestation was recorded which is indicated in the pollen samples by a decline in deciduous oak forest species (*Quercus faginea, Q. pyrenaica*). This change favours the expansion of taxa of the evergreen oak forest. *(Q. ilex, Q. coccifera, Q. suber).* The destruction of the deciduous oak forest was completed around 1070 BP, in other words 200 years after the Arab conquest of Morocco (in 681 AD). From this period on, the continuing high level of anthropic pressure favoured the extension of matorral shrub formations. The increase in pollen frequencies of the Cistaceae (especially of *Cistus*) testifies to the influence of fires on the vegetation dynamics.

DISCUSSION AND PERSPECTIVES

Selectivity in the recording of anthropic events by pollen sequences

The Holocene pollen sequences studied in Mediterranean countries have, in the majority of cases, shown signs of human intervention in the natural environment. Only a selection of anthropic events is recorded in the pollen sequences due to problems concerning pollen production and dispersal (which vary according to the type of plant) and the conservation of pollen in sedimentary sites. The events are as follows:

- Episodes of deforestation, in which the main sign in the pollen assemblages is a sharp fall in the arboreal pollen curves.
- Periods in which fields were not cultivated, which are rarely identified in the pollen sequences.
- Periods of reforestation, which can be indicated in pollen diagrams in several different ways. For example, in the Pyrénées, the policy of planting coniferous trees adopted by foresters at the beginning of the nineteenth century is indicated in the upper part of certain pollen sequences by an increase in the frequencies of *Pinus* and in the appearance of continual pollen occurrences of *Picea* (Saint-Pé-d'Ardet: Andrieu, 1991; Freychinède: Reille, 1993; La Restanque and Soucarat: Reille and Andrieu, 1994; Les Sagnes, Le Laurenti, Fournas, Le Serre, Gourg Nègre: Reille and Lowe, 1993) or by the appearance of a continuous *Eucalyptus* pollen curve, similar to that which can be seen in certain pollen diagrams of the Iberian Peninsula. (Charco da Candeira: van der Knaap and van Leeuwen, 1994).
- Periods of pastoral activity, which are generally indicated in pollen diagrams by an increase in the frequency of herbaceous and nitrophilous taxons, such as *Plantago lanceolata, P. coronopus, Rumex*, Chenopodiaceae and composites (Asteroideae and Cichorioideae).
- Periods of cultivation of various taxa:
  1) *Castanea* and *Juglans*, for which the first signs of cultivation are dated everywhere in pollen sequences in the Western Mediterranean to ± 2000 BP : this is the case in ex-Yugoslavia (2055 ± 60 BP in the Limski-LM5 sequence: Beug, 1977), in Italy (2130 ± 40 BP in the Lago di Ganna sequence: Drescher-Schneider, 1994; 1990 ± 50 BP in the Pian di Nel, Piedmont sequence: Caramiello *et al.*, 1994; 2050 ± 50 BP in the Agoraie sequence, Liguria: Cruise, 1990; 2050 ± 60 BP in the Canolo Nuovo sequence, Calabria: Schneider, 1985) and in France (2180 ± 90 BP in the Soulcem 2 sequence, in the Ariège Pyrénées: Jalut *et al.*, 1984).
  2) *Vitis* and *Olea*: the cultivation of these two taxa appears late in the Western Mediterranean. In France, the beginning of the cultivation of the olive tree is only dated in two sequences, that of the Etang de Berre (Provence) where it was dated from 1070 ± 70 BP (Laval *et al.*, 1991) and that of Marsillargues (Languedoc) where this event was dated to 1300 ± 60 BP (Planchais, 1982; Planchais and Duzer, 1978). In Portugal, in the Serra da Estrela, various episodes of cultivation of *Olea* were recorded and dated by radiocarbon datings: 1410 ± 35 BP (Candieira: Janssen, 1991), 1050 ± 60 BP (Lagoa Comprida 1: Janssen and Woldrinch, 1981) and 850 ± 90 BP (Lagoa Comprida 2: Janssen, 1991). In Morocco, the olive tree was first cultivated in 1080 ± 55 BP in the Tanakob sequence (Reille, 1977), 1070 ± 60 BP in the Marzine sequence (Reille, 1977) and 1010 ± 50 BP in the Abartète sequence (Reille, 1977). In Greater Kabylia (Algeria), the beginning of the cultivation of

Pays	FRANCE		
Réf. Biblio.	Planchais et Duzer, 1978	Planchais *et al.*, 1991	Planchais, 1985
Régions	Languedoc-Roussillon		
Sites	Marsillargues	Lattes	Canet-St Nazaire
CB = C. *Castanea*	D = 1300 ± 60		M = 700 ± 70
CC = C. *Cerealia*	1ère: D = 4760 ± 100 2ème: D = 2270 ± 70 *légèrement vieillie ?* 3ème: D = 1300 ± 60	Subatlantique: *non daté*	M = 700 ± 70
CJ = C. *Juglans*	1ère: D = 2270 ± 70 *légèrement vieillie ?* 2ème: D = 1300 ± 60		M = 700 ± 70
CO = C. *Olea*	D = 1300 ± 60		M = 700 ± 70
CV = C. *Vitis*	D = 1300 ± 60		M = 700 ± 70
DF = Déforestation	1ère: D = 4760 ± 100 2ème: D = 1300 ± 60	Subboréal: 3970 ± 90 <DF< 3730 ± 30	M = 700 ± 70
PA = Pâturage			M = 700 ± 70
RE = Reforestation			

Table 3.5. List of anthropic events recorded in the Marsillargues and the Canet sequences. (Languedoc-Roussillon, France)

Olea was recent: 300 ± 60 BP (Salamani, 1991).

3) Cerealia: the phases in the cultivation of cultivated Poaceae were frequently recorded in the pollen sequences in the Mediterranean basin from the Atlantic period onwards (around *ca* ± 8000 BP). The cereals that have been clearly identified as to their species are Rye (*Secale*) and buckwheat (*Fagopyrum*).
4) The Fabaceae: the cultivated plants belonging to this family included broad beans (*Faba*), lentils (*Vicia*), and chick peas (*Cicer*). As the pollen for this species is still generally unidentified, it appeared under the term of 'Fabaceae' or 'Leguminoseae' or 'Papiolonaceae'. However, the cultivation of Fabaceae is rarely recorded in pollen sequences (except in the Courthézon profile, in the Vaucluse: Triat-Laval, 1978). This is due to the fact that this family is made up of cleistogamic taxons, and therefore has a poor pollen dispersal.
5) *Linum:* the cultivation of flax is rarely recorded in pollen diagrams as this plant is entomogamous. Its pollen is, therefore, poorly dispersed.
6) *Citrus*: this term covers citrus fruit whose cultivation has only been located in recent pollen diagrams of the Middle East.

Problems of dating anthropogenic events

Anthropic events which have been illustrated by pollen profiles have rarely been dated using carbon dating or even using other forms of dating evidence (archaeology, historical documents). It is more often through stratigraphic correlation with other regional pollen sequences that anthropic events can be dated. The lack of information on the history and chronology of anthropization is largely due to national and international organisations' priorities in setting up and financing specific programmes. These deal predominantly with problems related to global climatic changes around the world. This state of affairs explains why, in certain areas, the history of the vegetation as well as the types of human interventions which took place in the natural environment remain unknown.

Correlating palynological and archaeological data: problems of scale

The information gathered through pollen data is essentially of value on a regional scale. In contrast, information gathered through archaeological data is of value on a local scale. It is therefore due to the fact that different anthropic activities are evaluated on the varying scales proposed by each of these two disciplines, that the correlation between pollen data and archaeological data often poses many problems (see also the discussion in Chapter 2).

The necessity for a multi-disciplinary palaeoecological approach

In order to get around these problems of scale, we suggest that the sedimentary sequences extracted from wet environments be studied from a multi-disciplinary palaeoecological perspective based on the following three approaches: palynology, of value on a regional scale; analyses of plant macroremains, fruits and seeds, of value on a local scale; and palaeoentomology, based on the study of insect sclerites, of value both on a regional and a local scale. The paleoenvironmental information brought together by these two latter approaches allows for greater precision in the definition of events recorded through pollen analyses, and may indeed bring to light new events. Research of this kind has already been successfully undertaken in Northern Europe by Gaillard and Lemdahl (1993, 1994).

From a methodological point of view, improvements could be made. They particularly need to be made in the resolution of sampling anthropogenic sections of Holocene sedimentary profiles. In the same manner, palynologists must refine, as much as possible, the palynological determination of anthropogenic taxons.

Moreover, the study of the modalities and chronology of anthropization in the Mediterranean should be the central theme of an international research programme. It is only with this type of programme that sufficient financial funding would be possible, allowing for optimal working conditions, the sampling (through coring) of sediment profiles, the studying of these from a multi-disciplinary perspective, and the systematic carbon dating of all recorded anthropic events. Priority should be given to new corings on sites in which previous studies indicate that anthropization of the natural environment was recorded but not dated. Finally, new sedimentary sequences should be sampled from sites lacking in historical data.

ACKNOWLEDGEMENTS

This research was financed by the EU within the framework of the 'Médimont', directed by M. Dubost (International Centre for Alpine Environment: ICALPE, Corte). We would like to thank him greatly for his assistance.

REFERENCES

Andrieu, V. (1991) *Dynamique du Paléoenvironnement de la Vallée Montagnarde de la Garonne (Pyrénées Centrales, France) de la Fin des Temps Glaciaires à l'Actuel.* Unpublished thesis, University of Toulouse.

Beug, H.J. (1975) Man as factor in the vegetational history of the Balkan Peninsula. In *Problems of Balkan Flora and Vegetation', Proceedings of the 1st International Symposium on Balkan Flora and Vegetation*: 72–7. Sofia.

Beug, H.J. (1977) Vegetationsgeschichtliche Untersuchungen im Küstenbereich von Istrien (Jugoslawien). *Flora* 166: 357–81.

Bonnier, G. (1990) *La Grande Flore.* Paris, Editions Belin, 4 volumes.

Bottema, S. (1974) *Late Quaternary Vegetation History of North-Western Greece.* Unpublished thesis, University of Groningen.

Bottema, S. (1980) On the history of the Walnut (*Juglans regia* L.) in Southeastern Europe. *Acta Botanica Neerlandica,* 29, 5/6: 343–9.

Caramiello, R., Siniscalco, C., Potenza, A., Mercalli, L., Allegri, L., Manfri, L., and Proposito, A. (1994) Pollen analysis and radiocarbon dating of a peatbog (Pian di Nel, 2256 m) in Orco Valley, Western Alpes, Italy. *Il Quaternario* 7, 1: 91–102.

Cruise, G.M. (1990) Pollen stratigraphy of two Holocene peat sites in the Ligurian Apennines, Northern Italy. *Review of Paleobotany and Palynology* 63: 299–313.

Drescher-Schneider, R. (1994) Forest, forest clearance and open land during the time of the Roman empire in Northern Italy (the botanical record). Evaluation of land surface cleared from forests in the Mediterranean region during the time of the Roman empire. *European Paleoclimate and Man 5*: 45–58.

Gaillard, M.J. and Lemdahl, G. (1993) Environmental and climatic changes at the transition Late glacial/Holocene in South Sweden based on pollen, plant macrofossil, and insect analyses: the example of Ångdala, Southern Scania. *Palyno-Nytt* 22: 8–10.

Gaillard, M.J. and Lemdahl, G. (1994) Late glacial insect assemblages from Grand-Marais, south-western Switzerland. Climatic implications and comparison with pollen and plant macrofossil data. *Dissertationes Botanicae* 234: 287–308.

Jalut, G., Esteban-Amat, A., Pages, P. and Mardones, M. (1984) Quelques aspects de l'action de l'Homme sur le milieu montagnard pyrénéen: conséquences phytogéographiques. Ecologie des milieux montagnards et de haute altitude. *Documents d'Ecologie Pyrénéenne* 3–4: 503–9.

Janssen, C.R. (1991) Degradation stages of vegetation. *Proceedings of the Peat Excursion of the Systematic-Geobotany Institute, University of Bern, Second Part: 'Serra da Estrela (Portugal)':* 39–58.Utrecht, State University, Laboratory of Palaeobotany and Palynology.

Janssen, C.R. and Woldrinch, R.E. (1981) A preliminary radiocarbon dated pollen sequence from the Serra da Estrela, Portugal. *Finisterra* 16, 32: 299–309.

Laval, H., Medus, J. and Roux, M. (1991) Palynological and sedimentological records of Holocene human impact for the Etang de Berre, Southeastern France. *The Holocene* 1–3: 269–72.

Planchais, N. (1982) Palynologie lagunaire de l'étang de Mauguio. Paléoenvironnement végétal et évolution anthropique. *Pollen et Spores* 24, 1: 93–118.

Planchais, N. and Duzer, D. (1978) Les pollens indicateurs de l'action anthropique aux alentours de l'Etang de Maugio (Hérault). *Comptes Rendus de l'Académie des Sciences de Paris* 287, D: 931–3.

Reille, M. (1977) Contribution pollenanalytique à l'histoire holocène de la végétation des montagnes du Rif (Maroc septentrional). *Bulletin de l'Association Française pour l'Etude du Quaternaire* 1, 50: 53–76.

Reille, M. (1991) L'origine de la station de pin à crochets de la tourbière de Pinet (Aude) et de quelques stations isolées de cet arbre dans les Vosges et le Jura. *Bulletin de la Société Botanique de France* 138, 2: 123–48.

Reille, M. (1993) New pollen analytical researches at Freychinède, Ariège, Pyrénées, France. *Dissertationes Botanicae* 196: 377–86.

Reille, M. and Lowe, J. (1993) A re-evaluation of the vegetation history of the eastern Pyrénées (France) from the end of the last glacial to the present. *Quaternary Science Reviews* 12: 47–77.

Reille, M. and Andrieu, V. (1994) Vegetation history and human action in Ariège (Pyrénées, France). *Dissertationes Botanicae* 234: 413–22.

Salamani, M. (1991) Premières données palynologiques sur l'histoire holocène du massif de l'Akfadou (Grande Kabylie, Algérie). *Ecologia Mediterranea* 17: 145–59.

Schneider, R. (1985) Analyse palynologique dans l'Aspromonte en Calabre (Italie méridionale). *Cahiers ligures de Préhistoire et de Protohistoire* 2: 279–88.

Triat-Laval, H. (1978) *Contribution Pollenanalytique à l'Histoire Tardi- et Postglaciaire de la Végétation de la Basse Vallée du Rhône.* Unpublished Thèse d'Etat, University ofAix-Marseille 3.

Van der Knaap, W.O. and van Leeuwen, J.F.N. (1994) Holocene vegetation, human impact and climatic change in the Serra da Estrela, Portugal. *Dissertationes Botanicae* 234: 497–535.

4. Reconstructing Vegetation and Landscapes in the Mediterranean: the Contribution of Anthracology

Jean-Louis Vernet

INTRODUCTION

Anthracology is the study of charcoal from archaeological sediments and soils. It has furnished a considerable body of data already not only on past landscapes but also on human impacts on those landscapes (Vernet, 1972).

In the Upper Palaeolithic in Cantabria, Spain, the gathering of wood was part of subsistence activities just like hunting (Uzquiano, 1992). The organization of the landscape into steppes, steppe-forest and riverside woodland made mobility necessary in order to collect the fuelwood necessary for daily activities. These activities do not seem to have had much impact on the vegetation.

A little closer to us in time, however, entire landscapes have disappeared due to the activities of people. In the Corbières coastal chain, for example, ecosystems rich in thermo-Mediterranean species, in particular the *Olea europea* of the oleaster variety (the wild olive tree), were progressively eliminated during the Neolithic, mostly by burning and grazing (Solari and Vernet, 1992). In other parts of the Languedoc, the Iron Age and Roman period were, like the Chalcolithic, periods of intense deforestation as human use of the environment for agricultural or industrial purposes intensified. The development of viticulture in the Roman period also had a profound effect. The oak forests, of both holm oak (*Quercus ilex*) and deciduous oaks, had their equilibrium modified in favour of the holm oak.

These opening remarks introduce the key issues in the study of people's impact on the Mediterranean environment: the nature and scale of this process through time, and of the imbalances, degradation and even desertification that can result. Can anthracology contribute to this study, considering that the Mediterranean ecosystem is complex and that we can only compare regions that are homologous? We must place considerable importance, therefore, on the chronology of human activity and its consequences for Mediterranean landscapes of varying latitudes: are we studying degradation, or desertification (Vernet, 1992, 1995)? Vernet (1991) provides a synthesis of these issues, whereas in this paper I shall concentrate on recent results from the sites of Font-Juvénal, in the Aude (Thiébault and Vernet, 1992), and Sallèles d'Aude (Chabal and Laubenheimer, 1994), as well as from several sites in the Alicante region of Spain (Badal *et al.*, 1994). Finally, the relevance of anthracology for our knowledge of medieval landscapes will be discussed, with particular reference to deforestation in the Pyrenees mountains as a consequence of smithing.

THE BASIS OF ANTHRACOLOGY

It might seem overambitious of anthracology to attempt to reconstruct past landscapes and people-landscape interactions given the emphasis of recent studies (as exemplified in this volume, and see especially Chapter 19) on a multidisciplinary approach integrating earth sciences, human sciences and archaeology. However, anthracology has an original contribution to make in terms of the perception of natural and humanly-affected ecosystems and the uses people have made of them. These considerations set the limits of the science of anthracology, which has fundamentally a diachronic approach.

For a long time the diachronic approach was not only sufficient but necessary because one of the priorities of palaeoecological studies was to build up a history of vegetation. This 'phyto-history' is now established, at least in its main characteristics, and sometimes in much greater detail, as in the case of southern France. We have to go beyond this and cope with the challenges of spatial anthracology and geo-anthracology if we are to progress to understanding people-environment relations.

Smart and Hoffman (1988) provide a synthesis of anthracology and its contribution to our knowledge of past vegetation, with particular reference to American examples. Their principal conclusions are closely akin to those obtained for the Mediterranean since the 1970s, as detailed especially by Chabal (1991, 1992, 1994).

The reliability of the information depends on the sampling done in the field. The first consideration is: what was the wood used for? While specific use will result in the selection of certain tree species for specific purposes such as for the construction of the framework of a building, the use of wood for fires will, over the long term, provide a charcoal sample that should be reasonably representative of the territory exploited for its wood.

The duration of wood collection is another essential point. A brief exploitation of the environment, such as that represented by a deposit in a hearth, is altogether insufficient for understanding the vegetation surrounding a site. In practice, the duration requirement is most often met if we include dispersed charcoal found in both primary and secondary (backfill) archaeological layers: they are often small fragments, collected through water sieving and flotation. This fragmentary and dispersed charcoal represents the sum of the exploitation during the occupation of the archaeological unit. Even if there is likely to be a certain bias due to preferences made in collecting the wood, over the long term such biases should be cancelled out. The 'mean anthracological image' thus obtained should be satisfactory from the point of view of the representivity of the vegetation present in the sample.

The harvest of wood is both a harvest of ligneous species and a sampling of the biomass. Within a given ecosystem the available ligneous biomass is not random, but depends upon the structure of the vegetation. In this way it has often been shown that twenty per cent of the ligneous species represent 80 per cent of the charcoal (Chabal, 1992), just as in present-day vegetation. This well known statistical law in economics and ecology (the Pareto law, or 'law of the strongest') is only refuted in imbalanced environments and always tends to re-establish itself. It is often observed in anthracology, except when sampling is insufficient or when we examine wood used for purposes other than as firewood.

It is also important to establish whether the combustion process and/or human actions have skewed the anthracological image of the vegetation. Of course it is impossible to prevent the anthracological spectrum giving a biased picture, if for no other reason than because there is a transfer of information from past vegetation to the anthracological diagrams. The causes of the over-representation of a given species are well known: the species may produce a higher biomass, and so more dead wood; people may collect it in greater abundance; it may leave a greater quantity of unburnt residues; its charcoal may be more resistant. Of all of these, combustion is an essential element. The state of fragmentation affects the expression of the relative proportions between tree species (Chabal 1991). A more delicate problem is the reduction of mass or of ligneous matter that can alter the proportions between species. Research concerning this question is in progress.

The interpretation of the resulting charcoal diagrams must be done with considerable caution. The proportion of a given species represented in the charcoal on an archaeological site does not actually tell us anything in absolute terms about the frequency of the species in the surrounding landscape. Having said that, though, the wooded landscapes prior to the beginnings of agricultural clearance (prior to the Middle Neolithic in southern France, for example) are probably rather well represented by the relative frequencies of the various species found on archaeological sites. In a severely cleared landscape, the frequencies of these same species are useful indicators of ecological imbalances, especially in terms of the representation of shrubs that benefit from clearing of fire. Noting the relative evolution of a species can show a variation in the area of wood supply. Thus at the important Gallo-Roman site of Lattes in Hérault, the relative rise in tamarisk charcoal after some six centuries of settlement indicates not the expansion of this species but rather the expansion of the wood supply area into wet lands (Ambert et Chabal, 1992).

THE VEGETATION SEQUENCE IN MEDITERRANEAN FRANCE

For the Mediterranean regions of France and neighbouring areas in general, anthracological results can be divided into four main biozones or phases (Vernet and Thiébault, 1987). These zones can be pushed back to 40,000 BP with the help of the data from the palaeolithic shelter site at the Pont du Gard (Bazile-Robert, 1981; Fig. 4.1). Anthracology reveals that relations between people and landscape were controlled by climate and natural changes in the vegetation up until the Later Neolithic. From this period onwards (the Chasséen culture in France), human influence is such that correlation with the vegetation reflects human activity very closely.

• Phase 1
This corresponds with the disappearance of birch *c.*13–12000 BP up until *c.*8000 BP, and is characterized by open vegetation of steppe type with pre-forest formations. In Sub-Phase 1a, these formations are dominated by Scots pine and juniper. In Sub-Phase 1b they are dominated by juniper and Scots pine along with a few deciduous oaks.

• Phase 2 develops between *c.*8500 and *c.*6000 BP. In this phase we see the regression of the juniper and the extension of deciduous oaks, along with a few holm oaks and some thermophilous species. This change is entirely due to climatic warming.

• Phase 3
This covers the period from 6000 to 4500 BP, which spans the Middle and Final Neolithic in the French cultural sequence, a period of prime importance for the evolution of society in terms of agricultural and social development, and the beginnings of the ensuing Chalcolithic. The vegetation changes are discussed in the following section on Font-Juvénal.

• Phase 4 is characterized by the formation of the present-

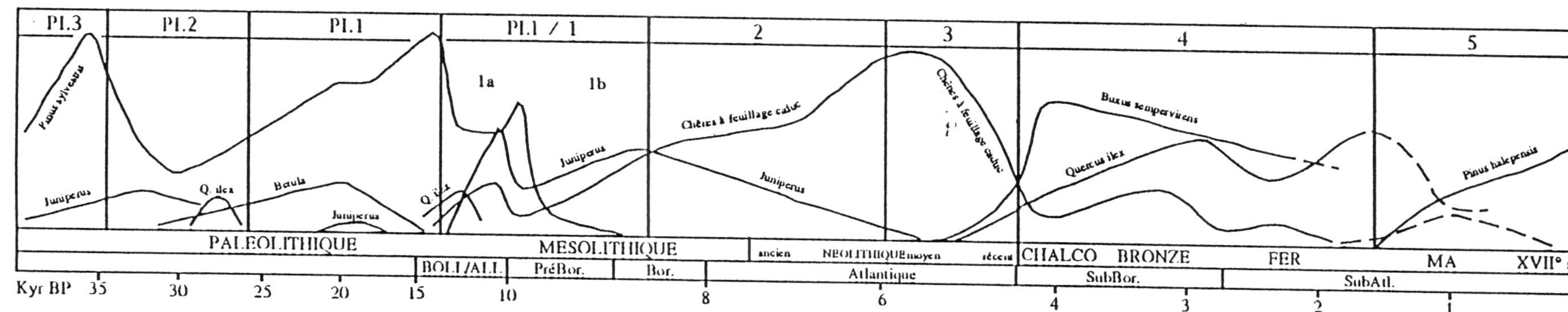

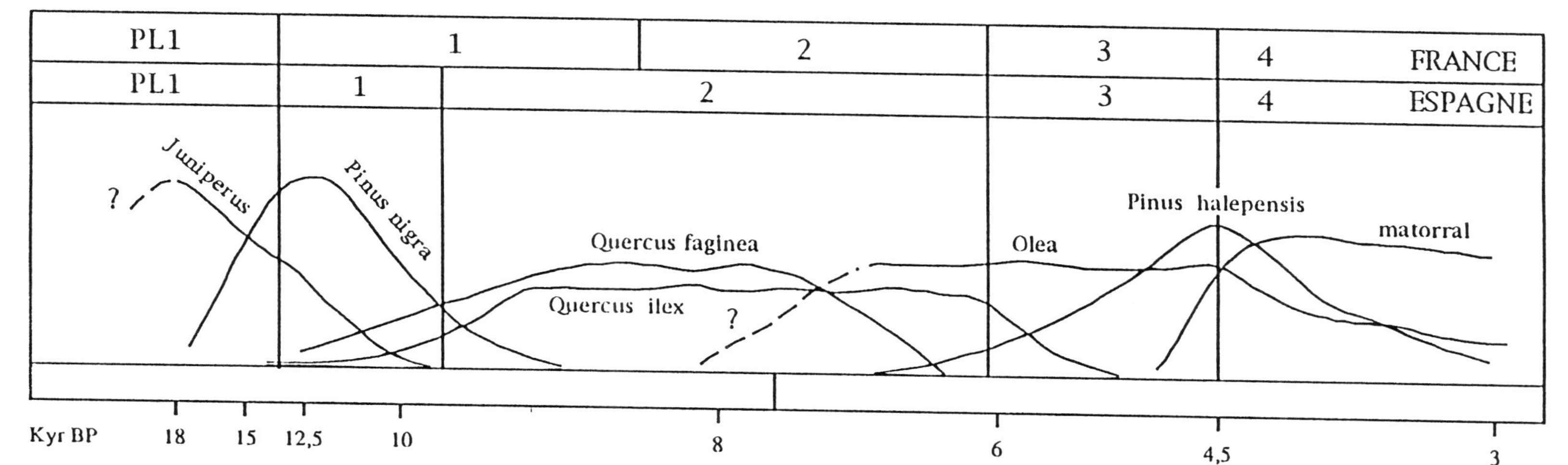

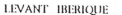

Figure 4.1. (above) Schematic representation of the eight anthracological phases identified in southern France spanning the last 40,000 years; (below) comparison between southern France and eastern Spain, showing that the oldest phases (1 and 2), climatically-determined, are not contemporary, whereas the following phases marking human impacts are broadly synchronous. (After Vernet, 1994)

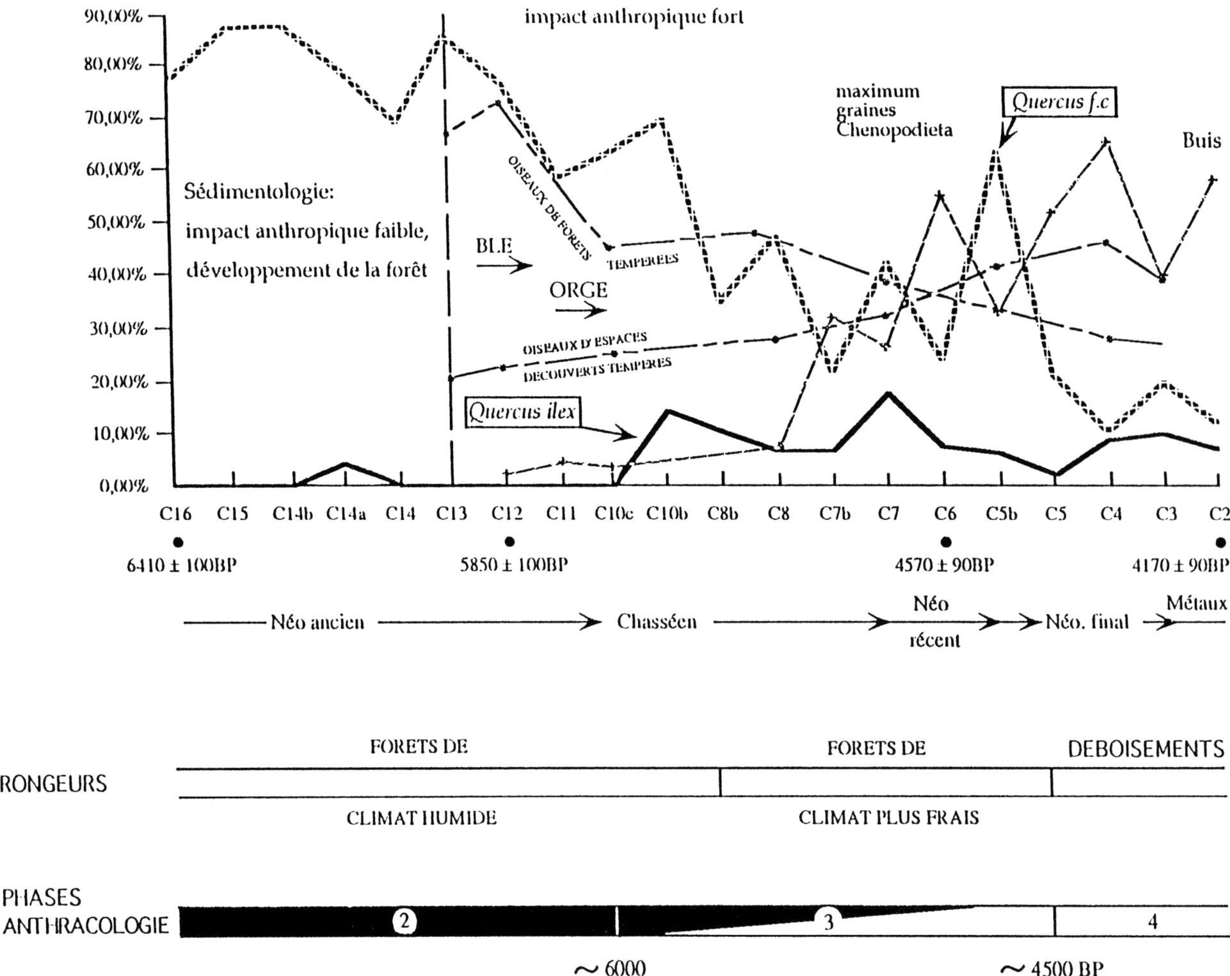

Figure 4.2. The palaeoecology of Font-Juvénal (Aude): the forest structured around the white oak starts to recede under the influence of Chasséen exploitation. Especially notable is the linkage between white oak/forest birds, on the one hand, and boxwood/open country birds on the other. (After Vernet, 1994)

day landscapes, for which the main markers are boxwood and holm oak. It starts with the beginning of metallurgy and continues to the present day, with the expansion of the Aleppo pine (Phase 5). As has been demonstrated in recent research, we can detect cycles of exploitation and fallow until modern times, the significance of which cannot be properly understood without resorting to documentary studies (Chabal, 1991; Durand, 1991).

THE SITE OF FONT-JUVENAL AND HUMAN IMPACTS ON ITS ENVIRONMENT

The rock shelter at Font-Juvénal (Conques-sur-Orbiel in the department of Aude) is a few kilometres north of Carcasonne, in the meso-Mediterranean stage of the holm oak. The site was discovered in 1970 and was excavated by J. Guilaine and his team up until 1981. There were more than 17 archaeological levels within a deposit 6–7 m thick, five of which belong to the Neolithic (Guilaine, 1988). The identification of more than 6200 pieces of wood charcoal furnished more than 42 taxons (Vernet, 1991; Fig. 4.2):

Assemblages of deciduous oak dominate during the Early Neolithic, until the end of the 'Epicardial' (*c.*6400–5800 BP). Sedimentology indicates low human impact and forest development. The impact of the first inhabitants of Font-Juvénal is difficult to discern. The image given of the site in this initial phase of settlement by the analysis of the charcoal is that of a stable environment, as yet little affected by people.

The first traces of *Quercus ilex-coccifera* and of boxwood appear with the middle neolithic Chasséen culture. At first, the frequency of deciduous oak remains relatively high (more than 50 per cent), and those of holm oak and boxwood relatively low (less than ten per cent for boxwood). This even with the increase in cereal (wheat and barley) cultivation at this time, we do not find the vegetation transformations noted on other sites of the same period. At Unang in the Vaucluse, for example, deciduous oaks disappear at the end of the Cardial (Early) Neolithic (Thiébault, 1988), and the same is true at the Baume de Montclus (Bazile-Robert, 1983), eradicated by the middle neolithic Chasséen farmers.

The boxwood curve at Font-Juvénal then rises progressively, reaching approximately 50 per cent by *c.*4500 BP. The holm oak curve remains relatively low, never reaching twenty per cent. Sedimentology shows the impact of human activity, for example in level 7 by great quantities of seeds of weeds of cultivation (Chenopodietea). The archaeozoological analysis shows that numbers of forest-dwelling birds declined at the same time as the frequency of deciduous oaks, and that numbers of open-country birds increased parallel with the increasing frequencies of boxwood and holm oak. The rodent fauna showed similar trends, testifying to the opening up of humid-climate forests, which were increasingly cooler from the Late Neolithic onwards.

With the Final Neolithic, and especially the Middle and Final Bronze Age, the frequency of deciduous oak drops to below ten per cent. Simultaneously, boxwood culminates at 40–60 per cent. In level 1, dating to 2390 ± 90 BP (not represented in the diagram), the frequency of holm oak even reaches forty per cent. The fauna confirms the extent of clearance, corroborating the boxwood and holm oak curves.

Phase 1 of the sequence described in the preceding section is not found at Font-Juvénal. The anthracological and radiometric data show that the origins of the settlement are 1500 years after the formation of deciduous oak forests, during the last period of stable exploitation of the forest, the second part of Phase 2 (Vernet and Thiébault, 1987). The upper limit of Phase 2 is particularly interesting, because in most instances it corresponds with the transition from the Cardial to the Chasséen Neolithic. During the Chasséen period, exploitation systems developed that have persisted through to modern times. (Boxwood is an excellent marker of the beginning of anthropic pressure on the environment, coinciding with the origins of the agricultural-sylvicultural-pastoral system, and was still widely used in the 'Caussenarde' traditions of southern France at the beginning of the nineteenth century: Durand-Tullou, 1972).

Boxwood also reveals the development of sedentary settlement systems in the Chasséen, with fixed villages and fields organization, in contrast with the more mobile systems of exploitation hitherto. At the same time, the management of the environment remained balanced until the middle of the Chasséen period, possibly related to the economic status of the site (Thiébault, 1991). The regression of the forest that generally characterizes Phase 3 seems to be of a short duration at the site, between 500 and 900 years. Phase 4 begins after *c.*4500 BP, characterized by maximum human impact, with the formation of *garrigues* and box tree stands.

FROM KILNS TO THE FOREST AND BACK

For more than 300 years the Gallo-Roman potters at Sallèles d'Aude used thousands of cubic metres of wood to stoke their kilns. We have chosen this example in order to illustrate that a detailed (high resolution) anthracological reading can inform on the nature and scale of crafts and industries in protohistory, and their impact on the landscape (Chabal and Laubenheimer, 1994).

The workshops at Sallèles d'Aude, which contain no less than fourteen kilns, are a very large establishment which functioned intensively from the first century AD to the sudden cessation of production at the beginning of the fourth century AD (Fig. 4.3). The kilns are not all contemporary, but it is possible with the help of archaeomagnetism to establish a schema of their evolution. The

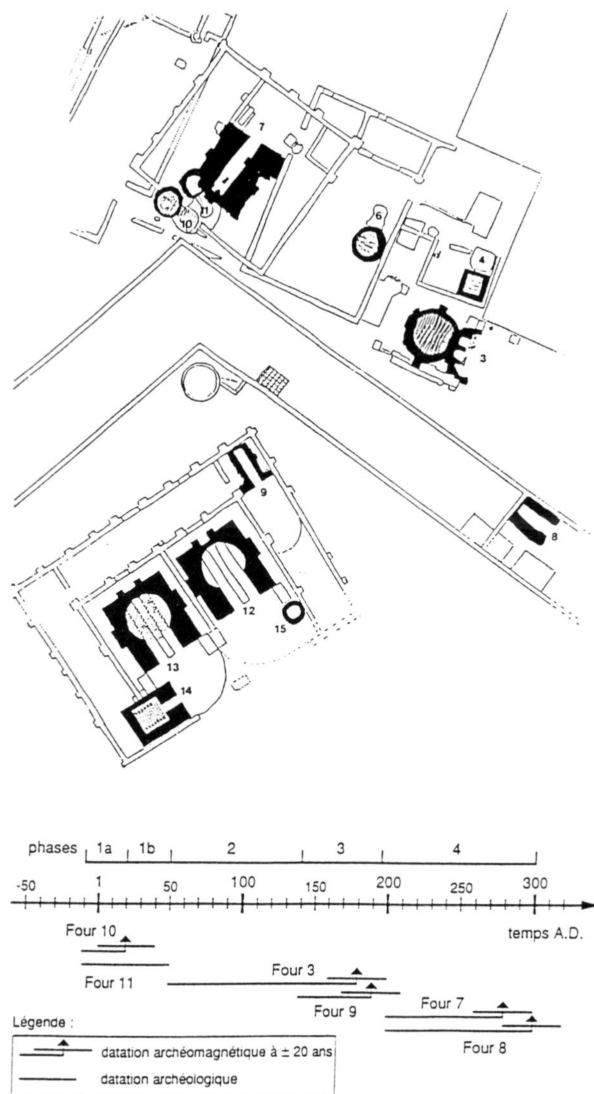

Figure 4.3. General plan of the Gallo-Roman potters' workshop at Sallèles d'Aude, with the kilns marked in black. (After Chabal and Laubenheimer, 1994)

workshop functioned for some three centuries with, however, changes in the number and size of the kilns, implying that there were fluctuations in the quantity of wood required. Through comparison with traditional cottage industries, we can estimate that one 'stere'of wood was required to fire two cubic metres of pottery. The workshop used small kilns at first, during the first twenty years of the first century AD, but large kilns were then built. between *c.*AD 20 and AD 50, attaining a capacity of 360 m^3 of pottery for 160 m^3 of wood. Later, with the recession of the third century, kiln capacities were reduced to 132 m^3 of pottery for 66 m^3 of wood.

The supply of fuel is the most vital constraint for potters, even more than of water or clay. The size of the kilns and the lifespan of the workshop imply an enormous consumption of wood, issues that were addressed by Chabal and Laubenheimer (1994) in their analysis of charcoal residues from the kilns and the site backfill..

The charcoal analyzed was taken from six kilns: 10, 11, 3, 9, 7 and 8. These cover all phases of activity except for phase 2, the phase of maximum activity, the study of which is still in progress. The results obtained on more than 3000 pieces of charcoal are, therefore, still preliminary. The charcoal is homogeneous and quite fragmented, from a few millimetres to a few centimetres, indicating burning in one or more firings. All the samples were water-sieved though a 4-mm mesh, with sub-samples extracted in the laboratory of at least 250 fragments.

At least 25 tree species were found in the kilns, of which some are of hard wood: deciduous oak (probably the white oak *Quercus pubescens*), holm oak, ash, and elm. The other ligneous species are represented in smaller numbers. Some of them are part of the Mediterranean oak forest or of damaged forms of it, such as Montpelier maple, strawberry tree, box tree, dogwood, juniper, pistachio tree, blackthorn, and laurel. Other trees present, such as common maple, alder, walnut, fir, and beech, require more humidity, and probably derive from the riparian woods that have been a major component of woodland vegetation in the south of France until the Middle Ages (Chabal, 1991; Durand and Planchais, 1982; Triat-Laval, 1978; Vernet, 1987). Alongside these taxons, the maritime pine must be an import because it requires acidic subsoil – the Corbières are the closest region. There are also four species that could have been cultivated: vine, olive, walnut and almond.

There is no correlation between the species found and either stratigraphic layer, period, the size of kilns, or individual kilns (Fig. 4.4).

Overall, we find that there are only half as many species represented as on a site where domestic firewood alone is analyzed. Moreover, the Gini-Lorenz concentration curve (Fig. 4.4) indicates 10/90 as opposed to the usual 20/80, indicating the equilibrium expressed by the Pareto law, from which few plant communities diverge (Poissonet *et al.*, 1973). This equilibrium is encountered in charcoal from domestic fires. These results indicate that the frequencies of species in the potters' fuelwood are not a reliable reflection of the natural environment in the wood supply area: the dominant species are completely over-represented. At the same time we can go further in our understanding of the wood supply and, therefore, of the landscape: the representation of the ten most numerous species through time shows a statistically-significant evolution that is also coherent in terms of the ecology (Fig. 4.4).

When the site was first occupied, plain or riverside tree species such as alder, ash and elm represent a considerable proportion of the wood used. The white oak is the most frequently encountered. Very quickly the proportions of ash and elm drop, disappearing completely. It appears, therefore, that a first phase of exploitation concerned mesophile or damp areas that can be found on the floodplain at the confluence of the Cesse and the Aude, some two km from the workshop. In a second phase deciduous oaks were the primary source. In the third phase, holm oak was dominant.

This tripartite sequence, ecologically quite clear, demonstrates successive intensive exploitations. The question that we must ask ourselves is whether this represents the use of several spatially-distinct areas, or a single area that underwent ecological transformations.

The two situations are in fact complimentary. Anthracological research on protohistoric sites in southern France has shown that, during the Chalcolithic and the Iron Age especially, large woods on the coastal and alluvial plains were destroyed (Chabal, 1991). The potters at Sallèles d'Aude initially exploited a low-altitude forest environment, more or less confined to riverside areas that must have coexisted with a deciduous oak forest beyond the plains.

Regional anthracological and palynological research also shows that the replacement of the deciduous oak forest by the holm oak was a consequence of deforestation (Triat-Laval, 1978). Cutting and repeated fires favour the holm oak more than the white oak, as it is better able to sprout from its stump. The holm oak was able in this way to fill in some of the gaps left by the white oak; deciduous oak practically never reappears. Even if the end of production was not linked to a shortage of wood – a hypothesis that remains to be verified – it is nevertheless clear that the location of the workshop, close to the abundant deciduous vegetation of the Cesse-Aude plain, must have been a determining factor for the potters: their site chosen was in close proximity to the three vital resources they required – clay, water, and wood. Based on results obtained in this manner and on spatial hypotheses, Chabal suggested a possible evolution of the landscape on a north-south profile around the site (Fig. 4.5).

Therefore, despite the very specific purpose for which the wood was selected by the potters of Sallèles d'Aude, their fuel allows for an adequate perception of their landscape. The slightly selective nature of their sample signifies that it was the arborescent species that were most used, in preference to subordinate shrubby species. The

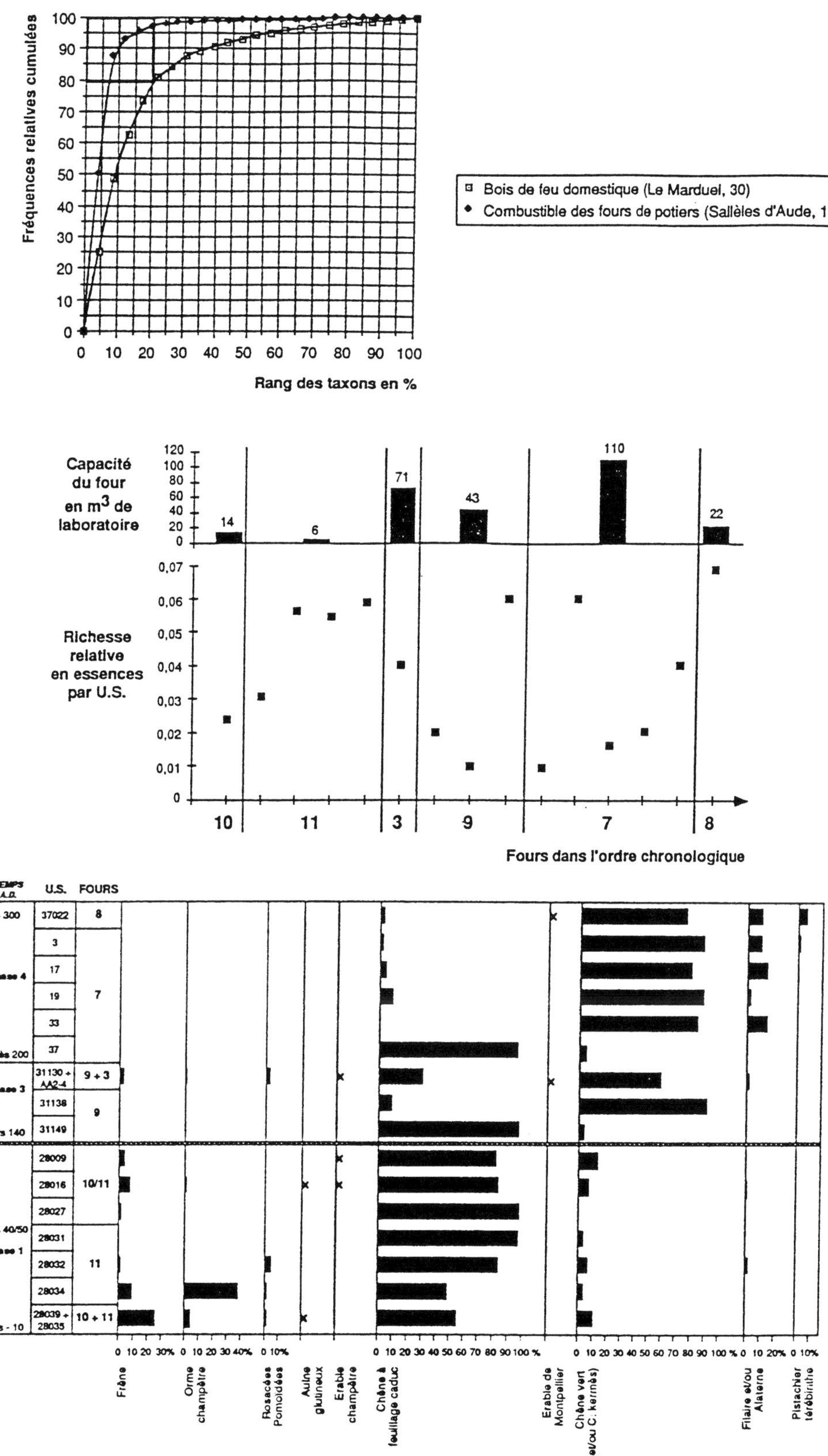

Figure 4.4. (top) Gini-Lorenz concentration curves for the charcoal from the Gallo-Roman kilns at Sallèles d'Aude (diamonds) and for domestic firewood from neolithic sites (squares): note the difference in the inflexion point on the curve – 10/90 for the kilns and 20/80 for the general case. (centre) Relative wealth in ligneous species ('richesses relative en essences par U.S.') in relation to the size of the kilns ('capacité du four en m^3 de laboratoire'). (bottom) The changing frequencies of the ten main tree species in six of the kilns at Sallèles d'Aude. (After Chabal and Laubenheimer, 1994)

potters' activity reflects their exploitation of their environment up to the point of the complete exhaustion of resources and the related transformation of deciduous oak forests into evergreen oak forests.

This research, despite its significance, also demonstrates the limits of anthracology, in terms of the uncertainties about the spatial variability in the resources exploited by the site's inhabitants and about the size of the territory from which they were derived. To go further, it would be necessary to adopt a systematic approach similar to that conducted in the Valdaine basin by Berger (1995): here, the integration of archaeological and palaeoenvironmental approaches informed on questions relating to the spatio-temporal dynamics of the soil, the waterways, the vegetation and agro-pastoral practices. The numerous geo-archaeological trenches and the comparison of multi-disciplinary data from each transect made it possible to consider the evolution of the geosystem in its globality. A differential signature was detected between the hills, where erosion was taking place, and the piedmont, which remained remarkably stable, supporting the phyto-geographic and historical analysis made by Barry and Le Roy Ladurie (1962).

EASTERN SPAIN

At the same latitude as Alicante, several prehistoric open air or cave sites (Cova Ampla, Cova de l'Or, Cova de Cendres) have yielded numerous charcoal remains, allowing for comparisons with the southern French data. While the archaeological chronology and cultural sequence are broadly similar, the ecological context is not the same – thermo-Mediterranean rather than meso-Mediterranean. This makes it possible to separate the roles played by climate and people in the transformations of the ecosystem.

The most complete results are provided by the sites of the Cova de Cendres and the Cova de l'Or (Badal *et al.* 1994). The first is a large shelter near Moraira on the coastal cliffs, which are covered by a matorral of Rosmarino-Ericion. The second is an inland shelter overlooking the Serpis valley, 650 m above sea level. Overall nearly 14,000 pieces of charcoal were analyzed, of which 10,000 came from Cova de Cendres.

At Cova de Cendres five 'anthracozones' have been distinguished:

1. Assemblages of black pine and juniper from an upper Pleistocene phase, attributed to Magdalanian settlement and dated to 12,600 BP (Badal Garcia, 1990).
2. After a long hiatus (epi-palaeolithic and mesolithic cultures are not present), Phase 2 begins *c.*7000 BP, characterized by three major assemblages. The first is the Mediterranean holm oak forest, including mesophile taxons such as *Pinus nigra* and *Quercus faginea*. We can estimate the time of the development of this Mediterranean forest between *c.*12,000 and 8000 BP. The second assemblage is a matorral of Querco-Lentiscetum characterized by the presence of *Olea europea*, probably the wild variety oleaster. The third assemblage is of riparian vegetation, with Fraxinus, Salix and so on. This phase represents the thermo-Mediterranean Holocene optimum, a mosaic of evergreen oak forests with a few mesophiles and a matorral of *Olea* (between *c.*10,000 and 6500 BP).
3. Between *c.*7500 and 6500 BP we can detect the beginning of an important phase of exploitation of the ecosystem, demonstrated by the presence of Aleppo pine and the strawberry tree, the remains of which increase considerably during Phase 4.
4. Phase CC4 is dated to between 6500 and 4500 BP and is dominated by charcoal from *Pinus halepensis* and *Olea europea* (the wild variety).
5. After *c.*4500 BP, assemblages from the matorral of *Erica multiflora*, rosemary and leguminous plants are dominant.

The Cova de l'Or provides comparable data, taking into account its ecological situation. Moreover, this research has been conducted within a multi-disciplinary framework including palynology, sedimentology and archaeobotany. This approach makes it possible to situate the limitations of the proposed interpretations which are, for all that, coherent from one field to another.

The Neolithic developed on the eastern coast of the Iberian peninsula from around 7000 BP. Its environmental context has been defined in part by anthracology and is composed of three main coexisting vegetations: evergreen oak forest, matorral of *Querco-lentiscetum* and riparian vegetation. If we are to believe the radiocarbon chronology, about 500 years after the introduction of agriculture and stock-breeding, a secondary vegetation developed in response to human impact. In this way the thermo-Mediterranean matorral of *Querco-lentiscetum* spread to the Cova de Cendres. Pollen analysis on non-anthropized sites shows that the evergreen oak forest receded after 5000 BP (Pons and Reille, 1988). This very general phenomenon is visible at Cendres, where this regression is accompanied by the development of the Aleppo pine (a consequence of the extension of agriculture and herding).

The Cendres sequence comes to an end in the Bronze Age, a period when vegetation suffered considerably due to the intensification of both agriculture and herding. The Aleppo pine recedes before a matorral of Rosmarino-Ericion, a transformation accompanied by intense erosive processes. As far as the olive tree is concerned, it is in these regions that it is the most precocious, encountered already in the warm phases of the late Würm (Badal, 1990). The behaviour of the olive tree during the Holocene is well understood now; the reference pollen site at Padul (Pons and Reille, 1988) shows that it follows a continuous curve from between 7840 ± 220 BP to 4450 ± 60 BP. Our results imply that this expansion since the Neolithic is clearly the consequence of human activity in these regions.

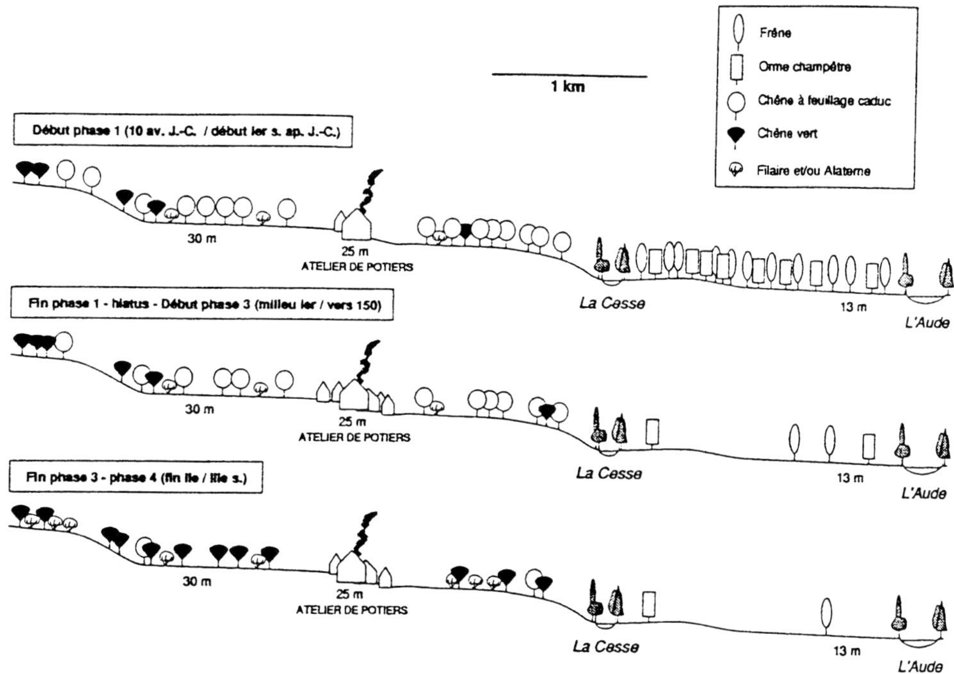

Figure 4.5. Probable sequence of exploitation of local fuelwood sources by the Gallo-Roman pottery at Sallèles d'Aude. (After Chabal and Laubenheimer, 1994)

Anthracological analysis reveals the nature of the plant landscape and which plants were used during the time the caves were occupied. In other open air sites (such as Niuet, in the Rio Serpis valley), high frequencies of *Quercus ilex-coccifera* continue even during the Late Neolithic. Contrary to the Cova de l'Or, which overlooks the Rio Serpis, Aleppo pine and olive trees are weakly represented. This difference is important as it is not fully understood; it could indicate a different system of settlement or land management.

It is clear that, in Spain as in southern France, the Mediterranean environment was exploited in a 'mosaic' system. In the Baza and Guadix basins, in the region of Granada, the charcoal and pollen data converge in showing the decisive role played by the Argaric peoples (in the second millennium BC) in the regression of the evergreen oak forests and their replacement by Aleppo pine and a matorral of Rosmarino-Ericion. The progressive destruction of the vegetation continued, resulting in a veritable 'desertification' with esparto grass steppes and halophilous formations in the centre of the basin (Rodriguez Ariza, 1992).

In the Ronda basin (Rodriguez Ariza *et al.*, 1992), the degradation of the environment was later. This delay may be linked to a strong megalithic presence in the mountainous areas, implying a mobile economy and a mix of herding and agriculture that resulted in little damage to the environment. Heavy degradation of the environment coincides with the development of the Tartesians (the Late Bronze Age), in the context of the rupture in the existing socio-political system. Agriculture underwent considerable development, intensifying in the most fertile areas during the first half of the first millennium BC, with specialization primarily in vines, olives, and cereals. The Iberians introduced few changes. The Romans brought about the most profound changes through irrigation, with agriculture transformed for the market economy.

Whatever regional problems still require clarification, it is already possible to make an interesting comparison between the different phases. In Figure 4.1 we show in a very schematic manner the evolution of marker taxons since 18,000 BP. We can see that Phase 1, marked by *Pinus nigra*, ends towards 10,000 BP or soon after, at the same time as evergreen oak and *Quercus faginea* expand. The interval is quite appreciable in southern France, where the replacement of cold-climate vegetation by broad-leafed trees, while often progressive, is not usually complete until 8000 BP. This delay is of course due to climatic factors. The beginning of Phase 3, however, is marked by strong anthropization (Aleppo pine and olive trees in Spain, holm oak and boxwood in France),and is more or less synchronous with the Middle Neolithic, the Chasséen.

THE ANTHRACOLOGY OF MEDIEVAL FORESTS

While anthracology and palynology have contributed enormously to our understanding of Mediterranean landscapes in the Neolithic, the Middle Ages remain rather poorly understood. Recent developments in medieval archaeology have given us access to new sources of information, complimentary to the traditional historical data that are often insufficient for direct research into the landscape (Durand, 1991). The study of four medieval sites in Languedoc provides an example of how anthracology and texts can shed light on each other (Durand et Vernet, 1987).

Most medieval historians normally consider that the most radical changes to the forest landscape in southern France took place between the tenth and the twelfth centuries. Ecologists, on the other hand, push back the primary development of the Languedoc landscape to the end of the Neolithic: the mesophile woods dominated by white oak disappeared between 4000 and 2000 BP and the garrigue, a regressive formation of shrubs, also began to develop at this time.

The medieval sites of Montagnac (1040 ±60 AD), Lunel-Viel (11th – 12th century), Laurac (eleventh and twelfth centuries) and Castelnaudary (fourteenth and fifteenth centuries) have provided abundant archaeological and anthracological data. At Montagnac, beech, fir, hazelnut, ash, elm, black poplar and so on are all represented. At Lunel-Viel, the same trees are found with a more markedly Mediterranean stamp (Aleppo pine, vine and so on are present). At Laurac, beech and hazelnut are abundant. Finally, on the later site of Castelnaudary, we find an opposition between mesophile species and Mediterranean species, with high frequencies of beech, fir, hazelnut and deciduous oak.

There is a remarkable consistency in the presence of mesophile trees such as fir and beech at all four sites. Two main hypotheses can be put forward to explain this:

- the waterways near to the sites in question may have carried tree trunks down from the mountains – rural society in the tenth to thirteenth centuries may have established trading practices that included wood supplies being brought from the hinterland;
- some mesophile woods may have survived in an exceptional manner during the Middle Ages, surrounded by low altitude xerophilous Mediterranean vegetation.

This last hypothesis seems at first sight to be the least likely. Beech, however, can be found to this day lower down than is the norm, as for example on the banks of the Larzac or in the Dourbie valley, where it is in association with riparian forests, while the nearby south-facing slopes are characterized by a supra-Mediterranean vegetation of pistachio trees.

Palaeoecological data provide some support for these observations concerning the present ecology of the beech: travertines from Valbonne near Pont-Saint-Esprit, from between 75 and 300 m in altitude, have furnished prints of beech leafs dated to *c.* 870 ± 50 BP, or from AD 1035 to 1255. Valbonne is, in fact, known for its atypical beech forests, which are generally explained either as medieval plantations or as relics of the Ice Age. Other reliable palaeoecological data show that beech did in fact flourish at the end of the last Ice Age in the Gardon Valley and other tributaries of the Rhone. At Valbonne the substratum, made up of Cretaceous sands, constitutes an excellent hydric reservoir that compensates for the dry Mediterranean climate. Moreover, the pollen diagram from Marsillargues, on the edge of the Etang de Mauguio basin, shows high frequencies of beech during the Middle Ages.

The documentary records, as far as we know, do not mention the intentional transport of wood from the mountains before AD 1250, and then only with respect to certain species such as chestnut that were used exclusively for important constructions such as ships for the royal fleet. In any case they do not concern rural society.

The hypothesis of mesophile vegetation such as beech and fir coexisting on favourable substrata, rich in water reserves, seems therefore to bear out. We must note, moreover, that beech stands and beech/fir stands appear in pollen diagrams towards the end of the Neolithic and disappear during the Middle Ages. Beech, however, only appears in charcoal samples in the Middle Ages, at the same time as its representation in the pollen record is diminishing.

The mesophile riparian forests seem therefore to have been cleared in the Middle Ages, between the tenth century and the end of the twelfth century. Some light is shed upon this by recent historical information (Gramain-Derruau, 1979). New lands were being developed along the rivers as early as AD 900–960. The development of these heavy soils was rendered possible by new agrarian techniques. The spread of the *paissière* mill made it possible to control the flow of rivers and to irrigate. Tools also were improved: the use of higher quality iron and the shoeing of horses made it possible to work the heavy soils.

THE MEMORY OF THE CHARCOAL BURNERS

The forges of the upper Aston valley in the Ariège functioned from 1473 to 1884. To supply them with charcoal required extensive cutting of the neighbouring forests. We tried to find out if the forges had overexploited the forest to the point of deforestation. Today the forest does not extend beyond 1700–1750 m above sea level. In the areas above the forest there are clearly identifiable remains of charcoal pits. Such pits are found everywhere in the pastures of the Aston valley, up to an altitude of 2200 m.

Anthracological analysis has been used on this type of archaeological site, and has demonstrated that their occupants exploited the resources at hand due to the steep incline of the land. The results make it possible to reconstruct the old high altitude resinous forest that was destroyed by four centuries of intensive cuttings. It has been possible in this way to prove the existence of an old pine forest above the beech forest, made up for the most part of Scots pine. It must be noted that the forestry documents from the 'Réformation de Froidour' (1670) are imprecise in this matter: they speak exclusively of 'wild pines' for the Haute-Ariège. This research also shows that fir existed up to a fairly high altitude (1970 m) especially on north-facing slopes. The 'Réformation' documents do confirm, however, the presence of this species in the upper Aston valley.

The perspectives opened up by this type of research are interesting, especially concerning research into the upper limits of mountain forests: the charcoal remains are big, unusually well-preserved, and can be radiocarbon dated. In this way a charcoal pit situated at 1740 m, in which Scots pine, mountain pine and birch charcoal was found, was dated to 580–895 AD. It is the first evidence for the exploitation of forests for metallurgy at such an altitude (Bonhôte and Vernet, 1988).

CONCLUSION

Concepts such as degradation and even more so desertification must be used with caution. Even in areas where diachronic studies have shown that deforestation was intense, such as eastern Spain, entire zones were rarely affected by neolithic populations. The concept of vegetation potential for these regions in the thermo-Mediterranean latitudes implies the existence of holm oak stands, even if there was also room for matorrals. In Spain, therefore, desertification can only be a localized phenomenon, undoubtedly reversible. In the latitudes of southern France, the vegetation was dominated by the 'pubescent' oak and mesophile trees such as the beech that thrived for a long time in riparian forests, though the holm oak played an important role on hillsides, in eroded areas, and in areas of hard limestone. To put it another way, the research shows that Mediterranean landscapes characterized by holm oak are secondary landscapes that have followed the Boreal-Atlantic climax characterized by white oak. At the scale of village settlement, field boundaries often show that, following the slow abandonment of agricultural land, particularly olive groves, the landscape was colonized by secondary vegetation characterized by Aleppo pine or, on more favourable soils, the white oak.

REFERENCES

Ambert, M. and Chabal, L. (1992) L'environnement de Lattara (Hérault): potentialités et contraintes. *Lattara* 5: 9–26.

Badal Garcia, E. (1990) *Aportaciones de la Antracologia al Estudio del Paisage Vegetal y su Evolucion en el Cuaternario Reciente en la Costa Mediterranea del Pais Valenciano y Andalucia (18000–3000 BP).* Valencia, University de Valencia, PhD thesis.

Badal, E., Bernabeu, J. and Vernet, J.-L. (1994) Vegetation changes and human action from the Neolithic to the Bronze Age (7000–4000 BP) in Alicante, Spain, based on charcoal analysis. *Vegetation History and Archaeobotany* 3: 155–66.

Barry, J.-P. and Le Roy Ladurie, E. (1962) Histoire agricole et phytogéographie. *Annales* 17: 434–47.

Bazile-Robert, E. (1983) La Baume de Montclus (Gard). Étude anthracologique. *Études Quaternaires Languedociennes* 3: 19–28.

Berger, J.-F. (1995) Facteurs anthropiques et naturels de l'évolution des paysages romains et protomédiévaux du Bassin valdainais (Drôme). In S. van der Leeuw (ed) *L'Homme et la Dégradation de l'Environnement* (XVe Rencontres Internationales d'Archéologie et d'Histoire d'Antibes): 79–114. Juan les Pins, CNRS.

Bonhote, J. and Vernet, J.-L. (1988) La mémoire des charbonnières, essai de reconstitution des milieux forestiers dans une vallée marquée par la métallurgie (Aston, Haute-Ariège). *Revue Forestière Française* 40 (3): 197–212.

Chabal, L. (1991) *L'Homme et l'Évolution de la Végétation Méditerranéenne, des Ages des Métaux à la Période Romaine: Recherches Anthracologiques Théoriques, Appliquées Principalement à des Sites du Bas-Languedoc.* Montpellier, Université des Sciences Montpellier II, PhD thesis.

Chabal, L. (1992) La représentativité paléoécologique des charbons de bois archéologiques issus du bois de feu. *Bulletin de la Société Botanique de France* 139: 213–36.

Chabal, L. (1994) Apports récents de l'anthracologie à la connaissance des paysages passés : performances et limites. *Histoire et Mesure* 9, 3/4: 317–38.

Chabal, L. and Laubenheimer, F. (1994) L'atelier gallo-romain de Sallèles d'Aude: les potiers et le bois. In *Terre Cuite et Société, la Céramique, Document Technique, Économique et Culturel* (XIVes Rencontres Internationales d'Archéologie et d'Histoire d'Antibes): 99–129. Juan les Pins, CNRS.

Durand, A. (1991) *Paysages, Terroirs et Peuplement dans les Campagnes du Bas-Languedoc (X–XIIe siècle).* Paris, University of Paris 1, PhD thesis.

Durand, A. and Vernet, J.-L. (1987) Anthracologie et paysages forestiers médiévaux. A propos de quatre sites languedociens. *Annales du Midi* 99: 397–405.

Durand-Tullou, A. (1972) Rôle des végétaux dans la vie de l'homme au temps de la civilisation traditionnelle (étude éthnobotanique sur le Causse de Blandas, Gard). *Journal d'Agriculture Tropicale et de Botanique Appliquée* 19, 6–7: 222–46.

Godron, M., Daget, P., Poissonet, J. and Poissonet, P. (1971) Some aspects of heterogeneity in grasslands of Cantal (France). *Statistical Ecology* 3: 397–415.

Guilaine, J. (1988) *Six Millénaires d'Histoire de l'Environnement: Étude Interdisciplinaire de l'Abri Sous-Roche de Font-Juvénal (Conques sur Orbiel, Aude).* Toulouse, Centre d'Anthropologie des Sociétés Rurales.

Planchais, N. (1982) Palynologie lagunaire de l'étang de Mauguio. Paléo-environnement végétal et action anthropique. *Pollen et Spores* 21: 73–118.

Pons, A. and Reille, M. (1988) The Holocene and upper Pleistocene pollen record from Padul (Granada, Spain). A new study. *Palaeogeography, Palaeoclimatology, Palaeoecology* 66: 243–63.

Rodriguez-Ariza, M.O. (1992) Human-plant relationships during the Copper and Bronze Ages in the Baza and Guadix basins (Granada, Spain). *Bulletin de la Société Botanique de France* 139, Actual. bot. (2/3/4): 451–64.

Rodriguez-Ariza, M.O., Aguayo De Hoyos, P. and Moreno Jimenez, F. (1992) The environment in the Ronda basin (Malaga, Spain) during recent prehistory based on an anthracological study of Old Ronda. *Bulletin de la Société Botanique de France* 139, Actual. bot. (2/3/4): 715–25.

Smart, T.L. and Hoffman, E.S. (1988) Environmental interpretation of archaeological charcoal. In C. Hastorf and Popper (eds) *Current Palaeoethnobotany*: 167–205. Chicago, Chicago University Press.

Solari, M.-E. and Vernet, J.-L. (1992) Late glacial and Holocene vegetation of the Corbières based on charcoal analysis at the Cova de l'Espérit (Salses, Pyrénées orientales, France). *Review of Palaeobotany and Palynology* 71: 111–20.

Thiébault, S. (1988) *L'Homme et le Milieu Végétal au Tardi et Postglaciaire dans les Préalpes Sud-Occidentales*. Paris, University of Paris I, PhD thesis.

Thiébault, S. (1991) Contribution de l'analyse anthracologique à la définition d'une identité du Chasséen. *Mémoire du Musée de Préhistoire d'Ile de France* T.4: 369–77.

Thiébault, S. and Vernet, J.-L. (1992) Végétations méditerranéennes et civilisations préhistoriques: le cas de Font-Juvénal. *Bulletin de la Société Botanique de France* 139, Actual. bot. (2/3/4): 441–50.

Triat-Laval, H. (1978) *Contribution Pollenanalytique à l'Histoire Tardi- et Postglaciaire de la Basse Vallée du Rhône*. Marseilles, University of Aix-Marseiiles III, PhD thesis.

Uzquiano, P. (1992) L'homme et le bois au Paléolithique en région Cantabrique, Espagne. Exemples d'Altamira et d'El Buxu. *Bulletin de la Société Botanique de France* 139, Actual. bot. (2/3/4): 361–72.

Vernet, J.-L. (1972) *Études sur l'Histoire de la Végétation du Sud-Est de la France au Quaternaire d'après les Charbons de Bois Principalement*. Montpellier, University of Montpellier, PhD thesis.

Vernet, J.-L. (1991) L'histoire du milieu méditerranéen humanisé révélée par les charbons de bois. In J. Guilaine (ed) *Pour une Archéologie Agraire*: 369–408. Paris.

Vernet, J.-L. (1992) (ed) Les charbons de bois, les anciens écosystèmes et le rôle de l'homme. *Bulletin de la Société Botanique de France* 139, Actual. bot. (2/3/4): 157–725.

Vernet, J.-L. (1995) Anthracologie, biostratigraphie et relations homme-milieu en région méditerranéenne.In S. van der Leeuw (ed) *L'Homme et la Dégradation de l'Environnement* (XVes Rencontres Internationales d'Archéologie et d'Histoire d'Antibes): 175–184. Juan-les-Pins, CNRS.

Vernet, J.-L. and Thiébault, S. (1987) An approach of northwestern Mediterranean recent prehistoric vegetation and ecologic implications. *Jounal of Biogeography* 14: 117–27.

Vernet, J.-L., Thiébault, S. and Heinz, C. (1987) Nouvelles données sur la végétation préhistorique postglaciaire méditerranéenne d'après l'analyse anthracologique. In J. Guilaine (ed) *Premières Communautés Paysannes en Méditerranée Occidentale:* 87–94. Paris, CNRS.

5. Some Examples of Climatic Reconstruction in the Mediterranean using Dendroclimatology

Frédéric Guibal

INTRODUCTION

In woody plants growing in temperate climates, annual growth involves a terminal shoot (apical growth) and the formation of a tree-ring (radial growth) resulting from periclinal divisions in the thin layer called *cambium*, located on the outer side of the trunk underneath the bark.

Ring width depends upon a number of factors internal and external to the tree. The external factors include soil, altitude, exposure, topography (constant factors in a tree's life), age, inter-individual competition, attacks from fungi, insects and other bark-eating animals, human intervention, seed production and climate-variable factors in a tree's life span. The role played by climate is essential, due to the year-to-year variations in the ring width. These variations are always similar on trees of the same species submitted to the same climatic conditions: temperature, precipitation, hygrometry, insolation, wind. This allows for the cross-dating of various wood samples and the elaboration of mean ring chronologies.

Dendrochronology is a means of dating of high precision and has thus been used extensively by archaeologists since its initial development by American researchers in the 1920s and by Germans in the 1940s (Baillie, 1982). Dendrochronology has also proved itself to be a palaeoenvironmental science of interest, because of its recording of changes in the biotope in which trees develop, using ring width and wood density series.

Palaeoenvironmental information obtained from the ring chronologies can be distinguished as to whether it shows marked variations in certain factors to the point of complete disruption of forests over a long period (that is, a century or more) or which reflect events the effect of which is felt over a shorter period (a maximum of one or two decades).

Several dendrochronological studies undertaken in Europe on large sets of wooden artefacts illustrating the history of ancient societies have made it possible to better understand, for instance, the transformations of the medieval landscape around the town of Lund (Bartholin, 1978), the changing exploitation of forests next to the neolithic trackways in the Somerset peat bogs (Morgan, 1984), and the structure of forest stands exploited during the Neolithic on the shores of Lake Constance (Billamboz, 1992, 1995) based on the diachrony of species used, the series of felling dates, medium-frequency variations in ring width and the age of the trees used. Some studies on subfossil trunks found on waterlogged sites (fluvial or lacustrine sediments, peat bogs, marshes and so on) revealed phases of natural regeneration, progressive or sudden decline which, when observed synchronously on several sites, reveal climatic variations on a regional scale (Baillie, 1979; Leuschner and Delorme, 1988).

Other research has revealed sequences limited to a few tree-rings, revealing past human activity or natural events the occurrence of which could have affected human populations. Examples of the former include the severe pollarding of hedge oaks in Brittany during the last five centuries in order to obtain extra fodder for herds (Guibal, 1988), or the cork harvesting at irregular intervals on cork-oaks used afterwards in the wharf construction of the antique port of Toulon (Guibal, 1992). Under the second heading, volcanic eruptions have been confirmed by high acid levels in Arctic ice cores (Baillie, 1991).

In the Mediterranean, the palaeoenvironmental factors the most clearly observed through tree-ring analysis are climatic: temperature and rain-fall. In all regions that offer seasonal climatic rhythms, ring width chronologies or wood density chronologies are amongst the most used 'proxy data' for acquiring quantitative climatic information relative to periods for which meteorological records are not available. Dendroclimatology is based on the analysis of the relationship between ring parameters (annual widths, wood density, stable isotopes) and climate for a period for which instrumental data from meteorological stations is available and then on the reconstruction of the climatic parameters that influence ring widths, wood density or stable isotopes.

This chapter does not aim, in any way, at being exhaustive but will present a few results from attempts at climatic reconstruction in the Mediterranean based on dendroclimatology, whilst also underlining the requirements and limitations of this work. We borrow largely from research undertaken by F. Serre-Bachet, J. Guiot, L. Tessier and C. Gadbin of the *Laboratoire de Botanique Historique et Palynologie*.

THE CONSTRAINTS OF DENDROCLIMATOLOGY

Climatic reconstruction based upon ring series requires series of wood samples (mean chronologies) and climatic parameters (meteorological data) of the highest possible quality.

Mean tree-ring chronologies must span a long period and be replicated by at least ten trees in order to obtain a chronology that is as representative as possible of a given ecological condition. Several chronologies must be built up in order to reflect several ecological conditions and several species must be taken into account in order to consider different ecological requirements: documenting different responses to climate according to species allows for a better reconstruction of climate (Serre-Bachet and Guiot, 1987). The reliability of a chronology depends on the number of trees used in its construction, whilst the length of the reconstruction depends on the chronology length.

Meteorological data series must be continuous and reliable; they must be carefully examined for missing information and for inhomogeneities. Any gaps must be filled in: for that purpose, it is necessary to have at least one complete series for one station. However, despite the length and the quality of available series, the location of meteorological stations in towns often far from the tree populations, especially those in mountainous regions, raises problems in tree-ring to climate investigations.

The common period between tree-ring and climatic series must be at least 50 years. This is due to statistical requirements and the need to have quite varied climatic situations represented within this period, for example:

- years marked only by a severe summer drought;
- years marked by a severe summer drought and a very wet spring;
- years marked by a severe summer drought and a late spring;
- years marked by a severe summer drought and a mild winter;
- years marked by a severe summer drought and a cold winter.

Also, climatic reconstruction using tree-rings is based on the assumption that the relationship between climate and growth has not changed over time within a given species (Tessier, 1989). This is one of the major drawbacks of the system, made even more acute when the reconstructions are made on chronologies built from tree-ring series from archaeological sites, for which the cambial age and the ecological conditions in which the trees grew are not known.

The analysis also encounters problems with the geographic scale represented by the reconstructed data. This scale depends upon the geographic origins of the tree-ring chronologies and the series of climatic data used. Temperatures are often of a regional nature, based on a point on a grid equal to 5° latitude and 10° longitude (Jones *et al.*, 1985); reconstructions of precipitation, more variable from one point to another than temperature, remain linked to specific meteorological stations (Serre-Bachet, 1988; Serre-Bachet *et al.*, 1992a; 1992b).

METHODS OF ANALYSIS

Reconstructions of climatic parameters are conducted in two stages:

- first, the relationships between tree-rings and monthly climatic parameters are analyzed; climatic parameters are considered for the biological year, this being from October prior to the growing period through September of the current year. The climatic parameters most frequently used during this stage are the total monthly precipitation and the average monthly maximal and minimal temperatures. After extracting the principal components from the climatic parameters in order to eliminate correlations between these variables, a simple or multiple linear regression is calculated in which the climatic parameters are the predictors (independent variables) and the ring width is the predictand (dependent variable). The result constitutes a response function (Fritts, 1976), which highlights the climatic parameters that are the most closely related to the ring width and makes it possible to identify the climatic parameter or parameters that may be reconstructed;
- secondly, a regression is calculated in which the ring width series are the predictor data and the climatic parameters, known for a given period, are the predictand; the result is a transfer function (Fritts, 1976). Groupings of climatic variables (e.g. average summer temperatures, total spring and summer rainfall) are frequent in order to improve the reconstruction of the climatic parameters most related to ring widths.

Ring width series cannot be used as raw data (1/100 mm) but are standardized beforehand in order to eliminate variations independent of the climate, such as tree age or competition between trees.

When calculating the response function and the transfer function, the model coefficients are first calculated over a calibration period that can be either continuous (a given sequence within the known climatic period) or discontinuous (random years drawn from the known climatic period). The stability of the function coefficients is then tested over a verification period that also can be continuous or discontinuous and made up of independent years: i.e. they are not used in calculating the coefficients (Guiot, 1989).

When calibrating the transfer function, there are as many partial coefficients as there are tree-ring chronologies. If the data estimated from these significative coefficients are themselves significantly correlated with the observed data, the same coefficients are used to estimate the climatic parameter or parameters over the verification period which is independent of the calibration period. If these estimations are also significantly correlated with the observed data, the climatic parameter or parameters are then estimated over a longer period and the reliability of the operation is statistically tested (Guiot, 1989; Serre-Bachet and Tessier, 1989; Serre-Bachet *et al.*, 1992a).

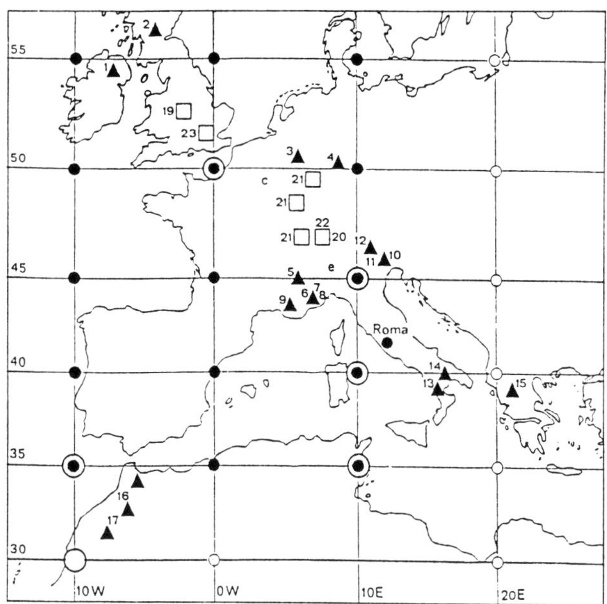

Figure 5.1. Location of proxy series used in temperature reconstruction for western and south-western Europe (tree-ring series: black triangles; historical archives: squares) and location of the temperature series reconstructed back to AD1500 (mean annual temperature: black dots; mean April to September temperatures: large and thick circles; grid points that have not been used: small and thin circles). (After Serre-Bachet, 1994a).

EXAMPLES OF RECONSTRUCTION

Temperature reconstructions in Western and South-Western Europe since 1500 AD (Serre-Bachet, 1994a; Serre-Bachet et al., 1991)

Seventeen tree-ring chronologies representative of the British Isles (*Quercus* sp.), Germany (*Quercus* sp.), the French Alps (*Larix decidua* Mill., *Abies alba* Mill.), Calabria (*Pinus leucodermus* Antoine), Greece (*Pinus nigra*), and Morocco (*Cedrus atlantica* Endl. Carrière) were used to reconstruct the annual and summer temperatures in sixteen points of the temperature grid established by Jones *et al.* (1985) for the Northern Hemisphere.

For statistical reasons, the analysis only gave significant results for the five following points: 50°N–0°W, 45°N–10°E, 35°N–10°W, 35°N–10°E (Fig. 5.1). The reconstructions are shown in Figures 5.2 to 5.6 expressed as departures from the mean of the calibration period: 1851–1969.

With the exception of point 35°N–10°E, the annual estimations fluctuate more than the summer estimations, both in high-frequency and medium-frequency. As regards the mean annual temperatures, a period characterized by a high number of years marked by negative departures from the mean is distinguishable between 1700 and 1800, in the middle of the Little Ice Age (Le Roy Ladurie, 1967) at latitudes of 50°, 45° and 40° whatever the longitude is. This period was preceded by a cold episode (1560–1590) and a warm episode (1610–1680). The estimated summer temperatures do not show any fluctuations corresponding to the Little Ice Age, but several fluctuations in the medium-frequency are synchronized with variations noted on the reconstructed annual temperature curves.

The cold episode known as the Maunder Minimum (1675–1715) shows up in the estimations of both mean annual temperatures and summer temperatures, with wider departures from the mean in the first than in the second. The episode is only noticeable in two of the ten curves: the annual temperatures at point 35°N–10°W and the summer temperatures at point 50°N–0°W. With a five per cent margin, the annual temperatures at point 35°N–10°W during the Maunder Minimum are higher than the mean for the period analyzed, while those at point 35°N–10°E are lower than this same mean. At point 35°N–10°W the beginning of the cooling does not start until 1703, while at four other points the temperature drop is centred on the period spanning 1687 to 1703.

Temperature reconstructions in Europe during the Middle Ages (Serre-Bachet, 1994b)

Seven long tree-ring chronologies representative of high altitude resinous species in Calabria and in the French and Italian Alps were used to reconstruct mean temperatures from April to September on the same points of the grid previously mentioned. Some of the chronologies are issued from standing trees only (*Pinus leucodermis* in Calabria, *Larix decidua* in the French Alps), while others are issued from standing trees and old buildings (*Larix decidua* and *Picea abies* Karsten in the Italian Alps). Only the results corresponding to point 45°N–10°E will be presented here, corresponding to the north of Italy, in as much as the seven average chronologies could be used in this instance as regressors. According to the number of regressors taken

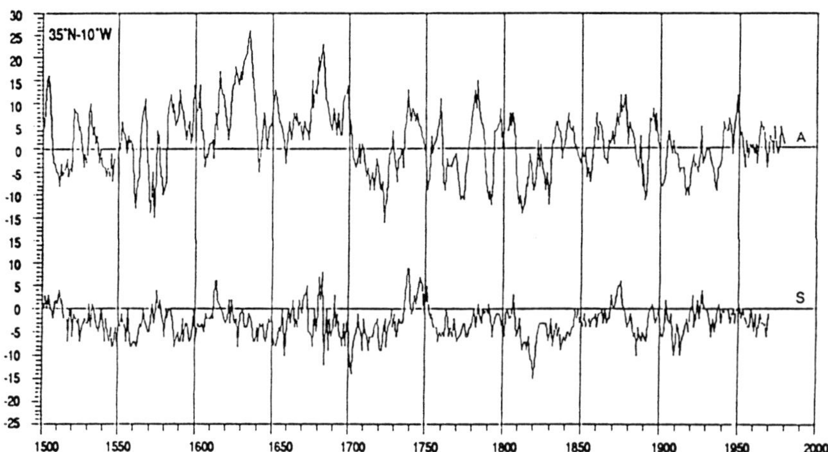

Figure 5.2. Mean annual (A) January to December and summer (S: April to September) temperatures reconstructed from tree-rings at the 35°N–10°W grid point. (After Serre-Bachet, 1994a)

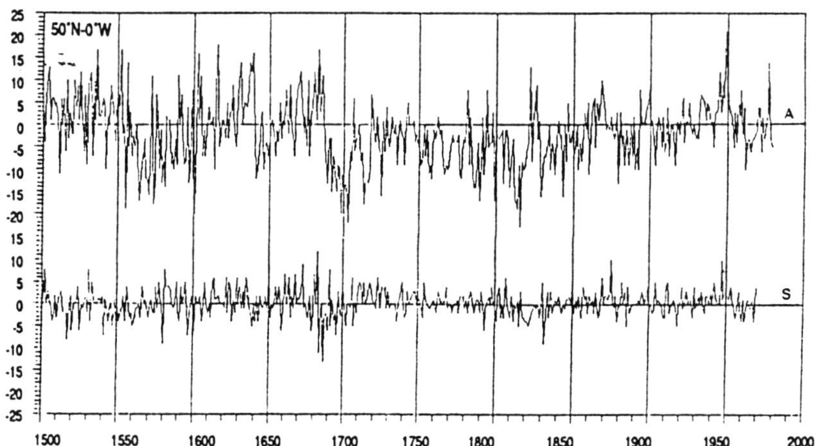

Figure 5.3. Mean annual (A) January to December and summer (S: April to September) temperatures reconstructed from tree-rings at the 50°N–0°W grid point. (After Serre-Bachet, 1994a)

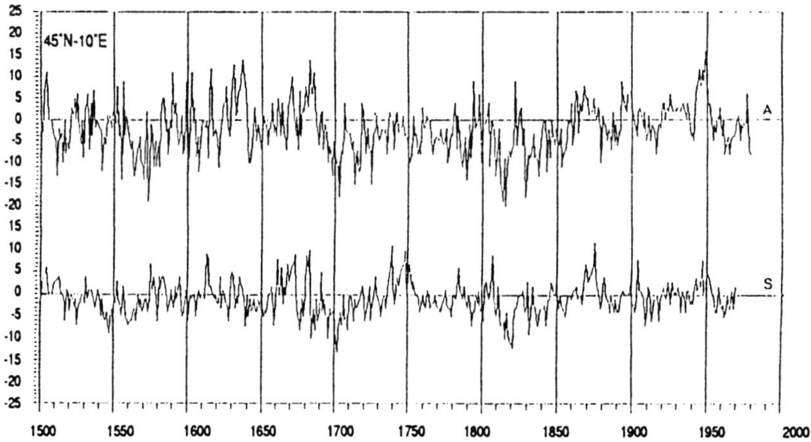

Figure 5.4. Mean annual (A) January to December and summer (S: April to September) temperatures reconstructed from tree-rings at the 45°N–10°E grid point. (After Serre-Bachet, 1994a)

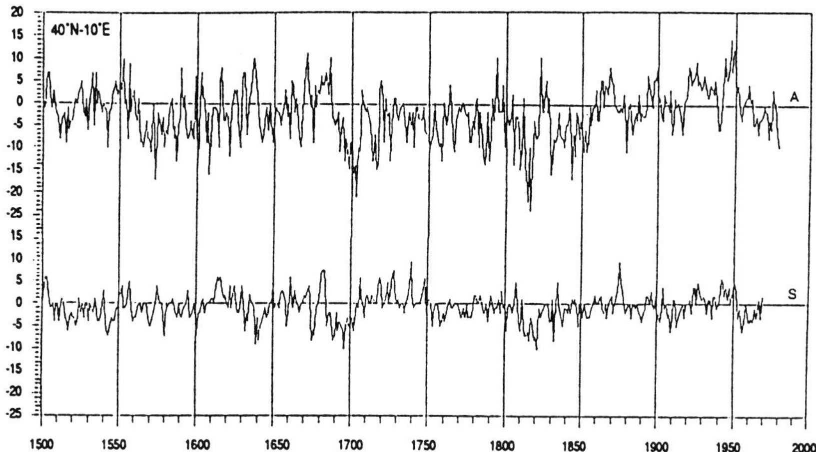

Figure 5.5. Mean annual (A) January to December and summer (S: April to September) temperatures reconstructed from tree-rings at the 40°N–10°E grid point. (After Serre-Bachet, 1994a)

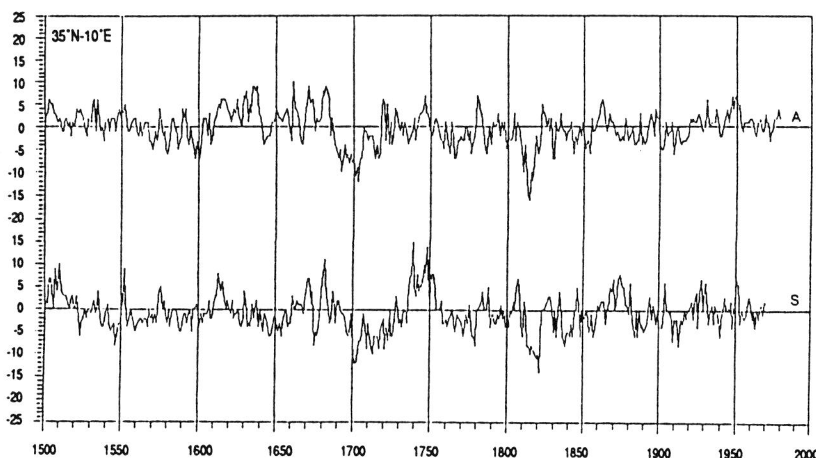

Figure 5.6. Mean annual January to December (A) and summer (S: April to September) temperatures reconstructed from tree-rings at the 35°N–10°E grid point. (After Serre-Bachet, 1994a)

into consideration, it was possible to plot out three curves of reconstructed data (Fig. 5.7).

The data estimated following the largest number of regressors presented the greatest inter-annual fluctuations (high-frequency), which is normal seeing as higher fluctuation is thereby explained.

Two types of negative departures from the mean make it possible to distinguish four periods: (1) two periods (970–1190) and (1600–1740) are characterized by deviations of more than 0.15°C from the mean for the period 1951–1970 and by high inter-annual fluctuations; two other periods (1190–1600) and (1740–1968) are characterized by deviations of less than 0.10°C from the mean and low inter-annual fluctuations. If we consider curve 7c to be more reliable in as much as seven regressors were used, it appears that high inter-annual fluctuations are the marker for the Little Ice Age.

The 970–1190 period shows up as cold and marked by high inter-annual fluctuations similar to the Little Ice Age. The period following it (1190–1450) is both warmer and more stable.

From this example we can see that the period known as the Medieval Warm Epoch (Lamb, 1988), supposed to have lasted from 1000 to 1300, was affected by both cold and warm episodes. Moreover, no warm episode seems to have affected the twelfth century. The climatic degradation after 1300 in western Europe mentioned by several authors (Lamb, 1988; Le Roy Ladurie, 1967) was not observed at point 45°N–10°E.

Precipitation reconstruction in Morocco since 1100 AD (Till and Guiot, 1990)

Forty-six tree-ring chronologies from Morocco cedars in the Rif and the Atlas mountains were used to reconstruct annual precipitation (autumn, spring and winter) for the

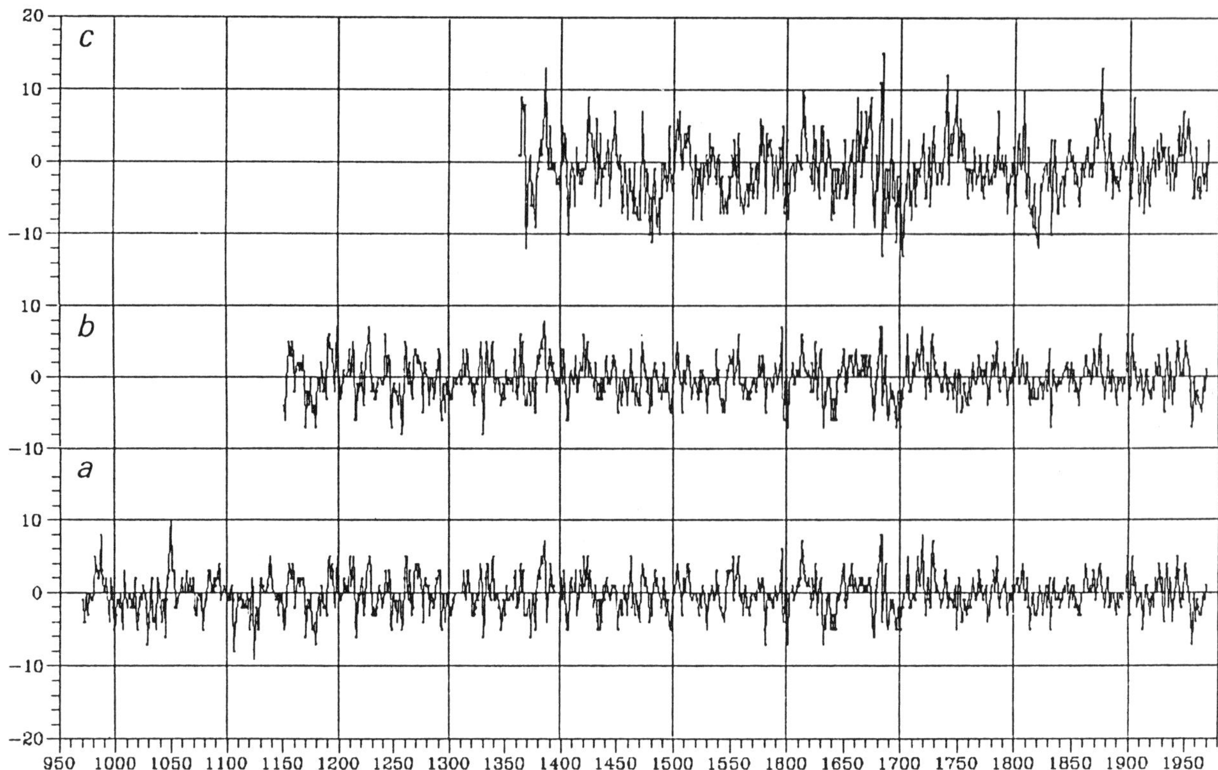

Figure 5.7. Reconstructed 45°N–10°E temperature anomalies (1/10°C) (April to September mean) relative to 1951–1970. Reconstruction on three (a: AD970–1969), five (b: AD1150–1969) and seven tree-ring series (c: AD1362–1969). (After Serre-Bachet, 1994b)

period from 1100 to 1979 in bio-climatic regions defined according to the annual precipitation (humid bio-climate: P 800 mm/year; sub-humid: 800 mm/year > P > 600 mm/year; semi-arid: 600 mm/year > P > 400 mm/year).

A high correlation prevails between the three series of annual precipitations reconstructed (r = 0,96 to 0,97). Figure 5.8 shows that during the Little Ice Age, the climate in Morocco was drier than it is today. While the actual mean annual precipitation for these three bioclimatic zones is respectively 1047 mm, 649 mm and 509 mm, they were equal to 1014 mm, 622 mm and 493 mm between 1500 and 1650. On average the rainfall is below average 48 years per century; the deviation from average is above a normal spread of twelve years per century; the length of a dry period (for which the deviation from average is more than a normal spread) never exceeds six years in the three regions.

Climatic fluctuations in Morocco have been compared with those in Europe and in the Sahel. No significant correlation has shown up concerning either alterations in the medium-frequency or characteristic years, between temperatures in Europe and precipitation in Morocco. Some winters described as very cold in Europe (Alexandre, 1987) correspond to humid years in Morocco (1143, 1151, 1173, 1253, 1276, 1323, 1326, 1354, 1361, 1364, 1408); while other years with cold winters in Europe correspond to dry years in Morocco (1126, 1210, 1219, 1234, 1303, 1317, 1339). Amongst the years characterised by a mild winter in Europe, there are three humid years (1279, 1357, 1362) and two dry years (1304, 1332). Drought in the Sahel is not linked to drought in Morocco: for example, the very dry years of 1947 and 1975 (Faure and Gac, 1981) and the drought of 1968–1985 in the Sahel are not contemporary with dry years in Morocco; the years from 1968 to 1971 in Morocco are even more humid than average; with the exception of parts of Morocco near the desert, no droughts were recorded between 1968 and 1979. Likewise, very humid years in the Sahel (1925, 1933, 1956, 1964) do not correspond with any particular climatic situation in Morocco.

Amongst the hypotheses put forward by the authors of this study to explain this absence of correlation are the following:

- The heterogeneous nature of the sources of paleoclimatic data renders it difficult to make a true comparison.
- The paleoclimatic variables that regulate the growth of trees are different in the different regions: while in Europe, the summer temperatures are often reconstructed due to their impact on diameter growth, the main factor that influences tree growth in North Africa is rainfall in winter and spring, while in the Sahel it is summer rainfall.

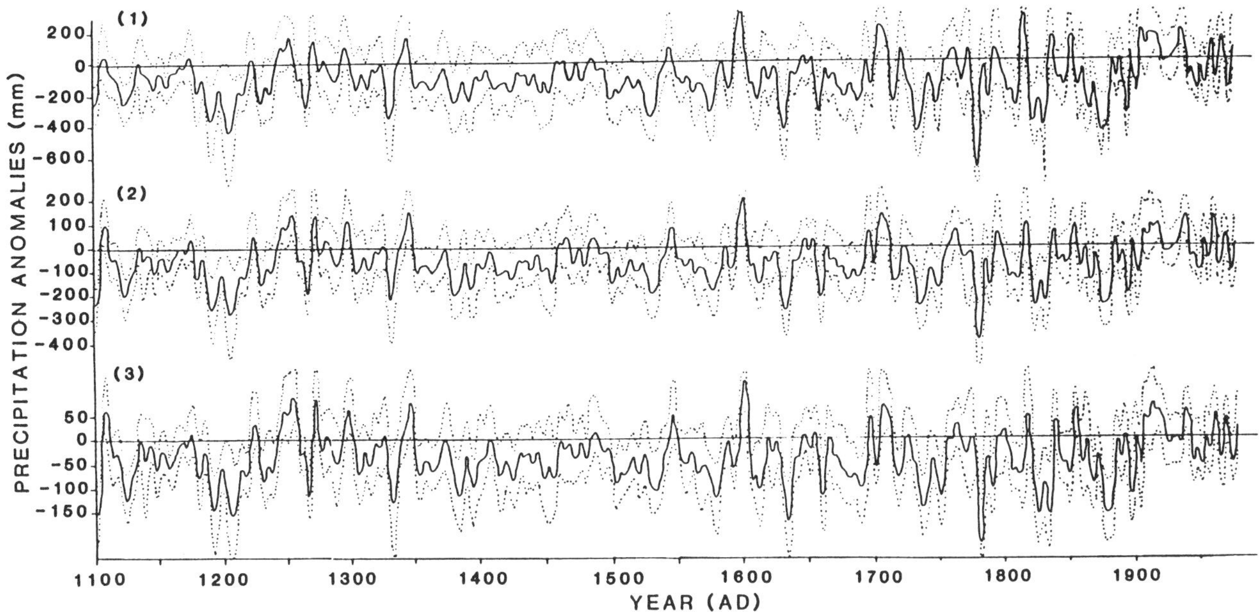

Figure 5.8. Morocco, smoothed reconstructed series of annual precipitation since AD1100 for the humid (1), subhumid (2) and semiarid (3) regions. Precipitation values are expressed as deviations from the calibration period mean in millimeters (1120 mm for the humid region, 689 mm for the subhumid region, 524 mm for the semiarid region). (After Till and Guiot, 1990)

- The climatic variations between each of these three regions are independent: a climatic fluctuation in one of these regions does not imply a simultaneous fluctuation in the others, especially considering the enormous difference in the climates of Europe, Morocco, and the Sahel.

CONCLUSION

While dendroclimatology displays certain advantages over other disciplines in the field of palaeoenvironmental research due to its annual resolution, it is subjected to some constraints, of which the main ones are related to the availability of long tree-ring series and long climatic series.

Another limit is linked to the ambiguous nature of the climatic information contained in ring-widths and in wood densities, insofar as other factors can also result in the formation of narrow tree-rings. For example, narrow tree-rings in Aleppo pine can just as well be caused by a very cold winter as by a very dry spring and lead to interpretations of years with dry springs instead of years with very cold winters.

The relationship between tree-rings and climate represents an average picture for the set of years taken into consideration. Dendroclimatology cannot reconstruct exceptional events for an unknown climatic period if these conditions did not occur during the period for which calibration and verification were established.

In order to obtain results that are as reliable as possible, the reconstruction offered by dendroclimatology must be reinforced by a geographic grid that is as close together as possible and therefore likely to demonstrate spatiotemporal variations. The results must also be compared with other proxy data, both on the local and the regional scale, most of which should be related to geophysical phenomena (i.e. formation and melting of snow-cover, frosts) or refering to phenophases or other signs of biological activity (i.e. blossoming and ripening of cultivated plants and trees, the beginning of the wine harvest).

REFERENCES

Alexandre, P. (1987) *Le Climat en Europe au Moyen-Age. Contribution à l'Histoire des Variations Climatiques de 1000 à 1425, d'après les Sources Narratives de l'Europe Occidentale.* Paris, Ecole des Hautes Etudes en Sciences Sociales.

Baillie, M.G.L. (1979) Some observations on gaps in tree-ring chronologies. In A. Aspinall (ed.) *Proceedings of the Symposium on Archaeological Sciences*, University of Bradford, Jan. 1978: 19–32.

Baillie, M.G.L. (1982) *Tree-Ring Dating and Archaeology.* London,Croom Helm,.

Baillie, M.G.L. (1991) Marking in marker dates : towards an archaeology with historical precision. *World Archaeology* 23: 233–43.

Bartholin, T.S. (1978) Dendrochronology, wood anatomy and landscape development in South Sweden. In J. Fletcher (ed.) *Dendrochronology in Europe*: 125–30. Oxford,British Archaeological Reports, International Series 51.

Billamboz, A. (1992) Tree-ring analysis from an archaeodendrological perspective. The structural timber from the South West German lake dwellings. *Lundqua Report* 34: 34–40.

Billamboz, A. (1995) Proxyséries dendrochronologiques et occupation néolithique des bords du Lac de Constance. *Palynosciences* 3: 69–81.

Faure, H., Gac, Y. (1981) Will the Sahelian drought end in 1985? *Nature* 291: 475–8.

Fritts, H.C. (1976) *Tree-rings and Climate*. London, Academic Press.

Guibal, F. (1988) Aspects de la dendrochronologie des habitations seigneuriales de Bretagne. *Wood and Archaeology*, PACT, 22, II.2 : 85–97.

Guibal, F. (1992) Applications de la dendrochronologie en milieu méditerranéen. *Actes des Rencontres Xylologiques*, Grenoble, 21–22 Feb 1991: 65–78.

Guiot, J. (1989) Methods of calibration. In E.R. Cook and L.A. Kairukstis (eds) *Methods of Tree-ring Width Analysis: Applications in Environmental Sciences:* 165–78. Kluwer Academic Publishers.

Guiot, J., Tessier, L., Serre-Bachet, F., Guibal, F., and Gadbin, C. (1988) Annual temperature changes reconstructed in W Europe and NW Africa back to A.D. 1100. *Annales Geophysicae*, special issue, XIII General Assembly of European Geophysical Society, Bologna, 21–25 Mar 1988: 85.

Jones, P.D., Raper, S.C.B, Santer, B.D., Cherry, B.S.G., Goodess, C., Bradley, R.S., Diaz, H.F., Kelly, P.M., and Wigley, T.M.L. (1985) A grid point surface air temperature data set for the Northern Hemisphere, 1851–1984. Washington DC, Department of Energy, Technical Report TR022.

Lamb, H.H. (1988) *Weather, Climate and Human Affairs*. London, Routledge.

Le Roy Ladurie, E. (1967) *Histoire du Climat Depuis l'An Mil*. Paris, Flammarion.

Leuschner, H.H., Delorme, A. (1988) Tree-ring work in Gottingen – absolute oak chronologies back to 6255 BC. *Wood and Archaeology*, PACT, 22, II.5: 123–32.

Morgan, R.A. (1984) Tree-ring studies in the Somerset Levels: the Sweet Track 1979–1982. *Somerset Levels Papers* 10: 46–64.

Serre-Bachet, F. (1988) La reconstruction climatique à partir de la dendroclimatologie. *Publications de l'Association Internationale de Climatologie* 1: 225–33.

Serre-Bachet, F. (1994a) Annual and summer mean temperature reconstructions from tree-rings in western and southern Europe since AD 1500 with special reference to the late Maunder Minimum. In B. Frenzel (ed.) *Climatic Trends and Anomalies in Europe 1675–1715*. Paläoklimaforschung Palaeoclimate Research 13: 265–74.

Serre-Bachet, F. (1994b) Middle Age temperature reconstructions in Europe, a focus on northeastern Italy. *Climatic Change* 26: 213–24.

Serre-Bachet, F. and Guiot, J. (1987) Summer temperature changes from tree-rings in the mediterranean area during the last 800 years. In W.H. Berger and L.D. Labeyrie (eds) *Abrupt Climatic Change. Evidence and Implications*: 89–97. Reidel Pub. Co..

Serre-Bachet, F. and Tessier, L. (1989) Response functions for ecological studies. In E.R. Cook and L.A. Kairukstis (eds) *Methods of Tree-ring Width Analysis : Applications in Environmental Sciences: 247–58.* Kluwer Academic Publishers.

Serre-Bachet, F., Guiot, J. and Tessier, L. (1992a) La dendroclimatologie. Pour une histoire du Climat. In *Les Veines du Temps. Lectures de Bois en Bourgogne*. Catalogue d'exposition: 93–119.

Serre-Bachet, F., Guiot, J. and Tessier, L. (1992b) Dendroclimatic evidence from south-western Europe and north-western Africa. In R.S. Bradley and P.D. Jones (eds): *Climate since AD1500*: 349–65. London, Routledge.

Serre-Bachet, F., Martinelli, N., Pignatelli, O., Guiot, J. and Tessier, L. (1991) Evolution des températures du Nord-Est de l'Italie depuis 1500 AD. Reconstruction d'après les cernes des arbres. *Dendrochronologia* 9: 213–29.

Tessier, L. (1989) Spatio-temporal analysis of climate tree-ring relationships. *New Phytologist* 111: 517–29.

Till, C., Guiot, J. (1990) Reconstruction of precipitation in Morocco since AD 1100 based on *Cedrus atlantica* tree-ring widths. *Quaternary Research* 33: 337–51.

6. Geomorphological Techniques in Mediterranean Landscape Archaeology

Antony G. Brown

INTRODUCTION

The natural landscape is a relative, culturally determined, concept. Not only do peoples have differing views of what is natural and what is not, but these views have generally changed over time (Mills, 1982). Although this affects how we conceptualise past nature-culture relationships, it does not prevent us from utilizing a battery of techniques derived from the natural sciences in order to reconstruct past landscapes. At its most minimal, landscape can be taken as the nature and spatial distribution of resources (positive and negative, the latter including hazards), but this does provide a definite human-orientated purpose for landscape archaeology.

This chapter aims to outline the many geoarchaeological methods currently used in the reconstruction of natural landscapes and their archaeological application in Mediterranean contexts. Because this is such a vast field of research which includes many different disciplines, it is impossible to be comprehensive, so examples will be restricted largely to those techniques and areas of the Mediterranean with which the author is familiar. There is an emphasis here on alluvial environments, not only because that is the area of specialism of the author, but because they are most amenable to landscape reconstruction using geomorphological and sedimentological techniques and their full potential has yet to be realised in the Mediterranean.

(GEO)ARCHAEOLOGICAL QUESTIONS

Any attempt to reconstruct landscapes has two components. The first is: what do we wish to know about the past, given that we cannot know everything ? All reconstructions are partial, so we need to decide which parts of the natural landscape have most archaeological importance. The answer to this will depend upon our archaeological interests and models. The second component is, given the present or near-future state of technology, and the nature of the site or landscape, what can we reconstruct? Sites and landscapes have different potential for environmental reconstruction. The answers to these two questions will vary from generation to generation even for the same site or landscape, as our archaeology changes and as new techniques become available. (The term 'site' is used here, and throughout this chapter, to refer to any location where geoarchaeological techniques have been, or could be, used which may or may not contain artefacts.)

It is worthwhile looking at the reasons for undertaking work on environmental reconstruction. The first is to predict (*sic* retrodict) past environmental controls on human activity, which may be geological, biological, or climatic. The second is to describe the impact of past peoples on their landscapes. The two reasons are obviously not independent, since it is the manipulation of natural resources that changes human environments and creates landscapes. It is important to take a wide view of what constitutes a resource, and to include space (i.e. land), plants and animals, soils, water and minerals. This presents a problem, because it is difficult to think of any natural substance that has not, at one time or another, been used by human beings for something. Even hazards are generally conceptualised as negative resources which affect human living conditions. In reconstructing human living conditions, archaeologists use many of the techniques associated with forensic science, and they share a common aim, which is to extract more and more information from the available field evidence.

Ideally, archaeologists would like to reconstruct most, or all, of the important resources available to a population at any one time and place. This would include aspects of the geological and geomorphological environment, the flora and fauna, and the climate, since these all have an effect upon human subsistence and wealth. In practical terms this would involve mapping the geology and landforms and reconstructing the past geological and geomorphological landscape through stratigraphy – what Butzer (1982) has termed the 'primary study components of geoarchaeology'. The basic skills needed are those of mapping and surveying the physical landscape, deciphering the local stratigraphy, and understanding site formation processes (Vita-Finzi, 1978). The reconstruction of local vegetation is of particular value, providing some idea of quantity or biomass (especially in semi-arid environments), what species were present and – more subtly – what was happening to the ecology, i.e. how was it changing ? The reconstruction of the faunal history would involve similar questions. Climate may also be reconstructed, because it affects not only resource type and availability but also living conditions. The data would also have to be reliably and precisely dated, preferably by independent means such as radiometric (e.g. ^{14}C or TL/OSL) or incremental means (e.g. tree-rings).

No site, or even set of sites, is ever likely to allow such a comprehensive approach, because the conditions favouring the survival of some evidence are precisely those that destroy other evidence. Just as there is a taphonomy of cultural evidence, there are major taphonomic controls on the survival of natural evidence. A second reason is that some organisms tell us much more about the environment that others due to their rather restricted, or particular, ecological requirements. It should also be remembered that, if we have no direct evidence of use, then we are technically only reconstructing potential resources: the presence of a butchered reindeer carcase is evidence of a resource, whereas a spring is a potential resource. As Zimmerman (1951) pointed out, resources are 'subjective, relative and functional'.

SURVEY AND GEOPROSPECTION PRIOR TO ARCHAEOLOGICAL SURVEY

The shift from expensive single-site digs to regional or landscape surveys that has occurred over the last decade has placed a new emphasis on surveying and geophysical prospection. As the survey of Troy by Zangger *et al.* (Chapter 10) illustrates, this non-destructive archaeology will in time become the routine first stage in any archaeological project. However, since this is not yet generally the case, it is timely to emphasize here the importance of geomorphological survey prior to the establishment of the size, boundary and sampling framework of the archaeological survey. If there is any rationale for the delimitation of survey areas, it is common to set the survey boundary according to some notion of the territory of a site or series of sites. There are several problems with this: firstly, it does not allow an objective test of the real area of influence of the site; second, there is a danger that important cultural or natural landscape features may be 'just over the border'; and third, if the area has no relationship to the topography, it means that important process chains, such as land use history and soil erosion, cannot be investigated in a way that is compatible with the archaeological field evidence. It is therefore more valid to delimit the area on geomorphological grounds, which may also have cultural importance, and it is certainly far more practical.

The techniques of geomorphological survey are well known and described in several texts and manuals (Cooke and Dornkamp, 1974; Gardiner and Dackombe, 1974). It is difficult to be precise due to variations between both surveyors and landscapes, but a trained geomorphologist might be expected to map between 0.25 and 1.0 km^2 per day. This makes it relatively cheap, especially considering the potential benefits, which include the recognition of new sites (especially if the surveyor is also archaeologically trained), the identification of sites suitable for geomorphological and biological work, and zonation of the land with respect to archaeological visibility and likely biases on archaeological survey and fieldwalking. Two Mediterranean examples will suffice: at at the site of Punic and Roman Leptiminus, Tunisia, preliminary geomorphological survey identified a coastal extension of the urban site onto a wave-cut platform on Tertiary sands which was subsequently proven by archaeological fieldwork (Brown, in prep.). Geomorphological survey of the Tuscania survey area in central Italy showed that one of the archaeological transects partially ran along a floodplain which was archaeologically sterile due to overbank alluviation. Such areas can either be included or excluded systematically if the geomorphological survey has been done prior to the establishment of the framework of the archaeological survey.

An invaluable aid to geomorphological survey is the use of vertical aerial photographs. These are valuable in the field and can also be analysed both conventionally using a stereoscope and digitally in the laboratory. An extension of aerial photography is modern remote sensing, which is becoming an important archaeological tool (as discussed in detail in Volume 4 in this series). The use of aerial photographs and satellite imagery has particular advantages in Mediterranean environments, as the sensitive (moisture-stressed) and discontinuous vegetation enhances differences in geology and soils.

There is now a wide variety of remote sensing techniques using different sensors and platforms. The most available data is visible and near-infrared imagery from satellites such as the Landsat series and SPOT. Due to its ground resolution (*c.* 100 m for Landsat, 25 m for Landsat TM and 10 m for SPOT if in spatial mode) it is most useful for mapping relatively large areas, although smaller features can be detected if their spectral contrast with the surrounding land is great enough. An important area of research is into new sensors, particularly sensors that can penetrate vegetation and soil. Infrared, near-infrared and microwave can only penetrate a few millimetres and so rely on vegetation and soil colour which can reflect depth of soil and the influence of structures (cf. crop-marks). These variations can be particularly useful especially if the sensors are aircraft-mounted and flown at low elevations (e.g. an airborne thematic mapper). Geomorphological work in Malaga province, Spain, using a Daedalus scanner giving a nominal ground resolution of 2 m, not only revealed soil spectral pattern due to geology, topography and erosion but also old field systems and structures (Payne *et al.*, 1994). A correlation was also observed between a transformation of reflectance and ground resistivity – both reflecting variations in soil depth.

New sensors will have a greater ability to penetrate soil and be all-weather. Synthetic aperture radar (SAR) which is on board ERS-1 is unaffected by cloud, but can only penetrate most soils a few millimetres except for pure dry sand. However, new SAR systems with different wavelengths may be able to penetrate several metres in suitable soils (Zangger *et al.*, Chapter 10 in this volume). Remote sensing and traditional geophysical techniques are rapidly converging. In addition to standard and relatively time-consuming ground-based geophysical survey (resistivity, magnetometry, shallow seismic and ground penetrating radar), airborne geophysical survey is becoming available. Generally mounted on a helicopter, this allows variable coverage and ground resolution.

Given the technical nature and expense of such survey techniques, archaeological projects contemplating such work require geophysicists and remote sensors on the team at the point of project formulation. The full benefits are as yet unrealised, but the day when soil can be imaged producing the equivalent of a bathometric map of soil depths are probably not too distant. These techniques all produce digital raster data and coupled with a global positioning system (GPS) can produce rectified data ideal for input into geographical information systems (GIS: see Volume 3 in this series).

RECONSTRUCTING ENVIRONMENTS FROM SEDIMENTS

Sediments are naturally complex and the specification of their meaning in terms of the conditions under which they were deposited or the causes of deposition does not spring automatically from sediment description or laboratory characterisation. In order to tackle the complexity of sediments and in order to be able to interpret their depositional environments, we can use the facies concept (Gilbertson, 1995). A facies is a regular set of deposits which are related together and controlled by systematic relationships between micro-environments. The alluvial facies therefore contains sediments formed by several micro-environments: cutoff, levee, backswamp, scroll-bars and point-bars. A non-rocky coastal facies may include sediments deposited in the lower, middle or upper beach, a storm beach, mobile foreshore dunes, a lagoon or slack, mudflats, a fossil cliff and raised beach. The different sediments that make-up the facies are produced by a set of micro-environments which are linked in together by the transfer of mass and energy.

The mapping of the geomorphology around a site not only produces a standardised description of the terrain but also indicates the spatial distribution of processes which may have affected site formation or destruction. Suitable sites can be cored. In the absence of test pits or excavation, coring still gives the most detailed data on stratigraphy without materially damaging the site. Much can be done by systematic hand-augering in transects or grids across suitable areas. Suitable areas are generally flat areas identified from geomorphological survey or remote sensing and include old lake basins, floodplains, and terraces. There are several examples of archaeological discoveries being made from systematic coring including the clay pit at Leptiminus and the palaeolakes associated with the sites of Rascino and Nepi in central Italy. Small portable power corers are available and have been used at several sites including Klithi in Greece (Bailey *et al.*, 1990). There is little doubt that archaeological surveys associated with large engineering schemes or involving coring will reveal well preserved buried sites and landscapes in many coastal areas of the Mediterranean.

Earth surface processes are classified according to the energy involved and the transporting medium, both of which affect sediment texture, structure and architecture (Tucker, 1982). In practise, it is essential for the archaeologist to 'get out of the trench' in order to appreciate the local and regional context. Despite some notable exceptions (Butzer, 1982; Vita- Finzi, 1978), this has not been stressed sufficiently in the environmental archaeology literature. For example, the implication for site interpretation, and future work, are different for a site located on an active alluvial fan, as opposed to a site located on a terrace remnant. There is a wide variety of geomorphological agencies responsible for site destruction and burial, related to the climatic and geological region. In Mediterranean and semi-arid environments, alluvial fan formation, gully erosion and deflation are most important. Tectonically-active areas such as the Mediterranean are generally of greater relief and so mass-movements (e.g. landslides, mudslides, mudflows etc.) are also common, as are coastal change, earthquakes and volcanic activity. Tectonic geomorphology is a developing sub-discipline (Keller and Pinter, 1996; Vita-Finzi, 1988) and potentially has much to offer archaeologists.

The identification of sedimentary processes is not always easy, especially with slope-related sediments (colluvium), where the processes may be alluvial (Newtonian flow), mudflow (non-Newtonian flow), or dry mass movements (gravity slides). Indeed, there is some doubt as to whether the term colluvium is necessary or useful (Boardman and Bell, 1992). However, in most alluvial and coastal contexts, the lithostratigraphy can be highly informative, providing an environmental history revealing environmental constraints and resources available to human societies.

Facies analysis is also applicable to culturally-modified sediments. An example is the work by Hunt *et al.* (1986) on the infill of Wadi Mansur in Tripolitania, Libya, which is closely related to the development of a wall-technology and changes in the farming system which may have triggered off accelerated erosion. The facies equivalent, if related to human rather than environmental processes, in the urban archaeological context is the Harris Context Model and work is underway on integrating the two approaches.

The lithostratigraphy of the sediments can also be used to identify sediment provenance. Although colour can indicate provenance, it is also very sensitive to reducing/oxidising conditions in the soil and iron mineralogy. Lithology can be traced using clast analysis of coarse deposits, heavy mineral analysis, thin sectioning, and analytical methods such as X-ray diffraction and X-ray fluorescence. As a general rule, finer sediments are more susceptible to post-depositional changes. These involve a loss of constituents through weathering and leaching, and the formation of new minerals such as secondary clay minerals. Also, where there are many different sources of material, resistance to weathering will control the clast lithology: in catchments which are largely on soft carbonate rocks such as chalk, the river terraces will generally contain only the resistant flint derived from the chalk formations.

In the last twenty years, new methods have been devised for provenancing sediments, one of which is magnetic susceptibility (Thompson and Oldfield, 1986). Variation in sediment iron mineralogy produces magnetic signatures which can be statistically differentiated. This use of sediment magnetic signatures to identify source rocks is really just an extension of provenancing using sediment mineralogy. In addition, topsoil is magnetically enhanced by soil processes, while subsoil and sediment are not. This has been used to distinguish between arable-field erosion and river-bank erosion, the balance of which is related to land-use (Brown, 1992; Foster *et al.*, 1990).

The description of sediment characteristics can also help us to infer the processes of deposition. This is of direct relevance as it concerns the environmental conditions at the time of human activity. There are two fundamental characteristics: the size and shape of grains; and the way the grains are related to each other – the fabric. Although complicated by the conditions of the bed, grain shape and grain density, the grain size of a deposit is mathematically related to the power of the transporting flow (flow competence), as indeed is the volume of material that can be transported (flow capacity). Equations which relate grain size to flow parameters can be used to estimate past river discharges, a procedure known as palaeohydraulic modelling.

While archaeologists rarely require quantitative estimates of this kind of environmental parameter, they do need to distinguish between different processes and this can be done using sediment architecture, sedimentary structures, sedimentary fabric, and particle size and shape. Grain or particle size, which is relatively easy to measure by a variety of methods, has been frequently used for this purpose through the comparison of the frequency distributions of particle sizes in deposits including contemporary sediments. There are several analytical methods, although the most common has traditionally been the use of descriptive (moment) statistics such as the mean, and measures of central tendency (the kurtosis or sorting) thought appropriate due to the assumed approximate log-normality of many grain size distributions. Discriminant functions for these statistics have been determined using modern environments and these have been applied to sediments on archaeological sites. A similar method is the use of process-sensitive bi-variate plots such as the CM diagram which plots the coarsest fraction (D1) against the median fraction (D50). Different clusters are believed to represent channel-lag, bedload, traction, pelagic and uniform suspended load (Brown, 1985; Passega, 1964). Other methods include the use of log-hyperbolic models (Bagnold and Barndorf-Nielson, 1980) and the log- skew Laplace model (Fieller *et al.*, 1992). This last method has proved valuable in detailing the infill history of the harbour at Lepcis Magna which involved both shoreline and lacustrine or lagoonal deposition (Fieller *et al.*, 1990). Polymodal sediments can be analyzed by separating out the Gaussian components (Middleton, 1976), or by multivariate similarity/difference methods (Brown, 1985).

The sedimentology literature and archaeological experience suggest some caution with grain size analysis, as many of these techniques seem to 'under-perform' in archaeological contexts. The reasons for this are probably three-fold. Firstly, grain size below the competence of the transporting medium is a function of grain type, availability and geomorphic history. Secondly, archaeologically-related deposits have frequently been disturbed and mixed, and may even have components present transported by completely different media. Thirdly, there do seem to be some fundamental particle size ranges determined by crystal size and fracturing (Pettijohn, 1949).

Similarly, grain shape (determined using Powers roundness index: see Briggs, 1977) is related to both the qualities of the materials (e.g. cleavage) and the energy of the transporting environment. While it is certainly possible to distinguish between extreme environments using shape and particle surface features, more subtle within-facies discrimination is often not possible, largely due to the reworking of sediments, especially in temperate slope-river systems. As a recent volume on archaeological sediments and soils illustrates, the most informative analytical strategy for both materials is the combined use of standard physico-chemical methods with micromorphology from thin sections (Barham and Mcphail, 1995; see Shiel Chapter 8 in this volume for further discussion).

Trace metal analysis has been shown successfully to highlight known sites (Bintliff *et al.*, 1992) and sites where metal-working took place will be surrounded by a zone of elevated metal values. The archaeological significance of this, however, is not always immediately apparent, and given its expense it is probably only valuable in the determination of function of indeterminate sites or the principal metals being worked at metal-working sites. In many ways soil phosphorous has the opposite problems: it is less well bound to the soil, and although it is generally elevated around sites, the causes (other than buried organic matter) are many and varied and difficult to specify using techniques available to most archaeologists, although intelligent data processing may help. Probably because most archaeologists come into very close contact with the soil, some understanding of soil processes and formation has long been advocated by environmental archaeologists. The study of palaeosols is particularly useful in Mediterranean contexts (see Shiel, Chapter 8).

DATING SEDIMENTS

Radiocarbon dating

This is the most important method for the reconstruction of Late glacial and Holocene environments and alluvial chronologies since it covers the last 50,000 years and is the most widely used. The basic method is summarised in numerous publications (Aitken, 1990; Gillespie, 1984; Lowe and Walker, 1984) and does not need to be reviewed here. The most common non-cultural sites for radiocarbon dating of Mediterranean environmental change are alluvial or lacustrine, and only rarely peat bogs. Some authors have used radiocarbon histograms to provide a chronology of Holocene alluvial events (Macklin and Lewin, 1993), but due to the non-linearity of the uncalibrated radiocarbon timescale, clusterings may occur which do not represent real-time clusterings. Stolk *et al.* (1989) have produced a computer program which corrects for this effect: it uses a 100-year moving average and shows that over 100 dates per 1000 years are required to get significant results. In addition to calibration problems, there are three further sources of potential error associated with the use of ^{14}C to date alluvial environments: reworked or old organic material; pedogenic factors; and rootlet contamination.

The extent to which these pose problems will obviously vary with the nature of the sample, and it is therefore necessary to consider the types of organics commonly found in floodplain and terrace sections that can be dated. Of most importance are wood, peat, organic mud, and charcoal, especially in drier locations. Wood and charcoal produce the most reliable dates, but if not *in situ* will only give a maximum age of deposition, which in the case of charcoal could considerably predate deposition. Observations of the exhumation of old tree stumps by natural riverbank erosion shows that the reworking, or incorporation, of old wood can occur; this may be particularly common in Mediterranean environments where decay can be limited by desiccation. Likewise, given the severe history of soil erosion typical in the Mediterranean, inwashed pedogenic carbon or charcoal fragments are common in lacustrine and alluvial sediments, potentially leading to date reversals. Contamination by younger organic matter is also common in Mediterranean sites and the deep penetration of roots from exposures and banks makes radiocarbon unreliable in many cases. One of the ways of overcoming problems of contamination is to date small quantities of carbon of known local origin such as identified macrofossils. This has been facilitated by the development of accelerator mass spectroscopy dating (AMS), where the ^{14}C is measured directly rather than its radioactivity. It is, however, less common to find sites with well preserved macrofossils in the Mediterranean than in northern Europe.

A more subtle problem with radiocarbon dating in Mediterranean environments is a bias imposed by the conditions favourable to preservation. If we take the case of alluvial sediments, exposures are provided by river incision and frequently organics are preserved at the base of the visible sequence. Lower organics are rarely obtainable and higher organics are destroyed by decomposition in the oxic zone. One result of this may be the large number of medieval dates recorded from such sections. For this and the other reasons cited, radiocarbon dating is less important for landscape archaeology in the Mediterranean than in northern Europe and there is a need for other, preferably sediment-based, methods.

Palaeomagnetic dating

Palaeomagnetic dating has been used for many years for fired archaeological materials, but can also be used on some natural sediments. From the remanent magnetic signature of the material, an estimate is made of (a) its polarity (i.e. normal or reversed) and (b) the position of the magnetic North Pole; these are compared with the known history of magnetic reversals and polar wandering, dated by other means. The most important characteristic of the sediment is that the natural remanent magnetism which is aligned to the ambient magnetic field must be locked into the grains at the time of formation or deposition.

In theory there are four ways this can happen. The first is thermo-remanent magnetism, which is formed as molten rock cools through the Curie point (i.e. volcanic rocks). All iron oxides demagnetise at the Curie point (675°C for haematite and 565°C for magnetite) and on cooling are re-aligned to the Earth's field. The second is detrital remanent magnetism, which occurs as ferromagnetic sedimentary particles settle in a column of water (e.g. lake sediments). The third is chemical remanent magnetism acquired when ferromagnetic oxides crystallise. The fourth is post-depositional remanent magnetism, where re-alignment occurs as sediments consolidate.

Recent studies have shown that lake sediments are often subject to chemical remanent magnetism after sedimentation and this may well be the most important mechanism for sedimentary rocks. The declination and inclination of the magnetic field at the time remanent magnetism was acquired can be measured using a magnetometer. At the scale of 10^5–10^7 years, polarity reverses, but during periods of fixed polarity there are shorter reversals called events; within these periods the wandering of the North Pole is also recorded. The remanent magnetism record can then be correlated with master curves from sites which have been independently dated and, because all magnetic events can be regarded as globally synchronous, the sediments can be dated quite precisely.

The most suitable terrestrial sediments other than lake deposits are aeolian or loess deposits. However, recent work has suggested that a remanent magnetism may be acquired by fine alluvial deposits (Batt and Noel, 1991; Clarke, 1992; Ellis and Brown, 1998). Although, in principle, overbank silts could acquire a detrital remanent magnetism, the lack of water column height and constant turbulence would seem to render this unlikely and it is more probable that the signal is caused by post-depositional chemical processes. If this is commonly found to occur and is not destroyed by reducing conditions (gleying), it could provide a valuable addition to the methods available for the dating of non-organic alluvial deposits and the calculation of sedimentation rates. Recent studies have shown that palaeomagnetic dating seems to work in two situations: firstly in relatively uniform sandy silts of overbank origin which have been rapidly accreted and relatively little bioturbated; and where the natural remanent magnetism is carried by detrital magnetic grains. These conditions are common in the Mediterranean, with its history of severe soil erosion and correspondingly high rates of alluvial deposition. Such sediments have recently been dated from small river valleys north of Rome (Brown and Ellis, 1996). The second situation is where palaeochannels have been abandoned and have a silt-clay infill deposited in organic-rich stagnant anoxic conditions, where the natural remanent magnetism is carried by iron sulphide minerals probably biogenically precipitated (Ellis and Brown, 1998). Magnetic properties such as anisotropy of susceptibility can also yield a wealth of information on sedimentary conditions and produce estimates of palaeocurrent direction and strength from suitable sediments, generally palaeochannel infills. Palaeomagnetic dating could also be extremely useful in conjunction with mineral magnetic studies of the dating of prehistoric topsoil erosion.

Luminescence methods

All materials that contain, or are exposed to, radioactive substances (such as uranium) are continuously bombarded by radiation. This causes ionisation and the trapping of electrons in the mineral. As radiation continues, trapped electrons build up and if they can be measured and the radiation dose rate is known, then the time elapsed since the radiation started can be calculated. This measurement is possible because, if the mineral is heated, it emits extra light above that normally emitted proportional to the electrons trapped – thermoluminescence (TL). If the heating is repeated, the extra light will not be given off, as electrons will not have had enough time to build up again. In addition to measuring the light emitted, the concentration of radioactive elements can be measured by mass-spectrometry.

Pottery is ideal for such dating, because firing reduces the TL signal to zero (as all trapped electrons are released) if the temperature is high enough. However, sunlight can also reduce the TL signal of sediments to zero, so the Mediterranean is far more suitable than northern Europe in this respect. Luminescence has been applied to river terrace deposits in Mediterranean-type climates outside the range of radiocarbon dating (Nanson *et al.*, 1991). It is therefore potentially of great importance for dating terrace-associated palaeolithic artefacts and sites. When first applied to alluvial sediments, doubt was cast over whether they had been sufficiently zeroed to give the date of deposition (Berger, 1984). Due to the dynamics of the fluvial system and the generally short period of exposure of the sediment, the thorough penetration of light for all grains cannot be assumed (Bailiff, 1991). However, Nanson and Young (1987) and Nanson *et al.* (1991) have produced TL dates from terraces of the Nepean river in New South Wales and from an alluvial sand below the floodplain of Coopers Creek in western Queensland which agree well with other dating evidence. Their conclusion is that, if the dates are from shallow sand flows deposited as sheets on floodplains, where residual TL and long-term sediment moisture contents can be accurately estimated, TL dating is reliable and can provide an excellent basis for alluvial chronologies.

A similar technique, optical stimulation luminescence (OSL), probably has a wider application to Mediterranean alluvial deposits and requires less sophisticated equipment (Bailiff, 1992; Huntley *et al.*, 1985; Rhodes and Aitken, 1988). Visible light can be used to stimulate luminescence in quartz and infra-red radiation with feldspars. As with TL, many factors affect the accuracy of 'apparent' luminescence ages, including mineralogy, light exposure before burial-darkening (Rhodes and Pownall, 1994), overburden, erosion, and the nature of the radiation dose. This last factor is itself affected by sediment water content. At present the method is being used in five river valleys in central Italy (Brown and Rhodes, in prep.). Another related chronometric method is electron spin resonance (ESR); its importance for geoarchaeology largely lies in the potential of this method for chronometric dating of flint artefacts in terrace deposits (Garrison *et al.*, 1981).

OTHER NEW METHODS

Potassium-Argon Series ($^{40}K/^{40}Ar$) dating is based on the principle that unstable potassium decays via two pathways to either ^{40}Ca or ^{40}Ar gas. The second pathway can be used to date volcanic or metamorphic rocks rich in potassium, if the mineral structure within the rock is tight enough to prevent the 'daughter' isotope, Argon gas, from escaping. The method is only of practical importance for ages over 100,000 BP. The most commonly used rock type for Quaternary applications is volcanic ash or tephra. Tephra layers can provide excellent correlation and dating over wide areas and a wide variety of sites (Dugmore, 1991; Long and Morton, 1987). Given the volcanic activity of the Mediterranean basin and the discovery of very thin ash layers at considerable distances from their volcanic sources, this method may have considerable potential for dating landsurfaces where sedimentation rates are high enough and mixing is limited.

Uranium-Series Disequilibrium dating has applications to the dating of calcites, common in the Mediterranean. The isotopes ^{238}U, ^{235}U and ^{232}Th (Thorium) all decay through complicated chains of intermediate isotopes to the stable lead isotopes. The Uranium-series method works on the basis that some of the isotopes are insoluble and others soluble in water. The insoluble ones, such as Thorium, will be present in sediments and accumulate on lake beds and the sea bed. The soluble ones, such as the uraniums, may be metabolised by organisms. The former are said to be unsupported, in that they have become isolated from the rest of the decay chain, while the latter, the biogenically precipitated, are supported. The measurement of the decay products of each can yield an estimate of the age of the material (Ku, 1976). Theoretically, carbonate-rich soils and tufas are suitable for this method, although as yet only speleothems and corals have received much attention.

Dendrochronological dating is rapidly becoming the most important method for dating archaeological sites in northern Europe, but it has yet to make as much impact in the Mediterranean. This is largely because of a lack of suitable material, but timbers are occasionally found, and if there is greater emphasis on buried sites (such as ports and waterfronts), then more suitable material will be found, allowing the determination of regional chronologies. Work on regional dendrochronologies is underway in several laboratories within the Mediterranean (see Guibal, Chapter 5 in this volume).

Amino-Acid Racemisation is only applicable to organic matter and as yet only to bone and shell, both of which tend to be well preserved in Mediterranean environments. Amino-acids in proteins can survive in bone and shell long after death. The original chains of amino acids (peptide chains) break down at a relatively slow rate, if trapped in the organic structure. One of the mechanisms of this diagenesis called racemisation occurs because there are two molecular patterns of chains with identical chemical composition but reversed configuration: the so-called L-isomer and D-isomer types. On death, the L-isomers are converted to D-isomers until both are in equilibrium so the D/L ratio is 1. The rate at which this happens is thought to be partially time-dependent. However, the rate is also temperature-dependent and varies for each amino-acid and from species to species. Largely because of the temperature dependence, it has so far only been used to erect an amino-stratigraphy which has been calibrated by radiometric methods (in particular uranium-series dating). Its major use so far has been in the dating of Interglacial raised beaches, but the dating of non-marine shells offers the possibility of direct dating of fossiliferous terrace deposits, and it is also an important method of cross-checking other methods for palaeolithic terrace sites.

MODELLING ENVIRONMENT AND ARCHAEOLOGY

A model is simply a hypothetical simplification of reality which in some way mirrors or reproduces the attributes or workings of a natural (in the widest sense) system in a way that we can understand. There have probably been more models of environment-culture relations derived from Mediterranean/Middle Eastern studies than for any other area. Obvious examples include Childe's oasis hypothesis, the fertile crescent and crop domestication, and site catchment analysis.

One of the most serious problems in trying to produce any model of culture- environment relations is the 're-inforcement syndrome', to use the term coined by Limbrey (*pers. comm.*). This can easily occur when specialists and archaeologists interact: the archaeologist asks the specialist (e.g. a palynologist) to analyse some material to see if it supports some particular hypothesis he/she has (e.g. regarding human impact), the specialist analyses the material and finds that, as in many cases, the result and interpretation are not clear-cut. The specialist may then be tempted to seek corroboration or support from the archaeologist, who in turn backs up his/her hypothesis with the superficially independent data of the specialist. This is a well known danger in forensic work and is an argument in favour of keeping the specialist to some extent 'in the dark', but this is not an acceptable practise in archaeology. In reality it is very difficult to decide when the task of putting together all the disparate lines of evidence strays over from hypothesis- or model-building into the reinforcement syndrome. Environmental models of cultural change, such as the relationship between soil erosion and Mediterranean populations, are particularly sensitive to this philosophical problem. Awareness of it should encourage researchers in Mediterranean landscape archaeology to make sure of the independence of their data when constructing such models.

Probably the most common models applied to Mediterranean landscape archaeology are those derived from the human geography of the 1960s and 1970s, such as rediscovered classical location theory, network theory, central place theory, core-periphery theory and so on. A typical example was Renfrew's (1975) use of Theissen's polygons to define the hypothetical territory of the twelve cities of ancient Etruria. These models have the advantage that they can, to some extent, be tested by analysing the trend of artefacts with distance from centres (Hodder and Orton, 1976). These models are also set for a new lease of life due to the ease with which they can be created and manipulated in vector-based GIS systems. However, the fundamental criticisms of them voiced by the new generation of human geographers (e.g. Massey, 1973) remain and should be taken on board by archaeologists before they become blinded by computer applications. This sort of modelling, if it includes environmental variables, includes them as a pull or push on location; in practice, physical phenomena such as springs or rivers are used in order to try and explain the spatial patterning of sites. This is a procedure which, despite being computerised, is essentially no different from the work done by Cyril Fox in the 1930s and it suffers from all the same oversimplifications and assumptions.

An alternative is to return to an earlier non-geographical approach which is that of archaeology as ecology (Butzer, 1982, see refs.). Since human survival and technological change depend upon resources, the availability and utilization of resources can provide the basis for models of cultural change, including population change, which may have spatial implications. An early and classic example is the ecological modelling of hunter gatherer mobility and settlement by Jochim (1976). More recent examples include the analysis of sites with crop remains into producing and consuming sites or of the 'downstream' analysis of the processing of agricultural products. These models have many limitations and in time will be revised or discarded, but they serve as vehicles for further research into environmental reconstruction and as such are essential.

Studies of historical landscape change have shown how complex changes in society are reflected in changes to the landscape (Astill and Grant, 1988; Walsh *et al.*, 1995). An example is models of the organisation and change of multiple states, or of village formation in early medieval Europe, and their landscape impact. The importance of these models is not their outcomes but the questions they pose. They engender a search to provide a full range of the resources of any particular landscape and the relationships between those resources and consumption. This search for the resource-based landscape is essentially the same as the functional definition of landscape given at the beginning of this chapter. The archaeological importance of landscape is fundamentally how it worked – what it produced and what labour was expended on it (the 'taskscape', to borrow Ingolds' 1986 term) and the 'resourcescape'. This approach fits well with the application of scientific methods and the philosophy of the natural sciences, as well as with the way environmental science is now going with its growing interest in landscape ecology and human impact on the environment.

CONCLUSIONS

There are four broad conclusions to this review, relating to the geoarchaeological input to landscape archaeology in the Mediterranean.

The first is that, for geoarchaeology to realise its full potential in any projects, it must be included at the initial stages of the selection and delimitation of survey area. This means that there must be a geomorphological input at the planning stage. It is not necessarily advantageous to have an area based on archaeological criteria, indeed it may be counterproductive. If, for example, soil erosion and land degradation are an important aspect of the project, then it makes more sense to delimit the area using catchment boundaries than on the basis of the 'guestimated' sphere of influence of a town.

Secondly, the techniques and specialists must be appropriate for the geology, timescale and budget. The vast majority of Mediterranean landscape projects are at least partially on limestone, and yet archaeological collaboration with karst geomorphologists is extremely rare. In some of these areas there is no soil at the surface and the only environmental archive may be in the cave system. The relative appropriateness of techniques changes as new techniques are invented and in the Mediterranean these exciting new techniques include remote sensing and OSL dating.

Thirdly, although the potential of alluvial archaeology has been realised in northern Europe (Brown, 1997), this is only in the process of occurring in the Mediterranean (Woodward *et al.*, 1995). The sites are undoubtedly there: ports, buried field systems, bridges and so on. Although it may be difficult to justify subsurface archaeological prospection when some standing remains are unrecorded, from an environmental perspective the value of buried sites is far greater and therefore allows a greater range of questions to be asked and possibly even answered.

Lastly, it is suggested here that the philosophical basis for environmental reconstruction is the reconstruction of resources and the impact that their utilisation had on the land. It seems difficult to see how environmental reconstruction cannot be functionally based, a conclusion with clear implications for landscape archaeology.

REFERENCES

Aitken, M.J. (1990) *Science Based Dating in Archaeology*. London, Longman.

Astill, G. and Grant, A. (1988) *The Countryside of Medieval England*. Oxford, Blackwell.

Bagnold, R. and Barndorff-Nielsen, O. (1980) The pattern of natural size distributions. *Sedimentology* 27: 199–207.

Bailey, G.N., Lewin, J., Macklin, M.G. and Woodward, J.C. (1990) The 'Older Fill' of the Voidomatis Valley, northwest Greece and its relationship to the palaeolithic archaeology and glacial history of the region. *Journal of Archaeological Science* 17: 145–50.

Bailiff, I. (1992) Luminescence dating of alluvial deposits. In S. Needham and M. Macklin (eds) *Archaeology Under Alluvium*: 27–36. Oxford, Oxbow Books.

Barham, A.J. and Macphail, R.I. (1995) *Archaeological Sediments and Soils: Analysis, Interpretation and Management*. London, Institute of Archaeology.

Batt, C.M. and Noel, N. (1991) Magnetic studies of archaeological sediments. In P. Budd, B. Chapman, C.Jackson, R.C. Janaway and B.S. Ottoway (eds) *Archaeological Sciences 1989 : Proceedings of a Conference on the Application of Scientific Techniques to Archaeology*: 234–41. Oxford, Oxbow.

Berger, G.W. (1984) Thermoluminescence dating studies of glacial silts from Ontario. *Canadian Journal of Earth Science*. 21: 1393–9.

Bintliff, J., Davis, B., Gaffney, C., Snodgrass, A. and Waters, A. (1992) Trace metal accumulations in soils on and around ancient settlements in Greece. In P. Spoerry (ed.) *Geoprospection in the Archaeological Landscape*: 9–24. Oxford, Oxbow Monograph 18.

Boardman, J. and Bell, M. (1992) *Past and Present Soil Erosion*. Oxford, Oxbow Books.

Briggs, D.J. (1977) *Sediments*. London, Butterworths.

Brown, A.G. (1985) Traditional and multivariate techniques in the interpretation of floodplain sediment grain size variations. *Earth Surface Processes and Landforms* 10: 281–91.

Brown, A.G. (1992) Slope erosion and colluviation on the floodplain edge. In M. Bell and J. Boardman (eds) *Past and Present Soil Erosion*: 77–87. Oxford, Oxbow Books.

Brown, A.G. (1997) *Alluvial Geoarchaeology : Floodplain Archaeology and Environmental Change*. Cambridge, Cambridge University Press.

Brown, A.G. (in prep.) The environment of Leptiminus. In J. Humphreys (ed.) *Leptiminus. A Roman North African City*. Michigan, University of Michigan Press.

Brown, A.G. and Ellis, C. (1996) People, climate and alluviation : theory, research design and new sedimentological and stratigraphic data from Etruria, Italy. *Papers of the British School in Rome* 63: 45–73.

Brown, A.G. and Keough, M.K. (1992) Palaeochannels and palaeolandsurfaces : the geoarchaeological potential of some midland (U.K.) floodplains. In S. Needham and M. Macklin (eds) *Archaeology Under Alluvium*: 185–96. Oxford, Oxbow.

Brown, A.G. and Rhodes, E.J. (in prep.) *OSL dating of alluviation in central Italy*.

Butzer, K.W. (1982) *Archaeology as Human Ecology*. Cambridge, Cambridge University Press.

Clark, A. (1992) Palaeomagnetic dating of sediments and its calibration. In S. Needham and M. Macklin (eds) *Archaeology Under Alluvium*: 43–9. Oxford, Oxbow.

Cooke, R.U., Dornkamp, J.C. (1974) *Geomorphology in Environmental Management*. Oxford, Clarendon Press.

Dugmore, A.J. (1991) International tephrochronological studies in the NE Atlantic region. Paper given to QRA annual discussion meeting, 3–4th January, 1991, *International Research Initiatives and Data-banks*.

Ellis, C. and Brown, A.G. (1998) The archaeomagnetic dating of palaeochannels. Some data from Hemington, East Midlands. *Journal of Archaeological Science* 25: 149–63.

Fieller, N.R.J., Flenley, E.C., Gilbertson, D.D. and Hunt, C.O. (1990) The description and classification of grain size data from ancient and modern shoreline sands at Lepcis Magna using log-skew Laplace distributions. *Libyan Studies* 21: 49–59.

Fieller, N.R.J., Gilbertson, D.D., Griffin, C.M., Briggs, D.J. and Jenkinson, R.D.S. (1992) The statistical modelling of grain size distributions of cave sediments using log-skew Laplace distributions: Creswell Crags near Sheffield, England. *Journal of Archaeological Science* 19: 129–50.

Foster, I.D.L., Grew, R. and Dearing, J.A. (1990) Magnitude and frequency of sediment transport in agricultural catchments : a paired lake catchment study in Midland England. In J. Boardman, I.D.L. Foster and J.A. Dearing (eds) *Soil Erosion on Agricultural Land*. Chichester, Wiley.

Gardiner, V. and Dackombe, R. (1974) *Geomorphological Field Manual*. London, Allen and Unwin.

Garrison, E.G., Rowlett, R.M., Cowan, D.L. and Holroyd, L.V. (1981) ESR dating of ancient flints. *Nature* 290: 44–5.

Gilbertson, D.D. (1995) Studies of lithostratigraphy and lithofacies: a selective review of research developments in the last decade and their application to geoarchaeology. In A.J.Barham, and R.I. Macphail (eds) *Archaeological Sediments and Soils: Analysis, Interpretation and Management*: 99–144. London, Institute of Archaeology.

Gillespie, R. (1986) *Radiocarbon User's Handbook*. Oxford, Committee for Archaeology Monograph 3.

Hodder, I. and Orton, C. (1976) *Spatial Analysis in Archaeology*. Cambridge, Cambridge University Press.

Hunt, C.O., Mattingly, D.J., Gilbertson, D.D., Dore, J.W., Barker, G.W.W., Burns, J.R., Fleming, A.M. and van der Veen, M. (1986) ULVSXIII: Interdisciplinary approaches to ancient farming in the Wadi Mansur, Tripolitania. *Libyan Studies* 17: 7–47.

Huntley, D.J., Godfrey-Smith, D.I. and Thewalt, M.L.W. (1985) Optical dating of sediments. *Nature* 313: 105–7.

Ingold, T. (1986) *The Appropriation of Nature*. Manchester, Manchester University Press.

Jochim, M.A. (1976) *Hunter-Gatherer Subsistence and Settlement. A Predictive Model*. New York, Academic Press.

Keller, E.A. and Pinter, N. (1996) *Active Tectonics*. Prentice Hall Inc. New Jersey.

Ku, T.L. (1976) The uranium-series method of age determination. *Annual Review of Earth and Planetary Science* 4: 347–79.

Long, D. and Morton, A.C. (1987) An ash fall within the Loch Lomond Stadial. *Journal of Quaternary Science* 2: 97–102.

Lowe, M.J. and Walker, M.J.C. (1984) *Reconstructing Quaternary Environments*. London, Longman.

Macklin, G.M. and Lewin, J. (1993) Holocene river alluviation in Britain. *Zeitschrift für Geomorphologie* 88:109–22.

Massey, D. (1973) Towards a critique of industrial location theory. *Antipode* 5: 33–9.

Middleton, G.V. (1976) Hydraulic interpretation of sand size distributions. *Journal of Geology* 84: 405–26.

Mills, W.J. (1982) Metaphorical vision: changes in Western attitudes to the environment. *Annals of the Association of American Geographers* 72: 40–63.

Nanson, G.C. and Young, R.W. (1987) Comparison of thermoluminescence and radiocarbon age determinations from late-Pleistocene alluvial deposits near Sydney, Australia. *Quaternary Research* 27: 263–9.

Nanson, G.S., Price, D.M., Short, S.A., Young, R.W. and Jones, B.L. (1991) Comparative uranium-thorium and thermoluminescence dating of weathered Quaternary alluvium in the tropics of northern Australia. *Quaternary Research* 35: 346–66.

Passega, R. (1964) Grain size representation by CM patterns as a geological tool. *Journal of Sedimentary Petrology* 34: 830–74.

Payne, D., Brown, A.G. and Brock, B. (1994) Factors effecting remotely sensed soil variation and near-harvest crop variation near Antequera, Southern Spain. In *Proceedings of the NERC Symposium on Airborne Remote Sensing 1993*. University of Dundee 20–21st December, NERC.

Pettijohn, F.J. (1949) *Sedimentary Rocks*. New York, Harper and Row, first edition.

Renfrew, C. (1975) Trade as action at a distance. In J.A. Sabloff and C.C. Lamberg-Karlovsky (eds) *Ancient Civilisation and Trade*: 3–59. Albuquerque, University of Mexico Press.

Rhodes, E.J. and Aitken, M.J. (1988) Optical dating of archaeological sediment. *La Chronologie* 1: 117–20.

Rhodes, E.J. and Pownall, L. (1994) Zeroing of the OSL signal in quartz from young glaciofluvial sediments. *Radiation Measurements* 23: 581–5.

Stolk, A., Hogervorst, J.J. and Berendsen, H.J.A. (1989) Correcting C-14 histograms for the non-linearity of the radiocarbon time scale. *Radiocarbon* 31: 169–78.

Thompson, R. and Oldfield, F. (1986) *Environmental Magnetism*. London, Allen and Unwin.

Tucker, M. (1982) *The Field Description of Sedimentary Rocks*. Milton Keynes, Open University Press, Geological Society of London Handbooks.

Vita-Finzi, C. (1978) *Archaeological Sites in Their Settings*. London, Thames and Hudson.

Vita-Finzi, C. (1988) *Recent Earth Movements: An Introduction to Neotectonics*. London, Academic Press.

Walsh, K., O'Sullivan, D., Young, R., Carne, S. and Brown, A.G. (1995) Medieval land use, agriculture and environmental change on Lindisfarne (Holy Island), Northumbria. In R.A. Butlin and N. Roberts (eds) *Ecological Relations in Historical Times*: 101–21. Oxford, Blackwell.

Woodward, J., Lewin, J. and Macklin, M.G. (1995) (eds) *Mediterranean Quaternary Environments*. Rotterdam, Balkema.

Zimmerman, E.W. (1951) *World Resources and Industries*. New York, Harper and Brothers.

7. L'Apport de la Micromorphologie des Sols à la Reconstitution des Paléopaysages (Application au Bassin Méditerranéen pour la Période 3000 AV. J.C./1800 AP. J.C.)

Nicolas Fédoroff et Marie-Agnès Courty

INTRODUCTION

Le sol, composante essentielle du paysage

En premier lieu, le sol doit être considéré comme un élément actif du paysage grâce aux multiples transformations physiques, mais surtout biologiques, biochimiques, chimiques qui s'y produisent et qui sont en équilibre avec les conditions environnementales externes (Bonneau et Souchier, 1994). De plus, le sol est un maillon essentiel du cycle de l'eau. Il faut aussi rappeler que la couverture pédologique forme un système continu couvrant tout le paysage.

A la différence des groupements végétaux, le sol constitue un élément relativement stable du paysage. Il est relativement peu sensible à l'action de l'Homme alors que les associations végétales le sont infiniment. Par ailleurs sa nature influe considérablement sur la composition de l'association végétale qu'il porte ce qui rend possible des reconstitutions végétales du passé.

Le sol, 'auto-mémoire et mémoire' paléoenvironnementale

Le sol possède une 'mémoire' qui enregistre les effets de son fonctionnement, mais aussi les impacts externes. Cette 'mémoire' malheureusement se vide progressivement et de façon différentielle avec le temps ce qui oblige pour les reconstitutions de paléopaysages à recourir à des paléosols, c'est-à-dire des sols enterrés dont la mémoire a été bloquée à un instant t_0.

Les causes de la sous-utilisation du sol pour les reconstitutions paysagères

En conclusion au paragraphe précédent, une reconstitution des paléopaysages, surtout si elle se veut dynamique, ne peut ignorer le sol. Néanmoins on constate qu'à l'heure actuelle, ces reconstitutions ignorent en partie, voire complètement, le sol étant réalisées essentiellement par des paléo-botanistes et des géomorphologues.

Par exemple, la dégradation des sols est inférée en s'appuyant sur des sens communs qui dénotent une méconnaissance du fonctionnement du sol (Rollefson, 1994; Runnels, 1995). Par exemple, Rollefson (1994) écrit: 'Les chèvres, capables d'arracher entièrement les plantes avec leurs racines, auraient peu à peu détruit la couche de protection des sols, laissant ceux-ci exposés aux effets du vent et de l'eau'; il continue: 'Les chèvres auraient ainsi lentement mais sûrement détruit les fragiles systèmes d'équilibre des sols dont la formation avait pris des millénaires'. Or il est connu que la régénération physique et biologique d'un sol à partir d'un matériel parental peut se faire très rapidement, en quelques mois ou une année (Tableau 7.1). Par exemple, les sols de polder aux Pays-Bas produisent des récoltes à hauts rendements trois ou quatre ans seulement après leur exondation. Le sol pour les archéologues et les géomorphologues est donc une boîte noire. L'état de surface du sol dont les pédologues (Bresson et Boiffin, 1990 pour les régions tempérées; Casenave et Valentin, 1989 pour les régions tropicales) ont démontré le rôle fondamental pour l'infiltration des eaux et donc pour le ruissellement et l'érosion, n'est pas pris en considération dans les études qui s'intéressent aux érosions du passé. L'érosion est estimée indirectement d'après la lithologie et l'épaisseur des sédiments. De plus, il est en général supposé qu'un dépôt sédimentaire calé par deux dates s'est mis en place de façon continue entre ces deux dates.

Pourquoi le sol pour ces reconstitutions, comme d'ailleurs dans d'autres domaines, est-il si largement sous-utilisé, voire ignoré ?

La faute en revient en premier lieu aux pédologues. En effet, pour l'essentiel, la pédologie a été et reste encore une science appliquée dont le but principal est d'augmenter et de rationaliser la production agricole. Par exemple, la 'mémoire' du sol n'a guère fait l'objet de recherches approfondies et systématiques. Par ailleurs, la pédologie n'est en pratique enseignée que dans les universités

	1 année avec travail du sol	1 à 10^2 ans	10^2 à 10^4 ans	10^4 à 10^6 ans
cohésion ou (et) degré de cimentation	sans cohésion et non cimenté, ex. loess	légère cohésion, ex. marnes	forte cohérence ou (et) cimentation moyenne, ex. calcaire crayeux	roches très cohérentes ou (et) fortement cimentées, ex. calcaires durs, quartzites
porosité initiale	élevée	élevée à faible	faible	nulle
nature des argiles	–	éclatement de la roche par gonflement des smectites	–	–
nature et abondance des minéraux altérables	–	très nombreux minéraux altérables, ex. sérécite	assez nombreux minéraux altérables	rares ou absence de minéraux altérables
présence de sels solubles	–	éclatement de la roche par remontée des sels (en climats semi-arides)	–	–

Tableau 7.1. Grille pour l'estimation de l'aptitude d'une roche ou d'une formation à régénérer un sol.

agricoles, rares sont les cursus en archéologie, écologie et en Sciences de la Terre dans les universités qui comportent un enseignement de pédologie.

Il faut aussi souligner que le sol est un milieu complexe, appréhendé par de nombreux spécialistes, altérologues, chimistes du sol, biologistes du sol et microbiologistes du sol qui communiquent peu entre eux. Le pédologue essaye de faire la synthèse de l'ensemble des résultats pour connaître, d'une part le fonctionnement et le comportement du sol et d'autre part sa genèse (son histoire).

La micromorphologie des sols

Pour la reconstitution des paysages, il est surtout fait appel à la 'mémoire' du sol. Cette 'mémoire' se présente dans le sol sous forme de minéraux et de corps spécifiques et surtout d'agencements des constituants du sol, appelés, *traits* et *assemblages pédologiques.* La plupart de ces traits et de ces assemblages ne sont identifiables qu'à des échelles d'observation microscopiques tandis que leur composition chimique n'est déterminable qu'en microanalyse.

La micromorphologie des sols dont l'objet d'étude est le sol non perturbé et par extension les formations superficielles aux échelles microscopiques par observation et microanalyse est évidemment particulièrement bien adaptée au déchiffrage de la 'mémoire' du sol.

Pourquoi la micromorphologie des sols, comme le sol, pour les reconstitutions paysagères, a-t-elle été sous-utilisée, voire ignorée ?

La micromorphologie des sols est pratiquée principalement par les pédologues, ce qui signifie que les remarques formulées à propos de l'étude du sol s'appliquent à la micromorphologie. De plus la micromorphologie des sols est une discipline récente, le premier ouvrage de base de la micromorphologie des sols, *Micropedology* de W.L. Kubiena n'a paru qu'en 1938. Ce retard est dû en partie à la difficulté de consolider des échantillons de sols et de sédiments meubles. Cette consolidation n'est devenue relativement aisée qu'avec l'apparition sur le marché après la seconde guerre mondiale des résines polyesters

Applications des méthodes et des concepts de la paléopédologie et de la micromorphologie des sols à l'étude des sols holocènes

La 'mémoire' des sols est un des objets d'étude de la paléopédologie. Malheureusement, les paléopédologues se sont presque exclusivement consacrés à l'étude des sols pléistocènes ou de sols encore plus anciens.

Pour ces paléosols, la micromorphologie des sols est considérée aujourd'hui comme un outil indispensable pour identifier les signatures des événements environnementaux, les interpréter et bâtir des chronologies événementielles et donc contribuer à la reconstitution des paléopaysages de cette période (Fedoroff et Goldberg, 1982).

Au contraire, l'Holocène a été longtemps considéré par les pédologues comme une période de biostasie au cours de laquelle le climat n'avait pas subi de variations notables et donc qu'il n'avait pas influé sur le développement des sols, seul l'Homme introduisant des modifications dans la formation des sols. Mais des études récentes dans le nord-ouest de l'Inde (Courty, 1990), dans le Haut-Khabbur (Courty, 1994) et dans le bassin de Vera en Espagne du sud-est (Fedoroff et Courty, 1995) ont montré que le développement des sols et des couvertures pédologiques a connu pendant l'Holocène autour de la Méditerranée et ailleurs des changements importants (Fig. 7.1).

La période, 3000 av. J.C./1800 ap J.C. envisagée dans ce travail suppose des reconstitutions de paysages à pas de temps très courts, d'une à quelques centaines d'années pour lesquelles les pédologues et les paléopédologues ne disposent pas d'outils vraiment appropriés. Une

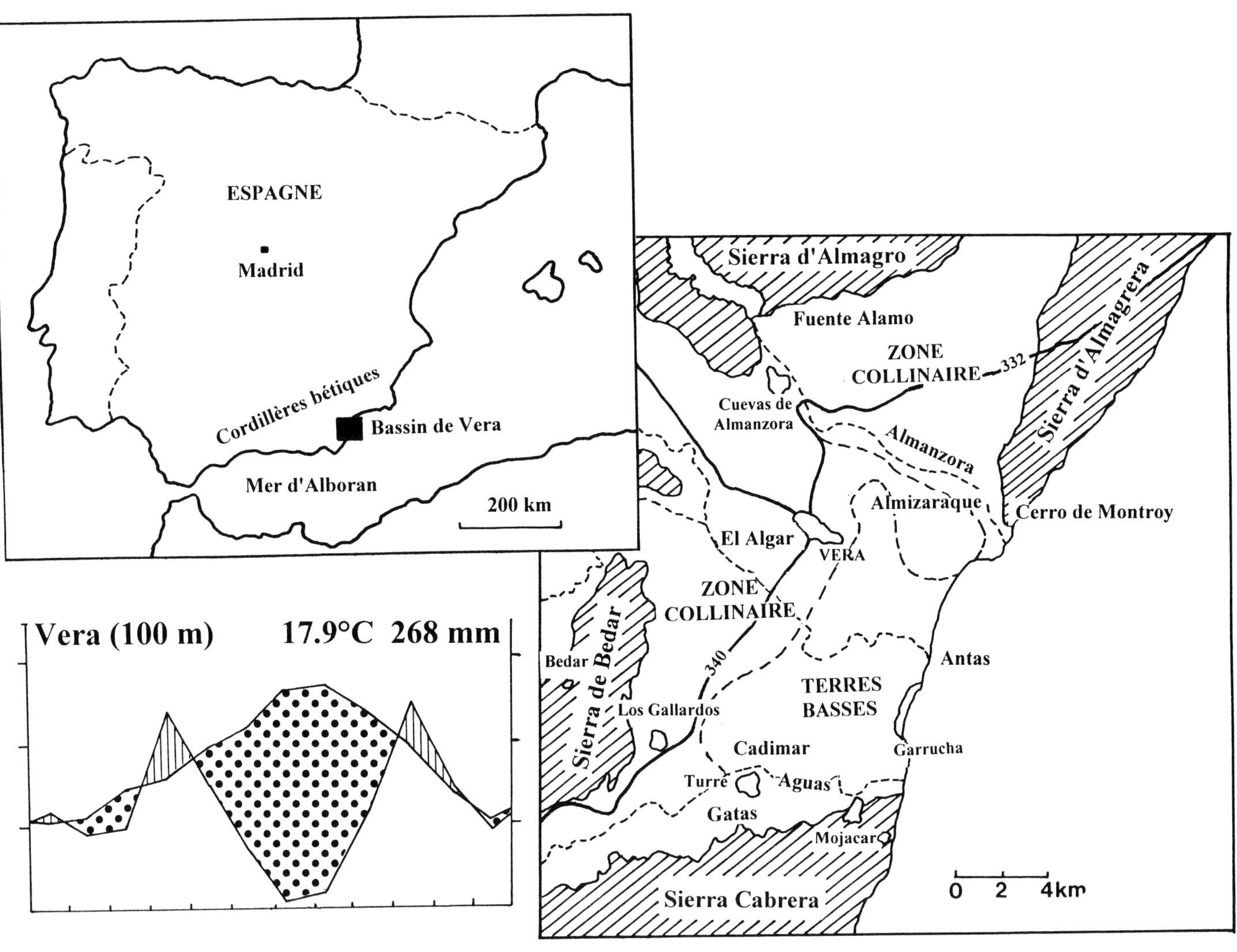

Fig. 7.1. Localisation et climat du bassin de Vera.

méthodologie nouvelle est donc à développer. Les crises caractérisées par des baisses de population, voire des disparitions et aussi des régressions culturelles qu'a connues le bassin méditerranéen au cours de cette période (Glassner, 1986; Tainter, 1988; Yoffee et Cowgill, 1988) résultent de l'avis général d'une surexploitation du Milieu par l'Homme qui provoque une dégradation de la végétation et des sols, responsables du déclenchement de l'érosion et d'une chute de la production agricole (Bottema et Woldring, 1990; Goldberg et Bar Yosef, 1990; Roberts, 1990; Thornes, 1987; van Andel et Zangger, 1990; Zangger, 1992). L'axiome de base qui a prévalu et qui prévaut encore est qu'un défrichement, suivi d'une mise en culture provoquent une érosion. Néanmoins plusieurs auteurs (Ballais, 1991; Ballais *et al.*, 1993; Provansal et Morhange, 1994; Vita-Finzi, 1969) constatent en Basse Provence et ailleurs dans le bassin méditerranéen que l'expansion agraire de l'époque romaine est une période de stabilité du couvert pédologique alors que la déprise rurale post-antique correspond à une érosion. Un effort particulier est donc demandé au pédologue pour séparer sans ambiguïté l'impact de l'Homme de celui des facteurs naturels sur les sols.

L'objectif de cette présentation est de: 1) proposer une méthodologie nouvelle pour la reconstitution des paysages autour de la Méditerranée pour la période 3000 av. J.C./ 1800 ap. J.C., puis d'en discuter la validité; 2) présenter un outil permettant de distinguer les impacts respectifs de l'Homme et des facteurs naturels sur le sol et le paysage. Enfin dans une troisième partie, nous appliquerons cette méthodologie à un cas concret, le bassin de Vera en Espagne du sud-est.

MÉTHODOLOGIE POUR LA RECONSTITUTION DES PAYSAGES HOLOCÈNES, PLUS PARTICULIÈREMENT POUR LA PÉRIODE 3000 AV. J.C./1800 AP. J.C

La méthode de reconstitution des paysages présentée ici repose sur: 1) une analyse systématique des sols enfouis sous les sites archéologiques et des couches de remaniement et d'abandon que ceux-ci renferment; 2) une approche mécaniste des processus pédologiques et sédimentaires; 3) l'établissement d'une chronologie événementielle; 4) la recherche pour les périodes et les régions où les archéologues trouvent des évidences d'activités agricoles, de signatures dans les sols de ces activités.

Cette méthode n'est donc valable que pour des régions abondamment pourvues en sites archéologiques. Elle suppose aussi pour le premier point une collaboration étroite entre archéologues et géo-pédologues. L'étude débute obligatoirement par des observations approfondies sur le terrain effectuée par le géo-pédologue lui-même. Elle se poursuit au laboratoire par un examen au microscope polarisant des lames minces taillées dans les échantillons prélevées sur le terrain. Cette étude micromorphologique conduit, d'une part à effectuer des analyses spécialisées complémentaires, et d'autre part à retourner sur le terrain pour des observations et un échantillonnage complémentaires.

L'approche de terrain

Sur le terrain, le géo-pédologue effectue: 1) une étude des sols enfouis sous les sites archéologiques et leurs abords immédiats; 2) un lever régional des sols et des pédo-sédiments; 3) des sondages dans les zones basses d'atterrissements et éventuellement dans les lacs.

Observations et échantillonnage sur les sites archéologiques

Cette méthode suppose que le géo-pédologue dispose préalablement à son intervention sur le terrain d'un inventaire régional des sites archéologiques. La valeur des reconstitutions paysagères par le géo-pédologue est étroitement liée à la qualité de cet inventaire. Cette valeur dépend de:

- La précision du cadre chronologique à la fois stratigraphique et culturel établi par l'archéologue. Un pas de temps aussi court que possible prenant en compte les phénomènes de sociétés pour lesquels le pas de temps est au maximum celui de la génération est à rechercher. Pour la période envisagée, 3000 av. J.C./1800 ap. J.C., un pas de temps de 100 à 300 ans pour la partie protohistorique doit être considéré comme satisfaisant alors pour la partie historique, ce pas de temps peut être réduit à quelques dizaines d'années.
- La qualité et du nombre de sites pour chaque période culturelle. Le site archéologique idéal pour de telles reconstitutions est une implantation humaine qui n'a pas perturbé le sol sur laquelle elle repose et qui a été enfouie instantanément sous une grande épaisseur de matériaux. Ce cas idéal est réalisé dans les khourgans (sites funéraires) du sud de la plaine russe. Au contraire, les sites archéologiques d'un faible intérêt sont, par exemple, les structures en creux ou des sites remaniés dont les objets sont éparpillés.

Les sites archéologiques de chaque période culturelle sont étudiés séparément. Ainsi pour une même période culturelle, t_0 à t_1 d'une région, il est procédé à:

- Une recherche, puis une description pédologique du ou des sols vierges enfouis sous chacun des sites. L'examen des matériaux de construction (briques crues et dans une moindre mesure briques cuites et tuiles) contribue aussi à la reconstitution de la couverture pédologique à cette période aux abords du site. On suppose que les matériaux pour les briques crues sont prélevés aux abords immédiats du site. Puis la couverture pédologique reconstituée est comparée à la couverture pédologique actuelle aux abords des sites et plus généralement à la couverture pédologique de la région. La couverture pédologique actuelle est soit donnée par une carte pédologique existante, soit levée spécialement.
- Un examen des couches de remaniement et d'abandon présentes dans les sites (étude faite en étroite coordination avec l'archéologue).

L'échantillonnage porte pour chaque période sur le sol vierge enfoui sous site archéologique; un profil est choisi comme référence, mais des répétitions sont vivement conseillées. Les horizons supérieurs sont prélevés en continu tandis qu'une attention particulière est portée au contact sol/matériel archéologique. Les couches de remaniement et d'abandon sont également échantillonnées; on prélève la couche elle-même et les contacts inférieurs et supérieurs. Il est conseillé pour établir une stratégie d'échantillonnage de consulter l'ouvrage de Courty *et al.* (1989).

Etude pédo-sédimentaire régionale

Il est indispensable de disposer pour la région étudiée d'une carte des sols et des formations superficielles aussi détaillée que possible. Deux possibilités existent, soit: 1) cette carte existe déjà; pour juger de sa précision, il est nécessaire de connaître le nombre d'observations au km^2 et de faire des contrôles au sol; 2) elle n'existe pas et des levers sont donc indispensables. Ces levers se font à l'aide de documents satellitaires et aériens avec un contrôle au sol pour chaque unité cartographique importante. Il est conseillé de produire une carte des unités de paysage selon Fedoroff et Courty (1995) qui a l'avantage de présenter les sols d'un point de vue évolutif (Fig. 7.2). A partir de la carte des sols, quelque soit son origine, il est possible de produire par simple compilation de données diverses cartes d'applications telles que carte de sensibilité à l'érosion, carte de potentialité à régénérer un sol, carte d'aptitude à la production agricole, etc. Pour chaque période, on compare les sols enterrés sous les sites archéologiques avec la carte des sols actuels ou des unités de paysage en vue de réaliser une première ébauche de la couverture pédologique existant à cette période (Figs 7.3, 7.4).

En complément, on recherche des coupes naturelles et

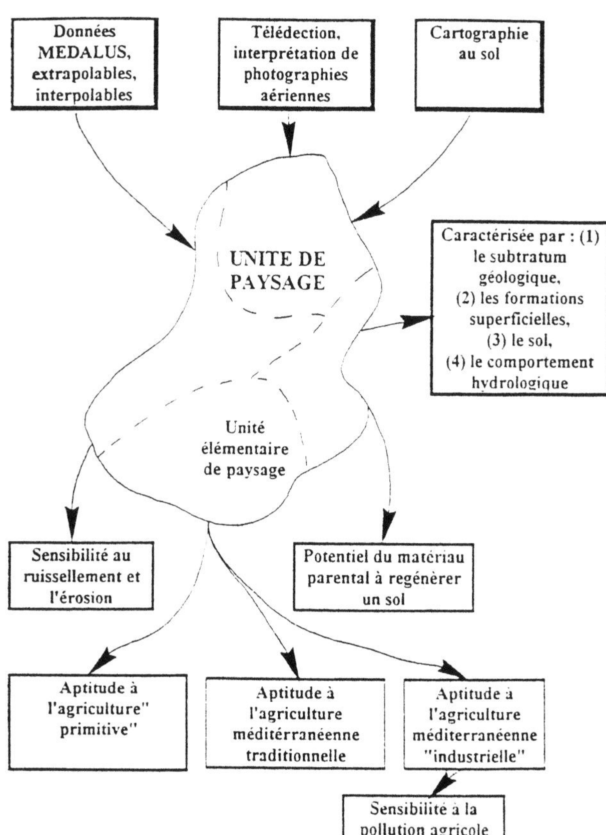

Fig. 7.2. Carte des unités de paysage. Mode d'établissement. Applications.

(ou) on fait creuser des tranchée à la pelle mécanique en vue de caractériser les pédo-sédiments ou les sédiments déposés en position basse au cours de la période envisagée, t_0 à t_1.

Les sols actuels seront seulement échantillonnés pour servir de comparaison aux sols enterrés sous les sites archéologiques. Par contre, les coupes seront échantillonnées systématiquement.

Sondages en zones d'atterrissements
Des forages en zone de sédimentation (comblements de vallées, de lacs) seront également réalisés en vue de suivre la ou les couches contemporaines de la période t_0 à t_1.

L'analyse micromorphologique

L'étude des lames minces sous le microscope polarisant taillées dans les échantillons non perturbés constitue la première étape des analyses de laboratoire.

Fabrication des lames minces
Les échantillons, préalablement à leur taille, doivent être imprégnés par des résines. Pour réussir la fabrication d'une lame mince, l'imprégnation doit être complète ce qui dans d'assez nombreux cas est difficile à réaliser. La réussite d'une imprégnation dépend: 1) du fait que l'échantillon au moment de l'imprégnation doit être sec; 2) de la fluidité de la résine; 3) de la montée de la résine qui doit se faire par capillarité le plus lentement possible (entre 24 à 48 h). Les lames minces doivent être de grande taille, par exemple 13 x 7 cm. Les divers ateliers de taille de lames minces de sols ont décrit leur technique de préparation de lames, citons par exemple Guilloré (1985).

Examen des lames minces
Il existe plusieurs manuels d'aide à la description de lames minces de sols (Brewer, 1964, 1976; Bullock *et al.*, 1985) qui malheureusement ne donnent pas d'interprétation des entités décrites. Par contre, l'ouvrage de Courty *et al.* (1989) destiné aux archéologues fournit des interprétations.

Nous donnons ci-dessous quelques exemples d'interprétation de lames minces.

- Identification de pratiques agricoles
  Les effets des pratiques agricoles modernes sur les sols aux échelles microscopiques sont assez bien connus (Jongerius, 1970). En particulier, les croûtes superficielles ont été inventoriées tandis que leurs mécanismes de formation sont bien compris aussi bien sous climats tempérés (Bresson et Boiffin, 1990) qu'en zones tropicales (Cazenave et Valentin, 1989). Leur vieillissement sur les terres en déprise a également fait l'objet d'études (Fedoroff et Courty, 1995). Les croûtes texturales internes et la prise en masse ont également été analysées ainsi que les effets des pratiques agricoles sur l'activité de la faune du sol (Ordaz, 1995). Dans les horizons non travaillés, des particules liées aux pratiques agricoles pénétrent sous forme de suspension et sédimentent sous forme de revêtements, mais le plus souvent de colmatages de vides (Fig. 7.5). Pour détecter les effets de pratiques agricoles du passé, il est évidemment indispensable que le sol cultivé ait été enterré brusquement.
- Mise en évidence d'incendies
  Ceux-ci sont identifiés par la présence dans la matrice du sol de charbons de bois, de carbone suie, de phytolithes et de fragments de sol chauffé. Les feux peuvent être classés en trois catégories: 1) feux d'origine anthropique (déforestation, gestion des pâturages, etc.); 2) incendies naturels; 3) incendies exceptionnels.
- Identification de phases arides
  Une phase aride se caractérise par un entassement d'agrégats arrondis, en général de provenances variées, en particulier d'horizons superficiels.
- Mise en évidence d'événements environnementaux abrupts
  La démarche est la suivante: 1) établir la séquence des attributs qui caractérisent la période avant l'événement, l'événement lui-même et le retour à des

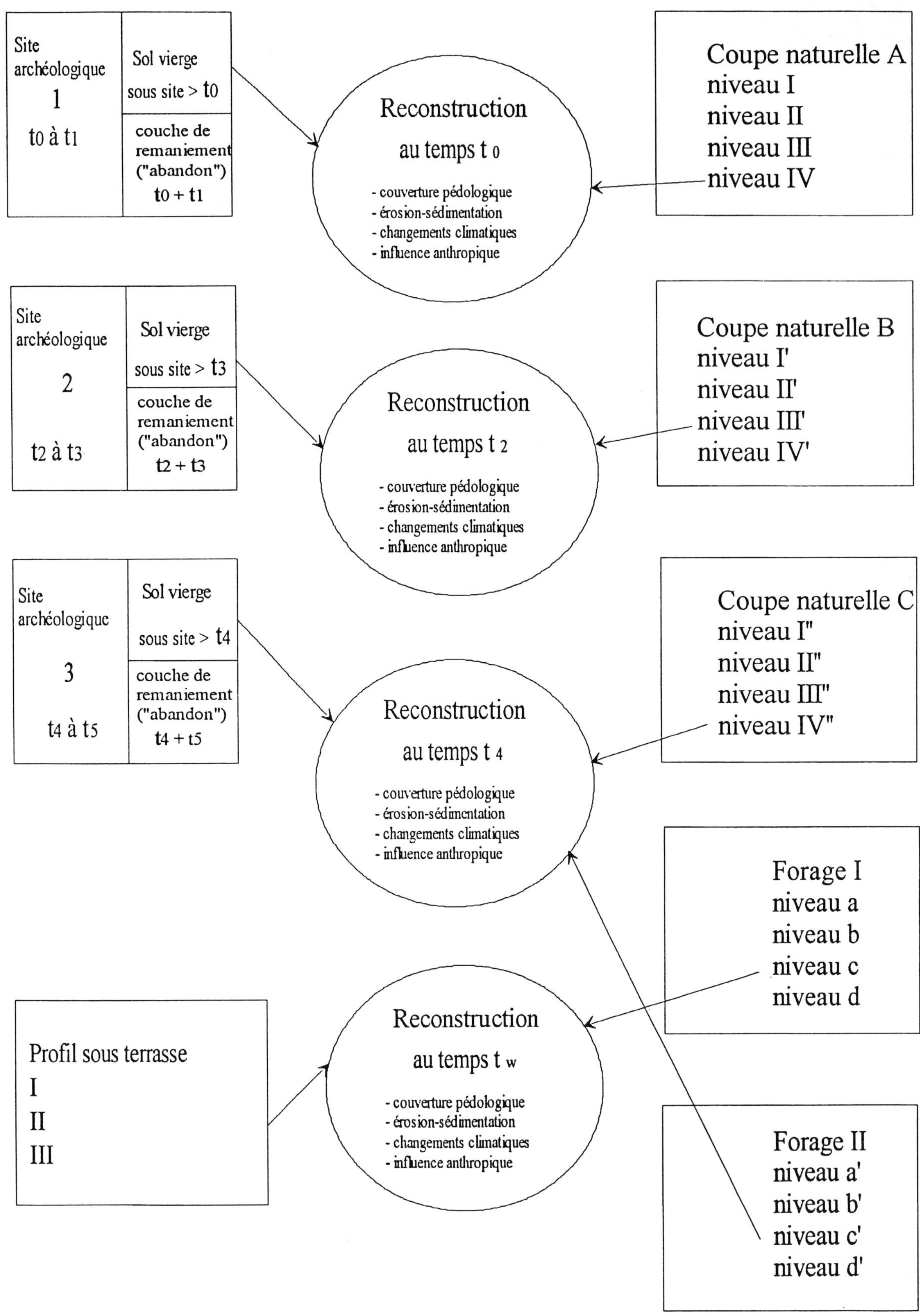

Fig. 7.3. Méthode de reconstitution des paléo-paysages.

Fig. 7.4. Photographie aérienne de la basse vallée de l'Antas.
a. Port de Garrucha. 1. Prise d'eau du canal d'épandage des eaux de crue. 2. Zone d'épandage des eaux de crue (La Esperanza). 3. Salars *de la Esperanza et de los Carros. 4.* Bancales *sur marnes et le horst de Garrucha. 5. Basse terrasses de l'Antas et los Amarguillos. 6. Lambeau de la haute terrasse de Cabezo Largo. 7. Affleurement de basaltes sur marnes.*

conditions normales; 2) déterminer le contraste existant entre les attributs des trois phases, ce qui permet d'inférer la soudaineté de l'événement; 3) apprécier la signification paléoenvironnementale des attributs liés à l'événement abrupt.

Un changement abrupt des conditions environnementales peut avoir un ou plusieurs des effets suivants sur le sol: 1) combustion de la végétation et des horizons humiques; 2) dénudation du sol; 3) érosion hydrique superficielle; 4) érosion et sédimentation éolienne; 5) saturation en eau d'un ou plusieurs horizons, accompagnée ou non de glissements de terrain; 6) gel profond du sol; 7) introduction de corps exogènes.

Les analyses complémentaires

Les techniques microscopiques, en particulier de microanalyses, ont connu un développement considérable (Fedoroff et Courty, 1994). L'outil de base reste la lame mince observée au microscope polarisant.

Méthode de reconstitution de paléopaysages

De telles reconstitutions supposent comme pré-requis un cadre chronologique à la fois stratigraphique et culturel à pas de temps aussi court que possible, prenant en compte à la fois les phénomènes de société pour lesquels le pas de temps est au maximum celui de la génération, et les

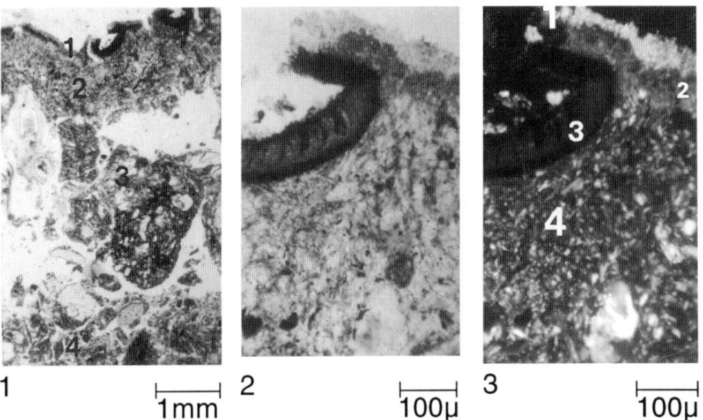

Photographie 1: Vue générale de la croûte à faible grossissement. On distingue de haut en bas: 1. une pellicule de surface continue, épaisse de 250 µm, formée de thalles cryptogamiques, 2. la croûte proprement dite, à structure massive, épaisse de 1 mm, 3. un sous-horizon à entassement de turricules de vers de terre, 4. un horizon à organisation excrémentale tassée qui se prolonge au-delà de la photographie.

Photographies 2 et 3: Vue de la partie supérieure de la croûte en lumière naturelle et lumière naturelle et lumière polarisée à fort grossissement.

On distingue de haut en bas: 1. une pellicule de cristaux d'oxalate de calcium, épaisse de 70 µm, à forte biréfringence, 2. une pellicule d'organismes chlorophyllien de couleur verte (sombre en noir et blanc), 3. latéralement un thalle, 4. la croûte minérale de surface, presque totalement décalcifiée.

Fig. 7.5. Morphologie d'une croûte de surface développée sur une friche ancienne.

facteurs climatiques que l'on croyait se modifier lentement avec un pas de temps de l'ordre de 10^3 à 10^4 (Berger, 1988). Mais des résultats récents ont montré que ces modifications pouvaient se produire en quelques dizaines d'années, voire en quelques années (Jansen et Veum, 1990). En effet, si l'on désire confronter l'impact respectif des événements anthropiques et naturels sur les sols et les paysages, il est indispensable de caler avec le maximum de précision ces événements à la fois temporellement et les uns par rapport aux autres.

L'interprétation des traits et des organisations recelés dans les sols enterrés sous les sites archéologiques permet de reconstituer le fonctionnement de ces sols avant l'occupation du site. Ce fonctionnement est indicateur des conditions environnementales, en particulier climatiques qui régnaient à cette période. Ces sols enterrés peuvent être vierges, ou renfermer des traces, soit de défrichement, soit de mise en valeur agricole. Dans quelques cas, les sédiments archéologiques eux-mêmes peuvent être prélevés en vue de caractériser l'évolution des conditions environnementales pendant les phases successives d'occupation du site.

La reconstitution du paysage caractérisant chaque période culturelle est réalisée en prenant comme base la carte des unités de paysage et en extrapolant pour chacune de ces unités les résultats ponctuels obtenus sur les sols enterrés sous les sites archéologiques et éventuellement hors des sites.

La précision de la méthode utilisée pour reconstituer l'évolution pédo-sédimentaire et évaluer les temporalités des impacts respectifs de l'Homme et des facteurs environnementaux sur les sols et le paysage dépend de: 1) la résolution du cadre chrono-culturel; 2) du nombre de sites archéologiques prospectés pour chaque période culturelle, de leur répartition spatiale et de leur degré de préservation; 3) du degré de calage par rapport aux périodes culturelles des sols enterrés sous les sites archéologiques et des sédiments; 4) du degré de conservation des enregistrements dans les sols enterrés.

Il ne faut pas aussi oublier notre capacité encore très limitée à analyser et à décrypter les signatures d'événements pédologiques et sédimentaires. Ainsi actuellement l'analyse d'un sédiment ne permet pas en général de conclure si celui-ci s'est déposé en une seule fois à la suite d'une pluie d'une intensité exceptionnelle ou au contraire s'il résulte d'un dépôt régulier pendant une longue période de temps.

Soulignons que les corrélations que l'on peut établir d'une région à l'autre pour un événement sont en général discutables, d'où la difficulté de juger de la globalité d'un événement.

Un exemple de cas concret: la reconstitution des paysages du bassin de Vera de 3000 ans avant J.C. à nos jours

L'Espagne du sud-est a été retenue en raison de son aridité, la plus marquée que l'on connaisse en Europe, qui crée des contraintes majeures au développement du milieu vivant, végétation et faune du sol. Les formes particulièrement spectaculaires d'érosion que l'on y rencontre, qui ont fait l'objet de nombreux travaux (Bork et Rohdenburg, 1981; Roquero, 1982; Thornes et Gilman, 1983). De plus, cette région au cours du dernier demi-siècle a connu une transformation radicale du mode d'utilisation des sols. L'agriculture méditerranéenne traditionnelle dépendante des précipitations a été quasi-abandonnée au profit d'une agriculture industrielle affranchie de la contrainte de l'eau grâce à l'irrigation au goutte à goutte. Le bassin de Vera au centre de cette partie de l'Espagne (Fig. 7.1) a été sélectionné en raison d'une forte occupation humaine depuis l'Age du Bronze particulièrement bien documentée (Castro *et al.*, 1994). Au cours de l'étude, il s'est avéré que le bassin de Vera possédait plusieurs autres avantages par rapport à l'objectif que nous nous étions fixés, à savoir que:

- il est possible de suivre pendant plus de trente ans l'évolution de l'occupation du sol ainsi que le développement de l'érosion grâce aux photographies

Séquence culturelle ou géologique	Erosion-sédimentation	Fonctionnement des paysages et des sols	Inferences sur le climat	Influence anthropique
Holocène ancien (10 000- 6000 B.P.)	quasi-absence d'érosion	stabilité des paysages, développement des sols, fonds des vallées marécageux; aggradation de gypse au cours de la phase aride	précipitations régulières et abondantes; une phase aride vers 8000 B.P.	-
Néolithique récent (6000-4300 B.P.)	érosion modérée sur les reliefs, incision des vallées	relative stabilité de la couverture pédologique	passage du régime à précipitations régulières au régime méditerranéen à pluies d'hiver	-
Chalcolithique (4300-3800 B.P.)	"	bonne stabilité structurale et de la couverture pédologique	climat méditerranéen à fort contraste saisonnier	faible
Crise de l'Algarique ancien (2300-1960 CAL B.C.)	érosion intense, très fortes incisions	feux, déstabilisation des sols, colluvionnement boueux; formation de bad-lands	crise climatique caractérisée par des sécheresses et des pluies torrentielles	négligeable
Algarique récent (1960-1550 CAL B.C.)	flux de sédiments faible	cicatrisation de la couverture pédologique	retour au régime méditerranéen	faible
Post-Algarique (1550-700 CAL B.C.)	flux de sédiments faible à moyen	stabilité des sols modérée	relative sécheresse avec faible pluies d'hiver	faible
Colonisation phénicienne, romaine à période wisogoth-byzantine	flux de sédiments modéré, érosion en rill et en nappes	faible stabilité structurale des sols, mais régénération rapide des sols	relative sécheresse, étés chauds	élevée localement
Période andalouse (718-770-1550)	flux de sédiments faible	stabilisation des paysages, recharge des nappes phréatiques	réchauffement, quelques rares événements pluvieux violents	modérée
Temps modernes (de la reconquête à 1950)	flux de sédiments en croissance avec l'extension des terres cultivées, liée à la démographie	érosion permanente des sols cultivés, corrigée par des travaux	-	croissance exponentielle
Révolution agricole (1950-1994)	ralentissement du flux sédimentaire avec la déprise agricole	érosion en griffes sur les terrasses en friche sur marnes, restauration lente de la structure	-	quasi-nulle sur les terres en déprise, intense sur les parcelles en ferti-irrigation

Tableau 7.2. La dynamique des sols et des paysages dans leur cadre géologique pour l'Holocène ancien et chrono-culturel à partir du Néolithique récent. (d'après Courty et al.*, 1994)*

aériennes dont les premières datent de 1957 et aux documents satellitaires;

- à l'heure actuelle, coexistent dans le bassin de Vera encore quelques parcelles cultivées de façon traditionnelle, des terrasses et des champs en friche et des parcelles irriguées au goutte à goutte dont beaucoup sont aménagées en serre froide;
- le bassin de Vera se situe entre deux sites instrumentés pour l'érosion et l'écologie de la végétation (El Ardal au nord et Tabernas au sud étudiés respectivement par Lopez-Bermudez, 1993 et Puigdefabregas, 1993; des travaux complémentaires sur ces sites ont déjà été publiés ou sont en cours de publication, par exemple, Sanchez et Puigdefabregas, 1994) appartenant au programme Medalus (Thornes, 1993) et dont les résultats peuvent être en partie interpolés au bassin de Vera.

Les recherches entreprises dans le bassin de Vera sur les temporalités depuis le Néolithique jusqu'aux temps présents des interactions entre les facteurs anthropiques et naturels sur la dynamique des sols et des paysages furent basées à la différence des études antérieures sur:

- le sol, plus précisément la 'mémoire' du sol, qui a été considéré comme l'objet d'étude principal (la 'mémoire' du sol est constituée des enregistrements dans le sol des impacts des activités humaines, comme ceux des facteurs naturels); les sédiments n'ont été envisagés que comme la 'symétrie inverse' des sols;
- le fonctionnement actuel des sols replacé dans la trajectoire à long terme de la dynamique des sols et des paysages, afin de comprendre comment le forçage anthropique récent modifie l'évolution naturelle.

Plusieurs sens ont été donnés au terme de désertification (Verstraete, 1986). Dans ce travail, nous nous limiterons à l'étude de la désertification du milieu physique, c'est-à-dire à la perte de fertilité des sols et de ses conséquences (Fedoroff et Courty, 1989). Le terme de désertification a fréquemment été employé pour le sud-est de l'Espagne et tout particulièrement pour le bassin de Vera (van der Leeuw, 1994). Nous avons essayé de répondre à la double question: 1) est-il logique de parler de désertification pour cette région ? 2) si la réponse à la première question est positive, quelle est la part de l'Homme dans cette désertification ?

Une échelle de temps aussi courte que possible, au mieux décennale et au pire millénaire, pour les événements naturels a été recherchée en vue d'assurer une compatibilité avec la temporalité des phénomènes sociaux ce qui implique un croisement systématique des données pédo-sédimentaires avec les données archéologiques (Tableau 7.2).

CONCLUSION

La méthode présentée suppose un travail de terrain préalable aux investigations aux échelles microscopiques, puis dans la plupart des cas, après les premières études au laboratoire un retour au terrain. Un pré-requis: la nécessité d'un cadre chrono-stratigraphique précis.

BIBLIOGRAPHIE

Andel, T.H. van, et Zangger, E. (1990) Landscape stability and destabilisation in the prehistory of Greece. In S. Bottema, G. Entjes-Nieborg et W. van Zeist (eds) *Man's Role in the Shaping of the Eastern Mediterranean Landscape:* 139–57. Rotterdam, Balkema.

Ballais, J.-L. (1991) Les terrasses historiques de Tunisie. *Zeitschrift für Geomorphologie,* Suppl. Bd. 83: 221–6.

Ballais, J.-L., Jorda, M., Provansal, M. et Covo, J. (1993) Morphogenèse holocène sur le périmètre des Alpilles. In Ph Leveau et M. Provansal (eds) *Archéologie et Environnement: De la Sainte-Victoire aux Alpilles*: 515–46. Aix-en Provence, Travaux du Centre Camille Jullian n°14, Publications Université de Provence.

Berger, A. (1988) Milankovitch theory and climate. *Reviews of Geophysics and Space Physics* 26: 624–57.

Bonneau, M., et Souchier, B. (1994) *Pédologie. 2 : Constituants et Propriétés du Sol.* Paris, Masson, 2e édition.

Bork, H.R. et Rohdenburg, H. (1981) Rainfall simulation in south-east Spain. Analysis of overland flow and infiltration. In R.C.P. Morgan (ed.) *Soil Conservation Problems and Prospects*: 293–302. New-York, Wiley.

Bottema, S. et Wolring, H. (1990) Anthropogenic indicators in the pollen record of the eastern Mediterranean. In S. Bottema, G. Entjes-Nieborg et W. van Zeist (eds) *Man's Role in the Shaping of the Eastern Mediterranean Landscape:* 231–64. Rotterdam, Balkema.

Bresson, L.M. et Boiffin, J. (1990) Morphological characterization of soil crust development stages on an experimental field. *Geoderma* 47: 301–25.

Bullock, P., Fédoroff, N., Jongerius, A., Stoops, G. et Tursina, T. (1985) *Handbook for Soil Thin Section Description.* Wolverhampton, United Kingdom, Waine Research Publications.

Casenave, A. et Valentin, C. (1989) *Les Etats de Surface de la Zone Sahélienne. Influence sur l'Infiltration.* Paris, Didactiques, Editions de l'ORSTOM.

Castro, P.V., Colomer, E., Gili, S., Gonzalez Marcen, P., Lull, V., Mico, R., Monton, S., Rihuete, C., Risch, R., Ruiz Parra, M., Sanahuja, M·E. et Tenas, M. (1994) Ecosocial dynamics : human and natural coevolution. In S.E.. van der Leeuw (ed.) *Understanding the Natural and Anthropogenic Causes of Soil Degradation and Desertification in the Mediterranean Basin. Vol.2: Temporalities and Desertification in the Vera Basin:* 85–141. Cambridge, Directorate General XII of the Commission of the European Union.

Courty, M.A. (1994) Le cadre paléogéographique des occupations humaines dans le bassin du Haut-Khabur (Syrie du Nord-Est). Premiers résultats. *Paléorient* 20/1: 21–59.

Courty, M.A., Fédoroff, N., Jones, M., Castro, P.V., Colomer, E., Gili, S., Gonzalez Marcen, P., Lull, V., Mico, R., Monton, S., Rihuete, C., Risch, R., Ruiz Parra, M., Sanahuja, M·E., Tenas, M. et McGlade, J. (1994) Environmental dynamics. In S.E. van der Leeuw (ed.) *Understanding the Natural and Anthropogenic Causes of Soil Degradation and Desertification in the Mediterranean Basin. Vol.2: Temporalities and Desertification in the Vera Basin:* 19–84. Cambridge, Directorate General XII of the Commission of the European Union.

Fédoroff, N. (1987) The production potential of soils : Part I : Sensitivity of the principal soil types to the intensive agriculture of north-western Europe. In H. Barth. et P. L'Hermitte (eds) *Scientific Basis for Soil Protection in the European Community*: 65–85. London and New York, Elsevier Applied Science.

Fédoroff, N. et Courty, M.A. (1989) Indicateurs pédologiques d'aridification. Exemples du Sahara. *Bull. Soc. géol. France* 8, T.V, n°1: 43–53.

Fédoroff, N. et Courty, M.A. (1994) Organisation du sol aux échelles microscopiques. In M. Bonneau et B. Souchier (eds) *Pédologie. 2: Constituants et Propriétés du Sol:* 349–75. Paris, Masson, 2e édition.

Glassner, J.J. (1986) *La Chute d'Akkadé. L'événement et sa Mémoire.* Berlin, Reimer.

Goldberg, P. et Bar Yosef, O. (1990) The effect of man on geomorphological processes based upon evidence from the Levant and adjacent areas. In S. Bottema, G. Entjes-Nieborg et W. van Zeist (eds) *Man's Role in the Shaping of the Eastern Mediterranean Landscape:* 71–86. Rotterdam, Balkema.

Guilloré, P. (1985) *Méthode de Fabrication Mécanique et en Série de Lames Minces.* Thiverval-Grignon, Département des Sols, I.N.A., P-G.

Jansen, E. et Veum, T. (1990) Evidence for two-step deglaciation and its impact on North Atlantic deep-water circulation. *Nature* 343: 612–6.

van der Leeuw, S.E. (1994) *Understanding the Natural and Anthropogenic Causes of Soil Degradation and Desertification in the Mediterranean Basin. Vol.2: Temporalities and Desertification in the Vera Basin.* Cambridge, Directorate General XII of the Commission of the European Union.

Lopez-Bermudez, F. (1993) El Ardal, Murcia, Spain. In J.B. Thornes (ed) *Medalus I. Final Report. Mediterranean Desertification and Land Use:* 433–60. London, Commission of the European Communities, European programme on climate and natural hazards.

Ordaz, V. (1995) *Impact de la Culture Intensive des Agrumes sur le Fonctionnement des Sols dans une Zone Tropicale du Mexique (Etat de Tabasco).* Paris, Thèse de l'Institut National Agronomique, P-G : Sols n°20.

Provansal, M. et Morhange, C. (1994) Seuils climatiques et réponses morphogéniques en Basse-Provence depuis 5000 ans. *Quaternaire* 5, 3–4: 113–8.

Puigdefabregas, J. (1993) Tabernas, Almeria, Spain. In J.B. Thornes (ed) *Medalus I. Final Report. Mediterranean Desertification and Land Use*: 461–503. London, Commission of the European Communities, European programme on climate and natural hazards.

Roberts, N. (1990) Human induced landscape change in south and south-west Turkey during the later Holocene. In S. Bottema, G. Entjes-Nieborg et W. van Zeist (eds) *Man's Role in the Shaping of the Eastern Mediterranean Landscape*: 53–67. Rotterdam, Balkema.

Rollefson, G.O. (1994) Le Néolithique de la vallée du Jourdain. *La Recherche*: 92–6.

Runnels, C. (1995) La Grèce ancienne, pays ravagé. *Pour la Science*: 92–6.

Tainter, J.A. (1988) *The Collapse of Complex Societies.* Cambridge, Cambridge University Press.

Thornes, J.B. (1987) The palaeo-ecology of erosion. In J.M. Wagstaff (ed) *Landscape and Culture. Geographical and Archaeological Perspectives:* 37–55. Oxford, Blackwell.

Thornes, J.B. (1993) (ed) *Medalus I. Final Report. Mediterranean Desertification and Land Use.* London, Commission of the European Communities, European programme on climate and natural hazards.

Thornes, J.B. et Gilman, A. (1983) Potential and actual erosion around archaeological sites in south-east Spain. In J. de Ploey (ed.) *Rainfall Simulation, Runoff and Soil Erosion*: *91–114.* Catena Supplement 4.

Vita-Finzi, C. (1969) *The Mediterranean Valleys. Geological changes in Historical Times*. Cambridge, Cambridge University Press.

Wainwright, J. (1994) Anthropogenic factors in the degradation of semi-arid regions : a prehistoric case study in southern France. In A.C. Millington et K. Pye (eds) *Environmental Change in Drylands : Biogeographical and Geomorphological Prospectives:* 285–304. London, Wiley.

Weiss, H., Courty, M.A., Wettersröm, W., Guichard, F., Senior, L., Meadow, R. et Curnow, A. (1993) The genesis and collapse of third millennium north Mesopotamian civilization. *Science* 261: 995–1004.

Yoffee, N. and Cowgill, W. (1988) *The Collapse of Ancient States and Civilizations*. Tucson, University of Arizona.

Zangger, E. (1992) Neolithic to present soil erosion in Greece. In M. Bell et J. Boardman (eds) *Past and Present Soil Erosion, Archaeological and Geographical Perspectives*: 87–103. Oxford, Oxbow.

8. Reconstructing Past Soil Environments in the Mediterranean Region

Robert S. Shiel

INTRODUCTION

For the visitors to the Mediterranean who penetrate beyond the beaches and bars, there is commonly a memory of blinding limestone, red soil and dark columnar cypresses. It is a bare, rocky landscape with monuments. To the more perceptive visitor these monuments are identified with civilisations centred in the Mediterranean lands – Greece, Rome, Palestine, Asia Minor, North Africa, Spain, Egypt. That the parched summer landscape could support these societies seems to require some view of a changed environment, and the two most popular views would be: 1) the climate has changed; and 2) soil has been lost. There seems to be little doubt that the climate of the Saharan region has become drier, and one only needs to experience a late summer downpour to see the red soil departing the hillsides. This leaves us with the problem of reconstructing the environment in which these societies operated, assuming that there probably has been both climatic change and soil degradation; the former will only be considered in so far as it acts with the soil in influencing the biotic environment.

DEGRADATION

Degradation is commonly viewed as a process which leads to loss of 'value'. Some care must be exercised over this definition for, on occasion, a 'degrading' process such as erosion may actually increase the productive potential of an area. This would be the case where old, heavily weathered and nutrient-deficient soil overlies less depleted materials. Equally, loss in one area is a prerequisite of deposition elsewhere – erosion of soil from the headwaters of the Nile was necessary before 'silt' could be deposited by the floods. Volcanic activity may be locally devastating, and cause climatic deterioration over a wide area, but introduces fresh, easily-weathered ash with a high nutrient content. Rotational land use also causes degradation, though in sophisticated agricultural rotations the depletion of soil quality during the exploitation phase is reversed wholly during the restorative phase: in slash and burn agriculture, recovery may not occur wholly, and the system progressively degrades. The removal of plant and animal products in long distance trade also constitutes degradation, and it may only be possible to retrieve the situation by a balancing import of manures and fertilisers – presumably causing a loss of these materials elsewhere. After these provisos, the major degradative processes must be stated as those leading to the loss of soil volume, or a change in soil composition or arrangement of that volume such that future productivity is relatively reduced. First we must have a clear view of what is 'good', before we can consider what is degraded. Although soil is a critical factor in determining biological activity, properties of the site – especially climate – are critical, and in fact the quality of identical soil cannot be considered to be uniform from site to site.

SOIL AND SITE QUALITY

The question of land quality has long excited landowners, landusers and politicians. In relation to economic production from land, this has led to the development of Land Use Capability Classification (LUCC) (Klingebiel and Montgomery, 1961) and Land Evaluation (FAO, 1976). In both of these, the degree of hazard – such as erosion risk – must be assessed and, based on the worst single hazard, a 'suitability' derived. The success of this depends very much on the quality of the physical data available and the skill and understanding of the user. The LUCC system compares the quality of a site to others within a geographic area – usually a country. The best quality land is considered to be capable of producing large, reliable yields of the whole range of crops that can be produced within the said area, without causing environmental degradation but applying the normal agricultural practices of the day. Thus flexibility of use is given priority over quality for a single crop or animal, an argument that is difficult to justify where specialism is desired. In such a case, land suitability classification is to be preferred – for one or more crops or animals.

The conceptual framework of such a scheme may be useful here, but must be adapted to societies in which there are severe technological constraints, a narrow range of species and, perhaps, different relative values attached to species, compared to ours. LUCC considers soil properties, slope, erosion risk, ease of management, climate and hydrology but ignores economic considerations such as proximity to market or the total area of land available; these factors will all have to be reinterpreted for our purposes. One major factor ignored by LUCC, which classifies land 'as is', is the extent of change over time. In the following section the potential for soil to change, or to be influenced by other environmental changes, is considered.

SOIL CHANGES

The most relevant changes for us to consider are those which affect the growth of plants; these are warmth, nutrients, light, air, water, support and an absence of toxins, pests and diseases (Brady, 1973). Animals require all of these with the exception of light, which is replaced by energy-rich food. The soil influences the nutrient, water and support for plants directly and is involved in air supply to roots, toxins, and pests and diseases.

Nutrients

In woodlands, the available nutrient supply is conserved by incorporation into the massive biomass, by retention on the soil's large exchange capacity resulting from the high organic matter content, and by recycling from depth by the deep roots. Also, woodlands minimise leaching by intercepting rain before it reaches the soil (Lockwood and Sellars, 1983); the soil's large organic matter content retains water well and there is relatively little opportunity for soil erosion from this environment. Soil nutrient content therefore changes slowly. Removal of woodland and its replacement by grassland increases nutrient loss significantly, but not to the same extent as use of land for annual crops or those, like vines, with only a partial soil cover. Replanting of grass or woodland only reverses changes in nitrogen content: the other available nutrients only accumulate if there is an atmospheric input, or if weathering of minerals releases nutrients into available form faster than they are lost.

Although legumes have been widely, and for long, known to increase soil fertility, and we now realise that this is due to nitrogen fixation, many of the sclerophyllous shrubs have associations with the nitrogen fixer *Frankia* (Kummerow, 1981). In order to minimise nutrient losses, the farmers can recycle wastes and sell high value products with a low nutrient content. Wine and oil are excellent examples of this last strategy, whereas wheat removes large amounts of nitrogen; animals remove phosphorus in bones, but the amount is relatively small. Rather than their direct effect on nutrients, it is the overgrazing that animals cause, leading to erosion, which results in most nutrient loss. It is unfortunate that in many areas rapidly-breeding sheep and goats are kept (Le Houérou, 1981). Nutrients can be imported from urban areas' wastes, from surrounding grazing land as manures, or by use of lime and manufactured fertilisers. Lime has long been used in temperate areas but was unknown to Roman authors (Russell, 1913), while fertilisers were only introduced in the nineteenth century AD.

The general trend, therefore, is that the concentration of mineral nutrients declines over time, except if there are massive introductions from outside as described, or by deposition of volcanic ash, alluvium or windblown materials such as loess. Old soils such as Alfisols, therefore, are base-depleted, while on slopes, river floodplains, volcanic areas and the fringe of glaciated areas, soils are rejuvenated – Entisols or Inceptisols. In areas with a marked dry season, calcium and magnesium rise by capillary movement to strengthen the enrichment of surface horizons with bases. It is only in areas with no marked wet period, during which rain falls in excess of water capacity, that mineral depletion does not occur – and salt concentrations can then increase to damaging levels. When soils are left bare for annual cropping, the surface is exposed to both wind and water erosion. Wind erosion is most damaging on soils with much silt and little clay, while water can erode any soil. Both mechanisms preferentially deplete the soil of nutrients and organic matter.

Available water

Between rainfall events, water is stored in the soil; that useable by plants – the available water capacity (AWC) – depends on soil structure, stone content, texture (particle size distribution), organic matter content and on rooting depth and intensity. Soils with much organic matter and a high proportion of fine sand and/or silt, with a fine system of pores through which water can be redistributed after rain and in which roots can grow, retain the largest volume of useful water (Bailey, 1990). A large AWC is a great advantage in a marginally dry area, but in arid areas has relatively little effect on growth (Specht, 1981). Water retained in the surface 5 cm is rapidly lost by evaporation after rain, and hence has little value to plants. Thus in areas with a very low rainfall, which occurs as numerous small events, vegetation will perversely be more xerophytic on soils with a large retention capacity (Alizai and Hulbert, 1970). In stony or sandy soils, a larger proportion of the water will sink beyond the zone of surface evaporation and hence be useful to plants. Trees growing in dry environments have an advantage over annuals in that their deep roots may tap water inaccessible to the annuals.

The distribution of rain through the year is also critical:

if it falls in the cool seasons (5–15°C), then it is relatively more valuable than if the same amount falls in the hot season (>15°C). Water falling in the cold season (<5°C) can only be stored for later use, but any excess will be lost by drainage. Woodland soils not only contain more organic matter than grassland or arable land; they are also better structured, hence water retention decreases when the vegetation changes from woodland through grassland to cropped land. In addition, cropped land is exposed to erosion, which preferentially removes the fractions which retain most water. The impact of changing vegetation on the water capacity of soil is therefore clear. Alluvium, loess and volcanic ash are all water-retentive, and can have a beneficial effect on AWC. In depressions the water table may approach the surface. This can be a clear advantage to trees, but if the water table comes within about 2 m, and there is no period of excess rainfall, then salt can accumulate to toxic concentrations. Water even closer to the surface results in toxins in the soil and an absence of oxygen. Removal of woodland can lead to a rise in water table, damaging crops growing on what appeared to be dry soil (White, 1979).

Toxins, pests and diseases

Even in dry areas, therefore, soil wetness of topographic origin can lead to toxins in the soil and these include ethylene and excessive sodium. Wetter areas have excess sodium as less, and ethylene more, of a problem. Plants vary greatly in their tolerance of both ethylene and sodium. Wetland rice normally grows in a flooded, ethylene-rich environment, which barley would not tolerate, while barley and dates will tolerate intense salinity which would kill beans or clover (Foth, 1978). Both these problems are amenable to modern techniques of management, but it appears that even today mismanagement is more likely to exacerbate than drainage is to minimise them. Pest and disease attack are often associated with stressed plants, and therefore are commonest in situations where water logging, salinity or nutrient deficiency occur. Many pests and diseases themselves prefer a moist habitat, and are therefore relatively advantaged by a wet environment. Changes in woodland will clearly affect the hydrologic and salinity conditions, as will removal of nutrients in arable cropping, but soil erosion now is seen to create a doubly deleterious effect, for not only does it deplete nutrients and AWC but it increases the risk of runoff-flooding in surrounding lowland areas. Following woodland clearance, reduction of rain interception and soil water storage and infiltration lead to increased peak flow in streams and widespread valley flooding without climatic change (Chapman *et al.*, 1987).

Reversibility of change

The changes described (nutrients, diseases) can be separated into those which are easily reversed – soil nitrogen content – or very difficult to reverse – soil erosion. Technology has recently allowed us to reverse nutrient loss instantly, at a price, but erosion still can only be halted, not reversed. Where technologies are unavailable, other strategies over land change must be sought – one possibility is to change the species grown from demanding to less demanding types. Cereals for example, are difficult to grow on discontinuous or stony soil, whereas permanent tree crops, such as fig, olive or almond, may flourish in this very environment. We have also seen here the varying timescales of change – nitrogen and organic matter content of soil can decrease rapidly, calcium and magnesium more slowly, while an Inceptisol may take millennia to become an Alfisol. Without the support of industrial technology, the replacement of nitrogen, for example, depends on nitrogen-fixing organisms, which replace nitrogen at a fraction of the rate at which it is lost from arable land. Hence, maintaining this nutrient's content in the soil requires a relatively large ratio of recovery area to cropping.

It is very unlikely that a change of vegetation or management will alter mineral nutrient content, unless the actual inputs are increased above outputs; weathering of existing minerals is unlikely to outpace losses such as leaching. Estimates of soil erosion rates vary: Le Houérou (1981) suggests it can reach 10 or more t/ha/annum (~1%) and this far exceeds the rate of replacement (~0.1%/annum). Arnoldus (1977), however, working in Morocco, suggests rates up to 2000 t/ha in a year; this constitutes total soil loss in a single season. The deposition of the eroded material leads to semi-permanent enrichment of flood plains; it is only where Oxisols are being eroded from plateaux that the existing soil may be buried under less valuable alluvium. This is a rare occurrence: even the Nile brings most of its alluvium from Alfisols in Ethiopia.

This leads one to consider the sphere of activity of soils. For a totally enclosed system, the only 'losses' occur to the atmosphere as gases and by conversion to insoluble or unavailable forms. This situation is unusual, most systems either gain or lose soil, or some of its components by fixation, leaching, erosion or removal in crops. Basin sites – such as the Po valley, Nile valley and delta or Rhône valley – gain, while steep hilly areas are net losers. This naturally leads to a consideration of the Mediterranean basin. It is necessary first to consider what the environment may have been without human interference. From this we can move on to consider how human activity has influenced soil properties.

SOIL FORMATION AND CHANGE IN THE MEDITERRANEAN BASIN

The Mediterranean environment

The zone between about 30 and 40° latitude experiences a weather system dominated by sub-tropical high pressure in summer and temperate westerly flow in winter. This results in a summer of clear skies and high temperatures, with only slight prospects of rain. During the other three seasons the movement of air masses introduces cool cloudy weather, strong katabatic winds and periods of intense, in autumn often thundery, rainfall. Köppen classified this pattern (Csa, Csb) as typical of Mediterranean zones, but with a large range in both winter temperatures and total rainfall (Köppen and Geiger, 1930).

In botanical terms, the rainfall is potentially very efficient, for it falls in seasons when the evaporative demand is also small. However, the year to year variation is very great – Bradbury (1987) suggests ± 75%. Thus, if temperatures are adequate, plants can photosynthesise actively with a relatively narrow transpiration ratio (the ratio of water used per gramme of dry matter fixed) (Russell, 1961). Also the water available in the soil is utilised much more efficiently by plants when the evaporative rate is small (Gregory, 1988). In areas which are cold (<5°C) during winter, photosynthesis will probably stop completely, and rain falling at such a time may recharge the soil reservoir, but is otherwise biologically inefficient. The intense precipitation can be very damaging, particularly if it falls as hail. Peak intensities can exceed 100 mm/hr, a rate which exceeds the infiltration rate of many soils. This can lead to runoff and, particularly if the soil is bare, severe soil erosion. Most erosion occurs from September to November, when soil is bare (Le Houérou, 1981).

The climate of the Mediterranean region is strongly water-limited in botanical terms. Even areas with a perhumid environment have a 1–2 month drought in summer (Di Castri, 1981) and, if irrigation or natural ground water are not available, then a large amount of solar energy effectively goes to waste. Plants which can either complete their life cycle in the short moist season, or which can tap deep water using an extensive root system, will be most successful. Crops such as the introduction maize, which grows in summer, will only be reliable if irrigated.

The Mediterranean Sea partly fills the remains of the basin of the Tethys Sea and occurs at the contact of the African, Asian and European plates, together with a number of p!atelets (Hsü, 1977). As a result of the plate collision, the sea is surrounded by relatively young mountains. Much of the sediments which now form land around the present Mediterranean were relatively recently part of the Tethys sea floor and, as a result of the shallow clear water in this sea, carbonate rocks are now common. The plate collisions and subduction result in much localised volcanic activity, seen today as Etna, Stromboli and Vesuvius, and which also appears in the geologic record as ophiolites. The core of the plates and platelets do contain large areas of old rocks, but owing to the massive orogenesis to which the area has been subject, the surfaces tend to be relatively recent (with the exception of parts of Lebanon).

This would normally create an environment of active rivers eroding the young rocks strongly and depositing sediments in their lower valleys. The mountains, however, are relatively close to the coast, and the coast itself is steep. The climate to the south is very dry, and even to the north rainfall is not exceptionally great. This results in few large rivers – Nile, Po, Ebro and Rhône – which have deltas and floodplains; many other streams are seasonal or disappear into the limestone, leaving a dry surface. The erosive force of these small or seasonal streams must not, however, be underestimated, for the steep landscape coupled with intense seasonal rain is potentially erosive. The wet autumn is often preceded by strong winds – Bora, Mistral, Levanter, etc. – which can fan destructive fires and then erode the dry and bared soil. The steep coastline results in much sediment being lost directly into deep water – there has been a sedimentation rate of ~20 cm/ 1000 yrs on the Mediterranean sea floor over most of the Quaternary (Stanley, 1977) !

Soil formation processes

Within this geomorphic environment the process of soil formation – controlled by climate, geology, topography, organisms and time (Jenny, 1941) – have proceeded. It will be noted that in the foregoing sketch of the Mediterranean, all but organisms have already been mentioned in shaping of the landscape. Several of these factors are also important in determining the agronomic qualities of soils already discussed; there is a strong interconnection between all the environmental factors. The vegetation (organisms) has acted to protect the soil from erosive forces, to add humus and to recycle nutrients as described earlier. For much of the Mediterranean area, the natural vegetation has been oak and pine woodlands, with shrubs and herbs restricted to areas with the shortest wet season.

This natural vegetation has the ability largely to restrict erosion, and therefore has permitted soils to persist over enough time for mature profiles to develop widely. Over much of the area these mature soils are Alfisols – those which are carbonate free but >35% base saturated and where there has been substantial transfer of clay from the A to B horizons. Where this process is less complete we have Inceptisols, in which there is a clear B horizon but little clay mobilisation or base depletion, and in the least developed situations – where the vegetation has not prevented erosion, or where fresh surfaces have been exposed by geomorphic forces – Entisols with only A and C horizons but no clear profile differentiation are formed. These last are often shallow profiles with rock near or at the surface (Soil Survey Staff, 1975). Within this scheme the familiar Terra Rossa is a rhodoxeralf (Duchafour, 1974; Chromic Luvisol in FAO/UNESCO system, 1974). A detailed modern soil map, or photograph, commonly presents a somewhat depressing picture of widespread Entisols (Lithosols, Regosols FAO/UNESCO); in fact the picture our tourist had of the Mediterranean – was this always the case ?

THE FORMER SOIL DISTRIBUTION

In reconstructing the past soilscape we must turn to the range of evidence available from documentary sources, from archaeological excavations, from geomorphology and sedimentology, palynology and edaphology. A thorough review is impractical, so I will restrict my comments to a set of type-examples which I hope it will be safe to extrapolate over much of the area.

Literary sources

Probably the most direct of the historic sources is Plato who, in *Crito* (c400 BC), recorded the massive recent loss of soil from Greek hillsides as a result of deforestation. He noted, too, that it would be difficult to retrieve the situation and that replacement of the trees would not be immediately successful. Herodotus (*c.* 500 BC) noted that the Zagros mountains, now deforested, were thickly wooded (Le Houérou, 1981), but Palestine sent timber to Egypt from 2600 BC and was still supplying it in 1000 BC (Naveh, 1973). That such losses of woodland due to Classical agriculture and clearance for building and industrial purposes was widespread, can be noted from the silting of harbours – notably Ephesus and Troy (Roberts, 1989) – which led to their subsequent abandonment. This alluvium survives as physical evidence of up-stream erosion, but in many places where the alluvium has not created such economic dislocation, it passed without comment until Vita-Finzi (1969) brought it to attention as his 'Younger Fill'. Since then, there has been a vigorous debate between the supporters of climate and humans as causes of erosion (Bintliff, 1992). The current view seems to be that catastrophic events of a climatic origin are responsible for most erosion (Gilman and Thornes, 1985) and Arnoldus' (1977) data supports this concept. His data is, however, for bare soil with no control measures, and this suggests that human activity may be a major stimulus to increased erosion, a view supported by Hunt *et al.* (1992) in Tuscany.

Archaeological excavations

The discovery of soil protected below monuments of known date gives a *terminus post quem* for erosion. Not only does the monument physically protect the underlying soil from erosion, but in limestone areas the overlying rocks of the monument saturate the percolating solution with carbonates and prevent dissolution of the underlying limestone (Trudgill, 1985). Burial of dated features under alluvium provides a *terminus post quem* date too for erosion, as does inclusion of artefacts within an alluvial deposit. It appears from archaeological investigations that soil was formerly more continuous, but that erosion has continued spasmodically to the present day. It has been suggested that, rather than intense use of land (De Planhol, 1976) being the cause of erosion, it has been the abandonment of erosion control features, such as terraces, which has led to catastrophic soil loss (Roberts, 1989).

It is hard, in view of Plato's comment, and observation of overgrazed karst, not to believe that both intense use and abandonment can lead to soil loss. The presence of dated artefacts in soil is itself a useful indicator of soil change. As these are added to the surface initially, though they may be incorporated subsequently by cultivation, then any accumulation of soil will lead to a sequence of progressively younger finds towards the surface. Slow soil accumulation will result in a great deal of mixing in cultivated soils, so that there is no clear sequence – only a trend in age, and deeply buried fragments will show clear wear. If no accumulation occurs, then all fragments will be present within the plough depth. A similar situation could occur as a result of soil loss by wind erosion, or even by non-catastrophic water erosion. Depressional sites, particularly if moist, are unlikely to be eroded, but on hillsides great care would be necessary in interpreting the distribution of finds within the soil profile.

Geomorphology and sedimentology

Vita-Finzi's (1969) 'Older Fill' certainly suggests that much erosion predates human interference – though there are indications from pollen in the last interglacial that the vegetation was being manipulated (West, 1968), presumably by humans. In the southern Argolid region of the Greek Peloponnese, van Andel (1987) has shown that, rather than one 'Older Fill', there can be in some valleys a complex sequence of fills dating back 300,000 years. These fills exhibit features of different types of erosional processes – grèzes litées, débris flows, colluvium, stream flood deposits and overbank loam – in all eight sequences ending in a developed reddened soil are recognised. The oldest deposits are early glacial (>35,000 BP), the next are postglacial (*c.* 4000 BP), there is no late glacial alluviation, then there are sediments of Roman to Byzantine date and the final sequence is modern. The indication from this is of long periods of stability punctuated by episodes of severe erosion. The form of the eroded material may itself be of value in indicating the nature of the erosive process. The 4000 year old deposit is mostly débris flow, indicating widespread sheet erosion, presumably from arable fields, whereas the Roman-period alluvium is stream flood deposits, indicative of gully erosion. The Byzantine alluvium is débris flow, and can be related to Byzantine field systems. The deposits are each up to 5 m thick, but become successively less thick and less extensive in subsequent events (Pope and van Andel, 1984; Zangger, 1992).

Explanations for these changes in extent may be progressive slope denudation, which concentrates all the moveable material into the valley floors, where soil that was formerly 30 cm thick over say 100 ha becomes a 6 m deposit of alluvium over 5 ha. In limestone areas vertical erosion of soil into grykes (solution voids in the limestone) may constitute a major source of loss (Trudgill, 1985) and, as it is only in rare situations that all the alluvium can be identified, a reconstruction by 'smearing' the alluvium back over the watershed is impractical. Erosion intensity due to water has a peak at ~250–350 mm annual rainfall because of poor vegetation cover. Perversely, steep slopes can suffer less erosion than gentle slopes, which are easier to cultivate (Bradbury, 1981).

Palynology and other biological indicators

During the glacial period, Mediterranean vegetation appears to have been a herb-dominated steppe with Artemisia and chenopods (Huntley and Birks, 1983). By the mid Holocene, this had been replaced with deciduous woodland, even at low levels in Greece, and in spite of the presence of *Quercus ilex* in the flora (Bottema, 1980). This may have been because of the lack of a summer drought, associated with a wetter Sahara, or because of the presence of thicker humus-rich soil and hence a greater water retention. The summer-dry evergreen woodland spread progressively north, possibly associated with increasing aridity. Part of this change may have been induced by human disturbance, and van Zeist *et al.* (1975) believe that, once the deciduous forest is cleared, regrowth will be either pine or *Quercus ilex*. Similarly, on eroded hillsides, deciduous oak, cedar or fir probably could not recolonise without a climatic change (Pons and Quezel, 1985). The maquis – shrubland – and garrigue – aromatic herbs – are held by Rackham (1982) to be dependent on human interference, but the existence of their local equivalents in the Southern Hemisphere suggests they may be natural. Pons (1981), however, indicates that shrubs are absent from the pollen record from Atlantic until Subboreal times, and Eyre (1968) agrees that some human interference has been critical in the spread of maquis and garrigue. The improved grazing that results from burning has probably long been influential in maintaining these vegetation types. It is notable that in the developed Mediterranean countries reduction in grazing has been associated with garrigue reverting to woodland (Le Houérou, 1973).

These vegetation changes have had a critical influence on soil resources. Apart from the erosion prevention due to woodland, its deep rooting recycled water and nutrients from depth. The open canopy of the shrublands, particularly after burning, not only facilitates erosion but allows leaching, and encourages clay mobilisation. The burning itself markedly reduces soil organic matter content and, although nutrients are released by burning, a substantial proportion is lost by wind removal of ash, by leaching or by runoff. The erosion of soil is itself part of a degradative spiral as the reduced water retention capacity renders the environment more arid, the vegetation more xerophytic, and further increases runoff and leaching. This will prevent species which are more water-demanding from re-establishing and, by reducing growth, further exacerbating soil degradation and reducing organic matter return.

One impact of reduced nutrient cycling under maquis and garrigue is that the loss of nutrients can lead to a more oligotrophic environment. This can be recognised both by soil and vegetation changes. The latter consists of a change from broad to narrow leaved habit as the site becomes oligotrophic. Vegetation on oligotrophic sites also tends to store nutrients in tubers and rhizomes – effectively recycling it within the plant (Specht, 1981). From this, an examination of vegetation change over time may act as a useful indicator of soil change. Under severely oligotrophic conditions, the soil may become distinctly acid: in this case, a heathland vegetation with *Erica spp* may develop. Similarly, changes from deciduous to evergreen habit may indicate changes in climate or soil water storage capacity as well as the impact of humans. These potential indicators of change require careful interpretation. Other indicators have been used but all require careful interpretation. An interesting example of this is the use of molluscs as indicators of open ground associated with colluvation (Hunt *et al.*, 1992). The effect of molluscs and numerous other indicators are discussed, mostly in a North European context, in Chambers (1993).

Edaphology

The soil distribution

Because soil formation is determined by the soil-forming factors described earlier, the distribution of soils within a landscape is highly ordered, and this order can be ascertained by the 'rules', if the principles of soil formation are understood. The geographic arrangement of soils is closely associated with the geologic structure of an area which determines parent material, slopes, elevation and the presence of ground water. In a pristine landscape, the vegetation is also strongly correlated with soil type, and a preliminary map of soil can be suggested from air photographs (Sevink, 1985). Subsequent mapping makes use of the geologic and topographic arrangement to locate parent material and wetness/thickness boundaries. Pit digging is then used to confirm the soil distribution. In an eroded or altered landscape, vegetation is a less secure guide – natural vegetation tends to be restricted to the less productive soils. Even where the soil is eroded, the expected pattern can be infilled using less eroded or altered sites to tie the speculation. Clearly this involves some creative mapping, but the remaining soil can provide clear evidence of the former distribution. This confirmatory evidence must be provided if others are to be convinced of the security of the data provided by a reconstructed map. A modern soil map – based on the soil distribution 'as is' – in fact holds at least part of the key to the past distribution, and can save much effort, if it can be relied upon as a basis. It would be misleading to use such a map in an archaeological context without making clear that it is unchanged (Kammermans *et al.*,

1985) or reconstructing what 'modern' eroded soils were (Sevink, 1985).

Monocyclic soils

The three major soil orders of the Mediterranean have already been outlined as Entisols, Inceptisols and Alfisols. The first are often formed in the remains of the last – i.e. in an eroded or depositional situation. The middle group consists of soils which have some stability over time but lack the argillation of the last group. A soil shown today as an Alfisol and which has, on examination, the classic profile of a silty A horizon overlying a clay-enriched, and possibly rubified B, is almost certainly a soil which has occupied that site for a substantial period (>10000 yrs) and which has only been subject to minor modification by human activity or nature. Davidson and Theocharopoulous (1992) noted that in Greece most Alfisols were on gentle slopes, while Entisols and Inceptisols were found on steeper slopes. This is perhaps not surprising, for on steeper slopes Alfisols could be quickly eroded to the other soil types. Conversely, a shallow, stone-rich, yellowish brown soil on a steep slope has almost certainly been an Entisol for some time, and will remain so as a result of slope-renewal even in the absence of human intervention. On a volcanic ash deposited *c.* 5000 BP, we would expect an Inceptisol, with a clearly differentiated B horizon, but no marked variation in soil texture with depth.

Complex and polycyclic soils

Such simple soils are perhaps the exception, rather than the rule, and Duchaufour (1984) described a number of major formation scenarios which occur in the Mediterranean, two of which – the development of complex soils and polycyclic soil development – are appropriate here. In complex soil development, a thin deposit of fresh material is deposited on an existing soil, such that both old and new material are involved in succeeding soil processes – this is distinct from a buried soil, where modern soil processes cease. Polycyclic soils occur where erosion of an existing soil and its subsequent redeposition render it the parent material of a new soil. Equally, one could argue that this would apply to a new soil developing in the B horizon of an eroded mature soil without transportation of the old B horizon.

Complex soils are likely to occur in areas where there has been deposition of aeolian material, much of it late glacial loess, thin volcanic ash deposits or Saharan dust. The last was noted in thick alluvial deposits in the Negev, Israel (Goldbury, 1986). All of this material is silt-rich, and deposition results in formerly fine textured soils seeming to have a coarse textured A horizon. This may be misinterpreted as an Alfisol, when in fact the soil is much younger. The large input of cations in the aeolian deposits will act as a rejuvenant on genuine Alfisols, and on eroded Alfisols will give the false impression of a complete profile. These issues are all of considerable pedological interest but, as far as soil as a productive material is concerned, all have operated to deepen and enrich the profile. Before emplacement, these soils would have been less productive than they are now, particularly the eroded soil.

Polycyclic soils will occur frequently at the base of slopes where colluvium collects. In this situation, erosion may mix the original soil with base-rich geological material or calcareous ground water, which leads to base resaturation of even strongly-decalcified materials. A classic example of this is the formation of Calcixerolls by the resaturation of eroded Chromoxeralfs (Terrae Rossae) in North Africa (Duchaufour, 1974). Similar situations will be expected where Alfisols are eroded on the northern shore of the Mediterranean – for example the multiple rubefied profiles described by van Andel (1987) in alluvium in Greece. Once again these soils are not devalued in agricultural terms by their polycyclic origin: in fact, they may have substantially better nutrient and water retention capacity than the degraded profiles from which they formed. The major problem is that their thickening and transportation, especially into superimposed stratigraphic sequences, catastrophically reduce the total area of deep soils. 'Plaggen' soils may be created by importing soil (Wagstaff, 1992). This may be confirmed, and the original site identified by examination of the soil matrix in thin section (Shiel, 1988).

It is in the area of truncated profiles, within which new profiles have developed, that the major degradative change in the Mediterranean has occurred. In these situations we see an A horizon of fine texture developing within the remains of, say, the B horizon of an eroded Chromoxeralf. As these soils are by definition thinner than their 'parent' soil, and often contain much loose or native rock (lithic subgroups), they are extremely difficult to cultivate, retain little water, and have a very limited capacity of supply nutrients. This leads to the problems discussed earlier of excess runoff, leaching, erosion and a more xerophytic vegetation.

Agronomic properties

In attempting to compare the soils, it is necessary not only to consider their pedological grouping, but also to consider their qualities in terms of the growth requirements of plants discussed earlier. The nitrogen supply is largely independent of soil type, but is largest in poorly drained soils with a large clay content under permanent woodland or grass. The amount can change so quickly with time, that initial differences can be neutralised by less than twenty years of arable cropping (Shiel, 1991). Cation content of many of these soils is substantial, and hence so is the soil pH. Alfisols are the most base depleted, though even they contain >35% bases on the exchange complex; they are frequently low in potassium. The aeolian inputs discussed above have increased the base saturation of such soils, but Alfisols with no evidence of such amelioration, or with a truncated profile, are likely to be marginally base deficient. This would only affect growth at very high output levels, and output in the pre-fertiliser era is more likely to have been nitrogen-limited. Care must be taken in assessing past nutrient content to allow for subsequent nutrient loss and/or amelioration. In order to ascertain the extent of input to the modern soil A horizon, it is necessary both to measure the cation composition of the surface and subsurface horizons and also to examine the mineralogy of the silt fraction to check for exotic inputs. Aeolian inputs are invariably widespread, so local detection must be extrapolated to cover over a wider district. The dating of input, and of any subsequent erosion, must also be assessed. Loss will have to be based on site-specific information.

The AWC also depends on organic matter, though in this case change with land use occurs somewhat more slowly than does that of nitrogen. Profile depth for rooting at the time of use is, however, critical in determining AWC, and for this the serious problem is to assess the depth of subsequent erosion, if any, and any change in organic matter or texture of the A horizon. The relatively large base status of these soils, and the clay content of the B horizons, assures a substantial AWC per unit of depth. The soil thickness and continuity are, however, more likely to influence profile AWC than does texture, carbon content or structure.

Management

Soils will be easiest to use if they are on a level site, are deep, stone free and silty, rather than clayey, and contain much organic matter and carbonate. From this we can imagine a soil sequence with increasing difficulty of management, until the point is reached when only permanent crops such as fig and olive justify the effort necessary to plant them, and finally when the land is only suitable for grazing or woodland. Excessive wetness can also be a serious limitation to plants and management. In the Mediterranean climate, this is most likely to be restricted to the winter period or to topographic hollows. Because of the rolling topography, widespread limestone and clay pervection, only a small proportion of soils will be naturally waterlogged unless they are in hollows. The better structure provided by large organic matter content and deep rooting would give marginally better drainage immediately after woodland clearance than is seen today under arable land use. The removal of woodland and loss of soil increase runoff, as described earlier, and hence topographic depressions will probably have become wetter and more flood-prone as land use intensity has increased. These very hollows may of course have also benefitted from silt deposited by floods. Such areas, and natural springs, would probably give the best summer grazing for livestock, certainly compared to eroded Terra Rossa on limestone (Shiel and Chapman, 1988).

Having then a map of the present soils, with a clear view of the qualities/deficiencies of each, it is practical to begin considering the extent to which they have changed over time. To achieve this we will need all the data presented so far, and may still be left with a considerable degree of uncertainty.

RECONSTRUCTION OF THE PAST ENVIRONMENT

Having developed an understanding of the evidence for change, and of the date of change in the soil type, we are in a position to consider a reconstruction of the past environment. This must be based on all the evidence available, so avoiding internal contradictions. It also must acknowledge the changes in climate, plants and animals available and the technology, population density and personal preferences to the local community. The three major soil types – Alfisol, Inceptisol and Entisol – will be examined first, after which the effects of the other changes will be considered.

Alfisols

The soils which show least evidence of change are the Alfisols with a well developed profile that has required long to form. Even within this group there is possible uncertainty as to whether the A horizon is original or a more recent, aeolian, addition. This may require detailed mineralogical investigation, but archaeological evidence such as superimposed monuments could help provide a *terminus ante quem* for deposition. If the A horizon can be firmly dated, then we are secure in our knowledge that there is only a limited range within which this soil may have altered. The other main changes of this type are the base status and organic matter content. Chemical tests of current base status are the only way of confirming what is now there but, if the land is subject to modern agricultural practices, it is probable that nutrient contents will have been amended. If this is the case, and if there is nearby unmanaged land with the same soil type, then extrapolation may be necessary. If on land that is not subject to modern management, and with reasonable certainty that there has been no aeolian input, the cation content can be safely considered to have only decreased modestly with time from Neolithic to present. Equally one cannot expect it to have been much larger in the Neolithic than it is now. The carbon and associated nitrogen contents will have been much more labile, and woodland soils may be expected to contain some three times the amount of old arable land. Because of the rapidity of change, organic matter could have passed through more than forty exploitation/recovery cycles since the Neolithic. Pollen analysis may help to confirm the regional vegetation, but it is undesirable to extrapolate this to individual fields. Conversely, continuity of apparent settlement, indicated by pottery, may again suffer from the problem that carbon and nitrogen cycles are relatively short.

Water storage in such soils is invariably good, though it does vary with carbon and structure. As such soils are likely to have had the largest AWC in the region, then only those which were irrigated or had high ground water could have been more productive. Management, too, is likely to have been easier than on other soils – though it may have followed a cycle, along with water and nitrogen, resulting from changes in organic matter.

Inceptisols

These have a well developed young profile and are somewhat more difficult to date on pedological grounds than are Alfisols. Here archaeological evidence can be very valuable in confirming a *terminus* either *ante* or *post* for deposition. If the soil is clearly of local geologic origin, or from loess, and there is no obvious local erosion/deposition, then the age is likely not to be postglacial. The development of a stable B horizon does take a substantial time, but Duchaufour (1984) suggests both fast and slow tracks; the decision between these must be based on the local environments. Generally a warm humid environment with easily weathered parent material will give much more rapid development than a cold or dry environment, particularly if the parent material is resistant. If an early date, with no evidence of a textural variation or of topsoil erosion, can be established for such soil, then we can be certain of a satisfactory nutrient supply, with the provisos for nitrogen described as in the Alfisol section, and AWC dependent largely on rooting depth and texture. Drainage may have deteriorated as a result of woodland removed, as described under Alfisols. These are potentially the most valuable soils available, though their surface, because of the lack of pervection, may be more clayey than Alfisols. The least valuable of the Inceptisols will be those with a relatively coarse texture – sandy loam for example. Such soils retain relatively little nutrients or water, so that plants growing on them in summer will suffer greatly from drought stress; because of the small clay content, they also retain little organic matter (Shiel and Chapman, 1988).

Entisols

These can be split into three groups: 1) recently deposited alluvium, colluvium or aeolian material within which there has been insufficient time for a B horizon to develop; 2) eroded Inceptisols or Alfisols from which A and possibly part of the B horizon has been removed and within which a new A horizon is developing, and 3) 'natural' Entisols which are metastable.

The first of these groups contains potentially very valuable soils which are nutrient-enriched and frequently can also have a large AWC. Those thickened with volcanic ash will, however, be initially deficient in nitrogen. Aeolian deposits can occur over any topography, but alluvium and colluvium occur at the base of slopes, frequently on relatively level surfaces. Such alluvial soils are potentially attractive because of the level topography, but may be seasonally very wet. As the wetness is worst from autumn to spring, cereal crops are impractical, as are permanent tree crops or fruit. It may be possible to use such land for short season vegetables, but unless flood prevention is guaranteed by levee construction, such sites are unsuitable for subsistence dependency. When viewed today they have often been drained and appear very attractive; before draining they may only have been suitable for rough grazing and hunting.

Those rejuvenated soils on slopes or on colluvium which do not suffer from drainage problems are without doubt exceptionally attractive agriculturally. Dating the rejuvenation of such soils can be a major problem. If unstratified artefacts are enclosed – as with Vita-Finzi's 'Younger Fill' – we have a *terminus post quem* date, but artefacts *in situ* will give us a secure date as a *terminus ante quem*. Volcanic events may themselves be securely dated elsewhere. Where there is no archaeological or literary record, the stage of profile development will have to be used as a guide to date. As this will depend on the original nature of the deposited material and on the weathering environment, such a study will require careful sophisticated analysis. If the deposit is shallow, it may be impractical to ascertain the extent of change since emplacement.

Entisols which have arisen through truncation of more-developed profiles will have many properties in common with the 'natural' Entisols on steep slopes – a shallow depth, stone near or at the surface – but strictly these are complex soils developed within the remains of an earlier profile. If the eroded soil was a terra rossa, then the 'parent material' of the 'new' soil will be already reddened. If the soil is not reddened, then distinguishing natural and truncated profiles may be difficult. Chemical testing may help to distinguish inherited B horizons now serving as a parent material, but in this situation comparison with nearby less-eroded profiles may help to provide supporting evidence. The soil pattern can be very useful in reconstruction at this stage: it may be possible to build up from nearby sites a clear picture of the regional soil pattern which will help to reduce the uncertainty – or at worst to suggest a maximum range for the degree of uncertainty.

It is in such conditions that dated archaeological features may preserve beneath them a more complete profile as described above. As eroded soils are commonly on slopes, examination of the downslope profiles is critical to ascertain if any deposits can be found. Monuments buried under metres of colluvium, or deep alluvial sequences, will help to confirm an hypothesis of downslope soil loss. On limestone, such deposits are likely to be absent because of 'vertical erosion', and even on other geological materials the presence of local deposition will depend on the nature of the local topography. Natural Entisols will probably have changed relatively little over time, and may only ever have been suitable for grazing and forestry. The truncated profiles may have been Alfisols or Inceptisols, with a profile sufficiently deep for arable cropping. Unless evidence of the types suggested above can be provided it would be safest to assume that the soil provided a rather better resource than today, but not too much better !

Assessing the past soil distribution

Having decided whether existing soils have metamorphosed, and if so having placed a tentative date on the change, we can begin to construct a distribution map of former soils. Because soils follow an ordered distribution, we can tentatively reconstruct a single soil series block from a modern Alfisol on a gentle slope, a modern polycyclic Entisol on colluvium nearer the base of the slope which has received eroded topsoil that has buried an Alfisol, the topsoil coming from the steeper phase of the Alfisol which is now a complex Entisol. A host of other scenarios can be conceived, and it is only detailed fieldwork that will permit the reconstruction of the former pattern. As the soil pattern is ordered, and the catenary sequence is not only generally simple but well understood and repeats itself over large areas with similar environments (Chapman and Shiel, 1993; Chapman *et al.*, 1987), such a reconstruction can be reasonably secure. The greatest degrees of uncertainty will occur where there are gently progressive changes in, say, topography; an abrupt change would always have signalled a boundary.

INTERPRETING THE PAST ENVIRONMENT

Soil evolution is only one part of the environmental change that has occurred, and it is critically important that any climatic, technological and social changes are also considered. Climatic changes can not only influence the risk of soil loss or even change its properties, but it also may lead to a change in the agricultural potential of the land (Chapman and Shiel, 1993). As water supply is the limiting factor to growth (Liebig, 1841) over the Mediterranean area, then changes in the atmospheric water balance will either amplify or minimise the effect of any soil change, and will alter the relative value of areas of land. Temperature changes will also affect the geographic range over which species are successful, though many which are not near the temperature limit will be unaffected (Chapman and Shiel, 1993).

Technological change in its broadest sense can include new species and new methods, as well as new equipment. The introduction of new species should be clear, but often related wild forms may confuse the pollen evidence. Macrobotanical remains may not clarify the issue, for products could be imported. Introduced species can make a major impact on the use of soil and its productive potential – for example, rice allows use of land which is otherwise too wet for conventional dryland agriculture, and may constitute a more cost-effective solution than draining an area of marshland. Drainage of low-lying areas (Shiel and Chapman, 1988) to create valuable level farmland is an attractive proposition, but required considerable hydraulic skills; levées may prevent seasonal flooding, but if water accumulates behind them they can be counterproductive.

A simpler technique to improve ease of use, at the cost of immense initial effort, is terracing. This acts to stabilise slopes and improves water retention in the soil. It has been argued that much soil erosion occurs when terraces collapse in periods of economic or military dislocation (Lehmann, 1993). Terrace remains will almost certainly persist and provide evidence of the former soil distribution – though this will be an anthropic, rather than a natural, soil. Unintentional, but nevertheless valuable, terraces develop where walls are built across land and soil accumulates at the base of the field. These require much less effort than steep-slope terraces (Shiel and Chapman, 1988), but Wagstaff (1992) suggests that on lateral terrace systems, soil may have been imported, a prodigious task. Stone clearance itself can provide evidence of soil changes, not only by preserving soil profiles beneath clearance piles or walls, but also by indicating a date at which clearance became necessary. Such necessity may result from a change in agricultural practice – towards growing annual crops – or occur because soil erosion led to exposure of stones, formerly buried by a deeper soil, or because the supply of land was inadequate.

This last requires some concept of either population pressure or land exhaustion: much more land is needed for a 'rotation' to counter pests and diseases and to facilitate nitrogen management (Shiel, 1991; 1994), than is cropped in any single year. Deciding which, if any, of these alternatives have been responsible for changes in land use will depend on the use of a wide range of archaeological and soil data for the surrounding area; it may also require climatic data, via say pollen analysis to exclude a climatic fluctuation. The labour-intensive use of apparently less-good land by a community requires a very careful consideration of the environmental data, because it suggests inefficiency.

Changes in tools and power sources also influence the type of soil that can be used. Sandy soils are easiest to cultivate, but are least water- and nutrient-retentive. Clay soils are unattractive to cultivate unless power is available, but do retain water and nutrients well. Their use may signal a technological change rather than the necessity to utilise difficult-to-manage soils. A change to a crop – for example wheat – that grows well on heavy land may be part of the reason. In cost-benefit terms, in fact the clay may be superior. A climatic change towards drier conditions would probably also precipitate increased interest in use of 'wetter' and heavier soils – or *vice versa* (Shiel, 1978).

Soil mores can have a major impact on land use strategy (Chapman and Shiel, 1993). Farmers have been inherently very conservative in their management and have also been bound by complex land tenure rules. Thus we have no reason to expect an 'efficient market' to operate in land use: even in the modern situation CAP operates to encourage or constrain not only those in the EU. In the historic period, we have records of vast flows of agricultural products across the Mediterranean region, carrying with them flows of nutrients and, where demand outstripped supply, encouraging use of sub-optimal land, which may then have suffered from severe erosion. Today we see a major dichotomy between the 'Developed' Mediterranean where land is being abandoned and the 'Developing' Mediterranean where population increase places huge stresses on the environment *via* fuelwood harvesting, clearance of land for arable use and increased livestock density (Le Houérou, 1973).

It is inconceivable that such pressures have not influenced use in the past. A good example is provided by the Ottoman invasion of large parts of the Mediterranean countries, bringing with it massive population movements, depopulation and a change to pastoral land use (Bracewell, in press). Unless these changes or limitations which either constrain or force use of land are well understood, our interpretation of the physical land use evidence may be erroneous. Intentional destruction of land by victorious powers is also a factor which must be considered. In the truly archaeological context we must accept that, because of our ignorance of social events, the conclusions we draw about the apparent use of the environment, and the effect of that on future users, may omit a major factor.

CONCLUSION

The problems of reconstructing past soil environments affected by a multitude of external factors varying to different degrees and at random intervals has made a modelling approach somewhat unreliable (Zangger, 1992). The problem that has befallen many attempts to explain soil change has been to simplify and to extrapolate *à la* Vita-Finzi. It is clear that both simplification and extrapolation can have catastrophic effects on the accuracy of the conclusions drawn but, at the same time, both are essential if an understanding between soil land use and environment is to be developed; it is the degree of simplification and the extent of extrapolation that are critical.

Simplification can only really be achieved by deciding for a given site which parameters are to be included, and any exclusion must be justified. Thus measurement of pH in an area dominated by carbonate rocks is somewhat fatuous, as would be measurement of sodium in an upland with 1000 mm rainfall. In order to simplify, it is essential that there is a full understanding of the parameters being excluded. It is inappropriate to apply a simplification developed for another situation without knowledge of the reasons for the original simplification. It is also wrong to assume that the land users of the past had a simple, efficient, subsistence economy (Ammerman, 1985). Certainly, difficult-to-produce commodities may have been preferred, for cultural reasons, rather than an easy to produce, boring, subsistence diet. As Flohn (1984) has indicated for many primitive societies, *reliability* is more important than average yield. This has been developed by Chapman and Shiel (1993) to suggest that zones near the climatic limit for a species are most unreliable – the geographic location of the climatic limit not necessarily being the same as today.

This also raises the distinction between land *capability* – what the land could be used for to maximise output – and actual land *use*. A complete spectrum is possible, from massive under-utilisation – which will tend to create a sustainable system – to over-exploitation – which invariably leads to degradation, often of an irreversible nature such as soil erosion. Information on the preferred requirements of species is often difficult to obtain: it is important not to be misled by requirements of modern hybrids. Similarly, the influence of soil and environment on management in prehistoric times is not the same as today. For these reasons, modern maps of soil and land capability are not necessarily reliable indicators of past quality; once again the simple solution fails.

The dangers of extrapolation in time and space have been all too clear. The processes leading to soil change may be universal, but their influence is wholly site dependent – for an example of a generalised approach, see the Revised Universal Soil Loss Equation (Renard *et al.*, 1991). This equation only relates a group of controlling parameters to one of the factors (soil quantity and properties) which influence growth and use of land. It is the next step in generalisation to land use – such as the LUCC approach – which requires even more skill and knowledge – as described above. The use of LUCC – which is a snapshot system – ignores change over time, changes in technology and products, so even this generalisation is inadequate for the objectives of archaeologists interested in past soil quality. These systems, developed elsewhere for other objectives, can be modified to suit local requirements, but all decision-making must be based on a wide range of locally-derived data and the user must be thoroughly conversant with the mass of complex interactions between the plethora of environmental, soil biological, and social influences.

REFERENCES

Alizai, H.U. and Hulbert, L.C. (1970) Effects of soil texture on evaporative loss and available water in some arid climates. *Soil Science* 110: 328–32.

Ammerman, A. (1985) Modern land use versus the past: a case study from Calabria. In C. Malone and S. Stoddart (eds) *Papers in Italian Archaeology* IV: 27–40. Oxford, British Archaeological Reports, International Series 243.

Arnoldus, H.M.J. (1977) Methodology used to determine the maximum potential average annual soil loss due to sheet and rill erosion in Morocco. *FAO Soils Bulletin* 34: 39–48.

Bailey, R. (1990) *Irrigated Crops and their Management.* Ipswich, Farming Press.

Bintliff, J.L. (1992) Erosion in the Mediterranean lands: a reconsideration of patterns process and methodology. In M. Bell and J. Boardman (eds) *Past and Present Soil Erosion.*: 125–32. Oxford, Oxbow Books, Monograph 22.

Bottema, S. (1980) Palynological investigations on Crete. *Review of Palaeobotany and Palynology* 31: 193–217.

Bradbury, D.E. (1981) The physical geography of the Mediterranean Lands. In F. di Castri, D.W. Goodall and R.L. Specht (eds) *Mediterranean-Type Shrublands*: 53–62. Amsterdam, Elsevier.

Brady, N.C. (1973) *The Nature and Properties of Soils*. New York, Macmillan, eighth edition.

Chambers, F.M. (ed.) (1993) *Climatic Change and Human Impact on the Landscape*. London, Chapman and Hall.

Chapman, J.C. and Shiel, R.S. (1993) Social change and land use in prehistoric Dalmatia. *Proceedings of the Prehistoric Society* 59: 61–104.

Chapman, J.C., Shiel, R.S. and Batovíc, S. (1987) Settlement patterns and land use in Neothermal Dalamatia, Yugoslavia: 1983–1984 seasons. *Journal of Field Archaeology* 14: 123–46.

Davidson, D.A. and Theocharopoulous, S.P. (1992) A survey of soil erosion in Viotia, Greece. In M. Bell and J. Boardman (eds) *Past and Present Soil Erosion.*: 150–161. Oxford, Oxbow Books, Oxbow Monographs 22.

De Planhol (1976) Le déboisement du Moyen-Orient. Etapes et processus. In *Collection sur la Désertification, Nouakchott,* 1972: 101–2. Dakar, Nouvelles Editions Africaines.

Di Castri, F. (1981) Mediterranean type shrublands of the World. In F. di Castri, D.W. Goodall and R.L. Specht (eds) *Mediterranean-Type Shrublands:* 1–52. Amsterdam, Elsevier.

Duchaufour, P. (1974) *Ecological Atlas of Soils of the World.* New York, Masson Publishing.

Duchaufour P. (1984) *Pedology*. London, George Allen and Unwin.

Eyre, S.R. (1968) *Vegetation and Soils : A World Picture*. London, Edward Arnold, second edition.

FAO (1976) *A Framework for Land Evaluation*. Rome, FAO Soils Bulletin 32.

FAO-UNESCO (1974) *Soil Map of the World*. Vol. 1 Legend. Rome, FAO-UNESCO.

Flohn, H. (1984) Selected climates from the past and their relevance to possible future climates. In H. Flohn and R. Fantechi (eds) *The Climate of Europe: Past, Present and Future*: 198–208. Dordrecht, D. Reidel.

Foth, H.D. (1978) *Fundamentals of Soil Science*. New York, John Wiley, sixth edition.

Gilman, A. and Thornes, J.B. (1985) *Land Use and Prehistory in South East Spain*. London, Allen and Unwin.

Goldbury, P. (1986) Late Quaternary environmental history of the Southern Levant. *Geoarchaeology* 1: 225–44.

Gregory, P.J. (1988) Water and crop growth. In A. Wild (ed.) *Russell's Soil Conditions and Crop Growth:* 338–77. Harlow, Longmans.

Hsú, K.J. (1977) Tectonic evolution of the Mediterranean Basins. In A.E. Nairn, W.H. Kanes and F.G. Stehli (eds) *The Ocean Basins and Margins*. Vol. 4A: 29–76. New York, Plenum Press.

Hunt, C.O., Gilbertson, D.D. and Donahue, R.E. (1992) Palaeoenvironmental evidence for agricultural erosion from Late Holocene deposits in the Montagnola Senese, Italy. In M. Bell and J. Boardman (eds) *Past and Present Soil Erosion*: 163–74. Oxford, Oxbow Books, Oxbow Monograph 22.

Huntley, B. and Birks, H.J.B. (1983) *An Atlas of Past and Present Pollen Maps of Europe: 0-13000 years ago*. Cambridge, Cambridge University Press.

Jenny, H. (1941) *Factors of Soil Formation*. New York, McGraw-Hill.

Kammermans, H., Loving, S. and Voorrips, A. (1985) Changing patterns of prehistoric land use in the Agro Pontino. In C. Malone and S. Stoddart (eds) *Papers in Italian Archaeology* IV: 53–68. Oxford, British Archaeological Reports, International Series 243.

Klingebiel, A.A. and Montgomery, P.H. (1961) *Land Capability Classification*. Washington, Soil Conservation Service Handbook 210 USDA.

Köppen, W. and Geiger, R. (1930) *Handbuch der Klimatologie*. Berlin, Borntraeger.

Kummerow, J. (1981) Structure of roots and root systems. In F. di Castri, D.W. Goodall and R.L. Specht (eds) *Mediterranean-Type Shrublands*. Amsterdam, Elsevier.

Le Houérou, H.N. (1973) Ecologie, démographie et production agricole dans les pays méditerranéens du Tiers Monde. *Options Mediterranée* 17: 53–61.

Le Houérou, H.N. (1981) Impact of man and his animals on Mediterranean vegetation. In F. di Castri, D.W. Goodall and R.L. Specht (eds) *Mediterranean-Type Shrublands:* 479–522. Amsterdam, Elsevier.

Liebig, J. van (1841) *Chemistry in its Application to Agriculture and Physiology*. London.

Lehmann, R. (1993) Terrace degradation and soil erosion on Naxos Island, Greece. In S. Wicherek (ed.) *Farm Land Erosion in Temperate Plains Environment and Hills*: 429–50. Amsterdam, Elsevier.

Lockwood, J.G., Sellars, J.G. (1983) Some simulation model results of the effect of vegetation change on the near-surfaces hydroclimate. In A. Street-Perrott, M. Bevan and R. Ratcliffe (eds) *Variations in the Global Water Budget*: 463–477. Dordrecht, D. Reidel.

Naveh, Z. (1973) The ecology of fire in Israel. *Proceedings of the Tall Timbers Fire Ecology Conference* 13: 131–70.

Pons, A. (1981) History of the Mediterranean shrublands. In F. di Castri, D.W. Goodall and R.L. Specht (eds) *Mediterranean-Type Shrublands:* 131–138. Amsterdam, Elsevier.

Pons, A., Quezel, P. (1985) The history of the flora and vegetation and past and present human disturbance in the Mediterranean region. In F. Gomez-Campo (ed.) *Plant Conservation in the Mediterranean Area:* 25–43. Dordrecht, Dr. W. Junk.

Pope, K.O. and van Andel, T.H. (1984) Late Quaternary alluviation and soil formation in the southern Argolid: its history, causes, and archaeological implications. *Journal of Archaeological Science* 11: 281–306.

Rackham, O. (1982) Land-use and the native vegetation of Greece. In M. Bell and S. Limbrey (eds) *Archaeological Aspects of Woodland Ecology:* 177–198. Oxford, British Archaeological Reports, International Series 146.

Renard, K.G., Foster, G.R., Weesies, G.A. and Porter, J.P. (1991) RUSLE – Revised Universal Soil Loss Equation. *Journal of Soil and Water Conservation* 46: 30–3.

Roberts, N. (1989) *The Holocene : An Environmental History*. Oxford, Basil Blackwell.

Russell, E.J. (1913) *The Fertility of the Soil*. Cambridge, Cambridge University Press.

Russell, E.W. (1961) *Soil Conditions and Plant Growth*. London, Longmans, ninth edition.

Sevink, J. (1985) Physiographic soil surveys and archaeology. In C. Malone and S. Stoddart (eds) *Papers in Italian Archaeology* IV: 41–52. Oxford, British Archaeological Reports, International Series 243.

Shiel, R.S. (1978) *The Effect of Soil Properties on Horticultural Crops in the North of Scotland*. Ph.D thesis. Aberdeen University.

Shiel, R.S. (1988) The soils. In A.M. Haggerty (ed) Iona: some results from recent work. *Proceedings of the Society of Antiquaries of Scotland* 118: 203–13, fiche A3-B4.

Shiel, R.S. (1991) Improving soil fertility in the pre-fertiliser era. In B.M.S. Campbell and M. Overton (eds) *Land, Labour and Livestock:* 51–77. Manchester, Manchester University Press.

Shiel, R.S. (1994) Rotational farming – a system misrepresented ? *Pesticide News* 25: 10–1.

Shiel, R.S. and Chapman, J.C. (1988) The extent of change in the agricultural landscape of Dalmatia, Yugoslavia, as a result of 8000 years of land management. In J.C. Chapman, J. Bintliff, V. Gaffney and B. Slapsak (eds) *Recent Developments in*

Yugoslav Archaeology: 31–44. Oxford, British Archaeological Reports, International Series 431.

Soil Survey Staff (1975) *Soil Taxonomy. A Basic System of Soil Classification for Making and Interpreting Soil Surveys*. Washington, US Government Printing Office, USDA Handbook 436.

Specht, R.L. (1981) Primary production in Mediterranean-climate ecosystems regenerating after fire. In F. di Castri, D.W. Goodall and R.L. Specht (eds) *Mediterranean-Type Shrublands:* 257–268. Amsterdam, Elsevier.

Stanley, D.J. (1977) Post-Miocene depositional patterns and structural displacement in the Mediterranean. In A.E. Nairn, W.H. Kanes and F.G. Stehli (eds) *The Ocean Basins and Margins*. Vol. 4A: 77–150. New York, Plenum Press.

Trudgill, S. (1985) *Limestone Geomorphology*. London, Longman.

van Andel, Tj.(1987) The landscape. In Tj. van Andel and S.B. Sutton (eds) *Landscape and People of the Franchthi Region*: 3–64. Bloomington, Indiana University Press.

van Zeist, W., Woldring, H. and Stapert, D. (1975) Late Quaternary vegetation and climate of south western Turkey. *Palaeohistoria* 17: 53–143.

Vita-Finzi, C. (1969) *The Mediterranean Valleys. Geological Changes in Historical Times*. Cambridge, Cambridge University Press.

Wagstaff, M. (1992) Agricultural terraces : the Vasilikos Valley, Cyprus. In M. Bell and J. Boardman (eds) *Past and Present Soil Erosion*: 155–162. Oxford, Oxbow Books, Oxbow Monograph 22.

West, R.G. (1968) *Pleistocene Geology and Biology*. London, Longman.

White, R.E. (1979) *Introduction to the Principles and Practice of Soil Science*. Oxford, Blackwell Scientific Publications.

Zangger, E. (1992) Neolithic to present soil erosion in Greece. In M. Bell and J. Boardman (eds) *Past and Present Soil Erosion*: 149–154. Oxford, Oxbow Books, Oxbow Monograph 22.

9. Energy Dispersive X-Ray Micro-Analysis and the Geochemistry of Soils and Sediments

John Grattan and David Gilbertson

INTRODUCTION

This contribution advocates the use of a Scanning Electron Microscope equipped with an Energy Dispersive X-ray Micro-Analysis (EDMA) for palaeoenvironmental research. Whilst an SEM equipped with a EDMA Probe cannot, in the 1990s, be regarded as particularly innovative, or high-technology, the application of an EDMA-based approach to palaeoenvironmental research is innovative. The approach has many advantages for studies in Mediterranean lands. Unfortunately the novelty of its application to geoarchaeological studies is such that we have to exemplify its utility by reference to an example from Scotland – specifically the study of lake and mire sediments from Borve Bog on the Outer Hebridean island of Barra. Although this is a part of the world which obviously does not possess Mediterranean ecosystems or Mediterranean climate, the problems that were addressed will be familiar to geoarchaeologists working in Mediterranean lands – for example, soil evolution and erosion, the impacts of deforestation and farming on ecosystems, the effects of volcanic tephra, the influence of mining and metal extraction on soils and water, and so on.

The great advantages of the approach are that: it can be used upon very small samples of deposits and can target particular sediment or other bodies seen in the field of view of an Scanning Electron Microscope; it enables extensive replication of analysis on very small samples; and it can be used to indicate the proportions of elements present with atomic numbers from and above sulphur.

SEDIMENT GEOCHEMISTRY AND ENVIRONMENTAL RECONSTRUCTION

In any study of accumulated sediment, the palaeoenvironmentalist makes the assumption that sediment composition and morphology will change in response to an alteration in the environment on a wide variety of scales. Traditional means of investigating such changes may employ studies of clast size, shape, provenance and orientation, or equally a study of the pollen retained and preserved, in each sedimentary facies. In the same way that these components can be observed to change in response to environmental modification, so the range of geochemical inputs to a sediment will also change. Hitherto, soil or sediment geochemical studies have been hindered, and discouraged, by the time necessary to carry out complex acid digestions, titration and so on, and by the limited range of elements which may consequently be studied. The application of EDMA to the study of accumulated bodies of sediment allows soil geochemistry to be added to the range of complimentary techniques available to the palaeoenvironmentalist.

The application of Energy Dispersive X-ray Microanalysis (EDMA) to the study of soil geochemistry makes it possible rapidly to determine the relative proportion of a great number of elements in any one sample, and to interpret this data in a meaningful way. The approach differs from conventional analysis by indicating the relative proportion of elements in a sample, but it does *not* provide information on the weight or concentration of elements per volume or weight of sample. It is therefore analogous to conventional pollen analysis, which also focuses upon the interpretation of relative changes in proportions present.

ANALYTICAL TECHNIQUE

The methodology is fully described in several papers (Charman *et al.*, 1995; Grattan, 1994; Pyatt *et al.,* 1995). The sediment is analysed by means of electron probe X-ray microanalysis. In the case study presented below, the system used a Link System 860 Series 2 Computer using a ZAF-4 program, which detected the presence and relative proportion of every element from and above sodium. These are detected by a lithium-drifted silicon director and passed on to a multi-channel analyser. Suitable areas for examination on each sample were selected for analysis using the microscope visual display monitor, and analysed at a magnification of 500 x for 100 seconds of live time at 20 *kv*. As a result of such factors, as the variable geometry of the sample faces to the X-ray beam, the quantitative accuracy of this procedure on biological samples may be restricted to ±10% (relative) of the true value (see Goldstein *et al.*, 1984; Pyatt and Lacy, 1988). To ensure accuracy, ten random areas were examined in each case, and three replicates were employed. Issues of replicability are addressed in Grattan (1994). The advantages of this analytical method can be best illustrated by a consideration of a case study presented in outline form below.

CASE STUDY: BORVE BOG

A 500 cm core was retrieved, using a Russian peat corer, from a basin peat which lay at an altitude of 65 m above sea level at the head of the Borve Valley (grid reference NF 677009) in the Outer Hebridean island of Barra. The geochemical study was complemented by a palynological study by Pratt (1992).

A wide range of environmental influences exists on the mire at the head of the Borve valley; many of these may have influenced soils or loch sediment deposition in the area. The mire is at the head of the valley only 3.6 km from the sea at Borve point, a distance which encompasses a wide range of soil types and landforms. The geochemistry of the core was established at 10 cm intervals and can be clearly divided into four chemizones (Figs. 9.1a and 9.1b). Outline notes on the elements identified are given in Table 9.1.

Chemizone BV1 (500–450 cm) – Interpretation: Late Glacial/Earliest Post Glacial conditions

Peaks in the proportion of K which occur at the base of this core have been found at the base of several long cores extracted from northern or western basins in Britain and which are conventionally interpreted as indicating cold conditions and intense solifluction (Atkinson and Haworth, 1990; Engstrom and Wright, 1984; Mackereth, 1965, 1966; Pennington, 1981a and b; Pennington *et al.*, 1972). The pattern of K presented in Chemizone BV1 might therefore represent two cold periods separated by an episode of warmer climate. In earliest post-glacial and preceding late glacial periods, with immature soil development and little soil stability or vegetation, sediments were easily transported by aeolian and fluvial processes. The proportion of K in the core might therefore be expected to decline as soils and vegetation cover evolved in the early Holocene. Subsequently, as soils and vegetation developed, the erosion of sediments would have become less likely and the thresholds at which erosion will occur are raised.

If these ideas are accepted, the pattern of K at the base of Borve bog could indicate the presence of two periods of recovery from glacial/periglacial conditions. The lowest may have been ended by a return to cold conditions, the second was ended by the evolution of soils apparent in chemizone BV2 above. Further evidence of climatic fluctuation is provided by the behaviour in the cores of Na and Mg. These two elements have been used as indicators of the oceanicity of past climates (Maitland and Holden, 1983; Waterstone *et al.*, 1979). The proportion of these elements in the core is seen to increase steadily from the base of the core upwards; this might reflect a change in the pattern of atmospheric circulation, from one where airflow over Britain originated in the continental interior to one where the airflow originated over oceans.

In brief, the pattern of elements in this zone may record the Windermere Interstadial and Loch Lomond re-advance, as experienced in the Outer Hebrides. The pattern of elements identified in this zone is strikingly similar to the pattern observed at Loch Hellisdale on South Uist and at Loch Lang on South Uist described by Bennett *et al.* (1990).

Chemizone BV2 (450–380 cm) – Interpretation: full Holocene conditions

The transition between chemizones BV1 and BV2 in this core is distinct, occurring at 450 cm. The elements which feature prominently in Chemizone BV2 suggest the operation of chemical processes in a developing soil, rather than the physical solifluction processes operating in an immature landscape inferred in zone BV1.

There is a sharp decline in the proportion of K at 450 cm from 27 per cent to two per cent and an equally sharp decline in Al and Si. The physical weathering processes which were characteristic of the environment in chemizone BV1 are no longer indicated by the geochemistry of the sediments above 450 centimetres. Instead, there are increases in the proportions of Ca, Na, Mg, Fe, Mn and S. These elements are not precipitated under cold conditions, nor are they commonly associated with the physical erosion of soils, or the chemical weathering of immature soils (Engstrom and Wright, 1984). They are, however, precipitated from organic soils in relatively warm, moist, conditions. It is interesting in this respect that calcium was deposited in the basin at 460 cm, twenty centimetres before Fe proportions in the core increase and thirty centimetres before the proportions of S increase. A mobilisation of Fe, Mn and S indicated at 440 cm depth might imply the existence of organic acid soils early in the Holocene history of the Outer Hebrides. The geochemical sequence detailed in BV2 suggests that the Holocene sediments initially laid down in the basin were base-rich, but that the subsequent environmental conditions experienced in the region led to the formation and deposition in the mire of acid organic sediments in a period still in the early Holocene.

Finally, the geochemical evidence indicates the existence of a sharp boundary between Late-Glacial and Holocene environments, that is between Chemizones BV1

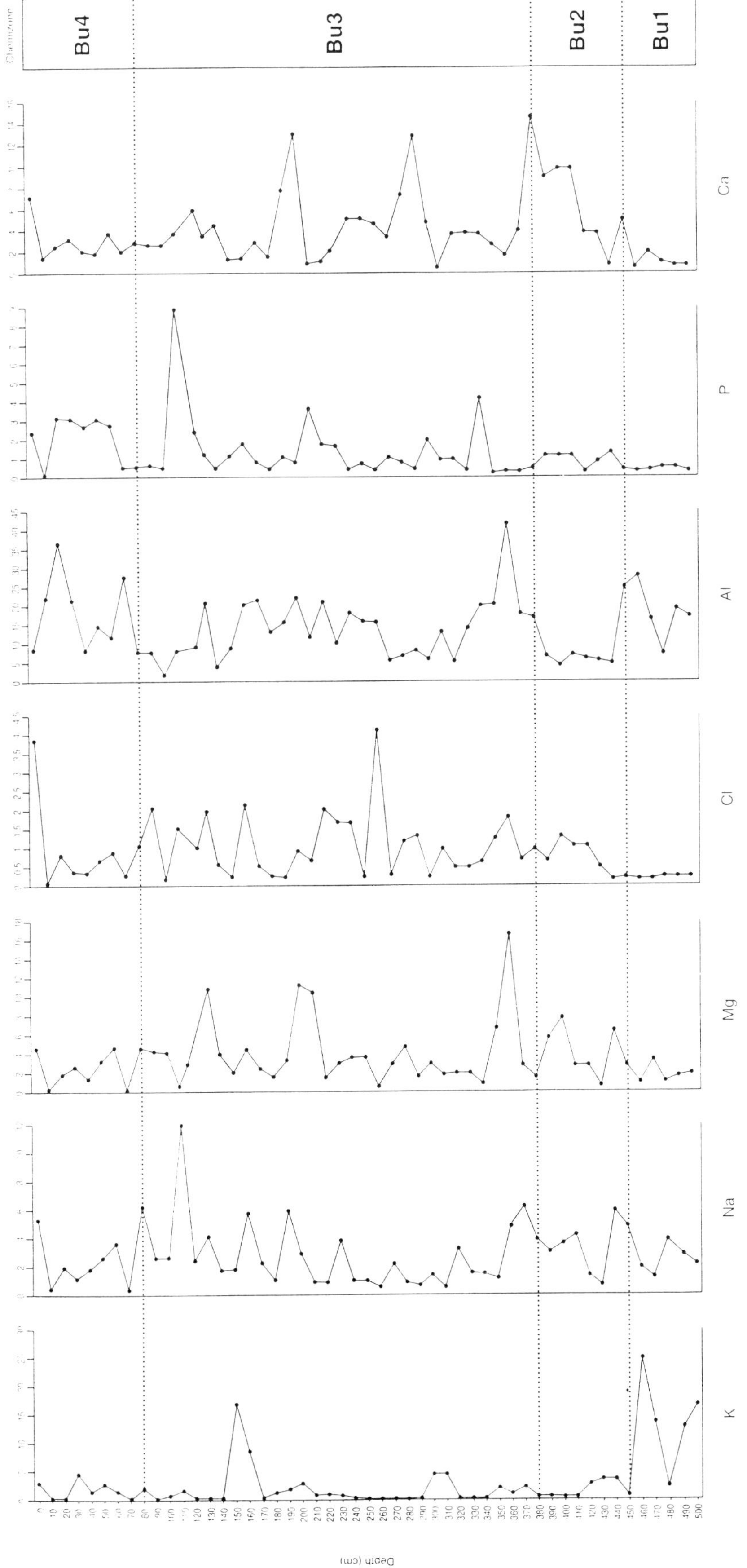

Fig. 9.1a. The geochemistry of Borve bog, Barra.

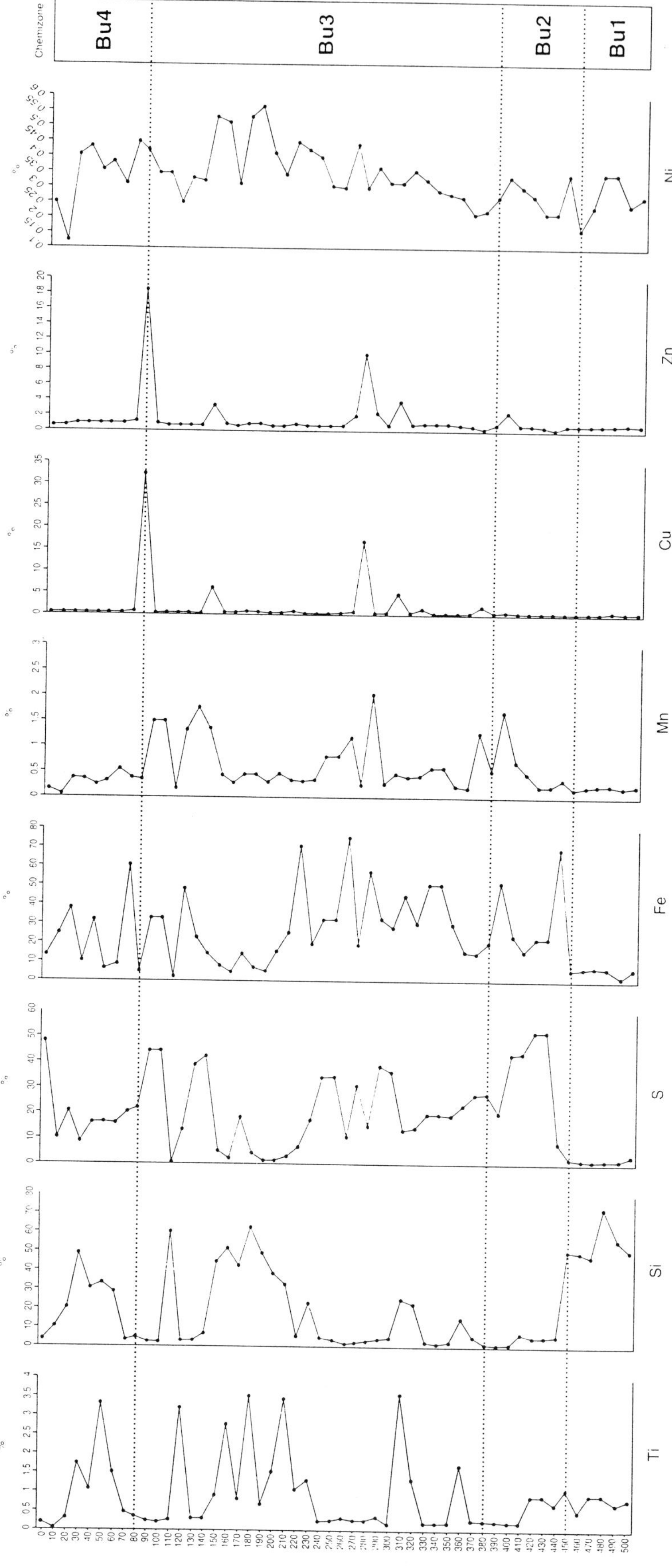

Fig. 9.1b. The geochemistry of Borve bog, Barra.

ELEMENT	SOURCES
Magnesium (Mg)	Often associated with mechanical weathering, the breakdown of chlorophyll in terrestrial and aquatic plants. Also precipitated in rain in exposed western environments.
Potassium (K)	A clastic mineral. Commonly used to infer episodes of soil erosion in a catchment.
Silicon (Si)	An abundant element. Can indicate, soil erosion and biogenic activity. It can be found in the silicified remains of aquatic flora and fauna.
Aluminium (Al)	An abundant inorganic element. Deposition can indicate soil erosion, the depletion of bases from a soil and the influence of the sea.
Sulphur (S)	Primarily associated with biological productivity in a lake, and often correlated with Si. However S can also be deposited in industrial pollution.
Chlorine (Cl)	Sea water, rainfall.
Titanium (Ti)	Commonly used to indicate mechanical erosion.
Calcium (Ca)	Present in some lake sediments as a clast, it can also be associated with humic and fulvic acids. Thus Ca concentrations in a core may indicate the deep weathering of a soil profile.
Vanadium (V)	A rare trace element and a component of several minerals.
Iron (Fe)	A common element. Can indicate the chemical weathering of a catchment soil, podzolisation and / or the acidity of catchment waters.
Nickel (Ni)	Nickel is a common element and has a variety of sources. It is difficult to interpret.
Sodium (Na)	Can indicate the depletion of bases in a soil but is frequently associated with climate and, in particular, rainfall intensity.
Copper (Cu) Zinc (Zn)	Background levels in most sediments, but peaks indicate industrial pollution. Can be used for dating.
Manganese (Mn)	Mechanical or chemical weathering. Where Mn dominates Fe, mechanical erosion is suggested, but where the opposite is true chemical weathering of soil profiles is implied.
Phosphate (P)	Many, can be sorbed by many elements in particular by iron. However can indicate a nutrient inwash and the activities of people.

Table 9.1. Geochemistry of Borve bog: possible sources of elements used in the analysis.

and BV2. This change is also apparent in the palynological evidence: pollen concentrations rose dramatically in the sediments associated with chemizone BV2, and the pollen suite was dominated by Cyperaceae, Gramineae, Ericaceae and *Sphagnum* (Pratt, 1992). This suite suggests the onset of a mire environment and base-poor soils and sediments, which are entirely in accord with the geochemical evidence described here.

Chemizone BV3 (380–80 cm) – Interpretation: Mid Holocene soil degradation and anthropogenic land-use

In this chemizone, most of the elements studied do not record long term changes in their proportion. No long term environmental change is indicated by the sediment geochemistry. However, short episodes of environmental change are indicated and these are, perhaps, mainly attributable to human activity.

It is possible that the episodic increases in the proportion of Ca detailed in this chemizone may indicate the disturbance and erosion of the calcareous dunes and machair three kilometres to the west on the Atlantic coast. Two such episodes can be identified. One, which begins at 300 cm, peaks at 290 cm, reaching twelve per cent, and returns to a low proportion by 220 cm. The second and shorter-lived episode begins and peaks at 200 cm and returns to a low proportion of Ca at 180 cm. This second episode is matched by changes in the physical characteristics of the core, in which finer mineral material, interpreted as sand blow from the coast, was found between 200 and 183 cm. The organic content in this part of the core was the lowest recorded. There appears to be no relationship between the high proportions of Ca in this chemizone and the proportions of S, Fe and Mn. The deposition of Ca in this chemizone, therefore, does not appear to have had an impact on the mire environment as reflected by the proportions of Mn, Fe and S, which otherwise might indicate acidity.

A past rise in pH levels in the mire is indicated between 210 and 150 cm by a consistent increase in the proportion of Si in the core and falls in the proportion of S and Fe. Other properties of the core are in accord with that interpretation of this geochemistry, for between 207 and 150 cm wood macro-fossils were found. Trees growing on the mire surface would indicate that the mire environment was drier and that soil pH had risen sufficiently for trees to grow.

If the increase in the proportion of K is correctly interpreted as the result of anthropogenic disturbance of the landscape, then it is possible that the major peak in the proportion of P detected between 150 and 120 cm may also reflect the utilisation of the landscape by people. Similarly, the observed increase in the geochemical indicators for acid conditions in the mire might be the result of increased water run-off, perhaps following a post-clearance episode. If this anthropogenic interpretation is further pursued, then the decline in the relative abundance of P at 170 cm could indicate a reduction in land use intensity. The palynology of this zone appears to support this interpretation. An increase in the proportion of Gramineae pollen at 140 cm corresponds with a major increase in the proportion of P in the core, from 0.5 to nine pe cent (Pratt, 1992). Although the interpretation of P in sediment geochemistry is problematic, it is often interpreted, when in tandem with other evidence, as evidence for human activity and an increase in the inwash of nutrients into a mire. Thus the peak in P between 130 and 140 cm and the corresponding increase in Gramineae may indicate ancient anthropogenic activity in the upper Borve valley.

Several peaks in Cu and Zn were detected in this chemizone. These elements are allocthonous to the valley sediments. The conventional interpretation for such increases is that they indicate the onset of industrial activity in Europe (Holdren *et al.*, 1984; Rippey *et al.*, 1982). In the remote western and northern parts of Scotland or Ireland, such deposition has been dated to the 1880s, but these episodes occurred at relatively shallow depths in loch cores (Rippey, 1990), whereas in Borve bog a prominent peak in Cu and Zn occurred at 270 cm, which is very deep to be ascribed such a recent date. This peak must considerably predate the Industrial Revolution. Perhaps the peaks at 270 and 300 cm have their origin in the use of metals in the European Bronze Age ? The source for these concentrations is an interesting research problem and in this respect it is interesting to note that a similar length core extracted from the Strath of Kildonan in Caithness also has a substantial peak in Cu at, curiously and coincidentally, a depth of 270 cm (Grattan, 1994).

Chemizone BV4 (80–0 cm) – Interpretation: recent human activity

Indicators of base input, soil erosion and anthropogenic activity (K, Ti, Si and P) dominate this chemizone between 60 and 30 cm, whereas above 30 cm elements which indicate acid conditions (S and Fe) are more abundant.

The increase in the relative abundance of K, Si, Ti and P between 60 and 30 cm suggests that a slight but significant disturbance of the upper Borve valley continued throughout the time period represented by this particular accumulation of sediment. The patterns of abundance of all four elements exhibit behaviour which can be interpreted as typical of dynamic or metastable equilibrium in the environment. In each case, a threshold appears to have been crossed at 60 cm. This was followed by a period of stability, when the increased proportions of these elements were maintained. The percentages of K, Si and Ti appear to cross a second threshold at 30 cm, where they decline. P may have crossed a threshold at 20 cm, following which the proportion of this element also declined.

Past human activity in the upper Borve valley may be the causes of these geochemical changes. The trend in the proportion of Ca in this zone does not suggest that the coastal soils were over being over-exploited and hence became vulnerable to erosion, as suggested in the earlier discussion of Chemizone BV3. A change in the character and practise of land-use may therefore have been the impetus for this inferred episode of greater exploitation of the valley head. The geochemistry suggests that the exploitation of the valley head has declined in recent years; this is in accord with the observations of Caird (1979) and Dodgshon (1988).

At 30 cm, indicators of acid conditions in the mire increase. These changes may be associated with the decline observed in the proportions of base indicators at this level in the core, or they may reflect a real increase in the acidity of the mire. The geochemical trends in the upper 20 cm of the core are difficult to interpret: the upper 15 cm of the core is obviously part of the active root zone of the current mire surface, and the influence of present day conditions on the geochemical trends in the core are obviously important. The obvious change in the trends of most elements in the core at 19 cm suggests that the acrotelm in the mire lay between 10 and 20 cm. The acrotelm is the upper sedimentary zone in which depositional processes are ongoing, in contrast to the catotelm, which comprises all those sediments which are considered to be geochemically stable, below the acrotelm (Ingram, 1978, 1987). An analysis of the chemistry of the acrotelm cannot be compared simply to the sediment chemistry of palaeo-sediments.

DISCUSSION: EDMA AND PALEOENVIRONMENT

The analysis of the sediment geochemistry of Borve bog has shown that the geoarchaeological application of EDMA has facilitated the reconstruction of general environmental trends and the identification of specific episodes of environmental disturbance in the upper Borve valley. The proportions of K, Ti, Si and Al can all be seen to 'behave' in tandem and to record short-lived episodes of landscape disturbance, as well as pointing to longer periods of time when these elements achieved a new 'equilibrium' indicative of persistent disturbance. These geochemical trends also help to highlight the nature of the 'forcing mechanisms' responsible. Episodes associated with the establishment of new equilibria may indicate climatic change, vegetational change, soil evolution, and human activity.

It is clear that EDMA is a powerful and versatile method by which the record of environmental change in any sediment accumulation may be examined.

TEPHROCHRONOLOGY AND VOLCANIC INFLUENCES ON THE ENVIRONMENT

Borve Bog has also been in receipt of tephra from Iceland. These tephra have carried on their surface a load of acid and often toxic substances which can have profound environmental impacts in certain situations (Grattan and Gilbertson, 1994). EDMA-based studies can sometimes detect these the palaeoenvironmental changes that were brought about by the airfall tephra (Grattan and Gilbertson, 1994; Grattan *et al.*, in press). This is because the approach can be applied to minute quantities of sediment. Potential past impacts may be detected where more conventional geochemical approaches might fail because of the need to process much larger weights or volumes of materials. The Mediterranean region can anticipate such investigations taking place in future years.

Recent advances in both theory and methodology have improved the value of tephrochronological studies in the Mediterranean area, already presenting a clearer picture of the impact volcanic eruptions may have had upon the Mediterranean environment. It is relatively simple to extract tephra from organic sediments following one of several techniques (Charman *et al.*, 1995; Dugmore, 1989; Pilcher and Hall, 1992) and accurately to ascertain the geochemical make-up of individual shards of airfall tephra (Dugmore, 1989; Hunt and Hill, 1993; Westgate *et al.*, 1995). It is therefore possible to ascertain the provenance of the eruption and accurately to correlate and date the sediments in which a tephra layer lies.

The environmental impact of volcanic eruptions around the Mediterranean has traditionally focused upon the spectacular eruptions of Santorini, with its supposed impact on Bronze Age civilisation, and on Vesuvius and its destruction of the nearby town of Pompeii. However, recent research has suggested that less spectacular volcanic events may also have had a significant impact upon the Mediterranean environment.

Mediterranean volcanic eruptions may emit large volumes of sulphur gases into the lower atmosphere and these may be concentrated to considerable effect and travel great distances. In 1783 AD, the Icelandic volcano Laki erupted, as did Vesuvius, Etna and Stromboli, and a cloud of dry fog was distributed around the Mediterranean and across Europe. This cloud, composed mainly of sulphur gases, brought crop damage, sickness to cattle, the destruction of insects, and asthma to many parts of Europe. In effect, it caused a severe natural environmental pollution event. Nor is 1783 the only year such phenomena are described. Camuffo and Enzi (1995) have studied the Italian historical record and discovered many records of dry acid fogs, volcanic eruptions, and crop damage and subsequent famine from all parts of Italy. No doubt these gas clouds were able to circulate around the Mediterranean basin.

It has now been recognised that distally transported acid gases and tephra shards are capable of causing environmental change far beyond the areas reached by obvious volcanic phenomena such as lava flows (Camuffo and Enzi, 1995; Grattan and Brayshay, 1995; Grattan and Charman, 1994; Grattan and Gilbertson, 1994). Volcanic influences may therefore extend over huge areas, as toxic volatiles may adsorb onto the tephra and be deposited with them (Rose, 1977). Tephra from Italian volcanic eruptions has now been found in Greece, and tephra from the intensively-studied Minoan eruption of Thera has now been found in Turkey, Greece and North Africa (Eastwood *et al.*, 1995; Keller, 1981; Stanley and Sheng, 1986; St. Seymour and Chistianis, 1995; Sullivan, 1988). The presence of tephra in basin sediments is the best indication that such influences may have been exerted upon a particular area/environment.

There is no doubt that the transport and deposition of volcanic gases dramatically extend the range within which one might consider a volcanic influence upon the environment to be likely, and this mechanism should be considered in palaeoenvironmental studies around the Mediterranean. In future, EDMA-based approaches can be anticipated to provide alternative sources of geochemical information on past environmental changes and their causes. And, because of their capacity to provide many replicate studies of minute samples, they are also likely to generate new ideas on the impacts of past volcanic eruptions on Mediterranean lands.

REFERENCES

Atkinson, K.M. and Haworth, E.Y. (1990) Devoke Water and Loch Scionascaig: recent environmental changes and the post-glacial overview. In R.W. Battarbee, Sir John Mason, I. Renberg and J.F. Talling (eds) *Palaeolimnology and Lake Acidification*: 123–30. London, The Royal Society.

Bennett, K.D., Fossitt, J.A., Sharp, M.J. and Switsur, V.R. (1990) Holocene vegetational and environmental history at Loch Lang, South Uist. *New Phytologist* 114: 281–98.

Caird, J.B. (1979) Land use in the Uists since 1800. *Proceedings of the Royal Society of Edinburgh* 77B: 505–27.

Camuffo, D. and Enzi, S. (1995) Impact of the clouds of volcanic aerosols in Italy during the last 7 centuries. *Natural Hazards* 11: 135–61

Charman, D.J., Grattan, J.P., West, S. and Kelly, A. (1995) Environmental response to tephra deposition in the Strath of Kildonan, northern Scotland. *Journal of Archaeological Science* 22: 799–809.

Dodgshon, R.A. (1988) The ecological basis of Highland peasant farming, 1500–1800 AD. In H.H. Birks *et al.* (eds) *The Cultural Landscape : Past, Present and Future*: 139–51. Cambridge, Cambridge University Press.

Dugmore, A.J. (1989) Icelandic volcanic ash in Scotland. *Scottish Geographical Magazine* 105 (3): 168–72.

Eastwood, N.J., Pearce, N.J.G., Perkins, W.T., Lamb, H.F., Westgate, J.A. and Roberts, C.N. (1996) Geochemistry of Santorini tephra in lake sediments from southwest Turkey. *Quaternary Science Reviews*, in press.

Engstrom, D.R. and Wright, H.E. (1984) Chemical stratigraphy of lake sediments as a record of environmental change. In E.Y. Haworth and J.W.G. Lund (eds) *Lake Sediments and Environmental History:* 11–67. Leicester, Leicester University Press.

Goldstein, I., Newbury, E., Echlin, P., Joy, D.C., Fiori, C. and Lifshin, E. (1984) *Scanning Electron Microscopy and X-ray Microanalysis*. London, Plenum Press.

Grattan, J. (1994) *The Impact of Icelandic Volcanic Eruptions upon the Ancient Settlement and Environment of Northern and Western Britain.* Unpublished Ph.D. dissertation, University of Sheffield.

Grattan, J.P. and Brayshay, M.B. (1995) An amazing and portentous summer: environmental and social responses in Britain to the 1783 eruption of an Iceland Volcano. *The Geographical Journal* 161 (2): 125–34.

Grattan, J.P. and Charman, D.J. (1994) Non-climatic factors and the environmental impact of volcanic volatiles: implications of the Laki Fissure eruption of AD 1783. *The Holocene* 4 (1): 101–6.

Grattan, J.P. and Gilbertson, D.D. (1994) Acid-loading from Icelandic tephra falling on acidified ecosystems as a key to understanding archaeological and environmental stress in northern and western Britain. *Journal of Archaeological Science* 21 (6): 851–9.

Holdren, G.R., Brunelle, T.M., Matisoff, G. and Whalen, M. (1984) Timing the increase in atmospheric sulphur deposition in the Adirondack Mountains. *Nature* 311: 245–8.

Hunt, J. and Hill, P. (1993) Tephra geochemistry: a discussion of some persistent analytical problems. *The Holocene* 3 (3): 271–8.

Ingram, H.A.P. (1978) Soil layers in mires: function and terminology. *Journal of Soil Science* 29: 224–7.

Ingram, H.A.P. (1987) Ecohydrology of Scottish peatlands. *Transactions of the Royal Society of Edinburgh. Earth Sciences* 78: 287–96.

Keller, J. (1981) Quaternary Tephrochronology in Mediterranean regions. In S. Self and R.S.J. Sparks (eds) *Tephra Studies*: 227–44. Dordrecht, Reidel.

Mackereth, F.J.H. (1965) Chemical investigations of lake sediments and their interpretation. *Proceedings of the Royal Society of London* B161: 295–309.

Mackereth, F.J.H. (1966) Some chemical observations on post-glacial lake sediments. *Philosophical Transactions of the Royal Society of London* B250: 165–214.

Maitland, P.S.and Holden, A.V. (1983) Inland waters of the inner Hebrides. *Proceedings of the Royal Society of Edinburgh* 83B: 229–44.

Pennington, W. (1981a) Records of a lake's life in time : the sediments. *Hydrobiologia* 79: 197–219.

Pennington, W. (1981b) Sediment composition in relation to the interpretation of pollen data. *Proceedings of the IV International Palynological Conference, Lucknow (1976–1977)* 3: 188–213.

Pennington, W., Haworth, E.Y., Bonny, A.P.and Lishman, J.P. (1972) Lake sediments in Northern Scotland. *Philosophical Transactions of the Royal Society of London* B264: 191–294.

Pilcher, J.R and, Hall, V.A. (1992) Towards a tephrochronology for the north of Ireland. *The Holocene* 2: 255–9.

Pratt, K. (1992) *Vegetational History of the Upper Borve Valley, Barra, Outer Hebrides*. Unpublished M.Sc. dissertation, University of Sheffield.

Pyatt, F.B, Grattan, J.P., Gilbertson, D.D. and Brayshay, B.A. (1995) Studies of loch-sediment chemistry and soil history from a 10,000+ year old core from Loch Hellisdale, South Uist, Outer Hebrides. *Scottish Geographical Magazine* 111 (2): 106–12.

Pyatt, F.B. and Lacy, D. (1988) An appraisal of atmospheric pollution by aluminium fumes emanating from smelter works in western Norway. *Environment International* 14: 407–16.

Rippey, B. (1990) Sediment chemistry and atmospheric contamination. In R.W. Battarbee, Sir John Mason, I. Renberg and J.F. Talling (eds) *Palaeolimnology and Lake Acidification*: 85–90. London, The Royal Society.

Rippey, B., Murphy, R.J., Kyle, S.W. (1982) Anthropogenically-derived changes in the sedimentary fluxes of Mg, Cr, Ni, Cu, Zn, Hg, Pb and P in Lough Neagh, Northern Ireland. *Environmental Science and Technology* 16: 23–30.

Stanley, D.J. and Sheng, H. (1986) Volcanic shards from Santorini (Upper Minoan ash) in the Nile Delta. *Nature* 320: 733–35.

St. Seymour, K. and Christianis, K. (1995) Correlation of a tephra layer in Western Greece with a late Pleistocene eruption in the Campanian Province of Italy. *Quaternary Research* 43: 46–54.

Sullivan, D.G. (1988) The discovery of Santorini Minoan tephra in western Turkey. *Nature* 333: 552–4.

Waterston, A.R., Holden, A.V., Campbell, R.N. and Maitland, P.S. (1979) The inland waters of the Outer Hebrides. *Proceedings of the Royal Society of Edinburgh* 77B: 329–51.

Westgate, J.A., Perkins, W.T., Fuge, R., Pearce, N.J.G. and Wintle, A. (1994) Trace element analysis of volcanic glass shards by Laser Ablation Inductively Coupled Plasma Mass Spectrometry: application to tephrochronological studies.*Applied Geochemistry* 9: 323–36.

10. Searching for the Ports of Troy

Eberhard Zangger, Michael E. Timpson, Sergei B. Yazvenko and Horst Leiermann

ABSTRACT

The paleotopography of the alluvial floodplain below the citadel of Troy (Hisarlik) is still disputed. Recently, it was suggested that one or several of the marshes and wetlands in the floodplain may represent silted-up basins which could have served as the long sought-after ports of bronze age Troy. To test this hypothesis and to generate the additional field data required to lead the discussion of the Trojan paleotopography towards a constructive solution, a short-duration, highly inter-disciplinary field study should be conducted. In this paper, the non-remote sensing, ground-based methods and components of such a project are discussed, including geomorphological mapping, systematic coring, micropaleontological analyses, identification of soils and their correlation through space and time, analysis of the paleoecology and paleoclimate, and technical reconstruction of the hydraulic system.

INTRODUCTION

No other city's fate has aroused as much general excitement and scholarly interest in Old World history as that of ancient Troy (Fig. 10.1). The earliest surviving written accounts in the western world, Homer's poems, revolve around the demise of this legendary city 3200 years ago. At first, the popularity of the oral traditions describing the end of the Heroic age may have helped to bolster the success of Homer's poetry, but soon the situation was reversed. The popularity of the *Iliad* and the *Odyssey* generated interest in the location and fate of the lost city. In the last century, the discovery by Charles Maclaren, Frank Calvert and Heinrich Schliemann of an extensive stratified settlement on the mound called Hisarlik, 25 km southwest of Canakkale in northwest Turkey, brought an end to the quest for lost Troy. This is the site generally identified with the city described by Homer – or at least parts of it. Many ancient Greek sources blamed the quarrel over Troy, apparently the biggest military engagement in the Aegean sphere at that time, for having caused the end of the heroic era – the watershed marking the boundary between the Bronze and Iron Ages. Greek and Roman generals made pilgrimages to the ruins of Troy, built temples to honour its memory, and sought to trace their family lineages back to Trojan ancestry. In medieval times, the war over Troy stood at the centre of many popular novels, despite the fact that knowledge of the Homeric epics was temporarily lost.

PERPETUAL PROBLEMS

Since large-scale excavations began at Hisarlik in 1871, the site has been subjected to an unusual degree of archaeological scrutiny, involving five excavation projects encompassing 26 individual years of excavation (up to 1997). Despite this impressive amount of scholarly dedication, the major questions surrounding the ancient city are as unresolved as they were shortly after Calvert and Schliemann first set their spades to it.

Some of the questions which emerged or re-emerged during the most recent excavations concern the size of the former city and the chronology of its settlement layers. The fall of Troy VIIa, marking the end of this once flourishing bronze age city, is a significant date for understanding the events during the so-called 'crisis years' around 1200 BC. At one point, the team of the current excavator, Manfred Korfmann, has stated that the fall of Troy VIIa might be placed around 1130 BC – considerably after the collapse of Mycenaean palatial society (Genz *et al.*, 1994: 341). Recently, however, this date has been adjusted to around 1180 BC (Brandau, 1997: 275; Zangger, 1994: 226).

Controversy also surrounds the actual size of ancient Troy. The British archaeologist John Bintliff (1991: 97), for instance, draws a picture of Troy VI as a fisherman's hamlet with a mere 100 inhabitants and no involvement in international commerce whatsoever, except as a fish market. According to Bintliff, Troy cannot be compared to a palatial

Fig. 10.1. Fortification walls of Troy VI.

residence such as Pylos, since the latter used to be a powerful administrative centre controlling an area many times larger than that belonging to Troy. In a similar vein, the former president of the German Archaeological Institute and excavator of Hattusa, Kurt Bittel, argues that 'the so-called sixth city of Troy is in reality a fortified chieftain's estate ("Fürstensitz") without any lower town surrounding it' (Bittel, 1976: 138). Korfmann too characterized Troy as a 'pirate's fortress' (Korfmann, 1986: 13) that was rather small in size. More recently, however, the excavators have considered Troy 'a residential and trading city of oriental style' (Korfmann, 1996: 30) and indeed 'one of the largest Aegean cities of its day' (Korfmann, 1995: 179). Since architectural remains of bronze age Troy emerge wherever archaeologists dig in non-erosional environments around Hisarlik, the 4th-century BC writer Hellanikos (F. Gr. Hist. 4,26a) may not have been entirely mistaken when he recalled that the city of Troy covered a number of different hills, with its citadel Pergamos crowning the tallest of them. Not surprisingly, the newly established National Park of Troy encompasses 61 known archaeological sites.

In 1992, the known extent of the city covered 100,000 m^2. Supposing that about one third of this area (= 33,000 m^2) was used for residential buildings (in addition to the citadel with its 5580 m^2) and taking into account the empirical value of 6.1 m^2 per person, Korfmann calculated a population of about 6000 (Korfmann, 1992: 138). Since 1992, however, the known extent of the city has at least doubled (to 200,000 m^2) if not tripled (to 300,000 m^2), but population estimates remained the same (Korfmann, 1995: 179). Provided the other parameters have not changed, the calculation of the population rate should now produce considerably higher numbers (12,000–18,000). The estimated population rate has not been raised, however, since it was previously argued that the available arable land around Troy was insufficient to feed the habitants of a large city (Korfmann, 1992: 138). The catchment of the city was estimated to have had a radius of seven kilometres, and an assumed 12.5% of this area was used for agriculture. Therefore, Korfmann calculated that the land could feed only about 6800 people. Supplies procured from the hinterland or conveyed by maritime trade were ignored. Moreover, the size of the catchment and the percentage of the arable land were taken from the work by John Bintliff, who estimated the total population of Troy to be a mere 100 – not a realistic figure from today's perspective. In his earlier work, Bintliff argued that today's fertile alluvial plains like the one at Argos used to be marshy grounds in the Bronze Age, unsuitable for agriculture (Bintliff 1977). More recent geoarchaeological studies have invalidated these ideas (Zangger, 1993: 84).

Considering the lack of investigations of late bronze

age sites in western Asia Minor, the question of how large an area the city controlled and how significant its influence on international trade might have been is virtually impossible to answer. Korfmann's graduate students argue that contacts between Mycenaean Greeks and the Black Sea region are not confirmed by archaeological evidence (Genz *et al.*, 1994: 344). Korfmann himself, however, states that, first, Mycenaean swords have been found in Georgia, Armenia, Rumania and Bulgaria (Korfmann, 1988: 52); second, 'people around the Aegean have been interested in the Black Sea region long before the Mycenaean period', and third, that Troy's significance rested precisely on this interest (Korfmann, 1994).

Another unsolved problem regards the two artificial ditches, about four metres wide and 2–3 metres deep, which were detected on the plateau south of the citadel by the geophysicist Helmut Becker during a magnetometer survey (Becker and Jansen, 1994). The inner ditch lies about 400 m south of the Troy VI fortification wall at an elevation of approximately 25 m above sea level (Jablonka *et al.*, 1994: 53). The excavators believe that this ditch was accompanied by a fortification wall marking the outer circumference of the city. The second ditch lies even farther outside the citadel and appears to be identical to the first one, but, at least initially, it was interpreted in a different fashion: it was not thought to have been accompanied by a wall and suspected to have been outside the former city (reconstruction in Eberl and Romberg, 1995: 24–5). The function of these ditches is anybody's guess. Because of their elevation and small size, it is certain that they were unrelated to any navigable watercourses which may have existed in the floodplain (Zangger, 1992: 211). Although Siebler, a former member of the project, declares that the inner ditch was already filled in by the time of the Trojan War (Siebler, 1994: 116), the excavators now regard it as an obstacle for approaching chariots, still visible during the eighth century. BC (Mannsperger, 1995: 350).

THE QUEST FOR THE PORT

The most controversial questions, however, regard the locations of the coastline, the ports of Troy, and the potential camp-site of the Greeks during the Trojan War (e.g. Bintliff, 1991; Kraft *et al.*, 1982; Luce, 1984, 1995; Rapp and Kraft, 1994; Zangger, 1992). Understanding the current discussion revolving around those issues requires a look at the research history of Troy.

Thirty years after the conclusion of Dörpfeld's two-year excavation campaign, the architect returned in October 1924 to conduct a reconnaissance in Besik bay (Fig. 10.2), apparently aiming to revive the German archaeological research in the Troad after World War I. Dörpfeld was accompanied by the archaeologist Martin Schede and by the Bavarian geologist and fund-provider Oscar Mey. All three men published the results of their investigation in individual reports (Dörpfeld, 1925; Mey, 1926; Schede, 1930), complementing the work produced by Alfred Brückner (Brückner, 1912, 1925) and Walter Leaf (Leaf, 1912, 1923). Re-examining these reports shows that many of the approaches taken by the recent excavation campaign rest on ideas developed seventy to eighty years earlier. These include the approach of Hisarlik via an investigation of Besik bay, conducting excavations on Besik Tepe, establishing the site of the port of Troy during the initial stage of the investigation and arguing that the port was located in Besik bay. Even the existence of a late bronze age graveyard in Besik bay, announced as a surprise discovery during the 1980s, was, in fact, nothing new, as it was known earlier this century (Brückner, 1925: 247).

Other valuable ideas already introduced by Alfred Brückner regard the significance of the marshes on the western side of the Trojan plain and of the two artificial cuts through the Yeniköy ridge connecting those marshes with the Aegean Sea (Brückner, 1925: 246). Brückner suspected that the distinctly-shaped Kesik marsh (Fig. 10.2 and Fig. 10.3) used to be the port basin of the classical city of Sigeion. The prominent 400 m-long and 30 m-deep artificial cut through the coastal ridge would then have been its entrance (Fig. 10.4). This idea was revived by Zangger, who argued that the Kesik marsh may well hide the long sought-after port of bronze age Troy, including the 'naval station' of the Greeks during the Trojan War (Zangger, 1992: 211). The excavator rejected this theory, alluding to 'strong arguments' from ancient philologists (Korfmann, 1993a: 45). Yet the ancient philologist John V. Luce was sufficiently impressed to present the Kesik harbour site as his idea (Luce, 1995: 211).

RECENT INVESTIGATIONS

The idea to stimulate new research about potential harbour sites in the Trojan plain fulfilled its purpose. Fourteen years after drilling investigations had begun at Troy, the sedimentologist Ilhan Kayan at last directed his interest to the marshes and cuts on the western side of the plain. The results of this recent investigation were presented in combination with a coastline reconstruction which differs significantly from the one published before (Fig. 10.2) – but still leaves a number of open questions. According to his observation the sea level at Troy rose by about two metres between 1000 BC and 1000 AD (Kayan, 1995: 216). Despite this relative sea level rise, the coastline regressed, due to the large amount of sediment deposited into the plain. This is a common phenomenon that has been observed elsewhere in the Aegean (e.g. Zangger, 1993: 67). What is unusual at Troy, however, is that prior to this period the relative sea level had dropped by about two metres (between 3000 BC and 1000 BC). The sedimentologist states that this bronze age fall in sea level 'accelerated the deltaic progradation and that most of the plain changed into land during this period' (Kayan, 1995: 217). Surprisingly, in his coastline reconstruction the rapid

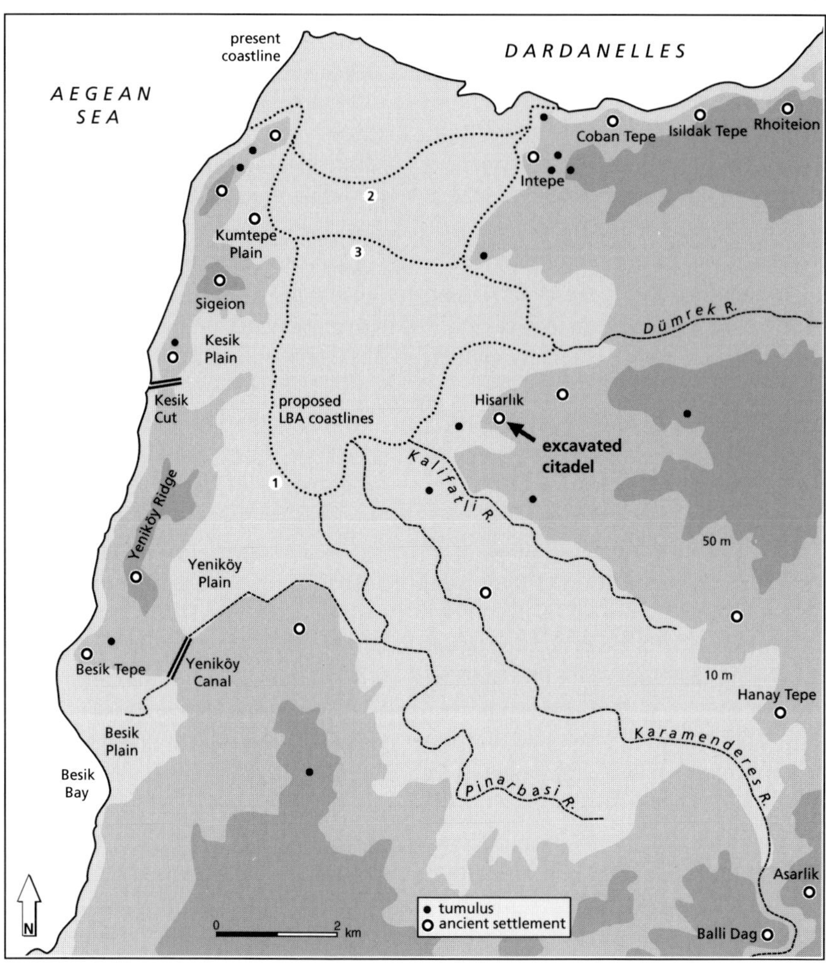

Fig. 10.2. Map of the plain of Troy with known archaeological sites, toponyms used in the text and river courses as recorded during the nineteenth century. Suggested positions for late bronze age coastlines are indicated as dotted lines and marked with numbers. 1. after Kraft et al. *(1982: 32), 2. after Zangger (1992: 211), 3. after Kayan (1995: 221).*

drop had the same effect as the subsequent rise. Both caused a moderate seaward movement of the shore (Kayan, 1995: Fig. 8). If, however, sedimentation rates are so high that they can compensate a sea level *rise*, a significant *fall* in sea level should have considerably accelerated the regression of the coastline. That such a fast regression apparently did not occur could be a hint at artificial interference with the hydraulic system. Anthropogenic control of the river sedimentation could have slowed down the sedimentation on the floodplain and thus the regression of the coastline. Another potential hint at the collapse of such an anthropogenic system could be the 'sharp change in the nature of sediments' in the floodplain observed by Kayan (Kayan, 1995: 231).

Inside the Trojan plain, the most landward possibility for a silted-up port is the Yeniköy plain, east of Besik bay. Kayan's drill cores revealed that this marsh was a marine embayment until the Early Bronze Age, and subsequently remained under water – even during the bronze age sea-level fall – since it was fed by the Pinarbasi stream rising at the south end of the plain of Troy (Kayan, 1995: 220). Between the Yeniköy plain and Besik bay, the coastal ridge drops to about 10 m above sea level. This low threshold is dissected by a canal running northeast/southwest. The canal was clearly not a navigable waterway, because it is too narrow and lies too high for that purpose. Kayan suspects that it was cut through the bedrock to drain the springs at Pinarbasi in order to prevent them from feeding the Yeniköy marsh (Kayan, 1995: 221).

There is no doubt that the canal was designed to direct water from the Karamenderes plain to Besik bay. If its whole purpose was drainage, however, a channel to the Karamenderes river would have sufficed. Thus, the real purpose of this construction remains enigmatic – and so does its date. Kayan cautiously states that the 'last use' of the canal was to drive a nineteenth-century AD water mill in the Besik plain. That such a massive construction was originally conceived and undertaken for this purpose is,

Fig. 10.3. During the 1960s the Kesik marsh (here seen from north) on the western side of the plain of Troy was drained and turned into arable land. Drill investigations have shown that the marsh used to be a marine basin during the Early Bronze Age. Later, it continued to be a depression filled with freshwater. Judging from its geographic position, this basin would have been an ideal port for bronze age Troy.

Fig. 10.4. The artificial Kesik cut dissects the 40-m high Yeniköy ridge. The bottom of the cut is now a field road, traversing the photograph from the lower right to the upper left corner. The light and dark macchia covers the north and south banks of the cut, highlighting its remarkable size.

however, economically irrational and rather unlikely. Peter Wilhelm Forchhammer, a geography professor at the University of Kiel, saw the canal when it was functioning and concluded that it must be of great antiquity. Rather optimistically, he hoped that nobody would assume that such a major construction was undertaken to drive 'the wheel of a humble water-mill' (Forchhammer, 1850: 20). To him, it seemed far more likely that an existing, silted-up, canal was cleaned and restored to be used for the mill. Korfmann, on the other hand, states that the canal definitely dates to the eighteenth century AD (Korfmann, 1993b: 28) – even though at that time, the date of construction was subject to debate as it is today. A Swedish engineer who examined the canal around 1790 remarked that 'everybody with even the faintest notion of engineering, would arrive at the conclusion that this construction is ancient' (Lenz, 1798: 22). The engineer himself dated it to the time of the Trojan War.

An outstanding candidate for a port inside the Trojan plain is the Kesik marsh due west of Hisarlik (Zangger, 1992: 207). Kayan states that before it silted up, this marsh could theoretically have been 'an excellent harbour', in particular since it appears to have been connected with the Aegean Sea through another artificial cut which dissects the coastal ridge (Kayan, 1995: 223). The surface of the coastal ridge rises to an elevation of 40 m in this area, while the highest point of the cut is at 13.7 m above sea level. Kayan's bore holes have revealed a 2–2.5 m thick layer of colluvium at the bottom of the trench. Thus, although the cut was an impressive 30 m deep, its bottom never came close to sea level. Tectonic movements are unlikely to have had a significant effect there, since bore holes in the Kesik plain have revealed coastal sand units from around 2000 BC at a depth equivalent to present sea level. Thus, Kayan believes that the cut was completely unrelated to maritime installations, something the British ancient historian John M. Cook (1973: 167) concluded some years ago: 'it seems to us clear that the work was never completed'.

Nevertheless, the cut could have been used as a dry slipway to transport ships between the Aegean Sea and the Kesik basin – as the German engineer and major Müller suggested in his report about the locality of the *Iliad*, published in 1798:

> 'Allein bey steilen, wenn gleich nicht hohen Ufern, war es eines Theils unmöglich, Schiffe von nur etwas beträchtlicher Grösse, so geradezu aus dem Wasser auf's Gestade zu ziehen, andern Theils würden selbige dabey sehr gelitten haben. Es wurden also Vorrichtungen erfordert, welche ersteres erleichterten, letzteres verhinderten. Dazu dienten Gräben, welches eigentlich in's Ufer gemachte Einschnitte waren, die allmählich (en pente douce) bis zum Wasser abliefen, und wodurch die Schiffe leicht, und ohne ihnen Nachtheil zuzufügen, heraufgezogen werden konnten.' (Müller, 1798: 139)
>
> (Translation: 'On low but steeply sloping coasts, it was almost impossible to beach ships without damaging them. Thus, installations were required which enabled the former and prevented the latter. For these purposes, channels were dug – actually being cuts into the coast – which gradually dipped towards the sea, and through which ships could easily be pulled without risk of becoming damaged.')

Kayan, however, points out that the lack of artefacts in trial trenches dug across the cut seems to indicate that it was not used in such a way. He advances the alternative explanation that the cut formed in a depression originally caused by a tectonic fault. Later, this natural passage was so frequently used by people commuting between the shore and the plain that the original valley deepened and widened. He overlooks the fact that such extensive commuter traffic would have produced a denser artefact scatter than the controlled lowering and rising of ships. Practical experiences gathered during numerous archaeological surveys tell that the number of surface finds increases in the vicinity of ancient roads and tracks.

The cut itself is too sharply defined, too straight, too large and too deep to be the result of some accidental trafficking. It is clearly a technical construction and was most likely designed to function as it now appears. It may not have been desirable to excavate the cut below sea level, to prevent saltwater from penetrating into the plain. The lack of artefacts in the buried paleosurface is not surprising, considering the degree of erosion that occurred in the area. Miocene sandstone is so prone to erosion that all remains of the classical city of Sigeion have disappeared from the coastal ridge.

Thus, despite the recent efforts to reconstruct the sedimentological history of the Kesik plain, many questions remain open. Kayan suggests that the Kesik plain could have been used as the port basin during the Early Bronze Age, but by the end of the Bronze Age it was probably silted up. Unfortunately, he does not discuss the depositional history of the plain after the Early Bronze Age. The radiocarbon dates (from marine shells) seem to indicate that it silted up after about 1300 BC In the stratigraphic cross-section through the Kesik plain, Kayan does not distinguish between 'swamp' and 'floodplain delta sediments'. Swamp sediments, however, might well conceal an ancient freshwater port basin. Finally, it is rather confusing that the Kesik plain appears as a marine embayment on the most recent reconstructions of Troy VI (Eberl and Romberg, 1995: 24–5), if it had silted up over 1000 years before.

Kayan ends his study with the conclusion that there is 'no evidence' that the basins on the landward side of the Yeniköy ridge have been used as ports in antiquity. On many occasions he refers to the lack of 'definite', 'clear', or 'most valuable or trustworthy' evidence. However, as always in archaeology, the absence of evidence is no evidence of absence – it should rather be taken as a challenge to change the methodology, the location of the search or the team of experts and to simply look harder. In erosional environments the chances of finding obvious or irrevocable evidence are minute. In order to even hypothesize how the now-destroyed landscape might have looked like in prehistoric times, one has to apply methods reminiscent of those used in forensic sciences.

In previous years Ilhan Kayan, Manfred Korfmann, George Rapp and John C. Kraft have unequivocally favoured the idea that the port of Troy was located in Besik bay (Korfmann 1991: 19; Kraft *et al.*, 1982: 40; Rapp and Kraft, 1994: 76), although there never was any 'definite' evidence to support this notion. Indeed, there is no 'conclusive' evidence that the archaeological site on Hisarlik is identical with the Homeric Troy. Only circumstantial evidence speaks in favour of this identification. Similarly, today there are numerous indications that the eastern side of the Trojan plain contained a complex hydraulic system, one that was most likely related to the ports of the city. These indications suffice to let the Besik hypothesis pale into insignificance. Kayan's closing remark that the theories advanced by Zangger (1992) lack 'the necessary proof' could be applied to any theory advanced by the excavators of Troy. Theories rest on arguments, not on proof. If new information arises which apparently contradicts existing theories, the latter have to be revised to fit the new data. As it turns out, the new data provided by Ilhan Kayan (1995) and insights gained during recent investigations of a late bronze age port system in Greece now permit a much more refined theoretical reconstruction of the paleohydrology of the Trojan plain.

ENVIRONMENTAL RECONSTRUCTION

In order to resolve the questions revolving around the canals and potential ports, it is clear that further paleoenvironmental studies are needed. We believe that after more than 120 years of traditional, palace-oriented, excavations at Troy, the time has come to supplement this work with a systematic investigation of its surrounding landscape, as has been so fruitfully applied elsewhere in the Mediterranean.

The sedimentological investigation of the plain of Troy began twenty years ago with a team composed of John Kraft, Ilhan Kayan and George Rapp – distinguished researchers whose pioneering work has paved the way for landscape reconstructions in the Aegean. Today, however, their approach resting exclusively on the sedimentological interpretation of drill cores no longer meets the standard required for landscape reconstructions. As these scholars themselves acknowledge, a wide array of new techniques is now available allowing far greater resolution and accuracy in landscape reconstructions. With respect to their investigation around Tiryns, Rapp and Kraft (1994: 85) conclude that 'the much more intensive study by Zangger (1991), based on a large number of drill cores, has provided a detailed picture of the environment and land use of Helladic people well beyond our previous work'. The same could be said about their study of the Gulf of Navarino, where they first detected an artificial stream diversion. A subsequent physical scientific study conducted in the framework of the Pylos Regional Archaeological Project was able to show that the redirected stream is just one component of a complex late bronze age port with a clean-water flushing mechanism (Zangger *et al.*, 1997a). It is quite conceivable that a succession of investigations by different geoarchaeological teams would lead to equally fruitful results at Troy.

At the outset of such a project, it is necessary to distinguish between the three different kinds of canals, cuts and trenches at Troy. First, there are the Yeniköy canal and Kesik cut dissecting the coastal ridge north and south of Yeniköy. Neither one of these constructions has ever been a navigable waterway. The Yeniköy canal is too narrow, while the bottom of the Kesik cut lies too high above sea level, as we now know. Second, there are at least two artificial ditches on the mound of Hisarlik which were found during a magnetometer survey (Jablonka *et al.*, 1994). Obviously, these narrow trenches are unrelated to the hydraulic system which might have existed in the plain. Why Manfred Korfmann consistently points out that Eberhard Zangger regards these as navigable watercourses remains enigmatic (Zick, 1997: 56) – they only have half the width of bronze age ships. Finally, there are paleostream beds and artificial canals inside the Trojan floodplain. These were described by many early travelers and scholars and still existed during the nineteenth century (Forchhammer, 1850: 20; Schliemann, 1880: 82; Zangger, 1992: 209). The senior author suggested that these now silted-up paleo-river courses inside the floodplain belonged to the port system at Troy – an idea initially rejected by Korfmann (1993a: 45). Meanwhile, however, the excavation team has also recognized the indications for navigable watercourses in the floodplain and now regards it as a possibility that a river port existed immediately below the citadel (Korfmann, 1997: 65). This interpretation is not new (Zangger, 1992: 146), but difficult to reconcile with earlier reconstructions, in which the sea was thought to have advanced all the way to the citadel.

To determine the purpose and possible interrelation of these features and to reconstruct the hydraulic system of the plain, a highly interdisciplinary study using state-of-the-art technologies from a number of natural scientific disciplines is necessary. This study must involve the application of several different remote sensing techniques at different altitudes, providing total-coverage information for the entire plain of Troy (Zangger *et al.*, 1997b). In this paper we concentrate on the ground-based methods to be considered, in particular on the contributions of geomorphology, soil science, paleoecology, geochemistry and hydraulic engineering.

GEOMORPHOLOGY AND PEDOLOGY

One of the first steps in a new investigation of the plain of

Troy would be the production of a geomorphological map which incorporates the information obtained by remote sensing, aerial photography, ancient and modern topographic maps, historic sources and ground checks. Based on this information, a team of earth scientists would conduct subsurface investigations, including coring and soil investigations, to determine the nature of the anomalies detected by radar and magnetometry surveys.

Recent landscape reconstructions in Greece and elsewhere have shown how much information about the paleoenvironment can be retrieved from examining the soils (e.g. Pope and van Andel, 1984; Timpson, 1992; Zangger, 1995). In order to obtain a detailed soil map, pedologists will examine the physical and chemical properties of the modern soils and the existence and degree of development of paleosols preserved in the alluvial sediments (e.g., Carter, 1993; Singer and Janitzky, 1986; Soil Survey Division Staff, 1993). Soil development involves a series of four interacting processes, consisting of additions, losses, translocations, and transformations, causing the differentiation of soil horizons. The quality and quantity of these processes depend on environmental factors including climate, parent material, and vegetation. Weathering and dissolution of primary minerals in the alluvial sediments result in mineral transformations and movement of the secondary weathering products to lower horizons. These processes manifest themselves in observable soil properties that can be determined in the field through close examination of the soils and sediments.

Describing soil horizons and their properties, therefore, not only provides initial insight into the processes and mechanisms involved in the development of soils, but also into the environmental conditions prevailing at that time. For example, weathering and movement of clay minerals from surface to subsurface horizons require many thousands of years. Thus, the observation of translocated clays in the soil B horizons implies long periods of landscape stability. The degree of soil development, the depositional environment, the nature of the soil parent material, and the physical processes involved in the formation of soils, can be determined through analyses in the particle-size distribution of the sediments and soils (Greenwood, 1969; Timpson and Foss, 1993). Because clay minerals weather in predictable sequences (Jackson *et al.*, 1948; Paquet and Millot, 1973), laboratory determinations of the clay fraction of the alluvial soils can be used to infer the conditions of weathering and therefore the regional climate (Timpson *et al.*, 1996). Subsequently, these soils will be correlated through space and time to determine – in relative terms – the periods of landscape stability and instability which occurred throughout the floodplain. Using this approach, it will be possible to develop a model of landscape evolution for the entire region (e.g. Foss et al., 1995; Mandel, 1994).

Since the Troad is known to have been seismically active in historic times (Rapp, 1982), the sedimentary record could also be examined for evidence of paleoseismic activity (Obermeier et al., 1990; Saucier, 1991). In the coastal plain region of South Carolina and in the New Madrid seismic zone of the central United States, subsurface injection features such as sediment dikes, and other seismically-produced sedimentary structures, including sand volcanoes and 'sand blows', have been found to document sediment liquefaction triggered by earthquakes (Obermeier et al., 1990).

Coring still represents an indispensable tool in environmental reconstructions, but it is important that core locations are established on a theoretical basis in order to reduce bias. An efficient way to investigate the subsurface stratigraphy of coastal plains utilizes cores that are placed at equal distances in straight lines across the floodplain (Zangger, 1993). Such cross-sections enable complete, unbiased coverage of the stratigraphy across the landscape. In the case of the plain of Troy, it is desirable to have several core cross-sections traversing the plain from east to west. To determine the paleoenvironment of subaqueous deposits found in those cores, it is essential to conduct detailed studies of the microfossil contents of the drill samples (e.g. Zangger and Malz, 1989). These investigations will be particularly useful to establish if and when the basins such as the one now concealed by the Kesik plain were once connected to the open sea.

PALEOECOLOGY

Archaeologists have long realized that knowledge of the vegetation history in their study areas is imperative to determine the degree of human impact on the natural environment, as well as past land use, and long-term changes in subsistence strategies. Obtaining continuous pollen records has therefore been a primary target of regional archaeological studies. The most recently investigated pollen cores from the Aegean are those taken from the Argive Plain in 1988 (Jahns, 1991, 1993) and from Osmanaga lagoon in 1993 (Zangger et al., 1997a). Both of these cores stem from regions of prime interest to Aegean prehistorians and both provide consecutive records of land use and vegetation changes extending back about 7000 years.

One of the challenges facing a palynologist in the Aegean is finding an appropriate site where continuous pollen preservation and sediment supply existed for a sufficiently long period of time. The most suitable depositional environments are marshes, swamps, lakes and coastal lagoons. In the dry and steeply sloping landscape of the Aegean, few such places exist. Gennett and Gifford (1982: 105) therefore postulate a hypothetical small, deep, spring-fed lake on the plateau 10 km east of Troy as the ideal source for recovering representative samples of the pollen from the vegetation of the surrounding countryside. There is no need, however, to establish such a hypothetical site, because wetlands abound within the alluvial floodplain of the Karamenderes and Dumrek rivers below Hisarlik. Even in historic times, the plain of Troy was regarded as swampy, and core analyses (Kayan, 1995; Kraft et al., 1982) have revealed that low-energy subaqueous environments existed within the plain at least since the Early bronze age. Considering the paramount interest in the archaeological history of the region and the rare presence of suitable pollen core sites, it is difficult to understand why a systematic paleoecological study has never been attempted. Given the abundance of marshes in the Trojan plain, several pollen cores might be taken, thereby enabling a reconstruction of spatial patterns of vegetation within the landscape as well as the discrimination between local and regional components in pollen diagrams.

The first and foremost task of pollen core analyses is the best possible identification of all pollen taxa found in the samples, combined with a thorough knowledge of ecological preferences of individual plant taxa. This aspect needs to be emphasized, because some previous pollen studies tended to focus on recognizing general groups of plants such as 'legumes', 'daisy-family' or 'oaks'. It is essential, however, to discriminate for instance between the pollen of deciduous and evergreen oaks, because these two species respond differently to human impact. Many crops (olive, walnut, flax, rye, corn) can be recognized in a pollen record and will therefore yield information about the extent and nature of agriculture and its historic development through time. Precise identification of weeds might help recognizing specific agricultural activities, such as grazing, farming and even crop rotation. It is interesting to note that inflorescences and roots of *Triticum durum* have been found in Troy I samples, possibly indicating that wheat was already cultivated at Troy during the earliest period of habitation around 3000 BC (Mulholland et al., 1982: 135).

An additional key element of high-resolution palynological analyses is dense core sample intervals providing high temporal resolution. Many important events in vegetation histories (for instance, forest fires and tephra layers from volcanic eruptions) have short time spans and might be overlooked, if the sample intervals are not densely spaced (see Bottema, Chapter 2). Furthermore, short sampling intervals help reduce the 'noise' and aid in extracting the main signals in long time-series. The anaerobic marsh environments in the floodplain are bound to contain ample remains of terrestrial plants that can be used to obtain a detailed radiocarbon chronology to date the vegetation history and to correlate changes in land use with historical events.

Another prerequisite of interpreting past vegetation changes on the basis of pollen records is a quantitative understanding of relationships between modern pollen production and the source vegetation. Thus far, interpretations of pollen counts in sediment samples from eastern Mediterranean countries are still problematic, since pollen counts do not necessarily reflect plant abundances in past vegetation. To establish relationships between the past pollen record and its source vegetation, modern pollen samples have to be examined quantitatively. In the temperate regions of Europe and North America, numerous studies have been conducted that quantitatively relate modern pollen assemblages to the source vegetation (Andersen, 1970; Bradshaw, 1981; Bradshaw and Webb, 1985; Heide and Bradshaw, 1982; Jackson, 1990; Webb, 1974; Webb et al., 1981; Yazvenko, 1991). Yet for the Aegean and, in fact, the whole of the eastern Mediterranean, the recent study of the landscape evolution of western Messenia (Zangger et al., 1997a) is the first attempt to quantify past vegetation – all previous studies have remained at a qualitative level (Bottema, 1974, 1980; Bottema and Barkoudah, 1979; Wright, 1972; Wright et al., 1967; van Zeist et al., 1970, 1975). Quantitative reconstructions of vegetation covers should provide a basis for assessing the proportion of land under cultivation and its changes through time.

Finally, fossil pollen samples should be compared with databases of regional vegetational records to find the closest modern analogs for the fossil assemblages and to accommodate pollen diagrams in the regional context. Such broad regional databases of modern pollen and vegetation data are available today, for instance for North America, central Europe, and the western Mediterranean.

GEOCHEMISTRY

Geochemical investigations are an essential part of the sedimentology, palynology, and pedology efforts. To test the hypothesis that some of the marshes in the plain of Troy may have been filled with water and connected to the sea, it will be necessary to determine and date the historical changes in the paleosalinity and paleoecology of the marsh deposits. The former depositional environment in the basins could be determined by measuring the sulphur and carbon contents of the sediments. If the marsh deposits conceal marine or brackish environments, the proportion of sulphur should be considerably above the values of the floodplain alluvium.

A coherent array of chemical testing, including determinations of carbon, nitrogen, and $\delta^{13}C$ should also be employed to analyze samples from the pollen cores (see Zangger et al., 1997a). Similar geochemical analyses can be conducted with soil samples. Organic compounds accumulate in the surface horizons of soils through the decay of plant remains, resulting in dark colours which mark the surfaces of buried paleosols. After burial, however, new additions of plant detritus cease and the organic compounds already present start to decompose, resulting in a gradual loss of the characteristic dark colour. Consequently, organic carbon content must be determined analytically to detect buried paleosurfaces more precisely.

Several other geochemical analyses have the potential of providing more information about the paleoclimate and environment in which a soil formed. For instance, quantifying the content and form of secondary iron minerals (such as hematite and goethite) can be used to assess the climatic conditions during soil formation (McFadden and

Hendricks, 1985). Also, determinations of the content, distribution, and composition of the primary and secondary carbonate minerals in soils can be utilized to model the processes and climatic conditions under which the soil formed (Mayer et al., 1988), because stable landscapes allow dissolution and movement of carbonates from surface to subsurface horizons. An initial assessment of the time frame needed for the soil's development can be obtained through field observations of the morphological expression of carbonate translocation (Gile et al., 1966). More precise information, however, requires laboratory analyses of these minerals.

Finally, insights into the paleoclimate and paleovegetation of the region may be obtained through measurements of the stable isotopic composition of carbon and oxygen in various soil components (Cerling et al., 1989; Grootes, 1993; Hays and Grossman, 1991; Kelly et al., 1991; Nordt et al., 1994).

URBAN PLANNING AND HYDRAULIC ENGINEERING

In traditional archaeological investigations, sites were considered as depositories of valuable artefacts to be retrieved from the ground. Today's regional archaeological projects have abandoned this approach (e.g. Cherry et al., 1991; Davis et al., 1997; Jameson et al., 1994; Snodgrass, 1987), and instead aim to consider sites as the settlement centres of dynamic and evolving societies whose fate and fortune depended largely on successful interactions with the natural environment. It is therefore necessary to incorporate the techniques of intensive survey and technical reconstruction of past urban planning in a regional archaeological study. However, no such study of the Trojan plain has been conducted since Forchhammer and Spratt surveyed and mapped the area in 1839. A century later, in 1924, many of the architectural remains recorded previously had already disappeared, including a 60 m-long stretch of what Thomas Spratt considered to be the fortification wall of Sigeion (Brückner, 1925: 242; Forchhammer, 1850: 22).

At Troy and Pylos, tumulus-shaped hills of bedrock have been identified, 'leftover'-remnants of the former surface which were spared destruction by modern agricultural practices (Kayan, 1995: 228; Zangger et al., 1997a). Considering the degree of surface destruction, many artefacts and architectural remains are likely to have fallen victim to erosion. Still, it would be better to conduct a systematic archaeological survey now: better late, than never. During this survey, particular attention should be paid to those areas where anomalies have been detected using remote sensing techniques to determine whether these lineaments correlate with structures visible on the ground.

Early hydraulic civilizations in Mesopotamia and Egypt were able to control annual river floods and turn them into a blessing for the economy long before the second millennium BC. Recent investigations of Mycenaean hydraulic engineering feats have shown that an impressive level of engineering expertise also existed in late bronze age Greece (e. g. Knauss, 1990, 1991, 1996). There is no reason to assume that ephemeral river floods limited the use of fertile alluvial soils in the floodplains around the Aegean. It is thus unlikely that the plain of Troy was a wasteland controlled by the floods of the Karamenderes river (as stated by Kayan, 1995: 232). More probably, the people at Troy stabilized their landscape to the extent that it could be optimally exploited for centuries. The large number of lineaments, abandoned channels, river quays, artificial canals, bridges, sand heaps and man-made ditches around Troy are strong indications that this was indeed the case. Even more, no other place has as many references to anthropogenic interferences with the hydraulic system as Troy – from classical times until the nineteenth century AD (e. g. Forchhammer, 1850: 20; Mauduit 1840: 132; Pliny, Nat. Hist. 5.30; Schliemann, 1880: 98). According to ancient mythology, the course of the Karamenderes River was actually determined by Heracles, thus its ancient name Skamander (skamma andros = 'man-made foam').

A WORKING HYPOTHESIS

The currently favoured approach of the excavation campaign to reconstruct the Trojan landscape on the basis of the Iliad (Mannsperger, 1995) bears many risks. Homer never mentioned the port at Pylos, the river diversion at Tiryns or the melioration of Lake Kopais. Even if Homer existed as an eighth-century BC individual, it would have been impossible for him to comprehend a hydraulic system which had collapsed five hundred years before. Therefore, the most promising approach to reconstruct the human interferences with the hydrological environment at Troy is through the cooperation with hydro-engineers – preferably those with a background in prehistoric technology. If modern engineers attempt to meet the goals of the past using the techniques available in the past, it may be possible to determine, at least approximately, the design of the infrastructure surrounding prehistoric and early historic cities. Common goals, fulfilled by common techniques, are bound to lead to common solutions. Prime examples for the methodology and potential of such technical reconstructions are the investigations of Mycenaean hydro-engineering (e.g. Knauss, 1991) and early iron age ports (e.g. Raban, 1997).

During the Pylos Regional Archaeological Project the collaboration between hydro-engineers and physical scientists from several different disciplines has unveiled the earliest thus far known artificial port in prehistoric Europe (Zangger, et al. 1997a). The system is highly sophisticated and reflects a level of engineering skill surpassing that of classical times. Its discovery proves that the hydraulic

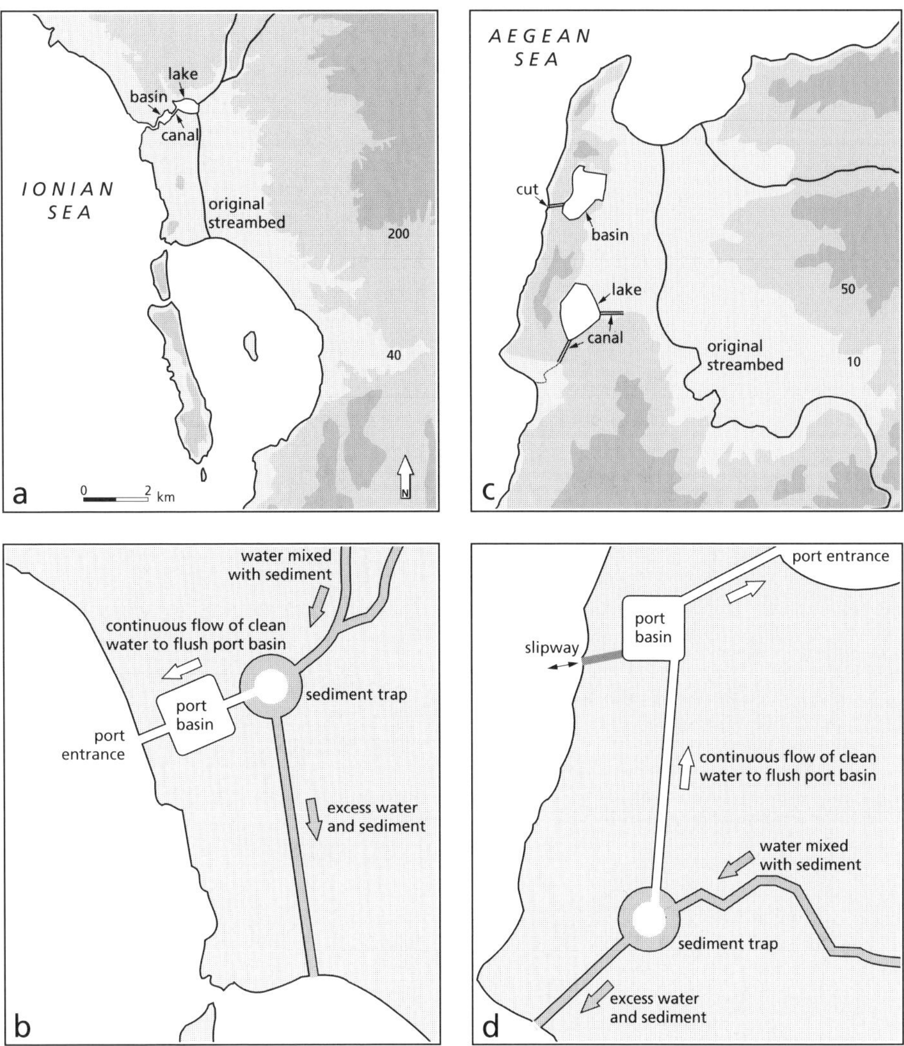

Fig. 10.5. During a recent geoarchaeological investigation around the Palace of Nestor on the southwestern Peloponnese, a complex hydraulic system was discovered (a). In one area a river was dammed to create an artificial lake. Sediment tranported by the river was deposited in the lake, while the clean water from the upper layers of the lake was used to flush an artificial port basin, thereby preventing it from silting-up by sediment derived from the sea (b). The remains of hydraulic installations at Troy (c) could have been components of a similar system (d).

expertise required for the complex domestic meliorations was also applied to maritime installations. About 4.5 km southwest of the 'Palace of Nestor' at Pylos, a cothon-type basin, 330 by 230 m in size, was artifically excavated about 500 m inland from the Ionian coast, connected to the sea by a paleochannel of a Pleistocene streambed (Figs. 10.5a, 10.5b). By itself, the entrance to the basin would have silted up after a few seasons – due to the large amount of sand transported along the coast by the longshore current. The architects who designed the port therefore constructed a flushing mechanism that prevented large amounts of saltwater (and sediment) from penetrating into the basin. The water required for the flushing current was derived from the nearby Selas River – by far the largest perennial stream of the region. Since the river itself also transports large amounts of sediment that would have filled the port basin, a sediment trap had to be constructed first. The river was thus dammed to form a lake 180,000 m^2 in size. When the river water reached the lake, it lost its energy and dropped the suspended sediment and bed load into the reservoir. From the surface of the lake a small current of clean water was directed through an artificial canal into the port basin, while the remaining water left the lake through the original streambed.

This system obviously demanded control of how much clean water was directed into the basin and how much dirty water was allowed to escape. When control was abandoned after the Mycenaean demise, the river, left to itself, chose the shorter course through the port basin, thereby filling it up almost immediately. Radiocarbon accelerator dates from auger cores have shown that the port was functional during the peak of the Mycenaean era,

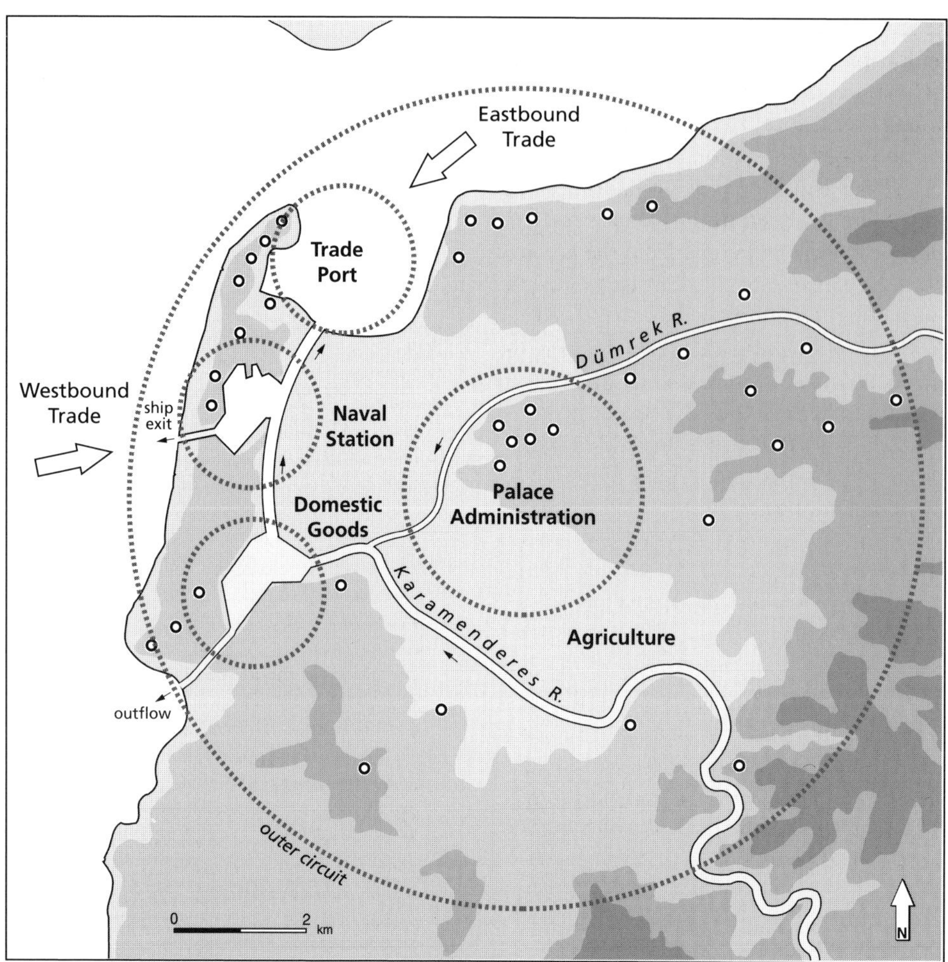

Fig. 10.6. This schematic model for the city of Troy illustrates how the floodplain below the citadel of Troy could have been used for port installations. The sediment-rich Dumrek and Karamenderes Rivers jointly exited into a lake at Yeniköy which could have been used for river traffic and for handling domestic goods. The canal toward Besik bay served as an outflow for excess water and sediment. Clean, sediment-free water was taken from the upper layers of the lake and directed north toward the basin at Kesik, which served as a 'naval station' either for military vessels or for westbound trade goods. Finally, the freshwater exited into the sea at Kumtepe, where there may have been the main port for trade with the Black Sea.

between about 1400 BC and 1200 BC. Its clean-water flushing mechanism, however, represents a standard-solution that was re-invented and widely applied in medieval Europe. All that was required to build such a naval installation was a floodplain, a stream feeding the floodplain and a low coastal ridge isolating it from the open sea – a typical landscape setting in the countries around the Aegean. A few engineers and about two hundred workers would have been able to build the system at Pylos in one to three years. Artificial port basins in Egypt, like the one of Birket Habu built under the rulership of pharaoh Amenhotep III., bear witness that constructions of this kind – even twenty times bigger than the basin at Pylos – were feasible using fourteenth century BC know-how and technology.

The knowledge about the port of Pylos, combined with the information provided by the recent subsurface studies along the Yeniköy ridge, now permit a refined theoretical reconstruction of the paleohydrology of the Trojan plain – one that might be used as a working hypothesis for future investigations. The port system at Pylos shows many similarities to the landscape at Troy and the remains of its hydraulic installations (Figs. 10.5c, 10.5d). The Yeniköy and Kesik plains represent silted-up basins and indeed remained wetlands until the 1960s. The former function of one basin, which now is the Yeniköy marsh, could have been equivalent to the lake and sediment trap at Pylos (Fig. 10.6). From this lake, sediment-rich water was directed through the artificial canal to Besik bay – an idea already advanced by the geologist Oscar Mey during his investigation of the sediments in the Besik plain (Mey, 1926: 19). At the same time, this lake may have been used as a river port for domestic goods. After all, most hydraulic installations fulfill more than one purpose (Leiermann, 1994: 18). Sediment-free water from the upper layers of the lake was directed towards a second basin, the 'naval station' at Kesik. This basin served as an interior freshwater port. It was generally preferred to keep vessels in freshwater to repulse worms and algae from the wooden hulls. The freshwater current continued to run toward the sea and exited near Kumtepe. Thus, saltwater – and the sediment carried by it – were prevented from entering the port system. Ships could enter or leave the Kesik basin by two ways. They could either sail into it from the north, or they could be pulled through the dry Kesik cut. In times of war, this additional exit permitted Trojan warships to circumvent naval attackers besieging the north coast. In peaceful times, ships travelling from and to the west were raised and lowered through the cut. Such a special service warranted extra high charges – and permitted a complete separation of the trade between the Aegean and Black Seas. Trade goods coming from and going to Aegean destinations were processed in the Kesik basin, while those from and to Black Sea cities were handled on the coast at Kumtepe. Keeping the suppliers separate from each other allowed the Trojans to dictate prices for goods in transit. In this way, the rulers of Troy would have ideally benefited from the favourable location of their city.

REFERENCES

Andersen, S.T. (1970) The relative pollen productivity and pollen representation of north European trees and correction factors for tree pollen spectra. *Danmarks Geologiske Undersøgelse, Række* 2, 96: 1–99.

Becker, H. and Jansen, H.-G. (1994) Magnetische Prospektion 1993 der Unterstadt von Troia und Ilion. *Studia Troica* 4: 105–14.

Bintliff, J. (1977) *Natural Environment and Human Settlement in Prehistoric Greece*. Oxford, British Archaeological Reports, International Series 28.

Bintliff, J. (1991) Troia und seine Paläolandschaften. In E. Olshausen and H. Sonnabend (eds) *Stuttgarter Kolloquium zur Historischen Geographie des Altertums* 5: 83–131. Bonn, Rudolf Habelt.

Bittel, K. (1976) *Die Hethiter. Die Kunst Anatoliens vom Ende des bis 3. zum Anfang des 1. Jahrtausends vor Christus*. München, C.H. Beck.

Bottema, S. (1974) *Late Quaternary Vegetation History of Northwestern Greece*. PhD dissertation, Rijksuniversiteit Groningen.

Bottema, S. (1980) Palynological investigations on Crete. *Review of Palaeobotany and Palynology* 31: 193–217.

Bottema, S. and Barkoudah, Y. (1979) Modern pollen precipitation in Syria and Lebanon and its relation to vegetation. *Pollen et Spores* 21: 427–80.

Bradshaw, R.H.W. (1981) Quantitative reconstruction of local woodland vegetation using pollen analysis from a small basin in Norfolk. *Journal of Ecology* 69: 941–55.

Bradshaw, R.H.W. and Webb, T. (1985) Relationships between contemporary pollen and vegetation data from Wisconsin and Michigan, USA. *Ecology* 66: 721–37.

Brandau, B. (1997) *Troia*. Bergisch Gladbach, Lübbe.

Brückner, A. (1912) Das Schlachtfeld vor Troja. *Archäologischer Anzeiger*: 616–33.

Brückner, A. (1925) Forschungsaufgaben in der Troas. *Archäologischer Anzeiger*: 230–48.

Carter, M.R. (ed.) (1993) *Soil Sampling and Methods of Analysis*. Boca Raton, Lewis Publishing.

Cerling, T.E., Quade, J., Wang, Y. and Bowman, J.R. (1989) Carbon isotopes in soils and palaeosols as ecology and palaeoecology indicators. *Nature* 341: 138–9.

Cherry, J.F., Davis, J. L. and Mantzourani, E. (1991) *Landscape Archaeology as Long-Term History: Northern Keos in the Cycladic Islands*. Los Angeles, UCLA Institute of Archaeology.

Cook, J. M. (1973) *The Troad – An Archaeological and Topographical Study*. Oxford, Clarendon.

Davis, J.L., Alcock, S.E., Bennet, J., Lolos, Y. and Shelmerdine, C.W. (1997) The Pylos Regional Archaeological Project, Part I: overview and archaeological survey. *Hesperia* 66 (3): 391–494.

Dörpfeld, W. (1925) Das Schiffslager der Griechen vor Troja. *Studien zur vorgeschichtlichen Archäologie, Festschrift A. Götze*.

Eberl, U. and Romberg, J. (1995) Troia. *GEO*: 14–38.

Forchhammer, P.W. (1850) *Beschreibung der Ebene von Troja*. Frankfurt a. M., Heinrich Ludwig Brünner.

Foss, J.E., Timpson, M.E. and Lewis, R.J. (1995) Soils in alluvial sequences: some archaeological implications. In M.E. Collins (ed) *Pedological Perspectives in Archaeological Research*: 1–14. Madison, Soil Science Society of America.

Gennett, J.A. and Gifford, J.A. (1982) Pollen Analysis. In G. Rapp and J.A. Gifford (eds) *Troy. The Archaeological Geology*: 105–16. Princeton, Princeton University Press.

Genz, H., Pruß, A. and Quack, J. (1994) Ein Puzzle, das uns nicht paßt. *Antike Welt* 25: 340–7.

Gile, L.H., Peterson, F.F. and Grossman, R.B. (1966) Morphological and genetic sequences of carbonate accumulation in desert soils. *Soil Science* 101: 347–60.

Greenwood, B. (1969) Sediment parametres and environment discrimination: an application of multivariate statistics. *Canadian Journal of Earth Science* 6: 1347–58.

Grootes, P.M. (1993) Interpreting continental isotope records. In P.K. Swart (ed) *Climate Change in Continental Isotopic Records*: 37–46. Washington, D.C., American Geophysical Union 78.

Hays, P.D. and Grossman, E.L. (1991) Oxygen isotopes in meteoric calcite cements as indicators of continental palaeoclimate. *Geology* 19: 441–4.

Heide, K.M. and Bradshaw, R.H.W. (1982) The pollen-tree relationship within forests of Wisconsin and upper Michigan, USA. *Review of Palaeobotany and Palynology* 36: 1–23.

Jablonka, P., König, H. and Riehl, S. (1994) Ein Verteidigungsgraben in der Unterstadt von Troia VI. Grabungsbericht 1993. *Studia Troica* 4: 51–74.

Jackson, M.L., Tyler, S.A., Willis, A.L., Bourbeau, G.A. and Pennington, R.P. (1948) Weathering sequences of clay-size minerals in soils and sediments I: fundamental generalizations. *Journal of Physical and Colloid Chemistry* 52: 1237–60.

Jackson, S.T. (1990) Pollen source area and representation in small lakes of the northeastern United States. *Review of Palaeobotany and Palynology* 63: 53–76.

Jahns, S. (1991) *Untersuchungen über die holozäne Vegetationsgeschichte von Süddalmatien und Südgriechenland*. PhD dissertation, Göttingen, Georg-August-Universität.

Jahns, S. (1993) On the Holocene vegetation history of the Argive Plain (Peloponnese, southern Greece). *Vegetation History and Archaeobotany* 2: 187–203.

Jameson, M.H., van Andel, Tj.H. and Runnels, C.N. (1994) *A Greeek Countryside: The Southern Argolid from Prehistory to Present Day*. Stanford, Stanford University Press.

Kayan, I. (1995) The Troia Bay and supposed harbour sites in the Bronze Age. *Studia Troica* 5: 211–35.

Kelly, E.F., Amundson, R.G., Marino, B.D. and De Niro, M.J. (1991) Stable carbon isotopic composition of carbonate in Holocene grassland soils. *Soil Science Society of America Journal* 55: 1651–8.

Knauss, J. (1990) *Kopais 3.* Berichte der Versuchsanstalt Obernach und des Lehrstuhls für Wasserbau und Wassermengenwirtschaft der Technischen Universität München, 63. Munich.

Knauss, J. (1991) Arkadian and Boiotian Orchomenos, centres of Mycenaean hydraulic engineering. *Irrigation and Drainage Systems* 5: 363–81.

Knauss, J. (1996) *Argolische Studien: Alte Strassen – alte Wasserbauten.* Berichte der Versuchsanstalt Obernach und des Lehrstuhls für Wasserbau und Wassermengenwirtschaft der Technischen Universität München, 77. Munich.

Korfmann, M. (1986) Troy: topography and navigation. In M. Mellink (ed) *Troy and the Trojan War*: 1–16. Bryn Mawr, Bryn Mawr College.

Korfmann, M. (1988) Ausgrabungen an der Bucht von Troia. *Tübinger Blätter*: 47–52.

Korfmann, M. (1991) Troia – Reinigungs- und Dokumentationsarbeiten 1987, Ausgrabungen 1988, 1989. *Studia Troica* 1: 1–34.

Korfmann, M. (1992) Die prähistorische Besiedlung südlich der Burg Troia VI/VII. *Studia Troica* 2: 123–46.

Korfmann, M.(1993a) Troia und Atlantis. Antike Welt: 45.

Korfmann, M. (1993b) Troia – Ausgrabungen 1992. Studia Troica 3: 1–37.

Korfmann, M. (1994) Die Schatzfunde in Moskau – ein erster Eindruck. *Antike Welt* 25.

Korfmann, M. (1995) Troia: a residential and trading city at the Dardanelles. In R. Laffineur and W.-D. Niemeier (eds) *Politeia: Society and State in the Aegean Bronze Age*: 173–184. Liège.

Korfmann, M. (1996) Troia – Ausgrabungen 1995. *Studia Troica* 6: 1–64.

Korfmann, M. (1997) Troia – Ausgrabungen 1996. Studia Troica 7: 1–71.

Kraft, J.C., Kayan, I. and Erol, O. (1982) Geology and paleogeographic reconstructions of the vicinity of Troy. In G. Rapp and J.A. Gifford (eds) *Troy. The Archaeological Geology*: 11–41. Princeton, Princeton University Press.

Leaf, W. (1912) *Troy. A Study in Homeric Geography.* London, Macmillan.

Leaf, W. (1923) *Strabo: On the Troad.* Cambridge, Cambridge University Press.

Leiermann, H. (1994) *Technische Rekonstruktion der Planung alter Städte.* Stuttgart, Karl Krämer.

Lenz, C. G. (1798) *Die Ebene von Troia.* Neu-Strelitz, Michaelis.

Luce, J.V. (1984) The homeric topography of Troy reconsidered. *Oxford Journal of Archaeology* 3 (1): 31–43.

Luce, J.V. (1995) *Archäologie auf den Spuren Homers.* Bergisch Gladbach, Gustav Lübbe Verlag.

Mandel, R.D. (1994) Holocene landscape evolution in the Pawnee river valley, southwestern Kansas. *Kansas Geological Survey Bulletin* 236: 1–117.

Mannsperger, B. (1995) Die Funktion des Grabens am Schiffslager der Achäer. *Studia Troica* 5: 343–56.

Mauduit, A. F. (1840) *Découvertes dans la Troade.* Paris.

Mayer, L., McFadden, L.D. and Harden, J.W. (1988) Distribution of calcium carbonate in desert soils: a model. *Geology* 16: 303–6.

McFadden, L.D. and Hendricks, D.M. (1985) Changes in the content and composition of pedogenic iron oxyhydroxides in a chronosequence of soils in southern California. *Quaternary Research* 23: 189–204.

Mey, O. (1926) *Das Schlachtfeld vor Troja: Eine Untersuchung.* Berlin; Verlag Walter de Gruyter.

Mulholland, S.C., Rapp, G. and Gifford, J.A. (1982) Phytoliths. In G. Rapp and J.A. Gifford (eds) *Troy. The Archaeological Geology*: 117–37. Princeton, Princeton University Press.

Müller (1798) Über das Lokal der Illiade. In C. G. Lenz (ed) *Die Ebene von Troja*: 132–43. Neu-Strelitz, Michaelis.

Nordt, L.C., Boutton, T.W., Hallmark, C.T. and Waters, M.R. (1994) Late Quaternary vegetation and climate changes in central Texas based on the isotopic composition of organic carbon. *Quaternary Research* 41: 109–20.

Obermeier, S.F., Jacobson, R.B., Smoot, J.P., Weems, R.E., Gohn, G.S., Monroe, J.E. and Powar, D.S. (1990) Earthquake induced liquefaction features in the coastal setting of south Carolina and in the fluvial setting of the New Madrid Seismic Zone. *United States Geological Survey Professional Paper* 1504: 1–44.

Paquet, H. and Millot, G. (1973) Geochemical evolution of clay minerals in the weathered products and soils of the Mediterranean region. In J.M. Serratosa (ed) *Proceedings of the International Clay Conference, Madrid. 23–30 June 1972*: 199–206. Madrid, Division Ciencias, CSIC.

Pope, K.O. and van Andel, Tj.H. (1984) Late Quaternary alluviation and soil formation in the southern Argolid: Its history, causes and archaeological implications. *Journal of Archaeological Science* 11: 281–306.

Raban, A. (1997) Near Eastern harbours: 13th-7th centuries BCE. In S. Gittin, A. Mazar and E. Stein (eds) *Mediterranean People in Transition – 13th to Early 10th centuries BCE.* Jerusalem.

Rapp, G. (1982) Earthquakes in the Troad. In G. Rapp and J.A. Gifford (eds) *Troy. The Archaeological Geology*: 43–58. Princeton, Princeton University Press.

Rapp, G. and Kraft, J.C. (1994) Holocene coastal change in Greece and Aegean Turkey. In P. Nick Kardulias (ed.) *Beyond the Site. Regional Studies in the Aegean Area*: 69–90. New York, University Press of America.

Saucier, R.T. (1991) Geoarchaeological evidence of strong prehistoric earthquakes in the New Madrid (Missouri) Seismic Zone. *Geology* 19: 296–8.

Schede, M. (1930) Anatolien. *Archäologischer Anzeiger* 44: 358–68.

Schliemann, H. (1880) *Ilios: The City and Country of the Trojans.* London, John Murray.

Siebler, M. (1994) Der allererste Weltkrieg. In M. Siebler (ed.) *Troia. Geschichte,Grabungen, Kontroversen*: 115–6. Mainz, Philipp von Zabern.

Singer, M.J. and Janitzky, P. (1986) Field and laboratory procedures used in a soil chronosequence study. *United States Geological Survey Bulletin* 1648.

Snodgrass, A. (1987) *An Archaeology of Greece: The Present State and Future Scope of a Discipline.* Berkeley, University of California Press.

Soil Survey Division Staff (1993) *Soil Survey Manual.* Washington, D.C., United States Government Printing Office, United States Department of Agriculture Handbook 18.

Timpson, M.E. (1992) *An Investigation of the Pedogenesis of Soils Developed in Quaternary Alluvial Deposits of Eastern Crete.* PhDdissertation,Knoxville, University of Tennessee.

Timpson, M.E. and Foss, J.E. (1993) The use of particle-size analysis as a tool in pedological investigations of archaeological sites. In J.E. Foss, M.E. Timpson and M.W. Morris (eds) *Proceedings of the First International Conference on Pedo-Archaeology*: 69–80. Knoxville, Tennessee.

Timpson, M.E., Lee, S.Y., Ammons, J.T. and Foss, J.E. (1996) Mineralogical investigation of soils formed in calcareous gravelly alluvium, eastern Crete, Greece. *Soil Science Society of America, Journal* 60: 299–308.

van Zeist, W., Timmers, R.W. and Bottema, S. (1970) Studies of modern and Holocene pollen precipitation in southeastern Turkey. *Palaeohistoria* 14: 19–39.

van Zeist, W., Woldring, H. and Stapert, D. (1975) Late Quaternary vegetation and climate of southwestern Turkey. *Palaeohistoria* 17: 53–143.

Webb, T. (1974) Corresponding patterns of pollen and vegetation in Lower Michigan: a comparison of quantitative data. *Ecology* 55: 17–28.

Webb, T., Howe, S.E., Bradshaw, R.H.W. and Heide, K.M. (1981) Estimating plant abundances from pollen percentages: the use of regression analysis. *Review of Paleobotany and Palynology* 34: 269–300.

Wright, H.E. (1972) Vegetation history. In W.A. McDonald and G. Rapp (eds) *The Minnesota Messenia Expedition: Reconstructing a Bronze Age Environment*: 188–99. Minneapolis, University of Minnesota Press.

Wright, H.E., McAndrews, J.H. and Van Zeist, W. (1967) Modern pollen rain in western Iran, and its relation to plant geography and Quaternary vegetational history. *Journal of Ecology* 55: 415–33.

Yazvenko, S.B. (1991) Modern pollen-vegetation relationships on the southeastern Caucasus. *Grana* 30: 350–6.

Zangger, E. (1992) *The Flood from Heaven. Deciphering the Atlantis Legend*. London, Sidgwick and Jackson.

Zangger, E. (1993) *The Geoarchaeology of the Argolid*. Berlin, Gebrüder Mann Verlag.

Zangger, E. (1994) *Ein neuer Kampf um Troia*. Munich, Droemer.

Zangger, E. (1995) Geology and the development of the cultural landscape. In S. Dietz, L.L. Sebai and H. Hassen (eds) *Africa Proconsularis. Regional Studies in the Segermes Valley of Northern Tunisia*: 57–83. Copenhagen, The Carlsberg Foundation and The Danish Research Council for the Humanities.

Zangger, E. and Malz, H. (1989) Late Pleistocene, Holocene, and recent ostracodes from the Gulf of Argos, Greece. *Courier Forschungsinstitut Senckenberg* 113: 159–75.

Zangger, E., Yazvenko, S.B., Timpson, M.E., Kuhnke, F. and Knauss, J. (1997a) The Pylos Regional Archaeological Project, Part II: landscape evolution and site preservation. *Hesperia* 66 (4).

Zangger, E., Leiermann, H., Noack, W. and Kuhnke, F. (1997b) A 21st century approach to the reconnaissance and reconstruction of archaeological landscapes. In P. N. Kardulias and Mark T. Shutes (eds) *Aegean Strategies: Studies of Culture and Environment on the European Fringe*: 9–32. Savage, Rowman and Littlefield.

Zick, M. (1997) Neuer Streit um die Wiege unserer Kultur. Bild der Wissenschaft 12/97: 52–58.

11. Case Studies from the Pontine Region in Central Italy on Settlement and Environmental Change in the First Millennium BC

Peter Attema, Jan Delvigne, and Berndt-Jan Haagsma

INTRODUCTION

This contribution intends to illustrate the importance of local environmental reconstruction for the interpretation of archaeological data. The data derive from field work that was carried out since 1987 as part of the Pontine Region Project (PRP). This project includes landscape and archaeological surveys of sample areas in the Pontine Region, about 60 km south of Rome in the province of Lazio (Figs. 11.1 and 11.2). Fieldwork before 1991 has been published in Attema (1993).

From the beginning, the strategy of the project was to combine environmental and archaeological field data – the topic of this contribution – with cartographical, historical, and ethnographical information. It was felt that these sources together would furnish a sound basis for diachronic reconstructions of the ways in which the varied landscapes of the Pontine Region were used in the past. The archaeological interest of the project is the development of Latial society from the Late Bronze Age to the Roman Imperial period (*c.* 1000 BC-AD 400).

Physiographically, three major landscape types can be delineated. The first is the dissected landscape belonging to the volcanic system of the Colli Albani, which borders the Pontine plain to the northwest. It is the landscape in which the Latin society of the Iron Age developed. The second is the Pontine plain, a *graben* filled with lagoonal deposits (notoriously marshy before the wholesale land reclamations of the late 1920s), separated from the Tyrrhenian sea by a system of beach ridges. In the history of sedentary settlement of the Pontine Region, this landscape was only put to marginal use. Thirdly, there is the zone of the Lepini and Ausoni mountains. Economic and political control of its foothills and slopes became increasingly important from early Roman times onwards.

The above characterization is, however, a highly simplified image of a far more dynamic and diverse reality. Naturally, the human activities were not limited to any one of the above-mentioned landscapes during the various episodes of the settlement history of the Pontine Region: human landscapes are not necessarily defined by the natural environment, nor are they equivalent to 'our' physiographic landscapes or 'our' regions. On the contrary, the archaeology and history of settlement and land use in the Pontine region reveal ever new combinations of landscape elements to be in use, over time resulting in a palimpsest of 'superimposed' landscapes. These were not only defined by functionalist categories (subsistence, technology, resources), but also by ideological ones (tradition, religion, power relationships), with environmental change affecting both.

Since the theme of the volume is landscape archaeology and environmental reconstruction, we present three case studies that illustrate the interplay between environmental and archaeological data in reconstructing and interpreting settlement and land use patterns in the first millennium BC. Case studies 1 and 2 are concerned with erosion and sedimentation episodes roughly pin-pointed in time using archaeological dating (ceramics) and radiocarbon dating. Case study 3 considers a pollen diagram in relation to a specific Roman Republican settlement pattern.

CASE 1: MUDFLOW SEDIMENTS NEAR THE SITE OF CARACUPA/VALVISCIOLO

Outline of the case-study

Some aspects of sedimentation in the survey area were investigated on a location in the plain beneath the Roman colony of Norba, near the Latin settlement of Caracupa Valvisciolo. An exposure in a foundation pit revealed mudflow deposits on top of colluvial deposits. This case of environmental change bears directly upon the landscape potential of this particular part of the plain. As such, it helps to reconstruct the local environment of the protohistoric settlement of Caracupa Valvisciolo. The exposure also contained features of direct archaeological interest.

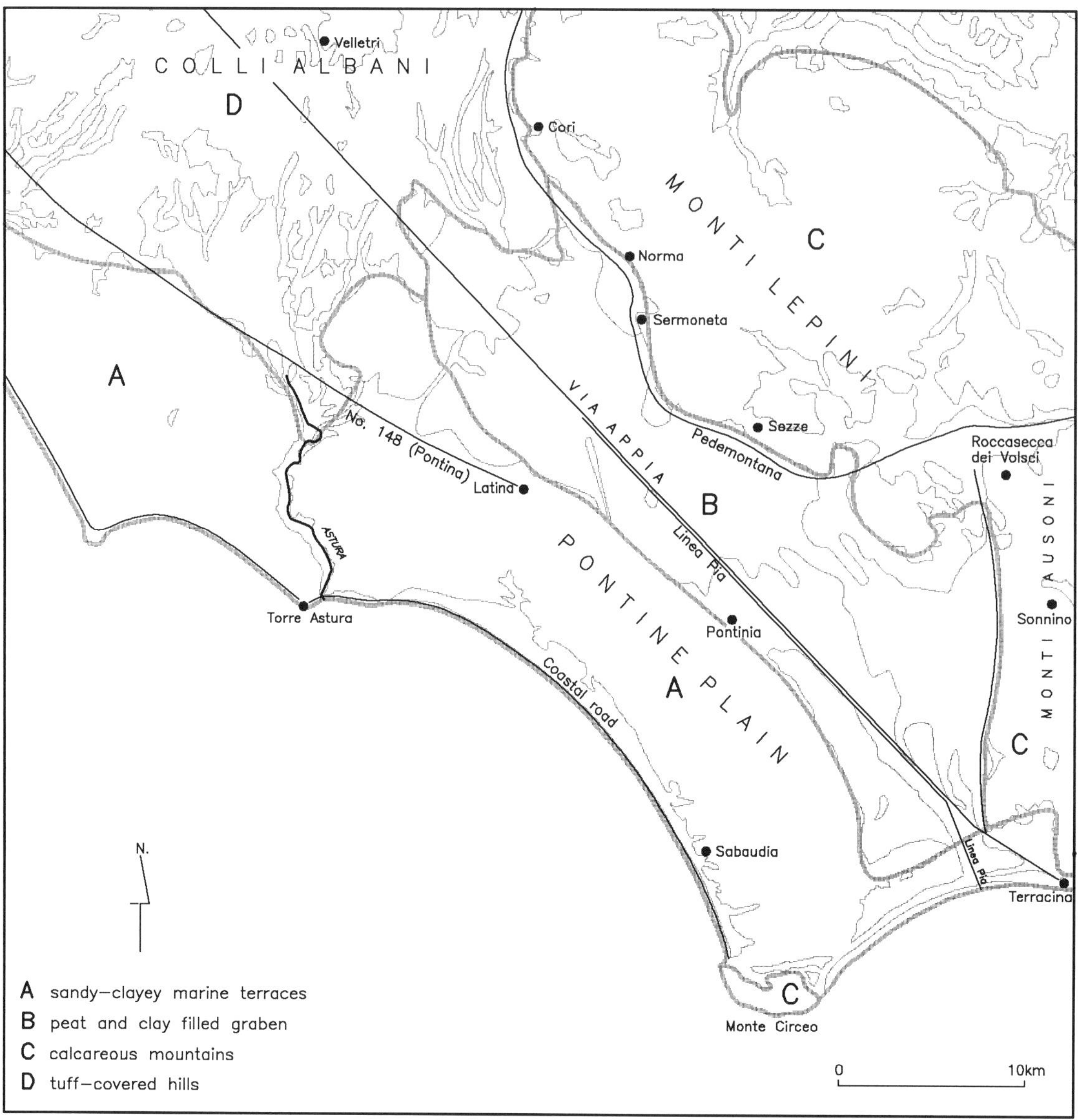

Fig. 11.1. Location map of Pontine Region Project (PRP) study area.

Location

The pit is situated to the north of the hamlet of Pontenuovo in the Contrada Trentossa, on a tongue of the alluvial fan emerging from the valley of Vado La Mola, southeast of Norma. The tongue is surrounded and underlain by colluvial deposits that cover the plain in a southeasterly direction. It forms a ridge with a length of 1 km and a width of about 300 m and protrudes up to 4 m above the surrounding landscape (Fig. 11.3). Hand augering revealed a layer of limestone gravel beginning at less than 0.90 m in the central part of the ridge. The gravelly sediment disappeared on the lower flanks of the ridge. The pit measured *c.*10 x 15 m, with a depth of 2.5 m, exposing the soil stratigraphy near the axis of the ridge. Three of the four sides were described (Fig. 11.4). A narrow trench had been dug to drain the pit into a nearby ditch. Both trench and ditch showed interesting phenomena as well.

Description of the soil profiles

To investigate the nature of sedimentation, primary attention was paid to the texture of the sediments. The lower part of the profile consisted of uniform reddish brown clay; in the upper part this clay was stratified with a varying content of gravel and stones. Layers with gravel between 0.2 mm and 5 cm and layers with stones larger than 5 cm are represented by different symbols in the profile drawings. Gravel and stones, all limestone, were moderately rounded. Sandy sediments are represented in the profile drawings by a separate symbol. The sand was hardly rounded and had a dark hue due to the high content of volcanic minerals. Darker soil material indicating organic matter, together

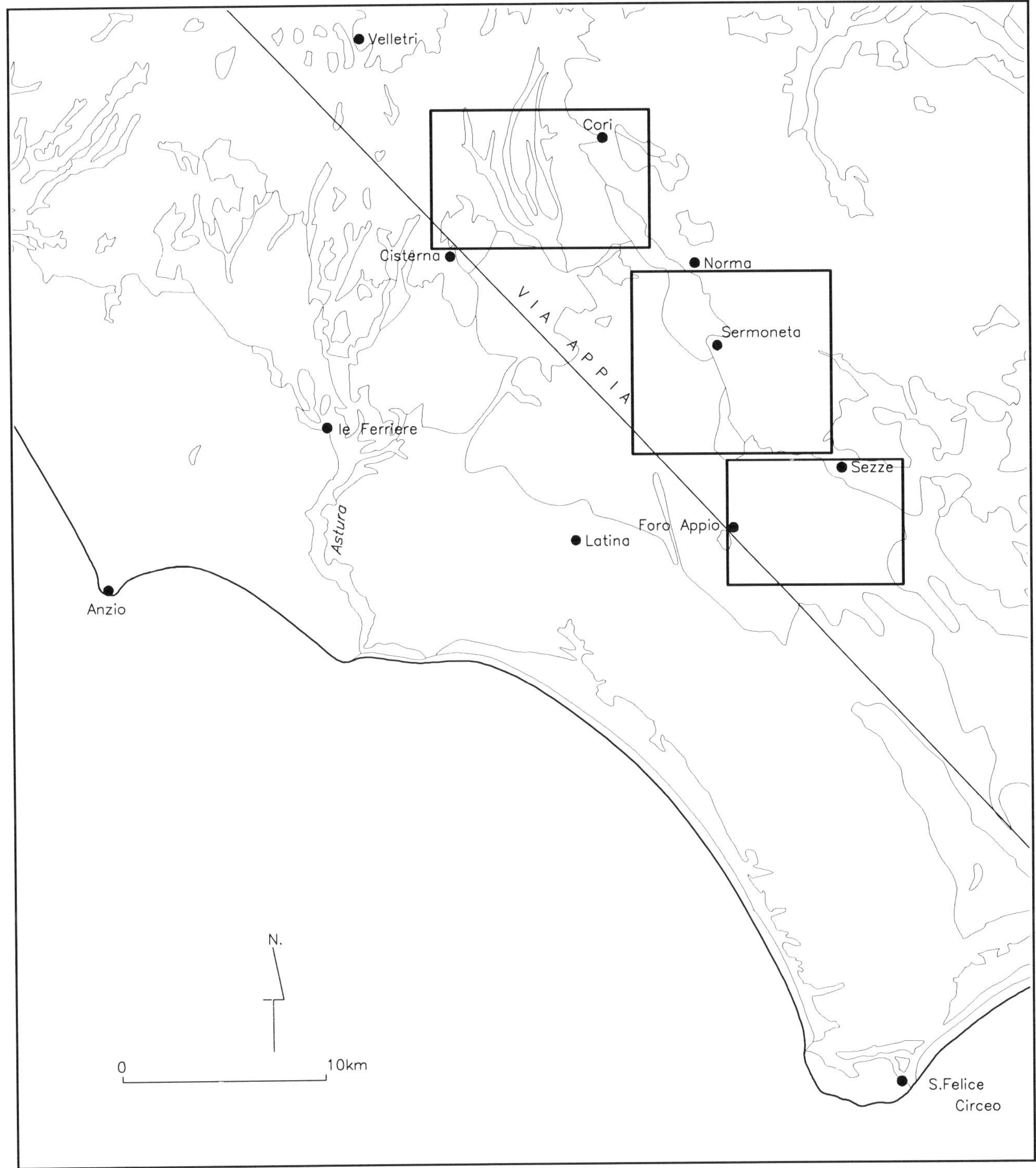

Fig. 11.2. Sample areas of the PRP in the study area.

with the recently ploughed or disturbed and somewhat darker topsoil, are also shown in the drawings. The letters denoting the separate layers do not correlate across the three sides of the pit (Fig. 11.5).

The sedimentation mechanism

The absence of sedimentary stratification and the oxydized colour in the lowest stratum visible in the pit are characteristic of colluviation (Sevink *et al.*, 1984). The sandy layer G and layer F in the northwest section (Fig. 11.5A), consisting of gravel and stones, indicates streamflow. The layers F and G may, in longitudinal section, be the fill of a gully. The sedimentation mechanism which resulted in loose gravel imbedded in a matrix of clay would have been a mudflow. A mudflow comes to

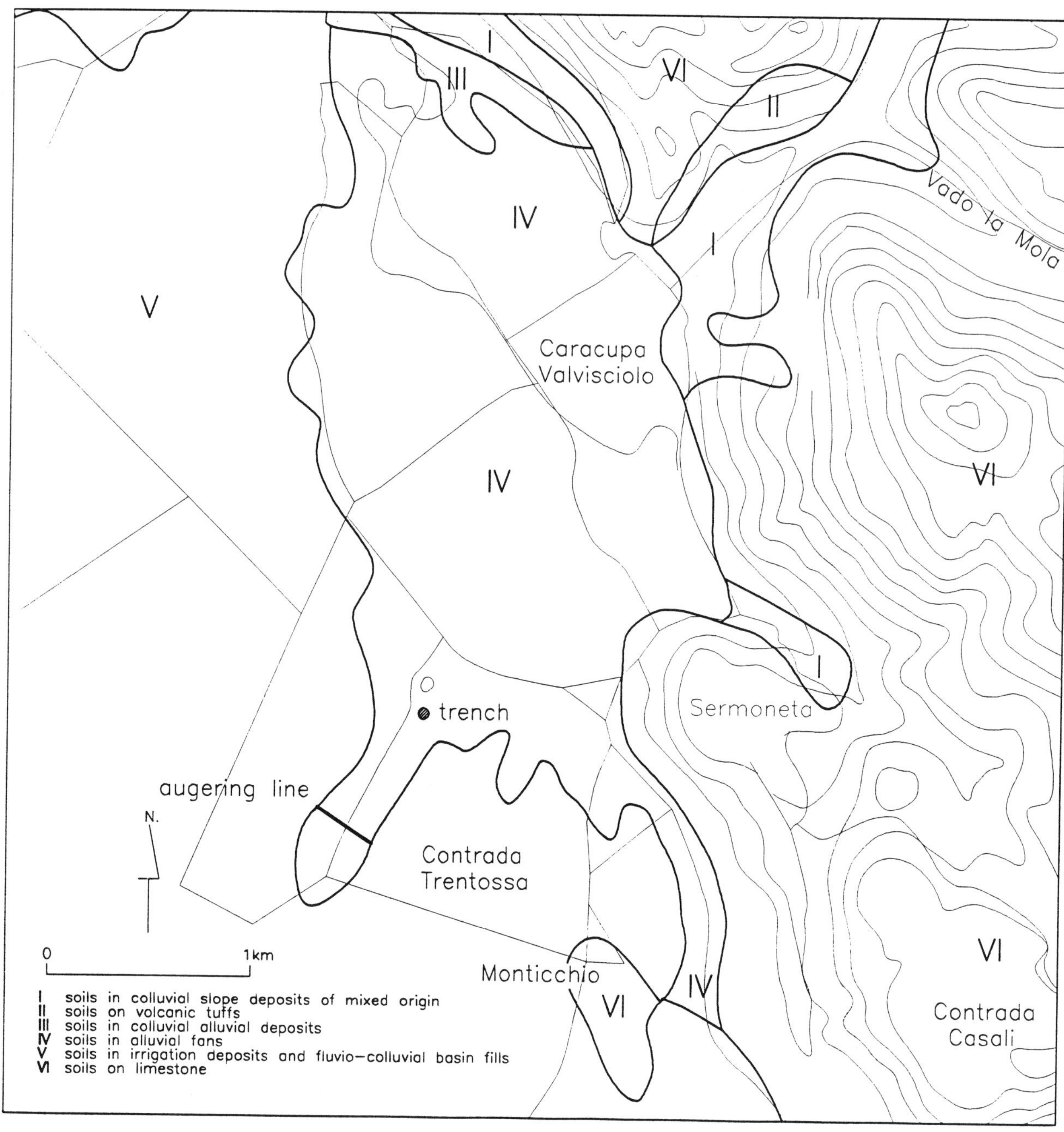

Fig. 11.3. Soil map of the Contrada Trentossa, showing the alluvial fan environment and the location of the investigated trench.

rest when the front of the mass has insufficient energy to continue moving downslope, in which case no selective sedimentation takes place. According to Costa (1984), mudflows move in a series of surges that deposit unstructured layers. Temporarily and locally they may, due to increased water content, transform into water flows. Mudflows and debris flows play an important role in the formation of the upper part of alluvial fans, especially in drier climates. The mudflows partly follow river gullies and spread out onto the alluvial fan surface in lobes (Beatty, 1974; Bull, 1977). The soil profile visible in the ditch, 101 m long, shows that the layers with gravel gradually become thinner and disappear from the profile down the flank of the tongue, with only the ploughzone still containing some gravel.

In a broader environmental context, the correlation between topography and sediment may be explained as follows. From the valley opening of Vado La Mola, some two kilometers away, mixtures of clay, gravel and water were thick enough to flow like tongues onto the slightly

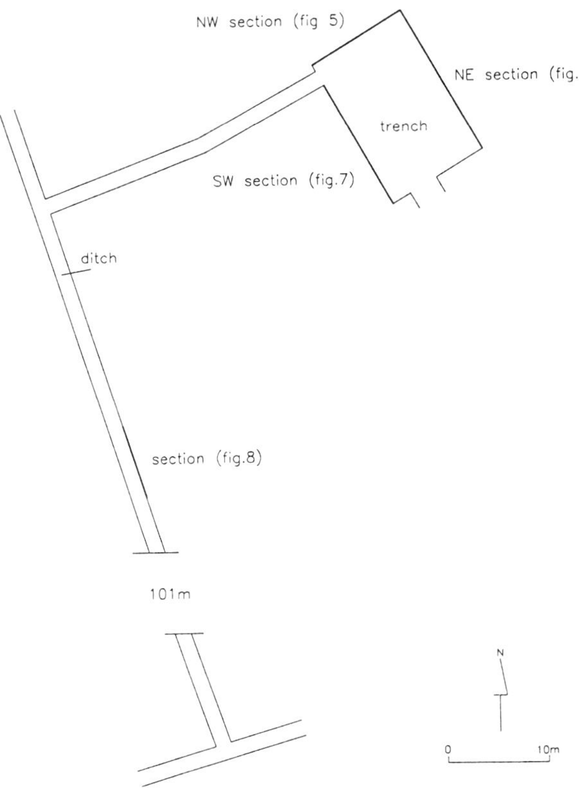

Fig. 11.4. Map of the Contrada Trentossa trench showing location of the sections of Figure 11.5.

sloping fan. At the point where a mudflow came to a standstill, fine material washed out at its sides. The transition between the soils in alluvial fans (IV) and the colluvium (V) can be interpreted according to this process (Fig. 11.3).

Landscape development

A change from colluviation to mudflow sedimentation, as shown by the sharp boundary in the pit, may indicate erosion of more and coarser material from the slopes in the hinterland. It is tempting to relate this change in sedimentation to human activities, because the mudflow can be dated to protohistory on archaeological grounds and a substantial protohistoric settlement, Caracupa/ Valvisciolo, was located near the valley opening, as has been attested by the archaeological survey. As a result of vegetational denudation of the mountain slopes, erosion would have increased and more material delivered to the river channel. From the seventh century BC onward, the need for wood (for building materials, fuel for kilns, fuel for iron smelting) would have steadily increased and also grazing will have had a serious impact on the natural vegetation. Possible (auxiliary) causes, such as climatic change or tectonic movements, however, should not be excluded. It is also possible that only the transport route of mudflows changed into this direction. Either case signifies, however, a change in the local environment of the Contrada Trentossa.

The darker colour of the clay layer beginning at a depth of 40–60 cm is caused by a higher humus content, corresponding to an old land surface. In Figure 11.6 the sedimentological and pedological chronology of the profiles is represented schematically. The lowest time boundary represents the transition to gravel containing mudflows. This process is relevant for all of the area that in Figure 11.3 is indicated as alluvial fan. Indirectly, the boundary may be indicative of a change in the environment from which the material originated. The second time boundary indicates a stable phase in the landscape. There are no clues yet as to how widespread this stable phase was over the region.

The archaeological interpretation

The pottery fragments collected from the various sections have been indicated in the drawings by numbers in the profiles and were published in Attema *et al.* (1990). The earliest fragments are of *impasto rosso,* dating to the seventh century BC. A number of fragments, including tiles, dates to the sixth century BC. To the fourth century BC and later belong a black glazed fragment and fragments of pottery and tile of depurated clay. Post-Roman ceramics do not occur in the sections. This corresponds to the surface finds collected during survey in the Contrada Trentossa. Sherds found in the lowest level of the mudflow sediment date to the protohistoric period (Fig. 11.6).

Layers F and G in the northwest section of the pit which, as stated above, most likely represent a longitudinal section of a gully fill, must have been deposited during or after the seventh century BC (Fig. 11.5A). The subsequent layers E, D and C in the northwest profile, and E and D in the northeast profile (Fig. 11.5B), which are regarded as mudflow sediments, were probably deposited towards the end of Republican times. In these layers both Archaic and Roman Republican sherds occur, whereas later material is absent. The fill of the gullies in the clay on the eastern flank of the ridge visible in the ditch may also be dated to this period on the basis of their ceramics. Sherds from both periods occur also in the upper strata, including the topsoil.

The degree of wear on the ceramics can be linked to stable and unstable periods. The sherds in the fill were, without exception, worn and rounded, which indicates transport by water, as does the texture of the sediments in which they were found. The degree of wear on the sherds in the upper layers, including the topsoil, varied, however, indicating that, during the first stable period with soil development, those sherds that are not worn were added *in situ* by human activity. These sherds were probably mixed with the worn sherds of the sediment by ploughing. Apart from the organic content of layers C and D in the sections in the trench, the homogeneous distribution of gravel and sherds in these layers points to ploughing.

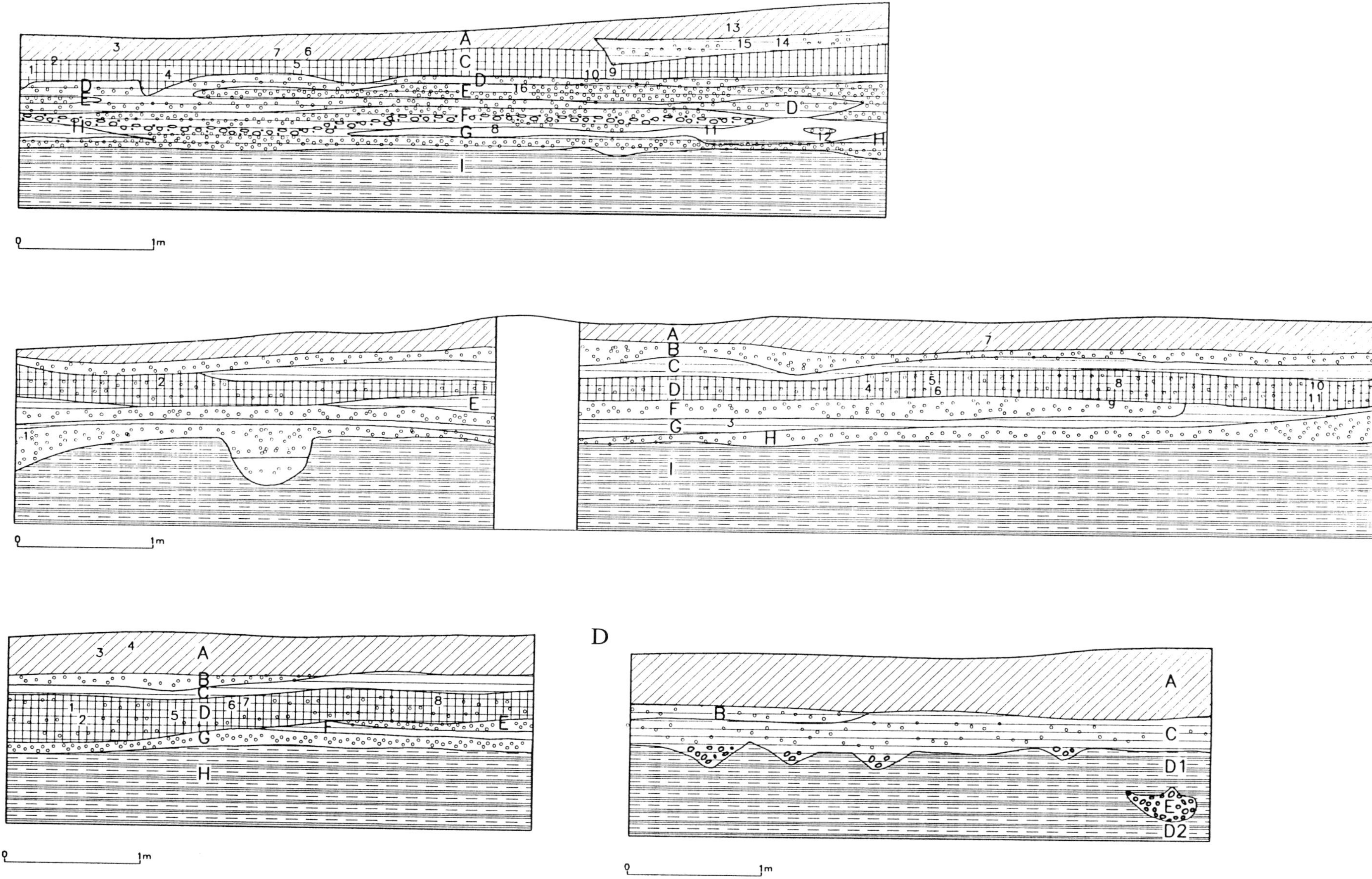

Fig. 11.5. Contrada Trentossa trench: A.northwest section; B. northeast section; C. southwest section; D. section from the wall of the ditch, showing furrow marks.

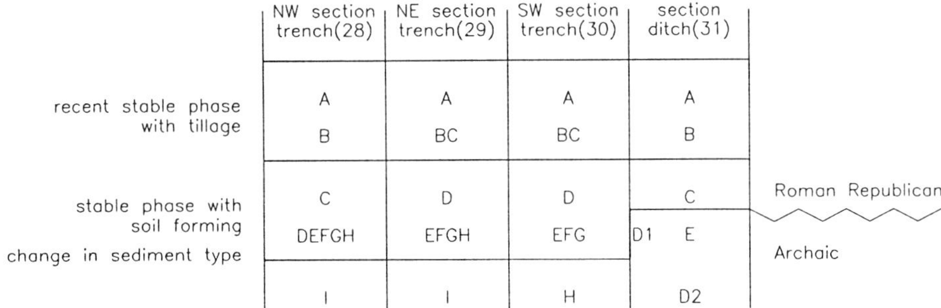

NW section trench(28)
NE section trench(29)
SW section trench(30)
section ditch(31)
recent stable phase with tillage
stable phase with soil forming
change in sediment type
A
B
BC
C
D
DEFGH
EFGH
EFG
D1
E
I
H
D2
Roman Republican
Archaic

Fig. 11.6. The sedimentological and pedological chronology of the trench and ditch sections.

Traces of cultivation of the soil in antiquity

Other indications of cultivation were noted in a section of the ditch profile (Fig. 11.5D). Over a length of 50 m in the northwestern part, V-shaped furrows can be seen in layer C cutting into the clay layer D. The gravel in the furrows is denser and coarser-textured than the remainder of the layer, which is characterized by an uniform distribution of gravel. The furrows are *c.*0.30 m deep and occur at irregular intervals of 1 m apart on the average. It is hard to explain these features other than through human activity (ploughing). In the southeast profile of the pit (not mapped) there were four of these V-shaped features, with a depth of *c.*0.30 m at intervals of *c.*0.75 m. Comparable soil features were mapped by De La Blanchère (1889: 199). The colour of the clay in these features is somewhat darker than in the layer underneath. Stratigraphically, layer C in the ditch may correspond to the organic layer observed in the sections in the pit (C and D in Fig. 11.5B–D).

A final indication of human activity was found in the gully and its fill in the northeast section of the trench. The gully cuts 0.60 m into clay layer I (Fig. 11.5B). It has steep straight sides and a fluvial fill. The almost vertical sides indicate that this is an artificial channel. The lower part of the fill consists of stratified layers of sand. The upper part consists of silts and clays with pebbles and gravel and is presumably a mudflow deposit, which may have eroded some of the fluvial deposits. The mudflow deposit spills out of the gully on either side. The form of the gully points to human construction, whereas stratigraphy dates it to pre-Roman times.

CASE STUDY 2: THE FLUVIO-COLLUVIAL DEPOSITS IN THE PLAIN OF ANCIENT SETIA

The fluvio-colluvial basin fill

Most of the soils in the Sezze survey area are mapped as being developed in a fluvio-colluvial basin fill. These sediments cover the plain from beneath Norma to the Sezze area and from the lower slopes of the mountains to the Via Appia. Unlike the large complex that occurs along the river Amaseno in the southeastern part of the Agro Pontino, the basin fill in this area extends longitudinally onto the plain. Near the modern Via Appia, the colluvial sheet splits into two tongues that cover the lagoonal deposits beyond the Via Appia in a southeasterly direction (Fig. 11.7). Towards the Via Appia, the deposit decreases in thickness. According to the latest publication by Sevink, Duivenvoorden and Kamermans on the soils of the Agro Pontino, the basin fills in the area of study all belong to the first and very extensive class of late Holocene sediments (Voorrips *et al.*, 1991: 41). It is stated that the upper few metres were probably formed under human influence, largely during early Roman times. The recent basin fill is described as predominantly fine to very fine textured, with a brown to reddish-brown colour. These sediments are thought to be connected to distinct artificial water courses, presently filled in with well-stratified sandy to gravelly sediments, with a high content of volcanic material.

Sedimentation mechanisms

The sediments in question were initially interpreted as irrigation deposits, that is, sediments from irrigation and drainage waters, running through humanly-made canals (Sevink *et al.*, 1984: 23). Later it was suggested that they represent colmatage deposits, sediments resulting from people redirecting river channels deliberately to silt up marshy areas (Sevink, 1985: 41). The highly varying thickness of the sediments is mentioned as evidence in support of this. Where the sediments extend into the marshy lagoonal area, beyond the Via Appia, their thickness is closely related to the distance to a canal or river.

From cartographical and historical sources, it is indeed likely that the many canals and ditches belonging to past reclamation schemes have played an important part in the sedimentation process. During these reclamations, waterways were diverted and dikes were thrown up. During periods of neglect, the ditches and canals silted up and the fine material carried by the inundating waters were deposited over large areas. There is no evidence as yet that sedimentation in the Pontine plain was provoked by human action. Although colmatage was proposed as a method to

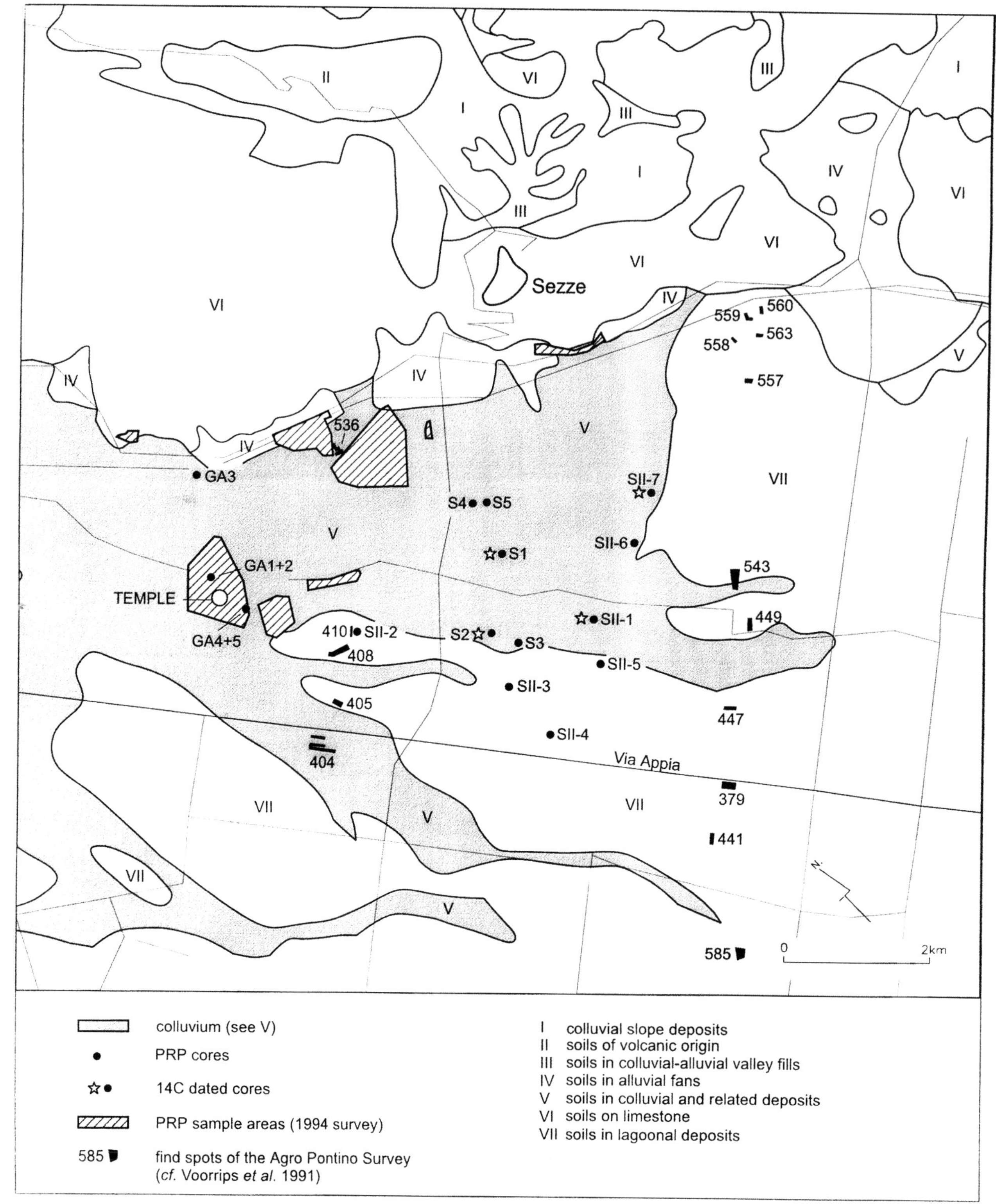

Fig. 11.7. Soil map of the Sezze area showing soil units and augering locations; see Postscript in text for detailed description.

reclaim land, it was never implemented (Attema, 1993: 50). On the contrary, silting up must have been a constant threat to the Via Appia Antica. From texts and cartography it becomes clear that, in the past, inundation rendered the Via Appia Antica impassable at places. Large parts of the Via Appia were at times covered by sediments (Attema, 1993: 42–3). Up to the fascist reclamation, sedimentation in the area must have been a poorly checked, on-going process of landscape change. Evidence from the pit near Contrada Trentossa indicates that the process intensified during the Late Iron Age, changing local conditions for settlement and land use. To investigate the age and composition of the colluvial sheet covering the plain beneath Sezze, and the impact of the cover on archaeological sites and environmental reconstruction in this part of the study area, a programme of hand augering was carried out to collect samples for radiocarbon dating.

Since the colluvial-alluvial sediments do not contain material suitable for radiocarbon dating and pollen analysis, samples of organic material were collected from layers underneath (in 1989, 1990 and 1994). It was found that at places colluvial sediments are separated from the lagoonal clay by a peaty layer varying in thickness and organic content. Unlike the substantial peat accumulation south of Sezze and in the area of Borgo Ermada, the peats here are very local as well as clayey. Sevink *et al.* (1984) discern two major areas of peat accumulation in the Agro Pontino: one south of Sezze – where peat deposits of 4 m thickness are common – and another near Borgo Ermada.

Radiocarbon dates

Fortunately, the samples S1 and S2 and SII-1 and SII-7 contained enough organic material for conventional ^{14}C dating (Figs. 11.7, 11.8). The samples used for dating were taken from the uppermost part of the layers underlying the colluvial sediments, thus providing local *post quem* dates for the formation of the deposit. The samples indicate that *c*.2000 BC the colluvium had not yet covered the landscape. Sherds found in the plough zone furnished at several places a possible *terminus ante quem*. Surface finds consisted of Roman Republican debris and possibly some earlier material as well. Further soil investigations were carried out on that part of the colluvial deposit that, according to the soil map, is related physiographically to the alluvial fans below Sezze. Surveyed fields in this area yielded much material related to Republican villas, whereas late Archaic material was found more widespread, but in much smaller amounts (Attema, 1993: 133–8). At places, the colluvial sediment contained ceramic fragments down to a considerable depth.

During the campaign of October 1990, more samples were taken in order to date the colluvium to the southeast. The results indicated that *c*.1800 BC, in the direction of the Pontine marshes proper, colluvium not yet covered the location of augering SII-1; the location SII-7 was not yet covered by 1000 BC. In both cases the actual date would have been considerably later, since the samples were taken at 0.15 m (SII-1) and 0.30 m (SII-7) beneath the colluvial layer (Figs. 11.7 and 11.8, and see the detailed descriptions at the end of this chapter).

Soil stratigraphy and surface archaeological remains

Further augerings were carried out near known archaeological features of Republican date. The cores at the Roman bridge known as Gli Archi (the river channel over which it was built is not visible in the present-day landscape) were taken in a field where much Republican material had been collected during survey. The colluvial clay contained archaeological material down to a depth of 1.05 m, allowing dating of the uppermost layer of the colluvium on this location. From 1.80 m downwards, the core showed a 2 cm thick sandy layer indicating fluvial activity, followed by another layer of colluvial clay.

Cores were also taken in front of the temple of Juno (GA4 and 5 in Fig. 11.8). The area is scattered with artefacts of late Archaic and Republican date. Ceramic fragments were found in the cores to depths between 0.85 m and 1.10 m. One core contained particles of charcoal from 1.10 to 1.50 m, but not enough for conventional ^{14}C dating. An excavation in 1985 (unfortunately not yet published) underneath the temple revealed a late bronze age/early iron age layer at a depth of *c*.1.50 m. In 1994 an intensive survey in the area around the temple was undertaken and further environmental research carried out. The preliminary results are given below.

Sedimentation rates

As stated, cores taken in the survey area at Sezze revealed peaty layers marking the transition between lagoonal and colluvial clays (Figs.11.7 and 11.8). These layers were radiocarbon-dated, providing *post quem* dates for the colluvium and *ante quem* dates for the lagoonal sediment. The ^{14}C dates range between the second millennium BC and the start of the first millennium BC. Therefore our environmental attention in the Sezze area is focussed upon the colluvial/alluvial sediments, as they may have had a direct impact on conditions of settlement and land use during the archaeological periods studied by our project.

Table 11.1 shows average sedimentation rates based on sediment thickness, *post quem* dates, and time elapsed since the dates given. It should be realized, however, that these rates have a limited relation to reality, based as they are on the unlikely assumption of a regular and undisturbed sedimentation. The method only calculates accumulation of sediments, and does not consider possible variations caused by soil erosion. However, the rates given, rough as they are, show considerable local differences. The rates at Monticchio and the Republican temple of Juno are disproportionately higher than the rates lower down the plain.

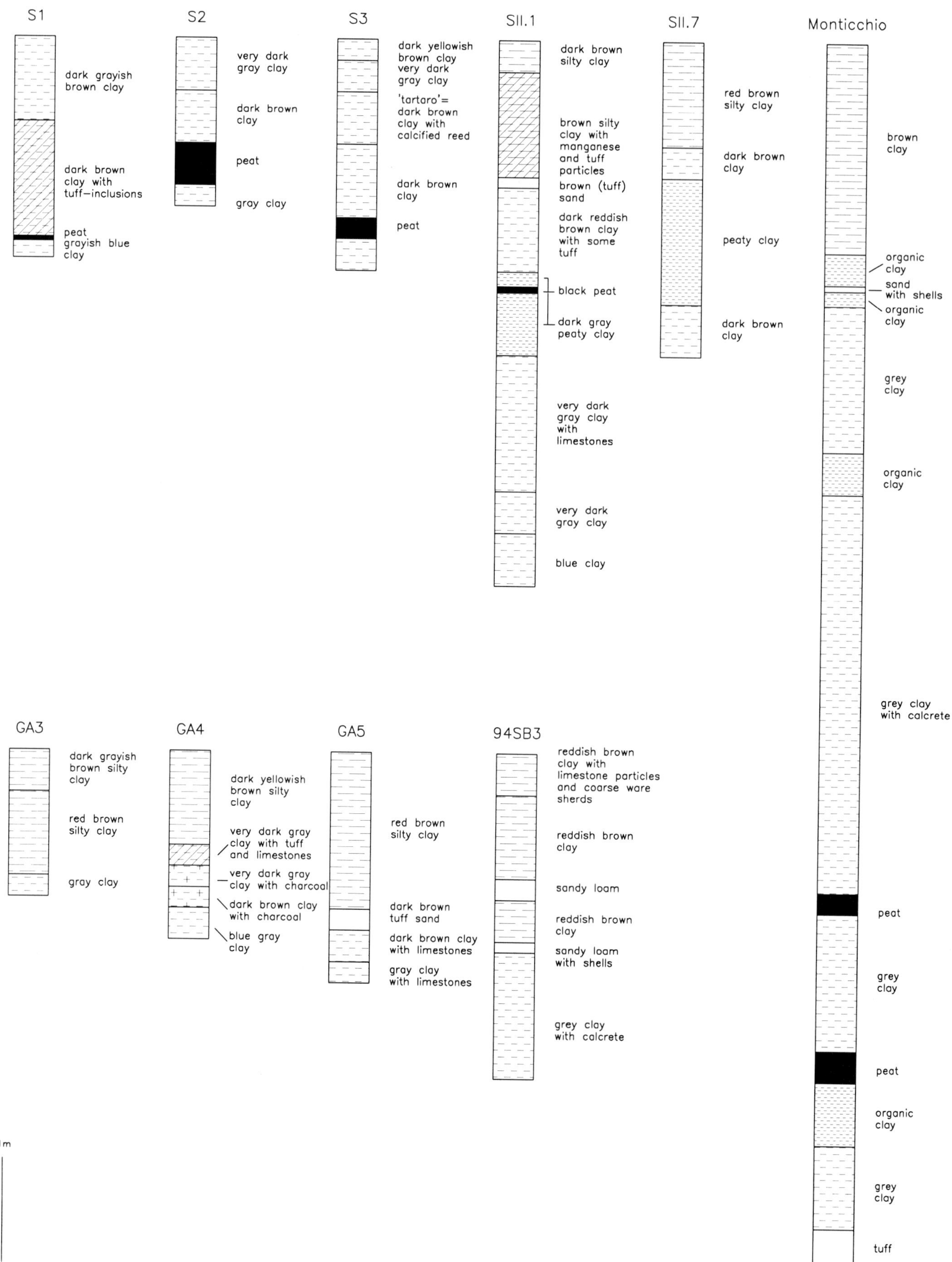

Fig. 11.8. Cores in the Sezze, Norba and Cori area; see Postcript in text for detailed description.

Cores	sample depth	calibration	GrN number	sedimentation rate (cm/100 yrs)
colluvium:				
sezze 1	180	4160±80 BP	GrN–18435	ca. 4.3
sezze 2	102	4220±100 BP	GrN–18436	ca. 2.4
sezze II–1	231	3735±100 BP	GrN–18439	ca. 6.2
sezze II–7	132	2760±110 BP	GrN–18440	ca. 4.8
temple core	150	1000 BC (archaeological date)		ca. 5.0
basin fills:				
Le Ferriere 92–1	110	500±50 BP	GrN–19560	ca. 22.0
Le Ferriere 92–II	140	585±50 BP	GrN–19561	ca. 24.0
Monticchio 2	226	2090±30 BP	GrN–18437	ca. 10.8

Table 11.1. Sedimentation rates of cores from the Pontine Region.

For Monticchio this is straightforward, since it is a local depression in which much sediment accumulated, as the Monticchio pollen core has shown (see Case Study 3 below).

The Juno temple, however, presents a particular case, possibly being situated on a fill of a former water course. Excavations by the Antiquario Comunale di Sezze and the Sopraintendenza per il Lazio proved the location of the temple of Juno to have a stratigraphy with, at a depth of 150 cm, a sandy layer (alluvial?) containing many bronze age/early iron age ceramics dating to *c.*1000 BC, and bones. This stratum was covered by an archaeologically-sterile layer consisting of reddish brown silty clay (colluvial) continuing below the temple for *c.*110 cm.. Our augerings in the immediate surroundings showed a 40-cm thick plough zone of reddish brown clay containing a large amount of Roman ceramics dating from the fourth century BC to the first century BC, followed by archaeologically-sterile colluvial clay. Set against the average sedimentation rates as shown in Table 11.1, the conclusion must be that a relatively large amount of sediment accumulated on this location from the Iron Age onwards.

Of course these data do not allow for a general hypothesis of sedimentation in a larger area, but still, the local stratigraphy of the temple suggests a period of increased sedimentation coinciding with the first human occupation in the area. On the other hand, the archaeological surveys in the area showed that the Roman Republican level in almost all of the area is not deeper than *c.* 40 cm below the surface, thus being part of the present-day plough zone. This means that, in the period following the Roman Republican period, relatively little sediment was added.

The exploitation of the Sezze territory in Roman times

A limited number of fields investigated in 1987 by the project, along a transect running from the Via Appia to the footslopes of the Monti Lepini to present-day Sezze, was indeed indicative of the strong relationship between landscape characteristics and pottery distribution in the plain of Sezze. On fields that were walked in the area of exposed lagoonal soils, almost no pottery was found in the topsoil. Fields on the colluvial soil units, on the contrary, often had substantial amounts of ceramic artefacts. These were almost invariably Roman Republican in date (Attema, 1993:133–8). The PRP archaeological field observations are corroborated by the evidence of the Agro Pontino Survey (Voorrips *et al.*, 1991: 126) from the same area. Both data sets show the presence of well-defined sites on or near the colluvial soils and the absence of clear sites on the exposed lagoonal soils. Where finds occur on the latter unit, they are suspect. The majority of findspots from the fields surveyed within the transect and sample blocks of both projects is again Roman Republican in date.

During the 1994 campaign of the PRP, an intensive survey was carried out on the colluvial soil unit. A total of 175 fields was walked, equalling 8.4 ha. During survey a total of 33,886 sherds was collected. Accounting for a mean coverage of 29 per cent of the fields, this results in a mean site and off-site density of 1.39 sherds per m^2. The preliminary results of the pottery analysis indicate that by far the larger part of the ceramics dates from the Roman Republican period, that is, within the period *c.*350–50 BC. Although the amalgamation of ceramic densities and artefact scatters into sites has not yet taken place, the fact that 95 fields out of 176 had Roman roof tiles and that ten fields had actual remains of constructions, may be taken as indicative of the immense building activity that took place during this period.

To this picture we should add the archaeological data that over time were acquired by the Antiquario Comunale di Sezze (Zaccheo and Pasquali, 1970, 1972) and the research in the area by Bruckner (1995). The publications of the latter concern substantial Roman villas and cisterns in the territory of Sezze, evidence for a developed Roman road system connecting the area with the Via Appia and the major transit sites along this through road, such as Forum Appi. The data available add up to an impressive wholesale infilling of the landscape following the foundation of the Roman colony of Setia that, according to

Velleius Paterculus (I,14), took place in the year 382 BC.

Pre-Roman remains in the Sezze territory

From the archaeological data it becomes clear that Roman colonization at a rapid pace turned the Sezze territory into a rural production area, probably specializing in the production of olive oil and possibly wine along the foot slopes of the Lepini mountains. Both ecological evidence and the site pattern support this view. The frequency and the distribution of sites in the surveyed fields, in combination with the data on the infrastructure, certainly prove a systematic reclamation and exploitation of the area to have taken place. But to what extent was this an exploitation *ex novo* ?

During the summer of 1985 a team from the Antiquario Comunale di Sezze excavated a votive deposit that was found within the perimeter of the temple. Votive gifts dating from the fourth century BC to the first century AD were recovered, tallying in date with the foundation of Setia in the beginning of the fourth century BC. In the Antiquario Comunale, however, there are also sixth-century BC terracottas on display that were found in a field opposite the temple site. These indicate that the temple site may have been in use well before the historical date of the arrival of the Romans. Together with the Late Bronze Age/Early Iron Age layer below the Roman temple, we have evidence for human activity on this site during most of protohistory, as is the case at so many other sites in southern Lazio. However, at variance with other sites with a protohistoric origin, pre-Roman settlement traces in the plain of Sezze are virtually absent. The exceedingly small amount of sherds dating earlier than mid-Republican times in the Sezze area would suggest that the area was only very sparsely settled in pre-Roman times, during a time when, in the northeastern part of the Pontine Region, large urban settlements existed. To what extent landscape change in the plain of Sezze is responsible for the under-representation of the pre-Roman period in the archaeological record is thus a crucial problem to be investigated further – it will only be solved by a progamme of intensive archaeological survey followed up by intensive augering or test pitting of the surroundings of the temple site.

CASE STUDY 3 : THE INTRODUCTION OF OLIVE CULTIVATION ON THE LEPINE HILL SLOPES; PALYNOLOGICAL AND ARCHAEOLOGICAL EVIDENCE

Introduction

Vegetational change, as represented in the pollen record of an augering site northeast of the Sezze-plain, is discussed in this section. The emphasis is on indications of human impact on the landscape, with special attention to evidence for agriculture, specifically the cultivation of olives and vines during the Roman Republican period. As already referred to in the introductory section of this paper, the cultivation of olive trees can be related to the remains of platforms that were built along the *pedemontana*, the road running along the foot of the Lepine hills. The PRP has mapped several of these platforms during recent surveys. These platforms are situated at fairly regular intervals and were built to carry edifices; at two of these sites, limestone press beds were found. Judging from both the masonry (polygonal masonry and *opus quadratum*, sometimes embossed), and the survey finds, we are definitely dealing with Republican structures. Theoretically, these may have been erected from the late fourth century BC onwards, coinciding with the fortifications of the Roman colonies of Norba and Setia. Assuming, however, a connection with the cultivation of olives, the platforms should be dated to the third and second centuries BC, implying that the hill slopes of the Monti Lepini became systematically exploited for the cultivation of cash crops from mid-Republican times onwards.

Location of the pollen core

The coring was carried out in a small basin with an undisturbed sedimentology between the Monti Lepini and a limestone hill named Monticchio (Fig. 11.9). The high amount of organic material in the soil suggested that the conditions for pollen preservation were quite favourable.

The basin from which the pollen core was obtained is filled with thick layers of clay. Two layers of peaty clay were struck, the first at 200–225 cm, the second at 930–1000 cm.

Method

The coring was carried out with a Dachnowski sampler. At a depth of 1134 cm, a hard layer of weathered tuff was reached, making further coring impossible. The sediment was cored in stretches of 25 cm, with 5 cm overlap. Samples of approximately 1 cm each were taken from the core at variable intervals, and prepared by the bromoform-alcohol flotation method (Brown, 1960).

Although reliable results require at least a pollen sum of 500 per sample, this proved hard to attain, especially in the lower sections of the core. The quantity of pollen in these sections is relatively low, possibly because of unfavourable preservation conditions.

Dates

The upper 120 cm of the core were disturbed by deep ploughing and therefore rejected. The lower sections of the core were not analyzed because of the low pollen content. Three ^{14}C datings were carried out by the Centre

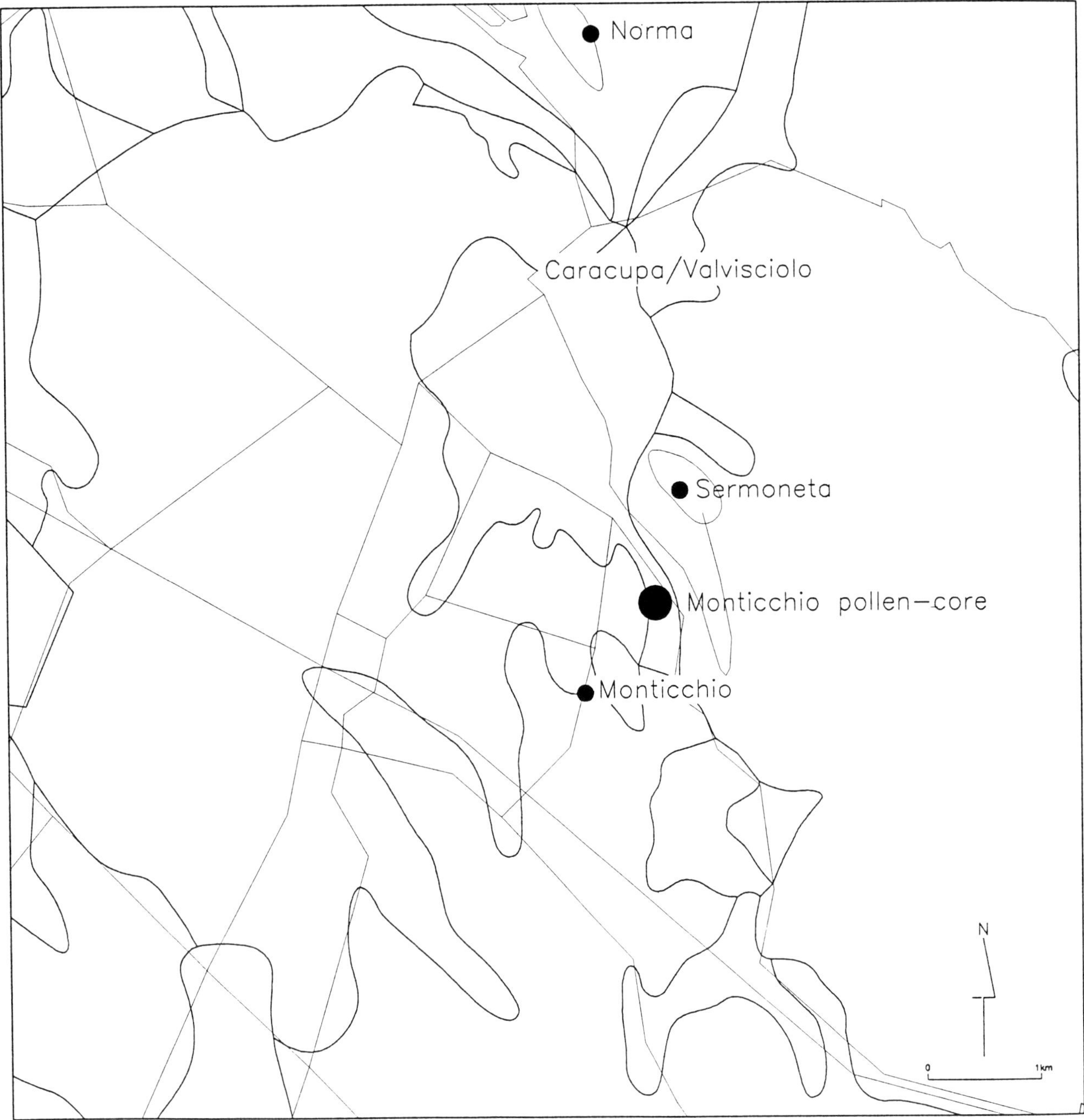

Fig. 11.9. Location map of the Monticchio pollen core.

of Isotope Research of the University of Groningen. GRN 18437 at 226 cm gave a date of 2090 BP ± 30, calibrated at 170–96 BC; GRN 16960 at 240–245 cm gave a date of 2240 BP ± 60, which was calibrated at 390–350 BC (Stuiver and Pearson, 1986); and GRN 18438 taken at 940–945 cm gave a date of 8015 ± 45 BP, calibrated at 6820–7056 BC (Stuiver *et al.*, 1986).

The diagram

The section of the core (Fig. 11.10) described here (between 130 and 340 cm) roughly covers the first millennium BC, inferred from radiocarbon dates and assuming a constant sedimentation.

The pollen sum includes trees, herbs and some ferns. Types that occur less than three times were not incorporated. The pollen is classified mostly on the taxonomic level of genus or family. In some cases a closer determination was made. For *Quercus*, two types are discerned, a deciduous type (*Quercus robur*-type) and an evergreen type (*Quercus coccifera*-type). Local waterplants such as *Myriophyllum* and *Isotes* (here interpreted as a waterplant) were also counted. Three pollen zones were distinguished.

- Zone I, from 340 to 300 cm, shows a high content of non-arboreal pollen. The values of *Polygonum aviculare*-type, *Ericaceae, Viburnum/Sambucus*-type and *Compositeae Tubuliflorae* are relatively high, although most significant is the massive increase of *Gramineae*. Most arboreal pollen decreases, especially types such as *Quercus robur, Quercus coccifera* and *Alnus*.
- Zone II is situated between 300 and 200 cm and is characterized by a peak in herbaceous pollen and relatively low percentages for trees. In subzone IIa (300–240 cm), *Cyperaceae* peak heavily and then disappear suddenly. *Caryophyllaceae* and *Chenopodiaceae* are also represented in relatively large quantities. The arboreal pollen still shows small percentages of *Alnus* and *Quercus robur*-type, whereas *Quercus coccifera*-type has totally disappeared. *Carpinus betulus* and *Ostrya/Carpinus orientalis* show a small peak, while *Olea* and *Juglans* appear for the first time. In subzone IIb (240–200 cm) *Alnus* increases rapidly. *Quercus robur*-type maintains its values at first but falls back later. *Quercus coccifera* increases again. In this subzone *Corylus* and *Olea* disappear. The non-arboreal pollen still is represented by a very high percentage of *Gramineae*. Also *Ericaceae* and *Cyperaceae* have small peaks.
- Zone III is situated between 200 and 130 cm. In this zone the arboreal pollen is well represented, especially by a large amount of *Alnus*. *Quercus coccifera*-type remains at a level of about five per cent, while *Quercus robur*-type continues to decrease. *Castanea* is also represented in this zone. Finally *Vitis* maintains an almost unchanging presence throughout the diagram, while *Cerealia* occur in negligible amounts. The non-arboreal pollen is still dominated by *Gramineae*, although in this zone a large variety of herbs is present.

Interpretation

In the first pollen zone, the low content of arboreal pollen, *Alnus, Quercus coccifera*-type and *Quercus robur*-type, suggests human activity. The cutting of wood was common in this period throughout Europe (Thirgood, 1981). The purposes varied from need for building-materials and fuel to need for land for grazing and agriculture. The increase of *Gramineae, Compositeae Tubuliflorae, Compositae Liguliflorae, Artemisia* and *Rumex acetosa* suggests an open landscape as a result of grazing, although part of the *Gramineae* could belong to local marsh vegetation.

In the second zone an open landscape type can be inferred from the diagram. *Gramineae* is predominant, although also relatively high values of *Compositeae Tubuliflorae, Umbellifereae* and *Caryophylaceae* are present. The peaking of *Cyperaceae* and the presence of some waterplants like *Typha latifolia* and *Myriophyllum* indicate a change in the water supply, although it is not clear if this means an increase or decrease of water at this location. The increase of *Carpinus betulus, Ostrya/Carpinus orientalis* and *Ulmus* could mean that the woods on the slopes of the surrounding mountains started to regenerate. At the end, however, they disappear again, making place for *Olea, Castanea* and *Juglans*. The high peak of *Olea* suggests strongly that these trees were planted. The presence of *Vitis* doesn't necessarily mean that it was cultivated. *Vitis* occurred in its wild form in the woods in the river valleys (Rikli, 1943). The relatively high percentages of *Vitis* in all sections of the diagram support this view, because the cultivated forms of *Vitis* normally do not produce a large quantity of pollen material. A sample taken at the surface of one of the present vineyards in the area resulted in a value for *Vitis* of only 0.8 per cent.

In the upper part of subzone IIb, a rapid succession of peaks of *Gramineae, Cyperaceae* and *Dryopteris* must be related to the formation of peat (peaty clay 225–200 cm).

In zone III, the arboreal pollen dominates: especially *Alnus* is present with high percentages. *Alnus* most probably must be interpreted as local, like the waterplants; possibly part of the *Gramineae* is local as well.

CONCLUSION

The first case study showed that a mudflow phase started in the Late Iron Age and covered the colluvial sediments that had accumulated earlier in the plain of the Contrada Trentossa. The mudflow sediments were cultivated in Roman Republican times, as is shown by *in situ* sherds, organic content and furrows visible at about half a metre's depth. This surface was then covered by sediments, which contain materials of Archaic and Roman Republican age (Attema, 1993: 129–31). The present-day ploughsoil contains both worn, very rounded, sherds and sherds having normal fractures, indicating that a second stable phase occurred in Roman times. In the Contrada Trentossa, the dating of part of the alluvial fan environment beneath the antique Roman colony of Norba, downslope of the protohistoric settlement of Caracupa/Valvisciolo, makes it possible to evaluate the potential of this landscape for the founding of Roman villas (a comparable example from northern Campania is given by Arthur, 1991: 42).

The mudflow sediments suggest that deforestation began in the mountainous hinterland in the Iron Age. This is the period in which settlement intensified in Lazio. During protohistory, the upper, older, part of the fan formed part of the catchment of the substantial protohistoric settlement of Caracupa/Valvisciolo (Attema, 1993: 157–80). Palynological research carried out at Monticchio, approximately 1 km south of the pit, reveals a sudden decrease of tree pollen in the tenth century BC (Haagsma, 1993).

The work by the French archaeologist De La Blanchère in the nineteenth century revealed traces of cultivation of the volcanic soils dated by him to antiquity, that are now covered by colluvial sediment (De La Blanchère, 1889: 122–4). Our research added examples of colluvial sedi-

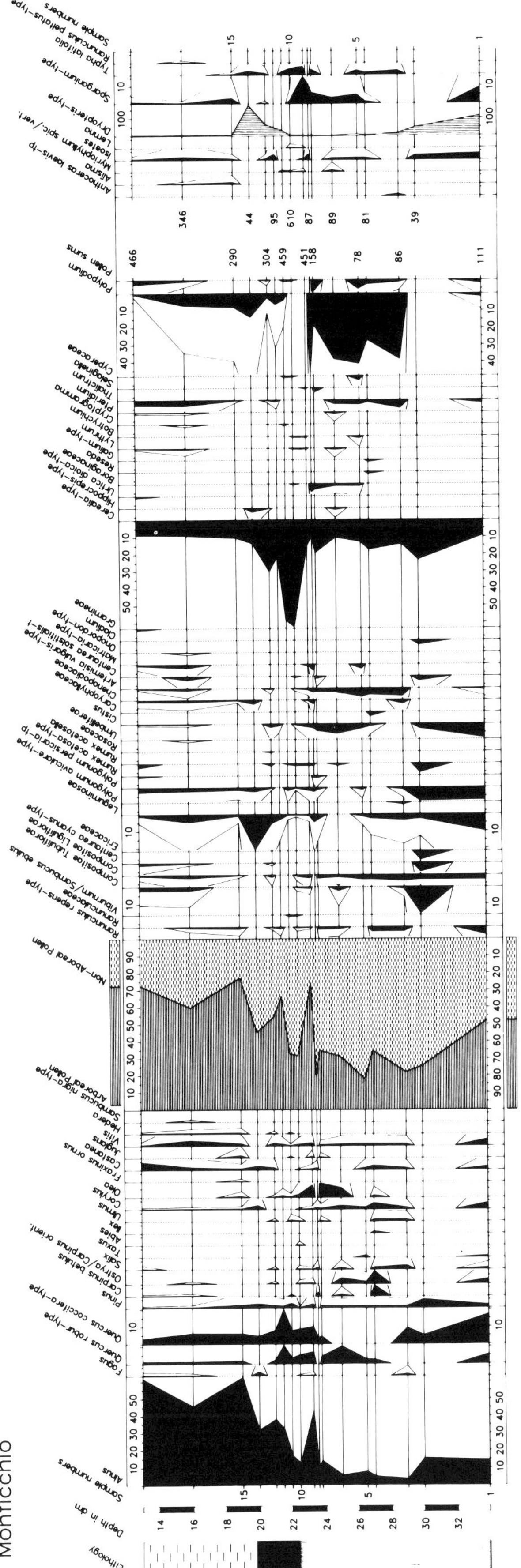

Fig. 11.10 Section of the Monticchio pollen diagram.

ments deposited on top of the Via Appia Antica (Attema, 1993: 96–7).

In the second case study, the 1994 survey in the plain near the Roman colony of Setia (present-day Sezze) revealed much Roman rural settlement, in date matching the Republican town and thus corroborating and complementing already available archaeological evidence on the area. The survey failed, however, to locate substantial earlier settlement on the plain. Excavation by the local museum in 1985, together with ^{14}C samples, pointed in the direction of a phase of increased sedimentation that preceded Roman settlement in the area, and which may have covered pre-Roman settlement. The excavation yielded proof of earlier settlement on the plain. It also showed the Roman Republican stratum to be separated from the pre-Roman Iron Age stratum by a thick sterile layer of colluvial clay. Sedimentation during pre-Roman times may thus have been responsible for the virtual absence of pre-Roman ceramics in the plough zone of the plain of Sezze.

Although not enough ^{14}C dates have been obtained yet to make generalizations, the colluvial sheet that covers the area beneath Sezze probably advanced slowly from the mountains in a southeasterly direction during protohistoric times. Pollen analysis indicates that marshy conditions prevailed before. Peat layers underneath the colluvial deposit that were found in a number of depressions support this assumption (Fig. 11.8). Radiocarbon dates taken from the top of these peat layers indicate that substantial colluviation started *c.*2000 BC. The colluvial silty clay contains volcanic minerals (augite, biotite), which means that the material originates in the volcanic Colli Albani to the north. The reddish brown colour of the sediment points to oxidizing circumstances during and after deposition. Contemporary with the phase of colluviation, some fluviatile sedimentation occurred, visible as lenses of sand or gravel.

This case study reinforces the supposition by Sevink *et al.* (1984) that the colluvial sediments were formed under human influence. As in the plain beneath Norba, colluviation in the plain beneath Sezze was an active environmental factor changing the conditions for settlement and land use. Those parts of the landscape that were covered by a colluvial sheet from protohistoric times onwards were settled and cultivated during Roman times, whereas indications for earlier settlement are few.

The third case study shows that it is very likely that most of the lower parts of the Pontine region had wet conditions during the whole of the first millennium BC. This means that at least these parts were not very suitable for the purposes of intensive agriculture. The pollen diagram provides no direct evidence for any agricultural activities that may be linked with the Archaic settlements of Caracupa/Valvisciolo and the Contrada Casali, or the smaller rural sites that occurred in the plain from the seventh century onwards. However, the land may have been used for extensive grazing by herds of cattle, in agreement with the openness of the landscape during most of the period covered by the diagram (De Grossi Mazzorin, 1989).

The diagram contains evidence for the cultivation of olive, walnut and chestnut in the third and second centuries BC. In this period the first Roman *villae rusticae* occur in the Pontine area, some located on the foothills of the Monti Lepini. Remains of a Roman villa dating to this period were found near the location of the core (Attema, 1993: 285, site 15). During this period, the elevated foothills and terraced slopes of the Monti Lepini will have been used for agriculture, especially the growing of olives.

Postscript: détailed description of the Sezze cores (Figs.11.7 and 11.8)

Augerings S2 and S3 yielded *post quem* dates for the colluvium of 4160 ± 80 BP (GrN-18436/Sezze 2) and 4220 ± 100 BP (GrN-18435/Sezze 1). Augering S2 was carried out in a shallow depression visible in field 13 of the Sezze transect. The core showed very dark gray clay (10YR 3/1) to a depth of 0.50 m and dark brown clay (10YR 3/3) to 1 m. A thicker peaty clay layer separated the 1 m thick colluvial deposit from the lagoonal deposit (0.40 m). This layer was sampled with a Dachnowsky auger. Augering S3 was carried out in field 10 about 1.25 km in the northern direction. The core contained dark yellowish brown clay (10YR 4/4) down to a depth of 0.20 m and very dark gray clay (10YR 3/1) to 0.50 m. Then the core showed a thick layer of dark brown clay containing 'calcified' reed (or *tartaro*), which continued to a depth of 0.95 m. The layer of dark brown clay continued to 1.60 m, but now without reed remains. Beneath this a layer of peaty material was found from 1.60 m to 1.95 m above the gray lagoonal deposit. The peaty layer was sampled for radiocarbon dating at a depth of 1.60–1.70 m (see also Figs. 11.7 and 11.8). It was thought that archaeological finds in the cores of our borings would provide a *terminus ante quem* for the deposition of the colluvial deposit. Core S4 contained, however, recent (though archaeologically-useful) dump to a depth of 0.50 m. S5 was more helpful. Surface finds of both Roman and (late) Archaic date continued in the brown colluvial clay in the form of small ceramic fragments to a depth of 0.80 m. Although the colluvial layer turned out to have a thickness of 2.80 m at this point, the layer was not undifferentiated. From 1.95 to 2.10 m and from 2.40 to 2.55 m, sandy layers occurred, indicating fluvial activity. The gray lagoonal clays were reached at 2.80 m without an intervening peat layer.

Augering SII-1 slightly to the southeast yielded a date of 3735 ± 100 BP at a depth of 2.30–31 m. The colluvial soil changed to organic clay at a depth of 1.80 m, followed by layers of clay with varying quantities of peat, from the first of which the ^{14}C sample was taken. The augering was continued till a depth of 5 m. Boring SII-7 yielded a date of 2760 ± 110 BP at a depth of 1.32–33 m. After 1 m of colluvial clay, a 0.30 m thick layer of organic dark clay was reached, followed by a peaty clay or peat from which the ^{14}C sample was taken. Clay layers with varying peat content continued to 2.80 m. Except for GA3, situated near the footslopes of the Lepini, all GA borings were carried out in the colluvial deposit: GA1 and 2 near Gli Archi – the remains of a Roman Republican bridge dated to the second century BC – and GA4 and 5 near the Republican temple dedicated to Juno and dated to the fourth century BC. Although a few archaeological finds were seen in the immediate surroundings of boring GA3, no material was encountered in the cores of the colluvial clay. GA5 had a sandy layer from 1.50 m to 1.70 m, whereas lower down, the colluvial clay contained calcareous fragments. At a depth of 2.00 m the gray lagoonal clay was reached.

REFERENCES

Arthur, P. (1991) *Romans in Northern Campania.* London, British School at Rome, Archaeological Monographs 1.

Attema, P.A.J. (1993) *An Archaeological Survey in the Pontine Region, a Contribution to the Early Settlement History of South Lazio.* Groningen, University of Groningen, two volumes.

Attema, P.A.J. (1995) Romeinse kolonisatie ten zuiden van Rome, de Sezze survey. *Paleoaktueel* 5: 67–70.

Attema, P.A.J., Delvigne, J.J. and Haagsma, B.J. (1990) Archeologie en landschapsontwikkeling, een case-study naar landschappelijke veranderingen in de Agro Pontino. *Tijdschrift voor Mediterrane Archeologie* 5: 18–28.

Attema, P.A.J., Haagsma, B.J. and Delvigne, J.J. (1997) Survey and sediments in the *ager* of ancient *Setia* (Lazio, central Italy). The Dark Age from a landscape perpective. *Caeculus* 3: 113–21.

Beaty, C.B. (1974) Debris flows, alluvial fans, and revitalised catastrophism. *Zeitschrift für Geomorphologie*, Suppl.Bd.21: 39–51.

Brown, C.A. (1960) *Palynological Techniques.* Baton Rouge, State University of Louisiana.

Bruckner, E.C. (1995) Forum Appi. *Quaderni del Dipartimento di Scienze dell'Antichità* 16 (Università degli Studi di Salerno): 189–221.

Bull, W.B. (1977) The alluvial fan environment. *Progress in Physical Geography* 1: 222–70.

Costa, J.E. (1984) Physical geography of debris flows. In J.E. Costa and P.J. Fleisher (eds) *Developments and Applications of Geomorphology*:268–317.Berlin, Springer Verlag.

De La Blanchère, M.R. (1889) Un chapitre d'histoire pontine, état ancien et décadence d'une partie du Latium. *Extrait des Savants Etrangers à l'Académie des Inscriptions et Belles Lettres*, Tome 10, 1ère partie. Paris, Académie des Inscriptions et Belles Lettres.

Dimbleby, G.W. (1985) *The Palynology of Archaeological Sites.* London, Academic Press.

Fenaroli, M. (1970) *Carta della Vegetazione Reale d'Italia.* Rome.

De Grossi Mazzorin, J. (1989) Testimonianza di allevamento e caccia nel Lazio antico tra l'VIII e il VII secolo a.C. *Dialoghi di Archeologia* 1: 125–40.

Haagsma, B.J. (1993) A pollen core from Monticchio in the Agro Pontino (South Lazio), a study on human impact in the Agro Pontino during the first millennium BC. In P. Attema*An Archaeological Survey in the Pontine Region, a Contribution to the Early Settlement History of South Lazio*: 249–55. Groningen, University of Groningen.

Meiggs, R. (1982) *Trees and Timber in the Mediterranean World.* Oxford, Clarendon Press.

Rikli, M. (1943) *Das Pflanzenkleid der Mittelmeerländer.* Bern, Huber, three volumes.

Sevink, J., Remmelzwaal, A. and Spaargaren, O.C. (1984) *The Soils of Southern Lazio and Adjacent Campania.* Amsterdam, University of Amsterdam.

Sevink, J. (1985) Physiographic soil surveys and archaeology. In C. Malone and S. Stoddart (eds) *Papers in Italian Archaeology* IV: 41–42. Oxford, British Archaeological Reports, International Series 243.

Stuiver, M. and Pearson, G.W. (1986) High-precision calibrating of the radiocarbon time scale, AD 1950–500 BC. In M. Stuiver and R.S. Kra (eds)*Proceedings of the 12th International Radiocarbon Conference*: 805–38. *Radiocarbon* 28.2B

Thirgood, J.V. (1981) *Man and the Mediterranean Forest. A History of Resource Depletion.* London, Academic Press.

Voorrips, A., Loving, S. and Kamermans, H. (1991) *The Agro Pontino Survey Project, Methods and Preliminary Results.* Amsterdam, University of Amsterdam, Studies in Prae- en Protohistory 6.

Zaccheo, L., Pasquali, F. (1970) Sezze, *Guida all'Antiquario e ai Maggiori Monumenti.* Sezze, Antqiarium Comunale Sezze.

Zaccheo, L., Pasquali, F. (1972) *Sezze dalla Preistoria all' Età Romana.* Sezze, Historia Selecta Setina 1.

12. Karst Dolinas: Evidence of Population Pressure and Exploitation of Agricultural Resources in Karstic Landscapes

Predrag Novaković, Helene Simoni and Branko Mušič

INTRODUCTION

The Karst is an area *c.* 500 km² in southwestern Slovenia enclosed by the Trieste Bay to the west, the Gorica plain and Vipava valley to the north, the Brkini hills to the east and southeast, and northern Istrian flysch hills to the south (Figs. 12.1 and 12.2). It is mostly composed of various limestones, with rare belts of dolomites, and forms a plateau which is more discretely elevated from the surroundings in its central and western part. The plateau itself is higher in the southern and southeastern part (*c.*500–600 m) and gradually falls towards the northwest into the Friuli plain.

Dolinas are among the most universal and typical geomorphological features in the karstic landscapes, and are especially frequent in the Dinaric zone (Fig. 12.3). The term *dolina*, which is found in South Slavic languages and local dialects, was introduced into international terminology by the first geographers that researched karstic landscapes in the territory of ex-Yugoslavia. Dolinas are defined as medium-sized karstic depressions. Their diameter varies

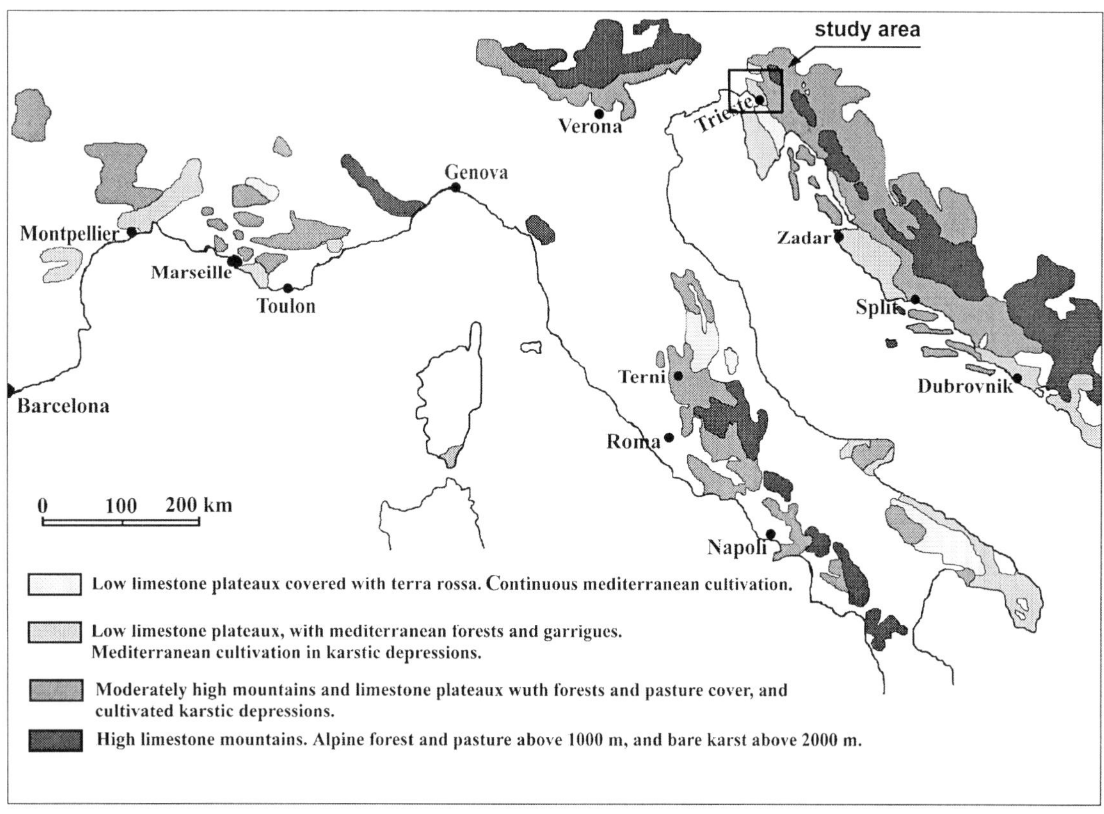

Fig. 12.1 'Paysages agro-karstiques' (after Gams et al., *1993: 60); study area shown as inset.*

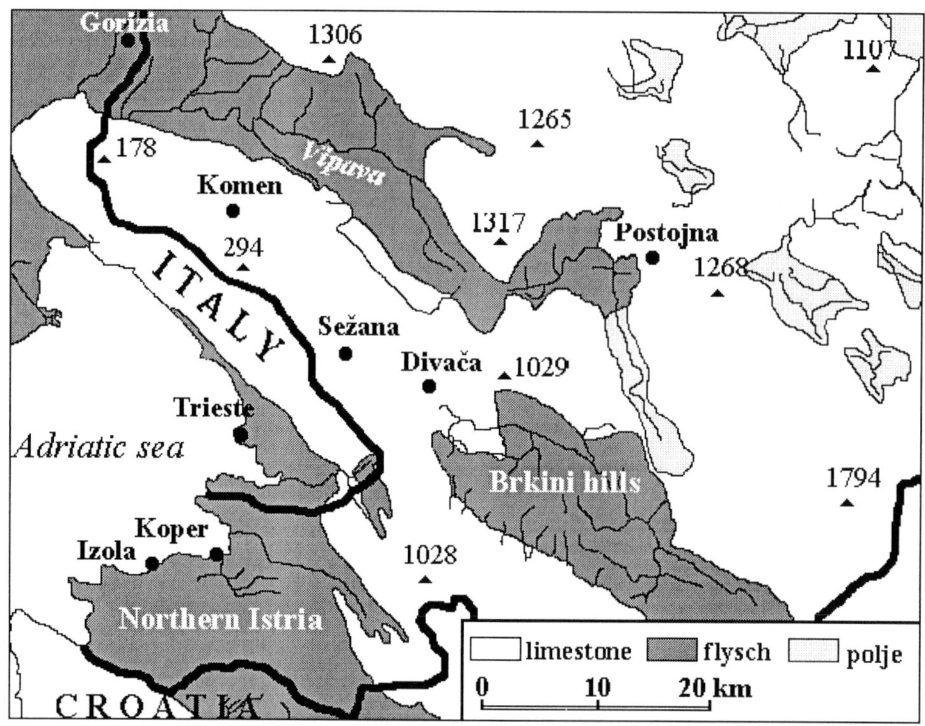

Fig. 12.2. The parental karst in southwest Slovenia: general geological map. (After Gams, 1987a: 5)

Fig. 12.3. Characteristic karstic landscape with dolinas: an example taken from Bela Krajina in southeast Slovenia. (After Cvijić, 1924: 417)

from 5 to more than 300 m, but most dolinas are between 20–50 m (Cvijić, 1924: 401). The ratio of depth to diameter is normally between 1:6 and 1:10. Their density depends on precipitation and geology and is very high on limestones, less on conglomerates, even less on dolomites. Another factor is the relief. They are more numerous on flat or leveled terraces and rare on slopes. In some areas of the Karst, their density exceeds 150 dolinas per km^2, while on the average, there are *c.* 50–70 per km^2.

Though many researchers studied dolinas very extensively, their origin and formation processes are yet to be clarified. Cvijić interpreted dolinas as areas lowered due to the drainage of rainfall and surface waters into the sub-surface rock (Fig. 12.4). There are other theories, too. According to one, dolinas are an integral part of the karst surface where, due to local conditions, lowering has been more extensive in some spots. Dolinas are also considered to have been formed by collapse and denudation processes (Šušteršič, 1994: 151). However, the present stage of knowledge cannot explain the origin of dolinas by merely one general cause (Bahun, 1969).

ECOLOGICAL CONDITIONS FOR AGRICULTURE IN THE KARST

The Karst climate is sub-Mediterranean (Gams, 1987a:

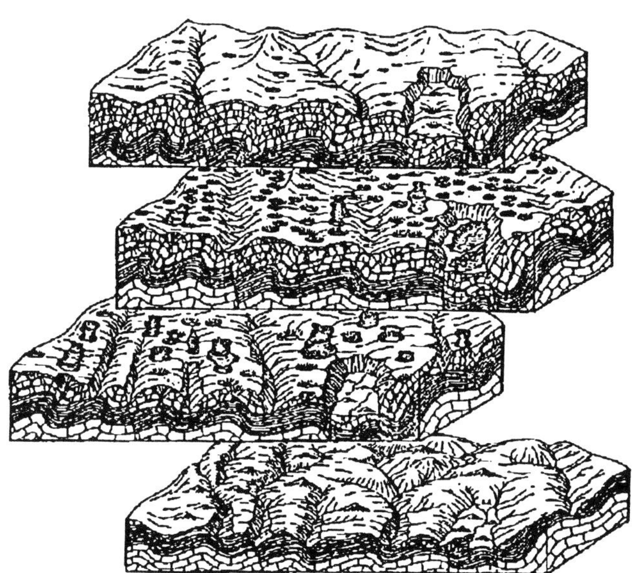

Fig. 12.4. 'The birth and death of the karstic landscape': the main stages of karstic corrosion. (Drawn by Cvijić, after Gams, 1974: 126)

95), with annual precipitation between 1200–1500 mm, and enhanced draughts in the summer (sometimes less than 100 mm/month). Mean July temperatures are 19–21.5° C, while mean January temperatures are 0.2–2.1° C. Microclimatological studies of dolinas have demonstrated temperature inversion during the night. The mean air temperatures of their bases are lower than the temperatures on their rims. The differences can vary from 4°C in February to 0.5°C in August (Gams, 1972).

Soil amount is unevenly distributed. Open land and steeper slopes normally have very thin layers, sometimes not enough to cover the bedrock. However, the soils are much thicker in the dolinas, sometimes more than 4 m. Dolinas' bases normally have soils richer in rubble. Such a soil is more aerated, lighter, and keeps warmth in autumn and winter, since rubble is a good heat conductor (Gams, 1972: 60). The most frequent soils in the Karst are rendzina, terra rossa, calcocambisols and washed calcocambisols (Lovrenčak, 1977: 443–9; Fig. 12.5).

The highly permeable limestones do not favour permanent surface streams. The only water-containing areas are at the interface of limestones with impermeable rocks. The lack of water is especially enhanced during the summer.

Among the climatic factors conditioning agriculture, a very strong northwesterly wind – the Bora – must be mentioned. It can blow for more than 40 days per year (sometimes for more than seven days continuously), predominantly in the colder seasons, and can frequently exceed velocities of 100 km/h. Its effect on crops can be disastrous, since it can blow away substantial amounts of soil from the open-land fields and decrease local air and ground temperatures in the winter period.

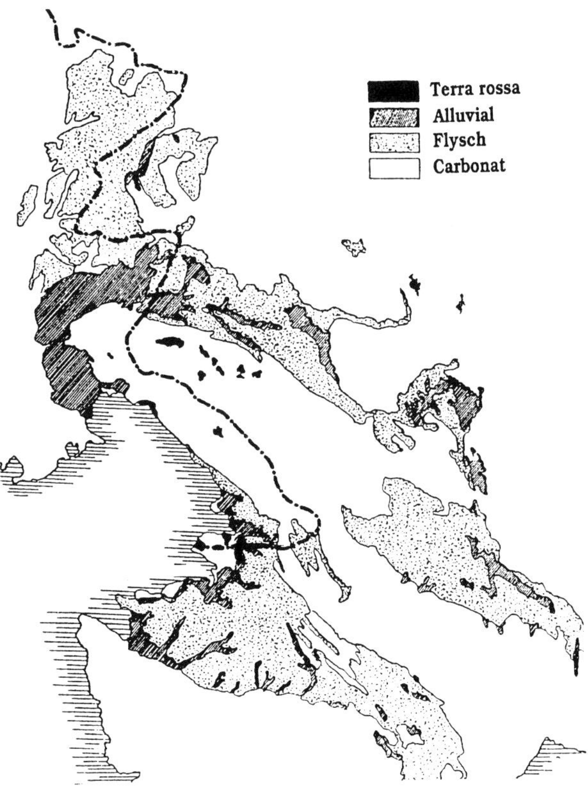

Fig. 12.5. General soil map of the Karst. (After Krš Slovenije, *Split, 1957)*

Deforestation is one of the human factors which have most influenced the ecological conditions in the Karst. In antiquity, the Karst had substantial tree coverage, predominantly oaks. However, from the second half of the first millennium BC, we can trace relatively extensive exploitation of the land and forests (Gams, 1990: 29–36). The first laws and regulations concerning forest exploitation in the Trieste hinterland date from the twelfth century AD. The extensive exploitation for timber, fuel, pastures and agricultural land lasted almost until the end of the last century, when the Karst landscape reached the maximum of its degradation. The impacts for agriculture included accelerated aeolic erosion, washdown of soil, lower humidity, and changes in microclimate and hydrology (Sauro, 1993).

Traditional agricultural strategies in Karst included: the keeping of sheep and goats by various transhumant and semi-transhumant strategies; the predominance of early and specialized crops (vine, olives, fruits); land improvements like stone clearing in the fields, meadows and pastures; various strategies of soil conservation (terracing for example); and construction of protective walls against animals, wind and so on (Fig. 12.6). All are well-known subsistence activities and strategies in the Mediterranean plateaus (or 'paysages agro-karstiques' as termed by Nicod, 1987: 98). To this we must include extensive agricultural use of all sorts of karstic depressions, especially the dolinas.

DOLINAS: AGRICULTURAL GARDENS

Dolinas, though relatively small plots of land, have acted in the past as, in effect, 'agricultural gardens', because they comprise natural reservoirs of fertile soils. A single medium-sized dolina may contain several hundred cubic metres of soil (Radinja, 1987: 131). They are also excellent shelters against the wind. They accumulate soil and have more moisture, but they require further improvements to be used efficiently for agricultural purposes.

Local people in Karst named 'worked dolinas' the improved ones (Fig. 12.7). The farmers normally dug a hole or trench at the bottom 10–15 m long, 2 m wide and 1.5 m deep, and filled it with several dozen cubic metres of stones collected from the bottom and the slopes (Radinja, 1987: 134). Then they scraped the soil from the surface and slopes and covered the whole bottom and raised it in this way. Another way to enlarge the field area was by constructing a scarp made of stones and filling it with soil (Gams, 1974: 178). The research of the collapsed dolina Drčivnik revealed a great amount of rubble, intentionally added to the clayish soil (Gams, 1987a: 111) so that the fertility of soil was augmented, its acidity decreased, the aeration increased and soil kept warm. Added stones also slowed down wind erosion of the topsoil. Almost all 'worked' dolinas were enclosed by one or two walls; they were the product of clearance and they further diminished the effect of winds and protected the crops from animals.

A typical village in the nineteenth century normally exploited more than 50 dolinas (Gams, 1987b: 118), sometimes even more than 100. In the case of the village of Krajna Vas, for example, nearly half of the dolinas were 'worked'. At an average density of 35 dolinas per 100 ha and a total area of 335 ha, this accounts for at least 50 'worked' dolinas exploited for agriculture by *c.*20 households before the First World War (Gams *et al.*, 1971). We can predict that a few thousand dolinas were 'worked' in the Karst alone. Their importance is further demonstrated by the fact that many of them had names denoting ownership, size, position, amelioration works, crops, trees, animals and so on: examples include Lesen du (wooden dolina), Bojin du (Bojin's dolina), and Pri Štirnci (Dolina near the little cistern).

Agricultural exploitation of the Karst reached its peak in the mid nineteenth century. Population pressure is especially evident from the beginning of the second half of the nineteenth century, mostly because of reduced child mortality (Verginella, 1990: 5–6) and the introduction of potato crops (Davies, 1988: 64, footnote 11). Due to the overexploitation of the land, the economy of individual households was very fragile and even smaller demographic changes could heavily affect individual families. Additionally, a land reform that ended traditional feudal landownership conditioned the fragmentation of larger estates: the average size of household property in a village near Trieste in 1886 was 1.6 ha (Verginella, 1990: 9). Small households were probably a reasonable answer to the circumstances, since they included various types of mixed agriculture, allowing many people to maintain minimal subsistence. However, as a result, the landscape was rapidly degraded by erosion, deforestation and livestock grazing.

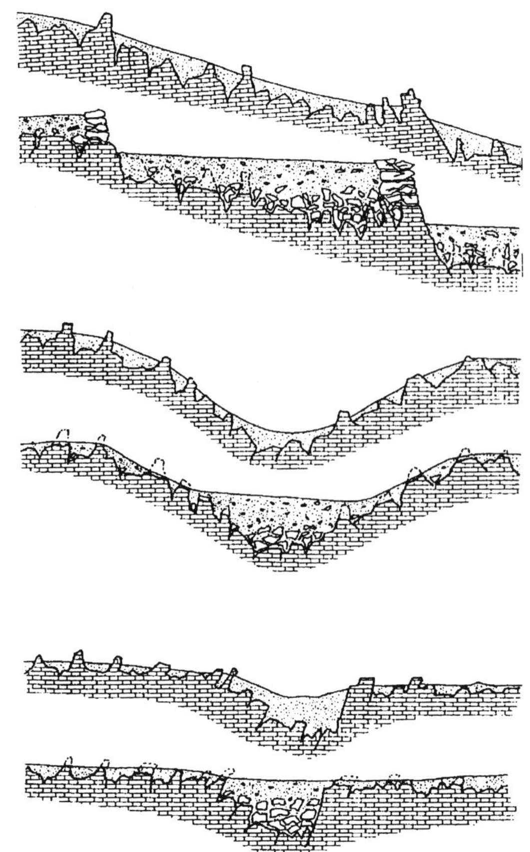

Fig. 12.6. Various types of ameliorations of agricultural land in the Karst. (After Gams, 1974: 178)

Agriculture has declined in this century, especially after the Second World War, because of a shift to industry and the tertiary sector. Besides, the establishment of a new border between Italy and Yugoslavia cut off many villages from Trieste, a long-standing central market. Consequently, most of the dolinas were rapidly abandoned. In the last decades, many of them have suffered severe changes. As they are small and mostly walled, they were difficult to exploit by mechanized farming. On the other hand, aided by the state, farmers started to improve their open land by digging out soil from the dolinas and spreading it on their fields (Habič, 1987b: 115; Radinja, 1987: 134). Radinja (1987: 131) estimated that the surface covered with soil from dolinas is at least ten times greater than the area from which it has been extracted. The result of these processes were hundreds of emptied dolinas.

CASE STUDY

The abandonment of traditional farming in the twentieth

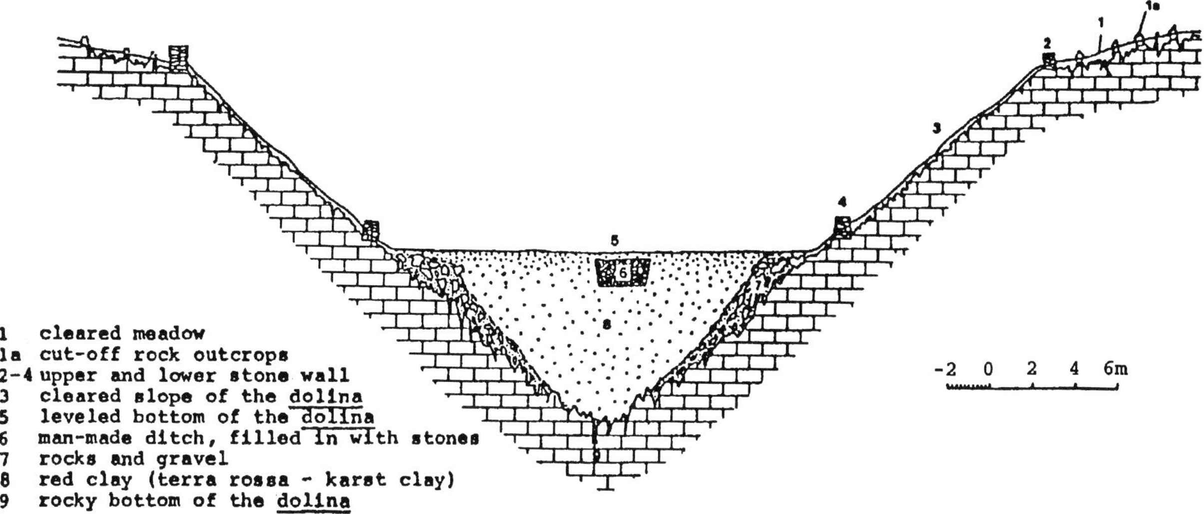

Fig. 12.7. Section of the typical 'worked' dolina near the village of Pliskovica in the northwest Karst. (After Radinja, 1987: 130)

century resulted in rapid afforestation, thus making archaeological research very difficult, especially systematic surveying. An archaeological survey conducted by the University of Ljubljana in 1974 (Slapšak, 1983, 1995) with the objective of reconstructing the economic basis for settlement in the past, included control visits of the sites and interviews with local people. Since it was more site-oriented, it left large parts of the landscape unsurveyed, since the methodology at that time did not include intensive systematic strategies.

Nevertheless, the evidence collected showed that the intensive settlement of the Karst belongs to the Bronze and Iron Ages. Earlier, the only significant sites are caves used as shelters and neolithic and eneolithic (chalcolithic) settlements. The bronze and iron age settlement pattern consists of numerous fortified hilltop settlements known as *castellieri* and some isolated stone barrows. The Roman period is characterized by a number of small villages predominantly in the lowlands, probably settled by indigenous people, a few villas on the better agricultural land, and a network of roads, which largely followed prehistoric routes. Numerous small villages that can be traced back to at least the fourteenth century mark the medieval settlement pattern; most of them have survived into our times. The medieval landscape remained almost unchanged until the mid nineteenth century, when land reform and the Vienna-Trieste railway line were introduced.

To a large extent, the natural conditions for agriculture, primarily the scarcity of water and the uneven distribution of soil, conditioned settlement in the Karst throughout antiquity and favoured the continuous occupation of the same locations from later prehistory to modern times. The same general pattern is followed after the period of the *castellieri*: the concentration of the settlements around the fertile plots of land. Various strategies existed to cope with the lack of water for animal including local and regional transhumance of flocks, and the use of ponds and seasonal streams. Some dolinas could serve this purpose too: the bottom was coated with a layer of stamped red loam, thus catching the rainfall (Habič, 1987a: 8). Cisterns were a major source of water from the Roman period onwards until the construction of aqueducts after the Second World War.

The process of emptying dolinas from the early 1980s onwards has not only destroyed many traditional agricultural landscape features in the Karst such as field boundaries and clearance walls (and the dolinas themselves in some cases), but has also had an important impact on the archaeological record, revealing many new prehistoric finds. The first reports came from the Regional Heritage Protection Office in Nova Gorica (Osmuk, 1993, 1994). Though the reports were very superficial, their increased number suggested that dolinas probably played a significant role in prehistory.

A few reconnaisance visits in the region had been carried out in the past by the authors prior to the more systematic archaeological survey in August 1995, when we surveyed nineteen dolinas (Fig. 12.8). Thirteen of them clustered in the area to the west of the Škocjan region were chosen as a sample likely to give insights into the exploitation of the dolinas in the region adjacent to the fertile Vreme valley, where a large amount of ancient settlement is known (A.N.S.I., 1975). Dolinas 1–13 (Fig. 12.8) were checked without regard to any previous information or knowledge on their archaeology. The rest (numbers 14–19) are dispersed in the north (Fig. 12.8) and were known from local archaeological reports. The majority of them (13 out of 19) had not been destroyed or emptied: some of them (2, 5–13, 18, 19) were covered with grass, while one (3) has been converted into woodland. On the other hand, six

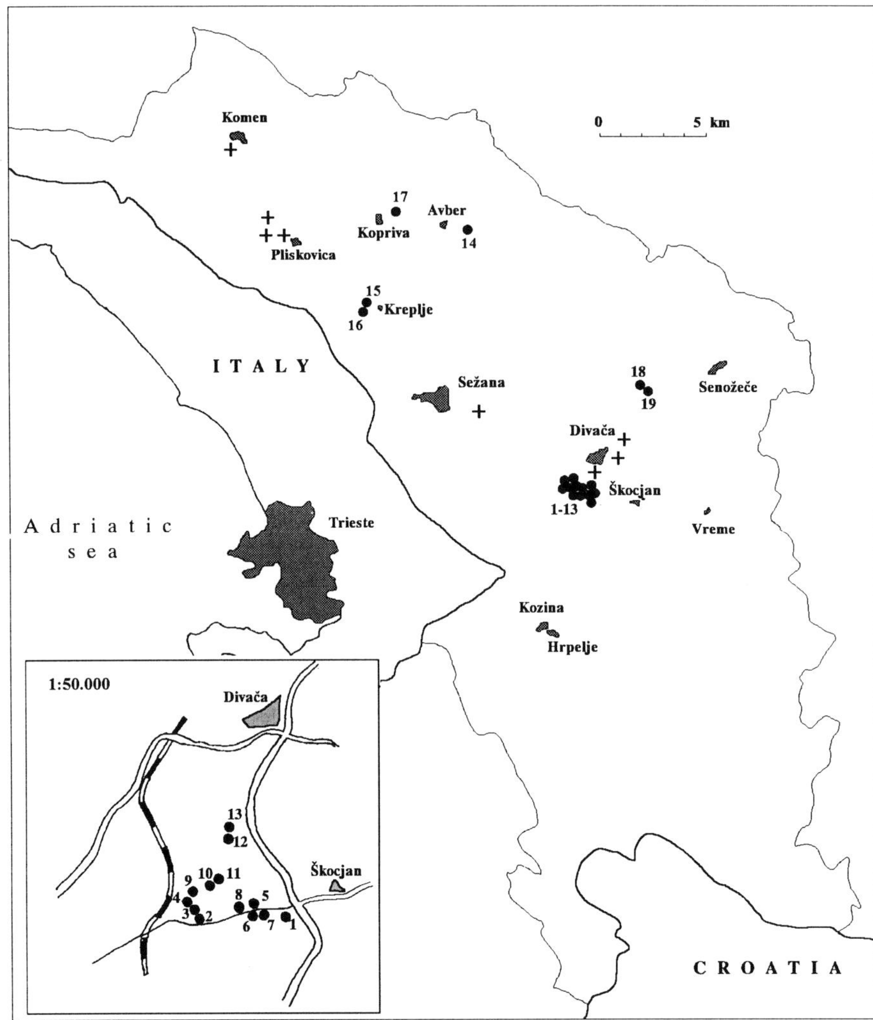

Fig. 12.8. Distribution of the dolinas with archaeological finds: • surveyed dolinas; + dolinas reported as containing prehistoric and Roman pottery. (After Osmuk, 1993, 1994)

dolinas (1, 4, 14–17) have suffered almost complete removal of their soil volume.

Different states of preservation called for different methods to be employed. First of all, at this stage our project was primarily aimed at clarifying the archaeological problems for more detailed research in the future, rather than attempting an exhaustive survey. Dolinas with no traces of agrarian use were intentionally omitted. The main features taken into consideration were signs of elaboration (enclosing wall, flattened bottom) and destruction (traces of digging, exposed outcrops of limestone bedrock).

Unfortunately, any remaining constructions, such as walls, could not offer any chronological indication, because most of them are relatively recent. The volume of the standing wall of Dolina 10 was measured in order to assess the volume of stone in such a construction. The wall was *c.* 250 m long and contained approximately 105 m^3 of stone.

Thus, different types of survey were used to discover archaeologically-datable material, mainly pottery, whether on or under the surface. Wherever a section of the slopes was visible, points were chosen around the dolina, each one situated at a distance of 5 m apart, and their surface was scraped to a depth of 5–10 cm all the way from the top to the bottom. Several grab samples were collected from the surface of the uncovered bottoms. In the dolinas with dense vegetation cover, a series of small test pits (measuring 30 x 30 x 30 cm) was dug and ceramics gathered up from the topsoil.

It is significant that fourteen out of nineteen dolinas produced ceramic material (Table 12.1). Nearly 50 per cent of our finds are dated to the Bronze and Iron Ages. Although we cannot ignore the fact that a certain bias was imposed by consciously collecting more prehistoric sherds whenever we came across them, it is still remarkable that prehistoric pottery outnumbers tiles and early modern pottery. This pottery is better identified as 'castellieri ware'. It consists of reddish-brown to black handmade, coarse, vessels, unevenly fired, thick and poorly cleaned, with a rough and porous surface that tends to be very fragile (Karouškova-Soper, 1983: 225–9). However, it is worth

Dolina	Survey Type	Total	Prehistoric	Roman	Mediaeval	Early Modern	Undatable	Tiles
1	G, SS	63	34	0	1	14	0	14
2	TP	6	0	0	0	0	1	5
3	TP	5	0	0	0	0	0	5
4	G	6	0	0	1	1	0	4
5	NS	0	0	0	0	0	0	0
6	TP	4	0	0	0	1	0	3
7	TP	0	0	0	0	0	0	0
8	TP	0	0	0	0	0	0	0
9	TP	2	0	0	0	0	0	2
10	TP	2	0	0	0	0	0	2
11	TP	7	0	0	1	1	0	5
12	G	29	0	0	4	18	0	7
13	TP	0	0	0	0	0	0	0
14	G, SS	10	1	3	2	0	1	3
15	G, SS	18	14	0	0	1	1	2
16	G	6	5	0	0	0	0	1
17	G	59	51	3	2	1	0	2
18	TP	0	0	0	0	0	0	0
19	TP, G	3	0	0	0	1	0	2

Table 12.1. Total amounts and chronological distribution of pottery recovered from dolinas.

Dolina	Total	Prehistoric	Roman	Mediaeval	Early Modern	Undatable	Tiles
	D/AF	D/AF	D/AF	D/AF	D/AF	D/AF	D/AF
14	10/5	1/0	3/0	2/1	0/2	1/0	3/2
15+16	24/16	19/13	0/0	0/1	1/0	1/0	3/2
17	59/12	51/8	3/0	2/1	1/1	0/0	2/2

Table 12.2. Chronological distribution of quantities of sherds found in dolinas and in adjacent fields.

noting at this point that fragments of the 'castellieri wares' are, at our present stage of archaeological knowledge, still rather undiagnostic in terms of their precise dates and typology

The Roman period was under-represented. Six sherds were discovered in total, three belonging to one thick-walled vessel in Dolina 14 and three very small and poorly preserved ones in Dolina 17. The medieval pottery belongs to the 'gray ware' and consists of sherds of medium thickness, dark coloured, with smooth, hard surfaces and many limestone and mica inclusions (Tomadin, 1992: 44–6). Glazed ware of the post-medieval (early modern) period and other sherds and tiles bear witness to the continuous use of dolinas until very recently.

A small-scale extensive survey with a surface grab collection was carried out in vineyards and meadows adjacent to Dolinas 14, 15 and 16, 17. The fields chosen lay in the immediate vicinity of the destroyed dolinas, and much of their soil was extracted from the dolinas. In fact, this operation comprises an important limitation of any survey in the Karst. In at least twenty cases recorded so far, archaeological artefacts were moved from their original location and redeposited elsewhere. If we take into account the fact that hundreds of dolinas were emptied and soil spread all over, this would present a major problem for all surveys in the open land surrounding the dolinas.

There was a notable coincidence in date range of the sherds from the dolinas and the nearby fields, although the quantity differed. The amount of material found in the dolinas was higher than that found on the adjacent fields. Prehistoric sherds clearly prevailed and the numbers of medieval and early modern sherds and tiles were extremely low in Dolinas 15, 16 and 17. Though more prehistoric ware was found in the fields, the difference with the post-Roman sherds and tiles was not so sharp. Medieval material was to be found in Dolina 14 and in the nearby field, whereas the only prehistoric sherd was located in the dolina (Table 12.2).

A mixed survey was conducted in Dolinas 1, 14 and 15. Material was collected from both the surface and subsoil, through grab sampling and section scraping respectively. Although the whole slope around each dolina was surveyed, the surface grab sampling proved more fruitful. Out of a total of 63 sherds and tiles in Dolina 1, 43 were spotted on the surface of the bottom (seven tiles, 27 prehistoric sherds, one medieval sherd, eight early modern sherds) and only twenty came from the slope surface (seven tiles, seven prehistoric sherds, five early modern sherds, one modern sherd), although the total circumference of it was more than 95 m. In Dolina 14, grab sampling revealed found six ceramics (two tiles, one prehistoric sherd, three Roman sherds), whilst the scraping produced only four ceramics (one tile, two medieval sherds, one undatable sherd). The slopes of Dolina 15 did not reveal anything and all sherds were spotted on the bottom.

Soil magnetic susceptibility was measured in Dolinas 1, 14, 15, 16, 17. A wall circumscribed their edges and pathways facilitated access, but no other human interference could be inferred except for soil removal. Pottery was the sole witness. The measurement of magnetic susceptibility was intended to complete the archaeological investigation by yielding insights into land use, since some layers of the topsoil showed clear traces of burning (Dolinas 14, 15, 16). Burning, as well as the decomposition of waste material, tends to enhance soil magnetic susceptibility (Clark, 1990: 101). Readings were taken from small holes dug to a depth of *c.* 15 cm on the bottom (Dolina 17) or the exposed profiles of the slopes (the others).

If we assume that all dolinas have similar soil structures, then the anomalies in magnetic susceptibility caused by the use of fire in the past will also appear in a similar way. Figure 12.9 displays the distribution of readings taken from all dolinas. The frequencies, to a large degree, are very close to the normal gaussean curve. This section was interpreted as background values. The mean value of all measurements is 2.6 x 10–5SI and the standard deviation 1.6 x 10–5SI. The value of two standard deviations (values higher than 5.8 x 10–5SI) was considered to be the limit between background values and anomalies.

Measurements revealed enhanced magnetic susceptibility caused by fire in Dolinas 14 and 16 (Figs. 12.10 and 12.11). Since anomalies in magnetic susceptibility are local in both cases, we excluded forest fire and assumed that human activities caused them (deposition of ash, burning waste, woodland clearance and so on). However, in the case of Dolina 14 we cannot exclude the existence of structures since later examination of the layer revealed one Roman sherd (and more Roman sherds were also found on a later occasion in the same dolina). In the case of Dolina 16, no datable material associated with the areas of higher magnetic susceptibility was traced.

DISCUSSION AND CONCLUSION

The crucial problem that we have to address is the occurrence of the prehistoric and Roman pottery. Since dolinas have never been studied in greater detail, the presence of artefacts in them was generally explained as a result of erosion from adjacent sites without this hypothesis ever having been checked. Our conclusions, however, proved to be completely different. All surveyed dolinas are on flat terrain with no slopes or steeper surfaces in the vicinity. Actually, the only slopes from where we can expect this movement to take place are the slopes of dolinas them-

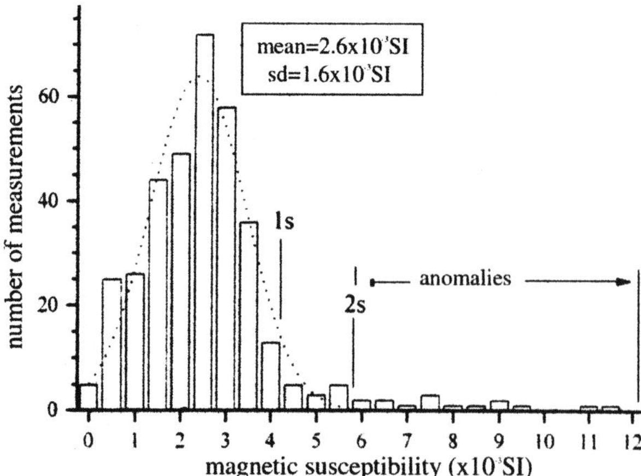

Fig. 12.9. Distribution of magnetic susceptibility readings taken from all dolinas.

selves. In all cases where we found larger quantities of sherds, these seemed to appear more or less evenly distributed on the bottoms and not clustered in one place.

Furthermore, in all of the surveyed and reported cases (more than twenty) of prehistoric pottery found in dolinas, there is no known archaeological site lying in the immediate vicinity from which the finds might be derived. The closest known sites are at least 1 km away. Only Dolina 17 is adjacent to an archaeological site, a Roman settlement. Nevertheless, we found only three Roman fragments. The fact that prehistoric pottery was found only in the dolinas where larger amounts of soil were extracted and deeper layers exposed, and only early modern and modern pottery was found in the upper layers and topsoil of the worked dolinas, supports the fact that many of the dolinas' bottoms have been raised in the last couple of centuries and thus layers with prehistoric and Roman pottery are buried underneath.

The mortuary use of a dolina is known in one case: a prehistoric cemetery discovered in the dolina Ponikve near Škocjan (Righi, 1982) with 92 cremation graves dated in two main phases: the tenth to eighth centuries BC and the third to first centuries BC respectively. However, this is an exceptional case: the dolina lies in the immediate proximity of the castelliere in Škocjan and at the centre of a wider archaeological complex that is extremely rich in sites from the neolithic to the medieval periods. Therefore, it cannot be taken as a typical example.

The occupation of dolinas in the Bronze and Iron Ages is, at the present stage of our knowledge, still very unlikely. Aside from numerous sherds, we did not find any other artefacts, like stone tools, flakes, querns, and daub suggesting habitation activities or house structures. However, the remains of prehistoric houses in some dolinas have recently been found in central Dalmatia. The excavation of one destroyed dolina near the village of Otišić (twenty km

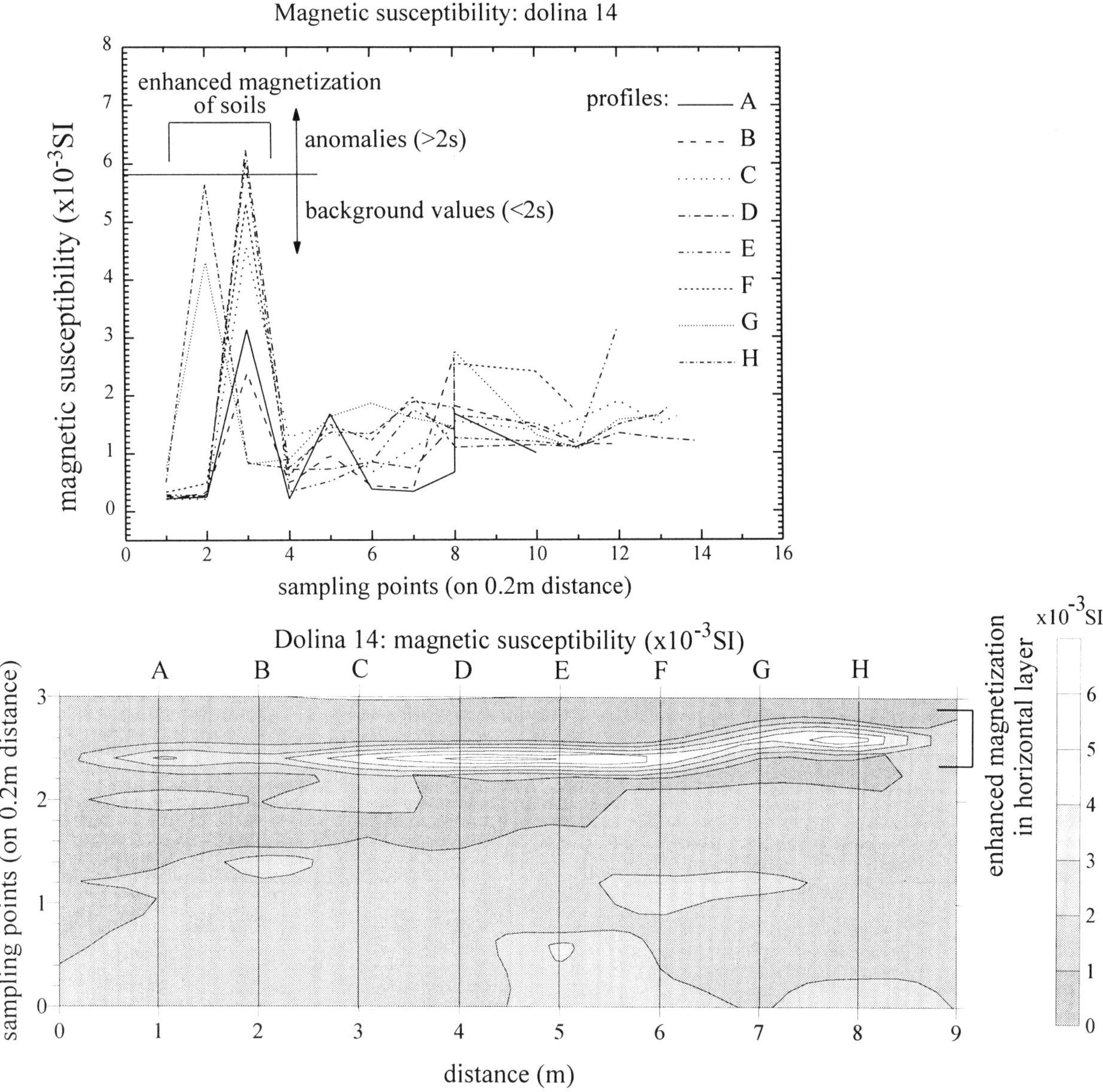

Fig. 12.10. Dolina 14: magnetic susceptibility readings.

northwest of the town of Sinj) revealed two periods of use: the prehistoric period and the fifteenth and sixteenth centuries AD. Beside the numerous pottery of the so-called Adriatic type of the Ljubljana Culture and the Early Cetina Culture (both belonging to the Late Copper/Early Bronze Age), five stone artefacts were found and the probable remains of houses in the central part of the dolina. Other dolinas in the vicinity revealed similar sherds. The excavators suggest that many dolinas on the plateau of Otišić were used for smaller houses in the Late Copper/Early Bronze Age and were part of a larger settlement complex (Milošević and Govedarica, 1986: 53).

At the moment, we do not have any finds suggesting similar use. The prehistoric sherds of our survey mostly belong to the Late Bronze Age and Early Iron Age, with the exception of one sherd from Dolina 17 dated to the Late Copper Age/Early Bronze Age. It was a piece of more refined pottery, brown in colour, with a 'winkeschnur' ornament typical for Ljubljana Culture (T. Greif, *pers. comm.*). The layer containing extensive traces of burning from Dolina 14 could be dated as not earlier than the Roman period according to the stratigraphic position of Roman sherds found in the section; only thorough excavation will prove the existence of structures.

However, it is reasonable to expect that most pottery in the dolinas reflects the intensity of their agricultural use. The prehistoric pottery belongs to the period of the most intensive settlement of the castellieri (the first millennium BC: Fig. 12.12) and the first traceable demographic pressure in the Karst (Gams, 1990: 29–36). Prior to the Late Bronze Age, the number of castellieri seemed to be lower (Karouškova-Soper, 1983: 170–5) and rather evenly distributed with regard to the fertile plots of land in the Karst. We can reasonably suspect that more intensive use

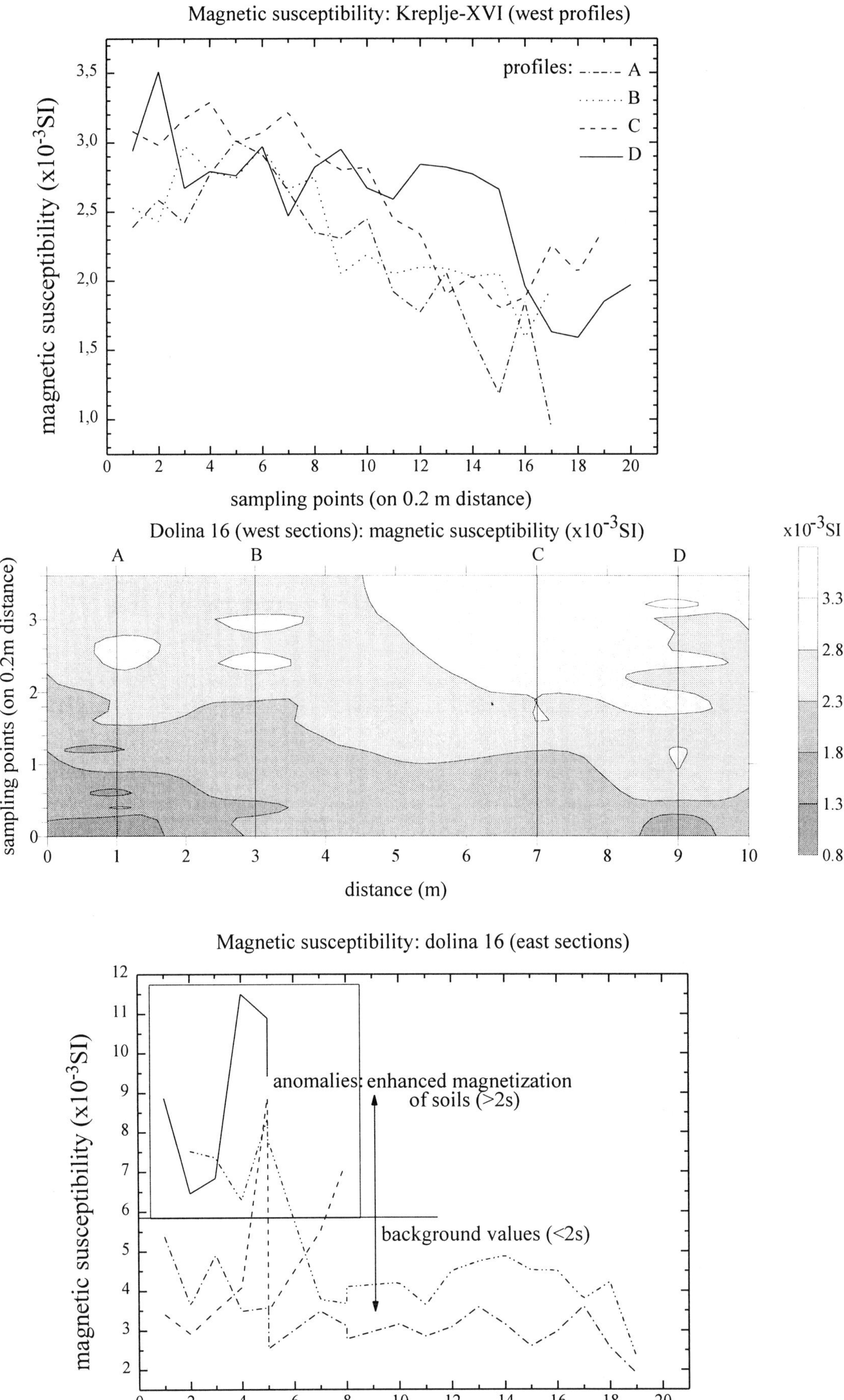

Fig. 12.11. Dolina 16: magnetic susceptibility readings.

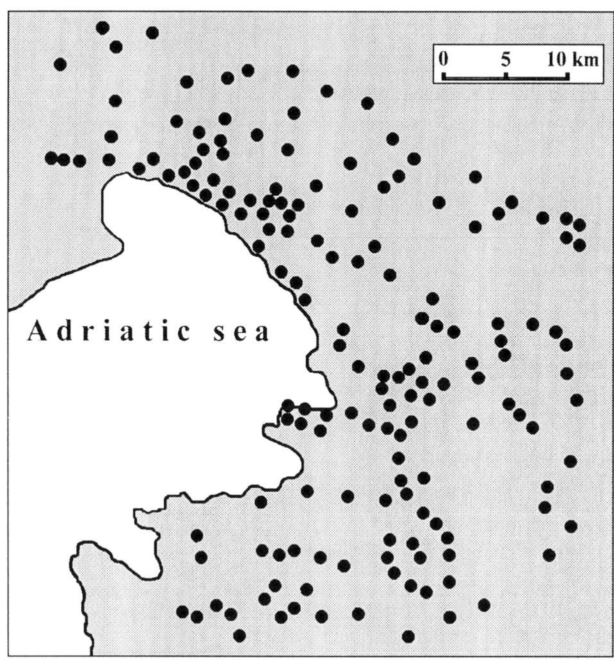

Fig. 12.12. Distribution of late bronze age and iron age castellieri in the greater Karst area.

of dolinas for agricultural purposes in prehistory began in the Iron Age (*c.* 800 BC) when more than 100 castellieri existed and exploited the Karst. Comparing their number, density and proximity to each other, their catchments rarely exceed more than 15 km^2 in this period (Karouškova-Soper, 1983: 171–2), which allows an average figure of only two per cent of agricultural land in their catchments.

The Roman period is clearly under-represented by the pottery found in the dolinas, even though people at that time tended to settle in the lowlands and less on hilltops. From this period, we know of villages and villas that exploited and cleared larger lowland areas close to the later medieval and modern villages: for example, there are numerous dolinas close to the Roman sites of Lokev, Sežana, Rodik, Povir and Kopriva (Slapšak, 1983). The case of Dolina 17 probably represents the best example of this kind. However, dolinas containing Roman pottery are still very few, partly because of the difficulties in recognising some of the local Roman coarse wares, which were very similar to prehistoric pottery.

Nevertheless, there remains the open question of how the prehistoric pottery actually came to the dolinas. Erosion accounts for the movement of finds from the slopes or rims of dolinas and only to a minimal extent, as explained above. Evidence for permanent or temporary occupation is also lacking. On the other hand, the agricultural use of dolinas could bring finds in various ways. Manuring is highly improbable, since the flocks of sheep and goat were mobile and were not animals used for the production of manure for arable land. Cattle was not common in the castellieri period, as is shown by the faunal remains from the Trieste karst (Karouškova-Soper, 1983: 201). This argument is more appropriate for the last centuries, when farmers turned to cattle grazing and farm enclosures were established to stall the animals.

However, we have seen that farmers improved soil quality by adding rubble, tiles (although never widely used in the Karst before our century) and other hard material they discarded as rubbish. It is difficult to say at the present stage of research if similar practices existed in prehistory as well. There is no reason to believe that the type of knowledge acquired today by the locals after years of daily contact with the land would have been unknown in antiquity. It is to be expected that the inhabitants of the Karst were well aware of the landscape and ways of improving it. Its strengths and weaknesses and their long standing occupation of it from the earliest prehistory onwards made it possible for them to adapt to environmental conditions and adjust the environment to their needs when this was possible. Dolinas have always played an important role in the economy of the Karst and the differences in type and intensity of use serve as indicators of long-term social and economic practices in the past. The mutual interaction between people and landscape led to certain decisions and activities that, even though not yet fully understood, reflect human perception of surrounding nature and a need to appease and manage, if not tame, it. Further research is needed, including excavation of dolinas as well as a more thorough investigation of the castellieri of the Karst, to fill a gap in the archaeology of this region and to answer many of the questions posed here.

ACKNOWLEDGEMENTS

We wish to thank Tatjana Greif for taking part in our survey; Miran Erič for the drawings; Božidar Slapšak and Peter Turk for discussing the work with us and for information regarding the use of dolinas; and Phil Mason and Rachel Miovič for proof-reading and improving the text.

REFERENCES

(Slovene titles translated in English)

ANSI (1975) *Arheološka najdišča Slovenije* (Archaeological Sites of Slovenia). Ljubljana, Državna založba Slovenije.

Bahun, S. (1969) On the formation of Karst dolinas. *Geološki Vjesnik* 22: 25- 32.

Clark, A. (1990) *Seeing Beneath the Soil. Prospecting Methods in Archaeology*. London, Batsford.

Davies, J. (1988) *Vzpon z dna* (Rise from Want). Ljubljana, Slovenska matica.

Cvijić, J. (1924): *Geomorfologija* (Geomorphology). Belgrade, Državna štamparija.

Gams, I. (1972) Prispevek k mikroklimatologiji vrtač in kraških polj. (A contribution to the microclimatology of the Karst dolinas and Poljes). *Geografski Zbornik* 13: 5–78.

Gams, I. (1974) *Kras* (The Karst). Ljubljana, Slovenska matica.

Gams, I. (1987a) Geographical karst review. In I. Gams and P. Habič (eds) *Man's Impact in Dinaric Karst*: 93–115. Ljubljana, University of Ljubljana, Department of Geography.

Gams, I. (1987b) Krajna vas. In I. Gams and P. Habič (eds) *Man's Impact in Dinaric Karst*: 118–23. Ljubljana, University of Ljubljana, Department of Geography.

Gams, I. (1990) Depth of Rillenkarren as a measure of deforestation age. *Studia Carsologica* 2: 29–36.

Gams, I. , Lovrenčak, F., Ingolič, B. (1971) Krajna vas: a study of the natural conditions and the agrarian land utilization in the Karst. *Geografski zbornik* 12: 221–6.

Gams, I., Nicod, J., Julian, M., Anthony, E., Sauro, U. (1993) Environmental change and human impacts on the Mediterranean karsts of France, Italy and the Dinaric region. In P.W. Williams (ed.) *Karst Terrains. Environmental Change and Human Impact*: 59–98. Cremlingen, Catena Supplement 25.

Habič, P. (1987a) The problematics of Karst water use and protection on the example of Unica near Postojna. In *Karst and Man. Proceedings of the International Symposium on Human Influence in Karst:* 7–18. Ljubljana, University of Ljubljana, Department of Geography.

Habič, P. (1987b) The Renčelica doline near Sežana. In I. Gams and P. Habič (eds) *Man's Impact in Dinaric Karst*: 115–7. Ljubljana, University of Ljubljana, Department of Geography.

Karouškova-Soper, V. (1983) *The Castellieri of Venezia Giulia, NE Italy (2nd-1st mill. BC)*. Oxford, British Archaeological Reports, International Series 192.

KRŠ Slovenije (1957) Split, publisher.

Lovrenčak, F. (1977) Prsti v Vrtačah Slovenije (Soils in dolinas of Slovenia). *Proceedings of the Jubilee Congress of Yugoslav Geographers, 15th-20th September 1976, Belgrade:* 443–9. Belgrade, Savez geografskih društava Jugoslavije.

Miloševič, A., and Govedarica, B. (1986) Otišić, Vlake – preistorijsko nalazište u vrtači I (Otišić, Vlake – prehistoric site in dolina I). *Godisnjak Centra za Balkanološka Ispitivanja ANU BiH* 24/22: 53–71.

Nicod, J. (1987) Aménagements agraires dans les petites dépressions karstiques.In *Karst and Man. Proceedings of the International Symposium on Human Influence in Karst:* 97–110. Ljubljana, University of Ljubljana Department of Geography.

Osmuk, N. (1993) Notes in *Varstvo spomenikov*: 193, 208, 297.

Osmuk, N. (1994) Notes in *Varstvo spomenikov*: 99, 107, 109, 171.

Radinja, D. (1987) Modern agricultural land improvement in Slovene Dinaric karst. In *Karst and Man. Proceedings of the International Symposium on Human Influence in Karst:* 123–35. Ljubljana, University of Ljubljana Department of Geography.

Righi, G. (1982) *La Necropoli 'Celtica' di S. Canziano del Carso*. Trieste, Monografie di Preistoria III degli Atti dei Civici Musei di Storia ed Arte, Trieste.

Sauro, U. (1993) Human impact on the Karst of the Venetian fore-Alps, Italy. *Environmental Geology* 21 (3): 115–21.

Slapšak, B. (1983) The Kras (Karst) Survey. In D.R. Keller and D.W. Rupp (eds) *Archaeological Survey in the Mediterranean Area*: 2201–2. Oxford, British Archaeological Reports, International Series 155.

Slapšak, B. (1995) *Možnosti študija Poselitve v Arheologiji* (Possibilities of the settlement studies in archaeology). Ljubljana, Arheo 17.

Šušteršič, F. (1994) Classic dolinas of classical site.*Acta Carsologica* 23: 123–56.

Tomadin, V. (1992) *Moggio Udinese: Scavi Archeologici ai Piedi della Torre dell' Abbazia di San Gallo*. Moggio Udinese, Commune di Moggio Udinese.

Verginella, M. (1990) *Družina v Dolini pri Trstu* (Family in Dolina near Trieste). Ljubljana, Zveza zgodovinskih društev Slovenije.

13. Archeologia Ambientale Padana: un Caso di Studio – la Pianura Padana Centrale tra il Bronzo Medio ed il Bronzo Finale (XVI–XIII sec.a.C)

Mauro Cremaschi

PREMESSA

La media età del Bronzo è per la pianura padana un momento di grandi cambiamenti ambientali, legati specialmente allo sviluppo della cultura terramaricola. Malgrado i cinque secoli che vanno dal XVI e XIII e ricadono nella cronozona Suboreale non vedano mutamenti di rilievo dal punto di vista climatico globale (Cremaschi, 1990–1991), la forte pressione demografica, le strategie di sussistenza basate essenzialmente sulla agricoltura intensiva e la pastorizia, produssero, in questa fase, rilevanti effetti sull'ambiente, specialmente a causa di una sistematica deforestazione.

Lo studio del paesaggio padano nell'età del Bronzo è oggetto di un progetto di ricerca, che vede implicata la Soprintendenza Archeologica dell'Emilia Romagna ed il Dipartimento di Scienze della Terra dell'Università di Milano ed è affrontato su scala regionale riguardando quel tratto della pianura padana centrale che comprende le provincie di Reggio, Modena e Parma (*c.* 2500 km^2) , a livello di mesoscala (250 km^2), per un'area campione corrispondente al basso bacino dell'Enza, tra Calerno-Brescello nella provincia di Reggio Emilia e, a livello di microscala, attraverso l'esplorazione di un sito specifico, la terramara di S. Rosa presso Poviglio.

A livello regionale e di mesoscala, è l'analisi geomorfologica e fisiografica che ha un ruolo prevalente ed è condotta con i tradizionali metodi del rilevamento geomorfologico e pedologico, mentre a livello di microscala l'indagine si è concentrata sull'esplorazione archeologica della terramara di S. Rosa di Poviglio, in cui, oltre al metodo di scavo stratigrafico, sono sviluppate ricerche paleoambientali sul campo ed in laboratorio che vanno dall'analisi sedimentologica e pedologica (specie micromorfologia) nonchè allo studio archeobotanico ed archeozoologico demandato a specialisti del settore (Bernabò Brea e Cremaschi, 1989).

LE TERRAMARE

Le terramare sono siti pluristratificati dell'età del Bronzo medio e recente, tipicamente circondati da un argine in terra e da un fossato. Furono scoperte già dall' inizio del XIX secolo perche' usate come cave di fertilizzante minerale (Bernabò Brea e Mutti, 1994), ed esplorate sistematicamente per tutta la seconda metà del secolo (Mutti 1993), il loro studio, abbandonato per più di mezzo secolo dalla fine dell'Ottocento fino agli anni '50, e' oggi di nuovo al centro dell'attenzione di numerosi studiosi italiani .

Dal punto di vista storico, le terramare si sviluppano a partire dal XVI secolo con abitati di piccole dimensioni fino ad un ettaro ed hanno il loro apice nel XIII secolo, che vede il moltiplicarsi dei siti e lo sviluppo di alcun e'estensione fino all' di 20 ettari, per poi estinguersi improvvisamente alla fine dello stesso XIII secolo (Bernabò Brea *et al.*, 1987).

Nella pianura padana centrale (Fig. 13.1) si conoscono *c.*200 siti terramaricoli con una densità di circa un sito ogni 25 chilometri quadrati. Si tratta di una concentrazione di insediamenti assai elevata, mai raggiunta fino allora, e non più ripetuta fino all' età imperiale romana, che ha implicato necessariamente un forte impatto antropico: la ricostruzione delle condizioni ambientali è pertanto utile per comprendere lo sviluppo della cultura terramaricola e le sue strategie di sussistenza.

TERRAMARE E RETE IDROGRAFICA

Qualora si intenda conoscere il contesto territoriale delle terramare ed eventualmente applicarvi analisi di Archeologia spaziale, finalizzate a generalizzazioni di carattere storico-paletnologico (Cardarelli, 1988), il primo problema da affrontare è se il territorio circostante è contemporaneo agli insediamenti.

La distribuzione dei siti quale emerge dalla carta di Figure 13.1 non è legata soltanto problemi di territorialità coevi ai siti stessi, quanto piuttosto alla evoluzione del reticolo idrografico. Come e' indicato in Figure 13.2 (Castaldini, 1987; Cremaschi, 1980; Cremaschi*et al.*, 1993),

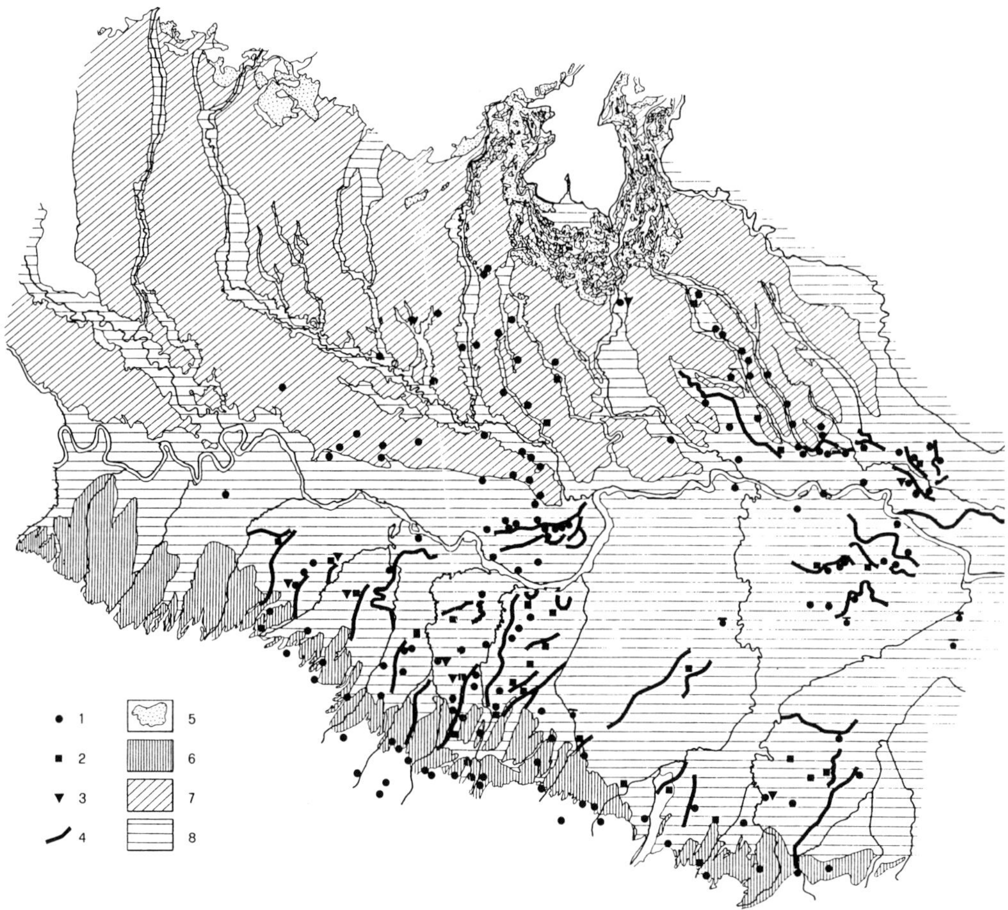

Fig. 13.1. Distribuzione delle terramare nel tratto centrale della pianura padana. 1. siti dell'età del Bronzo medio e recente; 2. terramare strutturate; 3. terramare con palafitte e palafitte perifluviali; 4. tracce di paleoalvei; 5. morene; 6. terrazzi pleistocenici; 7. livello fondamentale della pianura lombarda; 8. pianura olocenica.

gran parte della rete di paleoalvei che ancor oggi conservano evidenza geomorfologica e' di eta' romana o alto medievale e quelle piu' antiche sono sepolte. Le tracce di paleoalveo che sembrano precedere questa fase sono assai poche (Cremaschi, 1980), inoltre il criterio deterministico fino ad ora usato per l'attribuzione di un tratto d'alveo all'eta' del Bronzo, in funzione della sua relazione ad un vicino sito di tale eta', lascia oggi insoddisfatti in mancanza di una verifica stratigrafica puntuale.

I siti dell' eta' del Bronzo si trovano su isole, risparmiate dalla divagazione dei corsi d'acqua e dall' espandimento dei sedimenti di piana alluvionale. Qualora si voglia analizzare il contesto territoriale, al di la' del dato relativo al singolo sito, l'indagine si deve concentrare su quelle superfici che si configurano stabili, nel senso di Sevink (1985) almeno a partire dall'eta' del Bronzo.

A grande scala, e' pertanto difficile ricostruire il reticolo idrografico dell' eta' del Bronzo, poiche' l'estremo stato di frammentazione delle evidenze non consente di individuare le aste fluviali attive a quel tempo e tanto meno i loro caratteri geomorfologici e la loro tipologia.

STUDIO A MEDIA SCALA: L'AREA COMPRESA FRA CALERNO E BRESCELLO

Questa area ha un valore esemplare perche', gia' densamente insediata nel Neolitico e nel Bronzo antico, in essa sorgono sei villaggi terramaricoli, tra i quali Case del Lago e Case Cocconi, che per avere una estensione, rispettivamente di 22 e 15 ettari, si configurano come i siti di maggior rilievo del territorio terramaricolo .

L'area in esame (Fig. 13.3) si trova nella pianura reggiana, il substrato geologico e' costituito essenzialmente da una conoide tardo-pleistocenica di tessitura ghiaiosa ed i suoi lembi distali di tessitura piu' fine, che non sono stati sede di esondazione a partire dall' Olocene antico .

I suoli che si trovano su questo territorio sono inceptisuoli prevalentemente e relitti di alfisuoli, connessi a strutture neolitiche. La situazione e' assai simile a quella osservata a Casatico di Marcaria (Cremaschi, 1990), e si ipotizza che gli alfisuoli, presenti in gran parte dell' area almeno in eta' atlantica siano andati in erosione a partire dall'inizio del Subborelale e la situazione dei suoli attuali possa rappresentare quella gia' presente nel Bronzo medio.

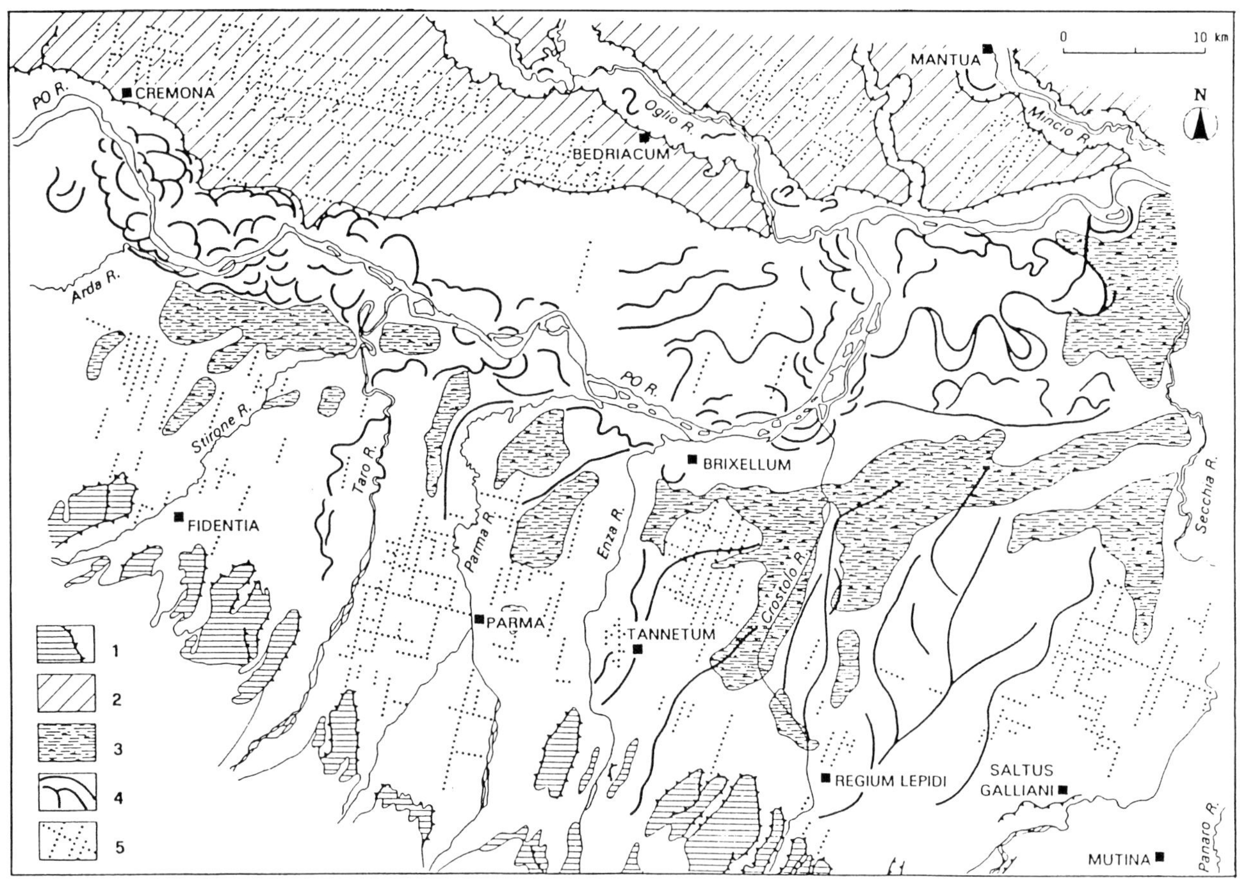

Fig.13.2. I paleoalvei e le aree palustri di età romana ed alto medievale nella pianura padana centrale. 1. terrazzi pleistocenici al margine appenninico; 2. livello fondamentale della pianura lombarda; 3. paludi e 'valli' medievali; 4. palealvei attivi in eta' romana ed alto medievale; 5. tracce di centuriazione .

La carta geomorfologica di Figure 13.3 evidenzia come la superficie stabile dell'area in esame risulti limitata dai paleoalvei di eta' romana e medievale del fiume Enza e del torrente Crostolo ad ovest e ad est, mentre a Nord dai coevi paleoalvei del Po e la zona valliva di eta' post romana, bonificata soltanto nel XV secolo A.D.

Come molte regioni dell'area mediterranea (Cremaschi *et al.*, 1994), l'area geomorfologicamente stabile risulta percorsa dalla centuriazione romana. Questa ha avuto un determinante impatto sui lineamenti fisiografici, i quali risultano allineati ad essa. Vi sono pero' delle significative eccezioni, che sono costituite dalle aree pertinenti alle piu' grandi terramare dell'area e le aree ad esse periferiche (cfr. Case Cocconi: Bronzoni e Cremaschi, 1990), le quali formano nuclei inglobati nella centuriazione, ma non distrutti da essa. Vi sono inoltre alcuni corsi d'acqua, che per essere sistematicamente associati alle strutture delle terramare stesse (Fig. 13.4), devono essere stati attivi nell'eta' del Bronzo. Questi corsi d'acqua sono incisi nella pianura, a differenza di gran parte dei corsi attuali che sono pensili ed hanno marcato orientamento Ovest-Est che contrasta con la direzione nordorientale degli assi della centuriazione romana e del reticolo idrografico attuale. Il perimetro delle terramare, di forma quadrangolare, risulta palesemente allineato con questi corsi d'aqua. Apparentemente le due terramare settentrionali, Motta Balestri e S. Rosa di Poviglio, non si accostano ad alcun paleoalveo conservato in superficie ed emergono dai depositi di esondazione piu' recenti, ma come verra' dimostrato dallo studio locale del sito di S. Rosa sono legate ad un antico corso dello stesso Po.

LA TERRAMARA DI S. ROSA DI POVIGLIO

Il sito si trova nella pianura olocenica del Po, da cui dista circa tre chilometri, a 20 m s.l.m., presso il punto di coordinate IGM 74 IV SO 44' 52' 37" 1' 52' 37", nella localita' di Fodico nel comune di Poviglio.

Gli scavi hanno carattere estensivo, sono diretti da M. Bernabò Brea (Soprintendenza Archeologica dell'Emilia Romagna) e dallo scrivente (Bernabò Brea e Cremaschi, 1990, 1995): ad oggi sono state condotte 15 campagne che hanno posto in luce circa 4000 m^2 dell'abitato.

La terramara si compone di due nuclei (Fig. 13.5) entrambi circondati da un terrapieno visibile sulla

Fig. 13.3. Carta geomorfologica della bassa val d' Enza. 1. conoide; 2. paleoalvei debolmente incisi; 3. paleoalvei marcatamente incisi; 4. dossi; 5a. drenaggi 'naturali; 5b. fontanili e depositi palustri; 6. limiti delle valli; 7. siti dell' età del Bronzo (a. in superficie; b. sepolti); 8. terramare; 9. assi della centuriazione romana; 10. curve di livello con equidistanza di un metro.

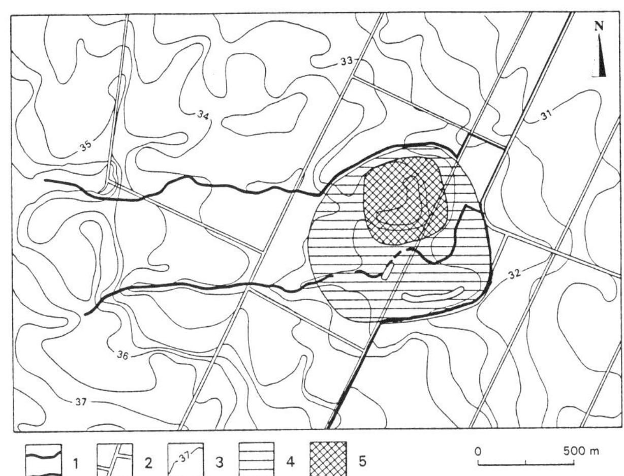

Fig. 13.4. La terramara di Case Cocconi. 1. drenaggi non modificati da interventi antropici; 2. strade e canali moderni, talora coerenti con la centuriazione romana; 3. isoipse con equidistanza 0,5 m; 4. recinto periferico della terramara; 5. estensione della terramara.

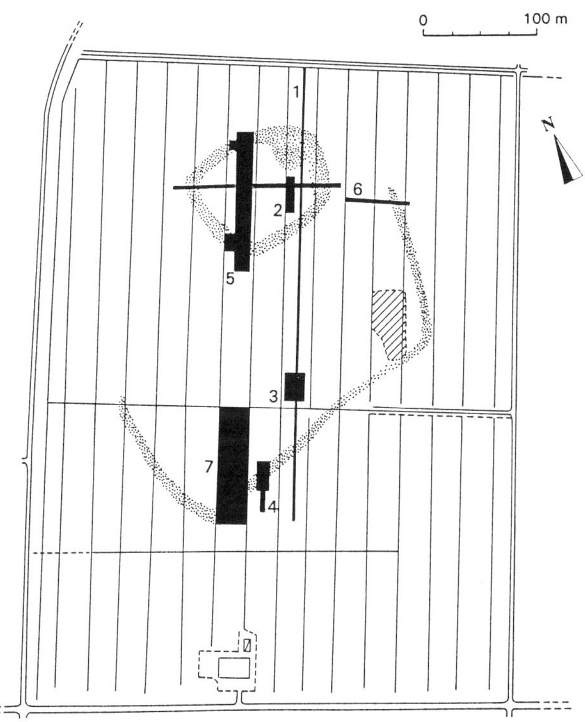

Fig. 13.5. La terramara di S. Rosa di Poviglio. Il puntinato indica la traccia dei terrapieni che delimitano rispettivamente il villaggio grande ed il villaggio piccolo. Le aree nere dall'1 al 7 indicano le aree esplorate fino ad oggi.

fotoaerea sottoforma di una fascia di terreno chiaro che contrasta con i suoli circostanti di colore scuro: l'abitato piccolo dell'estensione di circa un ettaro, e l'abitato grande dell' estensione di circa cinque ettari. L'indagine archeologica ha dimostrato che il villaggio piccolo corrisponde anche al nucleo piu' antico dell'abitato essendo fondato nel XVI secolo e che il villaggio si ingrandisce, attraverso grandi ristrutturazioni a partire dal XIV-XIII secolo.

L'analisi d'immagine, associata alla misura del microrilievo (Cremaschi *et al.*, 1994), rivela esternamente ai terrapieni, una depressione corrispondente all' antico fossato che circondava gli abitati. Il microrilievo mette altresi' in evidenza un rilievo artificiale determinato dalla stratificazione archeologica a ridosso dell'argine del villaggio grande, ma questo manca nel villaggio piccolo, poiche' il deposito e' stato in gran parte asportato dalla cava di terramarna attiva nel secolo scorso. Lembi di stratigrafia si sono conservati al margine dei terrapieni e all'esterno di essi.

L'interno dell' abitato piccolo all'interfaccia tra substrato sterile e lembi di stratificazione archeologica appare costellato di buche di palo, che formano una rete inestricabile dovuta alle numerose fasi di ristrutturazione che la terramara ha subito, all' interno delle quali si aprono numerosi pozzi magazzino e soprattutto alcuni pozzi per acqua, dalla caratteristica forma cilindrica, della profondita' di circa due metri. Questo fatto e' assai significativo, poiche' oggi la falda acquifera e' alla profondita' di pochi decimetri dal livello di campagna e lo scavo deve essere tenuto asciutto mediante pompe. Significa pertanto che la falda freatica nel Bronzo medio si trovava assai piu' bassa dell'attuale.

La stratificazione all'interno dell'abitato grande e', al contrario, perfettamente conservata (Fig. 13.6), e pur di modesto spessore registra due fasi di strutture abitative ed una fase di costruzione di una piattaforma in terra che si frappone fra le due fasi d'abitazione (Bernabo' Brea e Cremaschi, 1995). La fase abitativa piu' antica consiste di un edifici appoggiati su pali perfettamente allineati pertinenti a non piu' di due momenti di ristrutturazione. Lo studio dell' entisuolo su cui il villaggio appoggia e della ricca malacofauna, esclusivamente terrestre (*Retinella olivetorum*, *Cepea nemoralis*, *Macrogastra plicatula*, *Pomatias elegans*, *Monacha cartusiana* – det. A. Girot), evidenziano innanzi tutto un ambiente asciutto nonche' lavori di riporto artificiale di suolo per assicurare un drenaggio alla base delle strutture abitative. Anche nel villaggio grande vi sono pozzi per acqua che hanno le stesse caratteristiche e profondita' di quelli del villaggio piccolo. Particolarmente significativa inoltre la presenza di un piccolo corso d'acqua sinuoso, inciso nel substrato che attraversa parte del tratto scavato del villaggio e drena verso nord ovest. Esso risulta disattivato e completamente asciutto al momento della costruzione del villaggio, poiche' viene attraversato obliquamente dai filari di pali portanti le strutture e riempito dai butti provenienti dagli impalcati lignei, senza che in esso vi siano sedimenti trasportati o elaborati da acqua corrente o stagnante. Poiche' i corsi

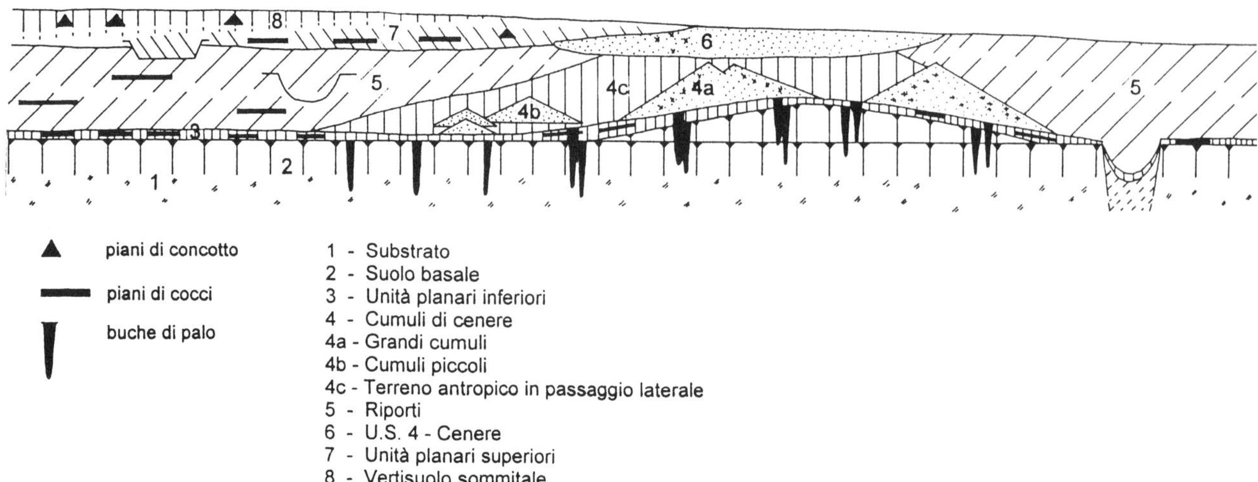

Fig. 13.6. Schema stratigrafico del villaggio grande della terramara di Poviglio.

d'acqua dell'area sono oggi pensili, il fatto di trovare all' interno del villaggio un corso d'acqua inciso dimostra che un marcato cambiamento negli equilibri idrogeologici.

I FOSSATI PERIFERICI DELLA TERRAMARA DI POVIGLIO

I fossati che circondano l'abitato terramaricolo sono fonti di informazioni preziose, poiche essi hanno agito da trappole sedimentarie sia durante l'uso dell'abitato che successivamente. Particolarmente significativo il fossato che e' stato osservato al margine settentrionale dell'abitato piccolo (Fig. 13.7). Questo e' alloggiato al margine di una depressione profonda circa tre metri dal piano campagna attuale e che corrisponde probabilmente ad un tratto del paleoalveo del Po. Il riempimento del fossato e' costituito alla base da sedimenti d'acqua corrente riza leuri al Bronzo medio, da scarichi del Bronzo recente e poi, da sedimenti di decantazione che culminano con un livello torboso contenenti materiali di eta' romana. Al di sopra vi sono due coltri di argilla dello spessore complessivo di due metri di eta' medievale. E' assai significativo il fatto che, tra la tarda eta' del Bronzo e l'étà romana si depositano non piu' di cinquanta centimetri di sedimenti, indicanti ristagno d'acque, mentre una sensibile accelerazione della sedimentazione, che porta al quasi completo riempimento dei fossati si ha soltanto in eta' alto medievale.

Il diagramma pollinico ottenuto per il riempimento di questo fossato (Ravazzi *et al.*, 1992; Fig. 13.8) indica un ambiente gia' sensibilmente deforestato nelle fasi del Bronzo medio e rimane tale sostanzialmente fino all' eta' romana, mentre contemporaneamente alle esondazioni altomedievali si ha la vera rigenerazione della foresta.

Lo studio del riempimento dei fossati e' importante per due aspetti. In primo luogo ha permesso di evidenziare la presenza, a Nord dell'abitato di una marcata depressione, che coincide con un paleoalveo sepolto. Il fatto di trovare un tratto di paleoalveo del Po inciso ad alcuni metri rispetto all'attuale livello di campagna spiega a livello locale che la presenza del drenaggio inciso che attraversa il villaggio piccolo, e dei pozzi da acqua, che indicano una falda freatica assai piu' depressa dell'attuale.

In secondo luogo da indicazioni sulla storia post deposizionale del sito. I fossati dopo l'abbandono del sito rimangono sede di acqua stagnante per lungo tempo, e solo molto piu' recentemente sono raggiunte dalle alluvioni del Po. Dal rilevamento pedologico di dettaglio e dall'analisi d'immagine e' stato evidenziato il limite delle piu' recenti alluvioni, identificate nella sezione del fossato, che seppelliscono soprattutto la parte nordoccidentale della terramara (Fig. 13.9).

TERRAMARE E *LAND EVALUATION*

La terramara di S. Rosa viene abbandonata alla fine del XIII secolo, come tutte le altre della regione. Lo studio del riempimento del fossato permette di escludere che tale evento coincida con fenomeni di dissesto idrogeologico vistosi, che sono invece registrati per l'alto medioevo. Una possibile ragione dell'abbandono dell'area puo' essere ricercata in una crisi di produttivita' del suolo connessa al crescere del numero e soprattutto dell'estensione degli insediamenti, indicati un sensibile aumento demografico, avvenuta nel XIII secolo.

Per stimare questa possibilita', si propone un tentativo di applicazione della *land evaluation* potenziale, per la stima della produttivita dei suoli, secondo metodi discussi altrove (Cremaschi, 1990). Pur riconoscendo l'ampio spettro delle fonti di approvvigionamento usate dalle comunita' dell' eta' del Bronzo, la valutazione verra' limitata alle culture cerealicole che ne costituirono la piu' importante.

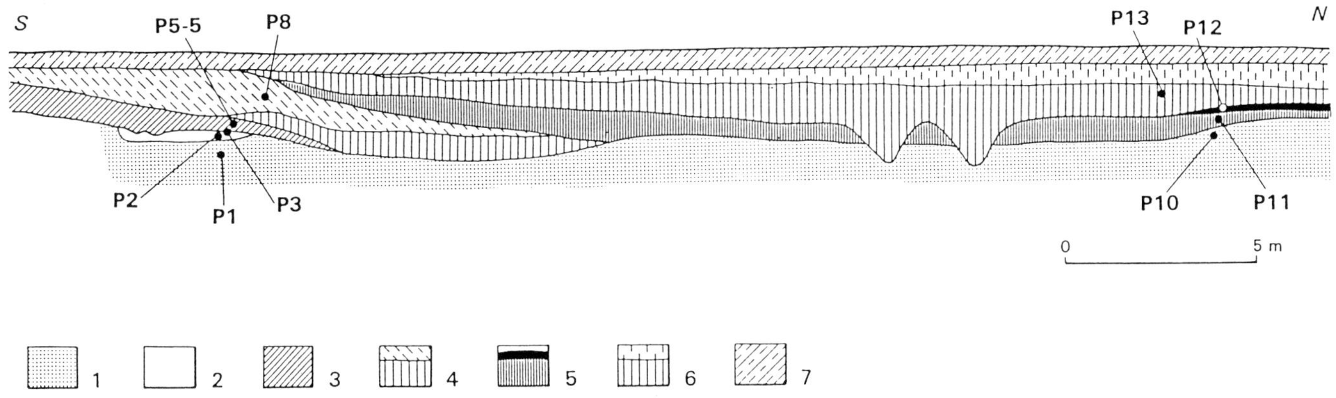

Fig. 13.7. Sezione stratigrafica del fossato Nord della terramara di Poviglio con ubicazione dei campioni palinologici (cfr. Fig. 13.8). 1. substrato; 2. piccolo fossato del Bronzo medio; 3. scarichi ricchi di sostanza organica; 4. ollasso dell'argine e sottostanti riempimenti del fossato; 5. depositi argillosi ricchi di sostanza organica con ceramica dell'età del ferro e torba con materiale di età romana; 6. depositi argillosi trasformati in vertisuoli di eta' medievale; 7. orizzonte arativo.

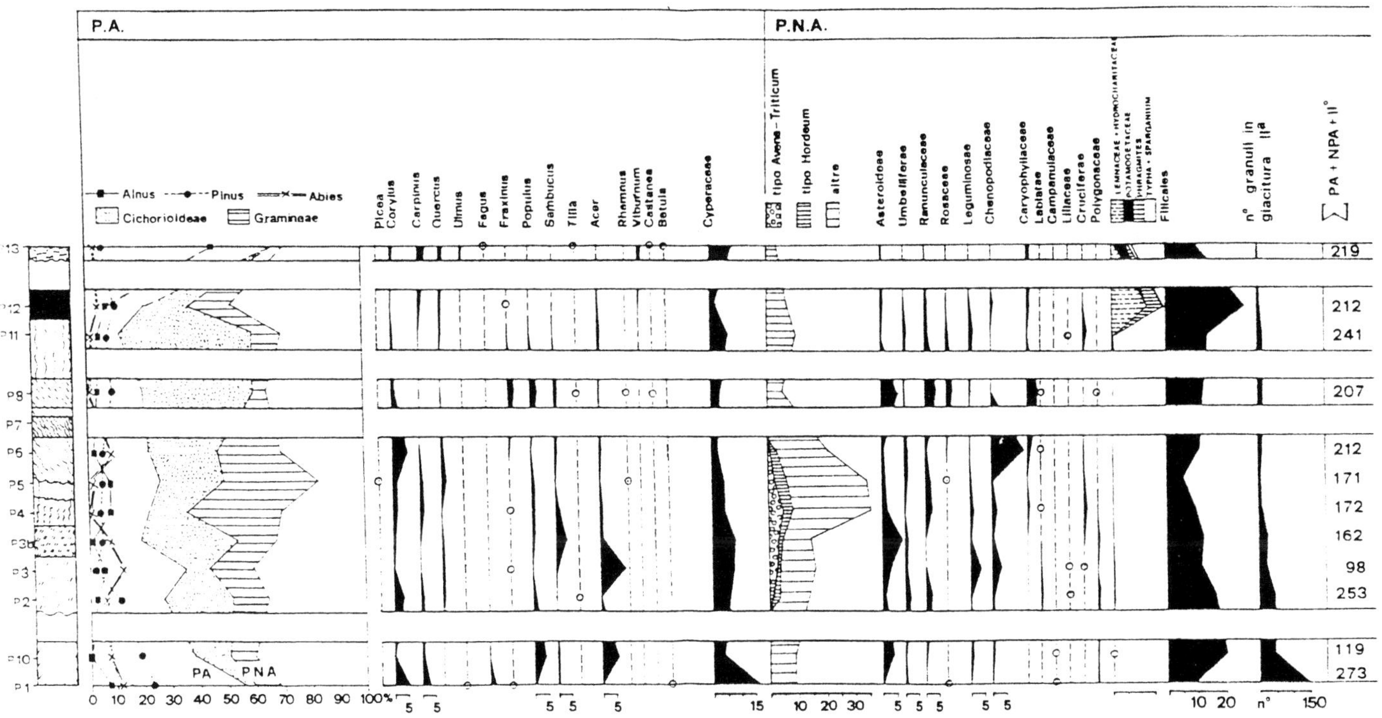

Fig. 13.8. Diagramma pollinico del fossato della terramara di Poviglio S. Rosa.

Come e' noto la valutazione richiede che vengano paragonati i *requirements* delle culture alle *qualities* dei suoli, tenendo conto della consistenza demografica e del livello tecnologico della popolazione cui tale valutazione e' applicata. Se le *qualities* possono essere valutate in modo relativamente oggettivo sulla base dei caratteri pedologici dell' area (Fig. 13.10), i *requirements* e le informazioni relative alle popolazioni richiedono ipotesi spesso costruibili soltanto su base induttiva.

Sulla base dei dati pollinici del riempimento del fossato di S. Rosa, viene stimato che il 34% dell'area fosse disboscato durante il Bronzo medio e che tale superficie salisse al 39% durante il Bronzo recente. Circa i *requirements* delle colture cerealicole, viene fatto riferimento a quelli relativi al grano tenero moderno, specie leggermente piu' esigenti di quelle in uso in eta' del Bronzo. Tenuto conto del livello tecnologico delle pratiche agrarie, il rendimento, stimato sulla base dell' agricoltura alto medievale, viene stimato 1 a 6. Il coefficiente pedologico viene calcolato a 0.9 per le classi di suoli a *suitability* pia' elevata, a 0.7 per i suoli di *suitability* 2 ed a 0.6 per i suoli con le maggiori limitazioni d'uso. Per calcolare la reale disponibilita' di grano, il rendimento effettivo viene diminuito di 1/6 per il grano da semina che viene stoccato e dimezzato, poiché si ipotizza una rotazione biennale nell' uso delle superfici disboscate per fini agrari. Circa la

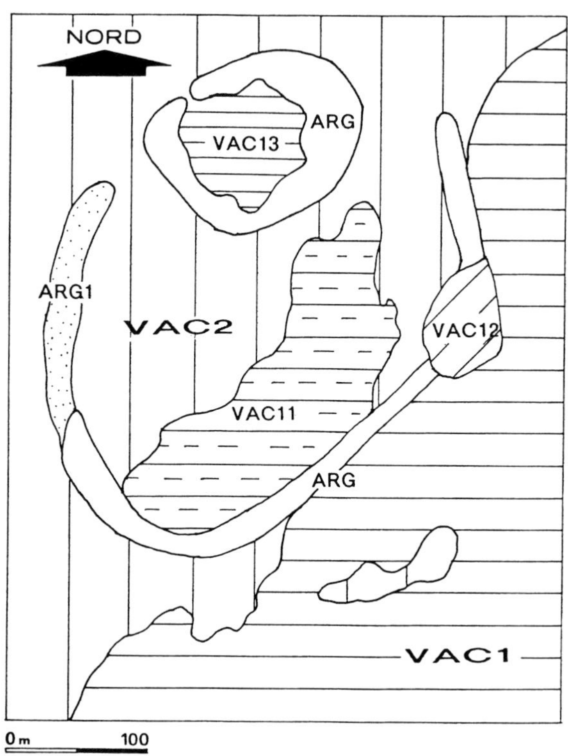

Fig.13.9. La serie dei suoli della terramara di Poviglio; la serie VAC2 corrisponde ai vertisuoli evoluti sulle piu' recenti alluvioni.

consistenza demografica dei siti terramaricoli viene stimata una presenza di 300 abitanti per ettaro di abitato del Bronzo medio, ridotta a 250 per i siti piu' ampi del Bronzo recente che avrebbero potuto comprendere aree non insediate al loro interno.

Fondata su queste premesse, la Figura 13.11 riporta i risultati della *Land Evaluation.* L'area in esame ha prevalentemente suoli poco evoluti – *xerochrepts* e *xererts* – generalmente adatti alla coltura del grano, i cui maggiori fattori di limitazione sono la tessitura argillosa, determinante a causa della tecnologia dell' epoca che non conosceva l'aratro metallico, e l' idromorfia del suolo legata anch' essa alla tessitura fine oppure alla presenza di falda vicino alla superficie. I suoli piu' adatti (S 1) senza limitazioni di uso sono il 28% dell' area, stessa percentuale hanno quelli con le limitazioni piu' severe. La disponibilita' viene calcolata per il Bronzo medio, per il Bronzo recente e per una ipotetica situazione di emergenza climatica, in cui le piu' abbondanti precipitazioni aumentino l 'incidenza del fattore limitante idromorfia sulla qualita' del suolo ed una diminuzione della temperature media annua influisca negativamente sulla stagione di maturazione del grano.

Confrontando il fabbisogno delle comunita' terramaricole con la disponibilita' di grano, appare che questa e' ampiamente in eccesso durante il Bronzo medio, mentre e' deficitaria per il Bronzo recente per aumentato

VALUTAZIONE					RISULTATO DELLA VALUTAZIONE			
CARATTERISTICHE	INTENSITÀ DELLE LIMITAZIONI				Aquic Xerochrepts (25%)	Typic Xerochrepts (18%)	Entic Chromoxeverts (40%)	Typic Chromoxeverts (17%)
	1	2	3	4				
profondità utile in cm	> 60	40-60	25-40	< 25	1	1	1	1
tessiture	FSA-FLA F FA FL FS	A AS AL L	S FS	S	2	1	2	2
drenaggio	buono moderato	imperfetto eccessivo	povero eccessivo	molto povero	2	1	3	2
$CaCO_3$%	0,5-1.5	15-20	< 0.5 > 20		2	1	3	2
rischio di inondazioni	basso	basso	basso	moderato	1	1	1	1

Fig.13.10. Unità pedologiche e loro attitudine alla coltura cerealicola nel basso bacino dell'Enza.

UNITÀ FISIOGRAFICA: CAMPEGINE-POVIGLIO (234 Km^2) *area deforestata:* BM h 16.500
BR h 18.700

Siti	*Superficie* BM	BR
Motta Balestri	h 2	h 2
S. Sisto	h 1	
Monticelli	h 2	h 9
Cocconi	h 3	h 22(?)
Case del Lago	h 2.5(?)	h 16
Elsa	h 1	h 1 (?)
Le Grazie	h 1	–
S. Ilario	h 1	h 1
	h 14,5	h 58
abitanti	300/h	250/h
FABBISOGNO DI GRANO ANNUO q	15.877,5 (23.925)	52.925 (79.025)
	BM Bronzo medio	BR Bronzo recente

Classi di suitability	*S1*	*S2*	*S3*
superficie occupata	28%	52%	28%
h BM	4564	8476	3260
h BR	5262	9735	3744
rendimento teorico q/h	6	6	6
Coefficiente pedologico	0,9	0,7	0,6
rendimento effettivo (grano annuo q)			
BM	24.646	35.600	11.736
BR	28.307	40.887	13.487
diminuito 1/6 per la semina / dimezzato per rotazione annuale			
	BRONZO MEDIO	BRONZO REC.	STRESS
DISPONIBILITÀ (grano annuo q)	29.993	34.450	27.992 (20.670)

Fig. 13.11. Risultato della land evaluation *potenziale condotta nel basso bacino dell'Enza.*

fabbisogno. Qualora si potesse dimostrare che alla fine del secondo millennio si sia verificato quel peggioramento climatico, da piu' parti ipotizzato (Cremaschi, 1990–1991), in questo periodo la fertilita' del suolo e la conseguente produzione di grano sarebbero state fortemente ridotte, rendendo il bilancio fra fabbisogno e disponibilita' drammaticamente deficitario.

La diminuita produttivita' del suolo, in un quadro di aumentata pressione demografica, potrebbe essere una delle cause che hanno prodotto il ben noto abbandono delle terramare centropadane alla fine del Bronzo recente

CONCLUSIONI

Le evidenze discusse indicano che l' idrografia nel Bronzo medio nella valle padana centrale era assai diversa dall'attuale. In una regione in cui i corsi d' acqua sono pensili ed arginati vi erano corsi d' acqua in chiara fase di incisione. Il fenomeno trova giustificazione nella storia del drenaggio padano a partire dall' ultimo ciclo glaciale.

Durante l'apice glaciale, per far fronte al forte abbassamento del livello marino, i corsi d'acqua padani sono in forte incisione, mentre al contrario, a partire dal Tardiglaciale e soprattutto nell' Olocene, la risalita del livello marino provoca il sovralluvionamento degli alvei. Tale sovralluvionamento non si e' ancora verificato in eta' del Bronzo ed avviene tardivamente, dopo l' eta' romana. Cio' significa che gran parte dell' idrografia nella piana olocenica e' recente e si e' sovrimpressa a quella piu' antica. A grande scala pertanto il paesaggio dell' eta' del Bronzo non e' piu' leggibile nella sua integrita'. Solo area di media estensione possono conservarlo.

Nell'area addotta ad esempio, si osserva una diretta correlazione fra idrografia ed impianti terramaricoli, che appaiono dove esplorati sistematicamente, siti fortificati eretti su terreno ben drenato. Il paesaggio che li circondava aveva destinazione prevalentemente agraria. L'applicazione della *land evaluation* potenziale all' area campione permette di formulare l' ipotesti che l' estinzione della terramare alla fine del XIII secolo possa essere legata all'impoverimento della risorsa suolo, dovuta all' eccessivo sfruttamento e forse ad un evento climatico sfavorevole, che puo' essersi sovrapposta ad altre ragioni di fragilita' del sistema da ricercarsi piu' nella vicenda storica che nel contesto ambientale.

RIFERIMENTI BIBLIOGRAFICI

Bernabò Brea, M. e Cremaschi, M., (1990) Les terramares del la Plaine du Po. *Actes du Colloque International de Lons-le-Saunier*: 407–17.

Bernabò Brea, M. e Cremaschi, M. (1995) L'indagine archeologica nelle terremare: gli scavi 1991–1993 nel villaggio grande di S. Rosa a Poviglio. *Memorie Museo Civico di Storia Naturale Verona, Sez. Scienze Uomo* 4: 309–23.

Bernabò Brea, M. e Muti, A. (1994) *Le Terremare Si Scavano per Concimare i Campi. La Nascita dell' Archeologia Preistorica a Parma nella Seconda Meta' dell'Ottocento*. Parma, Silva editore.

Bernabò Brea, M., Cardarelli, A. e Cremaschi, M. (1987) Le terremare dell'area centro-padana: problemi culturali e paleoambientali. In Preistoria e Protostoria nel Bacino del Basso Po, *Atti del Convegno di Ferrara 1984:* 147–91. Ferrara, Accademia delle Scima d'Ferrare.

Bronzoni, L. e Cremaschi, M. (1990) La terramara di Case Cocconi: strutture e materiali. *Padusa* 25: 173–226.

Cardarelli, A. (1988) L'eta' del Bronzo, organizzazione del territorio, forme economiche, strutture sociali. In AA VV, *Modena dalle Origini all'Anno Mille. Studi di Archeologia e Storia*: 86–127. Modena, Panini.

Castaldini, D. (1987) Evoluzione della rete idrografica centropadana in epoca protostorica e storica. *Atti del Convegno Nazionale Insediamenti e Viabilita' dell'Alto Ferrarese dall' Eta' Romana al Medioevo (Cento)*: 114–34. Ferrara, Accademia delle Scienze di Ferrara.

Cremaschi, M. (1990) Pedogenesi medio olocenica ed uso dei suoli durante il neolitico in Italia settentrionale. In P. Biagi (a cura di) *The Neolithisation of the Alpine Region*: 71–89. Brescia, Monografie di Natura Bresciana 13.

Cremaschi, M. (1991–92) (a cura di) Ambiente, insediamento, economia durante la media eta' del Bronzo. L'italia settentrionale. *Rassegna di Archeologia* 10: 145–88.

Cremaschi, M., Bernabò Brea, M., Tirabassi, J., D'Agostini, A., Dall' Aglio, P., Magri, S., Marchesini, A. e Nepoti, S. (1980) L'evoluzione della pianura emiliana durante l' eta' del Bronzo, l' eta' Romana e l' alto medioevo:geomorfologia ed insediamenti. *Padusa* 116 (1–4): 53–158.

Cremaschi, M., Ferretti, A. e Forte, M. (1994) Tecniche digitali e di visualizzazione in Geoarcheologia: il caso di studio della Terramara di S. Rosa di Poviglio. *Archeologia e Calcolatori* 5: 305–16.

Cremaschi. M., Marchetti. M. e Ravazzi, C., (1994) Geomorphological evidence for land surfaces cleared from forest in the central Po plain (northern Italy) during the Roman period. In B. Frenzel (a cura di) *Evaluation of Land Surfaces Cleared from Forests in the Mediterranean Region during the Time of the Roman Empire*: 119–32. Strasbourg, European Science Foundation.

Mutti, A. (1993) *Caratteristiche e Problemi del Popolamento Terramaricolo in Emilia Occidentale*. Bologna, Universita' di Bologna.

Ravazzi, C., Cremaschi, M. e Forlani, L. (1992) Ricostruzione della storia della vegetazione padana fra l' eta' del Bronzo e l' alto medioevo , in relazione all'intervento antropico. La successione pollinica del fossato della terramara di Poviglio. *Archivio Botanico Italiano* 67, 3/4: 198–220.

Sevink J., (1985) Physiographic soil survey and archaeology. In C. Malone e S. Stoddart (a cura di) *Papers in Italian Archaeology IV, Part 1, The Human Landscape*: 41–52. Oxford, British Archaeological reports, International Series 243.

14. Human Impact and Natural Characteristics of the Ancient Ports of Marseille and Fos in Provence, Southern France

C. Morhange, C. Vella, M. Provansal, A. Hesnard, and J. Laborel

INTRODUCTION

Southern Provence has proved to be a favourable location to study the relationship between people and environment. The landscape has been profoundly modified by human settlements for at least 5000 years. The research described here has called for collaboration between social and natural scientists. Above and beyond site studies, which are useful as chronological markers, this study seeks to address a set of questions about human impacts on land (Provansal 1995; Jorda and Provansal, 1996; Leveau and Provansal, 1993). We shall briefly review the research on inland Provence, in order to emphasize the originality of the studies carried out on the coast of Marseille and Fos.

The environmental history of inland Provence is that of a fragile natural environment whose development has been altered by humans since the neolithic period. Progressive deforestation and soil erosion have modified watercourses and have accelerated the silting up of alluvial plains. Both the prehistoric and historic periods have been punctuated by 'crises'. The Alpilles mountains and the edge of the Etang de Berre basin (see Fig. 14.1) were populated relatively early and underwent significant erosion *c.*3500–3000 BP. Such was not the case for the Sainte-Victoire or Sainte-Baume mountains. It was not until the Iron Age that the population density of the region became homogeneous, leading to a corresponding homogeneity in morphodynamic evolution.

Since the first millennium BC, three substantial periods of erosion have affected most of the sites in Provence: (1) during the Iron Age (the sixth to third centuries BC); (2) in the period of transition from classical antiquity to the medieval period (*c.*AD 500–800); and (3) in the early modern period (*c.*AD 1500–1850). These periods of rapid erosion were not necessarily contemporaneous with times of increased human activity. For example, the Roman period and the medieval period after the tenth century left few sedimentary traces.

The changes of water table level confirm the existence of hydrological variations across the region. They varied from positive in the Neolithic and later prehistoric periods to negative between 300 BC and AD 500. Similar oscillations have been found in alpine European lakes (Magny, 1992). However, the end of the Iron Age and the Roman period, as well as the medieval period and the twentieth century, are characterized by the reduction of flux in talwegs.

The impact of human settlements, whose effects on the Mediterranean regions have been established (Neboit, 1983), cannot be denied. The environmental history of southern Provence has been influenced by an interrelationship among natural factors, human factors and the fragility of the ecosystem.

METHODOLOGY

Two major ports, Marseille and Fos, have been studied in relationship to their natural environment (Fig. 14.1). The methods used have been applied for several years, for example in Carthage (Vitali *et al.*, 1992), in Phalasarna (Pirazzoli *et al.*, 1992), and Thronion (Niemi, 1990).

Founded by the Phoceans in the seventh century BC, Marseille harbour has remained continually active. Fos harbour, founded half a millennium later, disappeared in the High Middle Ages, and was only reactivated as an industrial port in the late nineteenth century. Beyond the socio-economic factors in these divergent histories, three important environmental questions can be asked: what part did the natural factors of each site play? what technological means did the inhabitants have to control these natural characteristics? and how did the construction of a city and a harbour affect the physical environment of these sites ?

Researches on the two sites have advanced unequally. The Marseille harbour has already been the subject of several articles (Morhange, 1994; Morhange *et al.*, 1996a, 1996b). In the case of Marseille, archaeological excavations have been carried out on dry land, facilitating stratigraphic analysis and altimetric measurement of the known ruins. In Fos, the site is submerged, a factor which constitutes a considerable handicap. In both cases, our research was performed in the geomorphologic context of the archaeological investigation, in collaboration with archaeologists and natural scientists in various fields.

The relationship between harbour sites and their natural environment has been analyzed primarily from two points of view. First, archaeological structures are used as clues to vertical sea-level relative variations (for example: Ambert *et al.*, 1982; Flemming, 1969; Pirazzoli, 1976). On some sites, analysis of fixed fauna allows for more precise estimations (Laborel and Laborel-Deguen, 1994; Morhange *et al.*, 1996b; Pirazzoli and Thommeret, 1973). This process is often used to complement markers of seismic activity around the Mediterranean (Bousquet *et al.*,1984 ; Pirazzoli, 1986). Secondly, archaeological ruins are used to mark lateral coastline displacements, whether due to progradation (coastline enlargement by sediment accumulation) (Bousquet *et al.*, 1987; Kraft *et al.*, 1980; Hoffmann, 1988; Lippmann-Provansal, 1987) or to coastal erosion (Oueslati *et al.*, 1987).

The research on Fos and Marseille has allowed for broader considerations of the relationship between the natural characteristics of a site and the technological capability of ancient societies to control and modify them.

Natural characteristics of coastal sites

The mobility of Provence's regional climate for the last 5000 years has been analyzed through its effects on erosion and hydrological variations in swampy grounds (Provansal, 1995). The climate determines the extent of erosion, and therefore of debris flows which silt up basins and cause coastline progradation. In Fos, the harbour was built at a climatically- and hydrologically-favourable time. The Rhône was lower than it is today, and it probably flooded less frequently. The alluvial plain of Arles was partially dry. However, from the fifth century AD onwards, the harbour moved eastward, and was then abandoned. These events were concurrent with a change in the hydrological and sedimentary dynamics of the Rhône delta. Increased flooding is confirmed by the increase in climatic humidity affecting Provence (Provansal, 1995) and the Alps (Jorda, 1992). Clues indicate that major streams of the Rhône moved eastward and had an increasingly important effect on the depositing of sand in the Fos harbour. The climate also determines the force of marine weather phenomena (winds, swells, and so on) and thus the fragility of coastal constructions.

The relative mobility of sea level introduces a constraint. We can distinguish between eustasy, land movements caused by tectonic or isostatic displacements, and mobility caused by harbour constructions (heavy loads, subsidence and so on). In Marseille, the subsidence is negligible when buildings are constructed on the Oligocene substrate. In Fos, at the edge of the Rhone delta, natural endogenous instability, either tectonic or isostasic, masks the specific impact of man-made constructions. Tide measurements show that sea level has risen twice as quickly in Fos than in Marseille since the turn of the century (two mm per year in the delta, in contrast with one mm per year in Marseille), an observation which reveals that the Rhône delta itself is subsiding.

Specificity of human impacts in the ports

The foundation of coastal colonies in the western Mediterranean in antiquity resulted in new types of settlements, soil management, and building along the coast. These changes provoked several specific types of impact (Delano Smith, 1979). Urban settlements increased runoff on the slopes, which caused silting up of the harbour. These modifications happened quickly and required additional forms of human intervention (harbour dredging in Marseille for example) or caused lateral displacements in Fos, the construction of docks, quays and so on reducing or accelerating erosion. Underwater sediments show the wide variety of types of human occupation in Marseille: shell middens from the Late Neolithic, sedimentary deposits on the harbour floor from the early Phocean (Greek) colony. According to Delano Smith (1979), it is important to differentiate between the town/ port of Marseille, where urban impacts have been inseparable from harbour development over time, and the outport (Fos), which is linked to the urban centre (Arles) by canal.

Sites for interactions among naturalists and archaeologists

Multidisciplinary collaboration is essential for a systematic study of the history of paleoenvironments in the coastal context. First, archaeology provides chronological markers which allow sedimentation rates to be calculated. It also gives information on sea level variations.

Second, marine biology provides essential data in two areas:

- Mean sea level variations are measured with precision on hard substrates, both natural and man-made, by using the upper limits of mid-littoral molluscan colonies. Sea level can be measured within five cm. Measurements using mobile fauna are much less precise. In Fos, the bio-indicators are indirectly indicative of sea level at the deposit location. They can convey the presence of a lagoon or a more or less open marine environment. These data provide a paleographic picture of the locations and types of different coastal environments, but they do not furnish precise altimetric measurements.
- The impact of human settlements is difficult to determine in the case of a vast open site such as Fos. We must distinguish between sedimentation caused by harbour constructions and natural deposits from the Rhône floods. The location of the canal which con-

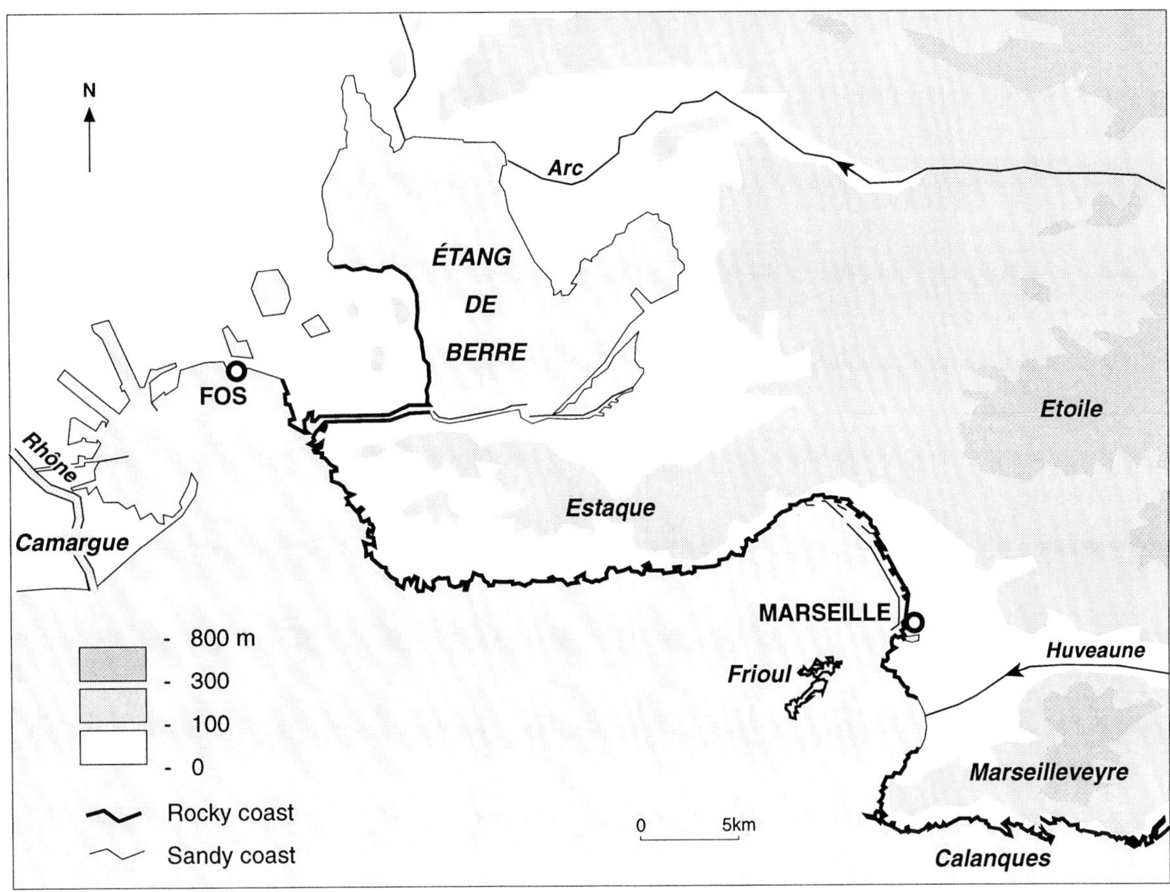

Fig. 14.1. The Marseille and Fos bays, southern France.

nected Arles to Fos should be identifiable from the presence of freshwater fauna.

Third, sedimentology and geomorphology provide a partial answer to two problems: sea level variations can be identified by sedimentary bodies, and human impacts can be evaluated in the same way as for a continental site. Changes in hydrological dynamics, aggravated by urban paving, and erosion of soil, are observed in the granulometric and mineralogical variations of the deposits. In a coastal environment, two types of restrictions must be considered. The mineralogy of the deposits can be altered by their exposure to sea water. Attention must be paid to neoformations and alterations specific to this environment (Chamley, 1971). Additionally, it is clearly much easier to evaluate human impact on a small site, such as the Lacydon in Marseille, than at the mouth of the huge Rhône drainage basin and the shores of an open gulf.

Overview of the physical geography of ancient harbour sites

Is it possible to suggest a systematization of the relationship between a natural environment and human modifications? An attempt is made here.

We differentiate between sites on rocky slopes and those on a low coastline. Among the first type can be found protected estuarine inlets, at the mouth of small drainage basins such as Marseille and Phalasarna, and more open bays at risk of silting up such as Troy (see Chapter 10), Pylo and Utica. Among the latter, we find ports built on the edge of deltas (Fos, Ravenna, Alexandria, Aquilea) and those at the mouths of rivers, characterized by sediment accumulations and swamps (Frejus, Ostia, Carthage).

Historically, it may be suggested that the harbours on rocky coasts were generally built at the time of the Greek and Phoenician expansion. These were commercial ports, whose activity was primarily maritime and not oriented toward inland agriculture.

On the lower coastlines, we see the development of large port cities such as Carthage and Alexandria; in other cases, we see merely the outports (Ostia/Rome, Fos/Arles). Development of lower coastlines has been easier because of a more favourable physical environment: reduced river flow and a less swampy environment due to a slightly lower sea level. However, from the fourth century BC, technological progress in the Hellenistic and Roman worlds made it possible to gain more control over less favourable environmental factors. This control was easier on rocky estuaries. It depended on the technical means available, on political choices, as well as on river flow. Utica and Troy were built on large rivers, so they rapidly became cut off from the sea. The harbour installations were thus progressively adapted to the changing shape of the coastline by dredging, empoldering, or moving the docks.

Ancient ports are thus remarkable sites in which to evaluate the limits of the human capacity to shape and modify a constantly fluctuating natural environment.

HUMAN IMPACT ON SEDIMENTATION AND COASTAL EVOLUTION IN THE LACYDON, MARSEILLE, SOUTHERN FRANCE

As we have seen above, the field of investigation of archaeological studies has recently widened towards the study of humanly-induced transformations of palaeo-environments. In that respect we have tried to link geomorphologists, biologists and archaeologists in the study of the north and east shores of the Lacydon, the ancient port of Marseille. The work of the archaeological team was followed for several months, measurements and sampling following closely the progress of the excavators. A multi-disciplinary approach allowed us to estimate the relative weight of human impacts upon coastal morphogenesis. We found that factors determining the evolution of shoreline were directly connected with the history of human settlement and urbanization from the initial bronze age village to Greek and Roman urban development.

The Lacydon is an estuarine creek, deeply indented into an Oligocene conglomerate. The creek is dominated by steep hills on both the northern (Panier Hill) and southern shores (Notre-Dame de La Garde) shores. On the east shore, several small rivers used to discharge into a coastal swamp (Fig. 14.2).

It is taken for granted that the city of Marseille was founded around 600 BC by Greek settlers coming from Phocea. On this site, two archeological excavations took place between 1992 and 1993: on the north shore on the site of the Greek harbour (Hesnard, 1994), and on the east shore, *extra muros*.

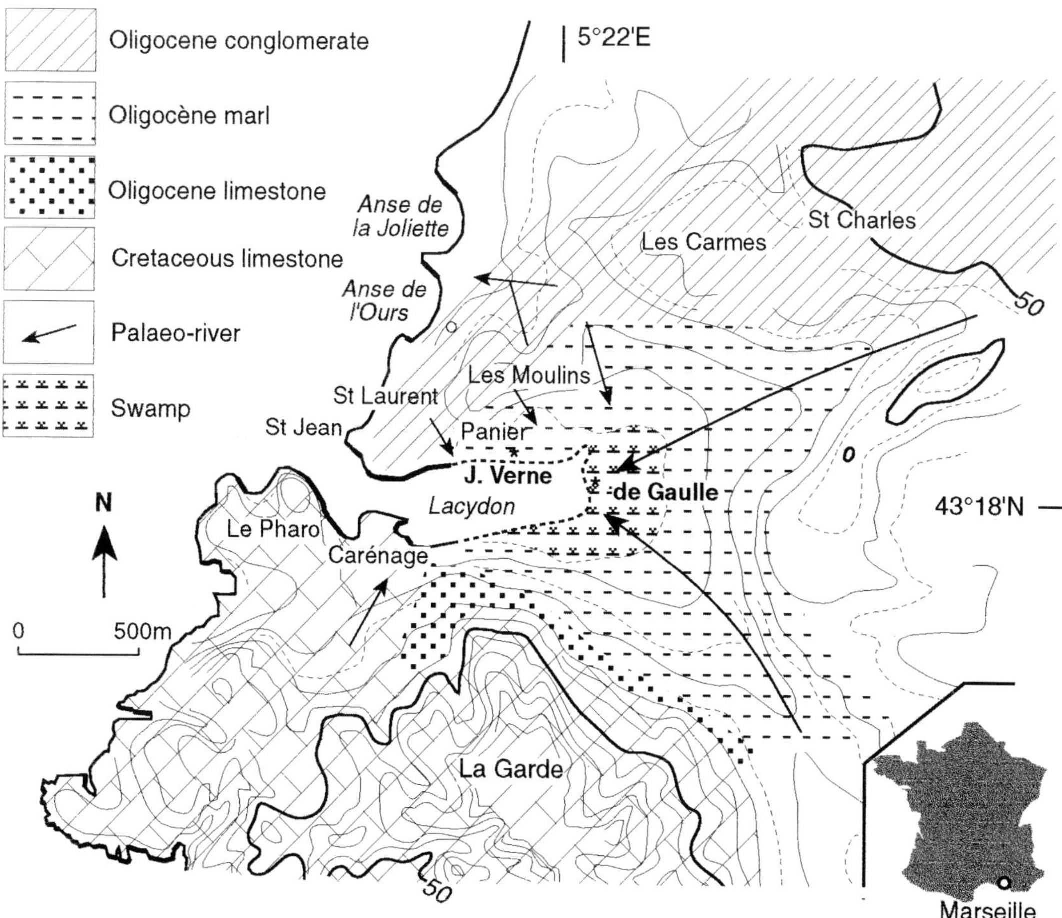

Fig. 14.2. Topography and geology of the Lacydon creek in Marseille; the coastline is approximate. (After Dellery and Gaudin, 1977)

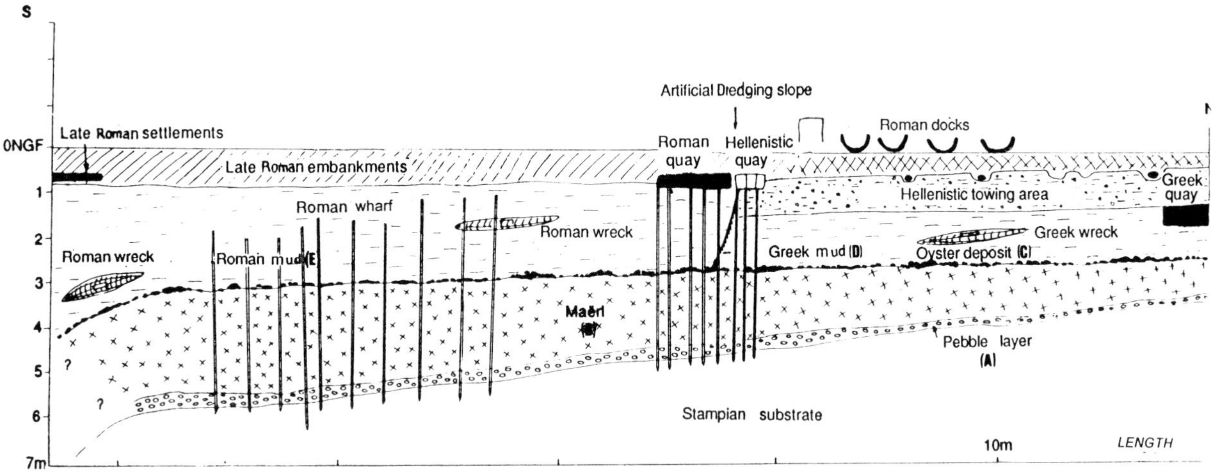

Fig. 14.3. Stratigraphic section of the north shore of the Lacydon, Marseille. See text for explanation of the lithology.

North shore of the Lacydon: Jules Verne Square

The north shore of the Lacydon creek is characterized by five sedimentary units (Figs. 14.3 and 14.4, and Table 14.1).

Unit A, a 30-cm thick deposit, overlying the eroded Oligocene, is the oldest marine sediment deposited in shallow water. It is defined by three important characteristics: (1) 50 per cent of sample weight consists of small Oligocene pebbles (mean diameter three cm), originating from the Panier hill nearby; (2) these limestone pebbles show traces of infra-littoral erosion such as *Cliona* perforations (boring sponges), as well as encrustations of coralline algae and oysters (*Ostrea edulis*); and (3) clay minerals of the argillaceous matrix do not indicate any impoverishment or alteration of smectites when compared with those from the Oligocene substratum (Perinet, 1977). Organic material of layer A was dated to 4600–4211 cal. BC.

Unit B is an algal biological marine deposit two to three m thick, caused by the accumulation of branching thalli of a free-living coralline algae (*Mesophyllum coralloides*). Such a biological deposit is widely represented in the Mediterranean and northern Atlantic, where it develops in frequently-renewed and well-oxygenated waters. It is called *maërl* by biologists and sedimentologists. Unit B was dated 3595–3246 cal. BC at its base, 2583–2188 cal. BC at the middle and 2020–1681 cal. BC at its top. This organogenic sediment ended at least 1200 years before Greek colonization.

Unit C is a layer of randomly-accumulated oyster shells which seals the *maërl* bio-accumulation. It is an anthropogenic or midden deposit, since the oyster (*Ostrea edulis lamellosa*) normally lives in open, deep, waters and the oyster valves (shells) are not found articulated in the deposit (Weydert, 1994). A number of such proto-historical middens is known in the Marseille basin (Courtin and Froget, 1976). The development of the oyster shell layer

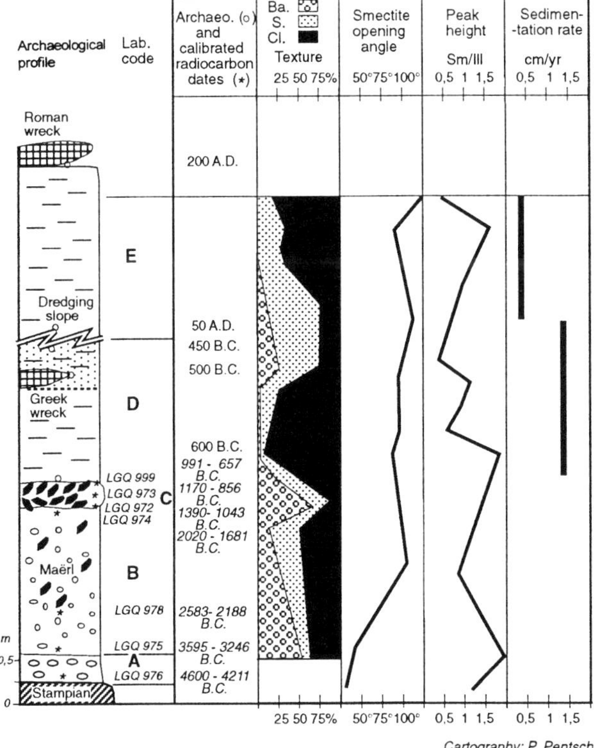

Fig.14.4. The north shore of the Lacydon, Marseille: archaeological profile, with granulometric texture (Ba=ballast, S=sand, Cl=silt and clay), clay minerals .(Sm=smectite, Ill=illite), sedimentation rate and dates.See text for explanation of the lithology. (After Morhange, 1994)

Layer n°	Thickness (metres)	Sediment type	Fossils	Date BP	Lab. N°	Calibrated or archaeol. Date	Interpretation
E	2.5	mud	marine			50–300 AD	Roman infilling
D	2.0	mud	marine			600–450 BC	Greek infilling
C	0.3	shells	marine	3000±130	LGQ 999	991–657 BC	Bronze age midden
			Ostrea	3180±130	LGQ 973	1170–856 BC	
				3340±140	LGQ 972	1390–1043 BC	
B	2.5	algal bio-accumul.	"Maërl"	3860±130	LGQ 974	2020–1681 BC	pre existing marine algal biocenosis
				4260±150	LGQ 978	2583–2188 BC	
				5010±140	LGQ 975	3595–3246 BC	
A	0.3	pebbles	marine	5930±200	LGQ 976	4600–4211 BC	transgressive gravel beaches

Table 14.1. Sediment description, northern shore of the Lacydon, Marseille. (After Morhange, 1994)

was not instantaneous, since scarce isolated shells were already present inside sediments of the upper part of unit B. Unit C, 0.30 m thick, was dated 1390–1043 cal. BC at its base, 1170–856 cal. BC, 0.15 m below its summit and 991–657 cal. BC at its top.

Unit D consists of black sandy muds about two m thick, containing a huge number of Greek artefacts dated from 600 BC at their base to 450 BC at their summit. Mean deposition rate was thus about 1.3–1.4 cm per year.

Unit E, separated from Unit D by a sharp boundary, consists of black sandy muds containing many Roman artefacts ranging from the first to the third centuries AD; it is interpreted as a dredging slope. Sedimentation rates are about 0.35 cm per year, three times slower than during the Greek period.

In both D and E, clay minerals show a strong degradation and impoverishment of the smectites, demonstrating their pedological origin and the importance of soil erosion inland.

The sequence is interpreted in terms of four major phases, as follows.

Neolithic (4600–4200 cal BC to 2583–2188 cal BC)

The marine sediments of Unit A and the base of Unit B are indicative of limited soil erosion according to clay mineral analyses (Jorda *et al.*, 1991). We believe, therefore, that vegetation cover inland was persistant throughout the latter period, without heavy human impact despite the presence of neolithic material. This is consistent with what is known of the neolithic morpho-climatic context of southern Provence, which was characterized by limited channel erosion in a naturally protected environment (Provansal, 1995).

First environmental event (2020–1681 cal. BC)

The first environmental event took place at the end of the neolithic period, around 2020–1681 cal. BC. The end of the maërl bio-accumulation may be explained by two factors:

- silting up: clay minerals contain degraded smectites of pedological origin, which indicate the end of the natural evolution of the Lacydon (Fig. 14.4);
- shell midden deposition, dated 1390–1043 cal. BC at its basis, seals the maërl bio-accumulation and possibly kills it. It is a biological event, linked to coastal settlement (a similar phenomenon was recently observed in Calanque de Port Miou, 30 km east of Marseille, where a stone quarry and the recent development of a yachting harbour led to deposition of gravel and mud, killing the maërl which was still well developed 25 years ago).

In the Lacydon, moderate sediment accumulation correlating with intense midden deposits suggests that human settlements and agricultural activity inland remained limited throughout the whole corresponding period. By contrast, an important centre of human activity was present on the northern shore of the Lacydon at least 1200 years before the Phocean foundation of Marseille. As far as we know, this is the first description of such a biological event linked to ancient human occupation of a Mediterranean littoral site.

Second environmental event (600 BC and later)

The great volumetric importance of land sediments can be explained by the urban foundation and growth of Massalia (the Greek colony of Marseille) since 600 BC, leading to landscape modification, harbour settlement, and increase of agricultural activity. Steep slopes induced a rapid erosive response inland, with abundant delivery of loose sediments (limestone, sand, conglomerates: Fig. 14.2). A regional climatic influence was recently considered to be the cause of increased runoff and accelerated erosion in southern Provence between 600 and 200 BC (Provansal, 1995). The lesser rate of sedimentation on the eastern shore of the Lacydon, outside city limits, is an indication, however, that Greek urbanization of the northern shores of the Lacydon created local conditions for this second event.

In southern Italy, Sicily and Greece, intense soil erosion

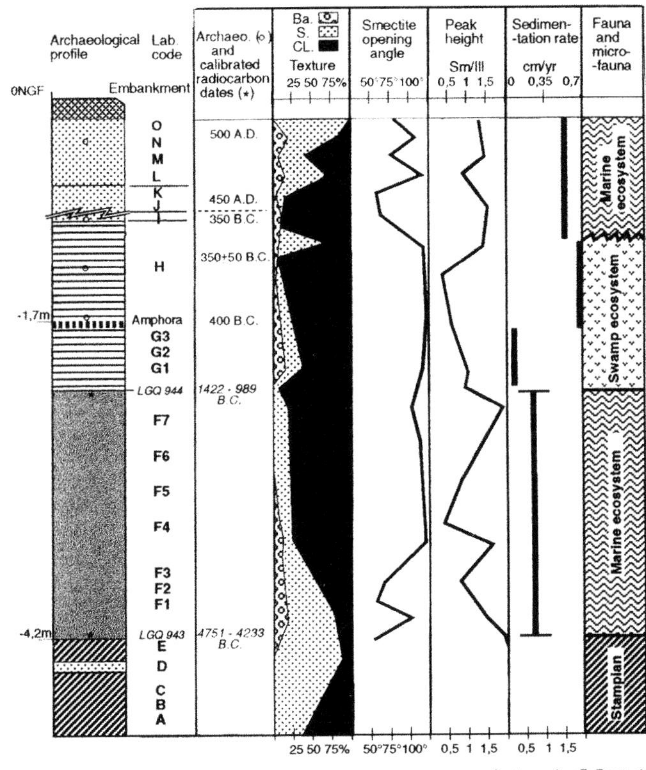

Fig. 14.5. The east shore of the Lacydon, Marseille: archaeological profile, with granulometric texture (Ba=ballast, S=sand, Cl=silt and clay), clay minerals (Sm=smectite, Ill=illite), dates, fauna and microfauna, and sedimentation rate. See text for explanation of the lithology. (After Morhange, 1994)

was induced by reduction of vegetation and bad agricultural practices, during the first millennium BC (van Andel *et al.*, 1986; Neboit, 1984). In Marseille, however, this event is not a mere 'speeding up' of erosion, but represents a new kind of morphogenic urban sequence, marked by large deposits of urban refuse of all kinds. The northern shore of the Lacydon was transformed into a huge waste deposit. Water quality was reduced, causing the development of pollution-tolerant species such as *Cardium exiguum*, *Amyclina corniculum*, and *Haminea navicula* (Arnaud and Leung Tack, 1971).

Roman times

Sediment composition suggests reduced water runoff or sediment supply. Strong degradation of smectites suggests that silting up of the harbour was mainly linked to increasing soil denudation inland.

This difference between the Greek and Roman periods can be explained by two factors: (1) a climatic factor – the first four centuries of our era appear in southern Provence to be a period of reduced morphological activity (Provansal, 1995); or (2) an urban factor – Greek sedimentary deposits are evocative of runoff eroding unpaved urban surfaces, whereas their Roman counterparts may be due to the action of rainwater flowing upon largely paved or cemented surfaces. Nevertheless, it must be pointed out that the Romans had to dredge the harbour around 50 AD, an operation which cut deeply into older Greek sediments (Fig. 14.3). The harbour, thus excavated, was again filled up later on, a fact already noted in the northeast corner of the Lacydon (Guery, 1992).

To summarize, we must emphasize the importance and the continuity of human coastal settlement during 4000 years. The Lacydon underwent a first, mainly ecological, stress during the Late Neolithic, resulting in the death of pre-existing marine biological assemblages. The true sedimentological event, inducing shoreline changes, began around 600 BC with the arrival of the Phoceans.

East shore of the Lacydon: de Gaulle Square

The archaeological excavations at de Gaulle Square display 5000 years of coastal sedimentary evolution in the bottom of the Lacydon. The rhythm and nature of these deposits differ from those of the north shore. The east shore is characterized by three superimposed sedimentary units (Fig. 14.5 and Table 14.2).

Units F1 to F7 consist of a series of fine-textured marine mud layers (Fig. 14.5: layers F1-F7), characterized by a muddy fraction increasing from the lower layer F1 to the upper one F7, due to the silting up of the bottom of the creek. Sedimentation rates vary from 0.09 to 0.38 cm per year. Their fauna corresponds to a calm-water, mud and sand marine community (*Venerupis aurea*, *Loripes lacteus*, *Gastrana fragilis*, *Cerithium vulgatum*, *Abra alba*, *Parvicardium exiguum* and *Cerastoderma glaucum*). The ostracod microfauna is characterized by lagoonal species

Layer n°	Thickness (metres)	Sediment type	Fossils	Date BP	Lab. N°	Calibrated or archaeol. Date	Interpretation
O to I	0.5	sand/mud	marine			AD 450	marine transgression
H to G	1.1	clay	freshwater			400–350 BC	littoral swamp
F7 to F1	2.0	mud	marine	3340±170 6010±240	LGQ 944 LGQ 943	1422–989 BC 4751–4233 BC	shallow and calm water sedimentation

Table 14.2. Sediment description, eastern shore of the Lacydon, Marseille. (After Morhange, 1994)

(*Cyprideis torosa, Loxoconcha elliptica*), but marine coastal species are also present such as *Loxochonca rhomboidea*, *Xestoleberis* spp., and *Aurila woodwardii*. From layer F1 up to F3, the clay minerals do not indicate any impoverishment or alteration of smectites between layers F1 and F3, but the deterioration of crystalline indexes of smectites deteriorate in layers F4-F7 reflects increasing soil erosion.

The far end of the creek was progressively filled up by clayey sediments deposited in a coastal swamp (Units G and H). A new biological element is the presence of fresh water ostracods (*Cyprinotus* sp.).

The G1, G2, G3 and H sediments are uniform and fine graded, with 65–85 per cent of clays, indicating a decantation process. Layers G1, G2 and G3 are grey coloured and sealed by broken pine branches and fragments of 'Massiliate' amphorae dated to around 400 BC. The sedimentation rate was about 0.04–0.07 cm per year. Layer H, dated about 350 BC, is greyish-yellow with white and rust spots, suggesting a pseudo-gley soil, characteristic of a temporarily-emerged sea-shore swamp.

Units I to O are dated to *c.*AD 450. Their macrofauna and microfauna, such as *Parvicardium exiguum*, *Cerastoderma edule*, *Cerithium vulgatum*, *Gibbula adamsoni*, *Venerupis aurea*, and *Posidonia oceanica,* are characteristic of stable marine muddy-sand biocenoses. About 80 per cent of the ostracods are coastal species (*Loxochoncha rhomboidea*, *Xestoleberis* spp., *Aurila woodwardii*). Freshwater microfauna is missing and the environment is typical of a shallow marine creek-bottom.

Deposits J and K are characterized by well-crystallized smectites relating to Oligocene clay minerals with a small amount of degradation.

Sediments L, M, N, and O are beaches near the late Roman mean sea-level: broken sea-shell sands are dominant.

Interpretation

The two sites, north and east, record the first human impacts in the same manner (slight degradation of smectites), indicating a moderate soil erosion limited to stream channels. This phase fits quite well with the climatic context described elsewhere in Provence (Provansal, 1995), but as time went by, the evolution of the two sites was different.

The increase of human activity in the Final Neolithic and the Bronze Age caused moderate soil erosion, reflected by fine grained sediments and altered minerals. The first ecological event (decline and death of the maërl bio-accumulation) happened during the Final Neolithic on the north shore, where the first settlement took place.

The foundation of Massilia, the Greek colony of Marseille, resulted in a dramatic acceleration of the morphogenic evolution of the north shore. The sixth and fifth centuries BC were marked by an increase in soil erosion, with large volumes of accumulated sediment. Chronologically this episode corresponds to an increase in fluvial sedimentation in Provence (Roux, 1991). In contrast, the sedimentary response on the east shore was attenuated and delayed.

From a period between 1422–989 cal. BC to about 350 BC the east shore also underwent a morphogenetic change, from a marine environment to a sea-shore tidal swamp. The low sedimentation rates in the swamps (about twenty times slower than on the north shore) may be explained by the distance from the city and the filtrating effect of the waterside forests upstream. Deposits were nevertheless sufficient to cause a marked progradation of the shoreline.

An important reduction of sedimentation on both sites can be detected during the Hellenistic and Roman periods, when erosion was more attenuated than during the preceding Phocean times. There is a possible coincidence with the morpho-climatic pause in Provence marked by runoff reduction or decrease in sediment supply.

At the end of the Roman period, marine beach sediments overlay the east shore swamps, reflecting a local retreat of the shoreline. This could appear paradoxical since sea level was gradually stabilizing around the present datum (Laborel *et al.*, 1994; Morhange *et al.*, 1996b). Here again, the scale and intensity of the sedimentary budget prevail over the movement of sea level proper in areas affected by human activity.

The differences in the evolution of the north and east shores of the Marseille bay can be attributed to different types of land occupation, urban on the north shore, peri-urban on the east one.

ACKNOWLEDGEMENTS

The authors are grateful to Dr. M. Bourcier (Station Marine d'Endoume de Marseille) for the determination of marine molluscan fauna, to Dr. P. Carbonel (Laboratoire CNRS de Géologie-Micro-paléontologie, Bordeaux) for help in the determination of the ostracods, and to Dr. M. Bouiron (Atelier du Patrimoine de Marseille). Dr. A. Murray (University of Virginia, USA) has kindly translated the French text into English.

REFERENCES

Ambert, P. M. and Maurin, G. (1982) Littoraux miocènes et Quaternaires du Languedoc occidental. *Comptes Rendus de l'Académie des Sciences Paris* 295, 2: 251–4.

Andel, T. H. van, Runnels, C. N. and Pope, K. O. (1986) Five thousand years of land use and abuse in the southern Argolid, Greece. *Hesperia* 55, 1: 103–28.

Arnaud, P. M. and Leung Tack, K. (1971) Faunes malacologiques du Lacydon antique et du Vieux Port de Marseille: comparaison écologique et remarques sur la pollution. *Tethys* 3, 1:105–12.

Bousquet, B., Dufaure, J.-J. and Pechoux, P.-Y. (1984) Connaître les séismes en Méditerranée, de la vision antique à la vision actuelle. In *Tremblements de Terre, Histoire et Archéologie* (IV° Rencontres Internationales d'Archéologie et d'Histoire d'Antibes): 23–37. Juan-les-Pins, CNRS.

Bousquet, B., Dufaure, J.-J. and Pechoux, P.-Y. (1987) Ports antiques et lignes de rivages égéennes. In *Colloque CNRS, Déplacement des Lignes de Rivages en Méditerranée*: 137–54. Paris, CNRS.

Chamley, A. (1991) *Recherches sur la Sédimentation argileuse en Méditerranée.* Mémoire du Service de la Carte Géologique d'Alsace 35.

Courtin, J. and Froget, C. (1976) La station néolithique de l'île de Riou. *Bulletin du Musée d'Anthropologie et de Préhistoire de Monaco* 15: 147–67.

Delano Smith, C. (1979) *Western Mediterranean Europe, a Historical Geography of Italy, Spain and Southern France since the Neolithic.* London, Academic Press.

Dellery, B. and Gaudin, B. (1977) Observations géologiques et géotechniques à l'occasion de travaux souterrains dans le bassin de Marseille. *Géologie Méditeranéenne* 4, 1: 55–64.

Flemming, N.C. (1969) *Archeological Evidence for Eustatic Change of Sea Level and Earth Movements in the Western Mediterranean in the Last 2OO Years.* Geological Society of America., Special Paper 109.

Guéry, R. (1992) Le port antique de Marseille. In Marseille grecque et la Gaule. *Études Massaliètes* 3: 109–21.

Hesnard, A. (1994) Une nouvelle fouille du port de Marseille, place Jules Verne. *Comptes Rendus de l'Académie des Inscriptions et Belles-Lettres* 1: 1–15.

Hoffmann, G. (1988) *Holozänstratigraphie und Küstenlinienverlagerung an der andalusischen Mittelmeerküste.* Bremen, Berichte aus dem Fachbereich Geowissenschaften der Universität Bremen 2.

Jorda, M. (1992) Morphogenèse et fluctuations climatiques dans les Alpes françaises du sud de l'Age du Bronze au Haut Moyen Age. *Les Nouvelles de l'Archéologie* 50: 14–20.

Jorda, M., Parron, C., Provansal, M. and Roux, M. (1991) Érosion et détritisme holocènes en Basse Provence calcaire, l'impact de l'anthropisation. *Physio-Géo* 22–23: 37–47.

Jorda, M. and Provansal, M. (1996) Impact de l'anthropisation et du climat sur le détritisme en France du sud-est (Alpes du sud et Provence). *Bulletin de la Société Géologique de France* 176, 1: 159–68.

Kraft, J. C., Kayan, I. and Erol, O. (1980) Geomorphic reconstructions in the environs of ancient Troy. *Science* 209: 776–82.

Laborel, J. and Laborel-Deguen, F. (1994) Biological indicators of relative sea level of co-seismic displacements in the Mediterranean region. *Journal of Coastal Research* 10, 2: 395–415.

Laborel, J., Morhange, C., Lafont, R., Le Campion, J., Laborel-Deguen, F. and Sartoretto, S. (1994) Biological evidence of sea-level rise during the last 4500 years, on the rocky coasts of continental southwestern France and Corsica. *Marine Geology* 120: 203–23.

Leveau, P. and Provansal, M. (1993) (eds) *Archéologie et Environnement: de la Sainte Victoire aux Alpilles.* Aix-en Provence, Université de Provence.

Lippmann-Provansal, M. (1987) Variations récentes du trait de côte sur les sites de Velia et Paestum (Italie méridionale). In *Colloque CNRS, Déplacement des Lignes de Rivages en Méditerranée*:115–24. Paris, CNRS.

Magny, M. (1992) Holocene lake-level fluctuations in Jura and the northern subalpine ranges, France: regional pattern and climatic implications, *BOREAS* 21: 319–34.

Morhange, C. (1994) *La Mobilité des Littoraux Provençaux: Eléments d'Analyse Géomorphologique.* Université de Provence, Faculté des Lettres et Sciences Humaines, PhD thesis.

Morhange, C., Hesnard, A., Arnaud, P., Bourcier, M., Carbonel, P., Chevillot, P., Laborel, J., Lafont, R., Provansal, M. and Weydert, P. (1996a) Anthropisation, sédimentation marine et morphogenèse sur la rive nord du Lacydon de Marseille depuis le Néolithique (chantier J. Verne). *Zeitschrift für Geomorphologie* NF 40, 1: 71–84.

Morhange C., Laborel J., Hesnard A. and Prone, A. (1996b) Variation of relative mean sea level during the last 4000 years on the northern shores of the Lacydon, the ancient harbour of Marseille. *Journal of Coastal Research* 12, 4: 841–9.

Neboit, R. (1983) *L'Homme et l'Érosion.* Clermont-Ferrand, Association des Publications de la Faculté des Lettres et Sciences Humaines de Clermont-Ferrand.

Neboit, R. (1984) Érosion des sols et colonisation grecque en Sicile et en Grande Grèce. *Bulletin de l'Association des Géographes Français* 499: 5–13.

Niemi, T. M. (1990) Paleoenvironmental history of submerged ruins on the northern Euboean Gulf coastal plain, central Greece. *Geoachaeology* 5, 4: 323–47.

Oueslati, A., Paskoff, R., Slim, H. and Trousset, P. (1987) Déplacements de la ligne de rivage en Tunisie d'après les données de l'archéologie à l'époque historique. In *Colloque CNRS, Déplacement des Lignes de Rivages en Méditerranée*: 67–86. Paris, CNRS.

Perinet, G. (1977) Sur la minéralogie des argiles de Saint-André Marseille. *Géologie Méditerranéenne* 4, 1: 47–54.

Pirazzoli, P.A. (1976) Sea level variations in the northwest Mediterranean during Roman times. *Science* 194: 519–21.

Pirazzoli, P. A. (1986), The early Byzantine tectonic paroxism. *Zeitschrift für Geomorphologie* NF 62: 31–49.

Pirazzoli, P. A. and Thommeret, J. (1973) Une donnée nouvelle sur le niveau marin à Marseille à l'époque romaine. *Comptes Rendus de l'Académie des Sciences Paris* 277, D: 2125–8.

Pirazzoli, P. A., Ausseil-Badie, J., Giresse, P., Hadjidaki, E. and Arnold, M. (1992) Historical environmental changes at Phalasarna Harbor, west Crete. *Geoarchaeology* 7,4: 371–92.

Provansal, M. (1995) The role of climate in landscape morphogenesis since the Bronze Age in Provence, southeastern France. *The Holocene* 5, 3: 348–53.

Roux, M.-R. (1991) Les sédiments de l'étang de Berre, témoins de la pression anthropique holocène? *Méditerranée* 4: 3–14.

Vitali, V., Gifford, J. A., Djindian, F., and Rapp, G. Jr. (1992) A formalized approach to analysis of geoarchaeological sediment samples: the location of the early punic harbor at Carthage, Tunisia. *Geoarchaeology* 7, 6: 545–81.

Weydert, N., (1994), le dépôt coquillier de la place Jules Verne à Marseille, étude malacologique et archèologique, DEA, Université de Provence, 1–56.

15. Developing a Methodological Approach to the Evolution of Field Systems in the Middle Rhône Valley

Jean-François Berger and Cécile Jung

INTRODUCTION

For the past ten years, archaeologists, geomorphologists and geoarchaeologists have been working together (in research groups such as the GDR 954 programme on Archaeology and Mediterranean Rural Spaces in Antiquity and the Early Middle Ages, the H11 Tricastin programme, and the Archaeomedes Project) on problems concerning land use and palaeoenvironments during historical periods in the departments of the Drôme and in the north of the Vaucluse. Recently, both palaeo-botanical and archaeo-botanical approaches have been integrated into this research programme, for example by J. Argant (palynology), S. Crozat (ethno-botany), and F. Magnin (malacology) and S. Thiébault (anthropology). This work has made it possible for us to propose a number of hypotheses about land management and ancient field divisions in this area.

The 'centuriation' or land division systems of classical antiquity were of course already well known: the Cadastre A and B of Valence in the Valence plain, as well as the Cadastre B of Orange in the Valdaine, the Tricastin and in the Orange plain. These centuriations were revealed in the 1950s and 60s by epigraphic and morphological evidence. The first research on the Cadastre B of Valence by Blanc (1953) was then refined by Chouquer and Odiot (1984). The Cadastre B of Orange was first identified by Piganiol (1962), and was then studied by Chouquer *et al.* (1994). However, only rarely have such centuriation systems been 'ground-truthed' by archaeological investigation.

The crossing of these areas by the line of the new *TGV Méditerranée* fast railway (Fig. 15.1) has provided an opportunity to make up this shortcoming and to progress in our understanding of the organization of these landscapes in historical times. First, map- and photo-interpretation were undertaken, under the direction of G. Chouquer, in the areas surrounding the route. These studies not only rendered possible the confirmation of the presence of cadastral grids but also revealed other ancient, medieval, and modern field systems, on a smaller scale linked either to ancient rural settlements or to medieval or modern population centres. Following this, research into agrarian structures and in particular ancient field limits was launched within a geographic area of about 100 km in length, between Saint-Marcel-les-Valence (Drôme) to the north and Caderousse (Vaucluse) to the south. A reconstruction of the crop types, the agro-pastoral rhythms and modes is also envisaged through the integration of palaeo-environmental research.

As this research is presently in progress, this chapter will concentrate more on methodological considerations than results.

MATERIALS AND METHODS

Geographic framework and scales of analysis

The route studied crosses different landscape units with varied geomorphological, pedological and hydrological characteristics: low-lying alluvial plains, Quaternary terraces, Quaternary alluvial Fans, marl and molasse piedmonts. It is also necessary to consider this territory on different scales (Figs. 15.2 and 15.3):

- an organization along the scale of the territory of the ancient city (Valence, Orange) which can encompass several different landscape units;
- a field system linked to the landscape units, most notably to problems and constraints of land use tied to palaeo-hydraulic dynamics requiring specific development (low-lying alluvial plains, damp basins, or certain Quaternary terraces) – this is illustrated by the work of Chartier in the town of Donzere (Drôme), who has demonstrated that strip fields with a drainage function occur in damp areas, and chequer-board systems elsewhere (Chartier and Chouquier, 1995);
- a field system within a 'terroir' or landscape unit such as a basin or hill slope – thus the marl basins of La Touche in the southern piedmont of the Valdaine basin

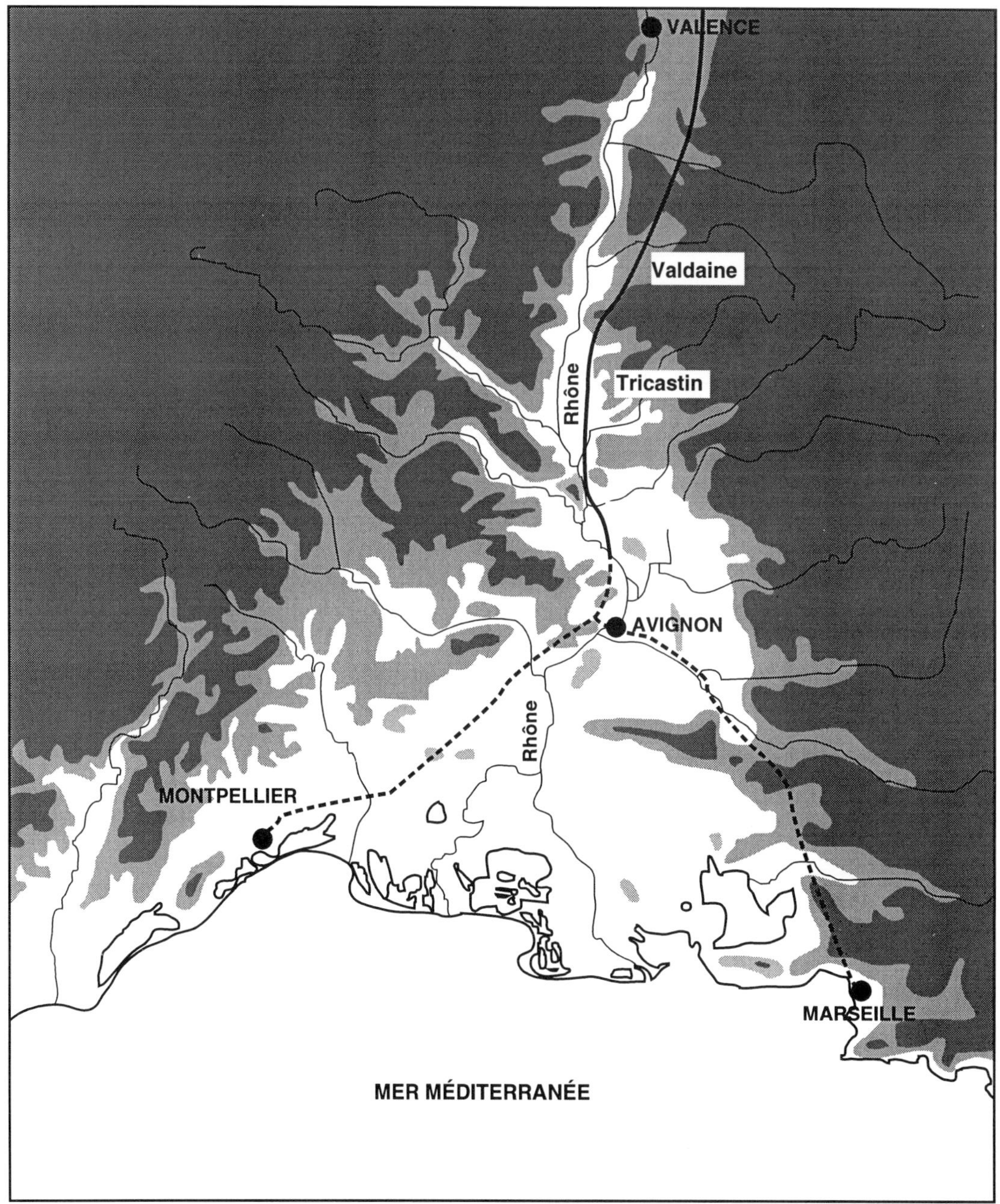

Fig. 15.1. The route of the T.G.V. Méditerranée *railway line, with the research area indicated by a solid line.*

form a sump into which drain a secondary system oriented along the Cadastre B of Orange or at a 45° angle to it (Berger, 1995a).

Operating methods

In the field, the following are done:

- observed traces of field systems are cross-checked by preliminary morphological studies; this can be repeated in order to discern their orientation;
- trenches are cut in order to recover dating material (pottery or charcoal);
- a micro-stratigraphic study is conducted to establish texture, structure, sediment colour, pedological characteristics (carbonaceous or ferro-manganiferous precipitation, traces of oxidation, and so on), as well as the presence of carbon, malacofauna and fragments of tiles or pottery;
- a ten-litre sediment sample is taken from each stratigraphic unit for anthracological, carpological, and malacological analysis. Sub-samples are taken for pollen and phytoliths.

The objective is to compare different phases observed

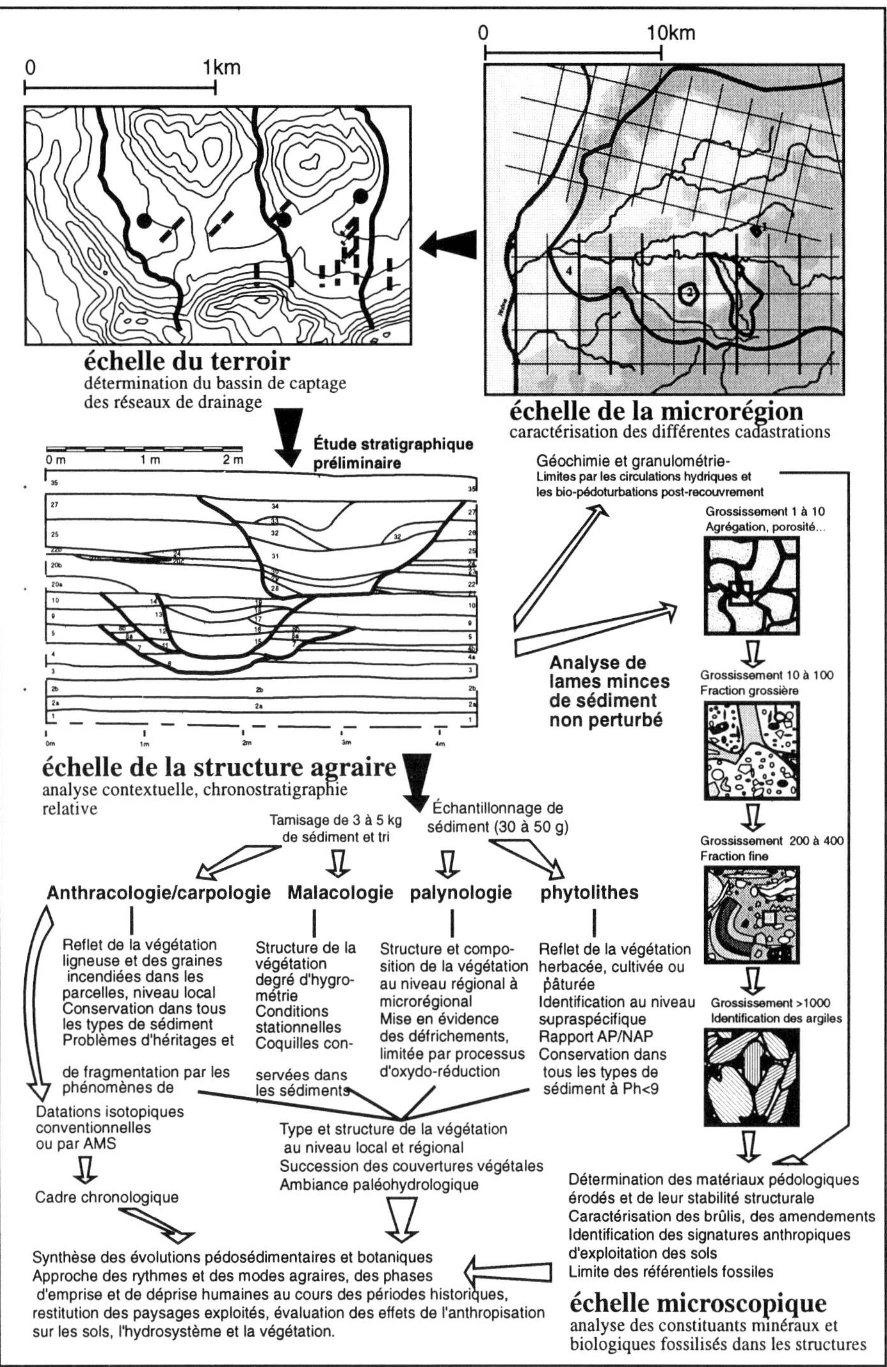

Fig.15.2. The different levels of observation involved in the project.

in the field through a microstratigraphic study and to compare the different pedo-sedimentological facies encountered by micro-morphological analysis, in order to construct the typology and diagnostic characteristics of the drainage systems. These observations will then be compared with the results of the various palaeo-ecological studies done in parallel with the geomorphological and pedological approaches. The contribution and limits of each of the palaeo-environmental analyses are shown in Figure 15.2.

In parallel, a study of ditches still in use or only recently filled in is planned, to allow us to construct a reference typology. We should then be able to calculate the rate at which ditches are filled and to establish the relationship between them and climatic and land use parameters determined by oral inquiry, archives and field observations.

PRELIMINARY RESULTS

The confirmation of morphological data

The transect formed by the TGV route gives us the opportunity systematically to intersect the field boundaries, fossilized or in use, identified by map and photo-interpretation. In areas with a thick sediment covering, systematic deep trenches allow us to identify boundaries not detectable by photo-interpretation. On the one hand, the constant confrontation of the theoretical grids of cadastral maps with the reality in the field allows us to validate their existence, better to apprehend their initial materialization (ditches, buried drainage systems, roads, hedges and so on) and, on the other, to make out their role and their function (drainage, irrigation, viability or protection from wind). A certain number of previously unknown field systems (Fig. 15.3) was discovered in the deep trenches, most notably in the Valdaine basin. Moreover, we can henceforth better apprehend the areas of good, or not so good, materialization of the Cadastre B of Orange on the ground. The intersection of these structures should also enable us better to date their implementation, use and abandonment. It must be noted that the dating proposed for field systems has been based on the measurements of the plots, on the dating of archaeological sites to which they apparently correspond, and on occasional excavations that cross the field boundaries (Fiches, 1993).

Following the preliminary field results, we frequently observed the perpetuation of field boundaries. Certain ancient ditches in the Tricastin plain aligned to the Orange B Cadastre, such as the 'Malalones' in the town of Pierrelatte (Fig. 15.4), were re-dug in the Middle Ages and in the modern period. (This was despite the raising of the level of the plain by alluviation.) Today, they are perpetuated in the landscape as active boundaries such as residual hedges and crop boundaries.

The validity and limits of the exploitation of ditches

Before going any further with the expectations of this research, it is necessary to recall the relevance of the study of ditches and the type of information that they can yield. First of all, a ditch functions as a sediment trap where abundant palaeo-environmental information is generally in a secondary position. It is therefore necessary to take into account the nature of the basin for the study of a true hydrographic network, in order spatially to replace the information collected: according to its position in the branching off of the network, it will yield information on the evolution of a few hundred square metres or of several square kilometres. In some ditches cut into alluvial cones in a piedmont, the filling is sometimes torrential, revealing the arrival of pedo-sedimentological material, following concentrated surface runoff often coming from far up in the hydrographic basin. This torrential activity modifies the initial profiles of the ditches, giving them the aspect of natural channels where sometimes only the base of the humanly-made structure is still recognizable.

We must always keep in mind that palaeo-environmental information does not survive whole, due to the numerous phases of cleaning out observed in the ditch sections. This is a taphonomic problem specific to the upkeep of drainage networks. First, in most cases, the information is obliterated for the initial period of exploitation, while information on the last phases of activity is well preserved, though the cuts of the primary ditches are invariably identifiable. Second, in some cases, the displacement of the modern ditch by as little as a few metres has meant that the initial phases are well preserved. Finally, in the best situations (areas of active sedimentation), geomorphological evolution has provoked a marked rise in the level of the ground through colluvial or alluvial sedimentation. The stratigraphic profile is dilated, and the various phases of digging are separated by layers of sediment sufficiently thick to protect the older levels from the more recent digging. This situation was encountered several times in the Tricastin (Fig. 15.4), but in each case the separation between phases concerned major cultural periods (Roman, medieval, modern), following neglect and an absence of upkeep in the surrounding plots.

Problems with dating ditches using the archaeological material found in them must also be mentioned here. Artefacts are relatively rare in ditches, and, when they are found, they do not necessarily give a coherent date. The alluvial matter in the ditches can contain material from sites older than the ditch further up the slope. We must therefore be very wary in using this chronological data. The presence of a structure covering the last filling layer of a ditch is much more reliable. It guarantees us of having an absolute *terminus post-quem*: thus at Les Bartraces, Bollene (Vaucluse), a hearth dated by pottery of the fourth to sixth centuries AD covers the sealing layer of part of the ancient irrigation system, indicating that the latter was no longer is use at this time (C. Markiévitch, *pers. comm.*).

Fig. 15.3. Map interpretation on a 1960 IGN map (scale 1:20000). Three ancient field systems can be identified: the southern limit of the Cadastre B of Orange, and two other networks, hitherto unknown, covering smaller surfaces (at the scale of a landscape unit) and which could be linked to rural settlements. Three ditches belonging to these new networks were cut across by the TGV line. All of them were used in antiquity, and two of them have been perpetuated as field boundaries.

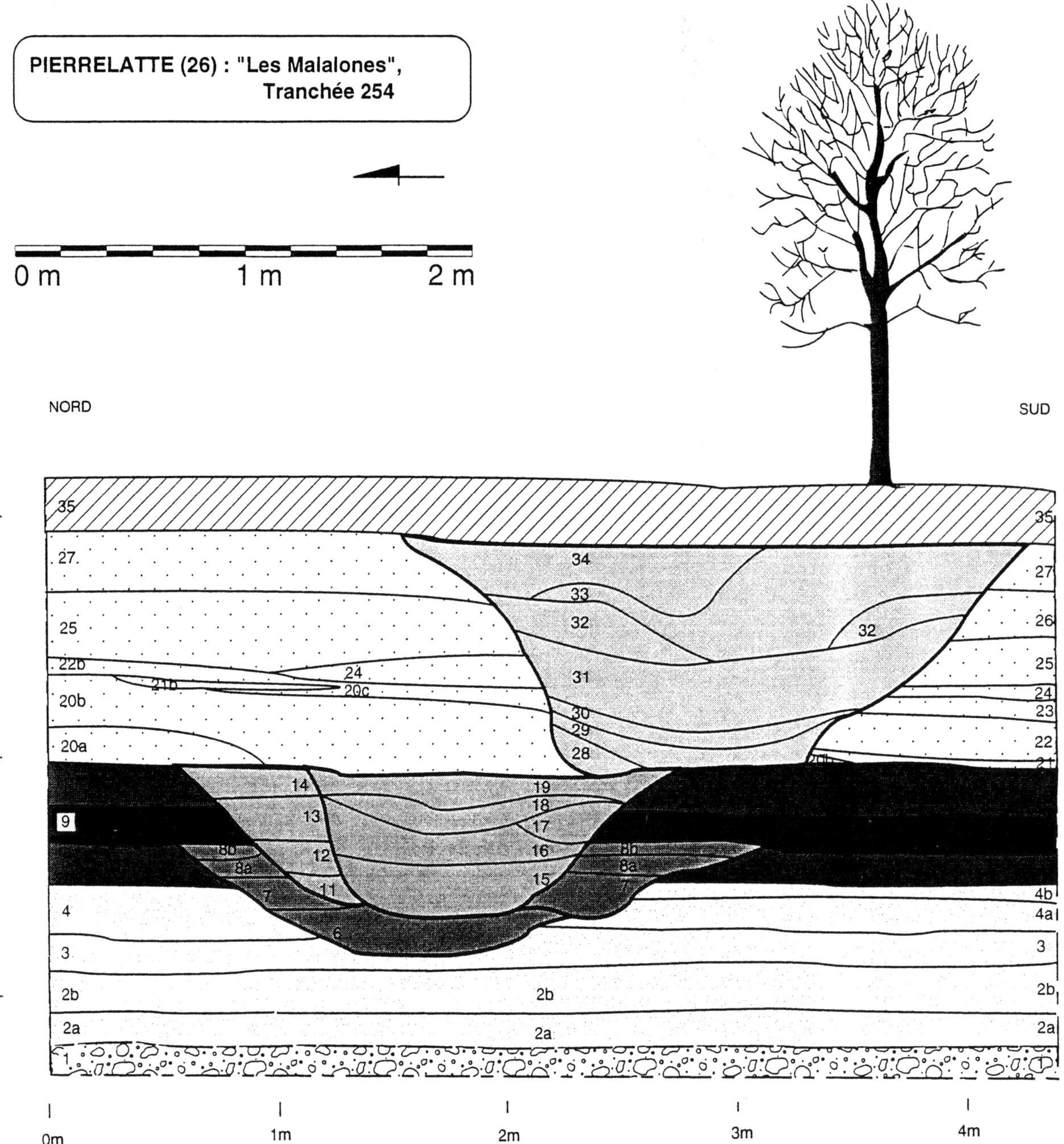

1- Graviers würmiens du Rhône, 2 à 4b- formations limono-argileuses alluviales du Rhône holocènes ancien/moyen, marquées par la pédogenèse, 5- sol limono-sablo-argileux brun foncé romain à tegulae et céramiques épars, 6 à 8b- unités sédimentaires colmatant un fossé de drainage romain indéterminé, 9 et 10- sol limono-argileux brun/noir à brun foncé riche en mollusques de milieu humide de la fin de l'Antiquité et du début du Moyen Age, 11 à 19, unités sédimentaires colmatant un fossé de drainage médiéval indéterminé, 20a à 27- formations alluviales sableuses peu pédogénéis ées, 28 à 34- unités sédimentaires colmatant un fossé de drainage ou d'irrigation moderne, 35- terre arable

Fig. 15.4. An example of the perpetuation of a field boundary. Despite the rise in level of the Tricastin plain due to alluvial silting, and some phases of neglect, the agrarian ditches continue to be oriented parallel to the decumanus *of the Cadastre B of Orange. There was a slight shift during historical times. This axis is still functional, taking the shape of a residual hedge.*

In most cases, it seems to be more pertinent to date these structures by the application of radiocarbon to samples of charcoal generated by agrarian practices contemporary with the functioning of the ditch.

The period in which agrarian structures were in use can also be determined in relative chronology, through acquaintance with the chrono-stratigraphic context, acquired by combining geomorphological, pedological and geochronological analyses. Certain pedo-stratigraphic indicators such as dark isohumic soils, vertics, and gley can be observed over wide areas and become relative geochronological indicators.

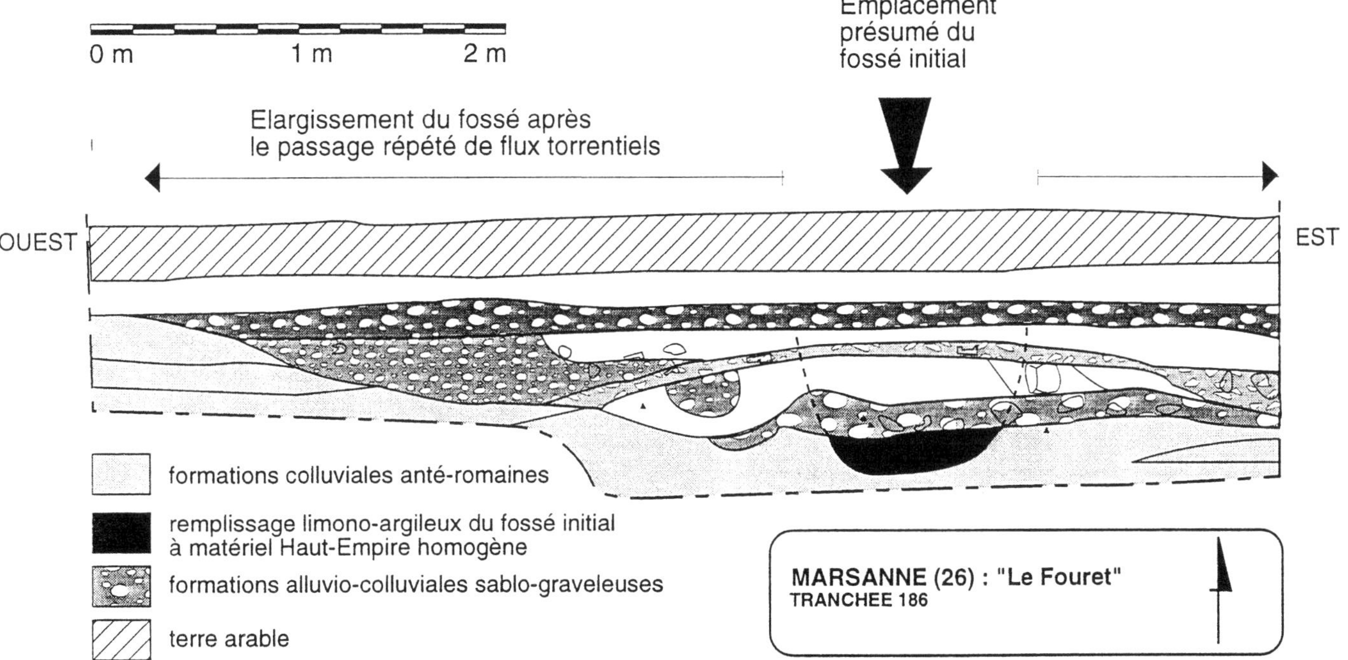

Fig. 15.5. An example of the modification of the profile of an ancient ditch caused by repeated torrential flow.

The reconstruction of agro-pastoral rhythms

Periods of increasing or decreasing human activity can be looked at by an integrated study of: (1) the microstratigraphy of transects cut across fossil field systems, which gives information on the rhythm of filling and clearing out of agrarian structures; (2) the chronological fixing of the various phases observed in the field; and (3) palaeo-environmental analysis, which indicates variations in the natural or anthropic environment.

The extrapolation of this data to the wider context of agro-pastoral rhythms would not be possible unless the results were confirmed over a wide geographic area, and in regions with varied environmental characteristics: topographically, pedologically and hydrologically, in order to avoid generalizations based on phenomena strictly dependent on local factors.

The results obtained concerning the phases of land use must then be compared with data concerning population dynamics obtained by the means of spatial archaeology, in order finally to broaden the history of field systems into that of a global historical view. The research conducted by Thierry Odiot (1995) in the Tricastin and by Jean-François Berger (1995a) in the Valdaine show that in the first century AD and in the first half of the second century AD, a large number of sites was founded, whereas in the second half of the second century and in the third century more and more sites were abandoned. These changes in population dynamics can be put into context in terms of profound changes in land organization and management. It should not be perceived as a period of decline or recession (Favory *et al.*, 1995). Preliminary results from the Valdaine basin indicate that the drainage network was neglected during an ill-defined period in Late Antiquity. People in Late Antiquity and the early Middle Ages (the sixth to the tenth centuries AD) seemed to prefer the limestone plateaus to the low-lying plains and the piedmont which had been more densely populated up until then (Odiot and Berger, 1995). Site indicators for this period are nonetheless infrequent and have a tendency to become even rarer between the eighth and the tenth centuries. During the Middle Ages (the eleventh to the thirteenth centuries), human pressure on the hillsides is attested to by the number of grouped settlements or *castra* (Bois, 1993). At this time, all of the landscape units were in use, and the settlement dynamics are similar to those of the early Empire. It seems that at this time new drainage networks were put in place, sometimes following the orientations of Roman field systems.

Agro-pastoral modes, technologies and mutations

The combined results of the palaeo-environmental research should make it possible to define agro-pastoral modes, be they monoculture, polyculture, or pasture. This data, put back into its chrono-stratigraphic context, will make it possible to look at agro-pastoral mutations. We already have information on the agro-pastoral rhythms in the Valdaine (Berger, 1995b), where we have noted extensive vine and walnut culture in the early Empire, whilst in Late Antiquity there is an extension of damp pastures probably tied to pastoralism. This research will try to confirm or to amend this change in land-use modes, and to fine tune its chronology, as well as to determine

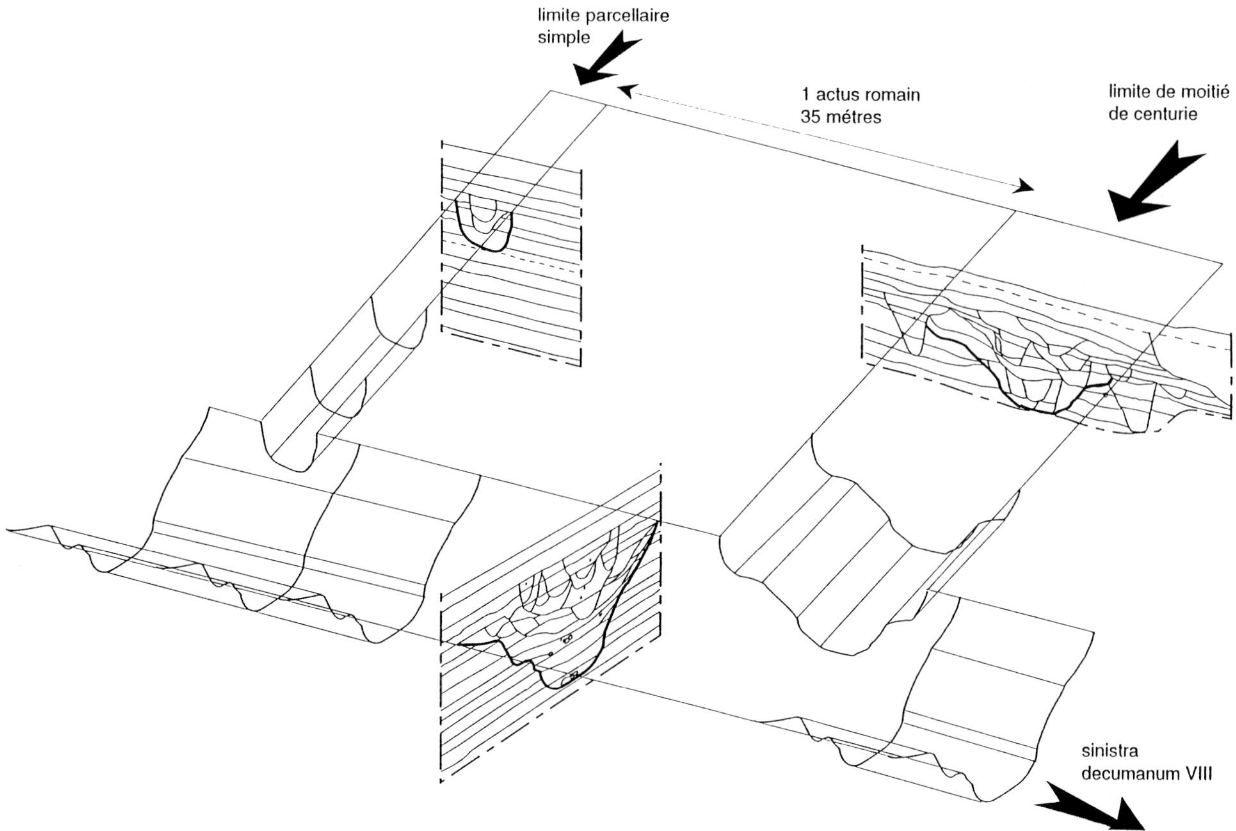

Fig.15.6. An example of ditch hierarchy in a Roman drainage network, within the framework of the Cadastre B of Orange (in the Tricastin plain, in the town of Mondragon).

whether or not it can be applied to a wider geographic area.

The study of ditches must also aim at reconstructing agrarian techniques used in Antiquity and the Middle Ages. First, the structure of the ditch gives an idea about drainage and irrigation techniques. Also, the dendritic organization of the drainage networks, from the small primary drains to the much larger central drain, sometimes taking the shape of a channelled river, is potentially reconstructable thanks to combined archaeo-morphological and geo-archaeological analysis. Hypotheses for the management of water based on a morphological study have already been proposed for the Tricastin plain (Chartier and Chouquer, 1995). A hierarchy was established between several drains in one plot at the locality of Le Duc in the town of Mondragon, based upon topographic and morphological evidence (Fig. 15.6).

Finally, the study of the contemporary morpho-pedological context of a ditch, when this is possible, can facilitate the identification of networks of ditches dug in landscape units that are not sensitive to hydromorphy, and that are intended only to drain excess water during heavy rainfall.

Moreover, the work done on the carbonized plant remains (wood, herbaceous plants, seeds) trapped in the sediments sealed in the ditches, can reveal several types of land use and agro-pastoral rhythms. We can envisage three processes.

The first would be the seasonal burning of fields resulting in burnt cereal grains and microcharcoal associated with phytoliths indicating the burning of herbaceous plants. These carbonized residues could also testify to the clearing of ditches by fire, during dry periods of the winter or spring as it is still done today.

The second would be the clearing of new land by burning, of plots temporarily neglected or of plots left to bush fallow (Boserup, 1970). The last two cases would indicate a re-colonization of the plot by heliophilous pioneer tree or shrub species, between two crops. This excludes the grazing of herds on such plots, as their presence would inhibit the development of woody vegetation. Pedo-anthrocological analysis, the identification of the species of burnt wood, is a determining element in the development of such hypotheses.

A third process could be the addition of ashes and charcoal to soil, a process of manuring which the presence of numerous rounded and worn sherds renders a possible hypothesis. The presence of totally allochthonous species of trees (streamside or hillslope species occurring in the plain, for example) may be an indication of soil being tranformed by materials containing charcoal. The study of the paleosols in association with these structures,

Fig.15.7. Bonlieu-sur-Roubion (Drome), Trench n° 585: a ditch oriented 23° east, dug into late glacial silt covering Wurmien gravel.

when they still exist, can give confirmation of such practices.

Reconstructing the agricultural value of ancient and medieval soils

Research in the Valdaine basin and in the Tricastin plain has shown that, for historical applications, present-day pedological maps are limited in value, and even misleading if they are not used in conjunction with research into the geomorphological and pedological evolution of the micro-regions in question (Berger, 1996). Pedological profiles are often rejuvenated by truncation, or by alluvial or colluvial sediment cover. In the best instances, stability has prevailed and the profile has evolved little since Antiquity; but then it may be that the intensification of farming practices has modified the agrological value of the soil in terms of increased stoniness, loss in fine fraction and in organic matter, degradation of structure, and so on.

Even landscape units considered to be stable since Antiquity such as Quaternary terraces may have undergone profound changes to their pedological cover. Drainage ditches have often trapped soil particles (pedological micro-aggregates) eroded during Antiquity. They are, therefore, precious elements for the reconstruction of lost soil coverage.

Figure 15.7 allows us to validate this reasoning. In the centre of the Valdaine plain (Drôme), the pedological map drawn up by Bornand (1967) indicates brown calcareous soils on a Wurmien substratum of gravelly-sandy alluvium. A section across a ditch that is probably ancient, and that is aligned to the Cadastre B of Orange, indicates that the soil eroded and trapped in Antiquity was different from present-day soils in texture (more argillaceous), in colour (reddish-orange), and in carbonate levels (high level of decarbonatation). Even before a more complete study of the micromorphology has been undertaken, it is possible to suggest that the soils farmed in Antiquity were similar to those found today on the same terrace a few kilometres upstream. Since Antiquity, a truncation has eliminated, either progressively or suddenly, the evolved soils that had developed on the alluvial terrace of Roubion since the end of the last Ice Age. Since then, a brown calcareous soil has developed over the sand and stones of the terrace that had been laid bare by erosion.

In the southern piedmont of the Valdaine Basin, the examination of a drainage ditch cut across a Wurmien alluvial cone (Fig. 15.8) equally indicates a strong contrast between present day soils (colluvial calcareous soils) and the ancient soil (dark brown decarbonated argillaceous soils of a vertic type). Here the rejuvenation of the soils is explained by a thick covering of alluvial-colluvial sediment, the origin of which can be sought in a succession of strong erosional phases starting in the middle of the Roman period.

The multiplicity of trenches excavated in the context of the TGV project, in varied landscape units, gives us the means to envisage reconstructing pedological cover contemporary with the functioning of the plots crossed, and rectifying the existing pedological maps.

Environmental constraints to human exploitation

Between the initial period of Roman colonization and the end of Antiquity, the Gallo-Roman farmer exploiting the low-lying alluvial plains and basin floors was faced with rising levels of groundwater and disturbances in the river system. From the beginning of the second Iron Age to the Augustan period, the general tendency was that of incision in the alluvial plains and a corresponding lowering of groundwater levels. This stability in the hydrological system made it possible to colonize and exploit the floodplains (Berger, 1995b; Bravard and *al.*, 1992; Starkel, 1983).

The point at which this tendency started to invert itself may be situated in the mid first century BC, even though the chronological markers drawn from geomorphological research differ according to the region studied (Bravard and *al.*, 1992; Gallay and Kaenel, 1981; Lamb, 1977; Magny, 1992; Potter, 1976; Vérot-Bourrély *and al.*, 1995). From that point on, disturbances in the functioning of the river systems caused a rise in the level of the alluvial plains due to thick layers of silt from flooding. This accelerated the sealing off, or even fossilization, of drainage and road networks. These hydrological crises must have played havoc with local land management and development policies. These phenomena were first noted in isolation in the lower Rhône valley, in the sediment from small pre-alpine rivers that have torrential discharge (Berger, 1995b). The Rhône plain around Orange, in which trenches were dug for the TGV project, is a concrete example of an area dependent on palaeo-hydrological fluctuations, not only in the Roman period but throughout the Holocene, during which time 5–8 m of sediment have been deposited. The tendency towards accretion accelerates during certain periods according to the chronological and palaeo-pedological markers already available. We must note the 50–80 cm of flood silt separating the levels of the early Empire from those of the later Empire (Fig. 15.9).

If these initial results are confirmed, we will need to reflect on the impact that these palaeo-hydrological phenomena may have had on land use and settlement in these low-lying lands, often considered to be the most fertile. What were the consequences for the economy of having the agricultural landscape instantly fossilized under tens of centimetres of silt? Is it possible to make a link between the abandonment of cultivated land cited in Antiquity (such as the AD 312 speech addressed to Constantine concerning the *pagus Arebrinus*: Latin Panegyrics, *Gratiarum actio Constantio Augusto* VIII.6–7), the social and economic situation of the Empire in the second and third centuries AD and the palaeo-environmental constraints discussed above?

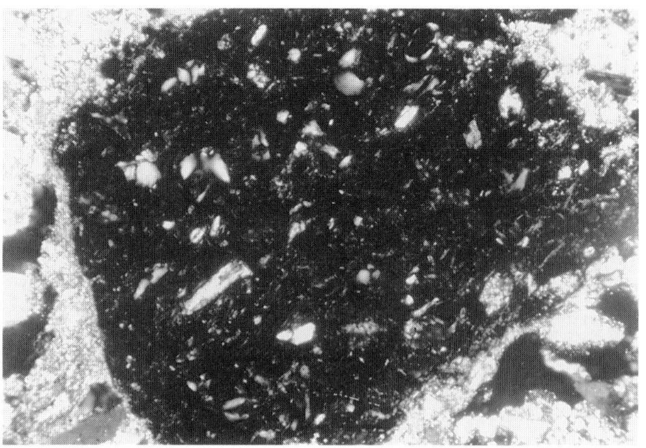

Fig. 15.8. Portes-en-Valdaine, (Drôme), Trench n° 17: view of a pedological aggregate (brownish-black soil) trapped in a Roman drainage ditch oriented on the lines of the Cadastre B of Orange. (Photograph taken with X200 polarising light.)

The characterization of the impact of agro-systems on historical landscapes

The information collected from the ditches testifies to an intensification of agriculture and associated erosion. The fill of the ditches comes from runoff from the surrounding plots. Observation of soil micro-aggregates trapped in the ditches should reveal the impact of agricultural activity on the structural stability of cultivated soils. The disintegration of a soil is very often linked to an intensification of exploitation (most notably of ploughing) and a shortening of time that fields are left fallow. This drastically reduces the level of organic matter, as well as that of clay in the upper horizons of the soil, leading to the progressive destruction of the organic-mineral complex, an essential element for aggregation and therefore for the structure of the soil. The presence of aggregates from deep horizons (B, Bc), in particular, is indicative of a strong truncation of cultivated soils.

The characterization of crop type obtained from carpological, palynological and anthrocological analyses, can also testify to the protection afforded by crops against rainfall erosion as measured against the EU Map of Susceptibility to Land Erosion of Mediterranean Europe: in the Valdaine, for example, Stéphane Thiébault has shown from the charcoal in diches cut into the Quaternary terraces and piedmont that the Romans planted vines and walnut trees (Berger, 1995b). Viticulture and arboriculture are the crop types that are the most sensitive to erosion phenomena, except when they are associated with other crops or protective grass cover. The drainage of plots set aside for pasture, as in the low-lying plains of Holland today, constitutes the form of agriculture that is the least sensitive to erosion.

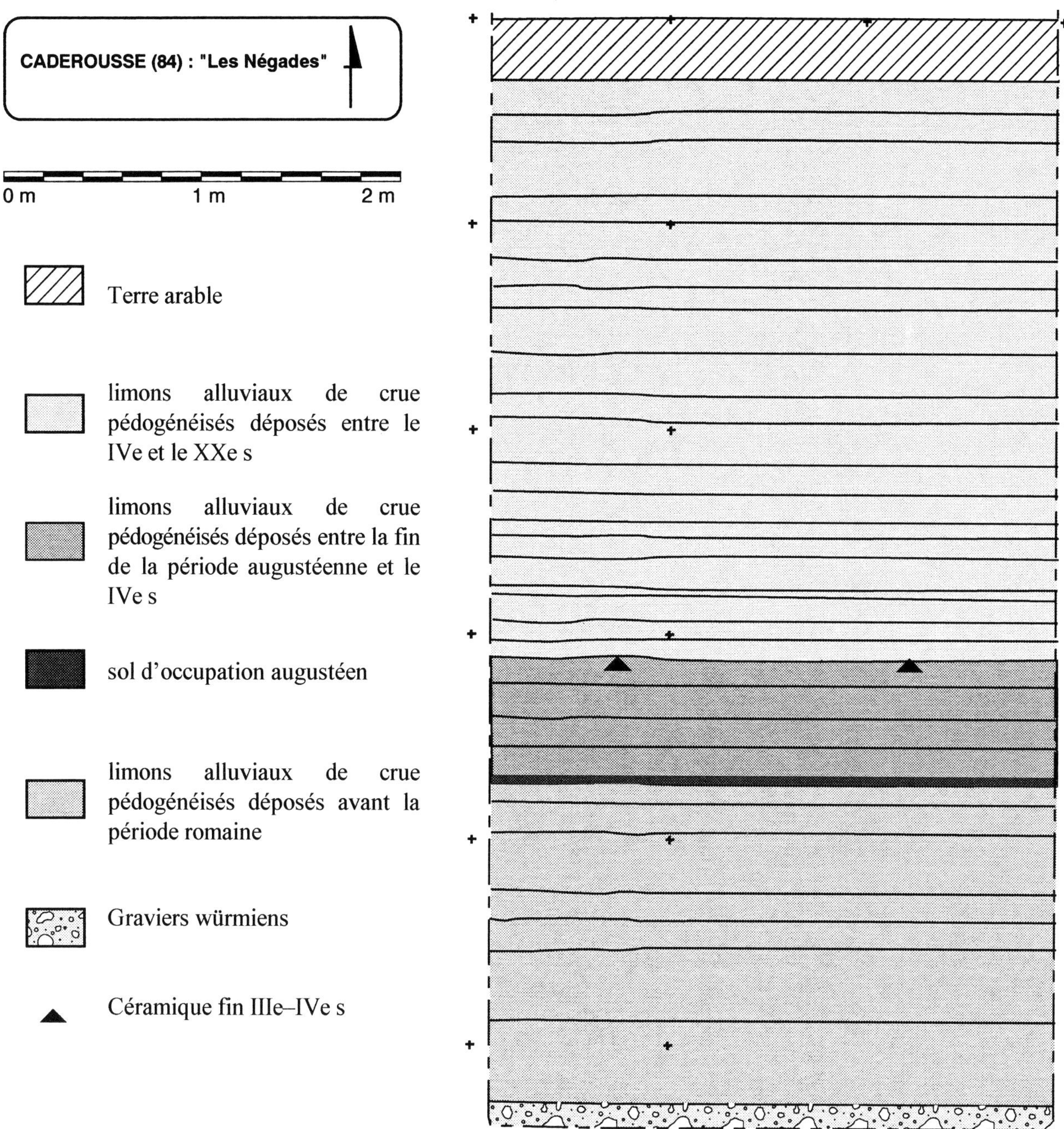

Fig. 15.9. Pedosedimentary sequence of the Orange alluvial plain showing sediment accumulation in the early centuries AD.

Specific work on the palaeo-hydrological and palaeopedological changes induced by drainage is done at the same time. This way of working is only possible in areas of active sedimentation, which allow for observations on previous soils, contemporary with and later than the drainage. Changes in the drainage conditions are perceptible in soils contemporary with the functioning of the drainage network: they often show signs of oxidation and porosity. A return to a hydromorphic environment, following neglect of the network also leaves pedological markers in terms of the reduction of sesquihydroxides and the closing up of soil porosity. Modification to the make-up of the malacology is also perceptible in the field: land molluscs are very sensitive to hydrological fluctuations and, as such, are complimentary to pedological analysis in revealing ecological modifications induced by agropastoral activity in the low-lying plains and basins. Thus Fréderic Magnin has shown through malacological analysis that the damp pastures and marshes of the piedmont and marl basins of the Valdaine expanded in late Antiquity (Berger, 1995b).

Joint research in palynology and anthracology illustrates the state of the forests in historical times. Intense clearing of forests and phases of re-colonization are perceptible in the diagrams built up by these two disciplines. They were based on information collected in the drainage ditches and in the paleosols that preceded and succeeded them.

CONCLUSION

The research project presented in this paper underlines the need to bring together morphological, archaeological and environmental data in order to reconstruct the history of agrosystems: their organization and development,their chronology, the systems of maintenances, and the farming practices which they supported. The systematic study of open drainage ditches is necessary in order to compare different phases noted in the initial microstratigraphic observations, and to develop a typology of the fills found in drainage structures. Certain facies observed fairly regularly (such as dark brown to dark grey layers of molluscs, enriched with more or less charcoal) already seem to be associated with a paludification of the drainage network, indicating, therefore, the neglect of proper maintenance of the ditches. The repetition of identical observations should allow the development of regional models concerning the phases of use of the drainage ditchesl. These phases are linked to phases of land development or to the abandonment of agro-pastoral systems, perhaps even transformations in agro-pastoral modes. The variety of pedo-sedimentological markers and of palaeobotanical or malacological combinations underlines the necessity to study the filling dynamics of drainage networks in terms of the interaction between processes linked to agro-pastoral activity and palaeo-hydrological processes. The analysis of sedimentological dynamics, together with the micro-pedological and petrographic verification obtained by micromorphological observation of stratigraphic units identified in the field, supply us with the means to place palaeo-ecological information trapped in ditches into a context that is favourable for its interpretation.

ACKNOWLEDGEMENTS

We wish to thank Thierry Odiot (S.R.A., Rhône-Alpes) who launched this project and kept it going, as well as Jean-Olivier Guillot (*T.G.V. Méditerranée* co-ordinator) and Valerie Bel (Section head for the T.G.V. in Drôme-Nord and the Vaucluse) for their confidence in us. We would also like to thank the archaeologists who excavated the sites, as well as the other members of our team: Alain Leroux, Françoise Launay, Jean-Claude Mège, Magali Truc and Nathalie Valour; the palaeo-environmentalists (Frédéric Magnin, Solange Farbos-Teixier, Stéphanie Thiébault) who did the analyses; Guilaine Macabeo who did the PAO; and Jacques-Léopold Brochier and François Favory for their comments on this text.

REFERENCES

Berger, J.-F. (1995a) Le bassin de la Valdaine. In S. E. van der Leeuw (ed.) *Understanding the Natural and Anthropogenic Causes of Soil Degradation and Desertification in the Mediterranean Basin. The Archaeomedes Project* 1: 160–280. Cambridge, EU DGXII.

Berger, J.-F. (1995b) Facteurs anthropiques et naturels de l'évolution des paysages romains et proto-médiévaux du bassin valdainais (Drôme). In S.E. van der Leeuw (ed.) *L'Homme et la Dégradation de l'Environnement* (Actes des XVes Rencontres Internationales d'Histoire et d'Archéologie d'Antibes): 79–114. Sophia Antipolis, APDCA.

Berger, J.-F. (1996) *Le Cadre Paléogéographique des Systèmes d'Occupation du Bassin Valdainais (Drôme) à l'Holocène.* Paris, Université de Paris I, Thèse de Doctorat Nouveau Régime.

Blanc, A. (1953) Les traces de la centuriation et les origines de la cité de Valence. *Revue d'Etudes Latines* 19, 1–4: 35–53.

Bois, M. (1993) *Le Sud du Département de la Drôme entre le Xe et le XIIIe s., l'Organisation du Terroir, Fortification et Structures d'Habitat.* Aix-en-Provence, Université de Provence,Thèse de Doctorat

Boserup, E. (1970) *Evolution Agraire et Pression Démographique.* Paris, Flammarion.

Bravard, J.-P., Verot-Bourelly, A., and Salvador P.-G. (1992) Le climat d'après les informations fournies par les enregistrements sédimentaires fluviatiles étudiés d'après des sites archéologiques, *Les Nouvelles de l'Archéologie* 50: 7–13.

Chartier, A. and Chouquer, G. (1995) Le rôle du parcellaire dans la gestion des flux d'eau. In S. E. van der Leeuw (ed.) *Understanding the Natural and Anthropogenic Causes of Soil Degradation and Desertification in the Mediterranean Basin. The Archaeomedes Project* 2: 286–90. Cambridge, EU DGXII.

Chouquer, G. and Odiot, T. (1984) Etude morpho-historique de la cité de Valence. *Dialogues d'Histoire Ancienne* 10: 361–96.

Favory, F. and Fiches, J.-L. (1994) *Les Campagnes de la France Méditerranéenne dans l'Antiquité et le Moyen Âge.* Paris, Documents d'Archéologie Française 42.

Favory, F., Fiches, J.-L., Girardot, J.-J. and Raynaud, C. (1995) Analyse statistique de l'habitat rural. In S. E. van der Leeuw (ed.) *Understanding the Natural and Anthropogenic Causes of Soil Degradation and Desertification in the Mediterranean Basin. The Archaeomedes Project* 2: 3–68. Cambridge, EU DGXII.

Fiches, J.-L. (1993) Critères de datation et chronologie des limitations romaines en Narbonnaise. *Revue Archéologique de Narbonnaise* 26: 99–104.

Gallay, K. (1981) Repères archéologiques pour une histoire des terrasses du Léman. *Archives Suisses d'Anthropologie Générale* 45, fasc.2: 129 -57.

Lamb (1977) *Climate: Past, Present, and Future.* London, Methuen.

Magny, M. (1992) Les fluctuations des lacs jurassiens et subalpins. *Les Nouvelles de l'Archéologie* 50: 32–6.

Odiot, T. (1995) La dynamique spatio-temporelle du front colonial en vallée du Rhône. In S. E. van der Leeuw (ed.) *Understanding the Natural and Anthropogenic Causes of Soil Degradation and Desertification in the Mediterranean Basin. The Archaeomedes Project* 2: 267–83. Cambridge, EU DGXII.

Odiot, T.and Berger, J.-F. (1995) L'occupation romaine au Bas-Empire dans le Tricastin. *Pages d'Archéologie Médiévale en Rhône-Alpes.*

Piganiol, A. (1962) *Les Documents Cadastraux de la Colonie Romaine d'Orange.* Paris, Gallia, XVIe supplément.

Potter, T.W. (1976) Valleys and settlement: some new evidence. *World Archaeology* 8: 207–19.

Starkel (1983) The reflection of the hydraulic changes in the fluvial environment of the temperate zone during the last 15000 years.

In K. J. Gregory (ed.) *Background to Palaeohydrology*: 213–35. Chichester, Wiley.

Vérot-Bourrély, A., Argant, J., Bravard J.-P. and Chaix L., (1995) Le paléoenvironnement du site de Gorge de Loup (Lyon IXe): les signes matériels de la dégradation d'après l'étude interdisciplinaire du gisement. In S.E. van der Leeuw(ed.) *L'Homme et la Dégradation de l'Environnement* (Actes des XVes Rencontres Internationales d'Histoire et d'Archéologie d'Antibes): 43–77. Sophia Antipolis, APDCA.

16. Progradación Fluvial y Cambios en la Línea de Costa en Época Histórica en el Golfo de Valencia (España)

Pilar Carmona

RESUMEN

Se estudian procesos de progradación fluvial y cambios en la línea de costa en época histórica en el Golfo de Valencia (Fig. 16.1). El registro geoarqueológico de la ciudad romana e islámica de Valencia ofrece datos sobre violentas inundaciones del río Turia. Se observan cuatro niveles de sedimentación : terrazas de arcillas y limos con suelos del tipo vertisol (early Holocene); limos, arenas y gravas de desbordamiento fluvial (época romana); limos

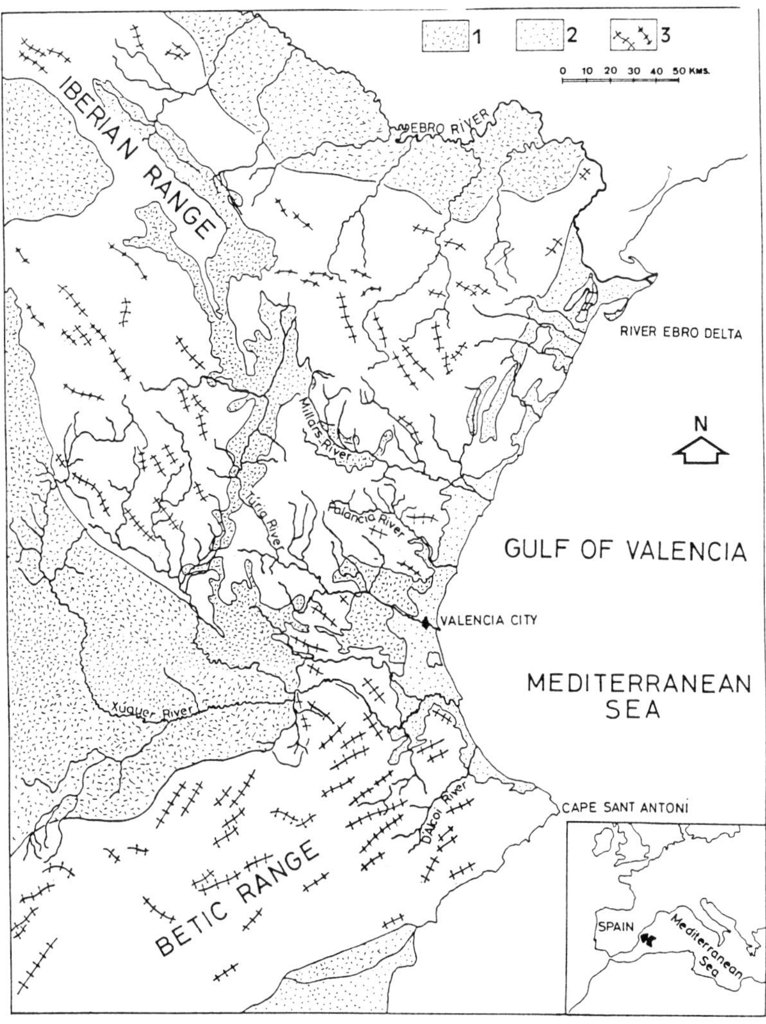

Fig. 16.1. Area de estudio y marco estructural: 1. Graben *terciario; 2. llanuras costeras cuaternarias; 3. plegamientos de los sistemas Ibérico y Bético.*

y arcillas orgánicas (marshes) en época visigoda y, finalmente, sedimentos de grano muy grueso (cantos grava y arena) en facies de barra de canal en época islámica. Estos depósitos de inundación corresponden a una fase de progradación continental y retroceso de la línea de costa de dos kilómetros de longitud. En la interpretación de estos fenómenos se contemplan variables de dinámica fluvial, erosión histórica en sistemas fluviales mediterráneos y dinámica y orientación del litoral.

INTRODUCCIÓN

En este trabajo se estudian procesos de progradación fluvial del río Turia y cambios en la línea de costa del Golfo de Valencia (Mediterráneo occidental) durante tiempos históricos (2300 BP hasta la actualidad). El estudio parte de anteriores investigaciones acerca de la formación y evolución de la llanura aluvial costera cuaternaria del río Turia (Carmona, 1990a, 1990b, *et al.* 1990). El método de trabajo seguido consistió en la realización de estudios estratigráficos, sedimentológicos y geomorfológicos en la llanura aluvial costera. Con estos datos se establece una secuencia cronológica de formación apoyada con dataciones absolutas de termoluminiscencia, carbono 14 y restos arqueológicos. Por otro lado se estudió la paleohidrología de los depósitos fluviales del registro geoarqueológico. Se realizó un análisis detallado de los rasgos geomorfológicos del área con trabajo de campo, interpretación de fotogramas aéreos y mapas topográficos con intervalos de curvas de nivel de un metro. Finalmente, los documentos históricos de archivos sirvieron para determinar formas y procesos del llano de inundación del río Turia.

Los rasgos geomorfológicos más destacados del área son : abanicos aluviales, terrazas, depósitos de inundación, paleocanales, ciénagas litorales, dunas costeras y playas. Las conclusiones de este trabajo aportan datos acerca de los procesos y evolución de los sistemas fluviales Mediterráneos en el Holoceno final y los cambios en la línea de costa.

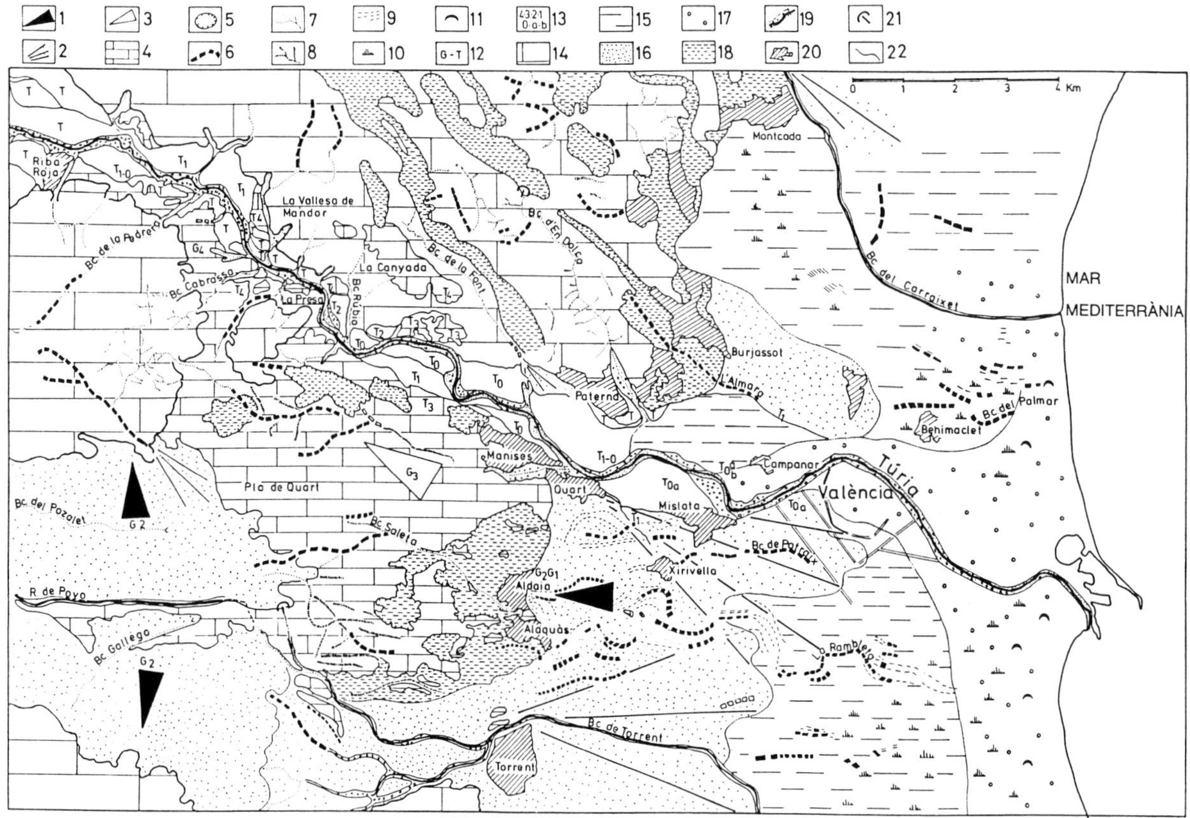

Fig. 16.2. Mapa geomorfológico: 1,3. glacis; 2. abanico aluvial; 4. costra calcárea; 5. dolina; 6,9. paleocanales; 7,8. escorrentía superficial y subsuperficial; 10. ciénagas; 11. restinga; 12. glacis y terrazas; 13. cronología niveles pleistocenos (4 y 3 pleistoceno inferior, 2 pleistoceno medio, 1 pleistoceno superior, 0 holoceno a, antiguo y b histórico); 14. calizas terciarias; 15. llanura aluvial, limos y arcillas marrones; 16, 18. limos, arenas arcillas y nódulos calcáreos rojos; 17. arenas limos llano inundación reciente; 19. canal fluvial; 20. poblaciones; 21. erosión regresiva; 22. contactos morfológicos.

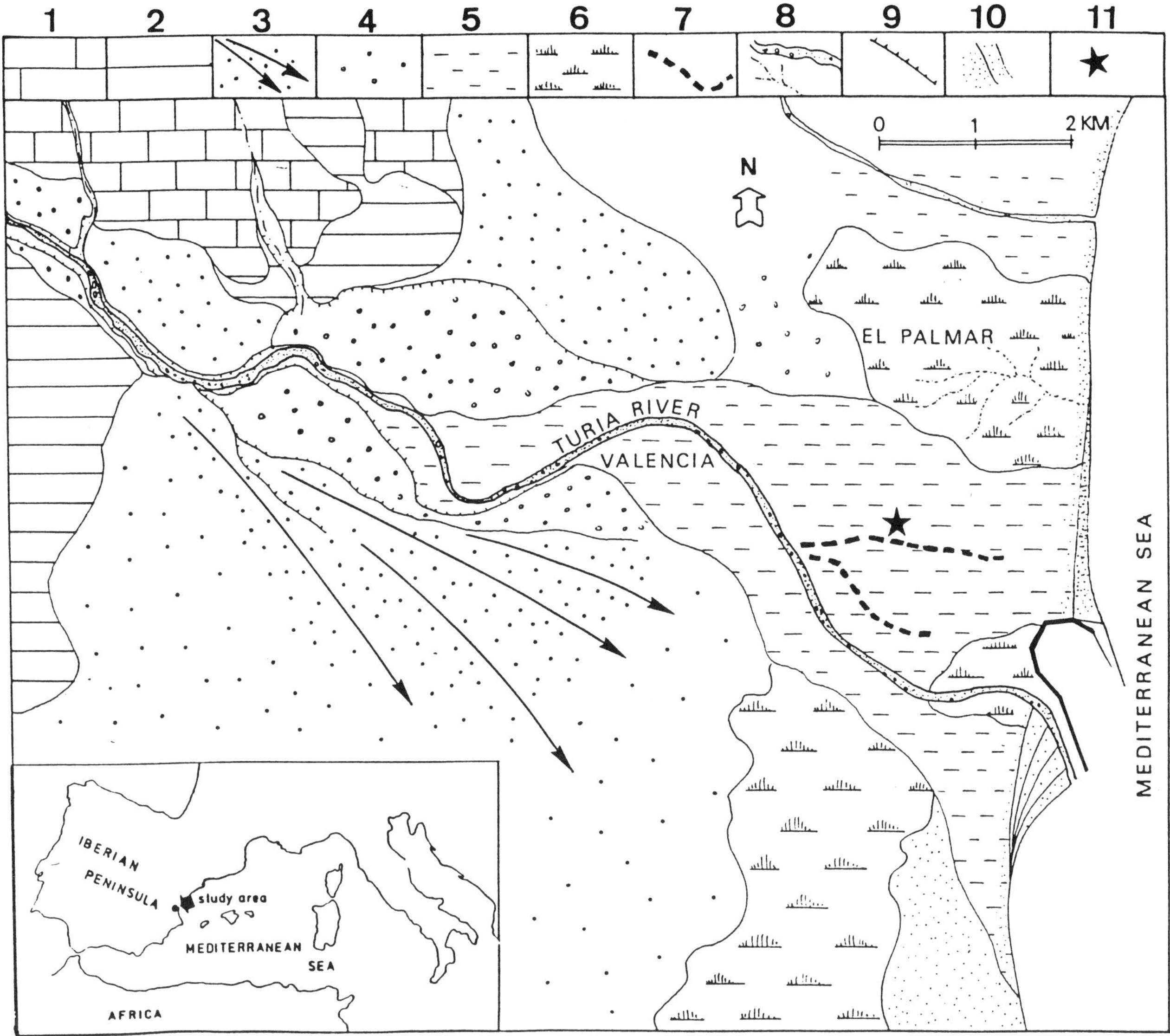

Fig. 16.3. Mapa geomorfológico de detalle: 1. calizas miocenicas; 2. pleistoceno medio; 3. pleistoceno superior; 4. holoceno antiguo; 5. holoceno reciente; 6. marismas; 7. paleocanales; 8. canales de río; 9. terrazas; 10. arenas costeras; 11. línea de costa 2300 BP.

DATOS GEOMORFOLÓGICOS

Desde una perspectiva geomorfológica el litoral presenta 2, 16.3 una amplia variedad de formas de acumulación pleistocenas y holocenas (Figs. 16.2, 16.3), abanicos aluviales, llanuras de inundación, terrazas, canales y paleocanales fluviales, ciénagas y lagunas litorales, cordones dunares y playas. Este litoral se caracteriza por un proceso de continua subsidencia, muy activa durante el Pleistoceno (Carmona, 1990a, 1990b; Carmona *et al.*, 1994; Goy y Zazo, 1974; Pérez Cueva, 1988; Segura, 1980; Simón, 1984).

Un abanico aluvial del Pleistoceno superior se despliega cuando el río entra en la llanura, su vértice está situado en uno de los ejes tectónicos distensivos que conforman el litoral. Tiene un perfil longitudinal relacionado con un nivel de base y línea de costa más alejada que la actual. Estas características morfológicas y la datación por termoluminiscencia de niveles de terraza nos permiten deducir que se depositó con el bajo nivel marino de la última glaciación pleistocena mediterránea. Está formado por materiales de cantos grava y arena fluviales, intercalados entre potentes niveles de limos y arcillas de tono rojizo con abundantes nódulos calcáreos (arrastres de paleosuelos rojos mediterráneos). Varios niveles de terraza escalonados y de época pleistocena están incididos en este abanico.

El canal actual está bordeado por una terraza de limos arcillas y arenas de tonos marrones con débil desarrollo edáfico, datada en el early Holocene (0a). Aguas abajo, esta secuencia fluvial holocena entierra (overlap) completamente las partes media y distal el abanico aluvial del

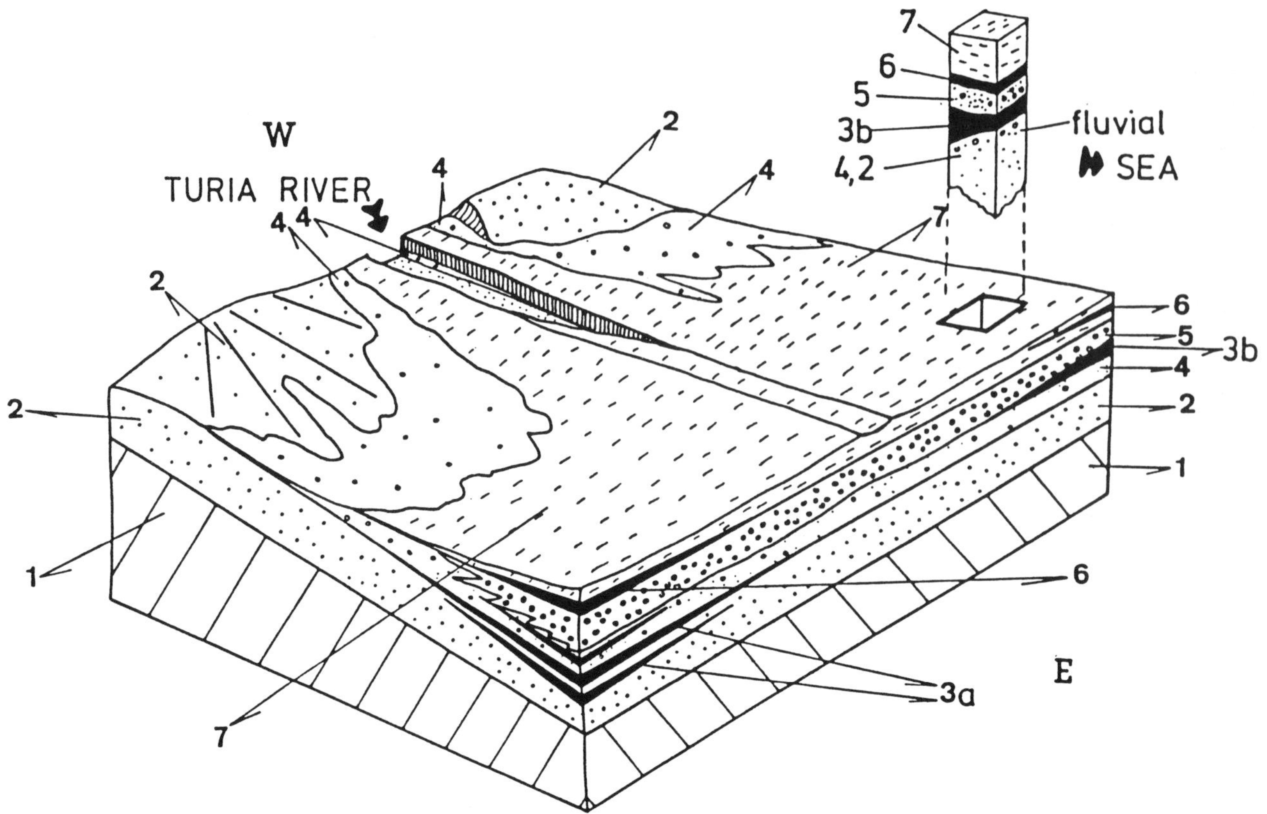

Fig. 16.4. Diagrama de columnas con los principales estratos de la llanura: 1. pleistoceno medio; 2. pleistoceno superior; 3a. laguna pleistocena; 3b. lagunas holocenas; 4. holoceno antiguo; 5. transgresión flandriana; 6. lagunas históricas; 7. holoceno reciente, inundaciones históricas.

Pleistoceno superior. Las facies terminales del abanico han sido identificadas en la plataforma continental (Goy *et al.*, 1987). Cerca de la costa, sedimentos del inundación del río Turia de época histórica (0b) entierran (overlap) el nivel del early Holocene. En el litoral, a ambos lados del canal, aparecen zonas deprimidas con ciénagas y lagunas costeras. Estas ciénagas están cerradas a la influencia marina por restingas que arrancan de la desembocadura del Turia.

Por lo que respecta a los procesos geomorfológicos actuales, durante la estación lluviosa todos los ríos afluentes al litoral pueden experimentar grandes crecidas e inundaciones que causan graves problemas a la población. En el mar, el rango de mareas en la costa mediterránea española es de menos de 20 cm. Los procesos que afectan a la dinámica costera son las olas y las corrientes litorales que son, por lo general, de norte a sur.

EVIDENCIAS DE SEDIMENTACION FLUVIAL HISTORICA EN EL REGISTRO GEOARQUEOLóGICO

El yacimiento arqueológico que ha proporcionado más información es la ciudad romana e islámica de Valencia. Fué fundada en el año 138 a.C. y los restos arqueológicos antiguos están enterrados bajo las construcciones de la ciudad moderna.

La ciudad está asentada sobre una terraza del early Holocene, situada en la llanura aluvial costera, a la orilla derecha del río Turia y distante varios kilómetros de la costa mediterránea (Fig. 16.3). Es posible que un pequeño paleocauce del río Turia rodease la ciudad por el sur.

La ciudad de Valencia, fue romano republicana en su origen, 138 a.J.C., alcanzó importancia en época romano imperial (I, II, III siglos d. J.C), permaneció varios siglos bajo influencia visigoda (siglos VI, VII) posteriormente bajo dominio islámico (siglos VIII hasta principios del XIII), hasta que fué incorporada a la corona de Aragón en el año 1238.

El estudio del registro sedimentario de más de 11 excavaciones arqueológicas (Carmona, 1990a, 1991; Carmona *et al.*, 1990) en el subsuelo de la ciudad permitió establecer la evolución geomorfológica del sistema fluvial del río Turia durante los últimos 2200 años (Fig. 16.5). Esta evolución puede deducirse de la interpretación paleohidrológica de sedimentos fluviales intercalados en el registro geoarqueológico. Distinguimos cuatro niveles sedimentarios (el estudio completo queda reflejado en las obras citadas, en este trabajo se presenta únicamente un resumen).

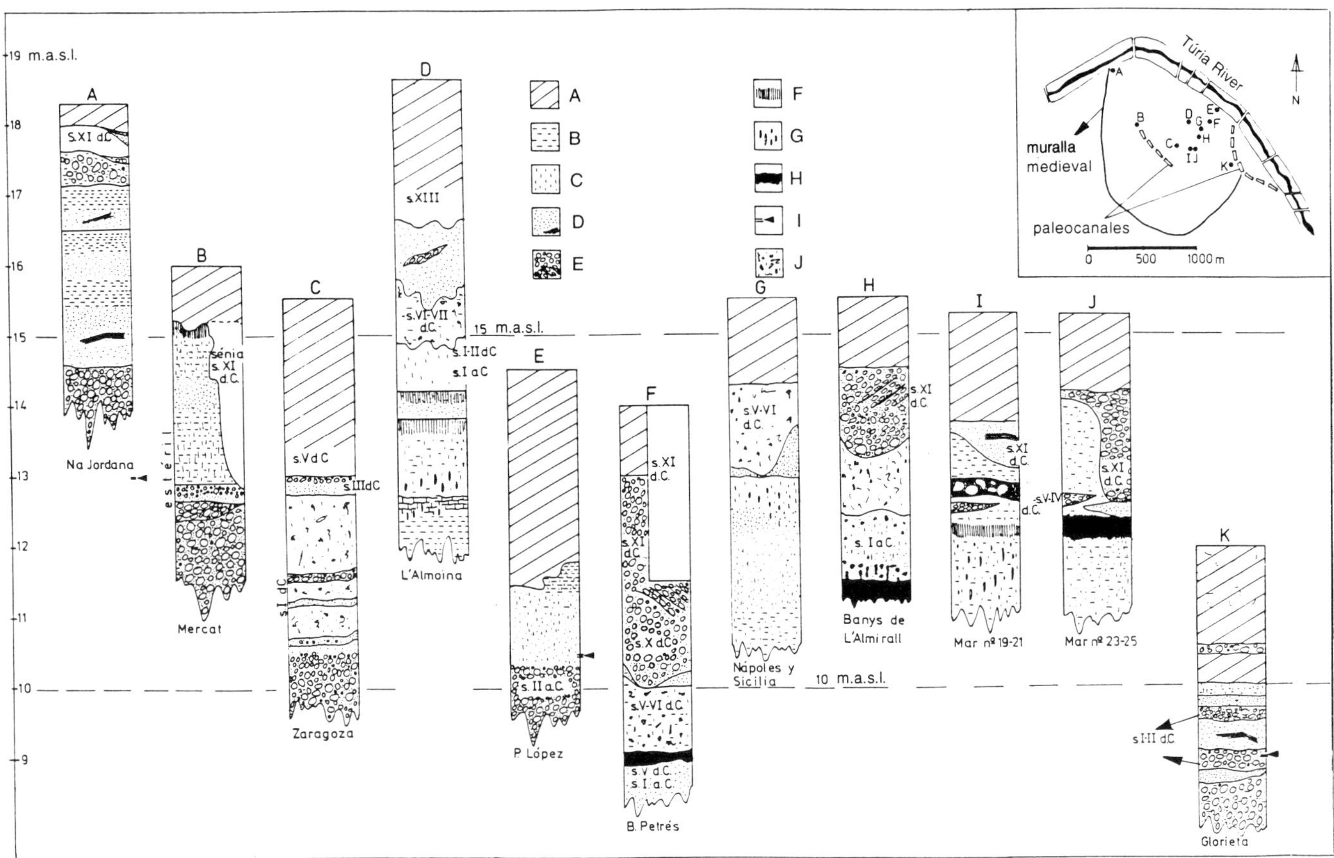

Fig. 16.5. Columnas estratigráficas registros geoarqueológicos estudiados: A. restos culturales recientes; B. arcillas; C. limos; D. arenas estratificación cruzada; E. grava y cantos estratificación cruzada; F. horizonte húmico; G. nódulos de carbonato; H. gley; I. cota lecho actual del río; J. antrópico.

El primero corresponde a los sedimentos de la terraza del early Holocene. Son arcillas y limos masivos de tono marrón oscuro, entre ellos, en algunas áreas de la ciudad, encontramos suelos del tipo vertisol; el ambiente sedimentario es de decantación en un medio de muy baja energía, posiblemente sedimentos muy finos tipo overbank y cuenca de inundación (Fig. 16.6).

El segundo nivel corresponde a sedimentos de inundación, aparece en todas las excavaciones de la ciudad de época romana, republicana e imperial (siglos II a. C hasta III d. C.). Este nivel se deposita en contacto erosivo sobre los sedimentos de la terraza holocena. El nivel tiene un grosor medio de decímetros, la textura es gruesa, arena de tamaño medio a grueso, masiva, y con bandas (10–20 cm) de cantos grava y arena con matriz arenosa. Hacia el sur de la ciudad, aumenta la potencia de este nivel (Fig. 16.7), ello es debido a la existencia de un paleocauce que rodeaba la ciudad por este sector. Estos depósitos de carga gruesa se interpretan como un aumento en la energía del medio, es posible que durante las crecidas la carga del lecho circule a través de brechas abiertas en la orilla del canal.

El tercer nivel es de época tardo romana o visigoda, siglos VI, VII, después de Cristo. Aparece en todas las excavaciones de este periodo en la ciudad, con potencia muy variable. Se trata de rellenos de depresiones o fosas excavadas en la ciudad de uno o dos metros de profundidad. El relleno sedimentario de dichas fosas es de textura muy fina, son arcillas negras o grises masivas, mezcladas con gran cantidad de restos antrópicos. Se interpreta un fuerte cambio en las condiciones hidrológicas, la energía del medio es mínima y no hay sedimentos de inundación violenta del río. El estudio micromorfológico de algunas muestras nos revela un ambiente sedimentario similar a ciénagas con fuerte interferencia antrópica.

El cuarto nivel se deposita durante los siglos X y XI, momentos álgidos de la instalación islámica en Valencia. Nuevamente, los restos arqueológicos contienen abundantes muestras de inundaciones violentas del río. Aparecen acumulaciones de uno o dos metros de potencia de arena y cantos grava arena, con matriz arenosa y con abundantes estructuras sedimentarias ('large-scale cross-bedding with pebbles'). Muchas casas, pozos y elementos constructivos de la ciudad son destruidos, reventados y cubiertos de grava, cantos y arena, formando a veces barras de canal fluvial ('fluvial channel bars'). Se trata de inundaciones violentísimas del río que rompe las orillas y deja depósitos muy gruesos en muchos puntos de la ciudad. Estas inundaciones son citadas en algunos documentos islámicos. En algunos áreas de la ciudad se observan depósitos semi-canalizados de subdelta de derrame (Figs. 16.6, 16.8).

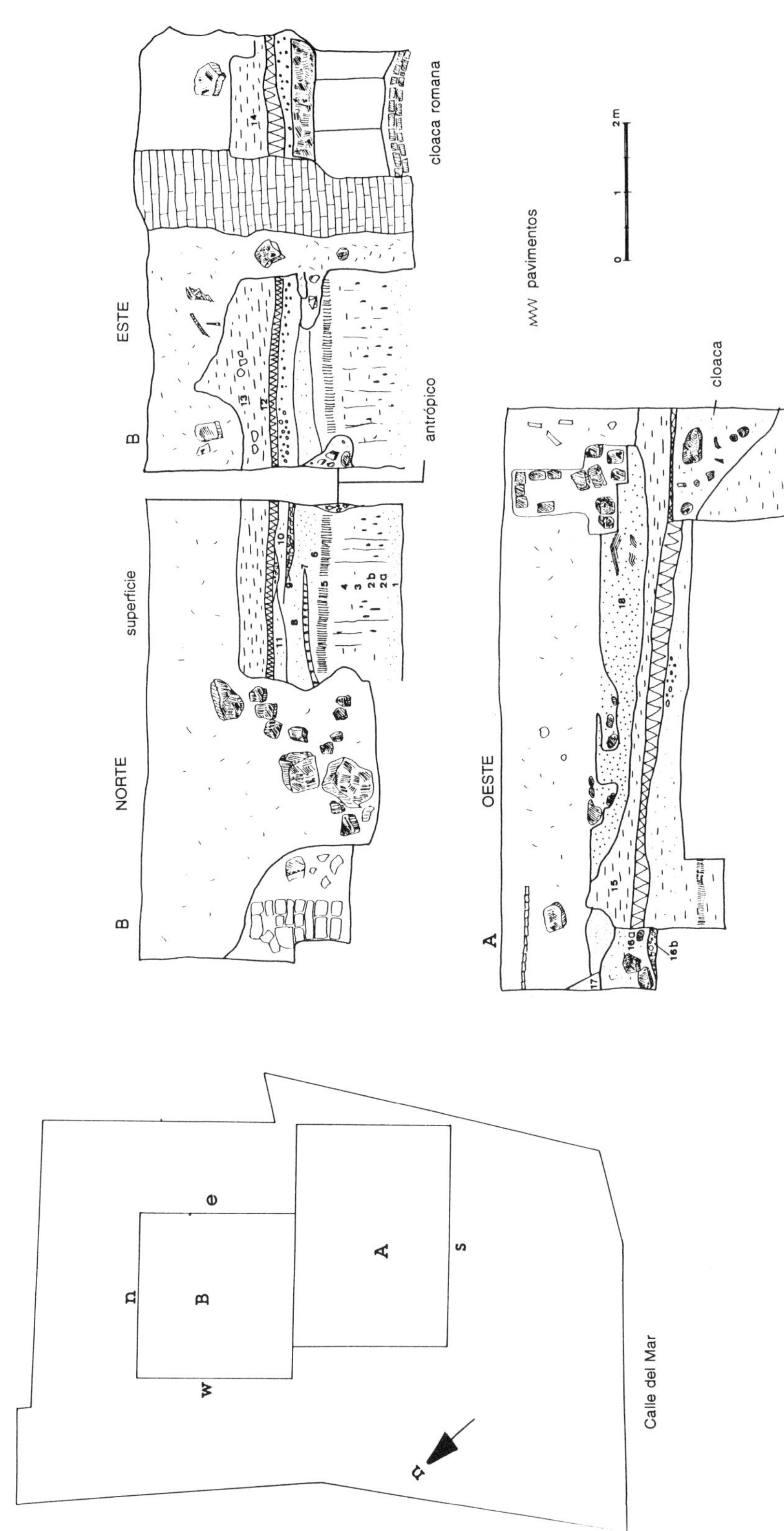

Fig. 16.6 Excavación de la Calle del Mar; los números corresponden a muestras sedimentarias analizadas: 1. limos arenosos; 2a, 2b. nódulos de carbonato, limos; 3. limos arcillosos; 3, 4. arcillas limosas; 5. arcillas, horizonte orgánico; 1–5. terraza Holoceno antiguo, no contiene restos antrópicos; 6–9, arenas limos y pasadas de gravilla, restos romano republicanos; 10, 11. limos arenosos; 12–15. arcillas grises, época visigoda; 18. arenas con estratificación cruzada, ripples de corriente, época islámica (siglo XI d. C.)

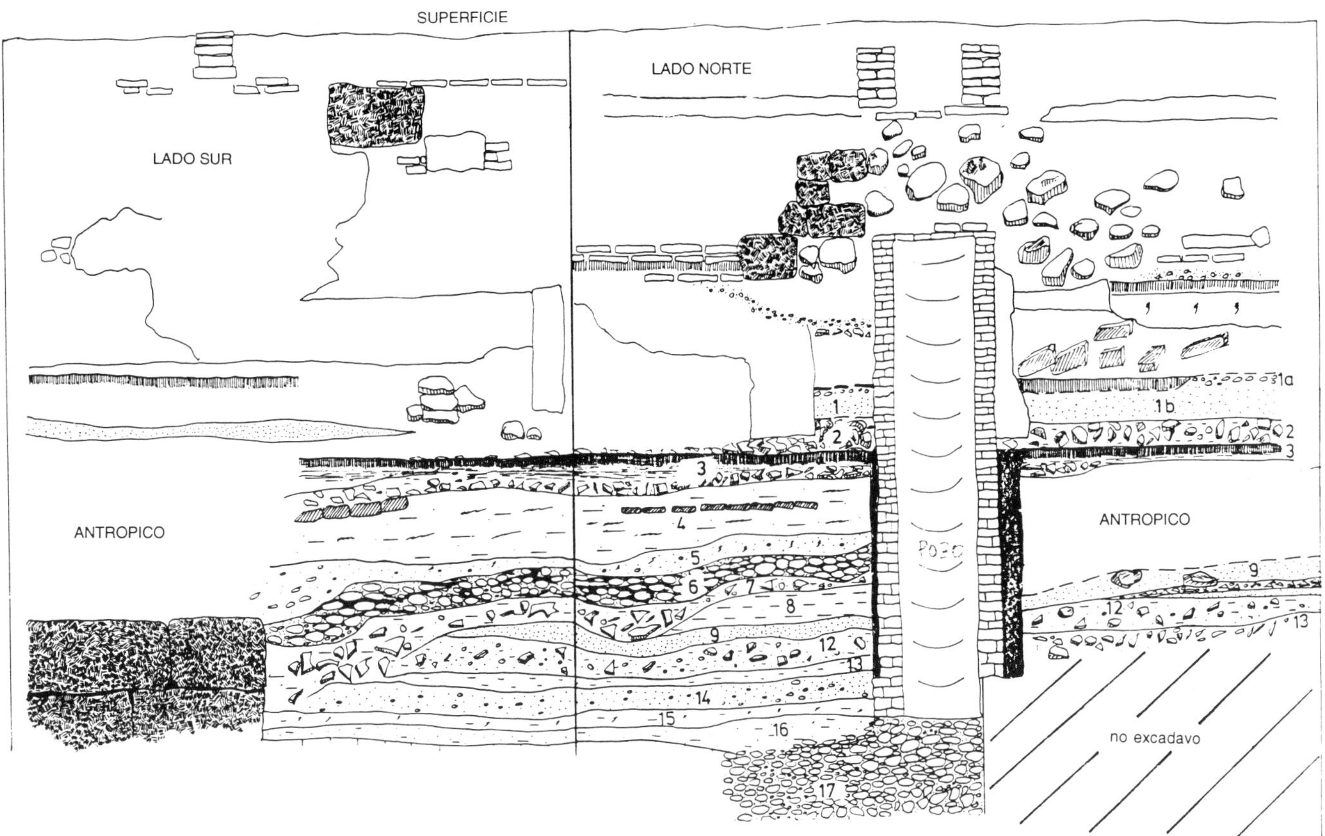

Fig. 16.7. Excavación Plaza de Zaragoza; los números correponden a muestras sedimentarias analizadas: 17, 14, 6. cantos grava y arena fluviales imbricados, matriz arenosa; 16, 9, 12, 5. arena y limo; 15, a3, 8, 7, 4. arcilla, limo y carbones; desde las muestras 17 a 4 los materiales son del siglo I d. C. al III d. C.; 2,3. pavimentos siglo III d. C.; 1a, 1b. arenas cantos y grava.

Con posterioridad y ya bajo el dominio de los reinos cristianos, en época medieval, las crónicas de la ciudad describen al menos cuatro episodios de fuerte inundación del río cada siglo en Valencia, destacando su poder destructor y las devastadoras consecuencias para la ciudad.

Los datos del registro geoarqueológico y las crónicas nos permiten reconstruir los rasgos geomorfológicos del llano de inundación del río Turia (Fig. 16.9), se trata de un río de morfología braided, lecho somero, orillas irregulares, carga sedimentaria gruesa y con procesos de fuerte inundación que rompen las orillas del canal y provocan cambios en su trayectoria.

PROGRADACIÓN CONTINENTAL Y CAMBIOS EN LA LÍNEA DE COSTA

Esta acelerada actividad fluvial tiene sus efectos progradantes en la línea de costa. Un registro sedimentario situado a dos kilómetros de distancia del mar en la orilla norte de un paleocanal del río nos muestra la siguiente secuencia (Carmona *et al.*, 1994; Fig. 16.10).

El corte tiene un total de 5 m de espesor, el techo está a 5 m s n m. Los 3 metros superiores (entre 5 y 2 m s n m) son capas de sedimentos fluviales de llano de inundación, limos y arenas de tono marrón claro, masivas que contienen abundantes restos de cerámica medieval e ibérico romana.

Debajo de estos limos arenosos fluviales se encuentra un nivel de potencia y textura variable. Por un lado (hacia el oeste) aparecen arcillas de tono marrón oscuro con abundantes restos orgánicos, que se interpretan como depósitos de ciénaga continental. Por otro lado hacia el este (lado de la costa) la textura consiste en una intercalación de bandas (centímetros de espesor) de arcillas grises con materia orgánica arenas masivas de tono blanquecino. Estos sedimentos rellenan la sección transversal de un pequeño canal en el centro del corte. En el fondo de dicho canal se acumulan gran cantidad de restos de madera carbonizada que fueron datados por C14 en el 2330 ± 65 BP). El conjunto puede interpretarse como un ambiente de ciénaga litoral.

Por debajo del nivel anterior entre las cotas (2,5 y 0 m s n m) aparecen sedimentos arenosos de dunas ('large-scale cross-bedding'), playas de arena ('sand planar cross-bedding') y depresiones interdunares (capas de arena y capas de arcilla de color negro con alto contenido en

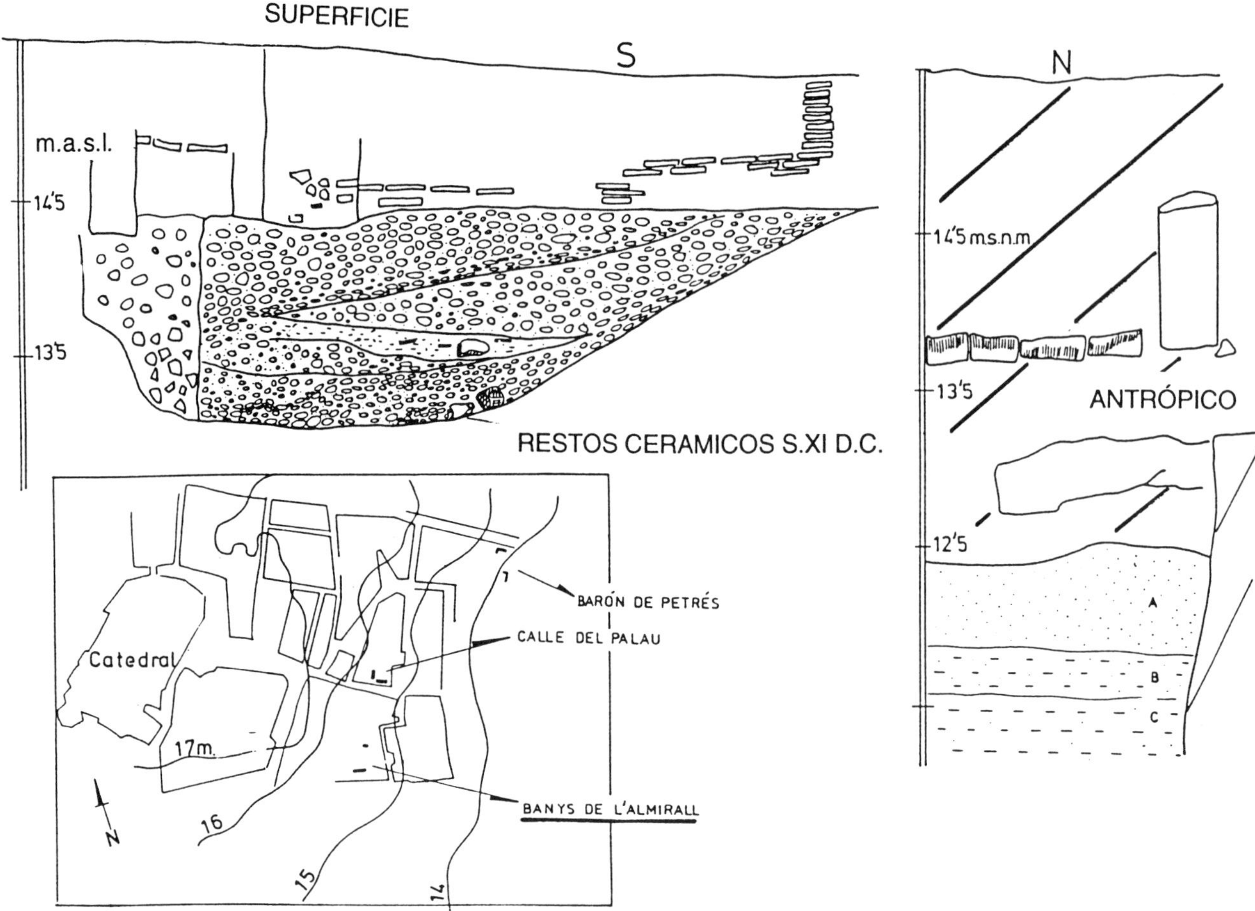

Fig.16.8 Excavación Banys de l'Almirall: a. arenas época romana; b,c. arcillas y limos holocenos, sin restos antrópicos; en el corte sur observamos un relleno de canal, cantos grava y arena con estratificación cruzada planar.

materia orgánica). El nivel en conjunto, se interpreta como un ambiente de línea de costa.

Entre las acumulaciones dunares y las de playa se encontraron abundantes troncos de árboles en muy buen estado de conservación y otros tipos de restos vegetales carbonizados (ramas, piñas etc). La datación por C14 de estos restos dió la cifra de 2295 ± 55 BP.

Esta secuencia sedimentaria nos permite deducir que nos encontramos en el punto donde se situaba la línea de costa en el momento de la fundación romana de la ciudad de Valencia. Los sedimentos fluviales de inundación que entierran esta línea de costa nos indican un importante proceso de progradación fluvial, de dos kilómetros de longitud y con varios metros de espesor. No se aprecian cambios altitudinales del nivel marino. Los datos de otros cortes sedimentarios costeros, nos indicaron que estos niveles de línea de costa se sitúan en techo del nivel trangresivo flandriense (Fig. 16.4).

Por otro lado, esta fuerte tasa de aporte sedimentario del canal del Turia tiene otros efectos geomorfológicos : el cierre definitivo de la restinga de la laguna de l'Albufera de Valencia, ubicada más al sur, con la formación de dos potentes alineaciones dunares, separadas por un surco interdunar. Estos dos cordones dunares pueden relacionarse con las fases de violentes inundación y su importante tasa de aporte sedimentario al litoral del río Turia.

CONCLUSIONES

Pensamos que para interpretar correctamente estos procesos hay que situarlos en contexto mediterráneo.

En el caso de Valencia, los dos episodios, romano e islámico, de violentas inundaciones y alta tasa de aporte sedimentario del canal, posiblemente están relacionados con procesos de deforestación en la cuenca del Turia por las prácticas agrícolas. Similares casos de acumulación fluvial han sido estudiados en el cercano río Júcar (Butzer *et al.*, 1983; Mateu, 1983). Durante el periodo visigodo (siglos VI, VII d.C.) se forman ciénagas en la ciudad, no se detecta ningún episodio de inundación del río. Esto debe interpretarse como un cambio en las condiciones hidrológicas de la cuenca. Este cambio ambiental ha sido detectado en áreas cercanas (Almansa), en el registro

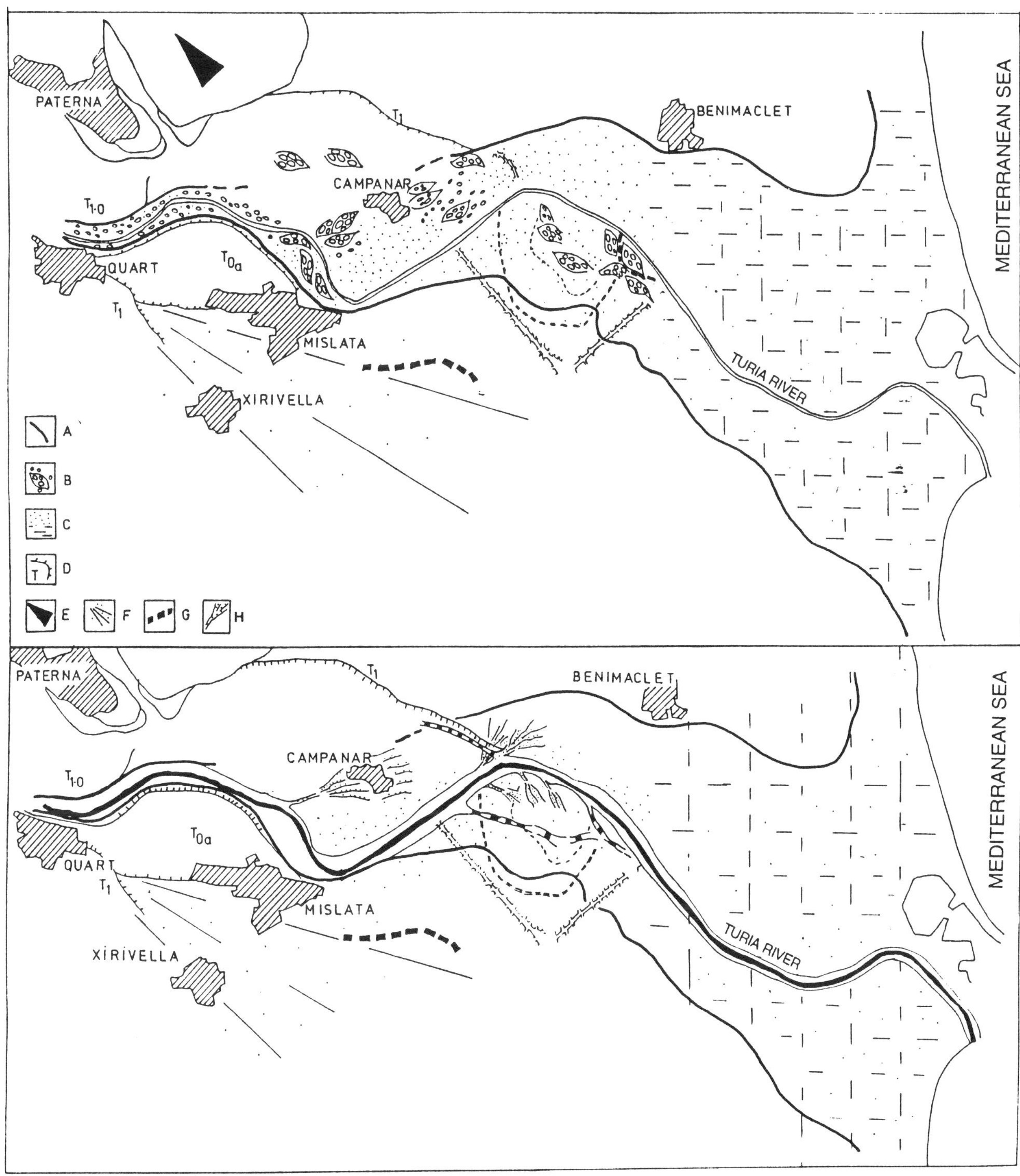

Fig. 16.9. Llano de inundación del Turia: A. límite área inundada; B. carga de canal; C. limos y arcillas; D. terraza; E. glacis; F. abanico aluvial; G. paleocanal; H. subdeltas de derrame.

polínico de un sistema endorreico, en el que durante el siglo VI d. C., el quercus predomina sobre el pino y la cobertura arbórea está en el 60 %, lo cual se interpreta como un episodio de recuperación de la vegetación debido al abandono de los cultivos extensivos de época romana (Dupré *et al.*, in press).

Se han multiplicado las investigaciones desde que Vita Finzi (1969), invocando causas climáticas explicó los depósitos del Late Holocene, desde entonces se ha mantenido un amplio debate en la explicación de esta morfogénesis Mediterránea (Bell and Boardman, 1992; Bintliff, 1982; Butzer, 1982; etc.). Mateu (1987), en una

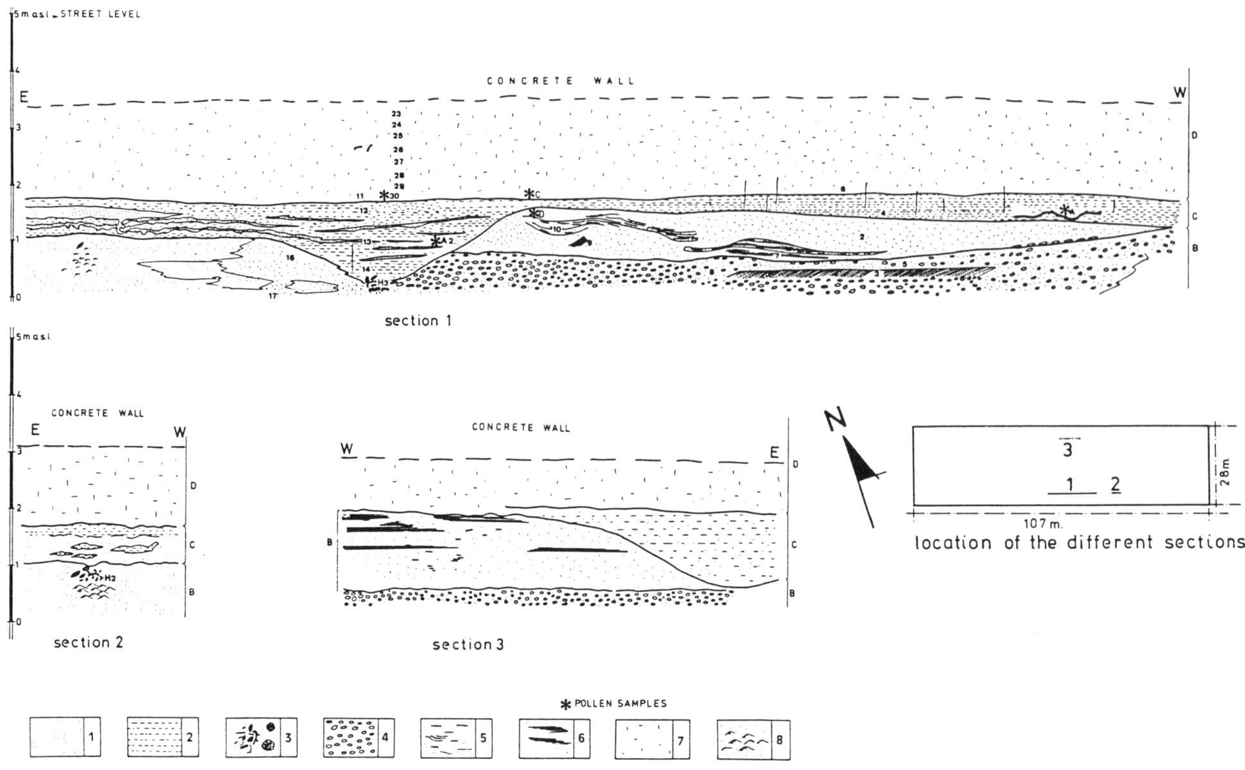

Fig. 16.10. Perfiles de las secciones: 1. arenas; 2. arcillas; 3. restos vegetales; 4. gravilla y cantos rodados; 5. estratos de sedimento orgánico y arcilla gris; 6. playas de arena; 7. arena masiva, cieno y arcilla; 8. ripples, a través de estratificación cruzada. La ubicacioń del corte está señalade con un asterisco en Fig. 16.3.

revisión del tema, señala las evidentes discrepancias cronológicas en los periodos de acumulación de una región a otra, y concluye que la complejidad de la realidad hace fracasar las explicaciones unilaterales y sobre todo los intentos de extrapolar las observaciones efectuadas en un punto a las grandes cuencas fluviales. En la interpretación de esta progradación fluvial en el ámbito de los sistemas fluviales mediterráneos, estamos de acuerdo con la apreciaciones de Bintliff (1993) que insiste en las complicadas relaciones que existen entre los procesos de las laderas y los rellenos de valle (valley fills).

Por otro lado, para la correcta interpretación de estos procesos costeros es necesario ubicar el fenómeno en el contexto de la dinámica litoral del sector.

Finalmente hay que tener en cuenta que todo el litoral es subsidente a escala de geológica, es posible que el sector norte muestre una tasa de subsidencia más alta, hay un yacimiento ibérico erosionado por el oleaje (Sanjaume *et al.*, 1996). En el sector de la ciudad de Valencia, el nivel de la línea de costa de época romana, está a cotas similares a las dunas y playas costeras actuales, por ello no podemos deducir ningún cambio en el nivel marino, ni tampoco procesos de subsidencia. Por otro lado, el tipo de depósitos estudiados, tales como dunas, no son indicativos de cotas de nivel del mar, y sólo pueden utilizarse como referencia en sentido amplio.

BIBLIOGRAFíA

Bell, M. y Boardman, J. (1992) (eds) *Past and Present Soil Erosion.* Oxford, Oxbow Monograph 22.

Bintliff, J.L. (1982) Climatic change, archaeology and quaternary science in the eastern mediterranean region. In A. Harding (ed.) *Climatic Change in Later Prehistory*: 143–61. Edinburgh, Edinburgh University Press.

Bintliff, J.L. (1992) Erosion in the Mediterranean lands : a reconsideration of pattern, process and methodology. In M. Bell y J. Boardman (eds) *Past and Present Soil Erosion*: 125–31. Oxford, Oxbow Monograph 22.

Butzer, K.W. (1980) Holocene alluvial sequences: problems of dating and correlation. In R.A. Cullingford *et al.* (eds) *Timescales in Geomorphology*: 131–42. Chichester, Wiley.

Butzer, K.W., Miralles, I. y Mateu, J.F. (1983) Las crecidas medievales del río Júcar según el registro geoarqueológico de Alzira. *Cuadernos de Geografía* 32–33: 311–32.

Carmona, P. (1990a) *La Formació de la Plana Alluvial de València. Geomorfologia, Hidrologia i Arqueologia de l'Espai Litoral del Túria.* Valencia, Institució Valenciana d'Estudis i Investigació.

Carmona, P. (1990b) Evolución holocena de la llanura costera del río Turia. *Cuaternario y Geomorfología* 4: 69–81.

Carmona, P. (1991) Interpretación paleohidrológica y geoarqueológica del substrato romano y musulmán de la ciudad de Valencia. *Cuadernos de Geografía* 49: 1–14.

Carmona, P., Dupré, M. y Sole, A. (1990) Reconstrucción paleoambiental del Holoceno en el registro sedimentario de la ciudad de Valencia. *Cuaternario y Geomorfología* 4:83–91.

Carmona, P., Dupré, M. y Belluomini, G. (1994) Coastal changes in the Gulf of Valencia (Spain) during the Subatlantic period. *Quaternaire* 5 (2): 49–57.

Déplacements des Lignes de Rivage en Méditerranée (1987) Paris, Colloques Internationaux du CNRS.

Dupré, M., Fumanal, M.P., Martinez, J., Perez Obiol, R., Roure, J.M. y Usera, J. (in press) *The Quaternary Lagoon San Benito (Valencia, Spain). Palaeoenvironmental Reconstruction of an Endorrheic System.* Valencia.

Goy, J.L. y Zazo, C. (1974) Estudio morfotectónico en el óvalo de Valencia. *Actas de la I Reunión Nacional del Grupo de Trabajo del Cuaternario*: 71–82. Madrid.

Goy, J.L., Rey, J., Diaz del Rio, V. y Zazo, C. (1987) Relación entre las unidades geomorfológicas cuaternarias del litoral y de la plataforma interna de Valencia (España): implicaciones paleogeográficas. *Geología Ambiental y Ordenación del Territorio* 2: 1369–1418.

Mateu, J.F. (1983) Aluvionamiento medieval y moderno en el llano de inundación del Júcar. *Cuadernos de Geografía* 32–33: 243–64.

Mateu, J.F. (1987) Morfogénesis mediterránea en tiempos históricos: limitaciones de un debate geoarqueológico. In *Estudios de Arqueología Ibérica y Romana* (Homenaje a Enrique Pla Ballester) S.I.P. Trabajos varios 89: 671–86.

Paskoff, R. y Oueslati, A. (1991) Modifications of coastal conditions in the Gulf of Gabès (southern Tunisia) since classical antiquity. *Zeitschrift Geomorph.* N.F. Suppl.-Bd. 81: 149–62.

Perez Cueva, A. (1988) *Geomorfología del Sector Ibérico Valenciano.* Valencia, Universitat de València.

Sanjaume, E., Rosselló, V.M., Pardo, J.E., Carmona, P., Segura, F., y López Garcia, M.J. (1996) Recent coastal changes in the Gulf of Valencia (Spain). *Z. Geomorph.* N.F. Suppl.-Bd. 102: 95–118.

Segura, F. (1990) *Las Ramblas Valencianas.* VAlencia, Universitat de València.

Simon, J. (1984) *Compresión y Distensión Alpinas en la Cadena Ibérica Oriental.* Teruel, Instituto de Estudios Turolenses.

Vita-Finzi, C. (1969) *The Mediterranean Valleys, Geological Changes in Historical Times.* Cambridge, Cambridge University Press.

17. The Integration of Archaeological, Historical and Paleoenvironmental Data at the Regional Scale: the Vallée de Baux, Southern France

Philippe Leveau

INTRODUCTION

The geoarchaeological work in the Vallée des Baux grew out of a collaboration between environmentalists and archaeologists working on historical periods. It began within the framework of a research project entitled Action Thématique Programmée: 'History of the Environment and of Natural Phenomena'. Inventory and survey programmes were carried out in collaboration with the Regional Archaeological Service of Provence-Alpes-Côte d'Azur (Leveau and Provansal, 1993a). These programmes were developed within the context of rescue archaeology. Subsequently from 1989 onwards, our team began their intervention in the Vallée des Baux, with a salvage excavation prompted by the development of a golf course in Mouriès. This collaboration was developed within the framework of a programmed excavation in the Vallon des Arcs and at the foot of the famous Roman mills at Barbegal. Subsequently these two experiences led onto a research programme on the Holocene in the whole of the drainage basin.

The Vallée des Baux is a favourable environment for such research in that it provides a well known functioning schema. The characteristics of a closed basin augured well for the survival of *in situ* sequences covering the Holocene. Cultural phenomena and major historical events allowed for a precise correlation between 'anthropogenic pressure' and the build-up of deposits. Finally, in as much as the closed basin is a characteristic Mediterranean landscape unit, it was possible to widen the scope of this research into one that combined archaeological and environmental approaches.

THE NATURAL CONTEXT AND THE RECENT HISTORY OF THE VALLÉE DES BAUX

The Vallée des Baux near Arles is a micro-region within Provence, amongst the 'closed basins' studied by Paul Ambert (Ambert and Clauzon, 1992; Figs. 17.1, 17.2).

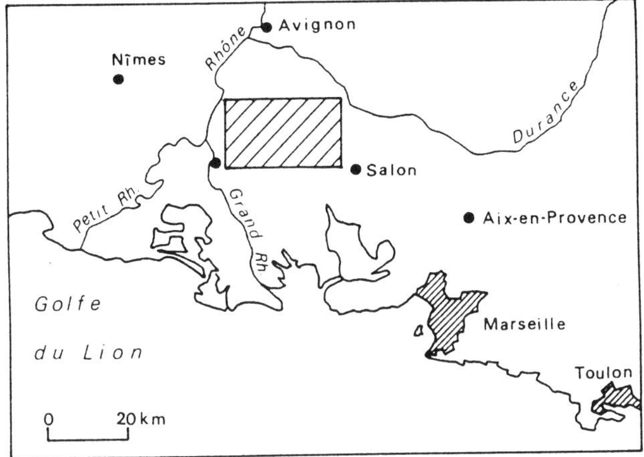

Fig. 17.1. The location of the Vallée des Baux study area.

Furthermore, this basin and its drainage catchment juxtapose three characteristic Mediterranean landscape units (Figs. 17.3). To the north, dominating the valley, are the Alpilles, a small limestone massif constituting a large water reserve, the resources of which were widely used in classical antiquity. The southern slopes of these hills, which are of soft rock, as well as the soils and Pleistocene formations, contribute to the sedimentary deposits that end up in the closed basin. To the south lies the Crau plain, a Pleistocene deposit left in an old river bed of the Durance. The permeable layer of pebbles that make up the plain are the remains of an arid landscape and a landuse system that has until recently remained essentially pastoral. Between these two formations (the Alpilles and the Crau), the Vallée des Baux is largely cut off from the Rhône valley and its delta by a narrow gully, and defined by the topography as a hollow, situated slightly under 20 m above sea level. Quaternary erosion has formed a number of ridges and basins, and alluviation has partially filled in the lower parts, presently situated at 1–3 m above sea level. In the absence of a structured hydrographic network, one can observe a multitude of diffused run-offs.

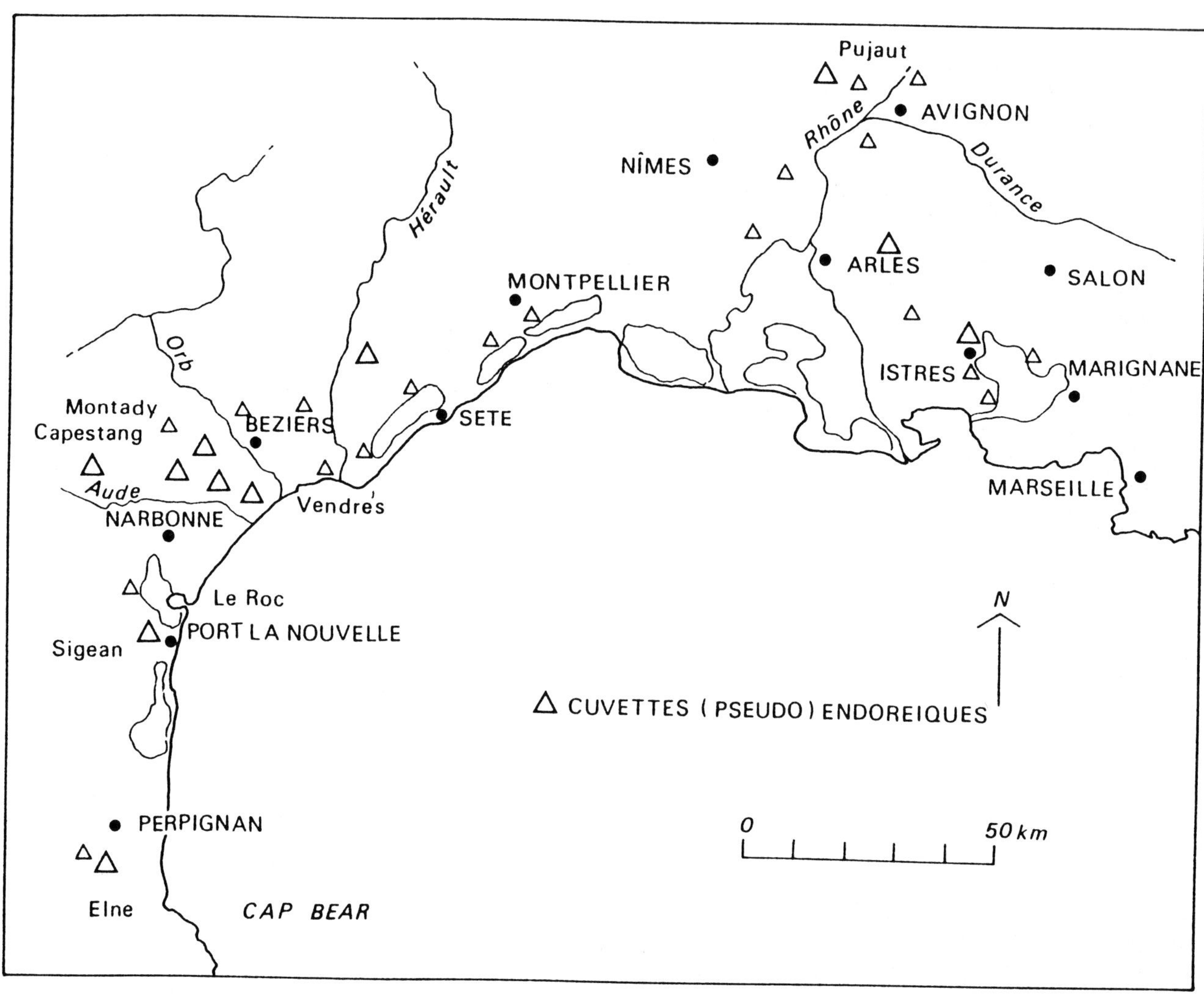

*Fig. 17.2. The closed basins (*cuvettes endoreiques*) along the Golfe-du-Lion. (After Ambert and Clauzon, 1992)*

Hydrological problems

Today the Vallée des Baux is covered in crops. Were the excess water not pumped into a canal that drains into the sea, the aquifer would rise and cover the bottom of the valley. The present-day use of the Baux marsh as a polder (Fig. 17.3: Marais des Baux) is an interesting implementation in the Mediterranean of a land use system widely used in northern Europe. With precipitation around 500–600 mm per annum and evaporation attaining 1200 mm, the hydrological balance proves to be negative. The natural tendency would result in the drying-up of the basin. The presence of an aquifer near the surface is due to the position of the valley below the Alpilles and its consequent runoff. There are also the additional contributions from the Crau aquifer (considerably increased by the presence of the Craponne Canal) as well as the natural drainage difficulties of the valley into the Rhône basin.

Various factors play an important role in maintaining water levels. In the summer, for example, artificial flooding is maintained: the Craponne Canal, built in the sixteenth century, along with the Boisgelin Canal, built in the eighteenth century, carried the sediment-rich waters of the Durance towards Arles. They irrigated the piedmont of the Alpilles and the Crau, with some of the water ending up in the bottom of the Vallée des Baux. These canals have significantly modified a hydrological system which extends beyond the Crau up into the Durance drainage basin. During the Roman period, aqueducts already made significant water transfers, the importance of which has been illustrated by Vaudour (1991). The major springs of the south face of the Alpilles were harnessed by Roman engineers.

Land use and the archaeological map

The choice of this region in order to carry out an interdisciplinary research programme is due to its wealth of archaeology and history. The important sites are markers for the study of the different phases of the valley's history, from the prehistoric funerary monuments known as the Fontvieille hypogeums (the most recent dates to the Chalcolithic) to the Barbegal mills and to the castle of Les

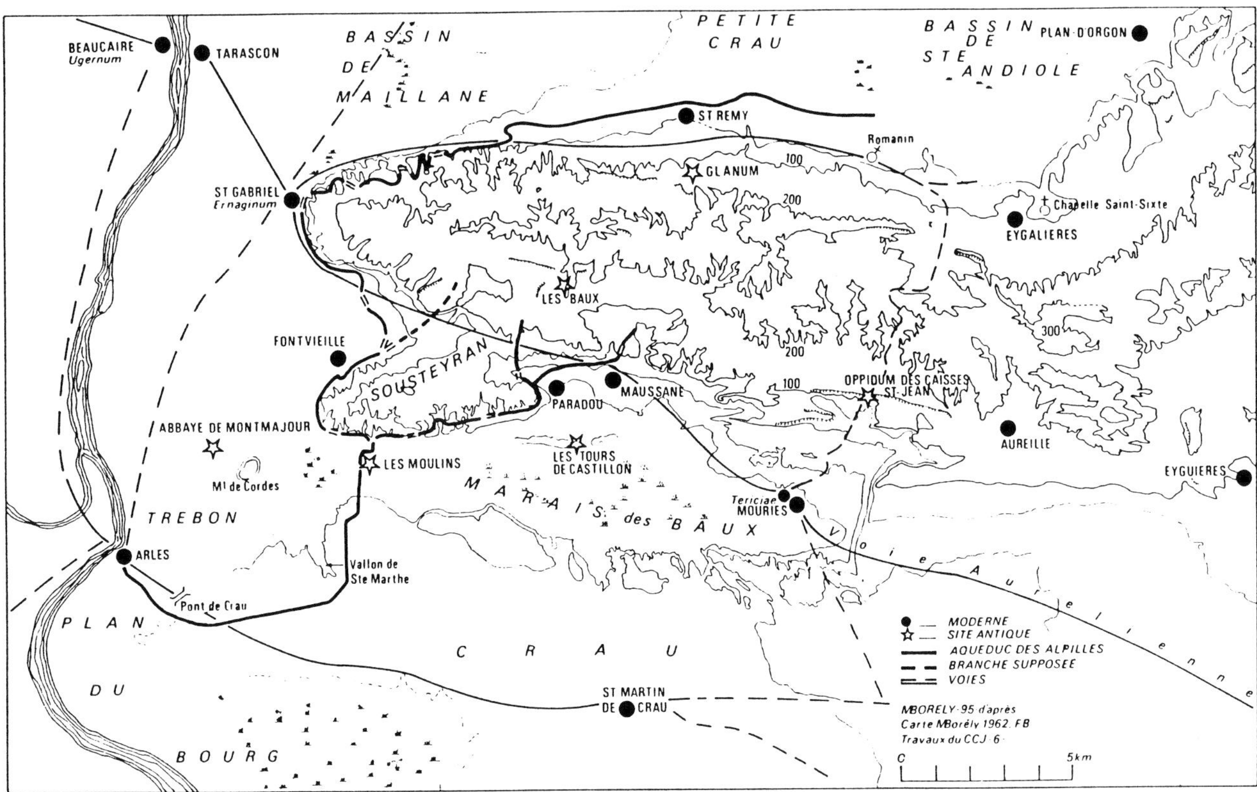

Fig. 17.3. The Vallée des Baux, showing topography, drainage, settlement and principal archaeological sites.

Baux. Recent research, however, has shown that next to these major sites there is a whole series of sites marking the land use of the Vallée des Baux during the Holocene.

The group of funerary monuments dating from the Late Neolithic and the Chalcolithic known as the Fontvieille hypogeums consists of long trenches covered by enormous stone slabs. Of all the megaliths of Provence and Languedoc, they can be distinguished by their size. Most of the hundred or so burials of this type are of relatively small dimensions. The dolmens of Provence and Languedoc are distinct in type from the two others defined by Sauzade (1990), those of the Alps and eastern Provence, as they are characterized by a long burial chamber with lateral dry-stone walls constructed in a pit. The Fontvieille hypogeums are cut into limestone and are up to 44 m in length, as in the case of the Grotte des Fées. In order to explain this complex of sites, ecological factors have often been invoked, notably the presence of rocky outcroppings and the type of the rock (molasse). Since the nineteenth century, researchers have considered them to be isolated on their outcroppings surrounded by water. It was considered that geographic isolation and the resulting weakening of outside contact would have favoured the creation of original megalithic structures, as in Malta, Sardinia and the Balearic islands.

Maps showing the distribution of neolithic, chalcolithic and bronze age sites generally give greater importance to the fringes of the present-day Baux and Grand Clar marshes. In as much as our research puts into question the permanence of the flooding within these zones, it has become necessary to re-survey the low-lying areas in order to check for the presence of prehistoric sites. The subsequent accumulation of sediments may have concealed prehistoric remains. Survey by M. Gazenbeek, however, has shown that the sediments were covering a varied landscape and that the burial monuments are therefore to be placed in a long series of sites dating to the Neolithic and Chalcolithic.

The wealth of finds relating to the Iron Age and the Roman period is equally as substantial. The *c.*30 known sites are distributed over the whole area: we must note, however, that only certain parts have been surveyed systematically. As in the rest of Provence and Languedoc, the Iron Age is characterized by the presence of perched or hilltop sites known as *oppida*. To the west we find Mont-des-Cordes with its iron age rampart and Le Castellet, occupied from the seventh to the second century BC (Poumeyrol, 1953). In the middle of the Vallée des Baux there are the settlements of Tours-de-Castillon (Tréziny, 1987–88) and the Castellas-de-Maussane (Tréziny, 1990) on either side of the Maussane/Paradou basin. Tours-de-Castillon does not seem to have been densely populated until some time in the second century at the beginning of Roman presence in the area: it was fortified at that time with a rubble stone wall, which was soon replaced by heavy stone masonry in the Hellenistic style. The site was occupied from the third century BC to the first or second century AD. To the east we find the Caisses de Mouriès, which can be divided into two sites: the *oppidum* of Des Caisses at the top of the hill and Servanne at the foot of the hill. We must also add to this list a shrine and funerary site at the Fontaine-de-l'Arcoule.

During the Roman period, the Vallée des Baux came under the administration of Arles. As early as the Augustan period, an aqueduct crossed the western end of the valley, bringing water from the Alpilles to Arles. Next to this bridge-aqueduct are the mills of Barbegal, which were dated until recent excavations to late antiquity (Leveau, 1995a). The Via Aurelia is to the north, in between the valley and the Alpilles. There has been a long-standing view that the countryside around Arles was under water and that communication was therefore only possible by raft (Benoit, 1940) – near the chapel of Saint-Gabriel, for example, on the site of the ancient town of *Ernaginum*, there are structures that have been identified as a jetty for small craft. This perception of the landscape, however, has been seriously put into question by more recent excavations. Firstly, the construction of the Barbegal mills has been dated to the Hadrianic period, with their functioning as an industrial establishment continuing up until *c.*AD 270. Secondly, the excavations have completely altered our understanding of the ancient landscape: in classical times: the Vallée des Baux was no more a backwater than in prehistoric times. Near the mill site there was an important settlement: funerary monuments were dismantled in order to consolidate the aqueduct in the later stages of its' functioning. Also, a villa contemporary with the mills was built a few hundred metres east of them (the Mérindole villa). In addition to the residential buildings there were also, and perhaps most importantly, agricultural buildings containing *dolia*, which were probably used for wine production. Directly to the north, excavations by Peter Bellamy and Bruce Hitchner revealed a cemetery dating to the seventh and eighth centuries AD. Moreover, the Mérindole site is not isolated: Gazenbeck's survey has shown numerous traces of contemporary rural settlements, despite the prior assumption that the landscape was flooded in classical times.

Surveys conducted above the valley bottom, at the foot of the Défends-de-Sousteyran and along the other hills that form the piedmont of the Alpilles, have shown that new sites appear during the fourth century AD and that sites abandoned in the late protohistoric period were then resettled. A series of salvage excavations near the church of Saint-Martins (mentioned in texts as early as the end of the tenth century) in the village of Paradou allowed an insight into land use starting from before the building of the *Via Aurelia* through to the end of clssical antiquity and into the early Middle Ages.

Our understanding of the medieval period is largely derived from a number of major texts such as the 'cartulaires' of the abbeys of Saint-Paul-de-Mausole, Montmajour and Saint-Victor-de-Marseille, the *Gallia Christiana Novissima* compendium for the diocese of Arles and Avignon, and the charter of the Maison des Baux. Despite the incomplete nature of these documents, they provide the means to study the distribution of rural churches and chapels as well as the *villae* (in the medieval rather than Roman sense) which comprised the settlement structure of the landscape. These texts, however, do not become substantial enough for our needs until the ninth or tenth century. Thanks to recent work on kaolinitic pottery from late antiquity and the early Middle Ages, survey work has started to provide useful indications regarding settlements around rural chapels, in isolated places and on or near the sites of protohistoric *oppida* (Le-Castellet, Les-Tours-de-Castillon, Mont-des-Cordes). Medieval occupation has also been revealed by the presence of fossil concentric field boundaries around Barbegal and elsewhere in the valley. Alongside the well-known fortified medieval sites such as Les-Baux or Montpaon, there are also sites on low-lying lands around the marsh (Saint-Martin, Paradou, Saint-Romain), and even on hill tops in the middle of the marsh (Barbegal, Notre-Dame-de-l'Ile). In the Middle Ages the marsh was most certainly not deserted: it was criss-crossed by channels, used for fishing and plant gathering, and in the dry season herds were brought there to pasture whilst the higher land was cultivated (O.Maufras and J. Palet, *pers. comm.*).

The first real attempt to drain the valley began in the seventeenth century. It was linked to the strengthening of the King's power: a delegation from Arles met Louis the XIIIth at Lunel and obtained the services of a Dutch engineer by the name of Van Ens. Royal power alone was to prove capable of overcoming the resistance of local interests, as well as in financing the works. These works were to take into account the varying interests of the three townships that shared the region. To the north, Tarascon wanted to drain the excess water coming off the Alpilles into the Duransole basin. To the south, the people in the Vallée des Baux also wanted to drain their excess waters. To the west, Arles wanted to protect its agricultural land from flooding caused by the draining of the Vallée des Baux and the Duransole basin as well as from the flooding of the Rhône. The work of Van Ens was justly lauded, as the marshes of Arles and Tarascon were drained (Waton-Chabert, 1963), but it was also short-lived: already by the end of the seventeenth century the installations were in a poor state of repair. The drainage of the Vallée des Baux was the first to be abandoned when the drainage works were demolished by the Prince of Monaco when he became Lord of Les Baux.

ARCHAEOLOGICAL SITES AND THE EVOLUTION OF THE ENVIRONMENT

The landscape and geoarchaeological problems that have been central to our research in the Vallée des Baux started to come together ten years ago. The problem of the depth of burial of archaeological structures was first posed in the course of a salvage excavation, the results of which rendered necessary collaboration between archaeologists and environmentalists.

Erosion in the Alpilles: Les Caisses-de-Servanne in Mouriès.

The first joint excavation involving both archaeologists and environmentalists was on the site of Servanne at Mouriès. The small valley of Servanne was to be developed into a golf course. It is at the foot of a limestone ridge upon which the *oppidum* Les Caisses-de-Servanne is situated. A salvage excavation directed by R. Royet revealed the presence of a group of iron age houses at the foot of the hill. This site had two distinct occupation periods: the first in the sixth and fifth centuries BC and the second in the second and first centuries BC. Underneath the apparently regular topography of today, deep trenches revealed an old *thalweg* several metres deep, fossilized by torrential and colluvial deposits. The archaeological material found in the filling allowed us to distinguish two torrential deposits, of which the first corresponds to the period in between the two periods of occupation of the site. The late iron age village was built on a *thalweg* that was no longer functioning. The filling of the remaining marginal channel was completed during another, post-antique, torrential period.

The geomorphological interpretation of this data was carried out by M. Jorda and M. Provansal (Jorda *et al.*, 1991). The torrential formations suggested that climatic conditions were different during the Iron Age from those of today: intense rainfall caused heavier run-off and greater erosion. This climatic situation is likely to have provoked serious change in the landscape, unless the soil coverage was not already made more vulnerable by agricultural activity tied to the presence of an important farming community. It was likewise observed that Roman land use, while being more intense, did not cause comparable erosion. It is necessary, therefore, to look for the primary cause for the reduction of torrential activity in a reduction in, and a better distribution of, the rainfall.

This example, which showed fairly clearly the need for reflection on the evaluation of bio-climatic parameters and social practices, was confirmed and strengthened by other work, most notably that done on the Gallo-Roman site of La Grande-Terre in Maussane.

The excavations at Barbegal, and the problem of the marshy nature of the Vallée des Baux

The salvage excavations at the Caisses-de-Servanne in Mouriès drew our attention to the climatic and human processes involved in the changes to the meso-relief on the southern slopes of the Alpilles. A few years later, excavations at the Barbegal mills provided further insights into the evolution of the valley bottom. The project was prompted by the desire of local townships to see a renewal in archaeological work on the Barbegal mills. One of our main objectives was to date the structures by digging trenches in an area not touched by Benoit's excavations in the 1940s. In his excavations, Benoit concentrated on clearing the structures on the hillside, stopping at the road that runs along the foot of the La-Pène secondary range. It was hoped that archaeological deposits would be preserved in the drainage ditch at the bottom of the mills, and that these deposits would provide material that would enable us to reassess the chronology of the monument.

Our excavations conducted in 1992 and 1993 provided the desired results, but they were also the starting point of a total re-evaluation of the landscape history of the valley. They revealed the superimposition of three layers, corresponding to three phases of settlement in this part of the valley (Leveau, 1995a). The composition of the top layer corresponded to the most recent history of the valley. The colour and texture of the sediments, and the molluscan fauna contained within them, showed that the layer had been deposited in a permanently wet zone covering the valley bottom in the late Middle Ages and the early modern period. This wet zone was the result of the building of a dam to protect the Arles plain from the flooding of the Barbegal marshes. The middle layer, deposited after the abandonment of the Barbegal mills, was made up of colluvial deposits dating to between the end of classical antiquity and the end of the Middle Ages. The sedimentological characteristics of these deposits showed that this area was not continually under water during this period: the water table would have risen only occasionally. The facies and geometry of the bottom layer, deposited during the functioning of the mills, showed that the water that activated the wheels exited the mills at around a metre's altitude. The characteristics of the pebbles deposited on the substratum attest to the absence of standing water in this part of the valley at this time.

The study of the depth of the archaeological structures proves that the monument was built on sediments deposited during a period of flooding. Jorda and Provansal have shown that the slow rise in the water levels in the valley during the Holocene was not a linear development. There were phases in which the water level regressed, notably during the Roman period. The time frame in which the mills were used (the second to third centuries AD) is contemporary with the drainage of the basin (Provansal *et al.*, in press; Fig. 17.4). The hypothesis that had been developed in the case of the Servanne site found an application here: there, just as here, the situation in the Roman period was the result of a combination of natural evolution and human intervention, this time in the development of wetlands.

The continuation of the excavations which, in 1993 and 1994, were to mark the end of this phase of the archaeological research programme, confirmed the robustness of the hypothesis regarding the progressive (and, in absolute terms, late) flooding of the Vallée des Baux. In 1993 the discovery and excavation of a cemetery near the Mérindole villa, at the mouth of a small valley that is presently dry and only a few hundred metres from the

Barbegal mills, gave the first confirmation of the inhabited nature of the valley in the late Merovingian period. The following year, while clearing the spoil tip left by Benoit's excavations, a few burials dating to the fourth and fifth centuries were discovered right next to the mills. It therefore became clear, contrary to what has been written since Benoit, that human occupation of the valley had not suddenly retreated to the north, abandoning the valley bottom in the face of the rising water levels. The new model made it possible to revise our understanding of the situations of the medieval sites to the east of the mills, such as the Tours-de-Castillon and the castle of Les Baux.

The importance of water in the medieval landscape remains unquestioned, however: the Abbey of Montmajour, for example, was an island in the middle of the marshes, the maintenance of which the monks considered very important (Stouff, 1993). In the archives studied by O. Maufras, the references to wetlands in the Vallée des Baux are frequent.

Nevertheless, it is necessary to put these data in their proper perspective, or rather to give them an historical dimension in order to re-establish the necessary conditions for a scientific approach to the study of past landscapes. Contradictory and ill-founded views of the landscape of the lower Rhône valley in the Roman period have been put forward. Thus in 1674 the flooding by the Durance of the low-lying areas between the Montagnette and the Alpilles seemed to support the hypothesis that a branch of the Durance went through this passage in the Roman period. Although this theory was abandoned it was replaced by another exaggerating the role of the Romans even more. The discussion of the Graveson and Maillane basin by a geographer serves to illustrate the problem (Hayez, 1978): 'starting at the Laurade and receiving waters from Eyrargues and Graveson, the Duransole ended up constituting a major water-way that ended up at Saint-Gabriel in the region of Arles. These very same Romans drained, channelled and brought also to this waterway water from the Rognonas marsh, thus creating the Laune (river) tributary of what was then called the River of Saint-Gabriel. The Romans also brought this waterway into communication with the Durance through the digging of a channel called Le Réal. This *rialis Durentiae* is attested in 1327 and 1469'. In the absence of excavations, cores, and field observations, such assertions, based entirely on the interpretation of archives, remain purely hypothetical.

CORING THE VALLEE DES BAUX: THE HISTORY OF THE DEPOSITS

A prerequisite for modelling the settlement archaeology is the study of sedimentation in the Vallée des Baux. Geomorphological analysis is essential for a proper understanding of the taphonomic processes by which ancient sites and land plots have been buried.

The starting point is the recent synthesis by Ballais *et al* (1993) of the filling in of the basin, based on observations made on the Barbegal site complimented by trenches dug mechanically at the foot of the mills and a little way to the east on the cone of the Crottes-d'Aubert torrent. These trenches were in essentially Holocene deposits, mostly dating to the protohistoric and historic periods. Previously, two cores had been extracted by H. Laval in the northeasterly part of the basin, probably directly to the south of the la Pène secondary range (Trial-Laval, 1978) and several trenches had been dug at the foot of the mills. This work was supplemented in 1995 by sixteen cores dug with a heliocoidal auger. The choice of places for coring was determined within a research strategy encompassing both archaeology (to understand modes of land use) and geomorphology (to develop a spatial model for the basin and understand the history of detritic and hydrological flux).

The locations chosen were the crossing points of the valley. To the west, two series of cores were undertaken in the Barbegal gully, one to the north of rock outcropping at the Mas d'Agard and one to the south of the Barbegal mills. Two cores were taken in the eastern part of the basin, in the area crossed by an ancient track and by the modern road south of Tours-de-Castillon. The main new information that came out of this work was that the basin has a lower topography to the east. Until now, geomorphological studies had only envisaged drainage to the west, but henceforth, the question of drainage must be posed in new terms. In a preliminary synthesis Bruneton (1995) proposes the following scheme: at the beginning of the Holocene, most of the topographic irregularities were filled in, almost exclusively by local sediment, but the eastern zone, which was considerably lower and lacustrine in nature, would have been differentiated at an early stage from the western zone, which may have been rather marshy but which would have flooded only rarely. It is in any case certain that the water rose very slowly here, with brief regressive periods. The level of the water descended considerably in the Roman period after reaching a maximum in the protohistoric period (though this maximum would have been lower than the levels reached during the modern period). Despite the regular extension of the palustrine zone, the difference between the two parts of the basin would have continued until the recent development of uniform conditions through land development: the creation of a wet or lacustrine zone in the sixteenth century, followed by the draining of the entire basin in the 1950s. Amongst the various possibilities, it is probable that a large part of the water in the basin drained to the east and not towards the Rhône and that in the Roman period an outlet may have been dug out in order to drain excess water through the Barbegal gully.

Pollen profiles were studied by H. Triat-Laval (1978) alone and later in collaboration with J. Médus (1994). The cores allowed V. Andrieu to renew the study with a narrow sampling mesh, benefiting simultaneously from progress

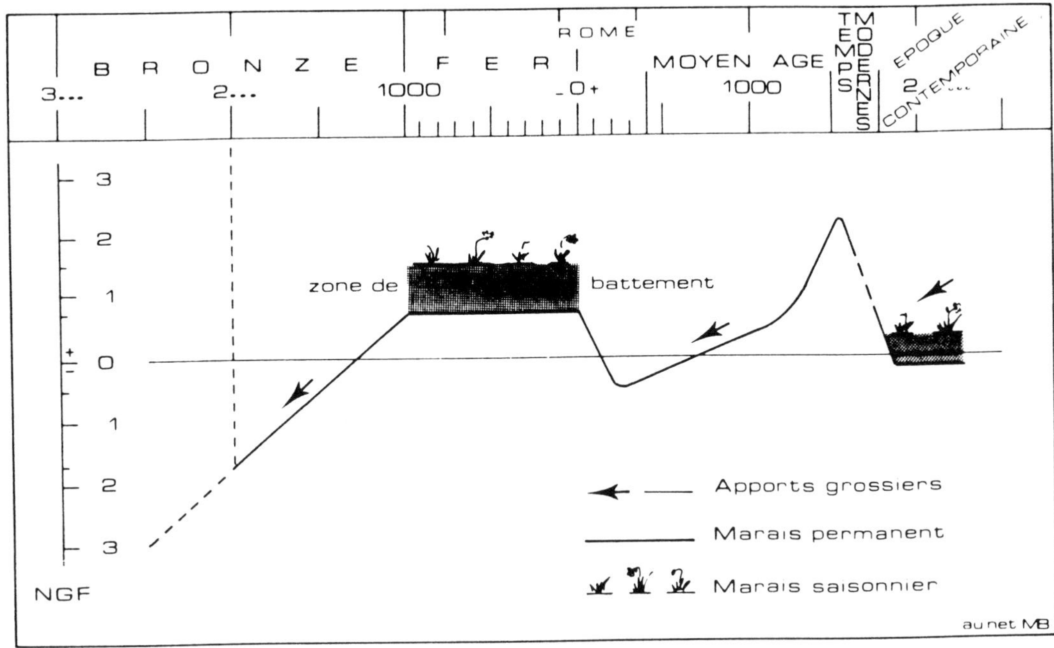

Fig. 17.4. The evolution of water levels in the Vallée des Baux in the past two thousand years. (After Provansal et al., *in press).*

in the treatment of sediments. In March 1996, three cores were thus analyzed: two from the centre of the marsh recorded the history of vegetation since the beginning of the Holocene, whereas the third, from the foot of the Barbegal mills, was characterized by a very segmented profile. However, though less interesting from the point of view of the history of the vegetation, this last core is of considerable interest in that it records a period of land clearance and pastoral activity associated with the lowering of the water levels in the marsh. Whilst being a wet zone favourable to pastoral activity, therefore, the Vallée des Baux may also have been a cereal-growing area. This finding is a good example of how paleoenvironmental research can provide important insights into settlement and land use.

ENVIRONMENT, LAND USE AND SETTLEMENT

The next step in our research consists of the integration of the paleoenvironmental and archaeological data from specific sites such as Servanne and Barbegal within a diversified regional model uniting the Vallée des Baux, the limestone massif of the Alpilles, the Crau plain, and the lower Rhône delta. Such a 'spatial system' is defined by geographers as the product of the interaction between central places, networks, appropriation units, administrative units, and land use (Pinchemel, 1988). The correct identification of successive spatial systems is, in effect, necessary in order to write the history of a regional society: establishments are distributed within a certain space, they generate their ring of fields that are served by a network of roads, which is in part determined by the integration of the micro-region into a larger space with wider horizons. These establishments grouped together to form political or ethnic units, the limits of which grouped together the *terroirs* and landscape units.

Within the region envisaged, present-day land use in the valley is determined by the distribution of settlement in large *mas* (farms), agricultural centres that coexist with villages such as Maussane, Mouriès, and Paradou that are the service centres. This form of settlement, tied to the integration of the region within an agricultural economy oriented towards commercialization, is not new: a close parallel can be made with the Roman period, for which a developed villa system has been revealed by archaeological surveys and excavations. In the Roman period, and from the beginning of the modern period (for the Middle Ages the question remains open), these forms of land use generated road networks, and more importantly channels for irrigation and for drainage. For the modern period, we have an abundant cartographic documentation; for classical antiquity, these networks can be reconstructed through the use of maps and air photographs, as well as through the observation of fossil traces on satellite images.

Interest in the agricultural use of water is not new. The position of springs has contributed to the location of settlements and cultivated areas. Likewise the use of the marshlands has varied according to the extension of the wet zone. Very early on, people must have modified the land to suit their purposes, but the Roman period marked a decisive and observable step in land development – drainage and irrigation works change scale considerably. The Romans did not invent either drainage or irrigation, but the integration of this region into the Imperial framework is marked by developments that are regional rather than local in nature. An analogous phenomenon happened in the modern period: the Craponne canal brought water for irrigation, and then in the eighteenth century the drainage of the valley began in earnest. The canals constitute strong lines within the landscape: on their margins, a network of irrigation channels has developed, while in the valley bottoms a drainage system is organized around a canal that starts at the Étang-du-Comte and leaves the valley at the Barbegal gully to join the canal from Arles to Port-de-Bouc, running parallel to the Rhône (Béthemont, 1972).

The important remaining question is what was happening in the Middle Ages. Until recently, the evidence available to understand the place held by sheep- and cattle-rearing within the landscape and agricultural life was limited to archaeozoological data on the consumption of various species (Goudineau, 1988). The documentation only becomes sizeable from the end of the Middle Ages, when transhumance was established. In the nineteenth century, sheep-rearing was still a dominant activity, and two types of tracks are clearly visible on the 1:80000 État-Major maps: first, tracks radiating out around the farms, and second, the major transhumance droveroads.

One of the major archaeological discoveries of the last few years has been that of ancient sheepfolds on the Crau plain. This discovery confirms the words of Pliny: 'the plains of stone in the province of Narbonensis are today filled with thyme; it is almost the sole revenue, thousands of sheep come here from distant lands to graze on the thyme' (*Hist. Nat.*, 21, 57). Without entering into detail, let us look at what it implies for our aims. The presence of tens of thousands of sheep on the Crau plain must have had an effect on the agricultural economy of its neighbouring regions: good relations between herds and crops must have been maintained by a network of droveroads to limit the wandering of the sheep. According to the texts, a system of this type existed in the Middle Ages. It is important to understand the characteristics of this network in order to see whether there was or was not continuity with classical antiquity. It is unimaginable that, during this period of Imperial control over regional life, some form of control over the movements of the transhumant herds did not exist. Various propositions have been put forward, for example by Badan *et al.* (1995) and Gros (1995).

Most of the research in landscape archaeology has examined the organization of surfaces that were generated in the Roman period with the development of two types of axis, the lines of communication between administrative centres (the Roman roads) and the lines of the centuriation systems that determined the dividing up of the land following the conquest. It is therefore important to study the way the Roman land developers – and their modern counterparts – reconciled regional logistics such as major roads and large scale agricultural projects with local roads and tracks serving farms and providing passages for herds, and hydraulic networks.

In the past 30 years, research conducted in the lower Rhône valley has revealed the existence of several centuriation systems of different orientations. M. Guy (1954, 1991) was the first to show evidence for a gridded network near Arles in the Crau: he calculated that the grid covered some 200 km^2. His results were taken up by F. Benoit (1964), who suggested a dating based on the integration of the town in the structure of land plots: he dated it to the Augustan period and considered it to be consecutive to the sharing out of the plots to the veterans of the VIth Legion. This centuriation was laid out directly in relation with a road from the period of the Greek colony of Massilia (Marseille) linking Entressen to Mouriès. Twenty years later, G. Chouquer located one of the Orange Cadastres, the A Cadastre, on the basis of place name evidence and of pottery fragments in the fossil bed of the Duransole river (Chouquer, 1983). This centuriation, put in place from a reference point (*locus gromae*) situated near *Ernaginum* (Saint-Gabriel), is limited on its southern side by a segment of the *via Aurelia* that runs along the south side of the Alpilles; it falls, therefore, within the northern part of Arles' territory. These field divisions are linked to problems in allotment and land development. In 1992 Chouquer identified a possible cadastre, called Arles A, corresponding to the orientations of the urban network of Arles. Identified in three areas, to the north of Arles, in the Crau (Saint-Martin-de-Crau) and in the Camargue, it should correspond with a second series of allotments (Chouquer and Favory, 1992). To this list we may add two recent proposals, one made by Faudot (1992) between 2° and 3° west, and another by Ferrando (1994).

These field grids overlap partially, and the inflation in the number of proposed identifications of cadastres poses a problem. For example, Assénat (1995) adds five new networks to those she had already proposed in 1993. Doubtless we should believe her when she writes (1995: 58) that she invented them! I have suggested that a moratorium should be put on the publication of new centuriation networks for southern France. The proposal has been approved by most specialists and by Chouquer in particular, who is increasingly sensitive to placing centuriation within long-term landscape history, and not limiting its study simply to structural traces.

However, if these centuriations really exist, then we must explain how they were elaborated. They maintain a relation with the reality of the regional landscape and in particular with the settling of the veterans of the VIth Legion around Arles and not in the Crau or on its margins as was suggested by Benoit (Leveau, 1995b). In the case of a centuriated system spreading across the south of the Alpilles, three solutions are possible: the zone in question was made up of marshes between the Crau and the Alpilles, but there could also have been an extension of land use due to drainage, unless the Vallée des Baux was in between two systems.

Today, research into the organization of agrarian systems in the Roman period must be embedded in a consideration of phases of agrarian development other than Roman (Gazenbeek *et al*, 1996). The spatial systems that make up the base of the landscape grid in the Baux basin and its surroundings are presently the subject of research using map and photographic interpretation by Fl.Mocci and by satellite imaging by M. Sintès. Satellite imaging has allowed us to observe a certain number of anomalies that seem to correspond with fossil structures. Circular structures correspond sometimes with a cross-roads, but can also correspond with an old agrarian centre of which these traces conserve the memory, as around Barbegal. It is probable that the more important settlements generated such structures. Their identification by an analysis of the Napoleonic field system should allow us to complete the map of settlements and cultivated zones. These field boundaries could, in effect, be in relation to medieval land use systems. Circular field structures could, however, have been generated by local topography (circular basins with radiating systems). In the Crau we find three types of field divisions: to the west, a small field system in appearance totally lacking in organization, bordered to the west and to the north by the edge of the plateau which has a structuring role; to the east, a larger and more regular field system with a strong north/northwest alignment; and further east again, another fairly regular field system follows a north/northeast orientation.

Drainage networks, sheep tracks and field systems answer to a logic that is often in contradiction with that of the road network. The present-day road network is characterized by the development of an east-west axis created by the road from Salon to Arles through Saint-Martin-de-Crau to the south of the Vallée des Baux. Its course is quite different from that of the Roman road, which went along the north of the valley and on towards Beaucaire rather than to Arles. The valley is presently crossed in two points by a north-south axis: to the west, the Barbegal gully was already crossed by the Roman aqueduct of Arles, and a bridge 160 m long with three arches was built across it in the sixteenth century; to the east, the road from Saint-Martin-de-Crau to Maussane coincides with a fossil road visible on satellite images to the south of the Tours-de-Castillon. This road formed a ford known to shepherds and hunters before the Marais du Comte was drained. Between the two points, a passage no longer in use ran from Paradou to Saint-Martin-de-Crau.

CONCLUSION

The research in the Vallée des Baux is a good example of what landscape research can bring to 'intersite' archaeology. This micro-region offered us the possibility of continuing the research into landscapes that we had commenced around the Étang-de-Berre. When this programme started ten years ago, its aim was to describe and understand a monumental Roman site, the Barbegal mills, and the aqueducts that supplied it with water. Through its repercussions, in orienting the research towards the study of the taphonomic processes that had buried the site at the bottom of the mills, the excavations brought us more and more towards the history of the landscape. The importance given to the spatial dimension led us to practice an 'off site' archaeology, which gave us a better understanding of the history of the region and which helped in the elaboration of salvage research strategies. The Arles plain and the western part of the Vallée des Baux are currently threatened by an Autoroute project, and the area will also be crossed by a pipeline. We hope that our work on 'off site' archaeology, the survey data, the excavations, and the map and photographic interpretation previously conducted, will facilitate these operations.

This research also has theoretical ambitions. The integration of data covering observable phenomena within spatial frameworks of variable size (local, micro-regional, regional) and variable chronological systems (geological, and long- and medium-term historical scales) requires an approach that integrates the notion of scales of space and time, that takes into account the notion of heritage, and accepts the principles of retrospective effect. This is why in presenting our findings we have often referred to a system widely used today in a number of social sciences, though not in history (Jollivet, 1992). In as much as the existence of strong contrasts between the landscape units within the region studied was favourable to modelling people-environment relations, the research in progress has led to the elaboration of a grid of systemic analyses of landscape dynamics that can doubtless be generalized to wet basins and plains across the Mediterranean (Fig. 17.5). Systemic models for the relation between people and environment have already been put forward (McGlade, 1995; Morch, 1994; Pinchemel, 1988: 12). The system we have presented here integrates a temporal variable, either in detailing the degrees in the capacity of a sub-system for action or retrospective effect on the sub-systems defined, or by introducing notions of complexity (as in the hydrological sub-system) or of evolution (as in the technical sub-system). This scheme allows for the evaluation of diversity in possible explanations of the situations observed at a given time, and for the organic development of research goals.

REFERENCES

Ambert, P. and Clauzon, G. (1992) Morphogenèse éolienne et ambiance périglaciaire: les dépressions fermées du pourtour du Golfe du Lion (France méditerranéenne). *Zeitschrift für Geomorphologie* N.F., suppl. Bd 84: 55–71.

Assénat, M. (1995) Le cadastre colonial d'Orange. *Revue Archéologique de Narbonnaise* 27–28: 45–55.

Badan, O., Brun, J.-P. and Congès, G. (1995) Les bergeries romaines de la Crau d'Arles. Les origines de la transhumance en Provence. *Gallia* 52: 263–310 .

Ballais, J.-L., Jorda, M., Provansal, M. and Covo, J. (1993) Morpho-

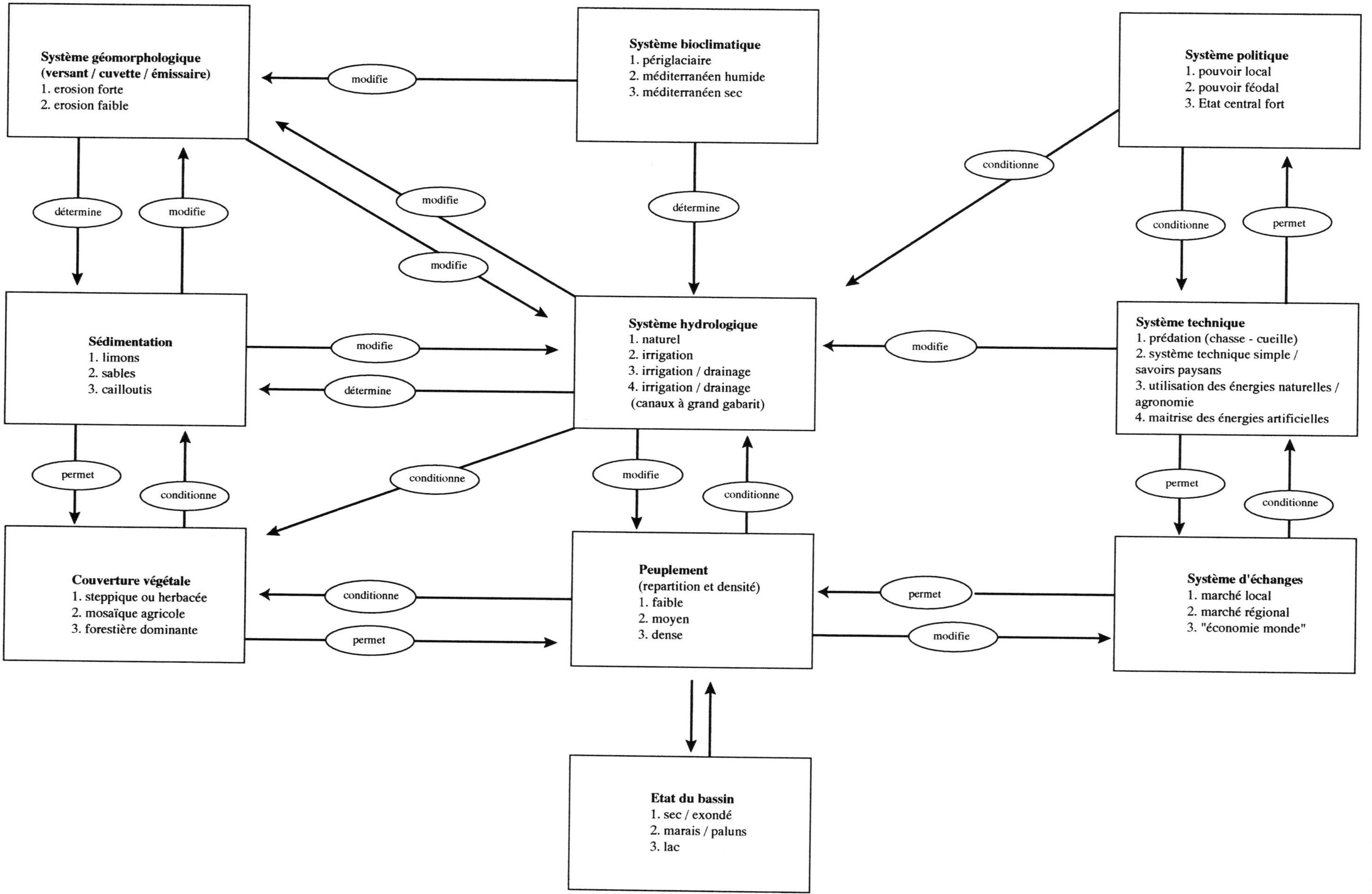

Fig. 17.5. Systematic modelling of people/environment relations based upon the research in the Vallée des Baux.

genèse holocène sur le périmètre des Alpilles. In P. Leveau et M. Provansal (eds) *Archéologie et Environnement: De la Sainte-Victoire aux Alpilles*: 515–46. Aix-en-Provence, Université de Provence.

Benoit, F. (1940) L'usine de meunerie hydraulique de Barbegal (Arles). *Revue Archéologique* 45, 1: 19–79.

Benoit, F. (1964) Le développement de la colonie d'Arles et la centuriation de la Crau. *Comptes-Rendus de l' Académie des Inscriptions*: 156–69.

Béthemont, J. (1972) *Le Thème de l'Eau dans la Vallée du Rhône. Essai de Genèse d'un Espace Hydraulique*. Saint-Etienne, Le Feuillet Blanc.

Bourilly, J., Mazauric, F. (1911) Note sur la Montagne de Cordes, près Fontvieille. *Bulletin Société Préhistorique Française:* 307–9.

Bruneton, H. (1995) *Stabilité et Instabilité des Environnements dans les Alpilles à l'Holocène*. Aix-en-Provence, Université de Provence, DEA de Géographie Physique, Option Géosystème Anthropisé.

Chouquer, G. (1983) Localisation et extension géographique des cadastres affichés à Orange. In M. Clavel-Lévêque (ed.) *Cadastres et Espace Rural*: 288–90. Paris, CNRS.

Chouquer, G. (1995) Aux origines antiques et médiévales des parcellaires. *Histoire et Sociétés Rurales* 4: 11–46.

Chouquer, G. and Favory, F. (1992) *Les Arpenteurs Romains. Théorie et Pratique*. Sophia Antipolis, APDCA.

Denizet (1929) *La Formation et le Dessèchement des Marais d'Arles; l'Œuvre de Van Ens*. Marseille, Imprimerie Nouvelle.

Faudot, M. (1992) Les réseaux cadastraux arlésiens. *Dialogues d'Histoire Ancienne*: 317–20.

Ferrando, Ph. (1994) Cantons de Châteaurenard et Tarascon. *Bilan Scientifique D.R.A.C.-S.R.A. Provence-Alpes-Côte d'Azur* 21: 167–8.

Gazenbeek, M. (1995) *Occupation du Sol et Évolution Environnementale depuis le Néolithique dans la Montagnette et la Partie Occidentale des Alpilles (Bouches-du-Rhône)*. Aix-en-Provence, Université de Provence, Thèse de Doctorat.

Gazenbeek, M., Leveau, Ph., Mocci, F. and Sintès, M. (1996) Archéologie des paysages, parcellaires et recouvrements sédimentaires sur le piémont sud des Alpilles. In G. Chouquer (ed) *Les Formes du Paysage* (*Les Formes du Paysage, t. 2, Colloque 'Archéologie des Parcellaires', Orléans, 28–30 mars 1996*): 113–29. Parris, Errance.

Goudineau, C. (1988) Le pastoralisme en Gaule. In C.R. Whittaker (ed) *Pastoral Economies in Classical Antiquity*: 160–70. Cambridge, Cambridge University Press.

Gros, P. (1995) Hercule à Glanum. *Gallia* 52: 311–31.

Guy, M. (1954) Traces du cadastre romain de quelques colonies de la Narbonnaise. *Etudes Roussillonnaises* IV-3: 217–38.

Guy, M. (1991) Prospection aérienne et télédétection des structures de parcellaires. In J. Guilaine (ed) *Pour une Archéologie Agraire*: 103–30. Paris, A. Colin.

Hayez, A.-M. (1978) Les Iles du Rhône du terroir d'Avignon au XIV siècle. *Etudes Vauclusiennes* 201: 19–23.

Jollivet, M. (1992) (ed) *Sciences de la Nature, Sciences de la Société*. Paris, CNRS.

Jorda, M., Provansal, M. and Royet, R. (1991) L'histoire 'naturelle' d'un site de l'Âge du Fer sur le piémont méridional des Alpilles. Le domaine de Servanne (Mouriès). *Gallia* 47: 57–66.

Laval, H. and Médus, J. (1994) Une séquence pollinique subboréal – subatlantique dans la vallée des Baux: changements de végétation climatiques et anthropiques de l'Age du Bronze à celui du Fer en Provence. *Arcs. Sci. Genève* 47: 83–93.

Leveau, P., and Provansal, M. (1993a) (ed) *Archéologie et Environnement: De la Sainte-Victoire aux Alpilles*. Aix-en-Provence, Université de Provence.

Leveau, P., and Provansal, M. (1993b) Systèmes agricoles et paysages du Nord-Est de l'Étang-de-Berre depuis le Néolithique. In C. Beck and R. Delort (eds) *Pour une Histoire de l'Environnement. Travaux du Programme Interdisciplinaire de Recherche sur l'Environnement:* 173–200. Paris, CNRS.

Leveau, P. (1995a) Les moulins romains de Barbegal, les ponts-aqueducs du vallon des Arcs et l'histoire naturelle de la vallée des Baux (Bilan de six ans de fouilles programmées). *C.R.A.I.* 116–144.

Leveau, P. (1995b) Colonie romaine et milieu naturel: Arles et les plaines du Bas-Rhône. In S. van der Leeuw (ed) *L'Homme et la Dégradation de l'Environnement (XVe Rencontres Internationales d'Archéologie et d'Histoire d'Antibes):* 245–62. Antibes, APDCA.

McGlade, J. (1995) An integrative Multiscalar Modelling Framework for human ecodynamic research in the Vera basin, south-east Spain. In S. van der Leeuw (ed) *L'Homme et la Dégradation de l'Environnement (XVe Rencontres Internationales d'Archéologie et d'Histoire d'Antibes):* 357–95. Antibes, APDCA.

Morch, H.F.C. (1994) Agricultural landscape: a geographer's consideration on the past. In J. Carlsen, P. Orsted, and J. Skydsgaard (eds) *Landuse in the Roman Empire*: 108. Rome, l'Erma di Bretschneider.

Pinchemel, P. and Pinchemel, G. (1988) *La Face de la Terre. Eléments de Géographie*. Paris, A. Colin (third edition).

Poumeyrol, L. (1953) Gallia Informations. *Gallia*: 112.

Poumeyrol, L. (1954) Gallia Informations. *Gallia*: 430–1.

Poumeyrol, L. (1960) Gallia Informations. *Gallia*: 305–6.

Poumeyrol, L. (1967) Gallia Informations. *Gallia*: 403

Poumeyrol, L. (1969) Gallia Informations. *Gallia*: 423.

Poumeyrol, L. (1972) Gallia Informations. *Gallia*: 518.

Poumeyrol, L. (1977) Gallia Informations. *Gallia*: 517.

Provansal, M., Leveau, Ph., Ballais, J.-L. and Jorda, M. (in press) Les moulins romains et le Marais des Baux. Archéologie et paléoenvironnements, de la protohistoire à l'époque moderne. In *L'Évolution du Milieu Physique durant la Période Historique sur le Pourtour de la Méditerranée, Ravello, 5–8 juin 1993.*

Sauzade, G. (1990) Les dolmens de Provence occidentale et la place des tombes de Fontvieille dans l'architecture mégalithique méridionale. In J. Guilaine and X. Gutherz (eds) *Autour de Jean Arnal*: 305–34. Montpellier, Université des Sciences et Techniques.

Stouff, L. (1993) La lutte contre les eaux dans les pays du bas Rhône. XIIe–XVe siècle. L'exemple du pays d'Arles. *Méditerranée* 3/4 : 57–68.

Tréziny, H. (1987–1988) *Gallia Informations* (2): 254–5.

Tréziny, H. (1990) *Gallia Informations*: 178.

Triat-Laval, H. (1978) *Contribution Pollenanalytique à l'Histoire Tardi et Postglaciaire de la Végétation de la Basse Vallée du Rhône*. Marseille, Université de Aix-Marseille III, thèse.

Vaudour, J. (1991) La notion de géosystème appliquée à l'étude des aqueducs antiques concrétionnés. In G. Fabre, J.-L. Fiches, and J.-L. Paillet (eds) *L'Aqueduc de Nîmes et le Pont du Gard*: 95–107. Nîmes, Consul Général du Gard.

Waton-Chabert, A. (1963) Historique du dessèchement de la région d'Arles, de la Durance à la mer. *Delta:* 10–14.

18. The Integration of Historical, Archaeological and Paleoenvironmental Data at the Regional Scale: the Étang de Berre, Southern France

Frédéric Trément

INTRODUCTION

An investigation carried out between 1987 and 1993 of settlement patterns and landscape development on the western side of the Étang de Berre, the lagoon system on the eastern side of the Rhone delta in southern France, forms the basis for a consideration of the integration of different methods of landscape archaeology on a micro-regional scale (Trément, 1994 and in press, a). It provides an example of a systematic, diachronic, and interdisciplinary study applied to a restricted area (100 km^2), in order to analyze as closely as possible the complex interrelations between social systems, geosystems, and ecosystems.

THE CHOICE OF THE MICRO-REGIONAL APPROACH

The archaeological map of the area in question has not been updated since the *Forma*. Nevertheless, a study carried out in 1973 under the direction of P.-A. Février (Vigoureux, 1973), the research of local scholars, and the surveys of Bouloumié and Soyer (1990), have shown the great potential of the area. It would be difficult to imagine otherwise, given the importance of the known sites, most of which have been excavated. These include the well-known protohistoric sites of Saint-Blaise and Ile de Martigues, the early prehistoric sites of Abri Cornille, Abri Capeau and Mourre Poussiou, the neolithic village of Miouvin, the iron age *oppidum* of Castellan, and the Roman port of Fos (mentioned in the Peutinger Tables) discussed in Chapter 16. These major sites, cited and used by archaeologists in their arguments about regional population, trade, the process of urbanization, and the relationship between Greeks and locals, appear to be completely isolated and incomprehensible on a micro-regional level. Thus it was necessary, at this level, to insert them into their contemporaneous rural context. By context I mean both archaeological context and also landscape context. The archaeological context was gained by means of survey and the landscape context through a series of interdisciplinary collaborations ('Actions Thématiques Programmées') in the area around the Étang de Berre, coordinated by Philippe Leveau.

The *oppidum* of Saint-Blaise was at the centre of the problem (Fig. 18.1). A detailed study of the bibliography of the site enabled me to rephrase a number of the questions formulated over the last few decades, including about salt production and the port of Saint-Blaise, first raised by Benoit (1965) then by Bouloumié (1984). A study of the local historiography has shown that the hypotheses advanced were influenced by a fanciful historical geography invented in the nineteenth century by the authors of the *Statistique des Bouches-du-Rhône*. In fact, the legend of a communication between the lakes and the sea during classical antiquity, based on an ancient tradition that Saint-Blaise was formerly a port on the Étang de Lavalduc, originated with N. Toulouzan (Villeneuve, 1824: pl. X, 9). Onto this imaginary historical geography was projected the medieval and modern image of the exploitation of salt in the lakes, reference to which can be traced back as far as 739.

The failure of archaeological excavations to prove these hypotheses has led to search elsewhere for answers, in this case at the bottom of the lakes, where the real questions have become: were the lakes always saline? were they salty during the period of occupation of Saint-Blaise? was the Étang de Lavalduc open to the sea at any other time? is the altitude of Saint-Blaise compatible with the hypothesis that it was a port?

Some time ago, P. Arcelin undertook a reconsideration of the site of Saint-Blaise, placing it securely within the framework of local indigenous population patterns (Arcelin, 1986). I propose to reduce the perspective even more and focus on a limited area but over a longer time period, changing the scale of the study in order to place the site in its territory (or at least its food-producing territory).

The choice of an intensive interdisciplinary and diachronic study of a geographically-reduced area implied

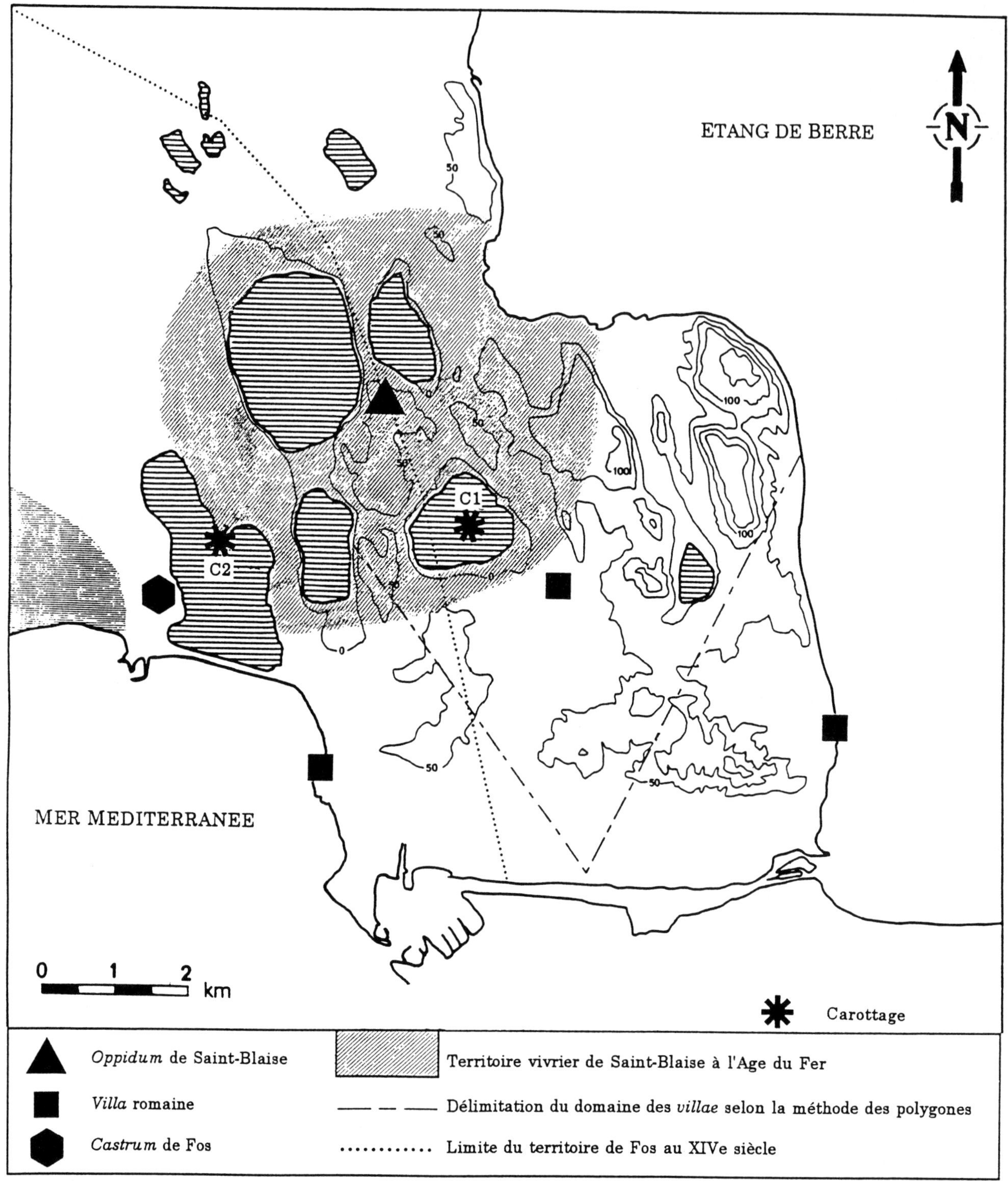

Fig. 18.1. The Etangs west of the Etang de Berre, showing the location of the main archaeological sites mentioned in the text, and of the pollen cores from the Étang de Pourra (C1) and the Étang de l'Estomac (C2), with the estimated territory of the Saint-Blaise iron age oppidum *shown in grey, the boundaries of villa estates (according to Thiessen polygon calculations) shown as dashed lines, and the boundary of Fos' territory in the fourteenth century shown as a dotted line.*

a collaboration between different specialists through reciprocal exchanges of information, while maintaining their independence. This process that could have resulted either in the integration of ideas or chaos, so it was necessary for each to define the major lines of inquiry. From the point of view of an historian or an archaeologist, the different aspects of the relationship between human beings and the environment can be approached from a triple perspective:

- the definition of a 'natural environment' in which the people exist and which conditions their activities – habitat and food production or other productive activities;
- the human exploitation of the environment – agriculture, stock rearing, hunting, fishing, craft production, industry (at this level the demographic factor is essential);
- the impact of these activities on the environment – deforestation, clearance, erosion, drainage, terracing and so on.

These three points of view are interlinked and interdependent: the humanized environment in turn conditions the human activities, which then result in new types of impact on the environment.

BACKGROUND AND METHODOLOGIES

The excavations at the prehistoric sites of Abri Cornille, Mourre Poussiou and Miouvin, together with the protohistoric and medieval sites of Saint-Blaise and the Ile de Martigues, have already allowed us to pose some questions about the relationship between people and environment. The animal bones, plant remains, molluscs and charcoal ecofacts, particularly from Ile de Martigues, have given us some answers for the Iron Age and the end of classical antiquity (Chausserie-Laprée and Nin, 1988). Surveys carried out some time ago have also given us some evidence, in an intuitive manner, of a clear correspondance between geology and ancient settlement types (Vigoureux, 1973). Finally, the work of historians has concentrated on medieval settlement (Lagrue 1988), medieval and modern salt exploitation (Balzano, 1987; Rolland 1940), and olive cultivation (Fabre, 1988).

The setting up of a series of interdisciplinary research programmes round the Étang de Berre gave me the opportunity to draw attention to the archaeological and palaeoenvironmental potential of the Saint-Blaise area. Three successive programmes were carried out: A.T.P. du PIREN: 'Histoire de l'Environnement et des Phénomènes Naturels': *Mobilité des Paysages et Histoire de l'Occupation du Sol des Rives de l'Etang de Berre, 1986–1988*; *Systèmes Agricoles et Evolution du Paysage depuis le Néolitique au Nord-Est de l'Etang de Berre, 1988–1990*; and Appel d'offre: 'Grands Projets d'Archéologie Métropolitaine': *Archéologie et Histoire de l'Occupation du Sol sur les Rives Occidentales et Méridionale de l'Etang de Berre, 1991–1992.*

From an archaeological point of view, the density and continuity of occupation allowed for the quantification of human impact on the environment, over a long, finely-calibrated, time period. From a paleoenvironmental point of view, the characteristics of the closed basins which are typical of this sector (size, negative altitude, watertightness, variability of the lakes, and salinity), make them, *a priori*, excellent recorders of climatic change, landscape change, and human impact on landscape through the Holocene. For these reasons, a team of students under the direction of Mireille Provansal carried out a study of several sectors which were both representative of the local landscape and also related to archaeological problems (Bertucchi and Pelissier, 1991; Bonnefoux, 1992; Iardino-Lamazou and Meyer 1987; Provansal *et al.* 1993).

It became necessary to increase the range of methods and intensify their application. A series of systematic surveys was therefore undertaken in order to study in detail the development of settlement patterns. These were followed by a research excavation of a Roman agricultural site dating to the early Empire, representative of the small dispersed settlements which complemented the villas of that period (Trément, 1997). Several sondages confirmed the validity of the interpretation of the surface finds, which could thus be 'calibrated'. The analysis of the faunal assemblage from the Soires excavation (Columeau, 1997), together with the study of the shellfish from the midden at Clapières (Trément and Brien-Poitevin, 1989), complemented the study of assemblages from the Iron Age and the High Middle Ages by Columeau (1993) and Brien-Poitevin (1993). A core sample was taken in the Étang de Pourra in 1989, in order to try to reconstruct the environment over a long time period. This core was studied by a geomorphologist from the Institute of Geography, together with two palynologists from the Historical Botany and Quaternary Palynology Laboratory and a sedimentologist from the Geosciences and Environment Laboratory (Laval *et al.* 1992; Fig. 18.2).

THE INTEGRATION OF THE DATA: STRATEGY, PROBLEMS AND LIMITS

Strategy of integration

The procedures adopted in the study area had to reconcile two different approaches to the environment corresponding with two different spatio-temporal scales: on the scale of an excavated site, the paleoecological and archaeological information is precisely calibrated in time but is only representative of a restricted area (the surrounding land, the territory) and is also biased by human selection processes; on a micro-regional scale, its evolution can only be seen as a whole, over a long period of time. This last type of approach has a double advantage. First, it allows us to understand the evolution of the landscape and the consequences of human action in a realistic fashion, rather than through specific analyses of archaeological contexts which represent an environment inevitably altered by human action. Secondly, the division of the study area into a series of independent basins created the possibility that different functions might be recognized in each, which could be related to differing local modes of occupation.

Two cases were investigated. The first shows that spatially-different human activities can be reconstructed on a micro-regional scale through comparative analyses of sedimentation in different basins (Fig. 18.1): the Étang de Pourra went through a phase of prolonged emersion, which seems to represent the combined effect of the climate in classical antiquity and the attempts by the owners of the nearby villa of Péricard (SM-34) to drain the lake and bring the land into cultivation. This event is not recorded in the adjacent lakes situated outside the villa's estate. On the other hand, the increased erosion in the twelfth century observed in the Étang de l'Estomac is perhaps related to clearances, initiated in this period, by the population of the *castrum* of Fos, whose territory surrounds the lake. These results show the potential of an interdisciplinary study of political and social space.

Conversely, the second case proves that, despite human intervention, the major variations in lake levels were primarily conditioned by climatic fluctuations: in effect, there was parallel evolution of the different lakes over the long term. If the ancient low water levels of the Étang de Pourra in antiquity can be explained by attempts at drainage, the same cannot be said for the low levels in the Étang de Lavalduc and the Étang d'Engrenier, the bottoms of which are at a height of 14.50 and 11.80 m above sea level respectively, which made drainage impossible with the techniques available at the time.In contrast, the high post-medieval levels of these latter two lakes can be explained by overspill from the Canal de Craponne; however, the Étang de Pourra, which received no artificial addition of water, also had a high water level at that period. Therefore, it seems likely that changes in water levels were largely the result of the dry climatic fluctuation in classical antiquity and the humid fluctuation of the Little Ice Age.

Dates, resolution and time scales

The integration of data from different disciplines is largely reliant on the ability to correlate the bioclimatic and anthropic chronological sequences. This correlation is extremely delicate on three counts, which are discussed below in turn.

The heterogeneity of the dating methods

The different dating methods used by the various disciplines are both qualitative and quantitative. Texts can provide absolute calendar dates. Excavation and survey give variable date ranges, but generally about 50 years, or indeed, as in the case of the treatments used here, about a generation. Geoarchaeological and archaeozoological data obtained from archaeological contexts are obviously dependent on archaeological dating methods. The geomorphological sections can also use artefacts as *termini*, but the chronological precision is very variable: for example, a deposit is referred to as being 'post-antique'. In the long core sequences, such as the one from Pourra, the absence of artefacts means that it is necessary to resort to other methods, such as radiocarbon dating or pollen chronozones. Two radiocarbon dates from organic material were obtained from the base of the Pourra core: 14800 BP ± 290 (Ly5254) at level 480 and 13180 BP ± 260 (Ly5263) at level 350. Taking into account the organic nature of the sediment dated, the dates probably need to be shifted forward one or two millennia (J. Evin, *pers. comm.*). This correction allows the base of the sequence to be situated in a late interglacial. The dating of the upper half of the core is dependent on the chronology of the pollen zones defined for Provence by H. Laval (Triat-Laval, 1978). In particular, it is based on the appearance and development of *Abies* pollen around 6500/6000 BP and *Fagus* pollen around 4700/4500 BP.

The discontinuity of cultural and bioclimatic sequences

Time is not recorded in a continuous and homogeneous fashion in archaeological and sedimentary deposits. The information conserved is partial and it is therefore necessary to take into account the inevitable gaps that occur: pauses in sedimentation for the geomorphologist, abandonment of occupation for the archaeologist. According to the palynologists, the end of the Pleistocene and the beginning of the Holocene are missing in the Pourra core (Laval *et al.*, 1992). A hiatus can also be envisaged for part of the upper sequence, where the appearance of *Fagus*, generally placed at the beginning of the Subboreal *c*.4500 BP, coincides with the expansion of *Quercus ilex* from level 130, whereas their development is usually separated in time. The sedimentary pause observed during part of the Iron Age and classical antiquity is also the reason for a relative lack of information about human activity and landscape change in this period. Erosion can also affect archaeological levels, but this increases the readability of the sites on the surface. In fact, survey is an excellent way to analyze the periods of settlement pattern change, when the conditions are favourable. This is true for the Saint-Blaise area, where the composition of the total finds assemblage (finewares, coarsewares and amphorae) has allowed a better understanding of the strong continuity of habitation from the Lower Empire to the beginning of the Early Middle Ages. Finally, the sampling of a stratigraphic profile introduces another level of discontinuity: it can help to mask certain details and thus lead to incorrect interpretations of continuity or change.

The differential chronologies of bioclimatic and anthropic processes

The developments studied by the different disciplines act

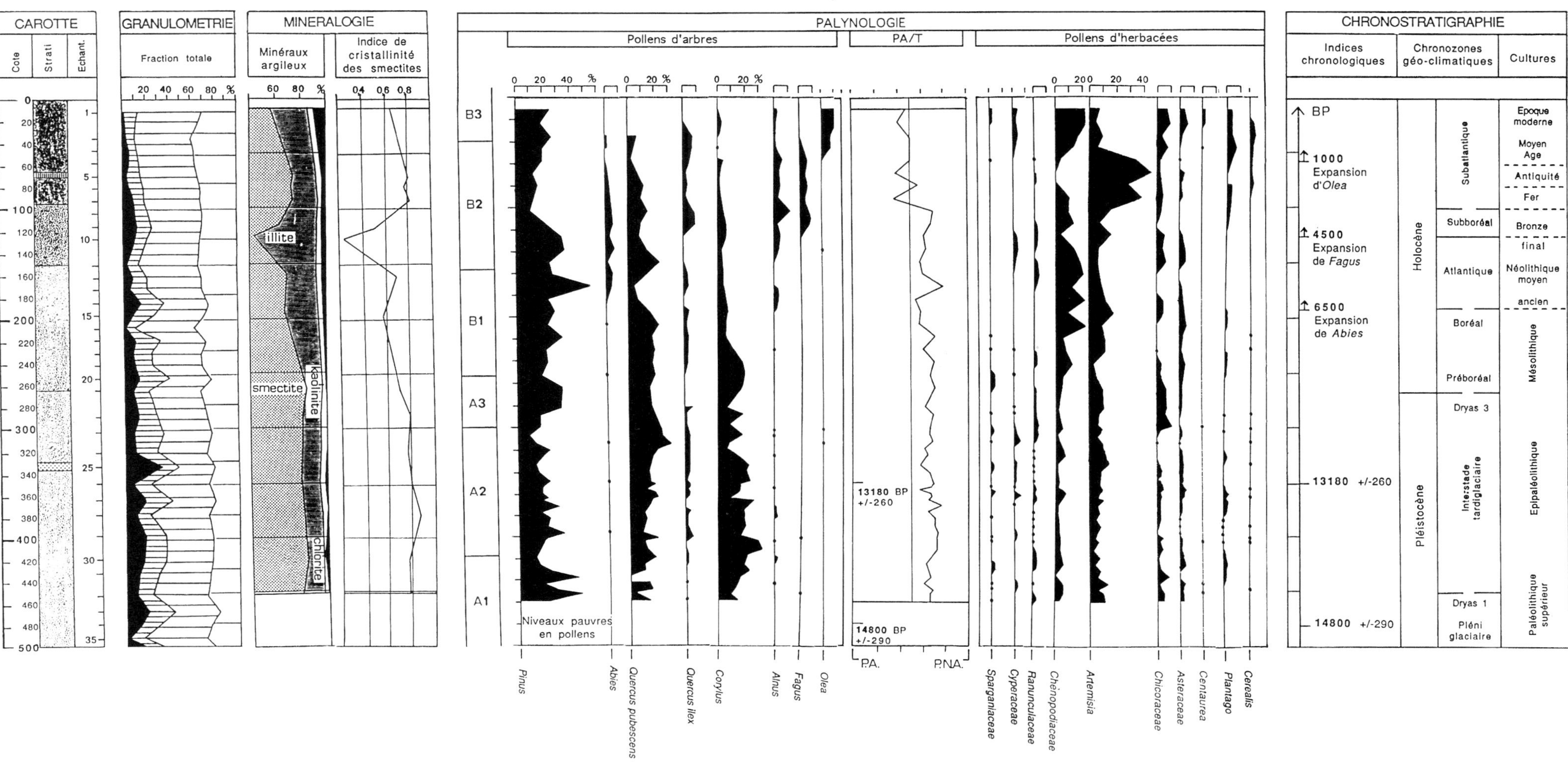

Fig. 18.2. Palyno-sedimentological diagram of the core from the Étang de Pourra

on very variable time scales. The distinction between 'geological time' and 'human time' is not one of chronological succession but of a difference in scale. Within the historical period, Braudel (1958) and Le Roy-Ladurie (1967) have distinguished different 'temporalities'. These temporalities combine their effects in a complex manner: for example, there is no strict parallelism between climatic and vegetation cycles — from the moment that humans interfered with the vegetation cover through clearance, agriculture and pastoralism, a new rhythm was imposed on it, thus increasing the complexity of the chain of causalities. For reasons explained in the earlier two points, the non-coincidence of bioclimatic and cultural temporalities with the scale of chronological resolution can lead to erroneous interpretations.

This is the case when one tries to relate the development of rural habitation in classical antiquity to historical references to invasions. Although the arguments can be accepted on a very general level — that of the Empire (though with many reservations) — it is inappropriate on a micro-regional scale. The perfection of a system of dating sites in bands of twenty years has allowed the recognition of developments in the study area outside of the conventional chronological framework, founded on a political and factual history with little relevance to the reality of the countryside (Trément, in press, c). The study of the Pourra core shows that there is no simple direct relationship between phases of agricultural expansion and the onset of periods of increased erosion. The consideration of 'cycles' and 'phases' has been enriched by integration with the concept of 'thresholds' (Provansal and Morhange, 1994).

Differential spaces and spatial scales

The above remarks could also be applied to the spatial dimension. The space 'perceived' through the techniques used does not obviously correspond with the space 'lived' by the inhabitants of that period. Also, it is necessary to split that which concerns the analytical techniques and that which deals with bioclimatic and anthropic processes. Several problems arise.

For example, the space perceived by the researcher is discontinuous and partial. For example, on the archaeological map, the urban and industrial zones and the transport infrastructure represent 'blank' areas, where information is either inaccessible or has been destroyed. Natural phenomena can also result in the disappearance (real or apparent) of sites: the Holocene rise in sea levels, the rise in lake levels, or erosive activity, affect to a greater or lesser degree the visibility of sites on the surface, leading to an over-representation of the most eroded sites and the masking of buried sites. Finally, sampling splits up the perceived space and makes it appear more mixed. In the study area only about 6600 ha out of a total of 10500 ha were available for survey; 34 per cent of this available area was surveyed, ten per cent in a systematic fashion. The site density varied from two to twenty per km^2 between the systematically surveyed and the less intensively surveyed areas. If the results of the surveys carried out in the different landscape units are compared, these differences are no more than about one to three, and are thus more likely to correspond to a real discontinuity of 'lived' space.

The second problem concerns the different spaces of bioclimatic and human processes. Archaeological evidence, ecofacts and palaeoenvironmental markers inform us about more or less extensive spaces. For example, to take two extreme examples in the domain of palynology, the *Pinus* pollen curve in the Pourra core reflects the evolution of pine forests not just in the study area, but in the whole region, as pine produces large quantities of pollen which can be transported a very long way, whereas at the other extreme, cereals produce a small amount of pollen which does not travel far, so is the most representative on a micro-regional scale (Janssen, 1966). There is a similar problem with ecofacts, since their presence in archaeological contexts is the result of selection through animal husbandry, mollusc collection or wood collection. In all these cases, it is only possible to learn about the qualitative evolution of the species consumed (animals, shellfish, wood) and not their overall quantity. For example, it is impossible to know what quantities of beef or mussels were consumed at Ile de Martigues in the second century, while the food consumption between the fifth and second centuries BC is relatively clearly understood (Chausserie-Laprée and Nin, 1988). Consequently, it is impossible to know the size of the herds and therefore the size of the pastures. Only through a comparison of data from different sites is it possible to illustrate the general or particular character of a phenomenon recognized on a site.

Returning to the example of Ile de Martigues in the second century, the palaeoecological and archaeozoological evidence clearly indicates the imbalance between population and resources, with the increasing importance of hunting, the diversification and intensification of shellfish collection, the growth of barley cultivation, and probably the extension of clearance. It is tempting to associate the increased food collection with the complete restructuring of the village at the beginning of the second century. The appearance of new needs can be explained by an increase in the local population due to the regrouping of hitherto-dispersed communities, or by real demographic pressure. However, a comparison with Saint-Blaise means that the second hypothesis has to be refined: the stability of the consumption structure at this site, confirmed by the lack of evidence for erosion in the adjacent drainage basin of the Étang de Pourra, shows a better balance in the exploitation of food resources (Columeau, 1993).

On a larger intra- and inter-regional scale, the question is to determine whether certain events are particular to the study area or illustrate processes happening on a larger scale. This question was applied to the forms of Roman habitation. The adoption of the descriptors used in the

Fig. 18.3. Landscape reconstruction of a closed depression (étang) *in the Late Neolithic. (After Trément, 1991).*

EU-funded ARCHAEOMEDES programme has allowed systematic comparison with the Beaucaire, Lunel, Tricastin and Vaison-la-Romaine areas (Trément, 1993b). This shows that there was a very similar form of occupation in the whole of the lower Rhône valley. The enlargement of the database to include the whole of Narbonnaise will allow new comparisons to be made (Favory and Fiches, 1988, 1994).

THREE EXAMPLES OF THE INTEGRATION OF DATA

It is not a question of presenting here a synthesis of the results acquired by the systematic integration of data from different disciplines, in the sector of Saint-Blaise (Trément, 1993a,1994, and in press, a). Rather, the intention is to show, through three examples from different time periods, how the information can be integrated and the limits of interpretation.

The Late Neolithic (Fig. 18.3)

The final neolithic/chalcolithic period provides an excellent example of the interaction of people and nature: there is plentiful archaeological data and the palaeoenvironmental data are relatively securely dated by the appearance of *Fagus* at level 130 and by a radiocarbon date.

One cannot speak of a 'natural environment' at this date, since the vegetation and soils had already been altered by the first farmers. On the plateaus and the slopes, clearance was undertaken at the expense of deciduous oak forests and pine forests, as the pollen curves of these plummet, while that of *Ulmus* is interrupted. This favoured, on the other hand, the expansion of evergreen oak, which is more resistant to edaphic conditions and tends to regrow from the stumps after forest fires. From level 120, the opposed development of the pollen curves of *Quercus pubescens* and *Quercus ilex* is a sign of increasing human intervention on the vegetation: henceforth cultivation formed an integral part of the landscape.

At this time, the lakes were at a relatively high level. On the south bank of the Étang d'Engrenier, a layer of black lacustrine silts, 1.50 m above the present lake level, has been dated to 4480 ± 280 BP (Provansal *et al.*, 1993: 255–7). In the Pourra core, the *Alnus* peak, the revival of *Chenopodiaceae*, and the variations in *Ulmus* and *Betula* pollen, also indicate a higher lake level, probably the result of the Subboreal climate deterioration. The Engrenier section shows that this humid phase caused marsh development in the whole depression (Provansal 1993: 258–60). This does not seem to have prevented frequent use of the edge of the lake: it seems that these zones, though difficult to occupy and exploit on a long term basis, were not considered unattractive, contrary to a widely-used but simplistic model (Triat-Laval, 1978: 266).

This period corresponds to an expansion of the settlement of Miouvin and a clear increase in the occupation of the lake zone. Several important sites have been identified on the low plateaus. The density of isolated finds around the edge of the marshy depressions suggests a complementary system of cultivation on the plateaus, together with an intensive exploitation of the food resources of the lakes. The appearance of a continuous curve of *Plantago*, together with a rapid rise in *Artemisia*, reflects an intensification of clearance, confirmed by the stone tool assemblage at Miouvin. In the geomorphological sections and the Pourra core, the increased occurrence of charcoal may be a direct sign of new clearances, and may also reflect the use of fire in the maintenance of pastures. The increase in *Alnus* and *Betula* can be explained by their ability to germinate well in ash. In parallel, the analysis of the faunal assemblage of Miouvin shows a growth in pastoral activities (ovicaprids, small cattle, pigs), fishing (fish bones), and the harvesting of shellfish (mussels, clams, oysters).

The balance in the number of sites through time suggests that we should neither overestimate the effect of humans on the environment nor underestimate the role of climatic factors in this period (Trément, 1998). For all that, one cannot help ascribing – at least in part – the increased erosion in the Subboreal to the speeding up of clearance at the end of the third millennium BC. The deposits accumulated on the slopes and at the bottom of the lakes abruptly change facies: they become finer, changing from silty sands to dark sandy silts rich in charcoal. The reoccurrence of sandy deposits became less frequent and less marked. In the Pourra core all the mineralogical parameters decrease sharply. The partially-decalcified orange-brown soil which developed on the slopes in response to the amelioration of the late glacial and postglacial climate was scoured off during this period. The Subboreal humid fluctuation certainly contributed its effects to those caused by human activity, but it is revealing that the fine fraction of the deposits, resulting from the action of diffuse streams on the soil cover, is systematically associated with cultivated plant taxa. The increase in charcoal in the deposits is a sign of the increased use of the practice of cultivation after scrub-burning, which is particularly damaging at the local scale to the stability of the slopes. The preferential location of habitations – and, it is reasonable to suggest, cultivation – in the zones most affected by erosion, especially the edges of the plateaus, explains why the attacks on the vegetation cover were occasionally devastating. Nevertheless, the whole forest cover was not threatened prior to the Iron Age: the impact of chalcolithic agricultural communities was selective and localized, characteristic of an agrosystem still very mobile and wasteful in its management of the soil.

The Iron Age (Fig. 18.4)

The Iron Age was an important stage in the evolution of the relationship between societies and the environment: the appearance of agglomerated settlements accompanied by demographic pressure led to an extension and a stabilization of the agrosystem.

During this period, the reversal of the arboreal/non-arboreal pollen ratio clearly indicates that human action on the forest was not just damaging but truly destructive, leading to a general diminution of the tree cover. This important change in the vegetation is characterized by a definitive decline in oak forest, a long-term diminution of pine woods, and an extension of the garrigue and arable and fallow land. At Ile de Martigues, the charcoal and molluscs confirm this image of an open environment, similar to the present-day landscape, where grasses and low shrubs predominate (Magnin, 1988; Thinon, 1988). The evolution of the lakes is more difficult to understand and date. The continuing occurrence of *Chenopodiaceae* suggests a relatively high water level in the Étang de Pourra. The thin shells of the cockles consumed at Saint-Blaise indicate their collection in a very saline environment, perhaps the sea but perhaps also the Étang de Lavalduc and the Étang d'Engrenier. The progressive lowering of the water level during the Iron Age perhaps caused an increase in salinity, therefore allowing the exploitation of salt (Stevenson *et al.*, 1993).

The Early Iron Age coincides with a relatively dense distribution of dispersed settlements around the agglomerated settlement of Saint-Blaise. The map of sixth-century BC occupation shows a concentric structuring of settlement within a radius of about three to five km. Consequently one can envisage that from this period there was a definitive stabilization of the agrosystem around the *oppidum*, through increasing population pressure. This situation seems to have lasted not much beyond the middle of the fifth century BC. The fourth and third centuries BC correspond with a marked contraction of settlement, despite the continuing occupation of Ile de Martigues. Throughout this period, a very strong correlation between the evolution of nucleated and dispersed settlements can be seen. On the other hand, the restructuring of the agglomerated settlements of Saint-Blaise and Ile de Martigues in the second century does not give rise to a resurgence of dispersed settlements similar to those of the Early Iron Age. Nevertheless, there is much more evidence for an increase in productive activities in the agglomerated settlements. This includes a diversification of the resources exploited, increasing storage capacity, an increase in indicators of craft activities, evidence for specialized functional spaces and signs of prosperity such as an intensification in commercial exchanges and the construction of the Hellenistic rampart.

The scarceness of dispersed settlements in the second century could be the result of integration within the agglomerated settlements of activities such as processing and storage which were previously spread throughout the land. The increase in data allows the agricultural system to be reconstructed. Palynological evidence reveals the start of a continuous curve of cereals, and an impressive

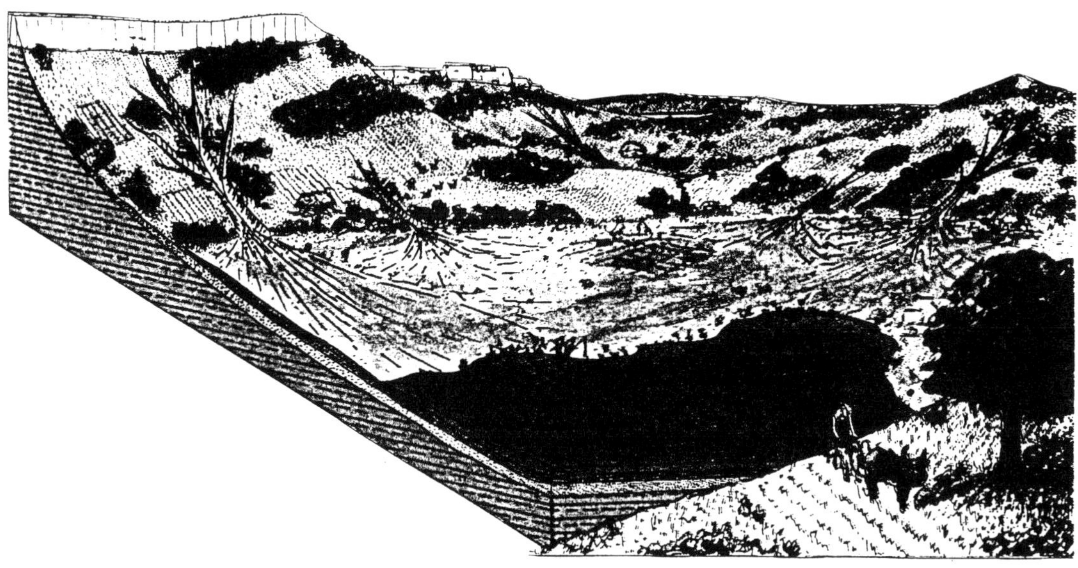

*Fig. 18.4. Landscape reconstruction of a closed depression (*étang*) in the Iron Age. (After Trément, 1991)*

expansion in *Artemisia*, indicating intense clearance and sowing. Archaeological finds (mills, presses) and in particular the archaeobotanical studies of the Ile de Martigues excavations confirm the increase in the growing of wheat, barley and millet, plus the appearance of not only olive and vine cultivation, but also linseed, and vetch (Marinval, 1988). Stock raising was a well-developed activity at Saint-Blaise, practised right through the Iron Age (Columeau, 1993). On the other hand, the lack of stability suggested by the stocking of beef within the village of Ile de Martigues forced a strong emphasis on hunting and shellfish collection (Brien-Poitevin,1993). The divergent evolution of these two sites and the grouping together of settlements suggest population movement rather than demographic expansion such as that witnessed in the Early Iron Age.

Paradoxically, the artificial transformation of the vegetation cover did not precipitate a severe erosion crisis such as that seen in the Late Neolithic. On the contrary, there is a positive inversion of all the mineralogical parameters in the Pourra core, with the increase in the smectite/illite ratio and the index of cristallinity of smectite, as well as a return to normal levels of organic material. This could be interpreted as the result of a direct abrasion of the living rock following the complete stripping away of the soil cover. However, this hypothesis is invalidated both by the preservation of evolved decarbonated soils on the limestone bedrock, which is borne out by anthracology, and by the slight accumulation of deposits comprising more than 80 per cent of fine silts and clays. It is more likely that there was a resumption of incision through the concentration of water run-off on slopes devoid of cultivation or else sheltered, either naturally through more favourable climatic conditions, or artificially by terracing.

The Early Empire (Fig. 18.5)

The Roman conquest did not cause a particular rupture in the evolution of the countryside, which was directly inherited from the previous period. In the Pourra core, the arboreal/non-arboreal pollen ratio was below 50 per cent, whilst there was a progressive decline in deciduous oak, hazel, and then beech. The evergreen oak was also subject to a slight decline, perhaps momentarily the victim of the extension of the agrosystem into areas which were previously garrigue (the slopes?). On the other hand, pine gradually continued to increase. As regards the herbaceous plants, the most remarkable event is the impressive double peak of *Artemisia*, which peaked at more than 40 per cent and thus alone is responsible for overturning the arboreal/non-arboreal pollen ratio. This episode coincides with a return to the mineralogical parameters present prior to human interference with the environment. The absence of Roman-period deposits on the slopes confirms the hypothesis of a stable and shel-

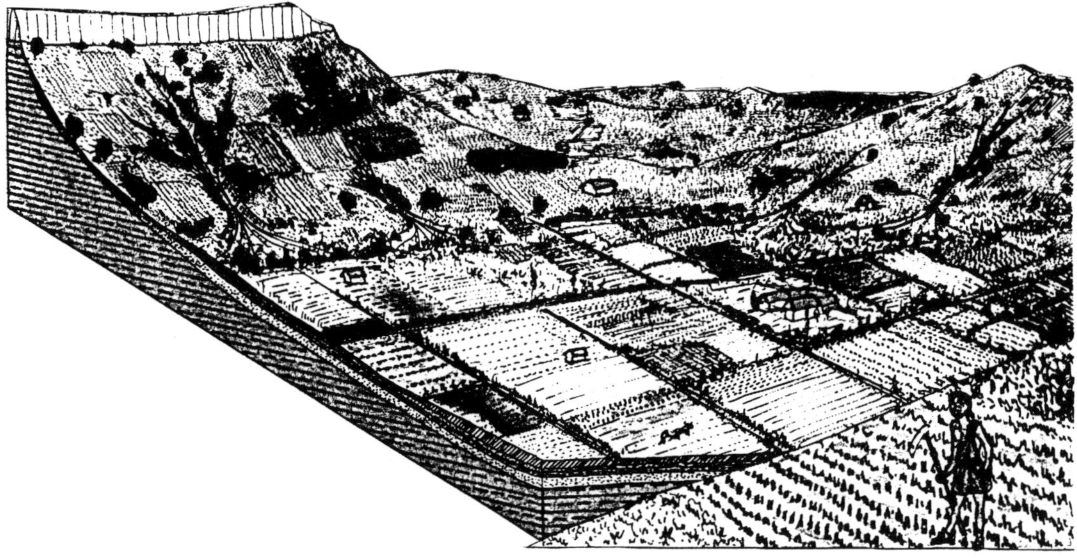

*Fig. 18.5. Landscape reconstruction of a closed depression (*étang*) in the Early Empire. (After Trément, 1991)*

tered environment. Yet, paradoxically, the lake sector had never been so deforested before.

The density of protohistoric occupation probably considerably mitigated the effects of Romanization on the countryside. Also, the positive influence of the dry climatic fluctuation in classical antiquity needs to be taken into account, together with the probability that the slopes were terraced. If the development of the villa economy implies the preferential cultivation of the lower land, which was less prone to erosion and well-drained thanks to lower lake levels, the remarkable density of small dispersed rural settlements suggests that the plateaus and the slopes were cultivated as well. The development of the agglomerated settlements of Fos and *Maritima Avaticorum* during the Augustan period suggests an increase in needs and greater human demands on the environment. Consequently, the measures taken by the Gallo-Roman farmers to conserve the slopes – the construction of small walls and terraces – were probably designed to stabilize or indeed favour the development of soil. Finally, the removal of stock to the Crau might have contributed decisively to the slowing down of the rate of erosion (Badan *et al.*, 1995).

The climatic factor probably favoured the drainage of the lower zones, the lowering of the lake levels in the Étang de Lavalduc and the Étang d'Engrenier, and the prolonged drying-out of the Étang de Pourra. The oxidation level observed in the latter at level 65 coincided with a momentary disappearance of *Chenopodiaceae* and *Cyperaceae*. It is tempting to link this phenomenon with a drainage channel found in this lake in the eighteenth century (Achard, 1787). This parallel seems more significant given the proximity of the Péricard villa (SM-34) and the 'archaeologically empty' Plan Fossan depression, suggesting that the basin was brought under cultivation by a villa estate. Such an enterprise would have allowed the villa owners to gain several hundred hectares of pasture or arable land. There are parallels for this type of activity in the area, for example, in the depression of Taillades (Fontvieille) (Leveau, 1993).

The Augustan period and the first decades of the first century AD saw a considerable increase in settlement density. As well as the spread of small establishments on the molassic plateaus of the central sector, previously occupied by the inhabitants of the *oppidum* of Saint-Blaise, there was the establishment of a network of villas in the southern hills, which had, until that point, remained unoccupied. This development was part of a general move to colonize the wetland zones as part of the expansion of estate economies. The newly-exploited lands were the heavy wet Bégudien marls, whose improvement required an appropriate technology. Locally, the problem of Romanization arises in the unequal distribution of the two types of habitation. The fact that villas are rare and restricted to the southern sector can be explained in different ways.

The first explanation relates to the natural and technological conditions. This period benefited from a combination of bioclimatic factors (the dry climatic fluctuation of classical antiquity) and technologies (new techniques of drainage and perhaps a renewal of plants and tools), which facilitated the extension of cultivation into the lowlands.

Secondly, there is a series of historical factors. The settlement patterns at the time of the conquest may have played a decisive role: the area of the extension of the small dispersed settlements corresponds exactly with that of the pre-Roman settlement associated with the Saint-Blaise *oppidum*, so consequently the villas were established in the unoccupied areas where land was available. Another factor may also be involved: that of the southward shift of the political and administrative centres – *Maritima Avaticorum* and the port of *Fossae Marianae* – after the conquest. The creation of a Latin colony at Martigues could have effectively given rise to a local aristocracy who invested in the neighbouring lands.

Furthermore, the original settlements – 'polynuclear' or 'dispersed hamlets' – spread out into the intermediary zones along the edge of the lakes and in the wet valleys. This can be interpreted as an attempt by the indigenous communities to improve new land by the collective employment of the techniques regularly seen in the working of the estates. The remarkable longevity of these forms of habitation, which lasted until the end of classical antiquity, is a sign of their undoubted success.

A reconstruction of the agricultural system has been attempted for this period, which has produced the greatest quantity of archaeological evidence. This reconstruction has taken into account:

- the paleoenvironmental data, which can inform us about the extent, the location and the potential nature of the crops;
- the ecofacts recovered from the various excavations, which allow us to trace the outlines of meat and shellfish consumption and indirectly to reconstruct the history of stock rearing and the exploitation of the lakes;
- the installations associated with the processing of agricultural products, mainly olive and grape presses, but also an amphora-manufacturing site (Sivier);
- the containers recovered from survey and excavation (*dolia*, *amphorae*, and other types of receptacle), which, to a certain extent, are able to give an idea of storage capacity and thus indirectly of production;
- the map of pottery scatters linked to cultural activity;
- and finally, obviously, the classification and distribution of settlement types.

A model for the villa estates in the southern sector can be proposed by incorporating the information from the map of settlement types, the geo-pedological data, the palynological and sedimentary data of the Pourra core, the map of pottery scatters associated with agricultural practices, and the distribution map of burial sites. The general impression is one of a heterogeneous countryside in which productive activities were closely dependent on natural conditions. The basic structures – those that are revealed through settlement analysis – fit very precisely into the principal landscape units determined by the topographic, pedological and hydrological conditions. The central sector, the molassic plateaus of Saint-Mitre, Fos and Istres, had small dispersed or 'polynuclear' settlements which appear to have been fairly specialized, either in olive cultivation (Fos) or in viticulture (Saint-Mitre). The southern sector, the Bégudien hills of Martigues, was dedicated to commercial cereal production, within an estate economy, but small dependent settlements may equally well have been involved in arboriculture on additional land.

CONCLUSION

Partial answers have been found to many of the questions asked, through more meaningful reformulation of them as the research advanced. The problem of salt at Saint-Blaise remains unanswered, but the understanding of this major site has nevertheless been advanced and from a new perspective. By combining the archaeological, historical and paleoenvironmental data it is possible to write a landscape history that permits the reconstruction of the evolution of a micro-region, concentrating on its specifics, while allowing the comparison with data obtained from a wider scale. The method implies the need to ask, right from the beginning, how representative is the information contained in the different archival sources: the soil, the subsoil, the texts. The integration of the experience of each discipline implies an initial independent analysis of the data, in order to avoid circular arguments. In this sense, it is not so much a matter of integrating the methods but of integrating the results. This is why I believe that landscape archaeology should remain simply one method within archaeology – it would be dangerous to try to establish it as a separate discipline.

REFERENCES

Achard, C.-F. (1787) *Description Historique, Géographique et Topographique des Villes, Bourgs, Villages et Hameaux de Provence.* Aix-en-Provence.

Arcelin, P. (1986) Le territoire de Marseille grecque dans son contexte indigène. *Études Massaliètes* 1: 43–104. (Actes de la Table Ronde d'Aix-en-Provence 16 Mars 1985: Le Territoire de Marseille Grecque.)

Badan, O., Brun, J.-P., and Congès, G. (1995) Les bergeries romaines de la Crau d'Arles. Les origines de la transhumance en Provence. *Gallia* 52: 263–310.

Behre, K. E. (1986) Die Reflektion archäologisch bekannter Siedlungen in Pollendiagrammen verschiedener Entfernung. Beispiele aus der Siedlungskammer Flögeln, Nordwestdeutschland. Niedersächsiches Landeinstitut für Marschen-und Wurtenforschung, Wilhelmshaven. In *Anthropogenic Indicators in Pollen Diagrams:* 95–114. Rotterdam, Balkema.

Benoit, F. (1965) *Recherches sur l'Hellénisation du Midi de la Gaule*. Aix-en-Provence, Ophrys.

Bertucchi, L. and Pelissier, M. (1991) *Étude Géomorphologique du Milieu Anthropisé de Quelques Bassins-Versants dans la Zone du Littoral de Fos et son Arrière-Pays*. Aix-en-Provence, Université de Provence, Institut de Géographie, Maîtrise de Géographie.

Bonnefoux, M. (1992) *Étude d'un Géosystème Anthropisé dans la Région des Etangs: le Littoral de l'Étang-de-Berre d'Istres à Martigues*. Aix-en-Provence,Université de Provence, Institut de Géographie, Maîtrise de Géographie.

Bouloumié, B. (1984) *Un Oppidum Gaulois à Saint-Blaise en Provence*. Paris, Dossiers d'Histoire et d'Archéologie 84.

Bouloumié, B. and Soyer, J. (1990) Prospections archéologiques en Basse-Provence. Itinéraires antiques et habitats. I, Étang-de-Berre. *Hamburgers Beiträge zur Archäologie* 13/14 (1986–1987): 119–237.

Braudel, F. (1958) La longue durée. *Annales E.S.C.* 4: 725–53.

Brien-Poitevin, F. (1993) Étude conchyliologique de quelques sites de l'Étang-de-Berre et la vallée de l'Arc. In P. Leveau and M. Provansal (eds) *Archéologie et Environnement: De la Sainte-Victoire aux Alpilles*: 285–300. Aix-en-Provence, Université de Provence.

Capeau, L. J. (1831) *Abrégé Chronologique des Documents Relatifs aux Étangs d'Engrenier et de La Valduc*. Aix-en-Provence.

Chausserie-Laprée, J.and Nin, N. (1988) (eds) *Le Village Gaulois de Martigues*. Paris, Dossiers d'Histoire et d'Archéologie 128.

Columeau, P. (1993) Le ravitaillement en viande, la chasse et l'élevage sur les rives de l'Étang de Berre. Essai d'une synthèse. In P. Leveau and M. Provansal (eds) *Archéologie et Environnement: De la Sainte-Victoire aux Alpilles*: 301–14. Aix-en-Provence, Université de Provence.

Columeau, P. (1997) Les Soires. Etude de la faune du Haut Empire. Pp. 60–61 in F. Trément, Un établissement agricole gallo-romain: le site des Soires à Saint-Mitre-les-Remparts (Bouches-du-Rhône). *Revue Archéologique de Narbonnaise* 30: 33–61.

Fabre, G. (1988) L'olivier et les moulins à huile à Saint-Mitre à la fin du XVIIIe siècle. *Provence historique* 152: 193–213.

Favory, F., Fiches, J.-L. and Girardot, J.-J. (1988) L'analyse des données appliquée à la typologie des sites gallo-romains dans le Beaucairois (Gard): matériel de prospection et environnement paysager: essai méthodologique. *Gallia* 45: 67–85.

Favory, F. and Fiches, J.-L. (1994) (eds) *Les Campagnes de la France Méditerranéenne dans l'Antiquité et le Haut Moyen Age. Etudes Microrégionales*. Paris, Documents d'Archéologie Française 42.

Iardino-Lamazou, A. and Meyer, J.-M. (1987) *Evolution Morphoclimatique et Anthropisation du Milieu dans la Région de l'Etang de Berre depuis l'Holocène*. Aix-en-Provence, Université de Provence, Institut de Géographie, Maîtrise de Géographie.

Janssen, C.R. (1966) Recent pollen spectra from the deciduous and coniferous-deciduous forests of northeastern Minnesota: a study in pollen dispersal. *Ecology* 47/5.

Lagrue, J.-P. (1988) *Le Château de Fos et son Environnement*. Aix-en-Provence, Université de Provence, Maîtrise.

Laval, H., Médus, J., Parron, C., Simonnet, J.-P. and Trément, F. (1992) Late glacial and Holocene climate and soil erosion in southeastern France: a case study from Etang du Pourra, Provence. *Journal of Quaternary Science* 7: 235–45.

Le Roy-Ladurie, E. (1967) *Histoire du Climat depuis l'An Mil*. Paris, Flammarion.

Leveau, P. (1993) Milieu naturel et histoire économique: Arles antique et son espace agricole. In P.Leveau and M. Provansal (eds) *Archéologie et Environnement: De la Sainte-Victoire aux Alpilles*: 485–514. Aix-en-Provence, Université de Provence.

Leveau, P. and Provansal, M. (1993) (eds) *Archéologie et Environnement: De la Sainte-Victoire aux Alpilles*. Aix-en-Provence, Université de Provence.

Magnin, F. (1988) Les mollusques terrestres. *Dossiers d'Histoire et d'Archéologie* 128: 97.

Marinval, P. (1988) L'alimentation végétale et l'agriculture. *Dossiers d'Histoire et d'Archéologie* 128: 92–3.

Provansal, M., Bertucchi, L. and Pelissier, M. (1993) Les milieux palustres de Provence occidentale, indicateurs de la morphogenèse holocène. In In P.Leveau and M. Provansal (eds) *Archéologie et Environnement: De la Sainte-Victoire aux Alpilles*: 249–66. Aix-en-Provence, Université de Provence.

Provansal, M. and Morhange, C. (1994) Seuils climatiques et réponses morphogéniques en Basse Provence depuis 5000 ans. *Quaternaire* 34: 113–8. (Colloque International de l'INQUA: Scales and Timing of the Quaternary Climatic Variations and Responses of the Environment)

Stevenson, A.C., Phethean, S.J. and Robinson, J.E. (1993) The palaeosalinity and vegetational history of Garaet el Ichkeul, northwest Tunisia. *The Holocene* 3, 3: 201–10.

Thinon, M. (1988) Approche anthracologique de l'environnement végétal de Martigues à l'Age du Fer. *Dossiers d'Histoire et d'Archéologie* 128: 68–9.

Trément, F. (1989) La région des Étangs de Saint-Blaise: pour une approche archéologique et paléo-écologique d'un milieu de vie. *Bulletin de la Société Préhistorique Française* 86, 10–12: 441–50. (Colloque G.M.P.C.A., Cité des Sciences et de l'Industrie de la Villette, Paris, 5–7 novembre 1989)

Trément, F. (1991) (ed) *Archéologie et Histoire du Paysage dans la Région des Étangs de Saint-Blaise*. Aix-en-Provence, Centre Camille Jullian, Exposition en 21 Panneaux Réalisée dans le Cadre de l'Année de l'Archéologie.

Trément, F. (1993a) Le secteur des étangs de Saint-Blaise: pour une approche archéologique et paléo-écologique d'un milieu de vie. In P. Leveau and M. Provansal (eds) *Archéologie et Environnement: De la Sainte-Victoire aux Alpilles*: 83–108. Aix-en-Provence, Université de Provence.

Trément, F. (1993b) Le secteur des étangs de Saint-Blaise: essai d'approche quantitative de l'histoire de l'occupation du sol. In P.Leveau and M.Provansal (eds) *Archéologie et Environnement: De la Sainte-Victoire aux Alpilles*: 165–82. Aix-en-Provence, Université de Provence.

Trément, F. (1994) *Histoire de l'Occupation du Sol et Évolution des Paysages dans le Secteur des Etangs de Saint-Blaise (Bouches-du-Rhône). Essai d'Archéologie du Paysage*. Aix-en-Provence, Université de Provence,Thèse de Doctorat Nouveau Régime.

Trément, F. (1997) Un établissement agricole gallo-romain: le site des Soires à Saint-Mitre-les-Remparts (Bouches-du-Rhône). *Revue Archéologique de Narbonnaise* 30: 33–61.

Trément, F. (1998) Prospection archéologique et démographie en Provence. Approche paléodémographique de la rive occidentale de l'Étang de Berre sur la longue durée. In J. Bintliff and K. Sbonias (eds) *Reconstructing Past Population Trends in Mediterranean Europe (3000 BC – AD 1800)*. Oxford, Oxbow.

Trément, F. (in press, a) *Archéologie d'un Paysage. Les Étangs de Saint-Blaise*. Paris, Documents d'Archéologie Française.

Trément, F. (in press, b) Prospection et chronologie: de la quantification du temps au modèle de peuplement. Méthodes appliquées au secteur de Saint-Blaise (Bouches-du-Rhône). In R. Francovich and H. Patterson (eds) *Extracting Meaning from Ploughsoil Assemblages*. Oxford, Oxbow.

Trément, F. and Brien-Poitevin, F. (1989) Les Clapières, dépotoir de la fin de l'Antiquité (Saint-Mitre-les-Remparts). *Notes d'information et de liaison de P.A.C.A.* 6: 114–6.

Triat-Laval, H. (1978) *Contribution Pollenanalytique à l'Histoire Tardi- et Post-glaciaire de la Végétation de la Basse Vallée du Rhône*. Marseille, Université de Aix-Marseille III, Thèse de Sciences.

Vigoureux, A.-M. (1973) *Inventaire Archéologique de la Région de Martigues aux Époques Préromaine et Romaine*. Aix-en-Provence, Université de Provence, Maîtrise dactyl.

Villeneuve, Comte de (1824) *Statistique des Bouches-du-Rhône*. II. Paris.

19. Geoarchaeology in Mediterranean Landscape Archaeology: Concluding Comments

Graeme Barker and John Bintliff

What we wish to do in this final paper is to summarize some of the key points of methodology and approach, and the major operational problems, that emerged from the papers, the discussions, and our own personal reactions to what we heard during the sessions and read in more detail in the pre-circulated papers. In so doing, we want to direct attention towards the central goal of the POPULUS programme: the future direction of regional field survey in the Mediterranean, and in particular here to focus on the role of regional environmental reconstruction – the special theme of the Aix conference – in this future goal.

THE STRUCTURE AND PHILOSOPHY OF GEOARCHAEOLOGY

During the conference, several alternative views were expressed about the way Geoarchaeology ought to relate to regional archaeological research. At one end of the spectrum were some archaeologists who advocated that they (the archaeologists) should enlist a battery of natural scientists and tap into their results for the purpose of understanding the environmental context of an excavation or survey record. At the other end of the spectrum were some geographers who proposed that they (the scientists) should run the regional archaeological projects, the head scientist being partnered by an archaeologist: the head scientist would know how to find the appropriate specialists and weld their results into the geoarchaeological context called for by his/her partner archaeologist.

It seems to us that neither approach allows geoarchaeology to fulfil its critical potential in the study of past landscapes. Both lack one fundamental component: where do we find the interpretative approaches for the human-landscape interaction that constitutes the prime reason these many specialists are working alongside each other ? In reality the only developed intellectual approach has to be a coherent sub-discipline of *human ecology*, neither a form of natural science nor a form of archaeology, but an integrated way of understanding humans in dynamic landscapes. In our view at least, all the specialists on a regional archaeological project need to put their specific research results into the wider framework that human ecology provides. Tony Brown raised the possibilities of this way of thinking when he discussed the concepts of 'resource-scape' and 'task-scape' as applied to the human use of landscape (see Chapter 6). We cannot look for a better intellectual underpinning to such an integrated ecological perspective than in the French tradition of historical geography that can be summed up in the 'Possibilism' advocated by Vidal de la Blache and Lucien Febvre.

It may be necessary, in the real world of budgets and logistics, to commence regional environmental archaeology traditionally, by employing the natural sciences to analyze the changing forms of the landscape, and archaeologists to analyze the changing landscape architecture and settlement forms imposed by successive generations of human hands. Subsequently, however, we must go further to more interesting questions, such as the utilization of landscapes in rational or irrational ways, or with high or low exploitation, or with narrowly-based or broad-spectrum economies. Such questions of human adaptation and choice take us into dynamic human ecology; and here the archaeologists and natural scientists have to look continually to rural anthropology and sociology for insights into the complex and varied ways people may have responded to constraints and opportunities made available by specific regional landscapes at particular phases of their evolution.

LANDSCAPES AND TIME

However, modern or early modern ethnohistoric parallels are merely a source of models, not a blueprint for claiming, for example, a continuity of land use and *mode de vie* in a given regional landscape. Indeed a second major insight that the conference gave rise to in our minds, was the weakness of a simple uniformitarian approach to the region.

Philippe Leveau in his paper on landscape reconstruction (Chapter 17) rightly exposes the problem of 'regressive analysis', where we take recent forms of landscape and push them back as likely givens for far older phases of the same region. The prime contribution to Mediterranean landscape archaeology of geomorphology and of related disciplines such as palynology has been to emphasize that the past was indeed 'another country', offering different contraints and opportunities to human populations compared with the present landscape, and with human populations in turn differentially equipped to respond to them in terms of their social institutions.

When many of us were students, we were taught a form of ecology where the regional environment was supposedly self-driven by some immutable law towards a 'climax community', but it is now generally admitted that all environments are unstable and historically contingent. The tendencies that appear fitfully towards community structure are being analyzed in terms of 'strange attractors' or gravity fields in chaotic/complex systems. We missed reference to these new frontiers of human ecology, although many contributors provided examples of appropriate landscape changes.

Some of the major landscape changes we can now detect in the Mediterranean region were the result of gradual long-term processes, others may have been caused by catastrophic events of short duration and very long recurrence intervals. The widespread application of dating techniques such as luminescence and palaeomagnetism in the coming years is likely to have an enormous impact in this respect: more refined chronologies seem likely to emphasize different rates of landscape change rather than uniformity, with profound implications for our understanding of human interactions with their landscape.

LANDSCAPE AND SPATIAL SCALE

Several chapters provide insights into the problem of spatial scale in environmental reconstruction. Bottema, for example (Chapter 2), warns us against overemphasizing ecofacts and other environmental evidence from excavated site levels without a due awareness of the range within which the plant or animal forms had operated. Sites are 'spots' on the map, and the environment on and immediately around a site can be quite unrepresentative of the regional environment. The same can be said of sample locations for pollen cores, snail samples and so on – the data may reflect a wide potential range of environments at ranges from a few feet to hundreds of kilometres from the sample spot. An archaeological settlement is a 'sump' containing many residues for geoarchaeological analysis, but the catchments of the various organisms that produced them – people, rivers, animals, birds, microfauna, pollen, plants, snails, and so on – obviously vary enormously, a basic truism all too often ignored when it comes to integration and landscape reconstruction.

It is also rather rare to find a region where the sample locations for environmental data are so dense and complete that we can confidently reconstruct the entire regional environment without the need of archaeological settlement research. Indeed during the conference several case studies were presented where very little was known of the history and prehistory of local human settlement to match a detailed but hardly total set of environmental sample points across the landscape. What must be called for in the future, surely, is a combined operation at the same landscape scale, where settlement history is as well-researched and understood as the changing face of the natural landscape. The only way to accomplish the former task is through the use of modern intensive archaeological surface survey, as is discussed in other volumes in the POPULUS series. On the positive side, we saw the remarkable results that can be obtained through such a combination in many case studies, for example those discussed by Attema *et al.* (Chapter 11), Novakovic *et al.* (Chapter 8), Vella *et al.* (Chapter 14), Leveau (Chapter 17) and Trément (Chapter 18).

In many regional studies of Mediterranean landscape history, there remains a tendency to locate archaeological sites in the landscape and then to treat them as dots in the reconstructed environment. Clearly such a view is too one-dimensional. Most of the time people living at these sites were working in the landscape outside of them, and to mesh the environment with the past societies using it, we must have some models of human ergonomics, of how people use space two-dimensionally. Kevin Walsh reminds us of this concept with his opening remarks on Site Catchment Analysis (Chapter 1). It is a very different picture of human impact or human reaction to the potential of landscape if, for example, we assume a radial exploitation territory of a 1 km or 2 km radius out from a site (where land types may be limited in variety), or in contrast give sites 'strip' territories that are long and thin and stretch across a wide range of different landscape types, perhaps as much as 5–6 km distance. Both types of territory occur in traditional parish or commune boundaries.

LANDSCAPE DEVELOPMENT AND AGENCY

Ever since the publication of Claudio Vita-Finzi's seminal study of Mediterranean alluviation (Vita-Finzi, 1969), the respective roles of anthropogenic and climatic causation of Mediterranean landscape development have remained highly contested (for example: van Andel and and Runnels, 1987; Barker, 1995; Bintliff, 1992; van der Leeuw, 1995; Lewin *et al.*, 1995). The case studies here (such as Chapters 7, 10, 11, 13, 14, 16 and 18) are typical in emphasizing the complexity of the evidence for vegetation and sediment changes sometimes being the result of climate, or human actions, or both in combination. One notable contribution of the papers was to highlight the need for much greater understanding of the range of 'anthropogenic' factors likely to impact on a landscape beyond the present simplistic models of vegetation clearance by people for ploughing or by goats – activities such as terrace building and abandonment (Moody and Grove, 1990; Wagstaff, 1992), fallowing changes, manuring, pastoralism (Chang, 1984), and charcoal-burning, for example – and of their potential signatures in the geomorphological, palaeoecological and archaeological record. The effects of similar processes may also vary, as Shiel points out in Chapter 8: erosion may be bad for one community but actually beneficial for a neighbouring community in a different topographical situation. Exactly the same can be said of the effects of small-scale climatic change.

In emphasizing the simplistic nature of current interpretative models, it is also worth noting that one of commonest themes running through the methodological papers that form the first section of this volume (Chapters 2–9), as was the case in the informal discussions at the conference, is the emphasis on the problems of contextual interpretation: taphonomy, taphonomy, all is taphonomy! The uncertainties of the methodological underpinnings of their discipline are emphasized by chapter after chapter, for example concerning links between present and past ecologies, or the efficacy of sampling procedures, or the robustness of standard analytical models. As in archaeology, so in dendrochronology, geomorphology, malacology, palynology, or whatever, there is currently as much art as science, and the chapters demonstrate a healthy awareness of the weaknesses of current methodologies, particularly regarding their sensitivity to recognizing, interpreting and measuring the effects of different kinds of human activities on the landscape.

LANDSCAPES OF VARIABILITY

Although some contributors to the conference called for global synthesis to summarize the grand timescale of landscape transformation under human influence, the consensus rather was to ask whether any historic or prehistoric landscape was ever a uniform environment – even under maximum human impact. When we analyze historic landscapes with excellent local detail, it is always the case that one parish or commune is slightly different from the next, that no one form of land use or vegetation type forms 100 per cent of the land surface. To expect whole countries or even wider geographical entities to follow a particular generalization of landscape type or land use type may therefore be illusory, and probably counterproductive of knowledge.

We might rather predict that all regional landscapes have been mosaics of environments and human usages at all times. The possibilities of each landscape will have interacted with the particular regional trajectory of human society in complex ways. To be sure, there will be trends which may or not be shared by adjacent regions, but prediction will probably be impossible given the input provided by local natural and human conditions. Perhaps Steven Jay Gould's 'Postdiction' is a better methodology, where we tease apart in retrospect the general trends and structures we understand, from the local perturbation and unpredictability we may describe but not necessarily be able to understand. Integrating the results of regional archaeological surveys provides encouraging signs that we can begin to compare and contrast the very different forms that Mediterranean regional landscapes appear to have taken, for example in response to Roman imperial expansion (Alcock, 1994; Barker and Lloyd, 1991; Carreté *et al.*, 1995; Cherry *et al.*, 1995; Potter, 1979), or as a complex set of outcomes from the interaction of core-periphery and neo-Malthusian structures (for example, in the Greco-Roman Aegean: Bintliff, 1997).

BIG ISSUES

Frequently through the conference we noted how regional investigations employing the techniques of landscape archaeology in different parts of the Mediterranean were raising the same major issues regarding human prehistory and history. One consistent theme for teams working in the central and western Mediterranean has been evidence for settlement shifts, population increase and agricultural intensification in the third millennium BC, and the extent to which these changes coincide with and are related to marked increases in the scale of human impact on sediments and vegetation and/or with climatic change. Regional inter-disciplinary projects are contributing as profoundly to our understanding of the impact of Romanization on the human and natural landscapes of the Mediterranean. As discussed above, another central concern is the relative impact of climatic fluctuations and human impact in terms of dramatic environmental change. Here, one significant weakness of current work is the lack of emphasis on investigating the prehistory and history of Mediterranean uplands (Barker and Grant, 1991).

Perhaps the greatest challenge for inter-disciplinary landscape archaeology in the coming years, however, will be to bridge the divide between the ecological approaches of the natural sciences to past landscapes, on the one hand, and the concerns of social archaeologists on the other with the interface between human actions and landscape, a concern that also emerges from the POPULUS conference on GIS (Gillings *et al.*, 1998). The 'mental maps' or perceptions of the ancient peoples of the Mediterranean about the world they inhabited obviously conditioned their relationship to their landscape, and their treatment of it. The implication is that, whilst geoarchaeology must be an essential component of inter-disciplinary landscape archaeology, it cannot by itself move from defining the 'resource-scape' and thence the 'task-scape' to understanding the human landscape in all its complexity. This brings us back to the point we made at the beginning of this chapter about the necessity for a mature and equal relationship between geoarchaeology as a natural science and archaeology as a human science in the investigation of Mediterranean landscape prehistory and history.

The Aix conference emphasized the enormous potential of effective partnerships between broad-based teams of geoarchaeologists and modern intensive survey teams in this endeavour. Reconstructing the history of Mediterranean landscape change certainly needs natural scientists to analyze the changing forms of the landscape, and archaeologists to analyze changing settlement morphologies and systems. To *understand* that history, however, in terms of the interactions between landscape and people, and the perceptions, choices and adaptations that have underpinned human actions, will need effective partnerships between broad-based teams of archaeologists, geoarchaeologists, historians, and anthropologists.

REFERENCES

Alcock, S. (1994) *Graecia Capta*. Cambridge, Cambridge University Press.

Andel, Tj. H. van, and Runnels, C. (1987) *Beyond the Acropolis: the Archaeology of the Greek Countryside*. Stanford, University of Stanford Press.

Barker, G. (1995) *A Mediterranean Valley: Landscape Archaeology and* Annales *History in the Biferno Valley*. London, Leicester University Press.

Barker, G., and Grant, A., (eds.) (1991) Ancient and modern pastoralism in central Italy: an interdisciplinary study in the Cicolano mountains. *Papers of the British School at Rome* 59: 15–88.

Barker, G. and Lloyd, J. (1991) (eds) *Roman Landscapes. Archaeological Survey in the Mediterranean Region*. London, British School at Rome, Archaeological Monographs 2.

Bintliff, J.L. (1992) Erosion in the Mediterranean lands: a reconsideration of pattern, process and methodology. In M. Bell and J. Boardman (eds) *Past and Present Soil Erosion*: 125–31. Oxford, Oxbow.

Bintliff, J.L. (1997) Regional survey, demography and the rise of complex societies in the ancient Aegean: core-periphery, neo-Malthusian and other interpretative models. *Journal of Field Archaeology* 24: 1–38.

Carreté, J.-M., Keay, S.J., and Millett, M. (1995) *A Roman Provincial Capital and its Hinterland: the Survey of the Territory of Tarragona, Spain, 1985–90*. Michigan, Journal of Roman Archaeology Supplement 15.

Chang, K. (1984) The ethnoarchaeology of herding sites in Greece. *MASCA Journal* 3: 44–8.

Cherry, J. F., Davis, J.L., and Mantzourani, E. (1992) *Landscape Archaeology as Long Term History: Northern Kheos in the Cycladic Islands*. Los Angeles, UCLA Institute of Archaeology, Monumenta Archaeologica 16.

Leeuw, S.E., van der (1995) (ed) *L'Homme et la Dégradation de l'Environnement: XVe Rencontres Internationales d'Archéologie et d'Histoire d'Antibes*, Juan-les-Pins, Éditions APDCA (CNRS).

Lewin, J., Macklin, M., and Woodward, J. (1995) (eds) *Mediterranean Quaternary River Environments*. Rotterdam, Balkema.

Gillings, M., Mattingly, D.M., and van Dalen, J. (1998) (eds) *Geographical Information Systems and Landscape Archaeology*. Oxford, Oxbow.

Moody, J., and Grove, A. T. (1990) Terraces and enclosure walls in the Cretan landscape. In S. Bottema, G. Entjes-Nieborg, and W. Van Zeist (eds) *Man's Role in the Shaping of the Eastern Mediterranean Landscape*: 183–91. Rotterdam, Balkema.

Potter, T. W. (1979) *The Changing Landscape of South Etruria*. London, Elek.

Vita-Finzi, C. (1969) *The Mediterranean Valleys: Geological Changes in Historical Times*. Cambridge, Cambridge University Press.

Wagstaff, M. (1992) Agricultural terraces: the Vasilikos valley, Cyprus. In M. Bell and J. Boardman (eds) *Past and Present Soil Erosion: Archaeological and Geographical Perspectives*: 155–61. Oxford, Oxbow Monographs 22.